A Chronology and
Glossary of Propaganda
in the United States

A Chronology and Glossary of Propaganda in the United States

Richard Alan Nelson

Greenwood Press
Westport, Connecticut • London

Library of Congress Cataloging-in-Publication Data

Nelson, Richard Alan, 1947–
    A chronology and glossary of propaganda in the United States /
Richard Alan Nelson.
      p. cm.
    Includes bibliographical references and index.
    ISBN 0–313–29261–2 (alk. paper)
    1. Propaganda—United States—History—Chronology. I. Title.
HM263.N44 1996
303.3'75'0973—dc20   94–47427

British Library Cataloguing in Publication Data is available.

Library of Congress Catalog Card Number: 94–47427
ISBN: 0–313–29261–2

First published in 1996

Greenwood Press, 88 Post Road West, Westport, CT 06881
An imprint of Greenwood Publishing Group, Inc.

Printed in the United States of America

The paper used in this book complies with the
Permanent Paper Standard issued by the National
Information Standards Organization (Z39.48–1984).

10 9 8 7 6 5 4 3 2

CONTENTS

Preface   vii

Introduction   ix

Selected Chronology of Propaganda-Related Events   1

A Propaganda Glossary   115

Selected References   277

Index   305

PREFACE

Americans have had a love-hate affair with propaganda since before the United States itself existed. The thesis of this book is that propaganda is as American as apple pie, with a long and indelible history. The right to persuade and communicate is enshrined in the First Amendment to the U.S. Constitution. The technologies and business aspects of mass media were perfected in America, where they were linked to marketing practices and messages that continue to shape culture around the globe. Today, the United States retains its position as the world's single largest producer of mediated communications. Less well known is the role played by literally hundreds of thousands of people who find employment in various "persuasion industries" through their work as advertisers, public relations practitioners, political consultants, government information officers, issues managers, marketing consultants, activists, and so forth. Individually and collectively, they are today's propagandists.

Knowledge is rarely neutral, often consciously shaped by these special interests and then unconsciously imbibed from our earliest childhood experiences as cultural "normality." More ominously, manipulation, misinformation, and deception are inescapably entwined with one's belief in the "truth." Propaganda also impacts on the level of public discourse by positively as well as negatively influencing the democratic process. Propaganda is thus common to how image makers influence, how educators teach, how sellers sell, and how elites govern. As the United States evolves into an uncertain, postmodern, information-based economy, propaganda's power to reach the masses becomes ever more essential to maintaining social cohesion in a multiculturally diverse society. As part of a series devoted to propaganda and American popular culture, *A Chronology and Glossary of Propaganda in the United States* is designed to serve as a comprehensive and inclusive finding tool that distinctively crosses over artificial barriers to open up new approaches to understanding a phenomenon that defines our time.

The book meets an immediate need for an easy-to-use resource that not only credibly defines the field but also stimulates new research. *A Chronology and Glossary of Propaganda in the United States* fills a long-existing gap in the literature by allowing readers to move beyond tangled webs of ideology and deliberate disinformation in order to hone in on precisely what they need to find. The clarification of what propaganda is (and is not) slices through the confusion surrounding the imprecise terminology and lack of historical background too often associated with its study.

The sweep of coverage is particularly remarkable. The first half of the book presents an extensive chronology of propaganda-related events in a detailed time line that places in historical perspective events and people important to understanding propaganda in America. The second section is an A-to-Z guide defining hundreds of important propaganda terms that are often used but generally ill-defined in context, such as "backdoor contact" and "spin doctor." A selected bibliography lists sources mentioned in the text. A combined name and subject index further facilitates access.

The author's independent analysis in *A Chronology and Glossary of Propaganda in the United States* sometimes draws on, and incorporates as fair use, limited quotes from copyrighted material. The sources are either fair use-paraphrased or cited by direct quote, as fully noted in the text. The group, Advocates for Self-Government, Inc., of Atlanta, Georgia, for example, gives blanket permission to quote from its excellent political definitions when acknowledgment such as this is noted. I am also grateful to on-line sources such as ACTIV-L, Factsheet Five, and other computerized "ethernaut" information providers whose work is made available freely through public domain, ShareRight, and similar mechanisms to researchers, activists, and media for unrestricted copying, reproducing, and other uses. Other noncopyrighted elements may be included without attribution, including pertinent descriptive and informational copy from documents, pamphlets, display exhibit notes, transcripts, and public domain materials such as those issued by U.S. and state government agencies. An occasional use of unrestricted public relations materials from private sources is also found within the text. This is limited to noncopyrighted publicity notes, marketing copy, sales catalogs, press releases, and other materials originally distributed by organizations for the specific public domain purpose of encouraging journalists, scholars, activists, and others to promote their works to wider external audiences.

This book is dedicated to Valoie Parent Nelson, the author's wife, who inspired its completion. Thanks also go to former colleagues and administrators at Kansas State University for suggestions and for a Bureau of General Research award which partially supported student assistance and travel in connection with this project. Extremism researcher Laird Wilcox was gracious with his help and advice, as was Don Vought of the U.S. Army Command and General Staff College, Fort Leavenworth, Kansas. Lance Speere and Jennifer Shakal provided professional consultation on copy preparation. The patience of the editors at Greenwood Press, especially Alicia Merritt and Lynn Zelem, proved legendary over the years in seeing this project into production.

Great efforts were made to avoid mistakes, but some are nonetheless bound to creep in due to human error and the dynamic nature of contemporary propaganda. Please send suggestions, corrections, additions, criticisms, and other comments to the author at the Manship School of Mass Communication, Louisiana State University, Baton Rouge, La. 70803-7202 USA. He can also be contacted by e-mail: rnelson@unix1.sncc.lsu.edu, voice: 504-388-2336, and fax: 504-388-2125.

INTRODUCTION

There is no question that the propaganda society we live in today derives from what went before, with the impulse to persuade others an indelible human trait. Scholars have traced the word propaganda to a Latin origin that had reference to the act of cultivating plant roots in ancient Roman gardens to make them multiply and spread rapidly. However, propaganda has evolved to mean cultivation of something with quite distinct properties—the human mind. Today, propagandists utilize print, electronic, and other media to carry their persuasive messages to individuals who taken together make up specialized and mass audiences. This wide ranging and systematic form of advocacy can be found in entertainment shows, news reports, public relations campaigns, educational programs, public information efforts, political communications, advertisements, and a myriad of other guises whose practitioners shy away from identification as propaganda conduits. This aversion to being known as a propagandist reflects the fact that the term has taken on a much more sinister popular connotation than advocacy alone. For many, "propaganda" implies the use of whatever means are at hand to influence others to believe in and act upon an idea—whether the source idea is true or not.

But dismissing something as mere propaganda is not so simple a task with two major complicating factors for those of us interested in better understanding the topic: (1) while propagandists often willingly lie, much of what they create is factually truthful and perceived as interesting or valuable by those who form the target audiences, and (2) advocacy communication has legitimate claims to legal protection from those who would actively censor controversial speech. This volatile mixture of social utility and potential harm is what makes the overall propaganda phenomenon so widespread and its impact so difficult to categorize.

In the pages that follow, you will learn more about propaganda, its history, and contemporary importance. The chefs of propaganda generally are most reticent when it comes to revealing the secrets of their recipes. But unless you are willing, like Eve and Adam, to take a bite out of the propaganda apple and also experience the consequences, there is no chance to fully know how propaganda shapes good and evil.

The story of propaganda is a remarkable one and displays a very human face.

As you will see, there certainly has been no shortage of those across the ages willing to speak out in order to promote their causes. Fortunately, the propaganda process also leaves behind media products that serve as documentary evidence useful for analyzing prior as well as current controversies. So even though individuals die, their ideas and created works often survive, calling out to us as living remnants of a very complicated—and bloodied—past. Artifacts of propaganda can be found from the first human cultures where monumental art and pictorial writing were used for political as well as commercial purposes. Beginning as early as 2,500 B.C.E. (Before Common/Conversion Era), the Sumerians, followed by the Egyptians, Babylonians, Assyrians and other ancient empires were using monumental art to reinforce the power of the state. Battle victories, not losses, are most pictured and recorded in the official archives.

The importance of military power led a number of thoughtful writers to write important books still read today. Chinese pundit Sun Tzu (mid-fourth-century B.C.E.) encouraged indirect use of deception in his *The Art of War*. The work survives despite the fact that the Chinese, who were the first to invent ink and paper made from wood, did not do so until more than four hundred years later (in the year 105 by our common calendar). Indian strategist Kautilya (321 to 296 B.C.E.) was another propaganda expert. His *Arthas´ästra* ("Statecraft") is a guide to understanding how elites maintain political control. The book stresses the use of espionage, persuasion and other arts of government manipulation. The Greek intellectual Plato is another key founder of propaganda studies. His Academy was an important center of learning established about 385 B.C.E., where scholars integrated ethical theory and practical politics. Plato's published dialogues record how the foundations of ancient democracy are connected with the emergence of professional communicators ("rhetors") skilled in using language to move other people to action. Aristotle, Plato's pupil and tutor to Alexander the Great, later established his own school at the Lyceum in Athens. Among Aristotle's masterworks is *Rhetoric*, which also remains a valuable introduction to propaganda techniques despite the passage of more than two millennia.

The dominant European and Mediterranean power of later antiquity was not that of the Greeks, but the Romans. As early as 59 B.C.E., they began posting daily events bulletins ("*Acta Diurna*") in busy public places, a precursor to newspapers and outdoor advertising. The posting of notices in convenient locations also proved an important persuasive and informational military tool during war or conflict. Rulers in the Roman empire and leaders of their successor states in Europe also extended the use of monuments, coinage, tapestry art, ritualistic appeals and other means to support their authority—practices that continue today.

Religious loyalties are critical to understanding the widespread use of propaganda, with three great world religions arising from the Middle East: Judaism, Christianity, and Islam. These "people of the book" have long shared a common belief in divine revelation and the importance of sacred writings stemming from the experience of Abraham, father of the Hebrews and Arabs. The Hebrew descendants, known as Israelites and Jews, historically intersect with most of the major powers at a variety of points in time.

These experiences have a unique impact on subsequent world developments, including the founding of America and shaping of its national attitudes. In 722 B.C.E., the northern kingdom of Israel was conquered by the Assyrians who forcibly relocated the population of the defeated nation hundreds of miles away in the Caucasus mountain region, giving rise to the legend of "the lost ten tribes of Israel." In the mid-sixth-century B.C.E., the Diaspora (or scattering) of the Hebrew people continued when the southern Israelite kingdom of Judah taken into captivity by the Babylonians. Fifty years later, only a remnant of Jews returned to Palestine from Babylon by order of Cyrus, founder of the Persian empire. The message of the Israelite prophets preserved in the *Torah* and other sacred writings that there is only one universal supreme being deserving of worship (Yahweh) collided with conventional views that there were many gods which needed to be appeased. The Jews' fiercely held belief in national independence also proved "troublesome" to those outside nations such as Rome which sought to impose their rule through force. For example, the crucifixion of Y'shua ben Joseph (the name means "help of Yahweh") in Jerusalem by Roman soldiers during the year 29 was largely a political decision taken in connivance with the Sanhedrin (the highest court and council of the ancient Jewish nation) to eliminate a political "agitator and heretic." However, many Jews and Gentile converts of the day came to believe he was the promised Savior or "prince of peace" believed to have fulfilled the Messianic prophecies. Others in the land of Israel continued to seek salvation and retribution through more violent means. In the year 70, the Jewish temple in Jerusalem was destroyed by the Roman General Titus after a horrific siege in which mothers were forced by starvation to eat their own children. Many of the rebels were brutally massacred, and thousands of other exiled Jews sold into slavery. By 132 to 135, the last major Jewish revolt against Rome under Bar-Cochba failed and Emperor Hadrian completed the forced removal of the people from Judea begun years earlier under Titus.

Undeterred by these setbacks in the Jewish homeland, subsequent followers of Y'shua ben Joseph (better known to history as Jesus Christ, from the Greek version of his name and the title *Christos* meaning the "Anointed One") believed he was a world savior miraculously returned to life as the son of the true God. At first a sect of Judaism, the universal message of God's love and redemption promulgated by these converts gradually evolved into the new religion of Christianity. The fervent evangelism of the early believers and their effective use of graphic symbols such as the fish and cross, helped build increased awareness of the faith. Believers were also aided by publication of the *New Testament*, a collection of letters, doctrinal commentaries, apocalyptic prophecies, and eyewitness accounts recording the life of Christ and his apostles, recorded in Hebrew dialects and in Greek (the widespread commercial language of the day). The propaganda message of the Christians reached out to rich and poor alike, but proved especially popular with the most down-trodden of society. By targeting the emotions and the hopes of the slave and oppressed lower classes, as well as gaining important support among the aristocracy, Christianity spread across the known world.

The last great Roman persecution of Christians began under Emperor Diocletian and his subordinate Galerius Caesar, who beginning in 303 instituted an eight-year long wave of brutality designed to exterminate the religion. A series of four edicts ordered all Christian property destroyed, demanded the surrender and burning of all sacred books, authorized torture to encourage apostasy, and decreed death for anyone continuing to profess their belief in the church. Later persecutions of Christians by fearful authorities in other countries only created new martyrs and failed to staunch the religion's growing (and potentially subversive) influence. With success, however, came schismatic splits that held special importance for the history of freedom and the subsequent formation of the United States.

The other great worldwide monotheistic religious movement is known as Islam ("submission to God"). It dates to the year 622 when the Arabian followers of Mohammed migrated with him (the *hegira*) to Medina in order to establish theocratic rule. Islam's leaders used calls to faith, scriptures (eventually collected in the *Qur'an, Qur-an, Quran,* or *Koran*), and the sword to gain converts. In 637, Jerusalem was captured by Muslim military forces. Later, in 933, the final version of the written Qur'an, still considered authoritative today by Muslims, was completed.

Much of what is now known of the writers of antiquity was preserved by Islamic scholars and the magnificent system of libraries they maintained at a time when most of Europe suffered through the "Dark Ages." For example, Al-Azhar University was founded in Cairo, Egypt, in 969. This center of learning predated its European counterparts by more than two centuries and continues to attract students from all over the world. A government official at the Arab courts of Granada, Morocco, and Algeria who later became the chief justice of the Mamluk sultans of Egypt, ibn Khaldun (died 1409), is now considered by many to be the father of modern historiography and sociology. Khaldun's masterwork is the *Muqaddimah*. Unlike most earlier historians who focused on propagandizing rulers and battles, the great Arab thinker recognized that events depend on many interrelated factors such as social customs, climate, superstitions, labor conditions, food availability, health practices, and so forth. Spurred by individuals such as Khaldun, Islamic civilization made many other contributions to science and the humanities, ironically paving the way for the rise of the West to its present prominence.

By being at the edge of Europe, Irish scholars also preserved important books that helped maintain historical links to past times. In 636, the southern Irish Church submitted to Roman Catholicism. But the widening schism between western forms of Christianity (dominated by the papacy in Rome) and those in the East (led by bishops in Jerusalem, Alexandria, and Constantinople) over who was most "catholic" (universal) eventually resulted in numerous secular as well as religious conflicts. A turning point in European history took place when Charlemagne was crowned by Pope Leo III in 800 as emperor of the restored "Holy Roman Empire" (which historians have dubbed "neither Holy nor Roman"). Charlemagne set a standard copied by other totalitarian rulers through underwriting great monumental construction and arts projects designed to reinforce acquiescence to his regime. Following his death, however, political instability reoccurred. By 1054, the break between the Eastern and Roman churches became permanent, and in 1095 the Crusades began as Christian soldiers from Western Europe invaded the Middle East to recover the "Holy Land" from the Muslims. The Pope sought to divert attention from domestic problems through the propaganda siren call of a divinely-inspired "noble cause." But the human result was a series of senseless wars noted mostly for their crass brutality which tragically prejudices public opinion against Arab peoples more than nine hundred years later.

The religious impulse bore other, less bitter, fruit. Beginning about 1200 and continuing for four hundred years, impressive cathedrals rose across Europe. These towering monuments to faith feature magnificently stained glass windows and other ecclesiastical art which visually reinforced Roman Catholic Church precepts to an impoverished pre-literate population. Similar use of icons in Orthodox areas of Central and Eastern Europe also strengthened the faith of the peasant masses there.

But what happened when the people began to think for themselves, challenging the right of the priests to alone communicate directly with God? Since church and the state were directly intertwined, asserting freedom of religion (or from religion) was a political act. By the thirteenth-century, Catholic authorities were moved to quell dissent. The leaders viewed reading of the *Bible* with suspicion, and denounced early translations. Members of the Council of Toulouse meeting in France in 1229 declared themselves in favor of censorship, warning, "We prohibit that any layman possess the books of the Old or New Testament translated into the common language." In 1233, King James I of Aragon ordered his subjects to turn in their Bibles to local bishops. Those who refused to cooperate in the book burning, including clergymen, were suspected of heresy. Intolerance reigned even in places thought to be fair. For example, in 1275 the first Statute of Jewry was enacted in Britain. Long before the rise of the Nazis, this anti-Semitic law confined Jews to certain locations, compelling them to wear a yellow badge, forbidding their ownership of land, and limiting their contact with other people. In 1290, King Edward I issued an even harsher edict which banished the Jews from England.

Forgeries of documents also were widespread, often created by religious zealots as powerful propaganda weapons in favor of papal claims. The *Donation of Constantine*, purporting to be an earlier letter addressed by Constantine the Great to Pope Sylvester I, was manufactured sometime in the mid-700s. What became known as the *Pseudo-Isidorian Decretals* were penned by an unknown forger in the ninth-century. These contain fictitious letters supposedly sent to early Popes by Clement (in circa 100) and Gregory the Great (circa 600). Along with other forged writings, the *Decretals* were long used to assert the continuity of the papacy as the inheritor of Roman civil powers until exposed as false during the Reformation.

The United States derives much of its culture from developments in Europe, particularly ones that originated in England. In 1066, a cross-channel invasion of Britain by William the Conqueror, proved successful when his Viking-descended forces arrived from Normandy in France to defeat the native Britons at the Battle of Hastings. Later abuses by the Crown evolved into a domestic power struggle. On June 15, 1215, *Magna Charta* ("Great Charter") was signed in Britain between nobles and King John. The Charter limited the powers of the Crown, forming the foundation for fundamental English rights, including trial by jury, equality before the law, and freedom from arbitrary arrest. Later versions of *Magna Charta* (most notably the 1297 agreement signed by Edward I despite the evil treatment of the Jews in his kingdom) reconfirmed these individual protections, providing a direct (if imperfect) legacy to the U.S. Bill of Rights.

This struggle between those favoring oppression and those favoring freedom is one of the dominant themes in human history. During the period beginning in the 1300s, the great religious and humanist cultural movement known as the Renaissance evolved in Italy and spread quickly to other countries. The thirst for knowledge was ironically aided by a great tragedy. Between 1348 and 1352, the Great plague killed an estimated one-third of the European population, giving rise to increased labor unrest, religious extremism, and other challenges to the established order. In 1381, unfair taxation and brutal exploitation of English peasants resulted in an uprising in Kent and Essex known as the Peasant's Revolt.

Leader Wat Tyler was eventually betrayed during an ill-fated parley with King Richard II, where he was brutally stabbed by the Mayor of London and then beheaded. Without Tyler, the worker rebellion was savagely repressed. Fifty years later, just across the channel, Joan of Arc, an illiterate teenager and feminist, headed a peasant army whose victories midwifed the nation-state of France. Church theologians of the University of Paris successfully urged that she be torched as a heretic. Joan, only 19, was burned at the stake, in part because she refused to stop dressing as a man. Exploitation by the monarchy and church continued in many locations, but the memory of freedom among the peasantry was never completely suppressed.

Communication developments also evolved in ways that gradually opened up social systems. Books ("codexes") began replacing scrolls by the year 360, with most of the early advances occurring in the Orient and Middle East. The first printed newspapers (748) appeared in Peking, China. By 765, pictorial printing was also found in Japan. Later, in 868, the first block printed book, the *Diamond Sutra*, was published in China. By 964, the Chinese are adept enough to publish an encyclopedia of 1,000 volumes, and seventy years later even invent a way of printing which uses movable type made of clay (attributed to Pi Sheng). During this time, writing technologies also spread westward after Chinese artisans in Samarkand taught paper manufacturing to their Arab captors.

Printing under these conditions, however, was not much faster than hand copying. The major problem involved the complexity of Chinese, Japanese, and Arabic written languages, particularly the large number of symbols involved. The West was also slow to adapt. Paper only entered wide use in Europe in the twelfth-century and not until 1400 did billposting become an accepted practice. Then something seemingly simple happened that ended up changing the world. To counter recurring debt problems, Johann Gutenberg of Mainz, Germany, between 1450 and 1456 perfected the printing press and movable metal type. This breakthrough allowed for mass printing of books, posters and other materials in the much simpler western alphabet symbols. At first a trickle controlled by the state, soon a deluge of independent publishing swamped Europe to influence domestic and overseas developments. For example, in 1477, William Caxton published the first known book printed in England, *Dictes and Sayings of the Philosophers*. His commitment to the new technology eventually lead him to publish about 100 different works, helping establish conventions of English grammar. The rapid spread of book publishing and typography in the half-century after Gutenberg began modern printing resulted in the appearance of over 35,000 book titles by 1501 with an astonishing distribution of more than 10 million copies.

In an attempt to discredit independent thought and halt the rising tide of heresy that eventually crested all across Europe in the Protestant Reformation, the Roman Catholic Church responded in 1478 by creating its Office of Inquisition. The most famous of these efforts to thwart Protestant religious subversion is the Spanish Inquisition established with the full blessings of King Ferdinand V and Queen Isabella I, rulers of Castile and Léon. Intolerance by the authorities for non-Catholic religions increased and Jews who refused to convert or go underground were victimized again by being expelled from Spanish-controlled lands. Propaganda emanating from all sides only enhanced the image of the Inquisition as an "all powerful, body-racking, mind-enslaving machine." The armed expeditions by Christopher Columbus, financed by Ferdinand and Isabella beginning in 1492, opened the vast lands and resources of the Western hemisphere to political, economic, and religious colonization by European powers. Led by Spain the exploitation of the Americas also resulted in massive suffering and death for the indigenous peoples unwittingly caught up in the racial and sectarian intolerance fueled by Old World disputes.

On October 31, 1517, a relatively unknown Catholic priest, Martin Luther, tacked a list of "95 theses" on his parish door in Wittenberg, a city located on the Elbe River in eastern Germany. The poster criticized sales of indulgences and other specific abuses witnessed by Luther. Unwittingly, this heartfelt act launched the Protestant Reformation which changed not only a corrupt church, but also the course of western civilization. Luther and other reformers articulated the view that Christians are going to be saved solely through God's grace rather than adherence to any ecclesiastical system of laws or program of good works. Their message was aided by the proliferation of printing presses in Europe which helped spread literacy to the common people. The lifting of ignorance and the resulting independence of thought were perceived by those opposed to change as a radical threat to royal governments and state religious unity. In 1521, the papacy instituted formal excommunication procedures against Luther, who fought back by using increasingly harsh, even scatological, language to attack his enemies. Luther's subsequent reputation is marred by his authoring of several virulently intolerant tracts, which while typical of the overt biases widely held in the Middle Ages, are prescient of the violence perpetrated during the later Nazi period in Germany. This prejudice is most noticeable in his *The Jews and Their Lies* (1543) where Luther gave up on the idea of mass conversions and urged the burning of synagogues, destruction of homes, confiscation of money, and suppression of Jewish religious books. "We must drive them out like mad dogs," he wrote, "lest we partake in their abominable blasphemy and vices, deserving God's wrath and being damned along with them."

Many of the other reformers engaged in their own excesses, with Protestants such as Calvin sometimes becoming as dictatorial as the Popes they denounced. Being outspoken also proved risky business, with numerous individuals still sentenced to torture and death by burning, hanging, or beheading for their controversial activities. For example, in 1536, English religious translator and pamphleteer William Tyndale was executed for heresy because his "radical" publications challenged state control over worship.

In 1540, the Society of Jesus was established by a papal bull entitled *For the Rule of the Church Militant*. Under founder Ignatius of Loyola, members of the Society (sneeringly labeled by opponents as "Jesuits") took on increasingly greater political influence. Between 1545 and 1563, at the Council of Trent, the Catholic Church reiterated its condemnation of Bible translations in the vernacular. It published an index of prohibited books, causing persons who possessed the outlawed works to face imprisonment or execution. By 1565, ecclesiastical commissioners in Britain caused the infamous Star-Chamber to issue a decree forbidding under very severe penalties "the publishing, the sale, and every part of the manufacturing, of any book" dealing with religious topics that the crown dislikes. The government even authorized warrantless searches of all suspected places for any such books.

The threats work in some locales, but as soon as one dissenter is silenced another rises up. In 1563, the classic anti-Catholic propaganda book, *Acts and Monuments of the Martyrs* by John Fox was first published, to document the Protestant case against the "Pagan and Popish persecution of the Church." That same year, the *Fogli d'Avvisi* appeared in Venice, a written newsletter of events that presaged the later *gazeta* (gazettes or newspapers costing only a small coin). And in 1564 another advance of note occurred: the pencil was invented using graphite discovered in England. (Today's "lead" pencils use a mixture of graphite and clay.)

By the 1600s, the sheer combination of widespread availability of information and the failure of straight repression forced proponents of various theologies and ideologies to engage in more reasoned intellectual argument. During the Counter-Reformation, the term propaganda was first widely activated after Pope Gregory XV created the *Sacra Congregatio de Propaganda Fide* (Sacred Congregation for the Propagation of Faith) in 1622 to bolster the Roman Catholic cause. Ironically, with the dawn of the so-called Enlightenment in the eighteenth-century, the historical excesses of the oppressors, reformers, and defenders provided ample fodder for opponents of all established churches.

As might well be expected, questions of freedom and duty stemming from the very real ideological conflicts chronicled above still hone contemporary debate about the rights of individuals versus those of governments and those of religions. The propaganda battles of the Old World were not simply transferred to the New World, but transfigured by what has proved to be a unique American experience. Indeed, it was in America that the volatile mix of faith and freethought, myth and hope, commerce and labor, objectivity and partisanship, principle and expediency, and individualism versus conformity most exuberantly blended into a special culture of influence and note.

A Chronology and Glossary of Propaganda in the United States

SELECTED CHRONOLOGY
OF PROPAGANDA-RELATED
EVENTS

1492—Sailing under the flag of Spain, Christopher Columbus leads his small fleet of ships across the uncharted Atlantic Ocean. Seeking a short route to the spice islands of the Orient, the expedition accidentally discovers the Western hemisphere. Treacherously ignoring the wishes of the people already living there (called Indians because Columbus mistakes them for residents off the coast of India), these "new lands" are soon exploited for their riches and opened to colonization by the leading European powers.

1536—The first European-language book printed in the Americas is published in Mexico City.

1611—The "Authorized" version of the Bible (better known as the King James Version) is published and quickly becomes the standard for the English-speaking world, including Britain's American colonies.

1619, August 20—The slave trade comes to the English North America when a shipload of blacks is brought by force from Africa and sold as cheap labor in Jamestown, Virginia.

1638-1639—The first English colonial press, is introduced into British North America by Stephen Day of Cambridge, Massachusetts

1640s—Fundraising via media emerges in the United States as Harvard College creates a development brochure, *New England's First Fruits*.

1641-1648—The periodic newsbook (proto-newspaper) evolves in Britain, free from government controls, an instance where the real public interest benefits from the disappearance of government-imposed public interest provisions. John Milton argues, in his now famous 1644 pamphlet *Areopagitica*, for freedom from parliamentary control of independent publishing. He warns, "Though all the windes of doctrin were let loose to play upon the earth, so Truth be in the field, we do injuriously by licensing and prohibiting to misdoubt her strength. Let her and Falsehood grapple; who ever knew Truth put to the wors, in a free and open encounter." Milton is thus among the first to advance the concept that freedom of expression is in the public interest, influencing others in England and colonial America.

1663—Rhode Island is the first British colony to provide for religious liberty in its charter.

1673—Regular postal service begins between New York and Boston.

1690, September 25—*Publick Occurrences Both Foreign and Domestick* becomes the first newspaper in British North America, but only one issue is published before it is shut down by colonial authorities.

1692—Witch trial hysteria dominates Salem, Massachusetts.

1704, April 24—The *Boston News-Letter* is founded as the first continuing newspaper published in the British North American colonies. In addition to news, slave trade advertisements are regularly featured.

1720s—The arguments for political liberty are advanced in *Cato's Letters*, written for British newspapers by John Trenchard and Thomas Gordon. These prove highly influential and become widely cited in the pamphleteer literature of colonial America.

1721—James and Benjamin Franklin publish the *New England Courant*.

1725—James Otis, who later becomes a leading propagandist for the American Revolution, is born.

1730s-1770s—Royal governors of this era warn headmasters in British North America that their schools are becoming "seminaries of sedition."

1732, May—The *Philadelphische Zeitung* is founded by Benjamin Franklin, the first foreign-language newspaper in British North America.

1734—From his parish in New England, Charles Edwards leads the "Great Awakening," a spiritual revival that stresses the dangers of eternal damnation because of humanity's corrupt nature. The movement influences the religious values of many Americans but is condemned as disruptive by others.

1734, August—The ever-active Benjamin Franklin advertises the sale of his version of the *Mason Book*, the first such book about Freemasonry published in the American colonies.

1734, November 6—Government representatives on Wall Street burn copies of John Peter Zenger's *New York Weekly Journal* to protest its attacks on the royal governor. Zenger is tried the following year in a celebrated court case designed to suppress his criticisms. Defense lawyer Andrew Hamilton successfully argues in favor of the fundamental right "of exposing and opposing arbitrary power," and Zenger's acquittal on free speech and free press grounds establishes truth as a defense against seditious libel in the British North American colonies. The *New York Weekly Journal* newspaper continues publication until 1751.

1737—Benjamin Franklin is named postmaster of Philadelphia.

1742—Faneuil Hall ("the cradle of American liberty") is built by Peter Faneuil in Boston and given to the city. During the Revolutionary War period, "radical patriots" use it as a meeting place.

1754—"JOIN, or DIE," a political cartoon by Benjamin Franklin showing a divided snake, appears in *Pennsylvania Gazette* urging British colonies to unite in fighting the French and Indian War.

1765—The Stamp Act by British Parliament demands revenue stamps be paid by those in the American colonies to help defray the funds needed to maintain royal troops in keeping order. The unpopularity of the new tax results in its repeal the following year. Nevertheless, resentments continue to escalate between the mother country and many residents of New England.

1770s-1780s—An estimated 40,000 Tory loyalists flee U.S. territory during and after the American Revolution to settle in the Canadian provinces of Nova Scotia and Ontario. Others return to Britain. This emigration shifts the demographics of Canada from French- to English-speaking, setting the tone for ongoing nationalistic sentiment concerned with avoiding American domination. Those Tories who remain in the United States often suffer from harsh and summary punishments meted out by the unforgiving victors.

1770, March 5—In an attempt to restore order, frightened British troops open fire on an angry populace in Boston. Escaped slave Crispus Attucks and several other colonists at the gathering are found dead. For many, this is the beginning of open rebellion. The "Boston Massacre" is popularized in a broadside poster, and the medium will become perhaps the chief instrument of communication during the American Revolution.

1772-1773—American radicals form colonial Committees of Correspondence to serve as a communications link and agitate for independence from Britain.

1773, December 16—Radicals disguised as Indians protest a new parliamentary tax by tossing British imports into the harbor in what is called the Boston Tea Party. The "patriots" prove expert at publicizing their grievances through such staged events and key organs of opinion (press, pamphlets, broadsides, and even music) to establish the agenda for debate, while simultaneously discrediting their loyalist opponents.

1774, spring—The British Parliament passes five measures meant to cement control over North America and punish the Massachusetts colonists for the destruction of private property at the Boston Tea Party and other dissident activities the prior winter. The Boston Port Act closes the port and orders the capital moved to Salem, the Massachusetts Bay Regulatory Act replaces elected officials with direct royal appointments, the Impartial Administration of Justice Act allows British subjects arrested in the colonies to stand trial in England, the Quartering Act requires colonists to provide housing and food for British troops sent to control them, and the Quebec Act extends the province southward and provides religious freedom to French-speaking Roman Catholics. The radical colonists see these measures as threats to their liberty and refer to them as the "Coercive and Intolerable Acts," spurring the call for America's first Continental Congress to seek redress of grievances.

1774, September—The Continental Congress meets in Philadelphia. In an address "To the Inhabitants of the Province of Quebec," the Congress lists five "invaluable rights"—including freedom of the press—that the colonies should preserve, even at the cost of the taking up of arms.

1775-1776—The Illuminati Order is founded in Germany by Adam Weishaupt, a professor of Canon law at Ingolstadt University. The Illuminati is later linked to political conspiracies involving other occult organizations, notably, the jacobinistic lodges of Grand Orient Freemasonry.

1775, April—First armed clashes occur between British army and American colonial militias at Concord and Lexington, Massachusetts.

1775, autumn—Two American armies, one led by General Benedict Arnold, invade Quebec hoping to make it the 14th colony in the simmering rebellion against the English crown. However, the Québecois are not persuaded by the American propaganda or military efforts, and a combined British-Canadian force turns the invaders back before reaching Quebec City on New Year's eve, 1776.

1776—*An Inquiry into the Nature and Causes of the Wealth of Nations* by Adam Smith is first published. Commonly called *Wealth of Nations*, the book provides the ideological foundation for laissez-faire capitalism and the Industrial Revolution.

1776, January—A relatively obscure journalist named Thomas Paine anonymously publishes *Common Sense* as a pamphlet. Although his ideas of limited government are not especially new, the understandable approach and comprehensive treatment are. Paine's impact on the average person is profound, even though he is criticized by many wealthy loyalist and revolutionist leaders alike (John Adams later calls Paine an "insolent blasphemer of things sacred and transcendent libeler of all that is good"). Within a year of its release, *Common Sense* sells between 150,000 and 500,000 copies (estimates are imprecise) in a colonial population of less than 3 million. Later, his published series *The American Crisis* (1776-1783) helps unite political idealism with the idea of economic advancement, providing comfort to those fighting during "the times that try men's souls." Paine is now regarded as the premier propagandist of his era for republican secular government in what would become America, Great Britain, and France.

1776, July 4—American rebellion against Britain results in a Declaration of Independence through action of the Second Continental Congress and issued by unanimous vote of representatives for the thirteen colonies constituting the United States of America.

1778, February—The French government recognizes U.S. independence.

1781, October—Forces under General George Washington compel British General Lord Charles Cornwallis and his army to surrender at Yorktown, Virginia, ending the military phase of the American Revolution.

1783—There are 35 newspapers in the United States with limited circulations, only 1 of which appears on a daily basis.

Also in 1783, revolutionary leader James Otis dies.

1783, September—A peace treaty between Britain and the United States recognizes the latter's independence. By November, English troops leave New York City.

1786—Steamships allow for the faster transmission of messages. Also in 1786, Shays' Rebellion, an insurrection by western Massachusetts farmers, is put down by government troops. The conflict is symptomatic of economic dislocations and discontent in the new nation.

1787—The first African Masonic Lodge in the United States is founded in Massachusetts by Prince Hall, a Methodist minister, antislavery activist, and Revolutionary War veteran. Boston's African Lodge No. 459 is one of the few Freemasonry orders still in possession of its original Royal Charter.

1787, September 17—Delegates from 12 states gather in Philadelphia to reform the Articles of Confederation; but instead complete a new Constitution of the United States. During the following nine months, controversy surrounding adoption of the federal Constitution. Proponents led by Alexander Hamilton, James Madison, and John Jay anonymously prepare a series of newspaper articles now known collectively as the *Federalist Papers* under the pen name "Publius" to sell Americans on the new Constitution. In keeping with the great traditions of political journalism, "Publius" draws on seminal works of philosophy, the experience of past statesmen, and a profound grasp of existing circumstances to articulate a vision of how a free and just government could be established. The Federalists support a more centralized government, while their anti-Federalist opponents warn against the undemocratic tendency to concentrate power. The debate results in compromises that satisfy no one entirely but masterfully balance the concerns raised by the various camps. As a result of its successful efforts "to refine and enlarge the public views," the *Federalist Papers* prove to be an articulate instrument of propaganda among opinion leaders, as well as a thoughtful political treatise of more lasting interest. In particular, the discussion of faction in the *Federalist Papers* numbers 10 and 51 (which concern the need to establish legislative neutrality) becomes a standard constitutional principle of the nineteenth-century. Judges long interpret Madison's views on factional politics and the Constitution as prohibiting special interest legislation in support of a particular class or group unless general benefits are also obtained.

1788, June 21—The Constitution becomes effective for the ratifying states when New Hampshire becomes the ninth state to endorse it.

1789—Claiming inspiration from the American experience, French revolutionaries overthrow the monarchy and promulgate a humanistic *Declaration of the Rights of Man and of the Citizen*.

1789, April 30—George Washington is inaugurated as the first president of the United States under provisions of the Constitution. Political candidates are among the first to see the promotional possibilities of specialty advertising, with an estimated 27 varieties of commemorative metal buttons produced during Washington's term of office.

1789, June 8—James Madison introduces in the U.S. House of Representatives a proposed Bill of Rights to modify the Constitution by adding individual protections against potential government abuse.

1789, September 5—Congress approves 12 constitutional amendments and sends them to the states for ratification.

1791—The largest city and media center in the United States is Philadelphia, with 53 printers.

In this year, construction work also begins at the site of the federal capital for the new nation on land carved out from Maryland and Virginia. In charge of the project is Major Pierre Charles L'Enfant who in gazing east over the Potomac River sees what others could not—stately avenues and broad boulevards replacing bottom land and bogs. According to Herbert Stein-Schneider ("Versailles on the Potomac," pp. 42-43):

Today, Washington, D.C., still bears the imprint of this Frenchman's imagination and of the site that inspired it, the royal town and palace of Versailles . . . . The Versailles palace was to be the center of the newly created capital city of the United States. This "palace," however, would not house an absolute monarch, but the true power of the democratic state, the representatives of the people of the newly liberated colonies. The center of Washington thus became the Capitol with its two legislative chambers, an idea derived from the constitution of John Calvin's Geneva in the sixteenth century and transmitted to America via the Puritan tradition of New England.

1791, December 15—Two of the proposed amendments to the U.S. Constitution fail, but 10 pass as the Bill of Rights is ratified by enough states for it to take effect. The package as adopted includes the First Amendment, which states "Congress shall make no law respecting an establishment of religion, or prohibiting the free exercise thereof; or abridging the freedom of speech, or of the press, or the right of the people peaceably to assemble, and to petition the Government for a redress of grievances."

1792—Thomas Jefferson, founds the Democratic-Republican party to perpetuate the principles he penned in the *Declaration of Independence*. He and his partisans begin organizing anti-Federalist political and fraternal groups (often referred to as reading societies).

That same year, the first women's suffrage book is published in the United States. *A Vindication of the Rights of Women, with Strictures on Political and Moral Subjects* by Mary Wollstonecraft Godwin is a reprint of a treatise first published in Britain in 1790.

1793-1794—The French Revolution "reign of terror" largely obliterates the *Declaration* of 1789. Unlike the United States, where individual and group civil rights are protected by constitutional limits on the state, the French adopt Rousseau's theory of the "general will" which says that after "the people" vote their parliament should hold unlimited powers to transform society. The radical Jacobins controlling France are thus free to order as many as 400,000 monarchists and other "counterrevolutionaries" shot, hacked to death, or taken to the guillotine, with thousands more humiliated through rape and plunder of their properties. Even Citizen Genêt falls out of favor. In order to avoid a French death warrant, he requests and is granted asylum in the United States.

1793, April 22—The new nation's first neutrality proclamation is issued and positions the United States as seeking a policy of "conduct friendly and impartial" toward other countries, particularly the opposing alliances led by Great Britain and France. The newly named French ambassador, Edmond Genêt, precipitates a diplomatic crisis by encouraging private American ships to seize British vessels in the name of France. Citizen Genêt is encouraged by the widespread popular enthusiasm of Americans for the French Revolution but misreads the desire of federal authorities to avoid conflict with Britain. Through his bumbling propaganda campaign, Genêt eventually squanders much of the goodwill he had inherited.

1794, August 7—President Washington is forced to send in militia to put down the Whisky Rebellion in Pennsylvania which is led by rioters protesting an excise tax on the alcoholic beverage.

1795—The hydraulic printing press is invented.

That same year, James Hardie authors his influential, encyclopedic work, *The American Remembrancer, and Universal Tablet of Memory, Containing a List of the Most Eminent Men, Whether in Ancient or Modern Times, with the Atchievements* [sic] *for Which They Have Been Particularly Distinguished: As Also the Most Memorable Events in History, From the Earliest Period Till the Year 1795, Classed under Distinct Heads, with their Respective Dates. To Which Is Added, a Table, Comprehending the Periods at Which the Most Remarkable Cities and Towns Were Founded, Their Present Population, Latitude, and Longitude. The Whole Being Intended to Form a Comprehensive Abridgment of History and Chronology, Particularly of that Part Which Relates to America.*

1796—The first competitive American presidential election campaign, is held.

Dominated by Federalist John Adams (the eventual winner) and Democratic-Republican candidate Thomas Jefferson, it proves a negative one conducted with widespread name-calling, accusational invectives, smears, and downright lies. George Washington's decision not to seek a further term of office is announced on September 17. In his *Farewell Address* the president urges future leaders of the United States to guard against "entangling political alliances." Washington's philosophy guides the nation for nearly 100 years, but after 1898 it is largely abandoned by twentieth-century political administrations committed to more interventionist policies. The first president's isolationist views, though expressed in eighteenth-century style, nevertheless retain great currency when, in speaking to Americans, Washington warns:

The nation which indulges towards another an habitual hatred, or an habitual fondness, is in some degree a slave. It is a slave to its animosity or to its affection, either of which is sufficient to lead it astray from its duty and its interest. . . . [A] passionate attachment of one nation for another produces a variety of evils. Sympathy for the favorite nation, facilitating the illusion of an imaginary common interest in cases where no real common interest exists, and infusing into one the enmities of the other, betrays the former into a participation in the quarrels and wars of the latter, without adequate inducements or justifications . . . and it gives to ambitious, corrupted or deluded citizens who devote themselves to the favorite nation, facility to betray or sacrifice the interests of their own country, without odium, sometimes even with popularity; gilding with the appearances of a virtuous sense of obligation, a commendable deference for public good, the base or foolish compliances of ambition, corruption, or infatuation. As avenues to foreign influence in innumerable ways, such attachments are particularly alarming to the truly enlightened and independent patriot. How many opportunities do they afford to tamper with domestic factions, to practice the arts of seduction, to mislead public opinion, to influence or awe the public councils! . . . Against the insidious wiles of foreign influence (I conjure you to believe me fellow citizens) the jealously of a free people ought to be constantly awake; since history and experience prove that foreign influence is one of the most baneful foes of republican government. . . . The great rule of conduct for us, in regard to foreign nations, is, in extending our commercial relations, to have with them as little political connection as possible.

1797—After a worldwide press and activist campaign to free the Marquis de Lafayette (led by his wife and two daughters, who voluntarily shared his dungeon for three years), the hero of the American Revolution is finally liberated from Austrian imprisonment.

1798—Political fears of secret societies are fueled by sensationalist accounts and the publication in America of John Robison's *Proofs of a Conspiracy against All the Religions and Governments of Europe, Carried On in the Secret Meetings of Free Masons, Illuminati, and Reading Societies, Collected from Good Authorities*. A mere seven years after the adoption of the First Amendment, Congress reacts by passing the Alien and Sedition Acts, which make it a crime for anyone to publish "false, scandalous or malicious" criticism of the Federalist administration. The government uses the acts to restrict free speech rights and to prosecute Democratic-Republican editors who castigate President John Adams' war policies. Congressman Matthew Lyon is sentenced to four months in jail and fined $1,000 for writing a letter to a newspaper criticizing Adams for "ridiculous pomp, foolish adulation, selfish avarice." These excesses ultimately turn the electorate against the Federalists. The Alien and Sedition Acts are never challenged constitutionally but rather expire in 1801, when no action is taken to renew them.

Also in 1798, lithography is invented by Aloys Senefelder.

1800—The American political party system emerges, using campaign tactics and mechanisms that evolve outside any provisions envisioned in the Constitution. The presidential campaign is dominated by an outpouring of propaganda attacking the private lives and character of the candidates. One anti-Thomas Jefferson pamphlet (*A Short Address to the Voters of Delaware*) even warns "that if Jefferson is elected, and the Jacobins get into authority, . . . those morals which protect our lives from the knife of the assassin . . . [will] be trampled upon and exploded." Jefferson eventually emerges victorious to complete a peaceful "revolution" transferring power to his faction, despite the strenuous efforts of the Federalists under John Adams and an electoral college tie with Aaron Burr.

Reflecting the growth of American media, Philadelphia has 81 printers by 1800.

1801—The American Convention for Promoting the Abolition of Slavery, and Improving the Condition of the African Race holds its Seventh Convention in Philadelphia.

Also in that same year, the Scottish Rite of Freemasonry officially organizes in the United States under the tutelage of Tory loyalist partisans, who were on the losing side of the American Revolution. Scottish Rite's roots go back to the early 1700s, when it was founded as a secret society in England by a clique of British philosophical liberals referred to as the Venetian party. Over time, Scottish Rite becomes a factor in the secession movement and is later reestablished as America's dominant form of Freemasonry.

1802—More than 25,000 miles of postal roads are established.

1804—States north of the Mason-Dixon line either forbid slavery or provide for its gradual elimination.

Also in that same year, the invention of locomotive trains points to future advances in transportation and communication.

1807—The Jefferson administration pursues a neutralist embargo policy toward Britain and France, which threatens the profits of New England shipping interests. The propaganda issued by these traders ("the moneyed speculators," led by the Tory "merchants of Boston and their hireling editors") seeks to deflect criticism and build coalition support for free trade by stressing the ruinous impact of the embargo on agriculture.

1808, January 1—A law abolishing the U.S. importation of slaves goes into effect. There are an estimated one million slaves living in the country.

1809—Thomas Paine dies, almost forgotten, but is eulogized by Thomas Jefferson as one who worked "to advance the original sentiments of democracy."

1810—Philadelphia has 168 printers.

1811—The first steam-powered printing press (invented by Friedrich Koenig) appears, soon revolutionizing the newspaper business in Europe and America.

1812—Angry British weavers smash their bosses' looms in the Luddite Rebellions in reaction to worker displacement caused by the introduction of new industrial technologies. "General Ludd's wives" lead one riot in Stockton, England, where two male workers, dressed as women, lead a crowd of hundreds to burn down a factory.

1812, June 18—Congress declares war on Britain to open blockaded ports for commerce and secure an end to the impressment (forced service) of American seamen on English vessels. "Uncle Sam" becomes a symbol of the United States.

1814—Following the burning of York (now Toronto), Canada, by Americans during the continuing War of 1812, British troops retaliate by invading the United States and torching Washington, D.C. The attack on nearby Fort Henry is commemorated by Francis Scott Key in *The Star Spangled Banner*. The Hartford Convention brings together prominent New Englanders who object to further war with England. The secretary for the convention is Theodore Dwight (1764-1846), an author, former member of Congress, and leading propagandist for the Federalist cause. The participants secretly meet to determine their options for peace and assert their right to secede from the national government should the need arise. The war ends in 1815, however, before such drastic action can be taken, thus further discrediting the Federalists. The convention also provides a precedent for future actions by pro-slavery forces in the South.

1816—The American Colonization Society is formed for the purpose of assisting former slaves to return to Africa. The country of Liberia is founded under its auspices in 1822.

1816, December 4—The Federalist Party's national influence ends after the disastrous loss by their candidate, Rufus King. The landslide election of James Monroe continues the "Virginia presidential dynasty" and ushers in a two-term "Era of Good Feeling" typified by a lessening of policy differences between Democratic-Republicans, Federalists, and other political factions.

1817—Harper Brothers begin publishing.

1820—The Missouri Compromise by Congress provides for Missouri's entry into the Union as a slave state.

Also in 1820, Philadelphia has 207 printers.

1823—President James Monroe proclaims the Monroe Doctrine warning Europe against interference in the Americas.

1824—The renewal of political rivalries results in four major candidates competing for the presidency, John Quincy Adams, Henry Clay, William H. Crawford, and Andrew Jackson. Although Jackson wins the popular vote, he falls short of an electoral majority. This throws the election into the House of Representatives, where Adams is finally selected. When Clay is named secretary of state in the new administration, Jackson's supporters denounce the "corrupt bargain," propagandize openly in opposition to the president's policies, and gear up for the next election.

1826—Anti-Illuminati feelings are rekindled with the disappearance of William Morgan, author of a book revealing organizational secrets entitled *Illustrations of Freemasonry*.

That same year, the American Missionary Society is founded in Boston.

1827, March 16—*Freedom's Journal* begins publication. The editorial policy attacks the "return to Africa" colonization programs favored by many prominent politicians such as Henry Clay. The antislavery movement eventually repudiates colonization in favor of assimilation.

1828—Supporters of Andrew Jackson, still bitter over the 1824 election (which they believe was stolen from them), organize what is now referred to as the first popular campaign. The American electorate undergoes mass mobilization through joyous mass parades celebrating Jackson's military prowess and emotional speechifying rallies complete with plenty of beer barrels, good food, and lively music. Campaign mementos made of glass, metal, ceramics, and other materials help remind the voters of their candidate's heroic exploits. Commemorative buttons provided to supporters feature a military style bust of Jackson on the front. Since many of the early settlers are farmers, they also receive practical specialty advertising gifts, such as rulers, yardsticks, calendars, and the *American Almanac*. These help Jackson cultivate an image as a man of the people, the "Second Washington," thus making a strong appeal for popular democracy. At the same time, "Old Hickory's" allies in Congress use their power of the frank to mail out impressive quantities of printed propaganda, at federal expense, attacking the "effete and corrupt" administration of John Quincy Adams. Such tactics work, and Jackson emerges victorious, with his strong leadership helping to build the modern Democratic party and revitalize the two-party system. Among his "kitchen cabinet" advisors is Amos Kendall, a writer and editor who is now often referred to as the "first presidential press secretary" (a term that did not exist in his lifetime). Kendall's effective publicity techniques (he wrote speeches, state papers, and press releases and conducted public opinion polls) are widely credited with the popularity that Jackson enjoys throughout his incumbency. The widespread use of song sheets such as *President Jackson's Favourite March and Quick Step* also contributes to building and maintaining his public image.

   Also in 1828, the first scheduled American passenger railroad (the Baltimore & Ohio) takes to the tracks.

1829—William Lloyd Garrison makes his first antislavery speech, at Park Street Congregational Church in Boston.

   Also that year, an Anti-Masonic party political organization is formed under the leadership of Henry Dana Ward, Thurlow Weed, and William H. Seward.

1829, September—African-American abolitionist David Walker publishes *David Walker's Appeal, in Four Articles; Together with a Preamble to the Colored Citizens of the World, But in Particular, and Very Expressly, to Those of the United States of America*, an 88-page pamphlet ardently urging slaves to resort to violence in order to be freed. It becomes one of the most widely read and circulated abolitionist tracts written by a black person. The text is modeled on the Constitution, using analogies to bring home the "degraded, wretched, and abject" condition of those in slavery's bondage. However, the arguments Walker advances create such outrage in the South that some state legislatures not only pass laws preventing his book's circulation, but also make it a crime punishable by death to introduce similar literature. In fact, Walker's essays are so powerful that a group of southerners puts a price on his head.

1830s—The first major use of posters in the United States for commercial purposes occurs during the presidency of Andrew Jackson. Traveling circuses, museum exhibits, and theatrical performances become more commonplace.

1830, April 6—The Church of Christ is established in New York state by the charismatic Joseph Smith, Jr., who serves as "the Prophet, Seer, and Revelator" of the "restored" religion. Controversy soon follows, particularly after Smith "translates" and publishes *The Book of Mormon*, scriptures that purport to tell the story of Israelite immigration and Christ's later visit to the Americas.

1830, June 28—Civil rights pamphleteer David Walker dies violently of mysterious causes near his Boston shop, a rumored victim of poisoning.

1831—The Choctaw Nation is forcibly removed from its ancestral homelands in Mississippi and sent to the Oklahoma reservation set aside by Congress for various Indian tribes. Horrendous winter conditions make the 500-mile walk even more difficult, with almost half the Choctaw people perishing during this "Trail of Tears".

    Also in that year, the Anti-Masonic party grows to become the first influential minor, or third, party in the United States. Anti-Masonic leaders introduce the technique of the national presidential nominating convention, which proves so successful that it is adopted by the major political parties over the next 12 months.

1831, April—Dissident Abner Kneeland founds a weekly newspaper devoted to religious free thought, the *Boston Investigator*. This evolves from earlier Universalistic publications that he edited, to become the nation's first nationally circulated news outlet for deist and atheist views.

1831, July 4—*America* is first publicly sung.

1832, January 6—The New England Antislavery Society is founded and soon becomes the American Antislavery Society. Numerous local affiliates help spread the society's moral and political doctrines, which arouse great passions, and even mob violence, in both the South and the North. The success of its propaganda eventually leads to splits between the more radical faction, typified by William Lloyd Garrison, and moderate elements seeking political and constitutional reforms. Garrison is best known as publisher of the *Liberator*, an influential and militant abolitionist journal. His impassioned convictions are echoed in the editorial found in the first edition: "I am in earnest—I will not equivocate. I will not excuse. I will not retreat a single inch and I will be heard!" The Nat Turner slave rebellion later that year leads the Virginia legislature to impose strict restrictions on abolitionist publications.

1832, May 21—The first national convention of the Democratic (officially Democratic-Republican) party convenes in Baltimore. Delegates nominate President Andrew "Old Hickory" Jackson for a second term, with running mate Martin Van Buren. Jackson favors "hard money" of gold and silver and turns against the financiers by vetoing a bill reauthorizing the central Bank of the United States. Instead, he asks for voter support at the polls. Jackson engages in a vigorous grassroots campaign, reaching out to what one opponent contemptuously calls "the unwashed masses," even though Jackson is simultaneously lambasted as "King Andrew the First." Broadside posters dramatically picture garish coffins to illustrate "Some Accounts of Some of the Bloody Deeds of Gen. Jackson," but Jackson's supporters organize "Old Hickory" clubs to hold public meetings, organize parades, and get out the vote. He is reelected in November despite the smear campaign against him, soundly defeating the National Republicans, led by Henry Clay.

1833—Mismanagement in Robert Owen's utopian community experiment at New Harmony, Indiana, leads Josiah Warren to begin writing, printing and publishing the *Peaceful Revolutionist*, a short-lived journal which fails to live out the year.

1833, September 3—Benjamin Day ushers in the "penny press era" of cheap newspapers that common people can afford with the *Sun* (New York City), the first daily sold for only one cent a copy.

1834—Editor Abner Kneeland is convicted of blasphemy in a Massachusetts trial for promoting free-thought atheistic and deistic challenges to religion through the weekly *Boston Investigator*. This "infidel newspaper" is condemned for circulating "moral poison."

Also that year, the Whig Party is established under the leadership of Henry Clay with a platform favoring a protective tariff, internal improvements, and a national bank.

1835—Anti-Catholicism continues to be promoted in propaganda literature such as *Six Months in a Convent* by Rebecca Reed and *Imminent Dangers to the Free Institutions of the United States through Foreign Immigration* by Samuel F.B. Morse. Although Morse is today best known as a portrait painter and inventor, at the time he is also a leading force behind the formation of the Anti-Popery Union.

1836—In a blow to the liberty of the press, editor Abner Kneeland of the *Boston Investigator* is again convicted of blasphemous libel by the Massachusetts Supreme Court for his promotion of democratic, secular humanism. Although Kneeland later turns the management of the *Boston Investigator* over to Horace Seaver and others, it continues to influence the entire free-thought movement and serves to inspire later leaders such as Robert Ingersoll.

1837—Illinois newspaper editor Elijah Lovejoy is murdered by proslavery fellow residents who object to his editorializing. Lovejoy's death commits others in the abolitionist cause to increase their support for the Underground Railroad, a clandestine group of individual activists helping escaped slaves flee north. Estimates suggest that between 500 and 1,000 blacks successfully make the trek each year, up until the time of the Civil War.

1838-1839—Americans in the secret society known as Hunters Lodges raid Canada in the mistaken belief that "oppressed Canadians" want liberation from British rule.

1839—Samuel F. B. Morse exhibits his electric telegraph in New York.

1839-1840—The Whigs fail to unite and so they pass over their more famous party leaders to choose as their standard-bearer a person who can be molded—someone with few enemies, a military record, and no particular policies. General William Henry Harrison of Ohio is selected in December by the Whig party as its presidential candidate, with John Tyler of Virginia as his running mate. With no election platform, the Whigs resort to blatant, sentimental propaganda to hype Harrison's exploits and western origins. Harrison is touted as a populist hero for leading the U.S. army forces in the 1811 Battle of Tippecanoe, where Shawnee chief Tecumseh was killed. Huge rallies, songfests, and lavish parades, complete with marching bands and giant buckskin rolling balls adorned with rhyming party jingles, are held in many states during 1840 by the Whig forces, who campaign on the slogan, "Tippecanoe and Tyler Too!" More than 200 different Harrison campaign ribbons are issued, supplemented by decorative medals, log cabin-design coat buttons, and an unprecedented barrage of other political novelties worn or displayed by supporters. Printed materials are equally plentiful. The *Log Cabin*, a party news sheet edited by Horace Greeley for the Whigs from May 2 to November 20, typifies the short-run, presidential election campaign newspapers issued during the period. When opponents try to label Harrison "the log-cabin-hard-cider candidate," his partisans begin distributing free hard cider to the crowds attending their events. Democrats, who had renominated the incumbent Martin Van Buren, blast the Whigs' resort to alcohol. They also attempt to point out the weaknesses of Harrison's claims (he actually was born into a wealthy farm family, never lived in a "log cabin," and proved rather incompetent as an officer), but this backfires because Van Buren has no military record. Democrats, depicting themselves as the party of virtue during a recession, in the end prove no match for the song and drink offered by the Whig mythmakers. An estimated 80 percent of eligible voters turn out at the polls. Although Harrison only has a 145,000 vote lead, in the electoral college he rides a landslide of 234 votes to 60 for Van Buren. Ironically, Harrison dies only a month after taking office and Tyler—who favors a different political agenda from the Whig leadership—becomes the country's first unelected president.

1840—The Free-Soil party is formed on a platform opposing the extension of slavery, while other conservative abolitionists form the Liberty party. The two political organizations merge in 1848 and by the mid-1850s are subsumed within the new Republican party.

1841—Growing influence of followers of Joseph Smith, Jr. creates a backlash typified by publication of *The Mormons; or, Knavery Exposed.*

Also that year, publisher James Gordon Bennett's *New York Herald* is the first American newspaper to begin a Sunday edition.

1843—Volney Palmer of Philadelphia opens the first advertising agency.

1843, October 13—B'nai B'rith is established as a Jewish Masonic secret society.

1844—Mormon leader Joseph Smith is murdered in the Carthage, Missouri, jail. The church organization he created splinters into several competing religious sects, with the majority following the leadership of Brigham Young.

In the East, Morse's telegraph is used between Baltimore and Washington, D.C., showing its potential to revolutionize communication.

Also in 1844, Democrats and Whigs both commit record sums to their presidential candidates, with each adopting the "hurrah" mass politics style of campaigning popularized by Jackson and Harrison earlier. A leading journal of that time, *Niles' Register*, reports that:

Standards are erected not only at places for holding elections—places of party meetings, and before public hotels, but hundreds are to be seen in every county at private residences towering far above the forest trees and decorated with the names, ensigns or flags of the partisans. Processions—standards—transparencies—bands of music—thundering artillery—burning tar barrels—and all the other para-phernalia of electioneering warfare are in active requisition.

Despite his effort at imagemaking, Whig candidate Henry Clay lacks the common touch and straddles the thorny question of admitting Texas as a slave state. Democrat James K. Polk forthrightly favors immediate annexation and is able to win the swing state of New York by more than 5,000 votes, thus capturing the presidency that Clay had so long coveted but never attained.

1845—English interests lay the first submarine telegraph cable across the English Channel. Later, British-controlled cables span the Atlantic to give that country great influence lasting more than a century over international information flow from Europe to the United States—especially during wartime.

Mid-1840s—Irish landlords fear the Molly Maguires, rebellious male peasants who dress in women's clothes to disguise their identities. The rebels' rejection of authority later influences American workers.

1846-1848—"Manifest Destiny" proponents in the North flood the country in the 1840s with literature designed to raise patriotic fervor for national expansion, culminating in the Mexican-American War, which is fought over the status of Texas and California. U.S. troops invade Mexico, eventually capturing Mexico City. The Mexican government capitulates by signing the Treaty of Guadalupe-Hidalgo on February 2, 1848, which cedes most of the disputed territory in return for $15 million.

1847—Failure of the potato crops leads to mass starvation in Ireland. The "Great Famine" results in new mass immigration to the United States.

The same year, the first adhesive postage stamps go on sale in the United States, featuring portraits of George Washington and Benjamin Franklin.

1848—A series of revolutions against the established order breaks out across Europe, aided by appearance of *The Communist Manifesto*. At first anonymously published, the work becomes so influential that its writers, Karl Marx and Friedrich Engels, emerge as intellectual leaders of the movement. Only a few months after publication of *The Communist Manifesto*, Orestes Brownson (described by Russell Kirk as "an American thinker of most remarkable talents, who . . . in 1840 was the original American Marxist") represents through his essay, "Socialism and the Church," and later writings those intellectuals expressing the American revulsion against envy as the basis for social action. However, nineteenth-century socialism in America is most identified with the widespread migration to the United States by German and other revolutionary believers in syndicalist doctrines forced into exile because their European revolts generally proved abortive. Over the next decade, the great tide of immigration to America is swelled by various ethnic groups seeking economic betterment, religious liberty, and political freedom. The emigrants provoke a violent reaction from Americans most threatened by social change, chiefly among those found along the populous Atlantic seaboard. Growing reactionary agitation seeks to exclude foreign-born citizens and Catholics from elective or appointive office.

1848, January 24—News of the discovery of gold in California spurs widespread interest, within a year bringing a horde of fortune seekers westward (the '49er Gold Rush). Later finds of precious metals in the far western territories further demonstrate the need for a more regularized coast-to-coast transportation and communication network and ensure conflict with the Native American tribes who inhabit the land routes.

1849—Latter-day Saint followers of Brigham Young in the intermountain West hold a convention to petition Congress to admit the State of Deseret (meaning "land of the honeybee," from *The Book of Mormon*). Opposition to polygamy, however, leads Congress to refuse and, the following year, instead to organize the territory of Utah. Mormons provide hospitality, to '49ers headed for the California gold fields, making Salt Lake City a regular overland stop for later pioneers.

The same year, Henry David Thoreau writes a famous essay, *On the Duty of Civil Disobedience*, which outlines his antiauthoritarian fear of democratic tyranny.

In upstate New York, the Order of the Star Spangled Banner is created, pledged to "preserve America for Americans." The order's "nativist" platform is centered on ridding the country of "immigrant corruption," particularly by "checking the stride of the foreign and alien, of thwarting the machinations and subverting the deadly plans of the Jesuit and Papist." Members of the order are bound to secrecy and serve as the nucleus for the spread of the Know-Nothing political movement during the mid-1850s.

1850s—Proslavery forces are active in the period up through the Civil War, issuing tracts and lobbying for support in Congress. In the South, states pass additional sedition laws criminalizing the publication of statements advocating the abolition of slavery. In many locations, no blacks or mulattos (whether slave or free) are permitted to be on the streets or hold assemblies of any kind at night.

In addition, the widespread usage of telegraphy by newspapers increases the speed and range of reports available to the general public, challenging the de facto control by government and military officials over information traditionally classified as intelligence.

1850, June 3-July 3—Governor John A. Quitman of Mississippi organizes delegates from nine states that are committed to maintaining the rights of slaveholders at a convention in Nashville. The threat of secession is taken seriously by President Zachary Taylor, who seeks Quitman's indictment by a federal grand jury (issued on June 21) for violating U.S. neutrality laws because of the governor's unauthorized and well-financed attempts to "liberate" Cuba from Spain. Taylor, on July 3, warns that those "taken in rebellion against the Union" will hang for treason. The following day, Taylor falls mysteriously ill and dies. Quitman is never prosecuted and becomes active in advancing the careers of fellow Mexican-American War veterans Jefferson Davis and General Franklin Pierce.

1851—*New York Times* begins publication.

1851-1852—Harriet Beecher Stowe's powerful propaganda novel indicting slavery, *Uncle Tom's Cabin*, sells 300,000 copies during its first year of publication, contributing significantly to the strengthening of the abolitionist movement.

1852, November—General Franklin Pierce, "a northern man with southern principles," is a dark horse candidate for the Democratic party nomination and goes on to win the presidential election. His campaign is secretly aided by financial backing provided by August Belmont, the U.S. representative of the Rothschild banking interests in Britain. With the failure of their candidate, General Winfield Scott, the dispirited and divided Whigs withdraw from the national scene.

1853, January 28—Abolitionist Wendell Phillips declares that "eternal vigilance is the price of liberty" in a speech to the Massachusetts Anti-Slavery Society.

1853, February—Early American suffragettes, Paulina Wright Davis and Caroline H. Dall, begin publication in Washington, D.C., of their magazine, *Una*.

1854—The Native American party (commonly referred to as the American or Know-Nothing party because its members are said to answer "I know nothing," to all questions) is officially formed by a faction of the northern Whigs. The organization is connected to a network of secret societies seeking to crush the power of the foreign-born in U.S. politics, especially through racist, anti-Catholic agitation against Irish immigrants. Sensationalist books such as *Popery! As It Was and As It Is*, by William Hogan, a former priest who turned against the church after his excommunication, provide valuable propaganda ammunition during the campaign. The Native American party is successful in electing six governors (including Henry J. Gardner of Massachusetts, who had the backing of a friendly legislature) and 75 congressmen in 1854, but the movement fails to overcome internal differences over the slavery issue.

Another nativist secret Masonic society, known as Knights of the Golden Circle, forms in Cincinnati, Ohio, to promote a new proslavery empire combining parts of the United States with new territories acquired through armed conquest of Mexico, the Caribbean, and Latin America, in concert with British interests. During the Civil War, many members join the Confederacy or become northern "Copperheads," engaging in pro-southern paramilitary espionage and propaganda.

Fearing an invasion, Spanish authorities emancipate most Cuban slaves, encourage racial intermarriage, and recruit the freed blacks into an armed militia designed to resist "gringo" aggression. Their fears of intervention are well founded. Public exposure occurs when James A. Bulloch, American captain of the *Black Warrior*, is arrested by Spanish authorities when his ship docks in Havana. The purpose of the voyage is as an advance party for the intended "liberation" of the island by up to 50,000 U.S.-based mercenaries. Bulloch's racist intrigues are sponsored by Governor John A. Quitman of Mississippi, who in turn is backed by a secret cabal of Masonic conspirators and New York financiers. The arrest sets off demands by Attorney General Caleb Cushing for a naval blockade of Cuba, and by Senator John Slidell of Louisiana for the repeal of U.S. neutrality laws. The crisis eventually dies down, but the so-called *Black Warrior* affair reflects the continuing desire of proslavery forces to extend their influence.

The Kansas-Nebraska Act of 1854 establishes two new territories under the new doctrine of "popular sovereignty," meaning that those who settle in each territory have the right to decide whether or not they sanction slavery. This contradicts earlier provisions of the Missouri Compromise which stated that slavery would not be extended to those parts of the West. The act brings strong believers in both options westward, with the strife resulting in "bleeding Kansas," which served as a metaphor for the national Civil War to follow.

Also in 1854, the temperance propaganda play, *Little Katy; or, The Hot Corn Girl*, enjoys a successful run. It tells a tragic tale of a young girl's death brought about by the alcoholism of her parents.

1854, February—Continuing sectional conflict leads to new political alignments, resulting in the formation of the Republican party, which is fused from the antislavery remnants of the Whigs, Free Soilers, disgruntled Democrats, and other parties.

1854, October 18—The Ostend Manifesto, declaring the right of the United States to control Cuba, is drafted in that Belgian city by Pierre Soulé (U.S. minister to Spain), in conjunction James Buchanan (U.S. minister to Great Britain), and John Y. Mason (U.S. minister to France). Their purpose is to aid America's "Manifest Destiny" and preserve slavery.

1855—David Hughes invents the printing telegraph. The same year, military adventurer William Walker invades Nicaragua with an armed company of men, overthrows the government, and establishes himself as that nation's president. The United States recognizes his new filibuster regime, but Walker makes the mistake of irritating Cornelius Vanderbilt, who controls Nicaragua's cross-country transportation and successfully maneuvers to force Walker from power.

1856—The new Republican party nominates explorer John C. Frémont ("The Path Finder"), who is noted for his exploits in California, as their presidential candidate under the banner of "Free Speech, Free Press, Free Soil, Free Men, Frémont and Victory." The American-Whig coalition chooses former President Millard Fillmore as their standard-bearer, while Land Reform party activists select Gerrit Smith to carry their message. However, voters are feeling jittery over the ongoing threats to the national government by sectional interests and radical advocates and decide that the compromise policies of Democrat James Buchanan offer the best hope for future peace and security.

Also in 1856, Virginia slave Henry Brown, aided by abolitionist James A. Smith, gains his freedom by secretly stowing away in a crate shipped through the mail from Richmond to Philadelphia.

1857—The Fenian Brotherhood, a body of Irish patriots and exiles, organizes in the United States to bring about Ireland's revolutionary independence from England.

1857, March 6—In a setback for the abolitionist cause, the Supreme Court holds in the *Dred Scott* decision that blacks could not be citizens of the United States The ruling comes as the level of pro-slavery propaganda intensifies. Books from enthusiastic apologists include *Cannibals All, or Slaves without Masters*, by George Fitzhugh of Virginia, which portrays the patriarchal-family-slavery model in the most favorable light, and *Slavery Ordained of God*, by the Reverend F.A. Ross, D.D., a Presbyterian pastor at Huntsville, Alabama, who takes the position that what is good for women is equally good for blacks.

1858—Voters in Illinois attend a series of entertaining public debates between Democrat Stephen A. Douglas and Republican Abraham Lincoln. The two candidates each seeks to persuade voters to cast their ballots for state representatives pledged to support him for U.S. Senator. Although the lesser-known Lincoln loses to Douglas in his Senate bid, he becomes a national figure in the process. The intellectual quality of the debates and their analysis of many of the country's most important issues results in widespread press coverage that impresses many readers. On July 31, in one of his most memorable statements, Lincoln observes: "With public sentiment, nothing can fail; without it, nothing can succeed. Consequently, he who molds public sentiment goes deeper than he who enacts statutes or pronounces decisions."

The same year, the first regular mail service, the Butterfield Overland Mail, is inaugurated between the East and West coasts.

1859—John Stuart Mill's famous essay in defense of individual rights, *On Liberty*, and Charles Darwin's challenge to conventional religious views about the nature of humanity, *On the Origin of Species*, are first published. These two controversial books prove to be immediate successes, but also have lasting intellectual and public policy influence.

1859, October 16—The U.S. arsenal at Harpers Ferry, Virginia, is seized by radical abolitionist John Brown and a company of 22 supporters hoping to incite a slave rebellion. The insurrection fails and Brown is hanged for murder and treason.

1860s—Beadle's "dime novels" glorify gun-toting "heroes" in the American West.

1860, May-November—The increasing instability of the national political scene results in another four-way presidential contest, which is overshadowed by the threats of secession and war. The Democrats split their support, with Stephen A. Douglas representing the national Democrats and John C. Breckinridge, the breakaway southern Democrats. The Republicans select Abraham Lincoln, while voters who favor none of the other candidates turn to John Bell of the new Constitutional Union party. On November 6, Lincoln is narrowly elected by the badly fragmented electorate. southern radicals see the results as devastating and accelerate their plans to divide the Union.

1860, December 18—The "Crittenden Compromise," which is intended to avoid war, by giving in to most of the southern radical demands and guaranteeing the legality of slavery throughout United States, fails in Congress only because delegations from a number of the seceding states refuse to take their seats.

1861—The telegraph connection is completed to California, making obsolete the short-lived Pony Express.

1861, February 4—The Confederate States of America is officially formed.

1861, February 18—Jefferson Davis of Mississippi is inaugurated as president of the new Confederacy.

1861, March 4—Abraham Lincoln takes office, with seven states already having seceded. The inaugural address is very carefully crafted to try to avoid saying anything that will spark a clash of arms, with Lincoln remarking that all Americans "are not enemies, but friends." The president hopes that leaders in the seceding states will reconsider and make efforts to come back into the Union. However, many of the reports on the speech appearing in northern and southern newspapers offer interpretations that deliberately distort his plain message of conciliation.

1861, April 12—The tinderbox of American division is lit when Confederate troops fire on the Union-held Fort Sumter in Charleston, South Carolina.

1861, April 12-1865, May 10—The American Civil War evolves into one of the most bloody in history. The conflict is also referred to as the "War between the States" and, by some of the un-Reconstructed (those who still feel the south morally was in the right), as the "War against Northern

Aggression." President Lincoln is vilified by some journalists but also proves adept at press manipulation. He drops choice news tips to friendly reporters, even rewarding many with money and political office. Lincoln also resorts to the first official U.S. government censorship of news media during wartime. The president claims an executive power, based on military emergency, to arrest and imprison journalists (along with other citizens) who are suspected of disloyalty. Northern state authorities actively move to shut down certain newspapers in an effort to stifle growing opposition to the war. Many of the trappings of contemporary journalism, such as the press conference, press pass, and author bylines, are further instituted by military leaders in order to censor battle reportage unfavorable to the Union. Lincoln also personally dispatches approximately one hundred special agents to Britain along with a ship load of foodstuffs for unemployed English cotton-textile workers to counter propaganda gains made by the Confederacy. In the North, the art of pamphleteering is advanced by the unceasing efforts of private organizations such as the Loyal Publication Society and the Union League Board of Publications. Despite free speech guarantees in the Confederate States' Constitution, publishers in the South also face rigid controls compounded by shortages of newsprint. Although still widely debated, a growing number of scholars see the Civil War in terms of a British empire-sponsored insurrection coordinated through a coalition of pro-slavery secret societies, Latin American expansionists, and financial interests which seek to weaken the United States' competitive threat to English interests.

1863, January 1—As a temporary war measure, President Lincoln issues an Emancipation Proclamation freeing the slaves in those states still in rebellion against the Union.

1863, July 13-16—Draft riots by New York City residents opposing involuntary war service in the Union Army leads to mob control of the municipality for four days. More than a thousand people are killed and $1.5 million in damage is incurred during the rioting.

1864—Despite a strong challenge from peace now advocates, a series of war victories strengthen Lincoln's hand and he is easily reelected. About the same time, the American Free Trade League is established by London insurance executive Alfred Pell (a descendent of Tory loyalist émigrés) through the efforts of his New York-based sons.

1865—Beginning with telegraphy, the forerunner of the International Telecommunication Union (ITU) is established to foster harmony between nations in the planning, use, standardization, coordination, and regulation of telecommunications through bilateral and multilateral agreements.

Work featuring the rascals "Max and Moritz" by German cartoonist Wilhelm Busch is published in a newspaper, inaugurating the basis for the modern comic strip.

1865, April 9—Robert E. Lee, the general-in-chief of the Confederate Army, surrenders his forces to General Ulysses S. Grant at Appomattox Court House, Virginia.

1865, April 14—Abraham Lincoln is shot while attending a play at Ford's Theater in Washington, D.C., by noted actor John Wilkes Booth, a southern sympathizer.

1865, April 15—Lincoln, the Union leader, dies just as battlefield successes are about to bring an end to the Civil War's carnage. The method of Lincoln's death and an apparent rush to judgment by authorities prompt continuing—and conflicting—stories about a conspiracy engineered by his political enemies. Andrew Johnson succeeds to the presidency, facing a Congress hostile to his efforts to carry out Lincoln's vision of a reunited America. Even before the fallen president is cold in the ground, a cult of adulation is fostered by northern radicals, who begin to promote the Lincoln icon as soon as he is dead, but gut his programs for national reconciliation.

1865, May 10—Confederate President Jefferson Davis is captured by Union troops.

1865, December 4—A "Joint Committee on Reconstruction" is appointed by President Johnson to plan for the readmission of southern states to the U.S. Congress. Johnson grants more news interviews during his term of office than any previous president but suffers from a highly negative press. The new president's efforts aimed at restoring the nation are continuously stymied by the radical Republicans who control Congress. They later fail by only one vote in an attempt to force him from office through trumped-up impeachment charges.

1866-1900—At the close of the Civil War, the full impact of industrialism and the importance of public opinion in the United States, begin to be felt. The nation becomes a fertile land for the growth of corporate America. The war cost the nation a great deal of money, encouraging westward expansion and speculative ventures. Kingpins (called by their enemies "Robber Barons"), who could generate big money—sometimes by bold stock fraud schemes and the ruthless treatment of their adversaries—take advantage of the situation to form trusts that have a substantial impact on the last 35 years of the century. In addition to capital, the nation's infrastructure begins to burgeon as local markets are displaced by national ones. The slow evolution from a rural-agricultural to an urban-industrial society demands that farm produce reach the urban industrial areas. This leaves farmers as the victims of the railroads, which favor corporate producers and often charge more for local shipment than for long-distance freight. In the midst of these new economic forces, government is, at best, a benign participant and often proves to be a pawn of the corporate builders.

1866—The Fenian Brotherhood seeks to mobilize sympathy in the United States by becoming more active in issuing propaganda. In the Fenians' case, they attempt to energize anti-British sentiment by staging an invasion of Canada with between 800 and 900 men, actually capturing Fort Erie in an uprising that Fenian leaders mistakenly hope will inflame annexationist sentiment in the United States.

1867—A group called the Patrons of Husbandry (better known as the Grangers) is organized by farm cooperative associations to pressure state governments in the Midwest to help alleviate problems of debt, stop falling crop prices, and lower the notoriously high transportation rates set by the railroad trusts.

That same year, the Ku Klux Klan is founded in Nashville, Tennessee, by General Albert Pike and others as a secret society designed to reverse the growing political challenge by advocates for black and Catholic civil rights. Pike is already a controversial figure. He played a key conspiratorial role in the Knights of the Golden Circle, served as supreme commander of Scottish Rite

Freemasonry in the South, engaged in war crimes perpetuated in the Civil War, and practiced Satanism. Within three years of its founding, the Klan grows to an estimated 550,000 members, who adopt white hoods and costumes to terrorize victims and protect the perpetrators' identity. The Klan conducts a series of fiery cross illuminations, church burnings, beatings, and lynchings which last through the end of Reconstruction. With the introduction of Jim Crow laws reestablishing white racism, the Klan is largely dormant until the popular success of the spectacular motion picture *Birth of a Nation* in 1915 boosts renewed interest in its creed.

1867, July 1—Most of the English- and French-speaking North American colonies controlled by Britain in lands north of the United States are formally integrated as provinces in a newly federated Canada.

1868—The typewriter is invented.

1869—The transcontinental railroad is completed, much of it built by Irish and Chinese laborers, with the driving of a ceremonial golden spike at Promontory Point, Utah. The photograph commemorating the event leaves out any evidence of minority participation.

Also that year, the Labor Reform party (later called the National Labor Reform party), becomes the first national working-class political organization in the U.S.

1869, March 4—Republican Ulysses S. Grant, famous as the general who finally brought victory to the Union Army in the Civil War, begins the first of his two presidential terms.

1869, September 1—The Prohibition party emerges from a temperance convention in Chicago with a mandate to seek a number of social and political reforms, including legislation prohibiting "the importation, manufacture and sale of all intoxicating drinks."

1869, December 10—The movement to bring the right to vote to American women receives a boost when Wyoming Territory becomes the first to grant full suffrage to its female citizens.

1870s—To pay for its over extension, the Union Pacific Railroad conducts a vigorous "Go West" promotion to further its business interests by encouraging settlers to form communities along the rail lines. Among those attracted are immigrants such as the Mennonites who seek religious and economic freedom. Pressure builds on the government from the rail interests and the increasing horde of settlers to end the "Indian problem" once and for all. More aggressive efforts to force Native Americans onto prison "reservations" are undertaken by the U.S. Army. A new series of "Indian Wars" results which demonstrate the courage and tenacity of the central and western tribes, who refuse to be assimilated at gun point. When diplomacy and military means prove incapable of defeating the Plains Indians, the U.S. Army encourages trainloads of hunters to wipe out millions of bison ("the buffalo slaughter") in order to destroy the natural food supply of their resourceful foes. By 1883, only a few thousand of the magnificent animals are left, ending the main lifeline to Native American independence.

Also in the 1870s, magazines first use color printing technology.

1870, January 15—The donkey symbol is first linked to the Democratic party in a *Harper's Weekly* political cartoon by Thomas Nast.

1872—First complete U.S. publication of *The Communist Manifesto* in

English, appears in a sensational weekly put out by sisters Victoria Woodhull and Tennessee Claflin, heads of New York Section 12 of the First International.

1873—Ezra H. Heywood's essay on *Uncivil Liberty* presents a famed human rights defense of legal and political equality for women and argues for an improved social environment based on equity and mutual respect.

1874—Farm, labor, and other economic interests who seek easy credit and inflation form the Independent National party, better known by its popular name as the Greenback party. About the same time, opponents, led by Alexander Mitchell and Lyman Gage, form the Honest Money League of the Northwest in Chicago as a propaganda agency seeking to force a contractionist credit policy by outlawing non-interest-paying government greenback currency first issued during the Civil War by order of Abraham Lincoln.

1874, November 7—The Republican party elephant symbol evolves from a critical political cartoon appearing in *Harper's Weekly* by Thomas Nast which compares its politics to those of a cumbersome, purposeless beast to indicate his disappointment with the "Grand Old Party (GOP)."

1876—Alexander Graham Bell perfects the telephone.

1876, June 25—Continued mistreatment of Native Americans by the United States government culminates in the Battle of Little Big Horn in Montana. All 265 men under the command of 7th Calvary leader George A. Custer are killed. Almost alone among newspapers of the day, the *Pilot* (located in Boston) declares Custer an ineffective military tactician who was outsmarted by forces with legitimate grievances. By campaigning in his publication, not only for the cause of his fellow Irish-Americans, but also in defense of the rights of blacks, Jews, Native Americans, and others who were oppressed, editor and owner John Boyle O'Reilly gains respect from many while incurring widespread censure from powerful enemies.

1877—Thomas Alva Edison invents the phonograph as an ideal aid for taking down dictation, one of more than 1,500 patents he is to receive.

A landmark Supreme Court ruling in *Munn v. Illinois* holds that state legislatures can regulate private property in the public interest. The case follows passage, in 1873, of a controversial bill by the Granger-controlled legislature in Illinois which set rates for farm grain storage in railroad warehouses.

Pittsburgh workers of the Baltimore and Ohio Railroad strike to protest a wage reduction, setting off a spontaneous wave of sympathy strikes in numerous cities across the country.

The Socialist Labor party is formed in the United States.

1878—George Eastman invents celluloid photofilm.

1879-1909—Charles Taze Russell cofounds the religious magazine *Zion's Watch Tower and Herald of Christ's Presence*. Later, Zion's Watch Tower Bible and Tract Society is formally incorporated in 1884 at Allegheny, Pennsylvania, with Russell as its first president. The Watch Tower Society, which originally is to be "nothing more than a publishing house," over time evolves into what believers call "God's organization, the only ark of salvation." Scores of local Bible study congregations (known as *ecclesias*) mushroom into existence in the East and Midwest as part of his rapidly growing, socioreligious movement. By the turn of the century, the work of

"Pastor Russell" becomes international. In 1909, he moves the society's headquarters to Brooklyn, New York.

1879—Millions of readers buy copies of Henry George's *Progress and Poverty*, which advocates a socialistic program to enact a single tax on individual property. George argues this will extirpate poverty by creating common ownership of land.

That same year, the incandescent lamp is perfected.

1881—Individualist anarchist Benjamin Tucker begins publishing *Liberty*, a magazine which provides a forum for authors who argue that people would be better off without government intervention in their lives. *Liberty*, which continues until 1908, presents provocative articles covering a wide range of public policy issues which are still with us today, such as the "evils of taxation, government schools and income redistribution," the quest for women's rights, and free trade.

1881, May 21—Clara Barton founds the American Red Cross.

1882—German radical Johan Most arrives in the United States, where he preaches communist anarchism and "the propaganda of the deed."

1883—Karl Marx dies in London. The American anarchist group known as the International Working People's Association, holds a convention in Pittsburgh, Pennsylvania, which issues its own manifesto calling for "equal rights for all without distinction of sex or race."

That same year, Joseph Pulitzer takes over the *New York World*, beginning the popular press era of sensationalized news.

1884—The fountain pen first appears and Paul Nipkow of Britain invents a scanning wheel which is critical to the development of television in Europe and America.

Also in 1884, Irish immigrant Samuel S. McClure establishes the first American newspaper syndicate.

In that November's presidential election, Republicans chide Democrat Grover Cleveland over his illegitimate child with the slogan "Ma, Ma, where's my Pa?" and Democrats counter by calling the Republican standard-bearer, "Blaine, Blaine, James G. Blaine, continental liar from the state of Maine." Although not the first political leader to grant interviews and provide inside information to journalists, following his victory President-elect Grover Cleveland begins the unprecedented practice of seeing a group of reporters regularly. Despite his overt disdain for the press, Cleveland recognizes its importance in influencing public opinion. From his practice of fielding questions from various reporters evolves the presidential news conference.

1885, May—Police and striking workers clash during the Haymarket Square Riot in Chicago. At a follow-up protest meeting called by August Spies, editor of Chicago's German-language anarchist newspaper, *Arbeiter-Zeitung*, a bomb is thrown into the crowd.

1885, September 2—Hundreds of Chinese laborers are murdered by Union Pacific Coal miners in the Rock Springs Massacre, triggering an upsurge in anti-Asian bigotry throughout America.

1886—Independent candidate Henry George runs on a "single tax" program for mayor of New York. National attention is drawn to the race. When George is favored to win against the Democratic party candidate, moneyed interests are successful in nominating the demagogic Theodore Roosevelt to serve as a spoiler. The three-way contest, scare propaganda against George, and ballot stuffing by the Democratic Tammany Hall machine end the Single Taxer's threat to form a national political party. George dies several years later. Roosevelt, though he also loses the election, earns loyalty points that prove useful in his later runs for public office.

1887—An American of German origin, Emile Berliner, receives a patent for a round gramophone disk as a replacement to Edison's more cumbersome phonograph cylinder. In addition, the Kinetoscope is marketed by Edison to show moving pictures in arcades.

The Interstate Commerce Act passes Congress with the support of farm interests, and invokes the notion of the "common good," to counter unfair railroad rates. The act lays the legal groundwork for public interest terminology in subsequent regulation, including controls on U.S. broadcasting. It also creates the Interstate Commerce Commission in an attempt to bring into check the rates charged customers by the railroads. However, some railroad executives actually welcomed it as a protective cover.

Acting contrary to previous U.S. government promises to respect Native American land rights, a large-scale movement of non-Indians onto Indian reservations begins following passage of the General Allotment Act. This effort to eliminate the so-called primitive and backward ways of life practiced by Indian peoples is popularly presented as a progressive demonstration of liberal democracy and Manifest Destiny, with proponents arguing that "Indians must be protected from the ravages of progress." However, the act effectively ends more than 260 years of treaty relations between the United States and hundreds of sovereign Indian nations.

1887, May 19—Charles B. Reynolds goes on trial in a New Jersey state court for the alleged crime of blasphemy because he distributed a pamphlet arguing against the infallibility of the Bible. Despite a state constitution clause that "No law shall be passed to restrain or abridge the liberty of speech or of the press" and an able defense by freethought spokesman Robert G. Ingersoll, Reynolds is convicted.

1887, November 11—Although who actually conspired to perpetrate the Haymarket Square bombing remains a mystery, eight men are convicted, more for their political beliefs than on actual evidence. Four anarchists, including newspaper editor August Spies, are hanged.

1888—The Kodak box camera and ballpoint pen first enter the commercial marketplace.

1889—The first corporate public relations department is established by Westinghouse to promote alternating current (AC) as the standard for the burgeoning electricity industry. The Edison Company, which favors direct current (DC), soon joins in this battle of corporate and industry image building by sponsoring a book, entitled *A Warning*, which is intended to scare readers by pointing to the State of New York's decision to use alternating current when administering capital punishment. Westinghouse's public relations head, former Pittsburgh newspaperman E.H. Heinrichs, in a successful attempt to win public acceptance and gain approval by governmental agencies, counters by subsidizing an opposing book on *The Safety of the Alternating System for Electrical Distribution*.

1890-1914—Populist sentiment has a lasting effect on American politics and society. The Progressive movement also strongly influences American culture, with historians commonly labeling this period the Progressive Era. These and other competing social forces seriously challenge the courts of the day to uphold the rule of law. According to Howard Gillman's *The Constitution Besieged* (1993, pp. 9-10):

The crisis in American constitutionalism that arose around the turn of the century becomes a story not of the sudden corruption of the law and judicial function, but rather of how the judiciary's struggle to maintain the coherence and integrity of a constitutional jurisprudence ultimately was derailed by the maturation of capitalist forms of production and the unprecedented efforts of legislatures to extend special protections to groups that considered themselves vulnerable to increasingly coercive market mechanisms.

1890-1898—Daniel De Leon, said to be the only American Marxist theoretician for whom Nicolai (V.I.) Lenin had any respect, becomes head of the Socialist Labor party. The party's influence in the period exceeds its vote-getting abilities, which peaks at 82,000 in 1898, after which splits in the movement draw attention to other socialist political vehicles.

1890—The widespread acceptance in the United States of nativist views and their use in stirring up the masses by propagandists for the existing order is typified by the remarks of Professor R.M. Smith who asserts (reprinted later in Roy L. Garis, *Immigration Restriction*, 1927):

An indication of the unfortunate effect of introducing so many men of foreign birth and belief into our social body is seen in the recent outbreaks of anarchism and socialism. These movements are always led and for the most part carried on by persons of foreign birth. Socialism and anarchism are not plants of American growth nor of Anglo-Saxon origin. They are not natural to the American mind; neither are they due to any deterioration in the condition of the laboring class in this country, and thus the fruit of despair and hopelessness in regard to the future. They are the importations of foreign agitators who come here for the purpose of making converts to their doctrines.

Also in 1890, John Boyle O'Reilly, a battler for civil rights in the United States, dies. Although the magazine was harshly critical of O'Reilly during his lifetime, the obituary in *Harper's Weekly* acknowledges that he "was easily the most distinguished Irishman in America. He was one of the country's foremost poets, one of its most influential journalists, [and] an orator of unusual power."

1891—Canadian Prime Minister John A. McDonald attacks a free trade proposal by the opposition Liberal party to lower tariff barriers with the United States, calling it "veiled treason" because of "the prospect of ultimately becoming a portion of the American Union." That same year, Charles Edward Coughlin is born in Canada.

1892-1900—Henry D. Traute, a matchbook salesman for the Diamond Match Company, at first fails to get a contract from William Wrigley, the Chicago chewing gum king. However, Traute finally obtains an unbelievable order for one billion matchbooks after threatening to give away Wrigley's gum to advertise Diamond matches. By the turn of the century, the advertising matchbook is widely used as a specialty communication item.

1892—The Homestead Strike against the Carnegie Steel Company becomes one of the most violent in U.S. history. Homestead proves to unskilled labor that corporate giants such as Carnegie are determined to resort to murder if necessary to destroy unions.

That same year, the first color photograph is published.

1892, February—Populists in the National Farmer's Alliance and Industrial Union, spurred by midwestern electoral successes, convene in St. Louis to organize the People's party. More than 1,300 delegates later gather in Omaha to nominate former Union General James B. Weaver, of Boonesville, Iowa, as the party's presidential nominee. Key figures at the convention include Kansas lawyer and politician Mary Ellen Lease, who is credited with coining the phrase "farmers should raise less corn and more hell," and Minnesota politician and writer Ignatius Donnelly, whose rhetorical skills lead him to be called "the greatest orator of populism." Weaver carries five states and garners 9 percent of the national vote in the November election.

1892, August 28—The Socialist Labor party (SLP) nominates the first openly socialist presidential candidate in U.S. history. The 1892 SLP ticket consists of Simon Wing for president and Charles Matchett for vice president.

1892, November—Democrat Grover Cleveland is elected to his second term as president.

1893—A contraction in available financing causes the Panic of 1893 and creates a severe business depression, leading many to reconsider the liabilities associated with industrial concentrations and the unbridled pursuit of wealth. Farmers and others champion financial reform. Congressional passage of the Safety Appliance Act is a landmark in consumer regulation, continuing efforts to limit corporate power.

The Antisaloon League is formed as a nonpartisan organization to spread temperance propaganda and exert political influence to suppress the manufacture and sale of intoxicating liquor.

The crusading *McClure's Magazine* begins publication. It features well-known writers who collectively become known as *the muckrakers*.

Printing presses and imprinting devices are developed that produce clear, colorful, long-lasting messages. Newspaper color presses are first used by New York City publishers seeking to make their product more graphically appealing during a long running and bitter circulation war. The emerging specialty advertising industry also benefits from advances in technology and mass production. At the World's Columbian Exposition in Chicago, Henry J. Heinz has trouble attracting visitors to his company exhibit and so hires some boys to hand out cards good for a free souvenir from his booth. As a result, the fair officials have to summon police to control the crowds lining up to receive a small key chain charm in the shape of a pickle and bearing the word "Heinz." By the end of the fair, Heinz has given away one million of the charms and become a household name.

1894—The first newsfilm in the United States is produced by Thomas Edison and his associates, who photograph a prize fight.

The American Railway Union under Eugene Debs strikes against the heartless practices of the Pullman Company, eventually encompassing a struggle by workers against 24 railroads, federal troops, and a U.S. court system that is biased against unions.

1895-1897—Radical J.A. Wayland begins publication of the *Appeal to Reason* in Kansas City, and it soon becomes one of the most widely circulated U.S. newspapers. In 1897, he moves publication to Girard, Kansas. The paper has a socialist slant and advocates radical notions such as state ownership of factories, an end to child labor, and women's rights. President Theodore Roosevelt is so angered by the editorial stance of the *Appeal to Reason* that he denounces it as a "vituperative organ of pornography, anarchy and bloodshed." Others call it the "Squeal of Treason."

1895—Membership in the American Federation of Labor approaches 350,000, and the National Association of Manufacturers (NAM) is established to serve as a federation of trade associations representing the interests of major American industrial businesses.

1895, May 5—The first color comic strip is "Hogan's Alley" (by Richard Outcault in Joseph Pulitzer's *New York World*), which weaves social commentary in stories about a captivating group of orphaned tenement youth in New York City. The unnamed central character becomes known as the Yellow Kid because of a printer's decision to color him that way. William Randolph Hearst soon buys the *New York Morning Journal* to compete with Joseph Pulitzer. Their two colorful Sunday comic inserts prove to be enormously popular, with Hearst boasting that his paper's section is "eight pages of iridescent polychromous effulgence that makes the rainbow look like a piece of lead pipe." An ego-driven personal feud between the news magnates escalates after Hearst lures Outcault away from Pulitzer with a higher salary. The resulting newspaper war between Pulitzer's *World* and Hearst's *Journal* over rights to the Yellow Kid leads to the term "yellow journalism" being widely applied to the brand of sensation-oriented publishing they practice.

1896—The first attempts at movie censorship in the United States stem from fears that the voluptuous exertions of *Delorita in the Passion Dance* would prove corrupting. Large black bars are added to the film to cover Delorita's more notable movements.

That same year, wireless telegraphy is patented by Guglielmo Marconi, and the Nobel Peace Prize is established by the will of Alfred Nobel, the millionaire Swedish industrialist who invented dynamite.

1896, April 23—The first official showing of projected motion pictures to a paying audience in the United States occurs at Koster & Bial's Music Hall in New York City. Featured is a program of short films using "Thomas A. Edison's Latest Marvel, the Vitascope," which the *New York Times* in its review the following day, finds "wonderfully real and singularly exhilarating."

1896, July 11-November 3—Populist William Jennings Bryan of Nebraska is selected as the Democratic party's presidential standard-bearer at their national convention in Chicago after delivering his passionate "Cross of Gold" speech. Bryan, known as "The Great Commoner," crisscrosses the country, giving over six hundred speeches attacking the trusts, railroads, and gold standard advocates. His Republican opponent, William McKinley, instead relies on a Wall Street-backed media campaign orchestrated by his manager, Mark Hanna. A former journalist, Hanna symbolically links McKinley to the flag and tirelessly pays reporters and clergymen to boost McKinley. For example, the Reverend Cortland Meyers warns his congregation that "The

Democratic Platform Is Made in Hell." What we would now call public relations is also used to place pro-McKinley and anti-Bryan messages in the nation's newspapers and magazines. For example, the *New York Times*, in a September editorial answers "yes" to the question, "Is Bryan Crazy?" Hanna dispatches 1,400 surrogate speakers throughout the country to discuss and distribute a series of pamphlets, many up to 40 pages long, issued by the Republican campaign. Workers' pay envelopes are stuffed with Republican party pamphlets and they are required to hear campaign pep talks during lunch time. Many find their labor contracts are rewritten to contain cancellation clauses threatening the loss of their jobs if Bryan wins. Not surprisingly, McKinley handily turns back the populist threat. The campaign also marks the widespread introduction of the modern-style, pinback lapel button as a specialty advertising political staple.

1897—The *New York Tribune* prints its first half-tone photograph, suitable for use in newspapers.

Also in 1897, labor union membership in the United States is less than 500,000.

1898—The United States sends warships and troops to occupy Spanish territories in the Caribbean and Asia, in a conflict popularly known as "The Spanish-American War." The U.S. Army, recognizing the power of public opinion, provides daily bulletins to the press. Among the famous journalists and writers serving as war correspondents are Stephen Crane, James Creelman, Richard Harding Davis, and Edward Marshall. Lt. Colonel Theodore Roosevelt organizes a cavalry regiment that, through the famous "charge up San Juan Hill," propels him further into the national political spotlight. Despite the popular image of Roosevelt as a man of action on horseback, he actually walks up the hill because his regiment's horses have not yet arrived in Cuba from Florida. Also neglected in the propaganda image buildup of Roosevelt as a war hero is the fact that he and his troopers were greeted at the top by a company of U.S. black cavalrymen who had arrived first. Highly patriotic short films released in 1898, such as *Tearing Down the Spanish Flag!*, excite audiences, while phony pictorial "news" accounts, typified by *The Campaign in Cuba* (really shot in New Jersey), show a flagrant disregard for truth. This visual power of "actuality" and "documentary" frees propagandists for the first time from a near-complete reliance on publications and the printed word.

1900—Union membership stands at 833,600, approximately five percent of the nation's total wage and salary workforce.

The first public relations firm, the Publicity Bureau, is founded in Boston by George V.S. Michaelis, Herbert Small, and Thomas O. Marvin, "to do a general press agent business."

Psychoanalysis emerges as a discipline with the international publication of Sigmund Freud's *Interpretation of Dreams*.

The Republican ticket of William McKinley and Theodore Roosevelt win the presidential election, defeating Democrats William Jennings Bryan and Adlai E. Stevenson. Eugene Debs receives nearly 100,000 votes for president under the Social Democratic party banner.

1900, July 1—The *International Socialist Review* debuts under the editorship of A.M. Simons, and vows to combat the predominant "utopian" socialism in the United States with a more "scientific" approach toward revolution. The publisher is Charles H. Kerr and Company, a socialist cooperative that publishes many important left-wing books and pamphlets.

1901—Marconi transmits telegraphic "wireless" radio messages across the Atlantic Ocean.

That same year, most of the leftist organizations in the United States outside the Socialist Labor party join to form the Socialist party, with a membership of approximately five thousand.

1901, April 19—The rebellion in the Philippine Islands is ended by proclamation after insurgent leader Emilio Aguinaldo is captured by American forces. The brutal suppression of the Filipino insurrection proves unpopular in the United States and fuels renewed public debate over American overseas empire building. The Anti-Imperialist League is especially active in issuing bitter denunciations of the army's use of torture to suppress the rebellion.

1901, September 14—Theodore "Teddy" Roosevelt becomes president after William McKinley is assassinated by Polish-American anarchist Leon Czolgosz at the Pan-American Exposition in Buffalo, New York.

1901, October—The *Comrade*, a monthly magazine begins publication in New York City to protest "the miasmas of commercialism" and herald a renaissance in socialism. The works of a number of important leftist writers, including poet and propagandist Morris Winchevsky, are featured. After four years, it merges with *International Socialist Review*.

1903—Charles Cooley's *Social Organization* is the first modern analysis of social communication.

Theodore Roosevelt becomes an advocate for corporate reform, possibly out of fear of losing a valuable portion of the electorate. He encourages farmers and other trustbusters to renew their attacks on big business combines. The enactment of the Bureau of Corporations Bill, which enjoys strong progressive and conservative support, establishes the U.S. Department of Commerce and Labor. This marks the beginning of an important era which sees the government become more proactive in the regulatory process.

McClure's Magazine exposes Standard Oil in a series of muckraking articles by Ida Tarbell.

Membership in the American Federation of Labor approaches 1.75 million workers.

1904—The Niagara Movement, forerunner of the National Association for the Advancement of Colored People (NAACP), is founded.

Labor union membership in United States tops two million, an indication of rising discontent among workers.

While working in the press bureau of the Democratic National Committee during the presidential election, Ivy Lee meets George F. Parker, another former newspaperman turned political publicist. The partnership of Parker and Lee, based in New York City, establishes one of the country's first public relations firms, a teaming that lasts four years.

Financier Jacob Schiff, of Kuhn, Loeb and Company in New York City, helps finance Japan in its war against Russia and then begins long-term funding of nihilist terrorist groups in Russia committed to the overthrow of the czarist monarchy and its policy of anti-Semitism.

1904, July 30—The *Boston Investigator*, a venerable organ of freethought established in 1831, ceases publication, with editor L.K. Washburn turning over the subscription list to the *Truth Seeker*.

1904, November 8—Theodore Roosevelt wins the presidency. Although the Socialist party has only 20,000 members, its candidate for president, Eugene Debs, gets over 400,000 votes.

1905-1919—Born out of disillusionment with Progressive Era reform movements and traditional labor unions, the Industrial Workers of the World (the "IWW" or "Wobblies") is founded by militant socialists bent on replacing the U.S. capitalist society with one controlled by the working class. By 1909, IWW members begin to attract widespread national attention through a series of selected free-speech fights which lead to mass arrests from coast to coast. For example, when Wobblies in Spokane, Washington, are thrown in jail for addressing pedestrians on street corners, hundreds more come west on railroad boxcars to help them. Wobblies take turns agitating and being arrested, overloading the jails and courts so severely that they eventually win the right to speak in public. This fierce commitment to social justice makes "worker solidarity" in the IWW a force to be reckoned with. Another early action is the creation of an educational bureau, which is divided into literature and lecture sections. Newspapers and periodicals are essential to the IWW propaganda effort, and the Wobblies publish an estimated sixty-six different newspapers between 1905 and 1919. The "One Big Union" also remains committed to fomenting revolutionary direct action through general strikes and violent sabotage. This leads to internal as well as external pressures. In 1913, over the opposition of Helen Keller, Walter Lippmann, and other leading socialists, a split in the movement results in IWW leader "Big Bill" Haywood and other militant left-wingers being expelled from the Socialist party.

1905—Radical novelists Upton Sinclair, Jack London, and others organize the Intercollegiate Socialist Society to promote the virtues of anticapitalism. With the uprising against the Russian czar, writer London becomes a propagandist for the struggle (which fails at that time) by signing a proclamation calling on American socialists to support the revolt and lecturing in various California cities about the need for change in Europe and at home.

1906-1908—Themes of corporate social responsibility and ethical behavior become increasingly commonplace in public relations statements. To avert an antitrust campaign, George Perkins of the International Harvester Company (IH), fights the U.S. government's Bureau of Corporations. He engages publicists George Parker and Ivy Lee to help him in the battle. The economics of mass production are explained in a series of IH-commissioned news stories which utilize a "benefits of largeness" theme and stress how corporations pay better wages than smaller businesses. The campaign proves so successful that the Roosevelt administration drops the case in 1908.

In one of the first issues management campaigns, the railroad industry hires the Publicity Bureau to fight a move by President Theodore Roosevelt to impose regulatory legislation on the industry. Public relations pioneer Ivy Ledbetter Lee also becomes the first publicity counselor for the Pennsylvania Railroad, with special attention to disputing the image that its industry leaders are heartless. The initial campaign fails and the Hepburn Act passes, Congress, in large part because Roosevelt takes his campaign to the people and wins the battle of public opinion. After this, the railroads reassess the use of publicity and start their own public relations departments. Lee continues working for the Pennsylvania Railroad, publishing a famous article in the November 1907 issue of *Moody's Magazine* that extols the virtues of railroads for employing hundreds of workers, carrying goods to markets, and making travel possible to an expanding West.

Ivy Lee is also appointed to represent the anthracite coal industry during a long and bitter strike, allowing him to showcase his new approach to the dissemination of information. As a former journalist, Lee is aware of the need to ease hostility between big business and the news media. Reporters are not permitted to attend strike conferences, so Lee breaks tradition by handing out reports after each meeting. Newsmen, who were unaccustomed to the free flow of information, find that this makes their job easier. Perhaps the most important development to come out of the coal strike, however, is Lee's now-famous *Declaration of Principles*, which was circulated nationally to newspaper editors and reads, in part:

This is not a secret press bureau. All our work is done in the open. We aim to supply news. This is not an advertising agency; if you think any of our matter ought properly to go to your business office, do not use it. Our matter is accurate. Further details on any subject treated will be supplied promptly, and any editor will be assisted most cheerfully in verifying directly any statement of fact. . . . In brief, our plan is, frankly and openly, on behalf of our business concerns and public institutions, to supply to the press and public of the United States prompt and accurate information concerning subjects which it is of value and interest to the public to know about.

1906—The Rand School of Social Science is established in New York City as a center for socialist education.

The first broadcast of spoken word and music together occurs from Reginald Fessenden's experimental radio station at Brant Rock, Massachusetts.

The Gannett media chain is founded.

1906, March—Emma Goldman, the dynamic exponent of communist anarchism, begins publishing the radical monthly magazine *Mother Earth* in New York City.

1906, April 24—William Joyce is born in Brooklyn, New York. Later, during World War II, Joyce becomes famous as the pro-Nazi radio propagandist "Lord Haw Haw."

1907—Though brief, the "Panic of 1907" economic depression proves to be one of the more disastrous in U.S. history.

Lee Deforest invents the audion tube, making possible voice transmission over wireless radio.

The word *television* is first used, in a *Scientific American* magazine article.

E.W. Scripps organizes the United Press news syndicate.

The first daily comic strip is H.C. "Bud" Fisher's "Mutt and Jeff," whose feature rights are purchased by William Randolph Hearst for his newspaper syndicate.

1908—Dr. Harry F. Ward starts the Methodist Foundation of Social Service, which subsequently changes its name to the Federal Council of Churches. The organization is attacked for Ward's support of communism and its promotion of a progressive, ecumenical agenda. Nevertheless, the influence of the council grows.

The American Telephone and Telegraph Company (AT&T) creates an issue advertisement to discuss the virtues of telephone service provided by a regulated monopoly. The conclusion of the ad emphasizes the bond between the company's interest and that of its customers: "The Bell System's ideal is the same as that of the public it serves—the most telephone service and the best, at the least cost to the user. It accepts its responsibility for a nation-wide telephone service as a public trust." This is part of the company's decision to placate public hostility and promote awareness of its policy.

1908, July 27-28—The newly formed Independence party meets in Chicago, where it acts to voice progressive causes. News magnate William Randolph Hearst serves as the keynote speaker.

1909, February 9—George Seldes is hired for $3.50 a week as a cub reporter for the Pittsburgh *Leader* newspaper.

1909, March 4—Republican William Taft succeeds Theodore Roosevelt as the new president.

Later that same month, the Board of Censorship (later the National Board of Censorship of Motion Pictures/National Board of Review of Motion Pictures) is founded. First financed by New York-based exhibitors, the board reviews productions for depictions of crime, violence, indecency, and immoral suggestiveness. By precensoring films prior to their screening, the major motion picture exhibitors and production companies seek to limit their legal liability, blunt the impact of vigilante groups, and stave off federal censorship laws.

1910-1917—The Mexican political system undergoes revolutionary convulsions, impacting American trade and public attitudes. The leading European rival powers, Britain and Germany, also actively compete during these years to influence public opinion in the United States.

1910—The Liberal party government in Canada of Prime Minister Wilfrid Laurier is defeated over another attempt at free trade with the United States. The victorious Conservative party campaigns with the slogan "No truck nor trade with the Yankees."

The same year, Walter Lippmann works to organize the first Socialist Club at Harvard University, and the Carnegie Endowment for International Peace is formed "to hasten the abolition of international war."

1911—*Pathé Weekly* introduces the first motion picture newsreel to the United States. The movie industry also releases several films that distort and exploit religion for commercial purposes. Roman Catholics are kept busy protesting such pictures as *The Nun*, *The Secret of the Confessional*, and *The Price of Ambition* (which shows a priest hugging and kissing another man's wife). Despite the strong Jewish presence in the industry, *The Yiddisher Cowboy* presents questionable ethnic images which have not entirely disappeared. Concurrent releases such as *A Victim of the Mormons* do little to build ecumenical cooperation. Even nonprofit groups are abused, in exposés such as *Organized Charities*.

In this same year, muckraking writer Will Irwin publishes a hard-hitting series of magazine articles on "The American Newspaper" in *Collier's* ("the national weekly"), proving that "freedom of the press" in many cities is illusory. Irwin exposes the often-secret ties between newspapers and powerful interests that are more concerned with controlling than reporting the news.

Labor conflict results in the use of dynamite in the disastrous McNamara affair, which unfortunately influences the American public mind to link all anarchists with terrorism. In truth, terrorism is rarely practiced by anarchists in the United States.

1911, January—*The Masses* begins publication, "with the special mission of propagandizing for the coöperatives movement." Among the products it advertises are Karl Marx Cigars. After floundering, the magazine finds a clear voice the following year under the brilliant editorship of Max Eastman. Contributors form a virtual "Who's Who" of left-wing intellectualism.

1912—Edward Mandel House publishes the novel, *Philip Dru: Administrator*, which presents a favorable view of conspiracies designed to promote "Socialism as dreamed of by Karl Marx." Later, "Colonel" House becomes President Wilson's most trusted advisor and serves on the U.S. delegation to the Versailles Peace Conference following World War I.

Under the Radio Act of 1912, the U.S. secretary of commerce is given licensing responsibilities as part of the nation's first comprehensive radio legislation.

With quasi-governmental backing, a national Chamber of Commerce is established to act as a spokesman for the business community.

According to Walter B. Rideout (*The Radical Novel in the United States 1900-1954*, pp. 98-99):

If 1912 marked the Socialist Party's greatest triumph at the polls, a very considerable part of that success belong to the Party's press, of which *The International Socialist Review* was only one representative; for in that year alone 323 [news]papers and periodicals of various shades of red were devoted to Socialism. Five English and 8 foreign-language dailies, 262 English and 36 foreign-language weeklies, 10 English and 2 foreign-language monthlies were creating an audience receptive to radical ideas. Because the rebels who had originally left De Leon's Socialist Labor Party to form their own political organization knew from experience how the S.L.P.'s National Executive Committee had been able to dictate policy partly through its control of a single official publication, the Constitution of the Socialist Party provided that its own National Committee should "neither publish nor designate any official organ." Out of the 262 English weeklies only one, *The American Socialist*, with a circulation of 60,000, was actually owned by the Party. The most important periodicals by virtue of the size of their distribution were the monthly *Wilshire's Magazine* (400,000) and two weeklies, *The National Rip-Saw* (200,000) and *The Appeal to Reason*.

The death in 1912 of radical newspaper publisher J.A. Wayland, founder of the *Appeal to Reason* based in Girard, Kansas, proves a setback. Despite his tragic suicide, the paper continues to be printed in eighteen regional editions reaching 760,000 subscribers (the largest circulation of any socialist periodical in the world).

1912, June 18—Republican party regulars are divided between loyalty to incumbent President Taft and the return to national politics of Theodore Roosevelt. Failing to capture the nomination, Roosevelt leads his followers into the new Progressive party (commonly referred to as the "Bull Moose party") which stands for direct primaries, votes for women, and other advanced policies.

1912, November—The split in the normally Republican ranks allows Democratic candidate Woodrow Wilson to be elected with only a plurality. Eugene Debs has his greatest popular success, setting a record percentage of votes cast for an American radical political party. He more than doubles the Socialist party vote in this presidential bid, polling over 900,000 ballots (approximately 6 percent of the total cast). A suffrage referendum held at the same time to give voting rights to women in Wisconsin is soundly defeated by the state's male voters, 227,054 to 135,736. Leading the antisuffrage propagandists are members of the brewing industry, who fear the addition of women voters will result in prohibition legislation.

1913—Congress passes the Federal Reserve Act, creating a privately controlled, quasi-public central bank as part of a series of "reforms," which are heavily promoted in the newspapers. Congressman Charles A. Lindbergh, Sr., is among the minority warning that the public has been duped by elite interests making up the "money trust." In passing other legislation that forbids "using appropriated funds for paying 'publicity experts,'" Congress attempts to ban lobbying by the executive branch.

The first package is sent via parcel post, enabling Americans to buy goods by mail.

The Anti-Defamation League of B'nai B'rith is formed in Chicago with the goal of combating discrimination against Jewish people. It becomes a leading research organization, publisher, and lobbying group.

American communist journalist John Reed is jailed for his role in instigating a strike by silk workers in Paterson, New Jersey. Subsequently he organizes a "strike pageant" in New York City's Madison Square Garden theater.

The Masses embarrasses the Associated Press (AP) through hard-hitting reportage, biting editorials, and telling cartoons concerning the latter's antilabor coverage of the conflict raging in West Virginia's coal fields. One particularly telling editorial cartoon, entitled "Poisoned at the Source," shows the AP emptying vials of "Lies," "Prejudice," and "Suppressed Facts" into a water reservoir used by unsuspecting sleeping cities below. Although the Associated Press sues for slander, the service quietly drops its suit two years later rather than face a trial that might reveal embarrassing facts about the news syndicate's business practices.

1913, March—Woodrow Wilson officially becomes president.

1913, July 30—The *Biblical Recorder* ("Organ of the Baptist State Convention of North Carolina") gives grudging praise to the success of the International Bible Students Association movement under the leadership of Pastor Charles Taze Russell:

The first [achievement] is its emphasis upon its peculiar doctrines. In this day when many Baptists and other Christians are relaxing their hold upon sound doctrine, the followers of Russell and other false teachers are making doctrine and the teaching of it the main thing of their work. And they are, therefore, succeeding out of all proportion to the merit of either themselves or their views. The second secret of the advance of Russellism lies in the aggressive and unwavering propagandism on the part of its promoters. They shrewdly use the secular press as the medium for their views. . . . Who ever heard of such a spirit of propagandism? Suppose Baptists had it; could we not soon conquer the world.

Russell is naturally media literate, and the amount of literature he circulates proves staggering. Books, booklets, and tracts are distributed by the hundreds of millions. This is supplemented by well-publicized speaking tours and a masterful press relations effort, which gives him widespread access to general audiences. A sermon column is translated into four languages and syndicated by telegraph to publications throughout the United States, Canada, and Europe. By 1913, Russell's views are appearing in three thousand newspapers with an estimated combined readership of between ten and twenty million persons each week.

1914—By publishing important documents in their entirety for the public record, the *New York Times* contributes to the move toward objective reporting.

Congress passes the Federal Trade Commission (FTC) Act which creates a new regulatory body to replace the U.S. Bureau of Corporations. An outgrowth of the Clayton Antitrust Act, the commission is set up to prevent large business concentrations. Considerable discussion revolves around definitions that could be used to distinguish "good" business concentrations and "bad" ones. For many years the FTC is typical of those agencies that protect corporations as much as they challenge them, with commission membership drawn from its own regulated industries. Soon after the FTC's creation, for example, it is populated with former National Association of Manufacturers members serving under the leadership of the avowedly probusiness Edward N. Hurley.

1914, January—The first truly million-dollar film enterprise, the *Photo-Drama of Creation*, is roadshowed by the International Bible Students Association to major European, North American, and Australasian theaters prior to the major battles of World War I. An estimated 20,000 screenings at about four thousand locations put heavy logistical and financial stresses on Pastor Charles Taze Russell and his supporters, despite their belief that motion pictures, "next to the power of the tongue, are the most powerful things in the world." The *Photo-Drama of Creation* tells the Bible story from Genesis to Revelation, drawing on advanced audiovisual technologies to adapt Russell's apocalyptic "end time" teachings to world conditions. It consists of a multimedia package of hand-tinted slides and moving picture films designed to popularize to a mass audience the scientific validity and prophetic fulfillment of the Bible at a time when religion is under increasing attack from "higher critics."

1914, January 25—Alexander Graham Bell and Dr. Thomas A. Watson, the same men who made the first telephone call (between two rooms) in 1876, now complete a live transcontinental phone connection from New York City to San Francisco.

1914, April—A peaceful strike by miners in Colorado seeking union recognition and job safety reforms results in fifty-three murders (including women and children) the day after Easter by overzealous strikebreakers employed by the Rockefeller family. The Ludlow Massacre redirects public sympathy to the miners, who until then had been portrayed as ungrateful, subversive socialists. Ivy Lee advises John D. Rockefeller, Jr., to visit

Ludlow with press in tow, tour the mines, talk with the workers, dance with their wives, and play with their children. Newsreels and photographic reports herald scenes showing the "humanized" Rockefeller as caring, sociable, and philanthropic. Lee supplements this effort with an ostensibly objective series of news releases issued by the Denver-based Committee of Coal Mine Managers under the title, *Facts Concerning the Struggle in Colorado for Industrial Freedom*. While wages, hours, and working conditions at the Ludlow mines see little change, the Rockefellers' much-maligned image as one of the most mistrusted American families is reversed by the news blitz and well-planned photo opportunities. Lee's successful campaign on behalf of the Rockefeller interests marks the culmination of earlier work to implement modern public relations techniques in industrial disputes.

1914, August 4—"Our Times of Troubles," historian Arnold Toynbee later observed, commences with the catastrophic events of the year 1914. Most notably, on this date Britain declares war on Germany, and World War I (the "Great War") begins in Europe. Britain aggressively pursues pro-interventionist policies, with its agents quickly cutting Germany's telegraphic link to the United States. At a disadvantage, Germany later attempts to buy the *New York World* newspaper to disseminate its views. The summary in the *Encyclopedia of American Facts and Dates* (edited by Gorton Carruth and associates, 1979, p. 431) is illustrative of how propaganda during the early stages of World War I tries to swing U.S. public opinion:

Atrocity stories, almost all of them later disproved, were circulated by both sides. Many rumors appeared in [the] American press and were believed because strict German and British censorship of all news dispatches from Europe had made all U.S. newspapers unreliable as regards the war. The most persistent rumor was that a large Russian army had left Archangel and, traveling by way of Scotland and England, joined allied forces on the western front. There was never the slightest truth in it, although U.S. newspapers carried many "eye-witness accounts" of bearded Russian soldiers in Glasgow or London or Calais.

1914, November 7—The first issue of the *New Republic* is published, ultimately serving as a "Who's Who" forum for academics and political commentators responsible for formulating twentieth-century American liberalism. Editor Herbert Croly is aided by Walter Lippmann and Walter Weyl.

1915—The National Americanization Committee in New York City, and the U.S. Bureau of Education in Washington, D.C., jointly distribute 150,000 copies of *America First*, a multi-lingual poster in a nationwide public relations campaign to attract immigrants ("Many Peoples, But One Nation") to schools offering English-language training and citizenship indoctrination.

Despite its title, the feature motion picture *The Battle Cry of Peace* creates anti-German hysteria. The widely screened commercial propaganda movie shows the militaristic Huns besieging New York City from the sea and reducing its towering skyscrapers to ruins.

Neon advertising signs begin to light up the night.

1915, January 2— An advertisement entitled "The Penalty of Leadership" by the Cadillac Motor Company is published in the *Saturday Evening Post*. The ad is notable as one of the first to combine image and issues. It advocates the need for maintaining high standards of manufacturing quality. However, the ad masks the fact that the original model 51 Cadillac is not very reliable.

1915, February 8—The official première of *The Clansman*, a blockbuster 2 hour and 45 minute motion picture glorifying the Ku Klux Klan (KKK), takes place at the opulent Los Angles theater owned by W.H. Clune. Based on Thomas Dixon's novel, filmmaker D.W. Griffith conceptualizes and directs the picture at a cost of $110,000. Soon retitled *The Birth of a Nation* for its New York opening, this feature film proves a technical landmark whose cast reads like a virtual rundown of everybody who was anybody in the early movie industry. President Woodrow Wilson is shown the film during a special screening in the White House and reportedly enthuses that it is "viewing history written with lightning." The quote is widely used in the publicity campaign to promote *The Birth of a Nation*, even though the phrase actually was created by Griffith himself after first receiving only a tepid reply from Wilson. In boldly picturizing an epic tribute to the Ku Klux Klan, *The Birth of a Nation*'s release also serves an important propaganda function. The intense social interest the movie generates leads to the KKK's revival as a potent national nativist political force striking out against blacks, Jews, Catholics, and foreigners. Although the NAACP launches a protest against *The Birth of a Nation*, the film proves a smash popular success.

1915, February 23—The Supreme Court declares that moving pictures are not constitutionally protected by the First Amendment in *Mutual Film Corporation v. Industrial Commission of Ohio*.

1915, May 7—A German submarine sinks the *Lusitania*, a passenger liner, off the Irish coast. Nearly 1,200 of those on board drown, including a number of prominent Americans. The sinking gives the British government an opening to unleash a barrage of anti-German propaganda in the United States designed to precipitate intervention in the European war. Although this immediate effort fails for a time, it does set up lingering Germanophobia. In a note presented to U.S. Secretary of State William Jennings Bryan on May 31, the British ambassador lies in declaring that the *Lusitania* was not armed. Americans are not told about the secret munitions shipments on board, nor that Winston Churchill, the First Lord of the British Admiralty, had commissioned a report speculating on the public opinion advantages that would accrue if a passenger liner with powerful neutral individuals aboard were torpedoed by the Germans. The British falsehoods are believed, and in combination with a series of subsequent public relations blunders by the Germans, gradually work to undercut proneutrality support in the United States.

1915, September 16—The U.S. military occupies Haiti and controls the country until 1934.

1915, November 19—IWW leader Joe Hill (the Americanized name of Joel Hägglund, born 1879 in Sweden) is executed (many say "murdered" on trumped-up charges) by Utah officials after a trial that is still the subject of much dispute. Hill, the "Wobblies' Troubadour," and another man whom the state never seriously sought, were accused with holding up a grocery store for a few dollars and then killing the owner. Most historians believe that Hill was framed on behalf of Utah's powerful mining industry, which feared his ability to agitate workers to seek meaningful reforms. His last words reportedly are: "Don't mourn for me. Organize."

1916—Internal disputes, the collapse of the Second International, and the impact of the war in Europe on American ethnic groups contributes to the decline of the Socialist party, whose membership falls to 83,000.

A group of major railroads form the Railway Executives' Advisory Committee to influence public opinion and coordinate press relations by the industry.

The Women's Bureau is founded by Mrs. George Bass of Illinois to organize feminine support for the Democratic party.

1916, May 27—President Wilson in a speech before the League to Enforce Peace, urges the creation of a League of Nations.

1916, October 31—Pastor Charles Taze Russell dies and his movement splinters. The majority follows leadership that evolves into the Jehovah's Witnesses organization.

1916, November—Republican Charles Evans Hughes from California is narrowly defeated by incumbent Woodrow Wilson in the presidential election. One possible cause: Hughes' overconfidence leads him to neglect advertising in his own home state, which is carried instead in a squeaker by Wilson on the campaign theme of "He kept us out of war!"

1917—Norman Thomas (1884-1968) and Roger Baldwin (1884-1981) establish the American Civil Liberties Bureau to provide legal assistance to antiwar conscientious objectors.

1917, February 24—The British Secret Service intercepts and decodes the so-called Zimmermann telegram, a message from the German Ministry of Foreign Affairs to the German ambassador in Mexico, which urges a possible German-Mexican military alliance against America. After first giving a copy to United States officials, the note is leaked to the press by British counterespionage agents. The resulting scandal proves very damaging to German-U.S. relations.

1917, February 25—The ocean liner *Laconia* is sunk without warning by German submarines. Journalist Floyd Gibbons' sensational report of the sinking (he deliberately chose to travel on a vessel likely to be torpedoed) is syndicated to the non-German world by the *Chicago Tribune*, accompanied by indignant editorial demands for the United States to enter the fight. Upon his arrival in London, Gibbons is unceasing in his lobbying and press efforts to put pressure on President Wilson and the U.S. Congress to declare war on Germany.

1917, March—Over 1,300 foreign-language newspapers are published in the United States. The German-, Yiddish-, and Polish-language presses each boast a circulation of 1 million readers, while the Italian press claims nearly 700,000.

IWW membership peaks at 100,000, aided by a series of "direct action" successes and dramatic organizing gains among harvest hands and other farm laborers.

1917, March-November—War hardships ignite a series of revolutionary disturbances which again rock the Russian empire. Czar Nicholas II abdicates and is succeeded by a democratic socialist government under Alexander Kerensky, which lasts only six months. Communist exiles begin returning during this chaotic period. Leon Trotsky (real name, Lev Bronstein), for example, leaves New York for Europe on March 17 aboard the S.S. *Christiana* with an entourage of 275 fellow revolutionaries. They are arrested by Canadian authorities when the ship docks at Halifax, Nova Scotia, but are released after five days when diplomatic pressure is brought to bear by Wilson administration advisor "Colonel" Edward M. House and a future Kuhn, Loeb and Company banking partner, Sir William Wiseman of Britain. Then, with aid from the Germans, Nicolai Lenin (also known as V.I. Lenin; real name, Vladimir Ilich Ulyanov), Leon Trotsky, and others return from exile to lead the Bolshevik Communists in the seizure of power in October and November. Although they number less than 100,000 in a population of many millions, the Bolshevik revolutionaries skillfully manipulate the situation to their advantage, dividing and conquering their opponents in order to form a Union of Soviet Socialist Republics out of the wreckage of the old Russian empire. Under Trotsky, a new, ruthlessly efficient Red Army is formed, which ultimately crushes all remaining armed resistance in a brutal, three-year civil war.

1917, April 6—The United States government declares war on the German and Austro-Hungarian empires and enters World War I on the side of Britain, France, and Russia. George M. Cohan's prowar song, *Over There*, soon becomes a popular hit.

1917, April 13—The Committee on Public Information (popularly known as the CPI or "Creel Committee"), America's first modern war propaganda agency, is created by executive order of President Woodrow Wilson. The committee's Foreign Section establishes offices in more than thirty countries, while the Domestic Section is responsible for influencing opinion on the homefront and monitoring the foreign language press. The CPI eventually issues more than six thousand press releases and directives to American newspapers in support of the government's commitment to participate in the European conflict. Evolving into an effective mass medium, the war poster is quickly taken up by the Creel Committee. James Montgomery Flagg's "I WANT YOU FOR U.S. ARMY" recruiting message delivered by "Uncle Sam" is among the most popular of the one hundred million patriotic posters and other publications that CPI distributes during its existence. Many other people later to become famous in advertising and public relations, including Edward Bernays and Carl Byoir, also begin working for the CPI.

1917, May—U.S. Secretary of War Newton D. Baker appoints Major Douglas MacArthur as his press officer. General John J. Pershing, in command of the largely paper American Expeditionary Force (AEF), arrives in Europe. Over the next two years, his press office, G-2D, over the next two years is expertly staffed by officers at the captain rank who include many prominent American field journalists and newspaper editors. Although they wear officers' uniforms and benefit from U.S. Army housing, food, and travel assistance, G-2D members have no military duties per se and are paid by their American press organizations.

1917, June—Senator Hiram Johnson of California makes the oft-quoted observation, "The first casualty when war comes is truth." Congress passes the Federal Espionage Act, which revives restrictions against dissenting American political expression and reimposes harsh penalties for those convicted of "seditious libel." Any newspaper running an editorial denouncing American involvement in World War I can be found guilty of attempting to obstruct military enlistment or causing disloyalty in the armed forces. This is vigorously applied against those whom the Wilson administration considers disloyal, including pacifists, socialists, dissenters, neutralists, Irish independence seekers, feminists, labor activists such as Eugene Debs, the leaders of the Watchtower Society (later the Jehovah's Witnesses), an unlucky movie producer of a Revolutionary War-era feature film considered too anti-British, and others harshly sentenced to lengthy jail terms. Over the coming year, federal police raid Socialist party headquarters in many localities and enter the offices of targeted publications, seizing manuscripts and business records. For example, in April 1918, U.S. government authorities move to forcibly suppress the radical monthly magazine *Mother Earth* (published by Emma Goldman). All told, as many as one hundred magazines and newspapers are barred from the mails and approximately 1,900 people are prosecuted for expressing political views forbidden by law. Intolerance and hysteria are boosted by bombastic prowar public relations campaigns mounted by the National Education Association, the Committee on Patriotism through Education (a division of the National Security League), and the National Board for Historical Service. The teaching of German is banned in many public schools, with the California State Board of Education declaring it "a language that disseminates the ideals of autocracy, brutality and hatred." Anti-German sentiment is whipped to so high a pitch that even the Hearst papers are moved to temporarily rename the popular "Katzenjammer Kids" comic strip, the Shenanigan Kids."

1917, November 2—Betraying a set of promises made to the Arabs and locked in a seemingly interminable war with Germany, the British government, through the Balfour Declaration commits itself to support Zionist interests in Palestine. This forms one of the legal (as compared to moral) foundations for the state of Israel.

1918-1919—The United States Brewers Association buys the *Washington Times*, a daily newspaper, to have a vehicle for its viewpoints in the national capital. Within a year, however, the business records of the association are seized as part of the 1919 U.S. Senate investigation into pro-German and pro-Bolshevik propaganda. More significantly, these documents also reveal the extent to which the organization attempted to block the women's suffrage and prohibition movements.

1918—The so-called Alexander Bill proposes that U.S. radio broadcasting become a government monopoly under the control of the military. This nearly becomes law.

1918, January 8—President Wilson delivers his dramatic "Fourteen Points" address to a joint session of Congress to outline his war aims. Largely authored by advisor Walter Lippmann, this effort is part of a broad "New Diplomacy" initiative by the American leader. Wilson seeks to construct a direct dialogue for lasting peace with the peoples of Europe that will bypass the old politics practiced by their governments.

1918, January 25, 26, and 28—Against the wishes of the governments involved, the liberal *New York Evening Post* runs a news series disclosing the contents of agreements describing the true war aims and "underhand bargains" negotiated by the Allied governments through secret diplomatic discussions. These are then reprinted by the newspaper in a pamphlet, *Full Texts of Secret Treaties as Revealed at Petrograd*. As the *New York Evening Post*'s editor, Oswald Garrison Villard, recounts (*Fighting Years: An Autobiography*, p. 340):

These vitally important documents were found in the Russian archives when the Bolsheviki took over the government and were promptly published in full in all of then existing Russian dailies. Every effort was made by the Allies to keep them out of the United States and to prevent our officials from reading or understanding them. Our great press associations were either too ignorant to appreciate their value, were unaware of the opportunity for one of the greatest scoops on record, or were too subservient to our government to undertake the publication; not even when I published them were they carried by the Associated Press.

1918, February—As the editors of *The Masses* await trial, John Reed and others put out a monthly magazine known as *The Liberator*, in which they defiantly proclaim their commitment to revolutionary action and hostility to "dogma and rigidity of mind."

1918, February 8—The official U.S. Army newspaper, *Stars and Stripes*, first rolls off the presses.

1918, May 8—George Seldes becomes a U.S. Army Captain on the staff of General Pershing's G-2D press section.

1918, May 16—Passage of the Sedition Act by Congress adds a new set of harsh penalties for those convicted of obstructing the war effort. Pacifists and socialists are again the main target. Because the IWW has strongholds in industries critical to the World War I effort, and also due to their refusal to sign no-strike pledges, the Wobblies are branded "pro-Kaiser" and relentlessly persecuted. One of the new twists in corporate issues management is the presence of Bolshevism as a scapegoat issue. This enables corporate representatives to claim criticisms of their business practices are unpatriotic and worker organizers as communistic. While government authorities turn a blind eye, the probusiness American Protective League begins actively promoting the use vigilante action to combat militant labor groups. Their "Down With Reds" and "Hang the Bolshies" crusade contributes to the nation's xenophobic mood, and results in some of the fiercest repression ever unleashed by big business in the United States. No wonder in wartime then that emboldened superpatriots undertake lawless attacks on union sympathizers. Soon a lynch mob, abetted by authorities in Butte, Montana, murders IWW organizer Frank Little. As Rideout later summarizes (*The Radical Novel in the United States 1900-1954*, p. 93):

Now the I.W.W. stand against the war and its continuation of strikes in wartime brought attacks from both the local vigilante committees and the Federal Government. After a protracted trial in Chicago on the charge of "spoken and written denunciation of war," Judge Kenesaw Landis sentenced nearly a hundred of the Wobbly leaders to prison terms which . . . totaled more than eight hundred years.

With most of the IWW leadership behind bars as a result of this mass show trial, the "One Big Union" movement is nearly crushed. The American Protective League campaign works so well for its beneficiaries that it continues into the 1920s.

1918, June 30—Eugene Debs is arrested and subsequently convicted for making antiwar statements in a speech he delivers in Canton, Ohio.

1918, July—The Wilson administration sends U.S. troops to join with those of Britain and France in a "military intervention" in Russia to combat the Bolsheviks (then cooperating with Germany), undercut anticapitalist propaganda, prevent Japanese occupation of Siberia, create support for a League of Nations, and achieve political objectives suitable to erection of a "new liberal order of the world."

1918, September 13—The "triumphal entry" of General Pershing's forces into the French town of Saint-Mihiel marks "the first great all-American victory" of World War I. News accounts detailing the attack are extensive and highlight the "courageous fighting." However, this coverage is based on a rewrite of briefing notes given the press before the action occurs. Several correspondents simply change the tense from "we will" to "we have" in dispatches sent to Allied news outlets. These fake newspaper accounts, rather than the facts on the ground, become history. According to George Seldes, who is on General Pershing's press staff at the time, the Germans abandoned the town in a systematic withdrawal and there was no fighting—no battle at all. All the historic accounts are total falsifications, he writes in *Witness to a Century* (p. 85), "based on the United Press—and perhaps other—news stories . . . [with] both the writers and the censors innocent of intentionally planning what should now be called one of the greatest hoaxes of all time."

1918, November 9—The democratic Weimar Republic is declared as the new government in Germany, replacing the monarchy.

1918, November 11, 11 A.M.—Despite short-term, sporadic fighting that continues briefly (215 U.S. soldiers are killed and 1,114 wounded that day), on most fronts the armistice ending the Great War takes effect. The stark silence, after years of bombardments, is for many an overpowering statement to the wastefulness of war. Jubilant civilians take to the streets (at least one million in Paris alone). Military discipline breaks down temporarily as soldiers of opposing nations, who only hours before were trying to kill one another, cross into the no-man's land to joyously fraternize, trade souvenirs, and express their relief. Official figures later recognize that 53,513 Americans gave their lives during World War I.

1918, December 14—President Wilson arrives in Paris as head of the American delegation to the peace conference. More than two million French citizens line the streets and rooftops straining to see "the new Messiah" and "well-doer of humanity" who promises an end to war.

1919—Victory overseas, however, fails to bring an end to domestic reform and concern over abuses by corporate America. As Louis Galambos (*The Public Image of Big Business in America, 1880-1940*, p. 193) notes: "The clergyman, the engineer, the farmer, the laborer—all found cause for distress in the immediate aftermath of the First World War." The year 1919 proves eventful for a number of reasons, especially the inauguration of Prohibition, banning sales of alcoholic beverages, which becomes the law of the land. Other propaganda-related landmarks of interest include:

The year sees publication of John B. Watson's *Psychology, from the Standpoint of a Behaviorist*, a pioneering book in terms of understanding human behavior. This occurs just as Edward L. Bernays realizes that he can build on his wartime experiences as a government propagandist to mold public opinion for profit. As Sigmund Freud's nephew, he pioneers in applying principles from psychology and the other emerging social sciences to the problems of mass persuasion. Bernays thus lays the scientific foundations for a new profession by becoming the first to define himself as "public relations counsel." His client list in private industry and government becomes a "Who's Who and What's What" register. Numerous women (including Bernays' wife and colleague, Doris Fleishman) also help advance public relations.

The Supreme Court rules, in the *Schenk v. United States* and *Abrams v. United States* cases, to uphold seditious libel convictions of two men prosecuted for publishing radical pamphlets. These landmark decisions in 1919 mark the first time the highest court fully addresses the issues of freedom of speech, the press, and political dissent.

The American Legion is formed to represent the interests of veterans. Cynics argue a hidden agenda behind the officer-bankers who organize the legion is to quell unrest among those whose experiences in the war horrified and radicalized them. Another national organization of importance, the American Farm Bureau Federation is also founded in 1919 and soon becomes a leading lobbying voice for agricultural interests.

The Radio Corporation of America (RCA) is established, with semisecret U.S. government assistance. About this time, the first experiments with short-wave radio also take place.

The Republican party creates a women's division under the directorship of Ruth Hanna McCormick Simms, daughter of party boss Mark Hanna.

1919, March—The first Congress of the Communist International (the Comintern) issues a call for immediate world revolution. The Third (Communist) International is also formed, resulting in splits among U.S. leftists, who create several new political organizations, including the Communist party (dominated by foreign-born Eastern European immigrants) and the harshly doctrinaire Communist Labor party (organized by native-born "revolutionary romantics" led by John Reed and Benjamin Gitlow). The estimated number of U.S. Communist party members of all factions is 35,000. Between 1919 and 1935, the Comintern holds seven world congresses. By the eve of World War II, Communist political parties are operating openly or clandestinely in dozens of countries, including the United States.

1919, May 30—A coalition of prominent British and American financiers, Fabian socialists (called that because they are members of the London-based Fabian Society), and others committed to a powerful new internationalized world order agree to establish the Institute (later Royal Institute) of International Affairs (RIIA, also known as "Chatham House") in Britain. Over the coming years, the work of John Maynard Keynes, Arnold Toynbee, Barbara Ward, and others of like mind is promoted.

1919, June 28—The Treaty of Versailles is signed in the Hall of Mirrors at Versailles, France, officially ending World War I.

1919, June 30—The Committee on Public Information disbands.

1919, November 7—Anti-Bolshevik opinion culminates in the first of several

"Red Scare" raids masterminded by Woodrow Wilson's U.S. attorney general, A. Mitchell Palmer. Over the next few months, the major communist groups are driven underground in this series of Justice Department roundups against suspected radicals. More than 6,000 immigrants in thirty-three cities are detained, tossed into "bull pens," and tortured into making signed confessions. Palmer displays his racist inclinations in declaring, "Out of the sly and crafty eyes of many of them leap cupidity, cruelty, and crime; from their lopsided faces, sloping brows, and misshapen features may be recognized the unmistakable criminal type." The anarchist movement in the United States is dealt a particularly harsh blow with the deportation to the Soviet Union of 556 radicals, including activist organizers and journalists such as Emma Goldman and her companion, Alexander Berkman, mostly on vague charges of "associating with communist groups." The National Popular Government League and other civil rights groups decry the excesses of the Justice Department, but America's "Hang the Bolshies" and "Down with Reds" outlook prevails throughout the decade of the 1920s.

1920-1929—The "Roaring Twenties" are characterized by get-rich-quick prosperity schemes, franker sexuality, widespread tolerance of speakeasy lawlessness, greater social mobility made possible by the automobile and education, and a national popular culture heavily influenced by the motion picture, radio, and sound recording industries.

1920—Union membership in the United States is reportedly at 4,961,000, totaling 17.6 percent of the nation's workforce.

The term public interest is first used in U.S. law with the Transportation Act of 1920, a supplement to the Interstate Commerce Act of 1887.

Upton Sinclair publishes *The Brass Check*, a pioneering exposé of the interest groups controlling the American press.

The wartime American Civil Liberties Bureau evolves into the American Civil Liberties Union (ACLU), intended to fight governmental civil rights and due process abuses as dramatized by the heavy-handed anticommunist raids of Attorney General A. Mitchell Palmer.

The Anti-Imperialist League disbands.

The National-Sozialistische Deutsche Arbeiter Partei (National Socialist German Workers party, often shortened to NSDAP, NS, or Nazi party) holds its first important meeting in Münich, Germany. Chief spokesman Adolf Hitler, at first largely ignored by mainstream political organization observers, successfully builds the Nazis into a major international movement with supporters (and opponents) in many countries, including the United States.

1920, April 29—Louise Bryant, herself a well-known radical writer, unsuccessfully corresponds with U.S. Secretary of State Bainbridge Colby, asking for help in restoring the passport of her husband, journalist John Reed (the letter is now in the National Archives). Reed, author of *Ten Days That Shook the World*, has his passport confiscated when U.S. officials discover him smuggling Soviet revolutionary material into the country. To avoid an indictment for treason, Reed flees America, but he dies of typhus in Moscow later in the year. His ashes are buried in the Kremlin wall, the greatest posthumous honor the Bolshevik regime can pay a foreigner. When later "rewriting" history, Soviet leader Joseph Stalin has the ashes and commemorative plaque removed in the 1930s.

1920, August 26—The Nineteenth Amendment to the U.S. Constitution is adopted, giving women the right to vote. Privately originated propaganda increases as numerous new pressure groups form in the 1920s to promote business, combat Bolshevism, and influence mass opinion. These are swelled by the newly enfranchised women voters.

1920, November—Republican Warren G. Harding, pledging to return America to "normalcy," wins the presidency (with running-mate Calvin Coolidge of Vermont) in a landslide over the Democratic ticket of James M. Cox and Franklin D. Roosevelt. Publicity for the Harding campaign is directed by advertising executive Albert Lasker, who is considered a genius of promotion. The first commercial radio station to offer continuous, regularly scheduled programming (KDKA, Pittsburgh, owned by Westinghouse) initiates the idea of broadcasting live coverage of the election. Although Harding adopts an old-fashioned, "front porch" campaign style that allows surrogates to do most of the work, he is the first presidential candidate to use the new medium. Lasker successfully humanizes Harding as "an old-fashioned, sage, honest-to-the-core middle westerner who could be trusted never to rock the boat." However, Eugene V. Debs, making his last presidential bid while campaigning from Atlanta Penitentiary, again polls nearly a million votes—reflecting an undercurrent of protest over the continuing government subversion of civil liberties. A few months later, President Harding, in an act of clemency, commutes Debs' sentence and those of other leftists imprisoned during the Wilson administration. Despite this gesture, Harding's administration is later seen as corrupt.

1921-1927—Nicola Sacco and Bartolomeo Vanzetti are convicted of a payroll robbery and murder in Massachusetts, more for their immigrant status and anarchist beliefs than any direct evidence of guilt. The case becomes a cause célèbre for liberals and radicals, who are outraged over the miscarriage of justice surrounding the men's trial, conviction and eventual execution in 1927.

1921-1931—The armed forces of Canada prepare to meet the threat of invasion by the United States. Colonel James Sutherland "Buster" Brown draws up Defense Scheme No. 1 which becomes the official policy of the Canadian Department of Militia and Defense. This outlines a scenario for a possible seizure of U.S. border towns in response to an American strike northward. Over a period of ten years, Canadian forces send a series of spying missions into the United States until the orders are finally canceled and burned in May 1931, the same year Canada largely becomes independent from Britain.

1921—Socialist party membership dwindles to 13,000. Following a more conciliatory policy, enunciated at the Third Congress of the Comintern earlier in the year, IWW leader Bill Haywood joins the Communist party. However, continuing harassment drives the various Communist factions further underground. By December 1921, they unite under a legal "above-ground" banner known as the Workers' Party of America and Haywood flees the United States for the Soviet Union.

1921, July 29—The Council on Foreign Relations (CFR) is established in New York as an independent sister organization to the London-based Royal Institute of International Affairs. Many of its founding members are connected with Kuhn, Loeb & Company, J. P. Morgan & Company, and other leading financial interests.

1922-1923—The American Relief Administration provides food aid to the Soviet government and saves the lives of an estimated six million children from starvation caused by the Russian civil war.

1922—*Reader's Digest* begins publication to reach a large general middle class audience, while the decline of socialism is reflected by the death of The *Appeal to Reason.*

   Walter Lippmann publishes *Public Opinion*, a book that influences many who are interested in understanding the phenomenon of mass society and political communication.

   WEAF radio in New York begins selling airtime to advertisers, setting a precedent for advertiser-supported electronic media.

   The Hays Office is set up by leaders in the motion picture industry to head off government censorship threats in response to a series of sex and drug scandals that rock the country. At about the same time, the popularity of Robert Flaherty's romanticized *Nanook of the North* breaks "with the purely descriptive" and establishes the documentary film as something beyond a camera recording total reality.

   Benito Mussolini takes power in Italy as the first Fascist party leader to head a government. Many Americans welcome his "strong hand" and encourage good relations between the two countries.

1923—*White America*, by Earnest Sevier Cox, argues that civilization is linked to ethnic cohesion and presents an intellectual defense of racism. That same year, Oklahoma is placed under martial law because of Ku Klux Klan terrorism. Cox's later efforts as an author, lecturer, and propagandist for state antimiscegenation and race registration laws lead him to support the black back-to-Africa nationalism of Marcus Garvey and influence political demagogues such as U.S. Senator Theodore Bilbo (D-Miss.).

   The first public relations book, *Crystallizing Public Opinion* by Edward L. Bernays, is published.

   Time, the first weekly news magazine, begins publication and becomes an overnight success.

   Vladimir Zworykin invents the iconoscope tube, which proves a major technical advance in television.

   Warren G. Harding dies mysteriously; Calvin Coolidge (R-Vt.) assumes the presidency.

1924—An alliance with LaFollette Progressives marks the last hurrah for the Socialist party, which is supplanted by other organizations and fades into a peripheral social and political role.

   J. Edgar Hoover is appointed as the first director of the U.S. Federal Bureau of Investigation (FBI).

   Cartoon serials such as Harold Gray's "Little Orphan Annie" incorporate political messages by promoting an ideology of individual self-help rather than the alternative of government aid.

   Imprisoned in Germany, Adolf Hitler dictates his political biography, *Mein Kampf* (translated as *My Struggle* or *My Battle*), to cellmate Rudolf Hess. In analyzing the success of British war propaganda and his adoption of anti-Semitism, Hitler outlines his theory of "the big lie," which says people more easily believe a large falsehood than a small one.

1924, January 21—Lenin dies in Russia. He is succeeded to power as secretary-general of the Communist party of the Soviet Union by Joseph Stalin (real name, Joseph Dzhugashvili) who quickly imposes one of the most ruthless dictatorships in history. Stalin (originally a nickname given him by Lenin meaning "Steel") aggressively supports international socialism through armed struggle and propaganda to spread the Communist party's "revolution without frontiers" to other countries (including the United States).

1924, October—The final issue of the *Liberator* announces that it is combining with *Soviet Russia Pictorial* and the *Labor Herald* to reemerge as the *Workers Monthly* (the "Official Organ of the Workers Party of America"), under the editorship of Earl Browder. At about this time, International Publishers is founded by Alexander Trachtenberg, the representative of the Comintern Publishing Department in the United States, to publish Marxist and Soviet works. These organizational changes reflect a consolidation in the American left, following the fragmentation of the IWW due to new internal disagreements (with some members moving into the communistic Workers' party) and the continuing emotional fallout from the harsh prison sentences meted out to leaders during the Wilson administration (even though commuted by President Harding prior to his death). Within a decade, the movement claims only 1,450 followers and a treasury of $29—a situation described as "flat broke members [in] a flat-broke union." Despite all attempts to fully destroy the IWW, the organization survives today, but not as an active union. Headquartered in Ypsilanti, Michigan, IWW supporters still are committed to seeking "industrial democracy," largely through efforts at public education.

1924, November—American voters endorse President Coolidge's performance in office by electing him to a full four-year term.

1925—Union membership declines to 3.4 million workers in the United States. Membership of the various Communist party organizations in the United States is placed at just sixteen thousand, with the Workers' Party of America changing its name to the Workers (Communist) Party of America.

The Communist regime in the Soviet Union early recognizes the propaganda potential of the motion picture medium, culminating in the release of Sergei Eisenstein's innovative docudrama, *Battleship Potemkin*. The film brings international acclaim to the Bolsheviks by presenting so powerful an account of the abortive 1905 uprising against the czar that many viewers fail to realize what they are seeing is a fictionalized interpretation.

Stuart Chase's book, *The Tragedy of Waste*, publicizes consumerism issues. Also at this time, the first scientific studies of attitudes measuring social distance (the degree of sympathetic understanding or closeness felt by a person toward other individuals and groups) are conducted by Emory S. Bogardus.

The Universal Negro Improvement Association (UNIA) is founded in 1925 by Jamaican immigrant Marcus Moziah Garvey (1887-1940) and becomes the dominant black organization in the United States on a platform of racial separation and a return to Africa. As early as 1923, the dynamic orator and charismatic leader Garvey expresses his views when he writes:

Hitherto the other Negro movements in America (with the exception of the Tuskegee effort of Booker T. Washington) sought to teach the Negro to aspire to social equality with the Whites, meaning thereby the right to inter-marry and fraternize in every social way. Still some Negro organizations continue to preach this race-destroying doctrine added to a program of political agitation and aggression. . . . Let the Negro have a country of his own. Help him to return to his original home, Africa, and there give him the opportunity to climb from the lowest to the highest positions in a state of his own.

An estimated one million blacks express a willingness to leave the United States under Garvey's leadership, but his opinions earn him many powerful enemies. In 1925, he is arrested on trumped-up charges and sentenced to five years' imprisonment, a sentence that is commuted in 1927 when Garvey is deported to Jamaica. Gradually, his organization atrophies in membership and influence. At his death in London in 1940, there is only a small circle of mourners to witness his passing. However, Garvey's emphasis on independence is renewed by later leaders associated with the Black Muslim movement such as Malcolm X and Louis Farrakhan.

1925, March—A twenty one-station radio hookup broadcasts President Coolidge's inauguration coast-to-coast.

1925, December 2—British government representatives admit in House of Commons debate that World War I atrocity stories appearing in the *Times* and other newspapers about Germans melting down the bodies of dead soldiers to turn them into animal feed were false. Other horrible allegations about Canadian soldiers being crucified, Belgian women suffering rape and hideous mutilation, and children having their hands cut off by "the Huns" are all similarly retracted during this period. These sensational revelations create widespread distrust of government and media pronouncements. One result, stemming from public revulsion at finding out about these wartime propaganda lies, is the growth of isolationist and pacifist sentiment in Europe, Canada, and the United States.

1926—The Ku Klux Klan is at the height of its influence, boasting of five million members and political influence connected to the election of fourteen senators and eleven governors. A U.S. Senate investigation exposes KKK excesses, while public revulsion and internal feuds cause the organization to decline.

The Zenith case holds that the U.S. secretary of commerce cannot deny a broadcast license under then current law. However, under the government-brokered antimonopoly Second Cross-licensing Agreement, AT&T is forced out of U.S. radio. The National Broadcasting Company (NBC), controlled by the Radio Corporation of America (RCA), eventually takes over AT&T's interests. This acquisition leads to creation of NBC's broadcast networks which dominate American popularity ratings for the next three decades.

The Book-of-the-Month Club is founded, helping dictate which authors are most likely to reach a mass audience.

Kodak markets the first 16-millimeter motion picture film.

1926, May—The first issue of the *New Masses*, an attempt to provide a "popular front" forum for liberal and radical thought, arrives on the newsstands. As time passes, the publication becomes more doctrinaire Marxist. By the 1930s, with the competing philosophy of fascism more accepted, the *New Masses* grows in intellectual influence as a "catalytic agent" for communistic revolutionary literature.

1927—A patent application for the first "electronic television system" is filed by Philo Farnsworth.

The first college course in "Public Opinion and Propaganda" is taught by Professor Harold Dwight Lasswell of the Department of Political Science at the University of Chicago.

The United Independent Broadcasters (UIP) radio network debuts, later to become the Columbia Broadcasting System (CBS). UIP has affiliates from St. Louis to Boston.

1927, February—A definition promulgated by a coalition of veterans groups states that "Americanism is an unfailing love of country; Loyalty to its institutions and ideals; Eagerness to defend it against all enemies; Undivided allegiance to the flag."

1927, February 23—Congress creates the Federal Radio Commission (FRC) with passage of the Radio Act of 1927, defining "broadcasting" and introducing the concept of the public interest to the electronic media. Although Section 29 of the act prohibits censorship by the commission, other provisions ban the use of obscene, indecent, or profane language.

1927, May 20-21—Charles Lindbergh, Jr., flies solo across the Atlantic, landing his *Spirit of St. Louis* airplane near Paris on May 21. The son of a former U.S. congressman who led a failed crusade against the "money trust," Lindbergh becomes an international celebrity and American hero.

1927, August 23—The Sacco-Vanzetti appeal efforts fail. The men's executions provide a continuing propaganda bonanza for leftist sympathizers seeking a mobilizing issue.

1927, October—The offices of the *Communist* magazine and party headquarters are moved from Chicago to New York. This typifies the decline in midwestern native radicalism and the leadership shift to the coasts.

1927, October 6—The first commercial feature-length motion picture with natural sound, *The Jazz Singer*, premières at Warner's Theatre in New York City.

1928—Left-wing "deviationist" followers of Leon Trotsky (the "Trotskyists") are expelled from the Workers (Communist) Party of America.

Former IWW leader Bill Haywood dies in the Soviet Union. In tribute, his ashes are placed in the Kremlin wall, making him the second American so honored.

The *Amos 'n' Andy* radio show debuts and becomes the first successful radio situation comedy. It is later attacked for its racism.

William Lear invents the car radio.

1928, May—Arthur Page, publicity director of AT&T, announces that the company's long-term campaign to win public confidence for the phone industry to be a monopoly is successful, but cautions that underlying suspicions of monopolies remain.

1928, July 12-September 1—The Comintern Sixth Congress is held.

1928, November—The election year advertising theme used by the Republican party ("A Chicken in Every Pot, a Car in Every Garage") during a time of prosperity propels Herbert Hoover of Iowa into the presidency.

1929, October—The John Reed Club is formed in New York by writers and artists associated with *New Masses* to "clarify the principles and purposes of revolutionary art and literature, to propagate them, to practice them." By 1934, there are an estimated thirty similar John Reed Clubs across the United States.

1929, October 24—The downward trend in stock prices results in a panic by investors. The Wall Street market crash triggers a worldwide depression.

1929—The League of United Latin American Citizens (LULAC) is founded in Corpus Christi, Texas, as a national organization to represent Mexican-Americans and their political interests.

The Workers (Communist) Party of America assumes the new designation of Communist Party of the United States of America (CPUSA), with William Z. Foster as its leader. Expulsions of left-wing and right-wing deviationists reduce its membership to around seven thousand. Foster's Trade Union Educational League abandons attempts to cooperate with the American Federation of Labor, changes its name to the Trade Union Unity League, and begins to build rival unions.

International Publishers distributes fifty thousand pieces of communist literature in the United States.

A Payne Fund study develops the "magic bullet theory" to explain the effects of mass media.

A massive international celebration, known as "Light's Golden Jubilee," honors Thomas Alva Edison's invention of the electric light bulb. This event is a public relations triumph for Edward L. Bernays and his clients, General Electric and Westinghouse.

The distinctive voice of *McClure's Magazine* is stilled as it ceases publication.

German Nazi political agitator Joseph Goebbels reflects in his diary that "Propaganda has only one object—to conquer the masses. Every means that furthers this aim is good; every means that hinders it is bad."

1930—Earl Browder replaces William Z. Foster as the U.S. Communist leader. The party's Seventh Convention reports that the "major problem" facing American Communists involves progressing "from a propaganda sect into a revolutionary mass party of action."

1930, March 6—Mass unemployment demonstrations in many major U.S. cities take place under Communist party leadership.

1930, March 31—Facing renewed threats from religious and government leaders during the first year of the Depression, a group of the largest film companies (The Motion Picture Producers and Distributors of America, Inc.) agree with industry lead lobbyist Will H. Hays to update their self-censorship efforts and adopt a nineteen-page *Code to Govern the Making of Talking, Synchronized and Silent Motion Pictures*. However, certain filmmakers continue to flaunt the voluntary Motion Picture Production Code edicts by the Hays Office, particularly in picturing sexual themes and other re-creations of stories "torn from the front pages" of contemporary newspapers. With network radio emerging as a major competitor, commercial moviemakers turn to crime-based theatrical releases, such as *Little Caesar* (Warner Brothers), which successfully exploit an interest in gangsterism. About this time, the first of the left-wing Film and Photo Leagues in the United States are also formed. These cooperatives operate outside the big studio system to produce politically-motivated "social documentaries," often recreating key incidents in anticapitalist labor struggles. While these are a form of class warfare propaganda, such independent films also form part of the docudrama tradition.

1930, May 9—George W. Fellowes is convicted in a U.S. District Court for illegally operating a radio station without a federal license. The Federal Radio Commission (FRC) targets Fellowes in order to ensure government control over broadcasting and to "stop every Tom, Dick, and Harry from getting on the air." That same year, Archibald Crossley creates the first radio ratings system.

1931—The FRC denies license renewal to John R. Brinkley's KFKB ("*Kansas First, Kansas Best*: The Sunshine Station in the Heart of the Nation"). The "goat-gland doctor," who operates a nationally-famed clinic and radio complex in the otherwise tiny town of Milford, Kansas, faced charges of "dishonest programming" because his populistic mix of unorthodox medical advice, political commentary, and musical entertainment offended the American Medical Association and state government figures.

The National Committee for the Defense of Political Prisoners is organized by U.S. radicals headed by novelist Theodore Dreiser.

The *Star Spangled Banner* becomes the official U.S. anthem.

1932—William Z. Foster publishes *Toward Soviet America*, a handbook of revolution issued during his presidential campaign. Foster and running mate James Ford receive 102,991 votes as Communist party ticket candidates; Socialist Norman Thomas posts 884,781 ballots. The big winner in November is Democratic party candidate Franklin D. Roosevelt, of New York who puts together a new electoral coalition to crush Republican incumbent Herbert Hoover.

1933—The American Society of Newspaper Editors adopts a statement on ethics known as the "Cannons of Journalism." At this time, the trend toward media consolidation is already evident in the U.S. press. Out of 1,142 cities of less than 100,000 population, 87 percent feature a one newspaper or one-company monopoly; only 163 such communities (13 percent) have two or more independent dailies.

James Beck, formerly solicitor general of the United States, rails against government "bureaucracy and its propaganda." He warns, "Publicity has become a potent factor in the growth of bureaucracy . . . which loudly vaunts its usefulness from the housetops by newspaper articles, reports, radio broadcasting and bulletins."

American union rolls in 1933 show under three million members.

1933, January 30—The legal appointment of Adolf Hitler as Chancellor of Germany is viewed with concern by anti-Nazis. Soon the National Socialists establish a Ministry of Propaganda and Public Enlightenment under Dr. Joseph Goebbels. This corresponds to an upsurge in anti-Semitic propaganda evident in the United States. Among the most prolific domestic propagandists parroting the Nazi line is Robert Edward Edmondson, who begins an active broadcasting and publishing crusade that reaches millions of Americans. According to Edmondson's subsequent rambling book, *"I Testify"* (p. 147), his business during the decade boomed: "Promoting patriotic power-publicity exposing the treasonable conspiracy of the anti-national Jewish Politico-Economic System that is seeking to overthrow The American Systems and substitute therefor the rabbi-proclaimed 'thoroughly Socialized Democracy,' which is Communistic." Alarmed by these developments, Jewish organizations in America pursue aggressive media relations campaigns and issue their own propaganda designed to arouse public opinion against the Nazi regime and its sympathizers.

1933, March—President Franklin D. Roosevelt (FDR) takes office and inaugurates his "New Deal" by delivering the first of a series of radio "fireside chats," in which he talks directly to the American people.

1933, July—The president of the World Jewish Economic Federation, prominent New York lawyer Samuel Untermyer, chairs the International Jewish Boycott Conference held in Amsterdam, which adopts anti-Nazi economic measures that he describes, in a speech broadcast over WABC radio, as a "holy war . . . that must be waged unremittingly" to bring Germany to terms.

1933, September 16—The entertainment industry trade journal *Variety* headline reads "Pinks Plan to Stalinize Studios," drawing attention to growing Communist party influence in the film industry.

1933, November 16—After more than a decade of ostracism, the U.S. government formally recognizes the Soviet Union with an exchange of ambassadors. An increase in pro-Soviet propaganda is soon evident in the United States.

1934—Congress establishes the Federal Communications Commission (FCC) as an expansion of the old FRC, with the authority to regulate radio, television, and telephone communications.

American isolationism is boosted by Nye Committee antiwar investigations held in the U.S. Senate. These subsequently lead to the enactment of neutrality laws that (unsuccessfully) seek to keep America out of "entangling" foreign wars.

International Publishers distributes 600,000 pieces of literature annually in the United States, including 80,000 copies of Joseph Stalin's *Foundations of Leninism*. The Communist Party USA claims to have 25,000 dues-paying members.

American public relations pioneer Ivy Lee dies.

After years of urging by his wife, Ruth Hale, and many others, Heywood Broun organizes the American Newspaper Guild as a unit of the Congress of Industrial Organizations (CIO).

In San Francisco, the nation's first general strike is called to show solidarity with striking longshoremen. Because they fear the socialistic "End Poverty in California" (EPIC) program promoted by Democratic gubernatorial candidate Upton Sinclair, virtually all the state's major businessmen, publishers, and Hollywood moguls support the incumbent Republican hack, Governor Frank Finley Merriam. To defeat muckraker Sinclair, Merriam becomes the first major candidate to turn his entire campaign over to an advertising agency. Concocting a classic "dirty tricks" campaign plan, airing clever broadcast political spots, screening faked newsreels, and saturating voters with alarmist propaganda slogans ("It's Merriam or Moscow!"), the Republicans eventually overwhelm the underfunded challenger.

1934, February 16—U.S. communists attempt to take over a Socialist party mass meeting being held in New York City's Madison Square Garden. The protest, over Austrian government persecutions of Viennese Socialists, is effectively disrupted and breaks up in disorder.

1934, April—The National Legion of Decency is established by Roman Catholic bishops (it is officially incorporated on October 28) to defend moral standards, rate motion pictures, boycott "offensive" films, and press for a movie industry crackdown under its own code (under threat of renewed lobbying for a federal censorship law). These efforts result in full-fledged enforcement of Hays Office dictums, changing the face of American moviemaking.

1935-1939—U.S. Communists abandon their attacks on the New Deal to concentrate on the growing fascist menace posed by Nazi Germany and its allies. This is known as the "Popular Front/People's Front" period. An estimated half of all American Communist party members reside in the New York City area, which is the country's leading center of radical activity. The Communist Party of the USA reports 31,000 dues-paying members.

1935—Army chief of staff General Douglas MacArthur appoints Alexander D. Surles to head the public relations branch of the army.

To stimulate the distribution of proletarian fiction and other Marxist works, the Book Union is formed as a left-wing book club.

George Gallup uses new social science research techniques to begin his commercial public opinion-polling organization.

Reality-based programs such as *Gangbusters* (1935-1940, NBC) and many later imitators begin airing on radio, often relying on the cooperation of police and other government agencies for access to case files. In 1935, NBC radio also lifts its outright corporate ban on the discussion of contraception and family planning on its air.

1935, February 1—The theatrical film version of *March of Time* debuts. Producer Louis de Rochemont's decisions to explain controversial events in dramatic "interpretive newsreel" fashion and declare reenactments as journalistically valid make him a successful figure.

1935, April—Leftist writers convene the first American Writers' Conference. Attendees deride Kenneth Burke's address suggesting that the revolutionary symbolism of the term *the people* would be more effective as propaganda in America than continued references to *the worker*. Out of this emerges the League of American Writers, which pledges, according to *New Masses* (April 30, 1935), to:

fight against imperialist war and fascism; defend the Soviet Union against capitalist aggression; for the development and strengthening of the revolutionary labor movement; against white chauvinism (against all forms of Negro discrimination or persecution) and against the persecution of minority groups and of the foreign-born; solidarity with colonial people in their struggles for freedom; against bourgeois distortions in American literature, and for the freedom of imprisoned writers and artists, and all other class-war prisoners throughout the world.

The Communist party apparatus controlling the John Reed Clubs deliberately shuts them down in order to consolidate literary efforts in the new league.

1935, May 27—Perhaps the most controversial of the early New Deal propaganda campaigns involves the National Recovery Administration (NRA). Partially on the basis of propagandistic excesses of its supporters, the National Recovery Act, which established the agency, is declared unconstitutional by the Supreme Court.

1935, September 8—A leading populist figure and one of the most powerful demagogues in American politics, U.S. Senator Huey Long (D-La.) is shot to death at the state capitol in Baton Rouge.

1935, October—President Roosevelt advises Americans not to travel in, or trade using, Italian or Abyssinian ships due to "war risks" connected with the Italian invasion of Ethiopia. The British government (through British Broadcasting Corporation control of transatlantic radio communication) refuses to allow Baron Aloisi, Italy's official spokesman, to speak directly to the American people.

Random House and International Publishers begin distribution of Emile Burns' *A Handbook of Marxism*, which rapidly becomes the standard introductory work for the prospective Marxist.

1936—The Olympic Games held in Berlin, Germany, despite the heroics of black American track star Jesse Owens, prove a propaganda triumph for the National Socialists. Germans air the contests live via radio and the new medium of television, with the world's first woman news anchor.

The Federal Theater Project in the United States created under the auspices of the Works Progress Administration. Controversy soon follows because many of the productions are written by activist playwrights attempting to inform and influence the American public about the causes and solutions to the Great Depression. Particularly innovative is *The Living Newspaper*, a series of New Deal stage productions that use slides, recordings, actual voices, and actors to bring political journalism into the theater. Most of the actors' dialogue is taken from newspaper articles, speeches, and government documents.

The Roosevelt administration also commissions the filming of a number of documentary films with strong social messages to mobilize support for New Deal policies, including Pare Lorenz's award-winning *The Plow that Broke the Plains*, which leads to natural resource conservation. Lorenz edits stock footage to create a memorable sequence showing how production overuse of the land in World War I helped cause the Midwest "dust bowl." In this film, composer Virgil Thompson works closely with Lorenz to incorporate music, adding strong emotional elements to the story.

The pro-neutrality World Peaceways organization, headquartered in New York City, becomes "one of the most efficient public-opinion coagulants in the country" through its "unique and effective advertisements, radio broadcasts, film activities, and newssheets." The effects of the Depression, the bold experimentation of the New Deal, and the rise of antifascism also contribute to making communism more acceptable to many Americans by the late 1930s. Indeed, U.S. Communist party leader Earl Browder's national presidential campaign concentrates on attacking the opponents of FDR. Browder's campaign slogan promotes the idea that "Communism Is Twentieth-Century Americanism."

1936, February 6—The Consumers Union of the United States is incorporated, with Colston Warne at its first president.

1936, July—Spanish military men led by General Francisco Franco rebel against the republic. They are aided by a coalition of Catholic churchmen, wealthy bankers, landowners, and agents for Hitler and Benito Mussolini. The

Spanish rebellion (usually referred to as the Spanish Civil War) takes on international aspects as a prototype of the conflict between the Marxist/socialist left ("Loyalists") and the fascist/conservative right ("Insurgent" supporters of Franco). Americans privately assist both sides, but the majority are attracted to the romanticism of fighting fascism. Many prominent intellectuals volunteer and travel to Spain, with Americans serving as enlistees in Loyalist republican military units such as the Abraham Lincoln Brigade. Soon after the fighting begins, Jane Anderson is captured in Madrid and held as a Nazi agent by Loyalist forces. The Georgia-born Anderson boasts a successful career as a journalist dating back to World War I, and her work is regularly published by the Hearst press. Noted also for her beauty and dazzling red hair, Anderson (who might now be called a right-wing feminist) is vulnerable because, after an earlier divorce, she gave up her American citizenship to remarry a Spanish nobleman and become the Marquessa de Cienfuegos. She is eventually released after pressure is brought by the U.S. government. Anderson's supporters include the Hearst-controlled media and Catholic Monsignor Fulton J. Sheen who, in one of his national radio broadcasts, calls her "one of the living martyrs." The war drags on until 1939, when the pro-Franco forces eventually take Madrid and extend their rule to all of Spain.

1936, July 23—The Hollywood Anti-Nazi League officially organizes to fight fascism through demonstrations, rallies, and the picketing of the German consulate in Los Angeles.

1936, August-1938, March—A number of "old Bolshevik" stalwarts are convicted for harboring anti-Stalinist views of Marxism in a series of Moscow "show trials." The staged nature of the proceedings raises doubts that create divisions among Communist party sympathizers in the United States.

1936, August 14—The National Union for Social Justice, headed by Catholic priest Charles Edward Coughlin, holds its first convention. Coughlin also begins publication of a weekly magazine of politics, religion, and commentary called *Social Justice*.

1936, November 3—A Democratic party presidential landslide reelects Franklin D. Roosevelt, who carries every state except Maine and Vermont. Thoroughly repudiated is the unscientific polling method used by *Liberty Magazine*, whose editors predict Republican nominee Alf Landon of Kansas will win based on a telephone survey which fails to take into account that only the well-to-do are likely to have phones during this time of depression.

1936, November 19—*Life* magazine, produced by Time Inc., hits the newsstands featuring many photographs.

1937—The Mutual Radio Network is formed. That same year, *Look* magazine appears, imitating *Life*'s distinctive pictorial format.

1937, April—The American Institute of Public Opinion ("the Gallup Poll") finds that 71 percent of those questioned believe U.S. entry into World War I had been a mistake.

1937, May—Despite efforts of U.S. communists to prevent its enactment, Congress passes the Neutrality Act, which bars the export of arms to belligerents as in Spain.

1937, June—The Second American Writers' Congress declares the sole task of the left "Literary Front" is not the overthrow of capitalist society but rather the defeat of fascism.

1937, December 12—Reflecting growing tension between the two nations, the Japanese sink the American gunboat U.S.S. *Panay* anchored in Nanking, China.

1938-1939—Alarmed by growing international influence of Germany, the U.S. Division of Cultural Relations is created in the Department of State to issue propaganda targeted at Latin Americans. A latecomer to international communication, the U.S. government officially begins short-wave radio broadcasts to Spanish-speaking audiences. The division's task is to portray the United States as a friendly brother nation in a common struggle against possible foreign aggression.

1938—The Foreign Agents Registration Act specifies that individuals and organizations engaged in disseminating propaganda or related activities on behalf of another country must file public reports with the U.S. Justice Department's Criminal Division. While the act includes exemptions for commercial, religious, academic, scientific, and artistic pursuits, it tends to be used arbitrarily as a way of controlling domestic dissent and limiting access to print and visual political materials produced outside the United States.

1938, August—At the urging of documentarist Pare Lorenz, the Roosevelt administration creates the U.S. Film Service to coordinate the production of motion pictures about national social problems that are neglected by the commercial industry.

1938, September—Congressman Martin Dies (D-Tx.) announces that the U.S. House Un-American Activities Committee (HUAC) will hold hearings in Hollywood investigating communist influence in the motion picture industry. However, these are soon canceled following attacks by the Hollywood Anti-Nazi League with the explanation that a "lack of funds and time" precluded follow-up for the time being.

1938, October 30—A *War of the Worlds* dramatization broadcast on CBS Radio by Orson Welles' *Mercury Theater* leads to a government investigation after it panics thousands of listeners who are already jittery about events in Europe. The production techniques used by Welles' troupe are carefully couched in realism and modernized for the radio medium, right down to news bulletin interruptions.

1938, November 9—Nazi thugs, encouraged by the Hitler regime, plunder Jewish shops and burn synagogues in cities across Germany in the so-called *Kristallnacht* ("Night of the Crystals"). News coverage in the United States reflects outrage over the events.

1939—Corporations active in the U.S. broadcasting industry as a whole earn 67.1 percent before-tax profits on their investments. That same year, the first experimental FM (frequency modulation) radio station goes on the air in New Jersey, based on technological advances of Edwin Armstrong; and the Radio Corporation of America (RCA) demonstrates television at the New York World's Fair.

The first American sales of mass-produced paperbacks occur in 1939. Pocket Books revolutionizes the publishing industry in the United States by mass-distributing eleven paperback book titles at the low cost of about 25 cents per copy.

Union membership rebounds to nearly eight million workers. The U.S.

Senate holds hearings detailing violations of labor free speech rights. In his book *America's House of Lords: An Inquiry into the Freedom of the Press*, New Deal "brain truster" Harold Ickes claims that lack of sympathy for unionism by the press ranges "from the polite unfriendliness of the dignified *New York Times* to the vociferous hostility of the reactionary *Los Angeles Times*."

1939, January 29—An end to U.S. isolation is demanded by U.S. communists, following the Moscow party line.

1939, April—Although slow to overtly portray Nazism in the early and mid-1930s, Hollywood moviemakers jump on the anti-Nazi propaganda bandwagon following the successful commercial release of Warner Brothers' *Confessions of a Nazi Spy*. In numerous films, they picture an America honeycombed with fifth columnists and spies.

1939, June—Congressional funding ends for the Federal Theater Project due to its perceived radicalism under director Hallie Flanagan. U.S. Congressman J. Parnell Thomas (R-N.J.), chairman of the House Un-American Activities Committee, asserts in news accounts that "Practically every play presented under the auspices of the National Theater Project is sheer propaganda for Communism or the New Deal."

1939, August—Congressman Martin Dies (D-Tx.) relaunches his attack on subversion in the film industry at a luncheon given in his honor by executives of Twentieth Century-Fox Film Corporation.

1939, August 23—A Nazi-Soviet Non-Aggression Pact clears the way for World War II. The political cynicism displayed by Joseph Stalin in coming to the agreement causes many long-time left intellectuals in the United States and Europe to repudiate their support of communism.

1939, September 1—Germany invades western Poland, and World War II begins in Europe. Later that month, Soviet troops occupy the eastern half of Poland. A Gallup poll released soon afterwards finds that 83 percent of Americans favor keeping the United States out of the European war. An Elmo Roper poll similarly reports only 2 percent are eager to declare war against Germany and just 12 percent are willing to aid the Allies short of sending troops.

1940-1942—Forged documents, planted news stories, doctored public opinion polls and increased numbers of covert actions are used extensively in America by the British Secret Intelligence Service (SIS) operation headed by William "Intrepid" Stephenson, the director of England's espionage network in the United States. These clandestine efforts are conducted with unconditional White House support and the personal approval of President Roosevelt. The refueling stop in British-held Bermuda for transatlantic flights becomes an important propaganda site, where all airmail between the U.S. and Europe is vetted by SIS agents. Targeting German-owned U.S. subsidiary companies and prominent Americans unsympathetic to the British cause, skilled forgers fabricate incriminating documents which are inserted in the post to be later "discovered" by FBI agents alerted by Stephenson's operatives. Among the victims of other elaborate SIS "dirty trick" schemes are patriotic isolationists such as Senator Burton K. Wheeler (D-Mont.), union leader John L. Lewis, and U.S. Ambassador to Britain Joseph Kennedy, father of the future president.

1940-1941—Colonel Charles Lindbergh, Jr., becomes the most prominent public leader of the isolationist America First Committee.

1940—Edward R. Murrow brings the European war into America's living rooms through emotional radio newscasts from Britain aired on CBS.

Leon Trotsky is murdered in his Mexico City home by an agent of Stalin. This further widens the gap between American communists loyal to the two sides.

George Seldes, despite a media boycott, starts the newsletter *Infact* as the first publication in the United States devoted entirely to press criticism.

The Smith Act requires the U.S. press to submit stories for censorship.

1940, February 21—Hollywood intellectuals, led by screenwriters Donald Ogden Stewart and Dorothy Parker, hold a mass meeting protesting anticommunist red-baiting by the House Un-American Activities Committee.

1940, August—Responding to growing concerns over the active promotion of communist ideology by members of the film industry, the Los Angeles, California, Grand Jury holds its own hearings.

1940, September 2—U.S. Communist party activists create American Peace Mobilization to keep the United States out of the European war.

1940, September 27—A "Tri-partite Pact" is negotiated between Germany, Italy, and Japan. This forms an "axis" cooperative agreement, seen by only some Americans as a threat to U.S. national interests.

1940, October 30—In a speech in Boston, President Franklin D. Roosevelt emphatically declares: "I have said this before, but I shall say it again and again and again: Your boys are not going to be sent into any foreign wars."

1941—The FCC rules in the *Mayflower* decision that U.S. broadcasters should not editorialize or otherwise advocate controversial positions. About this time, WNBT becomes the first commercial television station in the world.

Warner & Swasey Company, as part of its long running issue advertising campaign circulated in many business periodicals, creates an ad in 1941 titled, "Wonder What a Frenchman Thinks About?" This effectively uses the fear of Nazism to a foster patriotic commitment to American capitalism, replete with several glaring propaganda devices identified by the Institute for Propaganda Analysis (including band wagon, transfer, and card stacking). The ad voices the regret of the French worker in these words:

I wish I had been less greedy for myself and more anxious for my country; I wish I had realized you can't beat a determined invader by a quarreling, disunited people at home; I wish I had been willing to give in on some of my rights to other Frenchmen instead of giving up all of them to a foreigner; I wish I had realized other Frenchmen had rights, too; I wish I had known that patriotism is work, not talk, giving not getting.

1941, January 6—President Roosevelt proclaims his belief in the essential "Four Freedoms"—of speech and expression, of worship, from want, and from fear.

1941, April 19—The Fight for Freedom Committee is incorporated in New York City to arouse the American people into fighting Hitler. Arguing that the United States is already at war against the Axis powers, Fight for Freedom organizers soon establish local chapters across the country to hold rallies, place news stories, and agitate against isolationism.

1941, May—According to David Brinkley's *Washington Goes to War*, "over three thousand British businessmen, military officers, and Foreign Office officials [are] working in Washington to promote their country's cause. . . They [have] the satisfaction of watching, and helping to create, a shift in American opinion that ultimately [leaves] the isolationists and Anglophobes a powerless minority and [turns] England into America's most revered ally."

1941, June—The advertising firm of Batten, Barton, Durstine & Osborn (BBDO) is selected by the U.S. Navy to design a recruitment program for new enlistees.

1941, July 25—The United States government begins an embargo of strategic trade with Japan, freezing credits and refusing to sell American steel and oil.

1941, August 14—The Atlantic Charter is issued as a press release by President Franklin D. Roosevelt and British Prime Minister Winston Churchill, who meet at sea. This "joint declaration of peace aims" incorporates the "Four Freedoms" earlier articulated by FDR.

1941, September 8—A U.S. Senate Subcommittee of the Committee on Interstate Commerce, comprised of five isolationist senators (D. Worth Clark, chairman, [D-Idaho]; Homer T. Bone [D-Wash.]; C. Wayland Brooks [R-Ill.]; Ernest W. McFarland [D-Ariz.]; and Charles W. Tobey [R-N.H.]), begins investigating pro-British and anti-German war propaganda in Hollywood films. The California state legislature during this period also conducts its own investigation. Wendell Wilkie is appointed legal counsel and spokesman by the motion picture industry. The subcommittee is widely criticized as a pro-Nazi forum because testimony focuses on alleged Jewish control of American movies. Clark and the others are defended as patriots by Senator Gerald P. Nye (R-N.D.) and Father Charles Coughlin. The subcommittee recesses after two weeks of hearings and never reconvenes after the United States enters World War II. The hearings are published as *Propaganda in Motion Pictures* by the U.S. Government Printing Office in 1942, complete with a discussion of Senator Nye's exhortation (p. 54) that facts are needed on how many "propaganda films were the work in full or in part of refugee or alien authors, how many refugee or alien actors were cast in these pictures, how many alien writers have been financed by Hollywood and imported to Hollywood by the motion-picture industry, how many immigration visas have been arranged for motion-picture executives and by them."

1941, September 11—Aviator Charles Lindbergh, Jr. charges that "the British, the Jewish and the Roosevelt administration" want the United States to take up arms against Germany. He says Jewish organizations should oppose the prospect of war rather than "agitating" for it. Lindbergh denies being an anti-Semite but refuses to retract his statements.

1941, October 19—One of the most famous advertisements by the Fight for Freedom, Inc., organization appears in the *New York Times* warning, "In Hitler's Own Words: Shut up, Yank — learn to speak NAZI!"

1941, November 26—Hopes for a peaceful resolution of American-Japanese differences erode after the United States government issues a secret war ultimatum to Japan demanding its complete withdrawal from China and Indochina.

1941, December 5—A six-year-old state law prohibiting hate agitation and propaganda ("the Rafferty Act") is struck down by the New Jersey Supreme

Court as an unconstitutional abridgment of free speech. The justices unanimously hold that anti-Jewish remarks expressed at a German-American Bund meeting in June 1940 hosted by Nazi sympathizers did not constitute "a clear and present danger to the peace and safety of the state."

1941, December 7—Japanese aircraft carriers bomb America's Pearl Harbor naval base in Hawaii. President Roosevelt proclaims it "a date which will live in infamy."

1941, December 8—Congressman Hamilton Fish, Sr., (R-N.Y.), who had previously favored a nonintervention policy in foreign conflicts, takes the House floor to advocate retaliation for the sneak attack on Pearl Harbor. His speech marks the first congressional radio broadcast. The United States Congress votes for war against Japan (388-1 in the House; 88-0 in the Senate).

1941, December 11—Germany and Italy declare war on the U.S. This simplifies the choices facing the Roosevelt administration, with America joining Britain and the Soviet Union as allies against the Axis powers.

Recognizing that Americans will soon be expected to fight and die around the globe against formidable foes, the country quickly unites behind the war effort. Less than a week after Pearl Harbor, for example, U.S. songwriters copyright over 250 tunes with racist or insulting titles such as *We're Gonna Take a Fellow Who Is Yellow, and Beat Him Red, White and Blue* and *You're a Sap, Mr. Jap.*

In December, the U.S. Office of Facts and Figures (OFF) is founded as a propaganda monitoring agency under the leadership of poet Archibald MacLeish. Among the first to volunteer is communications scholar Wilbur Schramm.

With the U.S. entry into World War II, American documentary filmmaking is also stimulated by new federal funding as government agencies produce films to help unite the country behind the war effort. Many Hollywood studio veterans are also drafted into such media work. Major Frank Capra is commissioned by General George C. Marshall to create the *Why We Fight* "informational" documentary film series to explain the war to American military servicemen (commonly known as GIs, the shortened form for General Inductees). In these productions, Capra brilliantly incorporates animation, multiple narrators, recreations, and juxtaposed segments of Nazi and other materials. Capra's recutting of Leni Riefenstahl's National Socialist party rally films imposes a convincing anti-Nazi construction on motion pictures originally designed to glorify the Hitler regime, a classic example illustrating the power of editing and distortion in propaganda work. Working under Capra during the next five years in creating virulent and effective propaganda films are a number of talents, including Theodor Seuss Geisel, later known as Dr. Seuss, the author of beloved children's books.

1942—The Roosevelt administration moves to suppress domestic criticism of the war effort by ordering the post office to revoke mailing privileges for dozens of "subversive" publications such as Father Charles Coughlin's *Social Justice.*

The Advertising Council is established by the advertising industry to support the war effort. Volunteers at member agencies subsequently donate millions of dollars in creative time to publicize hundreds of organizations and positions on such wide-ranging issues as drunken driving prevention, savings bonds, social security, safety belt education, the U.S. Bicentennial, the United Nations, and world hunger problems.

Magnetic audio recording tape is invented.

1942, February—Racial fears of a fifth column uprising in California prompt the army to issue an order forcing the hasty relocation of 120,000 Japanese-Americans (many of them U.S. citizens) into inland concentration prison camps. President Roosevelt approves the intern action on national security grounds. A series of smaller camps are established for selected German-Americans and others suspected of disloyalty.

1942, February 12—Despite earlier help from the U.S. government in getting released from a Spanish jail, Jane Anderson begins broadcasting radio propaganda commentaries for the Hitler government.

1942, February 24—The Voice of America goes on the air to Europeans for the first time with a fifteen-minute program in German. This inaugural broadcast states: "The Voice of America speaks. Today, America has been at war for 79 days. Daily at this time, we shall speak to you about America and the war. The news may be good or bad. We shall tell you the truth." Similar programs in Italian, French, and English soon follow.

1942, March—Eugene Dennis of the Communist Party USA says support for the USSR should take precedence over the war in Asia. During this same period, the "Russia Is Our Ally" propaganda theme receives a drumbeat of government and media support.

1942, June 13—To make the war understandable to Americans, hundreds of employees engage in government public relations work (with 250 handling news releases alone) under the direction of veteran radio journalist Elmer Davis for the new U.S. Office of War Information (OWI), which is established by presidential Executive Order. Congress soon forces the merger of the Office of Facts and Figures into OWI, cutting OFF's budget in half.

1942, October—Voluntary sales of U.S. bonds raise only $10 billion during the first nine months of the war despite much publicity, involvement by famous Hollywood stars and sports figures, twenty-four-hour "radiothons," local fund drives, and general enthusiasm for the war effort. Government expenditures during this period are over $160 billion.

Communists in the United States urge an American "second front" effort to defeat the Nazis.

1943-1944—Government-sponsored broadcast propaganda is widely evident in patriotic radio programs such as *Treasury Star Parade*.

1943—The U.S. government forces NBC to sell its second (or "blue") radio network because of antitrust concerns. This network eventually becomes the American Broadcasting Companies (ABC).

Polish Jewish legalist Raphael Lemkin invents the word *genocide*, meaning the deliberate attempt to wipe out an ethnic or national group through mass murder and other means.

1943, May 22—The Communist International (Comintern) is disbanded, which is hailed as a step toward peaceful Soviet-American peaceful coexistence.

1944—The Roosevelt administration initiates sedition charges against a "Who's Who" roster of noninterventionist and anticommunist dissenters using "conspiracy" and "guilt-by-association" arguments. Some civil libertarians see in the proceedings an American version of the Soviet "show trials." The defendants are freed after the presiding judge dies and government prosecutors are forced to abandon the cases.

U.S. government and media support for the Soviet-U.S. alliance helps American Communist party membership reach 80,000.

The war years are good for the corporations making up the U.S. broadcast industry, earning them 222.6 percent before tax profits in 1944. These gains help underwrite the move of the radio networks into television. Sponsors begin to reserve time for after the war when commercial television restarts in United States.

1944, June 6—The Allied D-Day (short for Decision-Day) invasion of western Europe is launched.

1944, November—Franklin D. Roosevelt wins an unprecedented fourth presidential election. Democratic party bosses, secretly worried about FDR's declining health, successfully dump incumbent Vice President Henry Wallace from the ticket at the national nominating convention by portraying him as too liberal. The new vice president-elect is Senator Harry S. Truman (D-Missouri).

1944, November 24—The Allied Control Council, formed by the United States and its key military allies in the war to serve as a temporary government for liberated territories, issues Law No. 191 which orders the closing of all National Socialist media and the censoring of resurgent neo-Nazi ideologies. Responsibility for implementing these denazification directives is given to the council's Information Control Division, with orders to restore German communications services "as instrumentalities of democratic, peace loving society."

1945-1946—A notable advertisement of this era, reflecting the internecine battle within the rail industry, is one used by the Chesapeake & Ohio Railway—Nickel Plate Road to dramatize the fact that freight, and particularly agricultural produce, is given preferential treatment in transcontinental shipment. The headline of the advertisement makes the point: "A Hog Can Cross the Country Without Changing Trains—But YOU Can't!"

1945—The U.S. Federal Communications Commission (FCC) encourages the development of television, moving FM radio to another part of the electromagnetic band and giving part of the set-aside spectrum space to TV licensees.

Ebony magazine is founded, targeting the "Negro" audience.

Approximately 80 percent of U.S. newspapers are privately owned.

1945, January—Russian forces advance deeply into Nazi-occupied Poland, liberating the infamous Auschwitz prison camp. News accounts and photojournalistic images begin to explain the horrors that went on there.

1945, February 4-11—Yalta meeting in the Soviet Union between Roosevelt, Stalin, and Churchill attempts to clarify postwar policy. Roosevelt seeks to create cooperation with the Soviets, but the decisions taken there are seen by conservatives in the United States as a sellout to Communist expansion.

1945, March—U.S. Justice Department operatives raid the offices of a Communist-sponsored magazine, *Amerasia*, and find secret government documents in the files.

1945, March 22—The Arab League is founded. Its charter makes no provision for a public information department.

1945, April 12—Roosevelt dies; Harry S. Truman becomes president.

1945, April 25—The founding conference of the United Nations Organization (UNO or UN) starts in San Francisco, accompanied by a heavy proglobalist propaganda effort.

1945, May 8—VE-Day: World War II ends in Europe with the defeat of Germany and Italy.

1945, August 14—VJ-Day: World War II ends in Asia with Japan's surrender following the dropping of two atomic bombs at Hiroshima and Nagasaki by the U.S. Army Air Force. Official figures later record 292,131 Americans killed in World War II.

1945, September—An International Military Tribunal is set up at Nuremberg, Germany, to try the remaining Nazi leadership for war crimes.

1945, December 15—President Truman urges Chiang Kai-shek to accept Communists into his Chinese government.

1946—The end of the war removes the cause that temporarily united American documentary filmmaking, and government funding for these types of pictures is cut. Nevertheless, the army indoctrination film *Your Job in Germany*, released commercially by Warner Brothers as *Hitler Lives*, wins the Academy Award for best documentary short subject of 1945. The production attempts to discourage postwar fraternization by U.S. Army occupation forces, brilliantly caricaturing the alleged "inherent belligerency" of the German people. The picture is cowritten by Theodor Seuss Geisel and his wife. Their follow-up film, *Design for Death* (1946), wins an Oscar the following year from the Academy of Motion Picture Arts and Sciences.

CBS and NBC give the first American public demonstrations of color television. About this time, the FCC issues the so-called *Blue Book* which gives specific programming guidelines to licensees for the first time, further eroding broadcast First Amendment rights.

A Soviet spy ring is uncovered by Canadian authorities, raising questions about the possibility of similar spying in the United States.

1946, March—In the college town of Fulton, Missouri, Winston Churchill makes his now famous "Iron Curtain" speech warning against Soviet expansionism. Ironically, the phrase was first coined by German propagandist Joseph Goebbels and Churchill's remarks were widely panned by his contemporaries for being too hard-line.

1946, April 4—Member states of the Arab League charge it with formulating and internationally disseminating positive information (propaganda) about Arab peoples and issues.

1946, July 4—The Philippines receive its independence from the United States.

1946, July 17—The American China Policy Association, Inc., is founded to warn against "dangerous procommunist policies" followed by the U.S. government.

1946, October—*Plain Talk*, an anticommunist monthly magazine, is launched by Alfred Kohlberg.

1946, October 1—Twelve high-ranking Nazi leaders receive the death sentence at the Nuremberg War Trials, with seven other defendants given terms of imprisonment.

1946, November—"Tailgunner Joe" McCarthy is elected as a U.S. Senator from Wisconsin (R) on a strong anticommunist platform.

1946, December 18—President Truman proclaims a "hands-off" policy in China.

1947—The War Department in the Pentagon is renamed the Defense Department. As part of related reforms, the National Security Act of 1947 establishes the U.S. Central Intelligence Agency (CIA). Also created is the National Security Agency (NSA) to coordinate communication between various agencies engaged in security matters. The NSA's National Security Council becomes a forum for debate and a mechanism for policy analysis and development, delivering report recommendations to the president. By 1953 a new job title emerges as special assistant to the president for national security affairs, now known as the national security advisor. The NSA is subsequently used as a sort of private intelligence and covert action service for various administrations intending to circumvent congressional restrictions.

The University of Illinois establishes the Institute of Communication Research. Under the direction of Wilbur Schramm, this is the world's first behavioral and social science communication research center, and his appointment as the inaugural professor of communication also leads to the awarding of doctoral degrees in the new discipline.

1947, March 21—Responding to political pressure from members of the U.S. House Un-American Activities Committee (HUAC) and other anticommunists, President Truman issues Executive Order 9835 (the "Loyalty Order"), which creates secret "Loyalty Boards" to review the actions of federal workers. The order accelerates pressure for political orthodoxy and contributes to the post-World War II atmosphere of secrecy and fear in the government. Under its provisions, the attorney general is required to create a list of "subversive" organizations. Any federal employee associated (even peripherally) with such groups is suspected of unfitness to serve in the government. In total, more than 12,000 federal employees are eventually subjected to secret Loyalty Board proceedings.

1947, May 7—Hearings investigating communist influence in the motion picture industry begin under the auspices of the U.S. House Un-American Activities Committee. The HUAC hearings continue sporadically through 1953, leading to trial of the "Hollywood Ten"—writers and directors identified as uncooperative witnesses.

1947, September—The Cominform is established as a replacement to the old Comintern, which was abolished on Stalin's orders in 1943 during the height of the wartime Soviet-U.S. anti-Nazi alliance. This coincides with the publication of *The Cold War* by Walter Lippmann, a book in which he challenges "containment" policies against Russian expansionism advocated by George Kennen and the Truman administration. The term *Cold War* comes to identify the emergence of a new kind of "peaceful conflict" between the two superpowers after they realign into geopolitical blocs competing for international postwar dominance.

1947, October—Congress follows up on Truman's "Loyalty Order" by authorizing new procedures under which employees of sensitive agencies can be summarily dismissed for disloyalty. Any "written evidence or oral expressions by speeches or otherwise, of political, economic or social views" is enough to get a federal worker fired.

1947, November 24—More than fifty chief studio executives making up the

Association of Motion Picture Producers, responding to negative publicity created by the Hollywood Ten investigations, meet at the Waldorf-Astoria Hotel in New York. The "Waldorf Conference" decides to "not knowingly employ a Communist or a member of any party or group which advocates the overthrow of the Government of the United States by force or by any illegal or unconstitutional methods." Despite assurances that the industry leaders plan to "guard against the danger, risk, and fear" that innocent people will be hurt by their decision, the effect is to create a blacklist of hundreds of controversial leftists who are denied movie and broadcast work in the United States for more than a decade. The first to go on suspension without pay are writers of "dubious" political sympathies. Only Sam Goldwyn of Metro-Goldwyn-Mayer (MGM), Dore Schary of Radio-Keith-Orpheum (RKO), and Walter Wanger, a noted independent, dissent from the final statement.

1947, November 29—The United Nations Organization General Assembly proposes a "Plan for the Partition of Palestine" into Jewish and Arab states.

1948—Long-playing records (LPs) are invented and transistor radios go on sale, but the radio industry's high-water mark and biggest money year is followed by the erosion of its audience to television. The growing popularity of the new medium causes the FCC to temporarily "freeze" the allocation of new TV licenses while the commission rethinks its regulatory policies. This same year, *TV Guide* begins publication and serves as the most important print vehicle for industry publicists promoting programs and hyping celebrities to American audiences. The emergence of network television and federal antitrust intervention also alters the organization of the film business, resulting in a slow breakup of the Hollywood studio system. U.S. screens open up to independent films from domestic and foreign sources.

The United Nations Universal Declaration of Human Rights is adopted, including Article 19: "Everyone has the right to freedom of opinion and expression; this right includes freedom to hold opinions without interference and to seek, receive and impart information and ideas through any media and regardless of frontiers."

After postwar funding cuts, Congress resurrects the Voice of America to launch a worldwide anticommunist "Campaign for Truth" to counteract Radio Moscow's barrage of international propaganda broadcasts. National Security Directive NSC 10/2 also authorizes covert action and propaganda by U.S. intelligence services.

The *National Guardian* (later the *Guardian*), a weekly news voice for liberal issues and propaganda, is founded by Cedric Belfrage and James Aronson. Although Belfrage and Aronson are identified by critics as communists toeing the Stalinist line, the newspaper nonetheless publishes valuable inside information and analysis. Belfrage is able to tap contacts made from involvement in British intelligence during World War I and later experience at General Dwight D. Eisenhower's Supreme Headquarters of the Allied Expeditionary Forces (SHAEF) in post-World War II Europe, where he worked as part of the Psychological Warfare Division to "democratize" German news organs.

Whittaker Chambers, an editor for *Time* magazine, confesses to the U.S. House Un-American Activities Committee that he belonged to the Communist party during the 1930s. Chambers also testifies that Alger Hiss, the president of the Carnegie Endowment for International Peace and a prominent former U.S. State Department official, was also a member in that period. Chambers says he gave Hiss a number of secret federal documents to forward on to their Communist superiors. Hiss denies the charges, claiming he is a victim of red-baiting.

Harold D. Lasswell designs the "who says what to whom with what effect?" model of communication.

The Public Relations Society of America (PRSA) is established to promote professional development of the field.

With the support of both the United States and the Soviet Union, Israel is founded as a homeland for Jews, but soon finds itself engulfed in war with its Arab neighbors.

1948, September 24—Mildred Gillars, known to American GIs in Europe as "Axis Sally," pleads innocent at her trial for treason in Washington, D.C. Charged with broadcasting Nazi wartime radio propaganda, Gillars is convicted and serves twelve years in prison.

1948, November—The national presidential election is one of the most interesting in years, featuring a broad range of candidates. Truman defeats Republican Thomas E. Dewey of New York by an electoral vote of 304 to 189 (24,104,836 popular votes to 21,969,500). Campaigning as a prosegregationist, conservative, States' Rights Democrat, Strom Thurmond of South Carolina garners 1,169,312 votes, a little over two percent of all ballots cast. The liberal former vice president, Henry Wallace, runs under the Progressive party banner and receives 1,157,172 votes. Other radical candidates fail to attract much voter support, as follows: Socialist party, 139,009; Socialist Labor party, 29,061; and Socialist Workers party, 13,613.

1949—Claude Shannon and Warren Weaver publish *The Mathematical Theory of Communication*, including a seminal model describing the process of communication.

Radio Free Europe's short-wave service debuts, delivering news to Eastern Bloc countries from transmitters in Germany.

U.S. film distributors refuse to exhibit *Oliver Twist*, a film produced in Britain by the Rank Organization. Although faithful to Charles Dickens' novel, the Anti-Defamation League and other Jewish groups raise concerns over the potential of the Fagin characterization for anti-Semitic propaganda.

The Aspen Institute is established as a think tank to "revive the intellectual life of Germany." Following 1953, Aspen becomes more international in scope, with later reports linking it to the CIA.

Herbert Philbrick, who served for nine years as an FBI undercover agent while acting as a high-level Communist party operative, is the key government witness in a major federal subversion trial. Eleven leaders of the Communist Party USA are convicted and jailed for conspiracy to teach and advocate the violent overthrow of the U.S. government.

The Waldorf-Astoria Hotel serves as the meeting site for the Scientific Conference for World Peace, which is attended by Soviet delegates as part of a "peace offensive." Attacked by anticommunists such as Sydney Hook, the conference leads to the formation of the American Committee for Cultural Freedom as an opposition group.

Journalist Lewis Hill forms the Pacifica Foundation to promote alternative progressive viewpoints, using various media including radio.

The FCC changes its editorializing policies. Through the "Fairness Doctrine," the commission now allows American broadcast licensees to present editorial views in their regular programming on condition that time for opposing viewpoints also be made available.

Dragnet, a police program based on real-life events, begins airing on the NBC radio network, running until 1956. Fictional elements include the decision to "change the names to protect the innocent," as well as to minimize the lawsuits producers might face for invasion of privacy. The series is also successfully transplanted to television (1951-1959, 1967-1970, NBC-TV). The various incarnations of the series serve to propagate a progovernment "law and order" ideology.

The first cable television system is established.

1949, April—The North Atlantic Treaty Organization (NATO) treaty is signed.

1949, August 5—The U.S. State Department issues a "white paper" disclaiming any responsibility for the communist conquest of mainland China.

1950—The U.S. House of Representatives creates a Select Committee on Lobbying Activities (better known as the Buchanan Committee) to investigate the extent of organized special interests and their influence on Congress. The hearings fail to articulate what constitutes vital common interests that might collectively define the public interest. In other legislation, criminal penalties are enacted by Congress for anyone who "publishes" communication intelligence (COMINT) information.

The Federal Council of Churches changes its name to National Council of Churches.

Unionized workers in the United States comprise approximately 25 per cent of the total labor force.

Nine percent of all American homes (about 1.5 million) are equipped with TV sets.

Armstrong Circle Theatre (1950-1957, NBC-TV; 1957-1963, CBS-TV) first airs, basing many of its stories on contemporary news accounts. Although a journalist serves as host-narrator, the docudramatic style requires the use of actors and dramatic dialogue to recreate the events depicted.

Eric Blair, better known under his pen name "George Orwell," dies of tuberculosis in London. In a courageous 16-year career he alienates ideologues of both the left and right in Europe and the United States by brilliantly railing against the false promises of totalitarianism in hopes of engendering a "common sense" democratic socialism.

The Congress of Cultural Freedom (CCF), led by German-speaking Americans, holds an enormous rally in West Berlin to "defend freedom and democracy" in answer to communist government-sponsored jamborees held in East Berlin. Not until 1967 is the CCF revealed to be a CIA front.

1950, January 11—Senator Robert A. Taft (R-Ohio) accuses the U.S. State Department of being guided by leftists in carrying out American policy towards China.

1950, January 20—Following two trials and three years of complicated legal maneuvers, former U.S. State Department official Alger Hiss is convicted of perjury for his denials before the U.S. House Un-American Activities Committee that he spied for the Soviet Union. Hiss ends up serving a three and a half year prison term. Congressman Richard M. Nixon (R-Calif.) emerges as a national figure because of the sensational hearings. The case raises important issues about national security, civic loyalty, and the legitimacy of government authority in helping the jury come to its controversial verdict.

1950, February—Officials of the U.S. Justice Department and their counterparts from the British government's Scotland Yard reveal they have been cooperating in an investigation of a spy ring active in passing nuclear secrets to the Soviet Union. As a result of the probe, Americans Julius Rosenberg and Ethel Rosenberg are arrested by FBI agents for their alleged role in the plot.

1950, February 9—Senator Joseph McCarthy (R-Wisc.) makes his now-famous "numbers" speech in Wheeling, West Virginia, in which he charges that the U.S. State Department harbors many communists and is "riddled" with traitors. The post-World War II reemergence of isolationism soon culminates in the Subversive Activities Control Act of 1950, which sets the stage for a series of dramatic anticommunist hearings. On March 8, the Tydings Committee starts investigative hearings on State Department employee loyalty. Other proceedings chaired by Senator McCarthy in the early 1950s turn particularly abusive, and he is catapulted into national prominence. Critics call McCarthy's highly publicized personal crusade a political witch-hunt and the word *McCarthyism* enters the vocabulary to indicate any investigation where the primary purpose is to discredit the victims by besmirching their reputations through innuendo and alleging wrongdoing without actual proof.

1950, May—Alfred Kolhberg's *Plain Talk* ends publication and merges with the *Freeman*.

1950, June 25—North Korean forces equipped with Soviet-made arms cross the border into South Korea. American President Harry S. Truman receives UNO authorization to conduct a "police action" under U.S. military leadership to repel the invaders.

1950, fall—Over President Truman's veto, Congress passes the McCarran (Internal Security) Act, which requires members of the Communist party and "Communist fronts" to register with the U.S. attorney general. The act sets up the Subversive Activities Control Board (SACB) to monitor compliance. The law also permits the deportation of naturalized Americans if they join a communist group within five years of receiving their citizenship, restricts travel overseas by registered communists, and even prohibits entry into the U.S. of ex-communists. The FBI places the number of known American communists at 52,000. These efforts at the highest levels of government also accelerates similar efforts within the private sector. For example, the publication by former FBI agents ("American Business Consultants") of *Red Channels*, a book listing 151 alleged communists employed in the radio and television industry, leads to "political screening" which lasts for years: blacklisting of the accused by advertisers, advertising agencies, and broadcasters. At the same time, George Seldes' *In fact* newsletter ends publication, a victim of government harassment and false red-baiting.

1951—Hundreds of radio stations switch over to the disk jockey (dj) music format to make up for lost revenues as network radio declines. Movie attendance is also down in cities as Americans who can continue to switch their primary leisure time allegiance to programs airing on their local TV stations. There are now an estimated 15 million TV sets in the United States. About this time, the first experimental pay television system is demonstrated by Zenith. One of the major milestones in television journalism, *See It Now*, debuts on CBS-TV in 1951. Host Edward R. Murrow and producer Fred Friendly use an editorial technique that until now has been seldom used—the cross-cut interview. Lengthy, detailed question-and-answer sessions are filmed, but edited into short segments throughout the program. *See It Now* airs until 1958.

Radio Liberty short-wave broadcasts begin, targeting the Soviet Union.

The office of the United Nations High Commissioner for Refugees (UNHCR) is established at the outset of the Cold War to protect and assist refugees fleeing persecution.

1951, April 10—General Douglas MacArthur is removed from command of United Nations troops in Korea by direct order of President Truman. MacArthur returns to the United States and, on April 19, gives his famous "Old Soldiers Never Die" speech in an address to Congress. During 1951, a number of American prisoners of war in Korea prove unprepared for the psychological "brainwashing" horrors they experience in "political re-education" programs conducted by their captors. To bolster the Truman administration's foreign policy intervention in Korea and combat Soviet communism, *Why Korea?* (Twentieth-Century Fox-Movietone News) is distributed without charge by the American movie industry.

1951, July 25—Senate Internal Security Subcommittee (commonly known as the "McCarran Committee" after its chair, Pat McCarran, D-Nev.) hearings on communist infiltration of the Institute of Pacific Relations (IPR) begin and last for nearly a year.

1951, September 1—Israeli Prime Minister David Ben-Gurion issues a directive ordering that the Mossad be set up as an intelligence agency, independent of the Israeli Ministry of Foreign Affairs. The Mossad soon establishes itself as an effective service, with a network of agents in the United States and other countries.

1952—A record 6 million TV sets are sold in the United States. Largely due to the efforts of Frieda Hennock, the first woman member of the Federal Communications Commission, the FCC's Sixth Report and Order ends the TV station license freeze and provides for 242 channels set aside for the exclusive use of noncommercial educational television. To ensure program services for these new, independent educational stations and encourage a more active role by government, the Educational Television and Radio Center is created with funding from the Ford Foundation.

The critically acclaimed compilation documentary *Victory at Sea* (1952-1953, NBC-TV), detailing Navy exploits in World War II, draws on standard Hollywood techniques to highlight heroes and villains, editorially direct attention, and arouse emotion for less-than-neutral ideological purposes.

The Supreme Court reverses the 1915 *Mutual* decision and grants First Amendment protections to motion pictures in *Burstyn v. Wilson* (also known as *The Miracle* case, after the film involved in the litigation).

1952, March—According to Congressman Daniel Reed (R-N.Y.), the number of publicity people employed in all agencies of the federal government total

"23,000 permanent and 22,000 part-time" workers.

1952, June 20—Congressional hearings on the Institute of Pacific Relations end. The IPR's usage as a propaganda front to influence U.S. policy in Asia is confirmed by the Senate Internal Security Subcommittee in a report issued later in the year.

1952, June 27—Passage of the McCarran-Walter Act over President Truman's veto gives the government virtually limitless power to exclude or deport foreigners from the United States on the basis of vaguely defined ideological or public interest grounds. Most of those barred hold political beliefs or organizational affiliations contrary to the foreign policy goals of the administration in power, limiting access by Americans to opposing views and controversial ideas. Anticommunist books such as Herbert A. Philbrick's *I Led Three Lives* prove popular, and FBI statistics demonstrate that the attacks are working, with Communist party membership at under 25,000.

1952, July 11-November 4—Advertising executive Rosser Reeves of Ted Bates & Company masterminds the television campaign of Republican nominee Dwight D. Eisenhower, the first presidential candidate to recognize the importance of TV. Also brought in to help make Eisenhower a more polished media candidate is BBDO agency head Ben Duffy.

Eisenhower's running mate, Senator Richard Nixon (R-Calif.), takes to the airwaves, but not because he wants to. Soon after his vice presidential nomination, damaging news stories about Nixon maintaining a secret slush fund for personal use threaten his candidacy. Party leaders warn that they will kick him off the ticket unless Nixon can restore voter confidence. With nothing to lose, he buys national television time on September 11 to tell his side of the story. Although cloying and unctuous by today's standards, the speech works when he successfully diverts attention to a little dog— Checkers—that he accepted as a gift from supporters. Saying he would not give Checkers back as his daughters love the pup too much, Nixon gives the impression that his family has been impugned. He even says that his wife, Pat, wears "a Republican cloth coat," and they are not ashamed of that, either. Viewer response to the speech, aided by an orchestrated flood of letters to Republican headquarters, secures Nixon's political position.

The Republican party's (GOP's) effective use of Madison Avenue against the Democrats so angers retiring President Harry Truman that he delights in calling BBDO the home of "Bunco, Bull, Deceit & Obfuscation." In the fall elections, the Eisenhower-Nixon team goes on to handily defeat the Democratic party ticket headed by Adlai Stevenson of Illinois.

1953-1954—Guatemalan President Jacobo Arbenz, who moderately leans to the left, angers American business interests by seriously pursuing real land redistribution efforts designed to ensure a better life for his nation's citizens. This independent nationalism sets off alarm bells in official Washington, D.C. As the Eisenhower administration moves to overthrow the first (and to date, last) democratic government in Guatemala, U.S. State Department officials warn that the Central American nation

has become an increasing threat to the stability of Honduras and El Salvador. Its agrarian reform is a powerful propaganda weapon; its broad social program of aiding the workers and peasants in a victorious struggle against the upper classes and large foreign enterprises has a strong appeal to the populations of Central American neighbors where similar conditions prevail.

Cooperating in a CIA-engineered coup, which successfully ousts the elected Arbenz government, are the United Fruit Company and its public relations counsel, Edward L. Bernays. Military rule follows, leading to more than two decades of destabilization and ongoing violence against the nation's Indian population. Human rights groups estimate that more than 100,000 people have died violently since the change in regimes.

1953—The fiercely independent left-wing *I.F. Stone's Weekly* begins publishing, pointing to the news-behind-the-news by raising issues that undercut the certainties of establishment politics. Founder Isador Feinstein "Izzy" Stone's refusal to pander to any political faction and dogged pursuit of facts earn him high journalistic marks despite his radicalism. By 1971, during the height of the Watergate scandal, his publication becomes a biweekly with 70,000 subscribers. Stone's influence is magnified, as the *New York Times* later observes in its obituary tribute, "because so many of the readers were political activists, journalists and academics." The FBI closely monitors his activities but never publicly declares Stone a communist.

Hugh Hefner founds *Playboy* magazine.

Filmmaker Otto Preminger's *The Moon Is Blue* (United Artists) challenges the sexual mores of the day by depicting a teenager who is unhappy about being a virgin. The picture appears in theaters without a Motion Picture Production Code Seal and does good box office, the first major release to defy industry censorship in more than twenty years.

Burson-Marsteller, now one of the world's largest public relations firms, is founded as a joint venture by Harold Burson and William Marsteller. It will grow from 4 people working out of one office to a network of more than 2,100 people and forty-three offices worldwide.

The Voice of America becomes part of the U.S. Information Agency.

In Iran, the independent secular nationalist government of prime minister Mohammed Mossadeq, even though pro-Western and anti-Soviet, is overthrown by supporters of the shah with covert assistance from U.S. oil interests and the CIA.

After numerous political defeats, the Arab League establishes a Department of Information and Publications to target various audiences, including Americans.

1953, April—Grace Lumpkin testifies before the U.S. Senate Permanent Investigating Subcommittee that she wrote Communist party propaganda into her novel *A Sign for Cain* published in 1935, "after being told that Communist book reviewers would 'break' her literary career if she did not."

1953, May—KUHT-TV at the University of Houston becomes the first noncommercial educational television station in the nation to actually begin airing programs.

1953, June 19—Julius and Ethel Rosenberg are executed following their conviction as alleged communist spies.

1953, July 27—An armistice is signed to end the Korean conflict. Total casualties by members of the U.S. armed forces officially number 137,051, including 25,604 dead.

1954—Prince Bernhard of the Netherlands chairs a discussion group of leading international policymakers, backed by Rothschild and Rockefeller interests. The meeting of prominent business tycoons, bankers, politicians, media moguls, and educators is held secretly at the De Bilderberg Hotel in Oosterbeek, Holland. The aversion to publicity by high-ranking individuals (many from the United States) at this and all subsequent annual meetings fuels speculation by opponents of one-world government about a "Bilderberg Group" conspiratorial cabal. The ongoing semisecret liaisons by elite policymakers who become known as the Bilderbergers, always held in high-security lavish accommodations at various locations around the world, soon becomes a favorite target of conspiracy theorists.

There are an estimated 29 million TV sets in United States. The Army-McCarthy Senate hearings are televised, with Edward R. Murrow exposing Senator Joseph McCarthy's tactics on *See It Now* (CBS-TV).

1955—The modern U.S. civil rights movement is strengthened by the courageous action of one person. Rosa Parks, a black seamstress living in Montgomery, Alabama, refuses to sit in the back of a public bus as required by segregationist laws then in effect. She is arrested, but her protest is taken up by the Reverend Dr. Martin Luther King, Jr. He leads a nonviolent boycott of the bus system that focuses public attention on the issue, eventually leading to the enactment of national civil rights acts in 1957, 1960, and 1964.

The rock-and-roll era on radio begins with Bill Haley and the Comets' *Rock Around the Clock* reaching number one on the music industry sales charts.

Sixty-five percent of all American homes are equipped with TV sets, but the DuMont Television Network stops broadcasting due to competitive economic problems with the three other major networks.

Ultra high frequency (UHF) waves are produced at the Massachusetts Institute of Technology.

The controversial dramatic feature film about drug abuse by Otto Preminger, *The Man with the Golden Arm*, is released without Motion Picture Production Code approval.

The commercial and critical success of the *Village Voice* demonstrates a new style of alternative press.

Cedric Belfrage's support for communism leads to his deportation from the United States under the McCarran-Walter Act. For the next twelve years, he continues to write for the *Guardian* as "editor-in-exile" from Cuba, British Guiana, and elsewhere before retiring.

1955, February—*Armstrong Circle Theatre* begins its thirteen season run as the first continuing sixty-minute series to utilize the pure docudrama form on U.S. television. Executive producer David Susskind and producer Robert Costello set the guidelines for this unique format: "We aim to combine fact and drama—to arouse interest, even controversy, on important and topical subjects. . . . We can't use an idea only or a news story only, we must also be able to present some potential solution, some hope for your citizens to consider, to think about."

1956—Videotape is introduced to television by Ampex Corporation, presaging the end of many live national programs.

Liberty Lobby is founded by Willis Carto. The organization, based in

Washington, D.C., grows in influence to become a multimillion-dollar political information action operation, stressing America First populist themes through the *Spotlight* (a weekly newspaper), revisionist books, and other publications. By the late 1960s, more conventional conservative organizations disavow Liberty Lobby's "ultraconservative," anti-Zionist positions and the allegedly racist materials it distributes. The Anti-Defamation League of B'nai B'rith and liberal opponents such as columnist Drew Pearson publicly warn of Carto's "enormous political power" and label the Liberty Lobby a "neo-Nazi group," despite denials by Carto and other Liberty Lobby officials that all they advocate are nationalist constitutional policies, economy in government, low taxes, and nonintervention in the quarrels of other nations.

The Federal Bureau of Investigation begins a highly secret domestic spying and infiltration effort known as COINTELPRO (Counterintelligence Program) to track left- and right-wing political activist groups opposed to U.S. government policies.

Collier's magazine ends publication.

Transatlantic cable telephone service is inaugurated.

The presidential rematch of Dwight Eisenhower and Adlai Stevenson leads to the first extensive national U.S. television coverage of political campaigns. Eisenhower again wins.

1957—The first man-made satellites, *Sputnik I* and *Sputnik II* from the USSR, orbit the earth. This proves a propaganda coup for the Soviets and forces the United States to reevaluate its educational and technological priorities.

Leon Festinger publishes *A Theory of Cognitive Dissonance*, which convincingly demonstrates that people selectively interpret information and choose to ignore "inconvenient" facts and ideas that contradict their own attitudes, opinions, and prejudices.

1958-1963—Senator (later President) John F. Kennedy (D-Mass.) commissions 93 public opinion polls for private use.

1958—United Press and the International News Service combine to form United Press International.

1959-1960—A series of incidents occur in which Nazi swastikas are painted on Jewish graves and synagogue walls throughout West Germany and other European countries. Later, these widely publicized desecrations are revealed to have been part of a Soviet KGB-led disinformation campaign designed to discredit the West German government and weaken the western alliance headed by the United States.

1959—Scandals on radio ("plugola") and television (rigged quiz shows) force broadcasters to become more responsible for programs they air, undercutting advertising sponsor influence over content.

1959, January 1—The beleaguered dictator of Cuba, Fulgencio Batista, carts away several million dollars on a one-way airplane ride off the island. The following day, a rebel army led by Fidel Castro seizes power.

1960-1963—The House Un-American Activities Committee and Senate Internal Security Subcommittee investigate Pacifica Foundation radio programming for signs of disloyalty. Among the suspected intellectuals are Herbert Aptheker, Norman Cousins, W.E.B. DuBois, and Carey McWilliams.

1960—Registered professional lobbyists seeking to influence the U.S. Senate total 365.

An American U-2 spy plane is shot down over the USSR and the Cold War resumes.

The National Committee to Abolish the House Committee on Un-American Activities, later known as the National Committee Against Repressive Legislation (NCARL), is founded. The FBI soon targets the committee in attempts to "neutralize" its influence.

Major newspapers extend the use of computers for typesetting, but higher expenses and competition from television lead many owners to consider selling out or merging.

There are an estimated 85 million television sets in the United States, 10.5 million in Britain, and 1.5 million in France.

"Hollywood Ten" alumnus Dalton Trumbo garners an Academy Award for his work on *Spartacus* (Universal Pictures Company, 1959). He is the first of the blacklisted writers to once again officially receive on-screen credit for a U.S. motion picture studio production. The blacklist breaks down after scripts written by banned writers falsely credited to others (including one by Trumbo) receive Academy Awards in 1958 and 1959. Not until years later are the Oscars actually presented to their rightful recipients.

1960, September 26—The Nixon-Kennedy "Great Debate" is the first between major presidential candidates to be televised. Even though Vice President Nixon (R-Calif.) "wins" on radio, Senator John F. Kennedy (D-Mass.) "wins" the debate on television—proving the greater power of the new medium to politicians. In a very close race, Kennedy goes on to win the November election.

1961-1974—According to Gregory F. Treverton's book *Covert Action* (1987), "Of the thirty-odd covert actions undertaken by the CIA in Chile between 1961 and 1974, propaganda was the principal element of a half dozen. It was an important subsidiary part of many others."

1961—President Kennedy announces plans for the Peace Corps. White House Press Secretary Pierre Salinger soon convinces Kennedy to authorize the first live broadcasts of presidential news conferences. Prior to this, any recorded presidential news material was either off-the-record or subject to prior White House editing.

In a widely discussed speech, FCC Chairman Newton Minnow says televison is "a vast wasteland."

The American Institute for Free Labor Development (AIFLD) is set up in Washington, D.C., as a secret front, with field offices in most Latin American capital cities. While ostensibly an educational training institute in support of worker democracy, AIFLD's real purpose is to organize new unions or take over existing ones in such a way that these organizations will be controlled, directly or indirectly, by the CIA.

1961, April 24—President Kennedy states that he accepts full responsibility for the failure of the American-supported Bay of Pigs invasion of Cuba.

1962-1963—Tom Wolfe and Jimmy Breslin begin using "New Journalism" techniques in writing for the *New York Herald Tribune*.

1962—*Telstar I* sends the first transatlantic satellite television broadcast.

Red Nightmare (Warner Brothers, reissued 1965), with popular actors Jack Kelley and Robert Conrad, is produced under the personal supervision of Jack L. Warner and narrated by television star/producer Jack Webb. Such "educational" motion pictures help cement a long-lasting, formal alliance between the Hollywood studios and the Pentagon through such cosponsors as the Department of Defense Directorate for the Armed Forces and Educational Information.

Leaders of the Students for a Democratic Society (SDS) outline a series of goals in the *Port Huron Statement*, marking the beginning of 1960s "new left" college campus activism.

WBAI-FM, the Pacifica Foundation-owned radio station in New York City, criticizes J. Edgar Hoover and exposes unconstitutional activities by the FBI. For their efforts and exercise of constitutionally protected free speech rights, the station is subjected to political harassment from the Justice Department and FBI, bombing and arrest threats, and denunciations from the major commercial broadcasting networks.

1962, October—The Cuban Missile Crisis, a confrontation by the Kennedy administration with the Soviet Union over that nation's attempt to stockpile nuclear warheads in Cuba aimed at the United States, causes a full-scale military alert. The crisis ends when the Soviets withdraw their missiles and the United States stops its naval blockade of Cuban commerce.

1963—Following his return from Saudi Arabia and acceptance of more orthodox Muslim beliefs, Malcolm X ends his relationship with Elijah Muhammad and the Nation of Islam.

1963, August 28—The civil rights "March on Washington for Jobs and Freedom" draws over 200,000 participants. Martin Luther King, Jr., delivers his now-famous "I Have a Dream" speech.

1963, November 22—President John F. Kennedy is assassinated in Dallas, leading to numerous conspiracy theories. Television presents a three-day memorial dirge to the murdered leader in which regular broadcasts are suspended. Vice President Lyndon B. Johnson (D-Tex.) takes the presidential oath of office.

On that same day, writer and futurist Aldous Huxley dies of natural causes.

1963, December-1968, October—Reflecting the great concerns he has about how his policies are perceived, President Johnson commissions 130 public opinion polls for his private use.

1964-1965—Actual membership in various Ku Klux Klan organizations is estimated at 45,000. Gallup Poll survey takers find that 6 percent of Americans are "favorably disposed" to the Klan.

1964—The free speech movement erupts at Berkeley on the University of California campus.

In a major free speech victory, three Pacifica Foundation radio stations are awarded license renewals by the Federal Communications Commission following delays resulting from government-initiated investigations of their programming. The Commissioners issue a policy statement prohibiting probes of ideological ties and censorship of "provocative" programs.

A comprehensive Civil Rights Act is passed by Congress.

Martin Luther King, Jr., is awarded the Nobel Peace Prize.

The Palestine Liberation Organization (PLO) is established.

1964, August—A turning point escalating further American military involvement in the Vietnam conflict occurs with the Gulf of Tonkin incident.

The Johnson administration says that U.S. Navy destroyers "conducting routine patrols and intelligence-gathering in international waters" were attacked by North Vietnamese patrol boats. Only much later does evidence surface to indicate that no attack ever really occurred.

1964, November 3—In a very contentious election campaign, President Lyndon Johnson easily defeats the Republican challenge of U.S. Senator Barry Goldwater (Ariz.). The Democrats are joined by liberal Republicans who repudiate their nominee in successfully portraying (rather falsely) the conservative Goldwater as an extremist. Goldwater supporters, however, do get credit for the best bumper sticker (AuH_2O-64) based on symbols for the chemical elements gold and water.

1964, December 31—Malcolm X, head of the Organization of Afro-American Unity, charges in a speech delivered at the Hotel Teresa in New York City: "Never at any time in the history of our people in this country have we made advances or progress in any way based upon the internal goodwill of this country. We have made advancement in this country only when this country was under pressure from forces above and beyond its control."

1965—Thousands march 54 miles in 5 days, taking part in a triumphant demonstration on behalf of minority civil rights.

Edward R. Murrow dies of lung cancer.

The *Early Bird* communication satellite is launched.

The Highway Beautification Act becomes law with the support of antiadvertising groups. Their goal is to eliminate many of the 780,000 outdoor billboards adjacent to federal highways.

A Defense Department propaganda film *Why Viet Nam?* revives Cold War rhetoric and analyses.

American government officials decide to coordinate propaganda efforts in Vietnam under the aegis of the U.S. Information Agency and through a newly formed Joint U.S. Public Affairs Office (JUSPAO), directed by Barry Zorthian.

1965, February 21—Malcolm X is assassinated in New York City by gunmen linked to a rival black militant group.

1965, October 15-16—Demonstrations occur in cities across the United States, urging an end to continued American involvement in Vietnam. Several protesters publicly burn their draft cards in defiance of a law which went into effect on August 31 making it a crime to do so. Counterdemonstrations are also held by those favoring anticommunist containment in Indochina. Most of the news coverage, however, goes to the antiwar activists. The protests, draft board sit-ins, and other forms of civil disobedience evolve from staged "teach-ins" on Vietnam war issues held at hundreds of colleges and universities. Membership in Students for a Democratic Society (SDS) stands at 10,000.

1966—Black activists, such as Stokely Carmichael of the Student Nonviolent Coordinating Committee (SNCC), become prominent. "Hell no, we won't go!" and "Black Power" are popular militant slogans.

KSAN-FM in San Francisco and KPPC-FM in Los Angeles become "underground" progressive rock radio stations, with a format featuring album cuts, longer songs, satirical news coverage, and intelligent dj's.

Citizen groups are given legal standing to challenge broadcast license renewals in *United Church of Christ v. FCC*. Through the "Project to Combat Political Extremism" and follow-up "Racial Justice in Broadcasting" campaigns, the United Church of Christ (UCC) soon leads the way in efforts toward "cleansing the airwaves of scores of hate stations over the country."

Makers of the commercial feature film *Who's Afraid of Virginia Woolf?* (Warner Brothers) break most Hays Office rules. Nevertheless, industry censors at the Motion Picture Production Code give it a seal of approval as an exception. Public outcries over media sex and violence increase, putting pressure on the Hollywood studios to either accept federal censorship or create a new "voluntary" movie rating system.

The federal government's use of nonprofit foundations to secretly transmit funds for CIA field operations is first publicly revealed. Michigan State University's (MSU's) international program—financed originally by Rockefeller Foundation and later by Ford Foundation grants—is exposed as a hotbed of covert CIA assistance to the Vietnamese regime. MSU president John Hannah is later appointed by President Nixon to head the Agency for International Development (AID).

1967—Massive antiwar protests continue to occur across the United States. SDS membership tops thirty thousand.

The U.S. population reaches the 200 million mark.

Ku Klux Klan membership is estimated at fifty-five thousand.

The Congress of Cultural Freedom is revealed to be a European CIA front. The disclosures lead to changes in the organization's leadership, its renaming as the International Association for Cultural Freedom, and a shift in funding, with new monies from the Ford Foundation.

1967, June 8—A cover-up begins, masking the truth about the Israeli strafing and torpedo attack on the U.S.S. *Liberty* navy "spy" ship. Israeli pilots in American-made F4 Phantom jets repeatedly bomb, rocket and machine-gun the *Liberty* for twenty-five minutes while it monitors battlefield communications in the Middle East's "Six Day War." The findings of a Navy Board of Inquiry into the killing of 34 American servicemen and wounding of 171 more are suppressed on orders of President Lyndon Johnson. The official explanation offered to the American public calls the attack a "tragic mistake."

1967, November—Congress passes the Public Broadcasting Act of 1967, a law which establishes the Corporation for Public Broadcasting (CPB) based on recommendations made earlier in the year by the Carnegie Commission. A Carnegie report to the White House and Congress pushing for the new agency states that television for public use should be a nationwide undertaking. President Johnson endorses the report but believes the CPB should remain detached from the administration's direct political control. The phrase "public television" becomes a standard piece of broadcast terminology, largely replacing the notion of educational television.

1968—An estimated 78 million television sets are found in the United States, 25 million in the Soviet Union, 20.5 million in Japan, and 10 million in France.

1968, January 30—A Tet (New Year) offensive by Viet Cong rebels against Allied centers across Vietnam is a military disaster for the communists. However, the raids prove a public relations bonanza by raising new fears which undercut continued Western support for the South Vietnamese government. A total of 549,500 American troops are officially in Vietnam, marking the peak of U.S. involvement.

1968, February 11—White racism is condemned in a report issued by the President's National Advisory Commission on Civil Disorders ("The Kerner Commission"). The commission calls for massive aid to "Negro communities" in order to stave off further racial polarization.

1968, March 4—FBI officials issue a memo called "Counterintelligence Program: Black Nationalist-Hate Groups, Racial Intelligence," expanding COINTELPRO to forty-four offices. Specifically targeted is the Rev. Martin Luther King, Jr., for his alleged communist leanings in an effort to "prevent the risk of a 'messiah' who could unify and electrify the militant black nationalist movement." As the U.S. Senate Select Committee to Study Government Operations with Respect to Intelligence Activities (chaired by Senator Frank Church, D-Ida.) concludes in its 1976 final report:

> The Committee finds that covert action programs have been used to disrupt the lawful political activities of individual Americans and groups and to discredit them, using dangerous and degrading tactics which are abhorrent in a free and decent society. . . . The sustained use of such tactics by the FBI in an attempt to destroy Dr. Martin Luther King, Jr., violated the law and fundamental human decency.

This damning conclusion is reinforced by the FBI's refusal to make available to the Select Committee evidence on the more extreme disruption programs it used to undercut the black civil rights movement.

1968, March 31—In a dramatic television announcement, President Lyndon B. Johnson tells the nation that he is withdrawing as a candidate for renomination in order to concentrate on finding a solution to the conflict in Vietnam. This follows increasing dissent in the Democratic party and among voters and the media over the conduct of the war. When CBS news anchor Walter Cronkite visits Vietnam and concludes that a stalemate is the best that can be hoped for, President Johnson is reported to have told aides, "If we've lost Cronkite, we've lost middle America."

1968, April 4—The Rev. Martin Luther King, Jr., is killed by a sniper in Memphis, Tennessee. The assassination is followed by a week of rioting in the nation's urban ghettoes. On April 11, President Johnson signs the 1968 Civil Rights Act, making housing discrimination illegal, as a tribute to the slain black leader.

1968, June 5—Senator Robert Kennedy (D-N.Y.) wins the delegate rich California Democratic primary, giving him a good chance at the party's presidential nomination. Immediately after his victory speech in Los Angeles, however, Kennedy is felled by gunshot wounds and dies the following day. The public assassinations of two key leaders in so short a time results in extensive television coverage and a sense of national depression.

1968, August—Youthful protesters (calling themselves the Yippies) battle police at the Democratic National Convention in Chicago. The city's mayor, Richard Daley, orders National Guardsmen to join police in controlling the antiwar demonstrators. This effort at suppression erupts into seven days of generational conflict, which is later described as a "police riot" by the National Commission on the Causes and Prevention of Violence. The convention ends up nominating Vice President Hubert H. Humphrey (D-Minn.) for the presidency, against the backdrop of armed police and National Guard tanks rolling through the streets of Chicago. In a close election, Humphrey loses to Republican Richard M. Nixon. Following the inauguration of President Nixon in 1969, eight of the Yippie movement activists are charged with conspiracy for inciting the Chicago riots. The defendants include Abbie Hoffman; David Dellinger; Tom Hayden, cofounder of Students for a Democratic Society; and Bobby Seale, cofounder of the Black Panther party. The trial turns into a circus, with Judge Julius Hoffman repeatedly threatening the defendants and resorting to chaining a bound-and-gagged Seale to his courtroom chair. This exacerbates racial tensions and helps publicize Black Panther grievances. The FBI and the Chicago police respond with a show of force, conducting a predawn raid on Panther headquarters that results in the death of two Panther members. Although the "Chicago 8" are found guilty in their first trial, the convictions are overturned on appeal.

1968, November 1—To counteract criticism that children are being exposed to excessive violence and sex in films, a new industry ratings system takes effect in place of the discredited Motion Picture Production Code.

1969-1972—President Nixon commissions 233 public opinion polls for private use, including 153 during his 1972 reelection campaign.

1969—Campus unrest, with numerous antiwar and student power demonstrations, continues across the United States. The Weathermen faction splits off from SDS to foment revolutionary violence.

The emotional reaction in Europe and North America to Marcel Ophuls' documentary film on French collaboration in World War II, *Le Chagrin et la Pitie* (*The Sorrow and the Pity*, World Wide Pictures), points to continuing problems caused by postwar mythmaking. The film rips apart the notion that most people under the occupation resisted German rule and Nazi racial theories.

Posse Comitatus, a tax-resistance organization, is founded in Portland, Oregon, by Henry L. Beach, a retired dry cleaner and former member of the Silver Shirts, an earlier racist, pro-Nazi group.

The U.S. Supreme Court, in *Red Lion Broadcasting v. FCC*, rejects the metaphor of the radio or television station licensee as a speaker on an electronic soapbox, instead holding that the Federal Communications Commission's "Fairness Doctrine" rule gives the government the right to rid the airwaves of broadcasters deemed not to be serving the "public interest, convenience and necessity."

The Corporation for Public Broadcasting (CPB) establishes the Public Broadcasting Service (PBS) as an independent agency. The primary duty of PBS is to insulate public television from political control and carry out the process of interconnecting stations across the country by providing a common menu of programs.

Live television coverage of the first manned Moon landing gives a public relations boost to the space program.

The *Saturday Evening Post* ends weekly publication, a casualty of advertisers' shift to television.

1969, June 28—A New York City police raid on an unlicensed, homosexual night club in Greenwich Village known as Stonewall Inn leads to three days of rioting and the birth of the gay rights movement.

1970s—Many larger business associations and firms form new infrastructures to better understand the opinion environment and coordinate public policy efforts. Issues management and advocacy advertising enter the vocabulary, among the more widely discussed of new "boundary-spanning" functions used by corporations for adapting their policies to evolving expectations of social accountability.

A number of new TV series fail, ushering in a "second season" of new prime-time network offerings beginning as early as mid-January. Programmers resort to presenting a "third season" of reruns, pilot shows, and specials from mid-March through June. An analysis of A.C. Nielsen ratings data provides evidence that this last period in network schedules is a key "window" for docudramas to gain access to mass audiences that they might otherwise fail to reach.

1970—Garry Trudeau's "Doonesbury" begins syndication, continuing a tradition of blatantly political comic strips with controversial content dating back to "Little Orphan Annie," Al Capp's "Li'l Abner," and Walt Kelly's "Pogo."

An estimated 231 million television sets are in use worldwide.

ABC realigns its radio division by dividing into a number of "networks" featuring news, information, and entertainment formats demographically targeted to specialized audiences.

The Public Interest Research Group (PIRG) is formed through the leadership of consumer advocate Ralph Nader.

Alvin Toffler's *Future Shock* is published.

Advertising executive David Nolan devises an alternative to the conventional, but imprecise, left/right political scale, which dates back to the seating arrangement in the 1790s French Assembly. Dividing human behavior into "economic freedom" and "civil and personal freedom" categories, the Nolan Chart maps political orientation (classical liberal/libertarian, right/conservative, left/liberal, socialist and populist, and centrist) in terms of the amount of individual choice each "political family" allows.

The term *terrorism* first enters the index to the *New York Times*.

The Irish Northern Aid Committee is established in the United States and comes under FBI surveillance.

In seeking to influence Chilean elections, the CIA successfully provides press "guidance" that generates at least one editorial a day during the campaign that reflects views favorable to U.S. interests in *El Mercurio*, the leading daily newspaper in Santiago.

1970, May 4—During an antiwar demonstration, four students at Kent State University in Ohio are killed by National Guardsmen. This spurs more student street actions. The resulting "Seven Days in May" protests disrupt the nation's capital.

1971-72—A Weathermen bombing campaign occurs, war protests decline, and the SDS disappears.

1971—The U.S. Congress bans cigarette advertisements from airing on radio and television.

The voting age is lowered to 18 with final passage of the Twenty-Sixth Amendment to the U.S. Constitution.

Public Citizen, Inc., is founded by Ralph Nader to lobby for "public interest" causes.

Radicals burglarize the Media, Pennsylvania, office of the FBI, seizing more than a thousand secret documents that expose the illegal COINTELPRO spy program.

Look prints its final regular issue.

1972—Attacks by a coalition of activist groups allied with members of the Federal Communications Commission using Fairness Doctrine requirements to silence what are labeled "extremist broadcasters" are upheld in *Brandywine-Main Line v. FCC*. Writing in dissent, Judge David L. Bazelon warns: "It is beyond dispute that the public has lost access to information and ideas . . . as a result of a single blow of this doctrinal sledgehammer. . . . If we are to go after gnats with a sledgehammer like the Fairness Doctrine, we ought to at least look at what else was smashed beneath our blow."

An all-news radio format airs on stations in New York, Washington, D.C., and Los Angeles.

Life dies as a weekly publication.

Ms. Magazine, a forum for feminist writing, appears.

The first teletext systems, Ceefax and Oracle, are inaugurated.

The Outdoor Advertising Association of America designates the Florham-Madison Campus Library at Fairleigh Dickinson University in Teaneck, New Jersey, as the main reference depository for the industry.

The Office for Combating Terrorism is established as a special unit of the U.S. Department of State to coordinate government counterterrorism activities, particularly those taking place internationally.

The surgeon general issues a report on television violence.

A total of 113 political action committees (PACs) are registered in the United States.

1972, May 15—Alabama Governor George Wallace is crippled while seeking the Democratic presidential nomination in a near-fatal shooting by would-be assassin Arthur Bremer. Within hours, the Nixon White House seeks out "retired" CIA operative E. Howard Hunt to place George McGovern campaign literature in Bremer's apartment in order to damage the Democratic party front-runner. The plot is foiled, ironically, because the FBI proves efficient in sealing off Bremer's residence (according to an article not published until twenty years later, on December 6, 1992, when *New Yorker* magazine breaks the story in reporting about high-level conversations from previously undisclosed secret White House audiotapes still held under lock and key in the National Archives).

1972, June—White House operatives break into the Watergate complex in Washington, D.C., seeking confidential materials but are caught. The Watergate affair begins, with Bob Woodward and Carl Bernstein's *Washington Post* articles leading the exposé.

1972, November 7—President Nixon easily wins reelection over Democratic nominee Senator George McGovern (D-S.D.), carrying forty-nine states and ninety-seven percent of the electoral votes.

1972, November 8—Home Box Office begins airing pay cable programming.

1973-1983—College and university protests of the 1960s become almost nonexistent, although growing concern over environmental, antinuclear, and peace issues leads to a gradual reinvigoration of campus group involvement after 1981.

1973—A cease-fire is signed in Vietnam.

The criteria for determining obscenity are outlined by the U.S. Supreme Court in *Miller v. California.*

The summit meeting of the Non-Aligned Movement (NAM) heads of state calls upon developing nations to take concerted action in the area of mass communication to reduce their dependency on colonialist countries. This is seen as the birthplace of a proposed New World Information and Communication Order (NWICO), fostered by United Nations Educational, Scientific and Cultural Organization (UNESCO).

The Trilateral Commission is founded by David Rockefeller and others as a public policy organization to allow for high-level, unofficial discussions in relaxed settings by key leaders from finance, trade, diplomacy, and academic think tanks in industrialized North America, Europe and Japan. Critics see the commission as exerting undue influence as part of a shadow "world government" seeking greater international controls over national sovereignty.

KAYE-AM, a Payallup, Washington, radio station broadcasting ultraconservative and religious programs not found elsewhere in the Tacoma area, is forced off the air by the FCC in an acrimonious license renewal denial process, ostensibly over the station's failure to adhere to Fairness Doctrine, equal time and personal attack regulations. Supporters of station management argue that the real reasons have to do with the censoring of political ideas.

1973, January 22—The U.S. Supreme Court rules, in *Roe v. Wade*, that all then-existent laws prohibiting abortion violate a woman's right to privacy and are therefore unconstitutional. The ruling, however, leaves open questions about the extent of permissible state interest in the fetus as an unborn child, as well as the nature and scope of the right to privacy itself. The result is ongoing argument and political group activism from the increasingly militant "prochoice"/"proabortion" and "prolife"/"antiabortion" factions seeking to either defend or overthrow the decision.

1973, September 11—Chilean General Augusto Pinochet engineers a military coup against President Salvador Allende who is seen as taking the country too far to the left, interrupting Chilean democracy and marking the country as a human rights violator.

1974—The Committee on Public Doublespeak of the National Council of Teachers of English begins its annual award in "ironic tribute" to American public figures guilty of employing language that is "grossly deceptive, evasive, euphemistic, confusing or self-contradictory," a practice that is increasing in government, business, and the professions, where words are used to obscure, rather than clarify, and to conceal, rather than communicate.

Arab nations begin a coordinated program outlined in a confidential document, *Public Affairs Program for the Arab World*, to spend as much as $15 million annually employing a network of Washington lobbyists, influential lawyers, public relations experts, political consultants, and other specialists to shift American public opinion away from the Israelis.

Missiles of October on ABC-TV sets the standard for contemporary docudrama programming by scrupulously using news articles, personal diaries, transcripts, and other authenticated materials to faithfully depict events in the lives of President John F. Kennedy, Soviet Premier Nikita Khrushchev, and their key aides in a riveting recreation of the behind-the-scenes maneuvering taking place during the Cuban Missile Crisis of October 1962.

1974, August 9—President Richard M. Nixon is forced to resign because of political and legal difficulties caused by continuing news media coverage of Watergate revelations. Nixon is the first president to so give up his office. He is succeeded by his vice president, Gerald R. Ford (R-Mich.)

1974, December 14—Prominent newspaper columnist and foreign policy advisor Walter Lippmann dies in New York.

1975—Congress launches investigations of the Central Intelligence Agency, the Federal Bureau of Investigation, and other federal agencies in the "intelligence community." Testimony before the U.S. Senate Intelligence Committee reveals that the CIA owns over two hundred publishing front enterprises in the United States and abroad, including book, magazine, newspaper, and wire service outlets designed to influence public opinion. In addition, many more such media businesses covertly benefit from CIA subsidies.

The United Nations equates Zionism with racism.

The *Wall Street Journal* begins publishing via satellite.

Sony Corporation of Japan invents a half-inch videotape system (Betamax).

In an address to U.S. labor unions, Russian concentration camp survivor and noted historical novelist Aleksandr Solzhenitsyn warns:

> The Communist ideology is out to destroy your society. This has been their aim for 125 years and has never changed; only the methods have changed a little. What is ideological war? It is a focus of hatred. This is continuous repetition of the oath to destroy the Western world. Just as once a famous Roman Senator ended every speech with the statement, "Carthage must be destroyed," so today do the Communists repeat, "Capitalism must be destroyed."

1976—The Citizens band (CB) radio craze appears. With more than twenty million Americans experimenting with CB use, the FCC is forced to open up seventeen new channels (forty total).

Tricontinental Film Center, a distributor of noncommercial documentaries, is targeted in a U.S. Justice Department order to register as a "foreign agent" under the provisions of the Foreign Agents Registration Act of 1938.

Congress passes a Voice of America Charter which attempts to codify the importance of the radio service retaining "objective" and "balanced" news coverage while serving as a vehicle representing U.S. government interests.

Videocassette recorders are first sold in the United States.

1976, November—Jimmy Carter (D-Ga.) defeats Gerald Ford (R-Mich., the only appointed president in U.S. constitutional history) and a host of third-party candidates in one of the nation's closest elections.

1977—Deliberate attempts by an American Nazi group to provoke controversy through conducting a march in the Chicago suburb of Skokie, Illinois, leads to a national free speech confrontation. March organizers know that slightly less than half the community residents are Jewish, many of them survivors of the Holocaust. Donations drop when the American Civil Liberties Union sides with the Nazis on the fundamental principle that a community cannot deny political rights, even to an unpopular minority. Ironically, after generating widespread news coverage and winning their court struggle for the right to march, the Nazis opt not to parade.

Minister Louis Farrakhan becomes the National Leader of the Nation of Islam. His message of economic and social self-determination for African-Americans, anti-Semitic interpretations of history, and inflammatory racist style of rhetoric prove increasingly successful, as well as controversial.

Interactive videotext systems (PRESTEL and QUBE) appear.

1977, January 23—*Roots*, the eight-part miniseries based on Alex Haley's genealogical novel, begins airing on ABC-TV. This epic account chronicles, through the Civil War, succeeding generations of an actual family whose ancestors were originally brought as slaves to the United States from Africa. The widely viewed docudrama provides a powerful platform for reevaluating race prejudices. Because of fictionalizing and other problems in the docudrama genre, the National News Council encourages broadcast networks to demonstrate a greater commitment to historical accuracy and factual treatment of the historical subjects covered in future programs. The advice is largely ignored.

1977, March 5—President Carter appears with CBS newsman Walter Cronkite in a nationally televised phone-in program.

1978—The Institute for Historical Review is founded in Torrance, California, "to investigate the true causes and nature of war and to disseminate those findings" through "scholarship in the promotion of peace." The revisionist nature of many of its subsequent conferences and publications, especially those arguing that the Holocaust is an invention of Jewish propagandists, engenders international controversy. About this time, the docudrama miniseries, *Holocaust*, airs on NBC-TV. A Fairness Doctrine complaint about alleged anti-German bias in the program eventually is dismissed by the FCC.

1978, October 3—Radio Moscow begins its English-language broadcast service, targeting North America.

1979—Cable Satellite Public Affairs Network (C-Span) begins cablecasting proceedings of the U.S. House of Representatives, hearings, viewer call-in shows, analytic programs, seminars, and other political coverage. Foreign viewers tune into the network's televised congressional coverage through a U.S. Information Agency satellite link.

The United States becomes increasingly involved in El Salvador, overseeing the counterinsurgency war and directing much of that Central American nation's political life.

Father Charles Coughlin, the Catholic priest whose political activities in the 1930s and 1940s helped promote fascism in America, dies, largely forgotten.

Gallup Poll survey takers find that the proportion of Americans "favorably disposed" to the Ku Klux Klan has increased to 10 percent. The Klanwatch Project is established at the Southern Poverty Law Center in Montgomery, Alabama, to monitor and combat the activities of the KKK and other white supremacist organizations.

Writers, producers, historians, and others involved in producing and critiquing docudrama programs participate in a symposium hosted by the Academy of Television Arts and Sciences. Ethical concerns dominate the meeting. New sets of recommendations are proposed to deal with continuing problems of historical accuracy and how best to publicize alternative sources of information. Compliance is inconsistent, which is attributable to the lack of uniform standards.

Francis Ford Coppola's feature film, *Apocalypse Now* (United Artists), finally reaches American moviegoers. An analogy of what went wrong with the American involvement in Vietnam, *Apocalypse Now* presents powerful and disturbing images, which juxtapose napalming and surfboarding, being entertained by Playboy "Bunnies," and entering a psychedelic hell.

The United Nations Committee on Information is formed by a decision of the thirty-fourth United Nations Organization General Assembly to deal with two issues of ongoing debate: (1) the efforts made by the UNO to establish a new international information and communication order, and (2) the future role and functions of the UNO Secretariat's public information services. Growing political and ideological polarization is evident between those delegates most concerned about alleged "information and media imperialism" by developed nations such as the United States, Britain, France, and the Federal Republic of Germany, and the opposite views expressed by those who accuse the information services of the United Nations itself of engaging in a campaign of continuing "anti-Western propaganda."

1979, July 16—The tottering pro-U.S. authoritarian regime of Anastasio Somoza in Nicaragua is overthrown by rebels who occupy the capital city of Managua under the direction of Daniel Ortega, leader of the Sandinista National Liberation Front (FSLN). FSLN banners and flags hang from trees, power poles, and houses. Other Sandinista supporters march through the city singing revolutionary songs, carrying flags, and wearing the red and black FSLN colors. With aid from Soviet bloc and Cuban advisors, the Sandinistas develop Central America's most sophisticated intelligence operation. The Sandinista Front soon establishes a sophisticated lobbying and public relations campaign in the United States, while simultaneously hosting delegations representing the Palestine Liberation Organization, Iran, Libya, the Italian Red Brigades, and other controversial "progressive" forces.

1979, November 4—The U.S. embassy in Tehran, Iran, is seized by Muslim militants. The continued hostage standoff in Iran precipitates a crisis of confidence in American foreign policy.

1980—A total of 2,551 political action committees (PACs) are registered in the United States.

The Christic Institute is established in Washington, D.C. The institute soon proves controversial because of studies it publishes that allege illegal covert actions by agents of the U.S. government.

The Federal Communications Commission eliminates low-cost, ten-watt, Class D educational radio station licenses. This policy change encourages communities to establish more "professional" public stations but effectively precludes activists (most without the minimum of $50,000 needed to start a hundred-watt broadcast facility) from having a direct voice on the FM band.

U.S. communities with two or more competing daily newspapers decline to 172. Of that number, only 35 competing papers are actually controlled by different owners.

Defying the pundits who predict he will fail, media maverick Ted Turner launches his Atlanta-based Cable News Network (CNN). This pioneers as the first twenty-four-hour all-news television channel fed to cable systems nationwide via satellite.

The American-Arab Anti-Discrimination Committee is founded by former U.S. Senator James G. Abourezk (D-N.D.) in response to stereotyping, defamation, and discrimination against Americans of Arab descent.

The National Association for the Advancement of White People (NAAWP) is founded in Louisiana by former Ku Klux Klansman David Duke.

Several KGB-initiated disinformation coups, which are only unmasked later, prove the susceptibility of American and world media to cleverly planted false stories. One involves a forged Presidential Review Memorandum NSC 46, supposedly urging a tilt of U.S. foreign policy toward total support for the apartheid South African regime, complete with a program to monitor and divide American blacks to neutralize their political influence on this issue. Copies of the supposed document are widely circulated to black UNO delegates and U.S. news outlets. Subsequent denials by confused White House staffers prove so lame that they enhance the credibility of the forgery. In November, another forged document, this time purporting to be a State Department "dissent" paper, recommends what is called the "Zimbabwe option" in El Salvador. This suggests that the United States can limit Soviet and Cuban influence by aiding the Marxist opposition in order to wean them to the American side. A number of leftist newspaper and magazine columnists (unaware they are being manipulated in a Soviet disinformation campaign) encourage the Carter administration to heed the recommendations before the window of opportunity to influence the guerrillas is lost.

Commissioned by UNESCO, the published *Many Voices One World*: *Report of the MacBride Commission* (chaired by distinguished Irish statesman Sean MacBride) crystallizes the notion of communications and cultural sovereignty as basic human rights of all peoples.

1980, July-November—The Republican presidential slate of California governor Ronald Reagan and former Texas congressman and CIA director George Bush aggressively attack Democratic incumbents Jimmy Carter of Georgia and vice president Walter Mondale of Minnesota.

During the campaign period, nightly television newscasts on all the networks continually remind American viewers of their fellow countrymen trapped by Iranian radicals inside the U.S. embassy in Tehran. The daily repetition by ABC of the politically-charged slogan "America Held Hostage" and the drumbeat listing by CBS of the number of days in captivity help destroy Jimmy Carter's presidency. Connected with this are rumors that key Reagan campaign members (led by George Bush and William Casey) may have secretly made a deal with the Iranians and Israelis to delay the release of the hostages (in return for arms shipments) until *after* the presidential election. This is allegedly to prevent an "October Surprise" homecoming, which would be favorable to the Carter administration. Although the Iran-Contra hearings of the mid-1980s concern subsequent secret arms payoffs to the Iranians, it is not until 1991 that speculations publicly resurface about a possible (and vehemently denied) Bush/Casey "October Surprise" connection, a topic picked up with greater frequency following appearance of an op-ed article in the *New York Times* by respected former Carter foreign policy advisor Gary Sick.

The election of the Reagan-Bush ticket marks a shift to more conservative ideology. "Merger Mania" becomes the rage in American business, including the media industries, as corporate takeovers and buyouts become more common in the 1980s due to the favorable tax and legal climate created during the Ronald Reagan presidency.

1980, September 30—*Playing for Time* airs on CBS-TV. This docudrama recreates the strange, tension-filled experiences of an orchestra made up of Jewish inmates who are forced by their Nazi captors to play for other concentration camp prisoners on their way to the gas chambers in occupied Poland. Protests emerge over the casting of Vanessa Redgrave as the heroine, Fania Fenelon, since Redgrave is not Jewish and also because of her outspoken political support of the Palestine Liberation Organization.

1981—An estimated 40 percent of terrorist acts worldwide victimize Americans. The Anti-Defamation League of B'nai B'rith reports that 377 "anti-Semitic episodes," ranging from graffiti to arson, occurred in the United States during 1980, as compared to only 129 reported episodes in 1979. Membership in Ku Klux Klan organizations is estimated at 12,500.

The infamous El Mozote massacre in El Salvador points to savagery in that nation's civil war. Raymond Bonner, the *New York Times* reporter who documents the atrocities and the growing role of U.S. assistance to the regime, is removed from the Central America beat by the news organization after the Reagan administration and right-wing critics denounce him for biased reporting. Conservatives see also the growing grassroots and media influence of the Committee in Solidarity with the People of El Salvador (CISPES) as supportive of activities by an allegedly procommunist front. Between 1981 and 1986, fifty-two FBI field offices around the country assign agents to spy on CISPES officers, monitor meetings, and infiltrate the organization's other functions.

1981, February 19—Concentration camp survivor Mel Mermelstein files a $17 million lawsuit against the Institute for Historical Review and other codefendants for libel, injurious denial of established fact, intentional infliction of emotional distress, and breach of contract over a disputed offer of $50,000 first made in 1979 for proof that Jews were actually killed in gas chambers at Auschwitz, Poland. The suit leads members of the Jewish Defense League to demonstrate in front of the institute's offices, chanting "Never Again" and other slogans.

1981, November 17—*Skokie*, a two-and-a-half-hour docudrama airing on CBS-TV, fictionalizes the 1977 Nazi free speech controversy which dominated the news headlines in that year. Danny Kaye plays the fictitious composite lead character, Max Feldman, in director Herbert Wise's production.

1982—The Gannett Corporation's colorful national newspaper, *USA Today*, debuts as the first daily produced via satellite for a general readership.

A total of 3,149 political action committees (PACs) are registered in the United States.

The federal debt exceeds $1 trillion.

The Klanwatch Project of the Southern Poverty Law Center commissions a half-hour documentary film, *The Klan: A Legacy of Hate in America*. The production garners numerous kudos, including an Academy Award nomination.

Walter Raymond, a longtime CIA official accused by opponents of "specializing in psychological warfare, black propaganda, and manipulation of the press," is named to head the "public diplomacy" operations of the National Security Council.

1983-1988—Ernst Zündel, a Canadian of German birth, has charges brought against him under a previously unused "hate crime" law making it a penal offense to distribute information that the publisher knows to be false. Zündel's subsequent trials stem from books and pamphlets he sells on various conspiracy themes, especially from reprinting a booklet, *Did Six Million Really Die?* by Richard Harwood, which presents evidence countering the claim that six million Jews were Holocaust victims gassed to death by Nazis during World War II. Zündel's conviction in 1985, despite Canadian free press guarantees, is overturned on procedural grounds following an appeal. His second trial, beginning in 1988, creates a sensation with new forensic evidence challenging the credibility of Zyklon B usage based on "Prussian blue cyanide" samples taken at Auschwitz-Birkenau by independent U.S. "gas chamber engineer" Fred Leuchter. Despite the resulting uproar, Zündel is again found guilty on May 11, 1988, by the Canadian court.

1983—KAL 007, a Korean Airlines flight, wanders into Soviet airspace and is shot down, killing 269 passengers, including U.S. Congressman Larry McDonald (D-Ga., who is noted for his support of the John Birch Society). Doubts are immediately raised about whether the flyover is a deliberate spying attempt by the United States and Korea, a Soviet setup, or a tragic accident. Charges of disinformation are lodged against the Reagan administration and Soviet spokesmen by third parties.

If You Love This Planet, a National Film Board of Canada production that is critical of American environmental efforts to clean up pollution, is nominated for a Best Documentary Oscar by the Academy of Motion Picture Arts and Sciences. Screenings occur at the Los Angeles Filmex exhibition without a "foreign propaganda" label, despite U.S. Justice Department attempts to force it to be so registered.

Tom Metzger forms the White American Resistance (later, the White Aryan Resistance or WAR), a racist, neo-Nazi, activist group. The Anti-Defamation League of B'nai B'rith (ADL) estimates that various Ku Klux Klan and allied groups have a combined membership of eight to ten thousand individuals, who are active in about twenty states. The ADL says that for each robed Klan card holder, another ten Americans provide support through subscribing to publications, donating money, and attending rallies.

Bob Maynard becomes the first African-American publisher of a major daily newspaper, the *Oakland Tribune* in California.

1983, January 14—President Reagan issues "Management of Public Diplomacy Relative to National Security (SECRET)," National Security Decision Directive (NSDD) 77, which is subsequently declassified. The directive covertly orders the "organization, planning, and coordination of the various aspects of public diplomacy of the United States Government relative to national security. Public diplomacy is comprised of those actions of the U.S. Government designed to generate support for our national security objectives." Later allegations link this directive and related National Security Council efforts to Iran-Contra Affair public relations and money-laundering operations.

1983, June 3—Fugitive Posse Comitatus leader Gordon Kahl dies in a controversial Arkansas shoot-out with federal and state law enforcement officials.

1983, September—The Order is formed. Its goal is to promote a violent white revolution to restore racial supremacy in the United States.

1983, October—The U.S. Supreme Court turns down a petition to reverse the perjury conviction of former State Department official Alger Hiss.

1983, October 25—The Invasion of the small Caribbean island of Grenada by five thousand U.S. troops overthrows the nation's Marxist regime. Much of the deployment strategy is planned by a White House aide, Marine Lt. Colonel Oliver North. The press approach adopted by the military excludes media from the battle area for seventy-two hours, effectively muzzling critical coverage until after the field mop-up.

1984-1987—The Canadian government orders more than eight hundred confidential public opinion polls, averaging four surveys a week. The disclosures in late 1987 are a result of journalistic use of access-to-information laws. Canadian federal officials reluctantly comply by providing a list of subjects (but not the results). An unknown number of "sensitive surveys" are not included in the accounting, and remain closed to public scrutiny in the bureaucracy's computerized filing system. The full cost of these secret government surveys, all performed on commission by private research firms, is not disclosed although the estimated amount spent totals more than $64 million.

1984—More secret National Security Decision Directives (NSDDs) issued by President Reagan are used for various reasons, including an unpublicized national security exercise called "Rex-84 Alpha." This tests efforts coordinated by the Federal Emergency Management Agency (FEMA), National Security Council (NSC), and Department of Defense (DOD) to quell civil disorder, mass rioting, and terrorism should the federal government decide to invade a hostile Central American country such as Sandinista-led Nicaragua. Over the next several years, warnings to Nicaragua by the Reagan administration and racial and political discord in South Africa provide explicit moral issues encouraging expanded left-wing activism and propaganda. Nearly 150 college campuses are involved in protests.

Reverend Louis Farrakhan, the outspoken, Chicago-based, African-American leader of the Nation of Islam group, rises to national prominence by challenging historic economic and political power links between blacks and Jews. He is denounced as a "bigot," "racist," "anti-Semite," and "international ambassador of hate" for encouraging ethnic self-reliance, criticizing Israel, and supporting Jesse Jackson's presidential bid. Powerful groups such as the Anti-Defamation League of B'nai B'rith successfully wage a campaign that prevents Farrakhan from appearing on many radio and television programs.

A controversial video series called *Race* (later, *Race and Reason*), which is labeled neo-Nazi propaganda by its critics, begins production in Fullerton, California. Despite opposition, creator Tom Metzger successfully distributes the programs in more than thirty-five markets across the United States for screening via local cable public access channels. They air, despite legal problems for Metzger over his alleged instigation of more violent, direct actions against minorities by others. During this same period, Louis Beam (the self-styled "ambassador-at-large of Aryan Nations") establishes an electronic bulletin board to serve as a computer network for those supportive of white racism. Despite active news publicity, however, the network is never widely used.

Members of the Federal Communications Commission question the impact and constitutionality of the so-called Fairness Doctrine as it applies to the broadcast industry. The FCC continues other deregulation efforts, eliminating restrictive rules that previously prohibited broadcasters from directly sponsoring political debates.

The National Archives becomes an independent executive agency and is no longer run by the General Services Administration. Researchers estimate that while less than three percent of the seven million cubic feet of records generated each year by federal agencies need to be retained for historical purposes, their sheer bulk causes a huge backlog in selecting and filing. Each cubic foot contains about 2,500 to 3,000 pieces of paper, with permanence becoming a problem as records begin increasingly to be kept electronically and thus are more susceptible to computer editing and erasure.

The breakup of the U.S. telephone monopoly is completed by terms of the AT&T divestiture (known as the "Modification of Final Judgment") which creates openings for new long-distance carriers and sets up independent regional Bell Operating Companies (BOCs) for local calling. Included are provisions preventing the BOCs from offering "information services," including electronic publishing, until it can be shown that competition will not suffer.

1984, June-November—The Democratic party standard-bearer, Walter Mondale of Minnesota, selects Representative Geraldine Ferraro (D-N.Y.) as his running-mate. Ferraro is the first woman ever nominated for vice president by a major U.S. political party.

The Reagan campaign screens the eighteen-minute film, *A New Beginning*, in place of the traditional nominating speech at the Republican National Convention. Aired to a national audience on NBC-TV, this docudrama advertisement marks completion of the ongoing shift from verbal to visual rhetoric as the major persuasive component of American presidential campaigning. It is written and produced by advertising executive Phil Dusenberry of BBDO Inc. as part of the "Tuesday Team," which creates the Reagan-Bush reelection ads. The team is successful, as the Reagan-Bush campaign cruises to an easy victory over the Mondale-Ferraro forces.

Lyndon LaRouche garners nearly eighty thousand ballots and generates six million dollars in his presidential campaign as an independent Democrat.

The average "sound bite" of broadcast time given major presidential candidates in 1984 election coverage by U.S. television and radio networks lasts just thirteen seconds.

1984, June 18—Denver, Colorado, radio talk show host Alan Berg is murdered by members of the Order for his outspoken condemnation of white racism and equally fervent support of Israel.

1984, June 25—The office-library-warehouse of the Institute for Historical Review in Torrance, California, is destroyed by a firebomb loaded with napalm as part of a campaign of harassment and physical terrorism intended to silence the revisionist activists. The "Jewish Defenders," an alleged front group for the Jewish Defense League, assumes responsibility for the arson attack.

1984, September—The U.S. State Department denies a visa to Don Rojas, secretary to the International Organization of Journalists (IOJ) and its accredited representative to the United Nations, to visit the UNO headquarters in New York City. The decision is politically motivated because of outspoken criticism of "U.S. aggression" in Grenada by Rojas , a former press secretary to the Marxist prime minister Maurice Bishop, who was killed in connection with the military action on the Caribbean island by American forces.

1984, December 31—The U.S. officially withdraws from the United Nations Educational, Scientific and Cultural Organization (UNESCO), citing concerns over UNESCO's "ideological emphasis" and "attacks upon a free flow of communications."

1985—The U.S. State Department engages in an illegal, covert, propaganda effort to generate congressional and public support for President Reagan's Central American policies. The State Department's Office of Public Diplomacy for Latin America and the Caribbean begins awarding numerous contracts to outside public relations consultants to help "favorably influence" public support for the Nicaraguan Contra rebels. A secret National Security Council memo by Marine Lt. Colonel Oliver North to National Security Advisor Robert McFarlane, "Timing and the Nicaraguan Resistance Vote" (dated 20 March 1985), is publicly revealed as a result of the Iran-Contra congressional hearings in 1987. Such covert activities are held by the General Accounting Office, the investigative arm of Congress, to violate congressional restrictions that curb the use of federal funds for publicity or propaganda purposes.

Bill Moyers wins an outstanding interview/interviewer Emmy Award for a television episode titled *World War II: The Propaganda Battle*, airing on the Public Broadcasting Service (PBS) series *A Walk through the 20th Century with Bill Moyers*. Featured are Nazi film chief/documentarist Fritz Hippler and his American counterpart, Frank Capra. The nineteen-episode television series, now available on videotape, covers other topics of interest to propaganda students ranging from newsreels and public relations to charismatic leadership and political advertising.

Live Aid, the first global rock music concert organized for a cause, raises money for African famine victims.

The total number of billboards adjacent federal highways in the United States is estimated at 500,000—an average of 14 signs for every ten miles of pavement. Opinion polls continue to show strong public support for the outdoor messages, despite opposition to the industry from "beautification" groups.

1985, March—Following the death of Konstantin Chernenko in Moscow, the Soviet Union's Communist party chooses a lawyer, second secretary Mikhail Gorbachev, to take over leadership of the country as the new general-secretary.

1986—Exhausted cross-country Great Peace Marchers straggle into the nation's capitol without much impact on policy but set a new standard for computer-generated information. A fully equipped press bus provides reporters with information such as male-female marcher ratios and numbers of children involved, coast-to-coast participants, and births, marriages, and deaths on the march.

Media group owner Capital Cities Communications emerges with control of the ABC Television Network. Centralized ownership trends in other U.S. media also continue, with twenty corporations dominating the American magazine business and 72 percent of newspapers owned by outside firms.

The Deep Dish TV Network (based in New York City) begins programming innovative grassroots video services via satellite to cable public access channels around the United States. The network features documentaries, current affairs, and teach-in shows produced by radical, feminist, progressive, and other "unheard voices."

C-Span II begins cablecasting U.S. Senate proceedings and other alternative public affairs programming.

At least 130 million adults listen internationally to direct broadcasts by the Voice of America (VOA) at least once a week, according to a survey released by the USIA (an increase of over 11 million listeners from a similar survey in 1985). Not included in the figures are audiences for Radio Marti (broadcasting to Cuba), VOA Europe, or rebroadcasts of VOA programs on foreign radio stations.

1986, February—Federal investigators with the General Accounting Office (GAO) conclude that the publicity efforts of communications officers (COs), public affairs officers (PAOs), and public information officers (PIOs) on the federal payroll cost the taxpayers nearly a half billion dollars annually. "The responding agencies," says the report, "expected to obligate about $337 million for public affairs activities during the fiscal year 1985 with almost 5,600 full-time equivalent employees assigned to public affairs duties. In addition, about $100,000 was expected to be obligated in fiscal year 1985 for congressional affairs activities with almost 2,000 full-time equivalent employees."

1986, June 4—Former U.S. Navy intelligence analyst Jonathan Jay Pollard pleads guilty to spying for Israel and is sentenced to life in prison.

1986, November 3—First disclosures of the secret arms-for-hostages deal by the Reagan administration with Iran are published. The Iran-Contra controversy emerges from subsequent revelations about profits being secretly diverted by Marine Lt. Colonel Oliver North on White House orders to fund the Nicaraguan rebels, even though this violates congressional restrictions.

1986, December—Former Senator Paul Laxalt of Nevada, who serves as general chairman of the Republican National Committee, reports that $190 million was spent in congressional campaigns in 1986, with the major portion buying "30-second, mainly negative, mainly corrosive, mainly disruptive television commercials."

1987—The U.S. Supreme Court, in a 7-2 vote, strikes down a Louisiana state law requiring "scientific creationism" be taught in public school curricula.

Opponents of Judge Robert Bork's nomination to the U.S. Supreme Court conduct an unprecedented public grassroots lobbying campaign to prevent confirmation. Heavy news coverage results from updated releases of polling data and a steady stream of other media events designed to influence public opinion. Contact with senators is encouraged in broadcast and print ads, as well as through sophisticated computerized phone lists used to direct calls to targeted homes. Supporters of Bork, such as members of the We the People organization, are outraged and respond by charging that the anti-Bork forces "spent millions of dollars to conjure images and perceptions of a one man court turning back accomplishments of an entire nation. They lied. They threw ethics and integrity out the window. . . . They created a hate campaign to shape opinions that would suit their agenda." Anti-Bork groups, such as the American Civil Liberties Union and National Organization for Women, shrug off the criticism as sour grapes and say they were "clarifying the record" to encourage democratic citizen participation in a decision with far reaching social implications.

A study by the Postal Rate Commission (PRC) finds that 21 percent of nonprofit subsidized mail contains political advocacy. In separating political from nonpolitical mail in the study, the PRC terms political only those nonprofit pieces suggesting that some action should be taken on a political issue. It does not term political those mail pieces that merely discuss social issues. Most of the politically oriented mail is found to be of the action type, and "surprisingly little" of the alternative, educational discussion variety. At about this time, the Internal Revenue Service (IRS) proposes stringent restrictions on how much lobbying religious, educational, and other nonprofit groups can engage in to influence the making of government policies and laws. Tax legislation in 1976 guaranteed charitable organizations the right to lobby but put a financial ceiling on expenditures. The proposal sets out new definitions of lobbying that effectively eliminates most exemptions not previously counted in figuring the ceiling. This threatens the tax exempt status of many nonprofit sector groups by forcing them to choose between limiting their public issue advocacy or losing contributors. Widespread protests lead the IRS to withdraw the original proposal.

A Republican National Committee (RNC) effort to ensure "ballot integrity" by targeting heavily Democratic districts in three states where voters went by more than 75 percent with Mondale in the 1984 election leads to a lawsuit by the Democratic National Committee (DNC). The DNC charges that the Republicans are using the direct mailings to interfere with black voter registration, but the RNC contends that they are trying to clean up the rolls to eliminate phony vacant lot registrations and dead voters. In Louisiana, more than 31,000 letters are returned by the U.S. Postal Service because the addressee is not known at the designated address, and these are turned over by the RNC to state officials with a request to eliminate the names from the voter lists. The DNC calls this partisan and a smoke screen to hide the real intent, which is to scare minorities. An out-of-court settlement allows the Republicans to continue to practice in the future, but only with preclearance from the federal district courts.

Televised Senate Iran-Contra committee hearings feature dramatic testimony by Marine Lt. Colonel Oliver North. His demeanor and slide show about communist intentions to subvert Central America establish him as a hero to many. Conservative organizations send out millions of solicitation letters to capitalize on the strong public support that North receives as a result of the hearings. "Olliemania" demonstrates the importance of star personalities for causes and special interest organizations, with conservative groups seeing fundraising contributions shoot up 250 to 300 percent following his testimony.

More than $1.1 billion in free broadcast airtime and print advertising space is contributed by media to the Advertising Council's public service campaigns this year.

Friends of Animals, a national animal rights group, charges that the

ABC, CBS, and NBC television networks are refusing to run public service messages that ask consumers to boycott furs because broadcasters fear the loss of advertising revenues from furriers. Network spokesmen counter by saying that corporate policies prevent the airing of advocacy or issue-oriented commercials that take controversial positions.

The Fairness Doctrine is eliminated by action of the Federal Communications Commission in order to increase parity between free speech rights for electronic and print communicators.

Declines recorded in network viewer levels accelerate with the introduction of "people meters," which revolutionize the TV ratings industry.

Twenty-five publishing companies, including U.S. giant McGraw-Hill, announce they will stop supplying South Africa with books and journals as part of antiapartheid trade sanctions.

The theatrical release of Oliver Stone's controversial motion picture, *Platoon*, leads to a national reexamination of what the Vietnam conflict means to Americans.

"Operation Rescue" prolife antiabortionists, effectively adopt confrontational and media strategies perfected by earlier civil rights activists to focus attention on their cause and create pressure on their prochoice opponents to reluctantly respond. A leader of the movement to prevent pregnant women from obtaining abortions is former used-car dealer Randall Terry. His pamphlet, *Higher Laws*, announces the Operation Rescue campaign and presents the case that civil disobedience is necessary because

over 14 years of mostly education and political lobbying has gotten us virtually nowhere. . . . Over 20 million children are dead, and the situation is deteriorating. Euthanasia and infanticide are commonly practiced, school sex clinics are being established, and a political solution is as far away as ever. The truth is, we don't stand a chance of ending this holocaust without righteous social upheaval occurring across the country that "inspires" politicians to amend the Constitution.

The Pentagon says that the number of terrorist attacks in 1987 has reached the highest level since the United States government began keeping records twenty years earlier, with the curve of violence continuing upward.

The South African minister of defence, General Magnus Malan, acknowledges that the South African Defence Force underwrote publication and international distribution of thousands of booklets, *ANC: The Inside Story*, which seek to discredit the African National Congress (ANC). Following a demand for a retraction, General Malan says "Neither I, nor the Defence Force will apologize for acting against terrorists in the best interests of all our people. . . . Everything in the publication is the truth and reflects the real nature of the ANC."

1987, October 9—USIA's Express File is inaugurated to distribute information about the United States directly to journalists working for foreign news organizations (wire services, newspapers, magazines and broadcasters) in six European cities. The $2.5 million contract by the Reagan administration with United Press International (UPI) allows texts prepared by the U.S. Information Agency to be electronically transmitted on UPI's communications circuits. Official government statements, press releases, and news and feature articles on the Express File are clearly labeled as USIA material.

1987, December 2—In the case of *Palestinian Information Office v. Shultz*, U.S. District Court Judge Charles Richey rules against the American Civil Liberties Union (ACLU) and the Palestinian Information Office in a lawsuit challenging the legality and constitutionality of the State Department's order to close the PLO's Washington, D.C., communication center. The U.S. government position is upheld on appeal.

1988—Under orders from a federal court, the U.S. Information Agency creates new interim rules for reviewing and certifying documentary films that seek duty-free distribution status in foreign markets. Similar to prior regulations, which were declared unconstitutional by a federal judge, the new reviewing standards still allow government officials to impose a "propaganda" warning label on controversial motion pictures. Critics charge that the purpose of the rules is to give administration reviewers a way to effectively limit distribution of radical films in key markets abroad.

The Federal Communications Commission dismisses a complaint against Utah radio station KZZI for broadcasting a white supremacist talk show. Investigators find that the *Aryan Nations Hour*, hosted by avowed racist Dwight McCarthy, poses no "imminent danger of physical injury of the type that warrants action under federal court precedents." However, after a strong outcry and publicized boycott threats by advertisers to pull their support for other, more conventional programming on the station, the licensee reluctantly cancels the show after only two broadcasts.

Political extremist Lyndon LaRouche is convicted in federal court on eleven mail fraud charges and one count of conspiring to defraud the Internal Revenue Service. He receives a fifteen-year sentence. Government prosecutors allege that LaRouche and his operatives engaged in a criminal scheme to gain access to more than $30 million in unauthorized loans by misusing the credit card accounts of supporters who gave to his presidential campaign. The defendants deny the allegations, charging they are victims of a conspiracy to discredit the LaRouche movement and its ideology.

1988, June-November—The average sound bite given presidential candidates in campaign coverage by the broadcast networks declines to eight seconds. The lack of substance is highlighted when Republicans working to elect George Bush turn to "feel-good" commercials featuring patriotic themes supplemented by a series of highly effective "attack ads." These polispots play up voter fears about race and crime and help erase the large lead fumbled away by Democratic standard-bearer Governor Michael Dukakis of Massachusetts. The most famous of the negative advertisements features revolving-door imagery in telling the story of Willie Horton, an African-American man convicted of murder who brutally raped a Maryland woman while on parole from a Massachusetts prison. The controversial spot is made by a group of pro-Bush media and political consultants registered as the National Security Political Action Committee. Such groups must operate independently, but press accounts suggest that the $10 million TV push is given tacit approval of the Bush campaign, which goes on to capture the White House.

1989—Members of Congress vote down their own proposed pay raise, responding to grassroots opposition spearheaded nationally by a range of groups led by the fiscally oriented National Taxpayers Union, liberal Ralph Nader's Public

Citizen, and conservative activist Paul Weyrich's Coalitions for America. Proponents and opponents agree that the groups' strategy of taking the issue to the public via fax machines and a loose alliance of radio talk show hosts proves pivotal in mobilizing citizen opposition to the raise. Many broadcasters urge listeners to send their congressional representatives a tea bag in order to reinforce a no vote by symbolically harking back to images of the Boston Tea Party protest.

The Natural Resources Defense Council (NRDC) works with the public relations firm of Fenton Communications to warn of the harmful effects of the pesticide Alar on children. Even though NRDC's claims are based on questionable evidence, public opinion is so swayed by the campaign that apple growers are forced to stop using the product. The "Alar Scare" illustrates the power of modern public relations to manipulate media content and influence attitudes when competing information is limited.

In *Texas v. Johnson*, a U.S. Supreme Court majority holds that, under certain conditions, the burning of the American flag as a form of protest expression is regarded as constitutionally protected political speech.

The National Abortion Rights Action League (NARAL) embarks on a $2 million television, radio, and newspaper advertising campaign to rebut claims made by antiabortionists. According to NARAL executive director Kate Michelman, this is the first time paid prochoice television ads are broadcast. The spots feature a physician telling about the horrors of back-alley abortions. Planned Parenthood also distributes similarly emotional visuals free to the media in a videocassette labeled "for educational purposes only." Included is television news footage showing antiabortion demonstrators making racist remarks, discussing plans to set fire or bomb clinics, and taunting patients by yelling, "Dead baby! Dead baby!" while holding up models of aborted fetuses.

The Academy Award-winning motion picture, *Mississippi Burning* (Orion Pictures), is widely praised for its technical excellence and powerful acting, but also criticized for its highly distorted, pseudo-realistic glorification of the role played by FBI agents in winning civil rights for black Americans in the South. Critics point out that, in fact, the FBI carried out very direct, high-level covert activities designed to discredit the movement and its leaders.

BBDO Advertising develops the Emotional Development System to record emotional responses in copy-testing persuasive ad messages.

Independent journalist I.F. Stone dies.

Herbert Romerstein retires as head of the U.S. Information Agency's Office to Counter Soviet Active Measures and Disinformation.

Hoping to improve its public image in the United States, the Palestine Liberation Organization hires an expert on graphic design to convey its message through political poster art disseminated in universities and art galleries around the country.

International radio broadcasters air nearly thirty thousand weekly frequency hours per year, compared to about sixteen thousand in 1960. Leaders include Radio Moscow, on the air 1,810 hours per week; the Voice of America, 1,173 hours a week in more than forty languages (an estimated 127 million listeners per week, who send 400,000 letters per year); and the British Broadcasting Corporation, 756 hours a week (120 to 150 million listeners per week, who send 500,000 letters per year).

Argentina's intelligence agency openly conducts a political public opinion poll. That nation's secretariat for state intelligence issues a news release saying that its agents interviewed 2,800 citizens "on the street" to ask which presidential candidate they favored.

1989, February-May—The Central Intelligence Agency, acting under a directive signed by President George Bush only a month after taking office, launches a so-called covert operation to oust the regime of General Manuel A. Noriega in the forthcoming Panamanian presidential elections, to be held May 7, 1989. U.S. officials focus news attention on Panama in an attempt to put world pressure on Noriega. U.S. tax moneys also underwrite the opposition's organizing efforts, print anti-Noriega literature, and set up a network of clandestine radio and television transmitters. These efforts at subversion fail when candidates loyal to Noriega's independent policies win the election. Its inability over the next several months to covertly topple the government leads the Bush administration to explore a military option.

1989, May 31—The Bush administration renews China's "most favored nation" status, in effect signaling the Chinese government that there will be no U.S. trade or aid cutbacks even should China undergo further domestic repression or the imposition of martial law.

1989, June 4—The prodemocracy movement in China suffers a bloodbath as hundreds—perhaps thousands—of demonstrators are killed when army troops storm Beijing and retake Tiananmen Square. Dramatic U.S. television and radio news coverage focuses sympathy on the plight of those students leading the reform efforts.

1989, July—President Bush secretly dispatches two senior officials (Under Secretary of State Lawrence Eagleburger and National Security Advisor Brent Scowcroft) to China for high-level talks. After first denying that the meetings took place, the administration later admits they did occur.

1989, August 11-13—A major conference analyzing "Postmodernism and Propaganda" is organized in San Francisco by Media Alliance, the publishers of *Propaganda Review*. Jeff Cohen, director of Fairness and Accuracy in Reporting (FAIR), acquaints

conferees with the notion that the much touted 'balanced' view which is the stock and trade of U.S. media is, in fact, a powerful form of propaganda—centrist propaganda—the purpose of which is to maintain the status quo. It operates by limiting the debate to a narrow spectrum . . . located far to the right of center as was shown by FAIR's study of guests on *Nightline* and the *McNeil-Lehrer Report*.

In addressing the nature of contemporary propaganda, Fred Stout expresses "the view that we are in or at the cusp of a historic period characterized by differences in quality and extent of propaganda, and that to understand these differences is the unique task of propaganda analysis today." According to critic Ron Levaco: "We live in a society of spectacle, such that we can no longer even speak of reality since all experience is mediated. We are overloaded with information and short on knowledge, and there exists a sense of nostalgia along with a feeling that the game is over and civilization is coming to an end." Speaker Kathleen Tyner disagrees with the view that propaganda techniques today differ much from the past, but acknowledges the "extraordinary emphasis of style over substance."

1989, November 9—The Berlin Wall, long a symbol of the divided city, opens up. As residents freely mingle, the joyous atmosphere presages the unification of West and East Germany and the end of the Cold War.

1989, November 16—The slaying of six Jesuits, their housekeeper, and her daughter in El Salvador provokes international outrage. The massacre of the Catholic priests results in the conviction of two military men almost twenty-four months later—the only army officers ever convicted of human rights abuse in that country. U.S. complicity in the Salvadoran military's crimes is alleged.

1989, December 20—U.S. armed forces invade Panama ("Operation Just Cause"). The deployment of twenty-seven thousand American troops makes this the largest U.S. military operation since Vietnam. Using media censorship and access restrictions similar to those employed in Grenada in 1983, the Bush administration successfully directs press coverage into parroting the government line. A massive propaganda effort at home and in Central America includes the use of Army psychological warfare against Panamanian leader Noriega. He is subjected to loud blasts of heavy metal rock-and-roll music designed to drive him out of his Vatican embassy refuge. Although atrocities by American forces and the ineptitude of the Panamanian leadership installed by U.S. authorities are later revealed, the impact of the revelations is blunted by time and largely buried by the blur of news.

1990—The U.S. Postal Service estimates that Americans spend $200 billion each year on mail-order products. The service delivers more than a half billion pieces of mail per day, Monday through Saturday, which is equivalent to about two letters or packages daily for every person in the nation.

Combined participation in various Ku Klux Klan organizations, despite renewed media attention, continues to decline to less than four thousand members.

Socialist muckraker Mike Caddell upsets small-town residents of northeast Kansas when he converts a local community newspaper into *Alternative Index*, an ideological descendent of the *Appeal to Reason* with a masthead motto quoting the late publisher Joseph Pulitzer to the effect that "newspapers should have no friends."

The World Anti-Communist League (WACL) is renamed the World League for Freedom and Democracy. The league is reputedly at the center of an international network of conservative politicians, retired CIA and other intelligence operatives, ex-Nazis, and military and geopolitical strategists from many nations.

Nicaragua's leftist Sandinista National Liberation Front, which has held power since 1979, is defeated in free elections by the conservative domestic National Opposition Union (UNO) political party coalition backed by the United States. As part of the peace agreement, all ties to "irregular" groups are supposed to be severed by the various sides but the Sandinistas maintain much of their old network. Compromises made by new president Violeta Chamorro, for example, leave effective control of the military, police, and state intelligence in the hands of Sandinista leaders.

1990, April—Cuba denounces the propaganda broadcasts of TV Marti as unlawful interference in its domestic affairs. The Cubans hail a ruling by the

International Frequency Registration Board (IFRB) of the International Telecommunications Union (ITU), which holds that U.S.-sponsored TV Marti broadcasts to Cuba violate Regulation 2666. The regulation specifies that stations operating on frequencies in the 5060 KHz to 41 MHz bands (such as TV Marti) should use all technical means to:

- reduce to the "maximum extent possible" radiation over territory of other countries, and
- limit power to only that necessary to assure a national service of good quality "within the limits of its territory . . . unless an agreement has been reached previously" to the contrary.

However, the IFRB lacks enforcement authority, and the official American response disputes the IFRB and Cuban interpretations.

1990, April 23—Congress enacts the Hate Crimes Statistics Act requiring the United States attorney general to establish guidelines and collect data "about crimes that manifest evidence of prejudice based on race, religion, sexual orientation, or ethnicity, including where appropriate the crimes of murder; nonnegligent manslaughter; forcible rape; aggravated assault, simple assault, intimidation; arson; and destruction, damage or vandalism of property."

1990, June—Stanford University officials empower a ten-member student-faculty council to enact an antihate speech code known as "Fundamental Standard Interpretation: Free Expression and Discriminatory Harassment."

1990, August 2—Iraq invades Kuwait (claiming it as "the nineteenth province"). Despite the lack of a defense treaty with Kuwait, the U.S. government switches from a pro-Baghdad policy to lead UNO efforts in condemning Iraq and its president, Saddam Hussein. Sanctions are soon accompanied by an unprecedented deployment of U.S. troops—code-named "Operation Desert Shield"—into Saudi Arabia for "purely defensive purposes." The subsequent imposition of "press pools" and other restrictive controls by allied military authorities effectively tilt most media coverage in ways favorable to the U.S. government without having to resort to outright censorship.

The public relations firm of Hill & Knowlton (H&K) is hired by an expatriate Kuwaiti government front group called Citizens for a Free Kuwait soon after the Iraqi takeover of their country. Skillfully using a variety of techniques to build awareness and generate support for the client's objectives, Hill & Knowlton swings into action over the next several months with one of the most successful public opinion campaigns in history. For example, H&K distributes thirty video news releases (VNRs) to U.S. and international media, using a combination of videos smuggled out of occupied Kuwait and new footage, to help define key issues in the Persian Gulf crisis and stress the horrors of the invasion. The emotionally powerful stories are snapped up by television news operations hungry for visual images. The VNRs set a record for usage and successfully picture the pro-Kuwaiti story into millions of American homes. The public relations firm also repackages the videos and other pro-Kuwaiti material into a presentation "documenting" alleged Iraqi atrocities. Hill & Knowlton arranges to have these materials and "witnesses" presented in hearings before the United Nations Security Council, which then authorizes the use of military action to remove Iraq from Kuwait. Members of the U.S. Congress also are given a similar emotionally powerful presentation, most notably by a young woman (only identified as "Nayirah") during electrifying October 1990 testimony.

1990, October 3—German reunification occurs, with the former German Democratic Republic incorporated into an expanded federal state.

1991—The decline in newspaper competition accelerates. Only sixty-three communities in the United States now host two or more dailies, and most of these are controlled by the same company, so that just twelve are "separately owned, fully competitive rivals."

Court rulings allowing the local Bell Operating Companies (BOCs) to provide electronic voice and video services over their telephone networks set off an epic lobbying war on Capitol Hill, with cable companies and newspapers seeking to limit the impact of the potential new competition.

The top fifty U.S.-based public relations firms bill over $1.7 billion in fees.

According to *Advertising Age* magazine, Tokyo overtakes New York City as the world's advertising capital. For the year, ad firms in Tokyo bill $24.5 billion; in New York, $24.1 billion; in London, $12.1 billion; in Paris, $9.7 billion; and Chicago, $7.1 billion. The world's single largest agency, Dentsu, generates an estimated $1.45 billion in gross income.

The Article 19 International Centre against Censorship, headquartered in England, issues a report showing that censorship is the general rule rather than the exception in mass communication. In seventy-two nations (including the United States, Britain, and much of Western Europe) extralegal censorship is widespread. More than seventy journalists in twenty-one countries meet a violent death in 1991 because their writings are considered threatening.

Independently, the Reporters Committee for Freedom of the Press, based in Washington, D.C., charges the Bush administration with intensifying efforts to manipulate the flow of news. In its 1991 report, the committee cites 135 documented examples of administration censorship attempts to limit public access to information. While about half the instances are connected with "unprecedented restrictions on media" during the Persian Gulf War, the group states this "was not an aberration" but rather reflects "Bush administration information policy." However, President Bush signs a law limiting the United States Information Agency's power to classify American films as "propaganda," a designation that inhibits the international distribution of such motion pictures. The rules used by the USIA were previously declared by the courts to be largely unconstitutional, in part because the propaganda label was arbitrarily applied to films that contained ideas or opinions disliked by agency officials.

1991, January-March—U.S. public opinion polls report overwhelming support for President George Bush. They also show that most Americans do not like how the media are covering the Persian Gulf War. Entrepreneurs capitalize on the president's unrelenting focus on Saddam Hussein as a villain equal to Hitler by featuring an evil-looking picture of the Iraqi leader on specialty products ranging from golf balls to urinal target mats.

1991, January 13—Following the failure of diplomacy to achieve administration aims, the U.S. Congress votes favorably upon a request by President Bush for a war declaration authorizing the use of force in liberating Kuwait from Iraqi control (Senate, 52-47; House, 250-183). Antiwar peace forces in the United States are not so well organized and are marginalized by emotional "Support Our Troops" slogans and appeals.

1991, January 16—U.S. military forces, joined by coalition allies operating under a UNO mandate, attack Iraq with devastating high-tech strategic bombing, using the code name "Operation Desert Storm."

1991, January 17—U.S. aerial bombardment of Baghdad begins.

1991, January 19—Operated by members of the U.S. Special Forces psychological operations (PSYOPS) team, the radio network known as Voice of the Gulf begins broadcasting as part of an expanded propaganda effort in combination with literature drops and loudspeaker operations. Voice of the Gulf programming continues on the air nonstop until the end of the war. Sixty-six PSYOPS loudspeaker teams provide supplemental tactical support for every major ground unit throughout the land war, persuading and instructing thousands of Iraqi soldiers to surrender. More than 29 million propaganda leaflets (approximately twenty-nine tons) are also disseminated across Iraq and occupied Kuwait by coalition forces during Operation Desert Storm. According to numerous sources, including captured soldiers, these leaflets are extremely effective in convincing many Iraqis to cease resistance.

1991, February—The Republican National Committee mails 500,000 letters from U.S. Senator Alan Simpson of Wyoming urging recipients to sign preprinted letters and send them in accompanying preaddressed envelopes to local newspapers. The letters urge support for the troops in the Persian Gulf and denounce the media for giving "so much attention to the small number of antiwar protesters." These identical letters to the editor appear in dozens of newspapers across the country. RNC spokespersons deny that this is "press bashing," despite Simpson's claim that CNN Baghdad correspondent Peter Arnett is an Iraqi "sympathizer" who is guilty of making treasonous broadcasts.

1991, February 27—President Bush declares victory in the Persian Gulf War and announces a halt to combat after Iraqi troops are routed in their flight from Kuwait. The flush of victory is marred over the coming months, however, over the failure to remove Saddam Hussein from power and the breaking of secret U.S. commitments to the Kurds, who continue to suffer greatly in their quest for independence.

1991, July 10—President Bush terminates economic sanctions imposed on South Africa by the U.S. Congress under terms of the Comprehensive Anti-Apartheid Act of 1986.

1991, August—The editor of the Soviet newspaper *Rossiya* holds a press conference revealing that the Communist party in the United States regularly received $2 million a year from the Kremlin until 1990, with occasional annual supplements of $1 million or more.

1991, August-September—"Operation Rescue" protests in Wichita, Kansas, refocus national attention on the "prolife" movement's demands to end abortion.

1991, August 12—Anticipating a major national debate over health care, the American Medical Association launches a public relations campaign to polish the tarnished image of physicians.

1991, August 19-21—The failure of a short-lived coup by hard-line Communists opens up the process of democratization in Russia and encourages an end to Cold War thinking.

1991, September 30—A military coup in Haiti by U.S.-trained forces overthrows the popularly elected president, Jean-Bertrand Aristide, and results in renewed repression, torture, and killings. The American government undertakes a diplomatic and propaganda campaign to "restore democracy" and bring Aristide back to power.

1991, December—Black scholar and three time Communist Party USA (CPUSA) vice presidential candidate Angela Davis, noted historian Herbert Aptheker, *People's World* editor Barry Cohen, and approximately 900 other activists circulate an "Initiative to Unite and Renew the Party" during a tumultuous national convention held in Cleveland, Ohio. The dissidents urge organizational changes reflective of more "internal democracy," but they are rebuffed and purged as "factionalists" from their leadership positions by hard-line CPUSA Chairman Gus Hall and his allies. The dissidents regroup in a new organization known as "Committees on Correspondence," which is named after the radical organizations through which Samuel Adams and his colleagues of the pre-Revolutionary War era stirred opposition to British colonial rule.

1991, December 14—In anticipation of the two hundredth anniversary of the Bill of Rights, the American Bar Association releases public opinion poll results which show that fewer than one out of ten Americans know that the purpose of the first ten Amendments to the Constitution is to protect them from abuses by their own federal government.

1991, December 16—The United Nations General Assembly repeals a 1975 resolution condemning Zionism as a "form of racism and racial discrimination."

1991, December 26—The Soviet Union officially ceases to exist and is replaced by a Russian-led Commonwealth of Independent States (CIS). The KGB also is disbanded during the month, but its personnel and powers are largely subsumed under other continuing intelligence organizations headed by Russia's Ministry of Security (MBR).

1992—The U.S. Government Accounting Office (GAO) estimates that public information efforts by the federal bureaucracy now cost taxpayers at least $2.5 billion a year.

The U.S. Supreme Court, in *R.A.V. v. St. Paul*, holds that "hate speech" is broadly protected under the First Amendment.

Oliver Stone's feature film, *J.F.K.*, stirs controversy by reexamining the murder of President Kennedy and alleging a coup d'état conspiracy as the cause.

According to *We're Number One, Where America Stands—and Falls—in the New World Order*, by Andrew L. Shapiro, the United States ranks first among the major industrial nations in the world in time spent watching television, in per capita spending on advertising, in UNO Security Council vetoes since 1980, in *not* ratifying international human rights treaties, and in foreign military aid to developing countries. On the other hand, the United States holds the bottom rung in per capita publication of books and posted last in humanitarian aid as a percentage of gross national product.

1992, January 6—A *New York Times* op-ed column by John R. MacArthur, publisher of *Harper's* magazine and author of a forthcoming book on censorship and propaganda in the Persian Gulf War, reveals an interlocking connection between the Congressional Human Rights Foundation and the public relations firm representing the Citizens for a Free Kuwait organization. MacArthur suggests that widely reported horror stories about Kuwaiti babies taken from their hospital incubators and left to die by Iraqi soldiers following the invasion were "almost certainly false" and part of a "propaganda blitz" designed to incite war. The "atrocities" were repeatedly pointed to by President Bush during his successful campaign to get authorization to expel Iraq by military force, but the "refugee" source of the story (only referred to as "Nayirah" in earlier reports) is revealed by MacArthur to be the teenage daughter of the Kuwaiti ambassador to the United States. The suppression of her identity fuels speculation that she was persuaded, in the name of patriotism, to give false testimony. Corporate executives from Hill & Knowlton, as well as Kuwaiti government authorities, strenuously deny any wrongdoing or attempt to mislead.

1992, January—Democratic party presidential contender and Arkansas governor Bill Clinton faces a barrage of news stories about his alleged adulteries, largely fueled by lurid coverage in the national weekly newspaper, the *Star*. The fact that breaking political news about the Arkansas governor's problems did not originate in "the legitimate press" but rather in a sensationalist tabloid which uses "checkbook journalism" to pay for the information, is far more troubling to many critics than whether the reports are true.

1992, February—Former White House Counsel John Dean files a ninety-two page, $50 million libel and slander lawsuit against another Nixon aide, G. Gordon Liddy, and Len Colodny and Robert Gettlin (the authors of *Silent Coup: The Removal of a President*), for claiming Dean's wife was "an associate, member or intimate of a call-girl ring" and portraying him as a "traitor to his nation" whose "contritions are self-serving, ongoing historical fraud." Liddy and his codefendants countersue.

Representatives of the government of El Salvador and the Farabundo Marti National Liberation Front (FMLN) sign several accords to end the country's twelve-year civil war and begin the building of a democratic society.

1992, March—The FCC attempts to help the ailing radio industry by increasing the number of stations a person or company may own from twelve to thirty.

1992, March 11—Investigative journalist Manuel de Dios Unanue is shot at point-blank range in a crowded New York City restaurant. The brutal "censorship by assassination" effectively silences one of the country's leading Spanish-language muckrakers who pays the ultimate price for seeking to report the truth.

1992, April 5—More than 500,000 people participate in the March for Women's Lives in Washington, D.C., which is sponsored by the National Organization for Women, to peacefully demonstrate their prochoice position on the abortion issue. The feminist rally is the largest ever to take place in the nation's capital.

1992, May—Bush administration staffers distribute a draft supplement to the *National Industrial Security Program Operating Manual*, which OKs lying through the use of disinformation "cover stories" designed to mislead the public. Says the draft:

Cover stories may be established for unacknowledged programs in order to protect the integrity of the program from individuals who do not have a need to know. Cover stories must be believable and cannot reveal any information regarding the true nature of the contract. Cover stories for Special Access programs must have the approval of the Program Security Officer prior to dissemination.

Following subsequent publicity in *Scientific American*, the Pentagon denies that this draft is official policy.

1992, June—Various sources from the former Soviet Union, including newly declassified official state documents, reveal that hundreds of American prisoners of war (POWs) from World War II and the conflicts in Korea and Vietnam were secretly imprisoned in the USSR, assert that prominent independent journalists such as John Reed and I. F. Stone were actually paid "agents of influence" for the old Communist regime, and confirm that well-known industrialist and multimillionaire Armand Hammer served as a courier between the Kremlin and the Communist Party USA.

A court in Oslo, Norway, finds that activists in Greenpeace, the best-known international environmental group, used deception in fabricating earlier propaganda videos showing seals being brutalized and skinned alive in order to increase viewer support for their cause.

1992, July—The FCC adopts rules allowing telephone companies to transmit television programming to homes over phone lines, opening up new competition to cable companies.

1992, August—Democratic party headquarters across the United States are equipped with the Bill Clinton Interactive Kiosk, a 40-megabyte, Quick Time®-based, computer multimedia presentation that allows users to browse the campaign platform and hear what the candidate has to say about various issues.

1992, August 12-19—The last issue of the *Guardian* rolls off the press, stilling an important independent left-wing organ of "committed journalism."

1992, August 27—In a 4 to 3 ruling, Canada's Supreme Court declares the "spreading false news" law used to convict Ernst Zündel and other controversial revisionists unconstitutional. The judges hold the "hate crimes" provisions violate freedom of speech protections under Canada's Charter of Rights. The reversal encourages groups in Canada and the United States to find new ways to suppress the expression of similar revisionist viewpoints.

1992, September 8—A treaty known as the International Covenant on Civil and Political Rights takes effect in the United States after a fifteen-year ratification campaign. The covenant, which has the force of law, was originally signed by President Jimmy Carter in 1977, adopted by the U.S. Senate through a two-thirds vote on April 2, 1992, and deposited by President George Bush on June 8, 1992. Among its far-reaching—though legally untested—provisions, Article 20 of the covenant proclaims: "1. Any propaganda for war shall be prohibited by law. 2. Any advocacy of national, racial or religious hatred that constitutes incitement to discrimination, hostility or violence shall be prohibited by law."

1992, October—Haitian protesters accuse the *New York Times* and other mainstream media of functioning as "the public relations mouthpiece of the U.S. State Department" in its news coverage about the Caribbean island nation. The critics say that by denying the possibility of an internal Haitian solution, and by ignoring the ambiguous role already played by the United States, the U.S. media are framing stories to suggest that Haiti must once again bow to the traditional "necessity" of a U.S.-determined solution "for its own good." The Haitians point to a three-month tracking study, conducted from September to December 1991, in which U.S. officials comprised over 35 percent of the sources who gave information or commentary about Haiti in *New York Times* news articles. (Another 10 percent were unidentified diplomats interviewed on "background.") This "preferential sourcing" total is almost double the count of all Haitian sources—military, peasant, elite, and others—combined.

1992, October 15—Russian president Boris Yeltsin releases Kremlin documents and cockpit audiotapes from the KAL-007 airline incident, which indicate the deviation into Soviet airspace was accidental. As a result, many conclude that the "spy flight" news stories widely assumed to be true may well have been part of a lying propaganda campaign by the Soviets designed to cover up a Cold War atrocity.

1992, October 29—The *New York Times* reports that the general/historian overseeing the Russian government's military intelligence archives says his review of documents exonerates Alger Hiss from charges that the American diplomat spied for the Soviet Union. General Dmitri A. Volkogonov says the espionage accusations are "completely groundless" and that Hiss is "a victim of the Cold War" whose conviction "was a result of false information or judicial error." The eighty-seven-year-old Hiss and his supporters are heartened by these developments. Other historians and disinformation analysts, however, immediately are skeptical and question the basis for General Volkogonov's claims by raising doubts about his thoroughness and motives.

1992, November—The Anti-Defamation League of B'nai B'rith releases a study of Americans that reports that anti-Semitism has been in a slow decline over the past three decades, but that one in five adults continues to hold "deeply prejudicial" attitudes towards Jews. According to ADL National Director Abraham Foxman, 31 percent of those questioned in the especially commissioned public opinion poll believe that American Jews currently wield too much power and 35 percent say Jews exhibit greater loyalty to Israel than the United States.

The Democratic party ticket of Bill Clinton (Ark.) and Senator Al Gore (Tenn.) pulls ahead of incumbent Republicans George Bush (Tx.) and Dan Quayle (Ind.) to take the White House in an exciting three-way race enlivened by the independent candidacy of Texas billionaire businessman Ross Perot.

1992, November 13—Macon County Circuit Court Judge Jerry Patton sentences Black Liberation Radio operator Napoleon Williams to a three-year state penitentiary term on what many allege are "fabricated charges." Williams runs an unlicensed community radio station in Decatur, Illinois, which serves African-Americans in his housing project and focuses criticism on local police brutality, official corruption, and economic inequality. Using inexpensive hand-built transmitters, Williams is one of a growing number of "micro power" broadcasters who are providing real-life First Amendment challenges to "the information stranglehold imposed by the corporate media and enforced by federal regulation." Another notable "outlaw" is Free Radio Berkeley (5 to 15 watts on 88.1 FM in California). Such unauthorized micro-stations face continuing harassment by local police forces and legal attacks from the Federal Communications Commission and other agencies seeking to shut them down permanently.

1992, November 24—U.S. Senate Special Counsel Reid Weingarten publicly releases his committee's 156-page report into allegations that the Reagan-Bush campaign conspired with Iranian authorities to delay the release of U.S. embassy hostages until after the 1980 election. While finding that secret negotiations and a number of questionable "improprieties" did in fact occur, the panel found "no credible evidence to substantiate the accusation at the center of the investigation" that an "October Surprise" deal had been made. Rather, the report concludes, the Iranians staged the delayed release on their own initiative to show their contempt for President Carter and to further humiliate him. The cost of the Senate investigation is an estimated $75,000.

1992, December-1993, January—More than four tons of secret documents, photos, and recordings are discovered in Paraguay, meticulously documenting arrests and illegal incidents of torture and murder carried out by the political police under the fascist dictatorship of General Alfredo Stroessner from 1954 to 1989. The "archives of terror" stem from the country's Department of Police Investigations and the Technical Office for the Repression of Communism. The documents reportedly shed additional light on CIA collaboration with the regime, but critics fear they will be "sanitized" before being publicly released by the government.

1992, December 8—President Bush orders U.S. troops into Somalia, in an operation described as part of a UNO "humanitarian relief effort."

1993—The United States establishes dominance in the Third World arms business and reaches a 57 percent market share, up from 49 percent in 1991 and 13 percent in 1988. U.S. Defense Department and intelligence sources cited by the Congressional Research Service attribute the shift to the demise of the former Soviet Union and increased Mideast political strength by America in the wake of the Persian Gulf War.

Most of the large paperback publishing houses are owned by international media conglomerates based outside the United States.

According to the Institute for Policy Innovation, more than 40,000 paid lobbyists seek to influence legislation by the U.S. Senate.

Two national activist groups, the American Family Association (AFA) headed by the Reverend Donald Wildmon and Christian Leaders for Responsible Television (CLeaR-TV), launch a boycott of S.C. Johnson & Son Inc., makers of Johnson Wax and a wide variety of other household products. Johnson is targeted for its advertising sponsorship of television programs that contain pro-"lesbian innuendo" (*Golden Palace*) and "homosexual jokes" (*Love and War*).

1993, January 13—After spending eleven months and $1.3 million in taxpayer dollars, a U.S. House investigation chaired by Representatives Lee Hamilton (D-Ind.) and Henry Hyde (R-Ill.) releases a final report debunking "October Surprise" allegations as untrue. Crucial sources, states the report, turned out to be "utter fabricators" perpetrating a conspiracy theory hoax.

1993, January 20—William Jefferson Clinton (D-Ark.) takes office as the forty-second U.S. president since the ratification of the Constitution.

1993, February 15—The Lawyers Committee for Human Rights charges the former Bush administration with complicity in shielding military officers tied to the 1989 murder of six Jesuits in El Salvador. The Lawyers Committee backs up its charges with a 360-page report, entitled *A Chronicle of a Death Foretold: The Jesuit Murders in El Salvador*. According to Michael Posner of the Lawyers Committee, "The inaction of the U.S. government hindered a complete investigation," while the Salvadoran government "played a more active role in the cover-up than has been reported." The Lawyers Committee bases its findings on U.S. government documents withheld from the Salvadoran judicial system and investigators for the UNO-sponsored "Truth Commission," but which the group obtained through the Freedom of Information Act.

1993, February 26—The World Trade Center in New York City suffers from a terrorist attack involving an explosion that weakens the two structures and forces a mass evacuation. U.S. investigators find links to Islamic fundamentalist groups. Muslim spokespersons are critical of the broad-stroke propagandistic, "tar and brush," anti-Arab tone contained in many of the news accounts.

1993, February 28—A small army of agents from the Bureau of Alcohol, Tobacco and Firearms (BATF) raid a cult center controlled by the Branch Davidian religious sect near Waco, Texas. TV news cameras called in as part of a public relations ploy to enhance BATF's embattled image instead capture a horrific shoot-out that leaves four of the government assault team and up to six Davidians dead. Government officials lie about the purpose of the raid, the level of planning, their previous contacts with Davidian leader David Koresh, the extent and legality of his arms cache, and other key issues. New and completely unsubstantiated allegations made by government officials about supposed child abuse by the Davidians become a key focus of media attention to serve as an added, after-the-fact justification for the assault. Other propaganda, psychological warfare, and hostage tactic ploys completely fail to dislodge Koresh and his followers. Federal agents are the first to crack in the standoff. They move to forcibly end the embarrassing fifty-one-day stalemate on April 19 with a new armed attack, complete with specially equipped tanks, which succeeds in completely burning the Davidian compound to the ground. Koresh and more than eighty of his supporters, including many innocent children, are immolated in the deadly inferno. Eleven other surviving Branch Davidian members are subsequently arrested by government investigators to face murder and conspiracy charges. Despite Attorney General Janet Reno's "the buck stops here" posture, the political fallout coming from a critical internal Clinton administration review leads several BATF officials to resign over their role in the fiasco and cover-up. "Waco" becomes a symbolic rallying cry for those concerned about erosion of constitutional protections, including more extreme elements opposed to all forms of gun control.

1993, spring—The "New Generations of Resistance Tour" sponsored by the East Timor Action Network/US travels the country. A video produced by Paper Tiger Television during the tour, *East Timor: Turning a Blind Eye*, concentrates on U.S. foreign policy toward Indonesia and the role played by leading media in neglecting repression on the island.

1993, March—News accounts reveal previously secret documents admitting that continuous U.S. military surveillance of African-American civil rights groups actually dates back to World War I.

1993, March 2—Bill Clinton sends the first U.S. presidential Internet electronic mail message.

1993, March 5-7—"Speech, Equality and Harm: Feminist Legal Perspectives on Pornography and Hate Propaganda," a conference at the University of Chicago Law School, brings together race theorists, constitutional law scholars, and feminist legal theorists and activists to examine connections between harmful speech and conduct in the United States and Canada. One analyst calls the conference "a historic confluence of interest" which "may well signal a turning point in the history of social activism on behalf of women, people of color, gays and lesbians." Organizers from the Center on Speech, Equality and Harm hope that their efforts will "stand out as a watershed event marking the beginning of the end of an era of the toleration and constitutional sanctioning of harmful speech."

1993, March 15—The UNO-sponsored "Truth Commission" finds the U.S.-backed military in El Salvador and far-right death squads with ties to the army are responsible for 85 percent of the 25,000 civilian deaths in that country's civil war. After interviewing more than two thousand witnesses, the commission documents the army's massacre of at least two hundred unarmed peasants in the hamlet of El Mozote in 1981 (most recent estimates put the toll at seven hundred), and names Roberto D'Aubuisson, the deceased founder of El Salvador's ruling political party, as the mastermind behind the assassination of Catholic Archbishop Oscar Romero in 1980. The panel also details how El Salvador's joint chiefs of staff conspired to murder six Jesuit priests in the fall of 1989 and then covered up the crime. In El Salvador, the ruling ARENA party responds to the "Truth Commission" findings by introducing an amnesty designed to cover all military personnel named in the report. Leaders of the rightist party also launch a campaign to discredit members of the "Truth Commission," planting stories in the press to implicate Reinaldo Figueredo in a corruption scandal in his native Venezuela. While devoting ample coverage to abuses committed by the Salvadoran armed forces, the American press gives much shorter shrift to the role of the United States in bankrolling and directing the army. The architects behind the Reagan administration's Central American policy attempt to rebut the "Truth Commission's" findings but are somewhat undercut when audiences are reminded of the previous conviction of Elliott Abrams for lying to Congress about what the U.S. government was really supporting in the region.

1993, April 8—Police raid the San Francisco and Los Angeles offices of the Anti-Defamation League of B'nai B'rith, following earlier FBI sleuthing. Officials release hundreds of pages of documents suggesting that the ADL has long managed a widespread, nationwide "spying operation," with ties to government agencies in the United States, Israel, South Africa, and perhaps other countries. Files recovered by authorities during the investigation prove the ADL's local offices conducted surveillance on more than 12,000 individuals and 950 political organizations, labor unions, and news publications, cutting across the political spectrum. Many of the names that police found in the confiscated files are respected private citizens whose only observable "crime" is speaking out against political policies favored by the ADL. Speculation on how the ADL intended to use the information centers on possible leaks to friendly journalists and others, ironically leaving open the potential for defamation and character smears. Thomas J. Gerard, an experienced San Francisco police officer who also served on leave as a CIA weapons specialist in Central America (from 1982 to 1985), is a central figure in the revelations. In an interview with the *Los Angeles Times*, Gerard threatens to disclose illegal CIA support to Central American "death squads" if he is indicted and tried on the San Francisco spying charges. Gerard allegedly violated departmental policy and several laws by giving criminal histories and other confidential files to Roy Bullock, a San Francisco art dealer, an alleged undercover ADL intelligence source for forty years. These police records illegally ended up in the ADL database. Because of the possibilities of further embarrassments, behind-the-scenes negotiations are undertaken to quietly kill the story and drop the cases.

1993, April 19—A public opinion survey conducted by the Roper Organization for the American Jewish Committee finds that more than one in five Americans believe the Holocaust never happened and doubt that the Nazi government had a policy for mass extermination.

1993, April 22—The controversial United States Holocaust Memorial Museum is formally dedicated in Washington, D.C., as a powerful reminder of the hatred epitomized by Nazi Germany. Upon entering, each visitor receives an identity card of a Holocaust victim and follows what happened to that person when touring the various exhibits. Though it is primarily a memorial to the many Jews who lost their lives to the Nazis, organizers of the museum also document other groups of people who suffered under the Hitler regime.

1993, May 23—Nicaraguan Sandinistas are accused of participating in an international Marxist kidnapping and terrorist ring following a series of explosions emanating from a "car repair" shop outside Managua. The debris reveals a large illegal guerrilla arms cache containing tons of sophisticated weapons, hundreds of false national identity papers and passports, and other incriminating evidence. As part of the 1990 accord ending the civil war in Nicaragua, Contras and Sandinistas were supposed to destroy their arsenals. Elements of the Popular Liberation Forces of El Salvador (FPL), one of the five groups making up the umbrella Farabundo Marti National Liberation Front (FMLN), admit ownership of the weapons stored in Nicaragua. The failure of all the former belligerents to keep their promise raises new questions about the Sandinista party's past ties and possible ongoing links to leftist terrorist organizations in El Salvador and other nations, as well as renews doubts about President Violeta Chamorro's control over her country's army or intelligence operations. The impact also threatens to further spill over into neighboring El Salvador by undermining the precarious UNO-mediated peace process there.

1993, May 25-June 2—Guatemalan President Jorge Serrano Elias initiates an *auto-golpe* ("self-coup") to partially suspend the Guatemalan constitution, dissolve that nation's Congress, dismiss Supreme Court and Constitutional Court judges, and replace the rule of law with rule by decree. Government offices and officials with responsibility for human rights protection, such as the Human Rights Procurator's Office and the attorney general, are reportedly suspended or sought for arrest. These moves come in the wake of protests in the capital against corruption and attempts to impose a national identity card on students. Following widespread negative reaction to the Serrano regime's usurpation of power, the Guatemalan military overthrows his administration to install yet another new government. The "self-coup" may well have triumphed without the opposition of the communications media.

1993, June 8—According to the UNO report, *Discrimination Against Indigenous Peoples: Draft Declaration on the Rights of Indigenous Peoples*, "All doctrines, policies and practices based on racism and racial, religious, ethnic or cultural superiority are scientifically false, legally invalid, morally condemnable and socially unjust." As a result, says the study, "Indigenous peoples have the collective and individual right to be protected against ethnocide and cultural genocide, including the prevention of and redress for . . . Any propaganda directed against them." The term *propaganda*, however, is not defined in the human rights document.

1993, June 11—Anti-Racist Action (ARA) organizes a march in Toronto, Ontario, Canada, on the home of alleged "neo-nazi propagandist" Gary Schipper to protest his work coordinating "the racist and homophobic Heritage Front Hotline." Later, four arrests of antiracists are made on charges of mischief to property. ARA spokespersons say that the resulting property damage reflects "a disciplined and controlled demonstration of community outrage to fascist violence."

1993, June 12-13—U.S. aircraft conduct a second straight night of attacks on what Pentagon press officers describe as "military targets" and "two unauthorized vehicle sites" near the home of Somali "warlord" Mohamed Farah Aideed. In a nationally broadcast address, President Bill Clinton declares the U.S.-led assault is intended to send a "clear message" to Aideed and "to preserve the security of UNO peacekeeping forces" assigned publicly to aid those in the African country starving from widespread famine aggravated by civil war. Within twenty-four hours, a contingent of Pakistani United Nations soldiers in the Somali capital of Mogadishu take the lives of twenty demonstrators protesting the air raids on strongholds loyal to Aideed. The new round of shootings come in retaliation for a clash one week earlier in which Aideed's forces killed twenty-three Pakistani members of the UNO contingent. In a U.S. television interview, Aideed portrays himself as the defender of a civilian population suffering under UNO aggression.

1993, June 26—U.S. forces launch a cruise missile attack on the Iraqi government's principal intelligence command facility in Baghdad, ostensibly in response to an alleged assassination plot against former President George Bush made during his visit to Kuwait the previous April. President Clinton states that this "proportional response" has the intent of targeting Iraq's capacity to support terrorist violence against the United States and other nations and deterring President Saddam Hussein from engaging in such "outlaw behavior" in the future.

1993, June 28—The U.S. General Accounting Office, an investigative arm of Congress, publishes a series of reports detailing past deceptions and gross exaggerations by Pentagon officials concerning alleged Soviet threats.

1993, July 8—In the wake of the first United Nations World Conference on Human Rights for twenty-five years, Amnesty International's *1993 Annual Report* reveals an appalling picture of continued subjugation. During 1992, over 110 governments resorted to torture in their prisons or police stations;

prisoners of conscience were held in at least sixty-two countries; political killings were used by the state to exterminate opponents and "troublemakers" in forty-five countries; and opposition groups in some nations deliberately committed arbitrary acts of terroristic violence.

1993, July 15—A report issued by a special U.S. State Department panel headed by retired career diplomats George Vest and Richard Murphy criticizes some aspects of the American role in El Salvador's twelve-year civil war but clears the executive branch of charges it systematically deceived Congress about human rights violations. However, Senator Christopher Dodd (D-Conn.) calls the report "a whitewash" and Senator Patrick Leahy (D-Vt.) says it "glosses over [truth with] . . . the lies, half-truths and evasions that we came to expect from the State Department during that period."

1993, late July—Catholic bishops in Nicaragua—who received CIA funding in the Reagan years—call for "humanitarian intervention" by United Nations peacekeeping forces to restore stability to the country.

1993, August 10—The Farabundo Marti Front for National Liberation (FMLN) declares it has ended armed struggle in El Salvador, after giving up arms deposits hidden both inside and outside the country because of "the strong support the FMLN has among the Salvadoran people." FMLN spokesperson Juan Ramon Medrano states, "We are interested in closing the armed chapter once and for all, although we recognize that the subject will continue to be manipulated by government propaganda and the right-wing."

1993, August 13—A U.S. Court of Appeals rules that the federal government must preserve millions of electronic messages and memoranda under the same standards used for paper communications. The decision is hailed by historians and journalists, but opposed by the Clinton administration.

1993, August 31—Negotiations between Palestine Liberation Organization representatives and the Israeli government result in an agreement to establish limited Palestinian home rule. Jubilant supporters hope this will prove a "historic breakthrough," but substantial opposition exists to the deal.

1993, September—French Culture Minister Jacques Toubon threatens to veto the General Agreement on Trade and Tariffs (GATT) accord if it removes French limits on imports of American movies and television programs. Jack Valenti, president of the Motion Picture Association of America (MPAA) and the industry's chief lobbyist, pushes for continued U.S. support of liberalized audio-visual trade policies beneficial to Hollywood.

1993, September 30—The Central Intelligence Agency releases 277 declassified Cold War-era documents to reporters. "When the protection of certain information is no longer required," CIA head James Woolsey had told Congress two days earlier, "then we owe it to our citizens to work hard to disclose as much of that information as we can, consistent with our mission—warts and all." However, documents on twelve covert operations from before 1963, including the 1961 attempted invasion of Cuba at the Bay of Pigs, are not among those released. These will remain secret for at least two more years, CIA officials say, despite an earlier promise by Bush administration Central Intelligence Director Robert Gates that the declassified records would cover the Bay of Pigs operation and the 1954 Guatemala coup.

1993, October-November—Debate heats up on the North American Free Trade Agreement (NAFTA), a formal pact to reduce tariffs and other trade barriers between Canada, the United States, and Mexico, having broad social ramifications. Professional media, public relations, and lobbying campaigns mounted by pro- and anti-NAFTA forces become increasingly hard-hitting. On October 21, the Mexican television network Televisa SA abruptly cuts off live U.S. Senate Committee broadcasts when five Mexican citizens begin testifying against NAFTA. Sales of Texas billionaire Ross Perot's anti-NAFTA book, called *Save Your Job, Save Our Country*, increase as he completes travels to forty-three states and ninety-one cities as part of his intensely personal crusade to halt the agreement. Despite spending millions of dollars, Perot's efforts falter when he loses his highly touted televised debate with Vice President Al Gore on CNN's *Larry King Show*. After an impressive show of presidential "arm twisting," on November 17 Congress votes "yes" to NAFTA. Despite assurances from President Clinton that side protocols negotiated with Mexico will mitigate environmental and labor concerns, opponents continue their arguments that approval is going to negatively affect residents of the North American continent for decades to come.

1993, November—Khalid Abdul Muhammad, a close aide to Nation of Islam Minister Louis Farrakhan, charges in a speech delivered at Kean College in Union, New Jersey, that Jews are "bloodsuckers of the black nation and the black community" through their influence in media, government, and more conventional black organizations. Publicity about the anti-Semitic nature of the remarks by the Anti-Defamation League of B'nai B'rith results in condemnation of their content from leaders of the Congressional Black Caucus, National Association for the Advancement of Colored People, and other groups.

1993, November 1—Tough new rules regulating "900-exchange" telemarketers are adopted by the Federal Trade Commission. The regulations require detailed disclosure of the organization offering the service, the costs involved, and procedures to resolve billing disputes. Pay-per-call telephone services directed at children under twelve years old are prohibited.

1993, November 7—German police in Mannheim publicly announce the arrest a week earlier of a U.S. citizen who denies the Holocaust. Fred Leuchter, author of a forensic report that claims the Nazis lacked the technology to gas millions of Jews to death, is charged with inciting racial hatred and defaming Nazi concentration camp victims—crimes that carry a maximum sentence of five years in jail.

1994—The Anti-Defamation League of B'nai B'rith reports 2,066 anti-Semitic incidents for the year, a jump of ten percent since 1993 and the highest in the sixteen years since the organization began issuing its annual report. ADL civil rights director Jeffrey P. Sinesky warns that these examples of intimidation and "hate language" typified by increasingly shrill radio talk shows and violent rap music lyrics point to growing intolerance in the United States. However, FBI statistics for 1994 listing all hate crimes logged by police show a decline to 5,852 incidents from the 7,684 reported in 1993.

U.S. troops occupy the troubled Caribbean nation of Haiti and restore President Jean-Bertrand Aristide to power.

Just 6,500 lobbyists are registered under current federal law, despite estimates indicating that the actual number of individuals involved in influencing national public policy exceed 60,000.

1994, January 1—To coincide with the official implementation of the NAFTA accord, Zapatista National Liberation Army rebels launch an uprising against Mexican government forces responsible for neglect and repression in the impoverished southern state of Chiapas. The incident raises doubts in the minds of some potential corporate investors considering moving operations from the United States to Mexico.

1994, November 8—National discontent is evident in a sweeping political upheaval, with voters endorsing the Republican party's "Contract with America." The GOP seizes control of the U.S. House of Representatives, U.S. Senate, and a majority of the nation's governorships.

1994, December—Meeting in lame duck session, the U.S. Congress approves participation in the General Agreement on Trade and Tariffs (GATT), a far-reaching international trade treaty supporters contend is important to prosperity but which critics say will erode American national sovereignty.

1995, March 10—Edward L. Bernays, pioneer public relations counsel, dies at the age of 103.

1995, April 19—The Federal Building in Oklahoma City, Oklahoma, is destroyed by a domestic terrorist bomb. More than 100 people are killed in the explosion, including many children. False news accounts at first speculate on a possible Arab connection, but later stories devolve into concerns about extremist rhetoric by conservative talk show hosts and armed right-wing private militia groups angry at alleged excesses committed by federal law enforcement agencies.

1995, July-August—Congress begins controversial hearings into the botched Waco raid of 1993 and the Whitewater financial scandal in Arkansas, with Republicans attempting to embarrass President Clinton over his handling of the two matters.

1995, October 16—At least 400,000 (perhaps one million) people heed the call of Nation of Islam leader Louis Farrakhan for African-American men to gather on the mall in Washington, D.C., for a day of atonement, solidarity, and empowerment. This is the largest demonstration by people of color since the famed March on Washington led years earlier by Dr. Martin Luther King, Jr. However, because of Farrakhan's position on other racial and religious issues, the Million Man March becomes the center of controversy as well as celebration.

1995, October 31—At closed U.S. Senate Intelligence Committee hearings, new CIA director John Deutch reveals that counterintelligence expert Aldrich Ames, who actually served as a Soviet spy inside the Agency during the 1980s, helped recruit dozens of Russian informants. These dual agents systematically planted disinformation used to mislead Reagan and Bush administration defense policy makers and news analysts.

1995, November 4—Israeli prime minister Yitzhak Rabin is assassinated at a peace rally in Tel Aviv's Kings Square. The confessed killer, Jewish law student Yigal Amir, tells authorities the killing is meant to halt the giveaway of land to Arabs in the U.S.-mediated Middle East peace process.

1995, December—The first of more than 60,000 NATO and Russian troops under U.S. command begin entering Bosnia to enforce a brokered peace deal agreed to by leaders of the warring factions in the former Yugoslavia.

1995, December 6—The Conference Committee on Telecommunications

Reform of the U.S. House of Representatives votes to impose far reaching "indecency" restrictions on the Internet and other interactive media, including large commercial online services (such as America Online, Compuserve, and Prodigy) and smaller Internet Service Providers such as Panix, IDT, the Well, Echo, and Mindvox.

1995, December 19—Regulation of lobbyists is tightened under a new law signed by President Clinton which goes into effect on January 1. The law mandates how lobbyists report the specific issues they are working on and the amounts they are paid by their clients to do so. Those who contact congressional aides and executive branch officials are also now included in the definition of lobbying. In conjunction with new rules limiting gifts to members of Congress, proponents of the lobby reform law say it will force many lobbyists to publicly disclose their activities for the first time and lessen the impact of monied interests on government policy.

A PROPAGANDA GLOSSARY*

ACTION GROUP—A LOBBYING/LOBBYIST and information organization capable of mobilizing affiliate groups, volunteer supporters, and NEWS coverage in favor of, or in opposition to, a particular bill, nominee, or ISSUE.

ACTIVE MEASURES—Practices that include the recruitment of agents in other countries; penetration and control of supposedly independent organizations, which are useful for PROPAGANDA purposes; the spread of DISINFORMATION *(DEZINFORMATSIA)* to drive a wedge between allies, such as between the United States and Europe or the Industrialized West and the THIRD WORLD; covertly-sponsored demonstrations, strikes, and TERRORIST actions that are damaging to competing governments; character assassination against unfriendly foreign leaders; and assassinations of particularly troublesome foes, usually in a way that focuses the blame on one's enemies. See also COVERT.

ACTIVISTS—When part of a community feels it is not being dealt with fairly, this generates outrage. Those individuals most motivated to become involved in social and political causes are, by definition, activists, who usually organize themselves collectively in public policy groups. The Heath/Nelson Model of Activist Movement Development, by Robert L. Heath and Richard Alan Nelson, was first published in their book *Issues Management: Corporate Public Policymaking in an Information Society* (1985, pp. 204-223). This model points to five key phases:
- *Strain:* a MOVEMENT gets its impetus from a desire to change some condition, resulting in the formation or coalition of INTEREST GROUPS.

---

* NOTE: Terms listed in CAPITAL LETTERS (with the exception of acronyms) indicate a cross-reference in the glossary.

- *Mobilization:* the stage in which a movement must begin to marshal its power resources (including access to media).
- *Confrontation:* that moment when interest groups or coalitions attempt to force a corporation or government agency to recognize their importance as STAKEHOLDERS by meeting their specific demands.
- *Negotiation:* when contacts occur in a variety of forums (both private and public) in which each side in the controversy seeks to leverage power to reach an accommodation that maximizes its own advantages and minimizes its losses.
- *Resolution:* the stage of the PUBLIC POLICY PROCESS that determines how society will be adjusted to accommodate the results of discussion and negotiation.

To gain support and put pressure on legislators, activists regularly highlight the impact of the fear, anger, and harm they feel. For NEWS MEDIA, outrage makes the best story. If the organization responds openly by forging community alliances, sharing critical information, involving activists in planning as part of advisory panels, increasing local investment, and otherwise building trust, then the conflict can be minimized. Business, labor, professional, and other interests have also responded by aggressively setting up their own varied FRONT GROUPS/SATELLITE ORGANIZATIONS and POLITICAL ACTION COMMITTEES (PACs). However, if those under attack make the mistake of STONEWALLING or otherwise fail to bring about CONFLICT RESOLUTION through effective ISSUES MANAGEMENT efforts, the breakdown will feed suspicion and exacerbate the amount of attention given the allegations. Lawmakers often respond by caving in to activist pressures, often in ways unfavorable to the activists' target (particularly when doing so plays to POPULAR OPINION so as to ensure their reelection). Moreover, because legislators ultimately determine the policy agenda and control the budgets, appointed members of regulatory bodies are not immune from the sway of activist influence. When an activist group or coalition fails to change through democratic methods, the group may dwindle or resort to increasingly aggressive intimidation measures that devolve into TERRORISM. The more fanatic of the antichoice "rescuers," for example, are ZEALOTS who attempt to prevent women from obtaining abortions and other health care services by blockading entrances, harassing patients as they enter the clinics, stalking doctors, sabotaging facilities through fire-bombings, and committing other acts of violence.

ACTUALITY—An explanatory audio quote (usually brief) containing on-the-scene sounds and interviews edited to appear in a radio NEWS report. The equivalent audio-visual DOCUMENTARY element in television journalism is known as a sound bite. See also VIDEO NEWS RELEASE (VNR).

AD HOMINEM ATTACK—Generally refers to appeals based on prejudices rather than reason. Includes dismissing a proposal or argument out of hand merely because one dislikes the person who advocates it. See also SLIPPERY SLOPE.

ADVERTISING—Advertising is a planned communication activity, which is paid for by an identified sponsor and utilizes controlled messages carried by media to persuade audiences to engage in a voluntary transfer of goods, services, or ideas. As a result, advertisements—unlike conventional NEWS RELEASEs issued by PUBLIC RELATIONS (PR) firms—are generally not edited or changed by media GATEKEEPERS before they reach their intended target audience. Understanding the content and pervasive influence of advertising in the modern world remains an important task since, for better or worse, advertising is an integral and influential part of our lives. The advertising process encompasses the consumer domains of:

- *Industrial technology*, from which issues an endless flow of new products,
- *popular culture*, which is embedded with applied psychological appeals and conventions through which socialization occurs, and
- *the media*, which unify the flow of symbols, images, and motivational messages that audiences choose to "decode" from what they see or hear.

See also ADVERTISING COUNCIL, ADVERTORIAL, ADVOCACY ADVERTISING, COMMERCIAL SPEECH, DIRECT-RESPONSE (DR) ADVERTISING, FACT SLINGING, FEDERAL TRADE COMMISSION (FTC), FOUR P'S OF THE MARKETING MIX, GROSS RATINGS POINTS (GRPs), HOT SWITCHING, ISSUE ADVERTISING, MEDIA/MEDIUM, POLISPOTS, PUBLIC SERVICE ANNOUNCEMENTS (PSAs), PULLOUTS, REACH, and SPECIALITY ADVERTISING.

ADVERTISING COUNCIL—A not-for-profit association of ADVERTISING professionals who volunteer their creative efforts to craft PUBLIC SERVICE ANNOUNCEMENTS (PSAs) on behalf of more than thirty national, nonpartisan, nonsectarian clients a year. Because many media professionals rely on the Advertising Council imprimatur in deciding who gets airtime or space, its decisions play a pivotal role in determining which "PUBLIC INTEREST" voices are heard. Literally millions of dollars of free PUBLICITY are donated each year by broadcasters and publishers to Advertising Council clients, who only pay for the actual cost of materials and are selected, after rigorous review, from hundreds of applicants. Originally started as the War Advertising Council during World War II, today the organization continues to work closely with the federal government and allied agencies in supporting programs, ranging from Savings Bonds to the UNITED NATIONS ORGANIZATION, that help shape national policy. Other clients include the Red Cross, the National Alliance of Business, and the National Committee for the Prevention of Child Abuse.

ADVERTORIAL—The integration of ADVERTISING and editorial materials into one NEWS-like package designed to enhance credibility, either as: (1) a paid column, ad page, or commercial reflecting the views of a sponsoring organization on political, economic, social, and/or PUBLIC INTEREST issues (rather than through a more overt, conventional product sales message); or (2) a paid special section appearing in a targeted publication or broadcast in which the advertiser exercises editorial and commercial message control in an informative sales supplement created to emulate the editorial style of the surrounding media content. See also ADVOCACY ADVERTISING and INFOMERCIAL.

ADVOCACY ADVERTISING—Issue-oriented ADVERTISING messages targeted to clearly defined audiences—including grassroots mobilizations—that are designed to advocate, induce, or discourage a specific kind of action on the part of a social, corporate, or governmental entity. Most advocacy ads seek to promote an organization's beliefs or positions on a controversial matter of public policy. See also ADVERTISING COUNCIL, ADVERTORIAL, FACT SLINGING, and ISSUE ADVERTISING.

ADVOCACY JOURNALISM—News reporting that rejects the concept of objectivity by incorporating political opinion and analysis within stories rather than separating personal interpretation into editorials and signed "commentary" columns. See also NEW JOURNALISM.

AGAINST THE MAIL—Votes and openly-stated positions on ISSUEs that are taken by legislators despite the expressed wishes of their constituents and contrary PUBLIC OPINION polls.

AGENDA SETTING—The role played by MASS COMMUNICATION media in establishing the salient ISSUEs and images to which the collective public reacts is a controversial one. Agenda-setting theory states that the menu of NEWS and other information made available to audiences by media decision-makers ultimately defines what is considered significant. The question then becomes how agenda setting influences the importance subsequently attached to the images and events thus presented. Although much of the research to date has concentrated on proving a causal relationship between NEWS MEDIA coverage and perceptions of political issues, it seems clear that even the most mundane commercial television ADVERTISING may have a great impact on popular culture as well. Donald L. Shaw and Maxwell E. McCombs observed in *The Emergence of American Political Issues: The Agenda-Setting Function of the Press* that:

Considerable evidence has accumulated that editors and broadcasters play an important part in shaping our social reality as they go about their day-to-day task of choosing and displaying news. . . . This impact of the mass media—the ability to effect cognitive change among individuals, to structure their thinking—has been labeled the agenda-setting function of mass communication. Here may lie the most important effect of mass communication, its ability to mentally order and organize our world for us. In short, the mass media may not be successful in telling us what to think, but they are stunningly successful in telling us what to think about.

Agenda setting is linked with the TWO-STEP FLOW (MULTI-STEP FLOW) theories of communication, which assume that definable groups of "opinion leaders" pass along and amplify media themes to less informed audiences. One PROPAGANDA MODEL (HERMAN AND CHOMSKY) asserts that the agenda is set for elite media before newsrooms perform their GATEKEEPER

function. See also BROADCASTING, DEEP POCKETS SPENDING, HATE
CAMPAIGN, HIDDEN AGENDA, JOURNALISM/JOURNALIST, MEDIA
BIAS, MEDIA EFFECTS, POLITICALLY CORRECT (PC), SALIENCE,
SPIN CONTROL, and SPIRAL OF SILENCE.

AGENTS/AGENCIES OF INFLUENCE—According to Ladislav Bittman,
author of *The Deception Game* and other major works describing how nations
utilize DISINFORMATION (*DEZINFORMATSIA*) based on his personal
experiences working in cooperation with the Soviet KGB (*Komitet po
Gosudarstvennoy Bezopasnosti*), agents of influence include:

Disguised voices in foreign governmental, political, journalistic, business, labor,
artistic, and academic circles. While agents of influence may incidentally transmit
intelligence, their overriding mission is to alter opinion and policy in the
interests of (the country they hold true allegiance to). No activity of the KGB
abroad has higher priority than its efforts to manipulate the thought and action of
other nations by insinuating such agents into positions of power. . . . Normally...
the agent of influence conceals his true motivation and his servility.

Entities serving the same purpose, such as a FRONT GROUPS/SATELLITE
ORGANIZATIONS, are agencies of influence.

AGENTS PROVOCATEUR—Intelligence agents and other operatives who
"defect" to or infiltrate competing groups under false pretenses. The purpose of
agents provocateur is to mislead, disrupt, and provoke nefarious actions by the
individuals and organizations they target. Examples from history include:
  • FBI agents inciting violence by pretending to be gung-ho Ku Klux
    Klan members in order to further publicly discredit the KKK; and
  • CIA and MOSSAD ("INSTITUTE") spies planting TERRORIST
    bombs and otherwise stirring up unrest in Moslem countries in order
    to link Islamic fundamentalists with TERRORISM in the public
    mind.
  • Pinkerton Detective Agency strike-busting operatives who join labor
    unions to incite illegal acts in order to undercut sympathy for the
    workers and bring about police intervention that is favorable to
    corporate management interests.

AGITATION—The interpersonal use of emotion and persuasion to arouse
dissatisfaction, stir up unrest, and violently mobilize individuals for social
change. Communists tend to see it as the person-to-person propagating of a
few ideas to many people. As nineteenth-century American abolitionist
Frederick Douglass observed:

If there is no struggle, there is no progress. Those who profess to favor freedom
and yet deprecate agitation are people who want crops without plowing up the
ground. They want rain without thunder and lightning. That struggle might be a
moral one; it might be a physical one; it might be both moral and physical, but it
must be a struggle. Power concedes nothing without a demand. It never did and
never will. People might not get all that they work for in this world, but they must
certainly work for all they get.

See also ACTIVISTS, AGITPROP, FREE SPEECH, MARCH OF PROVOCATION, POLEMIC, TWO-STEP FLOW (MULTI-STEP FLOW), and WHISPERING CAMPAIGN.

AGITPROP—Agitational propaganda is a term that was popularized by Soviet ACTIVISTS and dramatists. It has the objective of inciting rebellion and gaining popular support for revolutionary objectives through interpersonal experience, such as is found in the performance of radical plays before workers in their factories. For example, V.J. Jerome, the cultural head of the American Communist party in the 1930s and 1940s, articulated the view that "agitprop drama was actually better drama because Marxists better understood the forces that shaped human beings, and could therefore write better characters." See also INDUSTRIAL THEATER.

A-I-D-C-A FORMULA—A persuasive communication format analyzing how effective the message is in attracting *Attention*, building *Interest*, creating *Desire*, reinforcing *Credibility*, and inducing *Action*. This is sometimes referred to instead as the A-I-D-A formula, with the credibility step considered inclusive within the other elements.

AMERICA BASHING—Selective negative interpretation of American governmental policies, economic activities, and/or cultural practices designed to elicit the expression of unfavorable opinions about the United States. See also JAPAN BASHING.

AMERICA FIRST—Patriotic slogan resurrected by the proisolationist America First Committee of 1940-1941 which sought to keep the United States out of World War II. It continues to be widely used in appealing to nativist sentiment, particularly by RIGHT-WING/CONSERVATIVE groups opposed to internationalist influence on American foreign policy. See also ANGLOPHOBE and ISOLATIONIST.

AMERICAN EXPEDITIONARY FORCE (AEF)—American military troops assigned to the European theater in World War I. The military PRESS section was known as G-2D.

AMERICAN PARTY—Name of several political parties in U.S. history, most closely associated with the "Know-Nothing" movement of the 1850s and renewed far-right efforts beginning in the 1970s. See also POPULISM/POPULIST and RIGHT-WING/CONSERVATIVE.

ANARCHISM/ANARCHIST—An antiauthoritarian movement centered around the belief that a desirable voluntary social order could emerge in the absence of the coercive monopoly of the state. The word anarchy derives from the Greek *Avapxia*, meaning "without a ruler." There are nearly as many definitions of anarchy as there are anarchists, although a common thread is the desire by anarchists for the creation of a utopian society without compulsory government. Anarchists reject all involuntarily imposed ruling authority (no "divine rights") and advocate the removal of "existing, arbitrary social institutions." Whether this is to be achieved through peaceful evolution, a change in human nature, or revolutionary violence is a much debated point among anarchists and critics. Some anarchists shun all electoral activity. Others are simply militant unionists who would disavow all labels. Anarchism is a lively field, with a growing body of literature and increasing numbers of adherents. Unfortunately for the broad diversity of insurgent viewpoints represented within their decentralized socialist philosophy, the terms *anarchy* and *anarchist* have become value laden, which means that people readily identify anarchy with particular ideological, social, and historical images stored in various information database sources and in their subconscious minds. Progovernment opponents in America seeking to maintain the dominant social order have successfully poisoned the public mind by linking anarchism and its reformist impulse with social chaos. Rather than being understood as heroic freedom fighters for a socially responsible and autonomous humanity, anarchists are seen by the great majority of people as either threatening ("bearded, bomb-throwing radicals") or irrelevant ("pipe-smoking armchair idealists"). However, while anarchists are often popularly associated with the notion of violence, more often than not they are victims of it. For example, Emma Goldman ("Red Emma"), who was subsequently deported from the United States for her views in the post-World War I anticommunist roundups, defined anarchism as "the philosophy of a new social order based on unrestricted liberty and the theory that all government rests on violence and is therefore wrong, harmful and unnecessary." Remaining truer to the ideal of FREE SPEECH than her critics, she later also outspokenly condemned the excesses of Soviet-style communism. See also ANTIAUTHORITARIANISM, AUTONOMIST, BOURGEOIS, COMMUNISM/COMMUNIST, DIRECT ACTION, DYSTOPIA, GLOBALISM, and SOCIALISM/SOCIALIST.

ANCHORS—(1) The key linkages by which persuaders bridge their interests with the concerns of the target audience. Because changing minds is much more difficult than mobilizing predispositions, the persuader seeks shortcuts. By couching the propaganda with allusions which play on preexisting attitudes, behaviors, beliefs, group norms, opinions, and/or values, the persuader takes advantage of mental building blocks or "anchors" already in place. (2) The in-studio electronic newscasters who serve as "hosts" of a particular program (known in Britain as "NEWS readers").

ANGLOPHILE—Literally, "England lover," or a person whose emotional, financial, and political commitments to English culture and government are overriding factors in urging support for the United Kingdom in any conflict between that nation and its enemies of the moment. ISOLATIONISTs, for example, have condemned key U.S. State Department INTERVENTIONISTs as Anglophiles for their slavish imitation of British dress, accent, and willingness to commit American resources (even when American interests may well be harmed) to assist England in conflicts ranging from World War I to the more recent Falklands/Malvinas War with Argentina. See also ANGLOPHOBE, AMERICAN EXPEDITIONARY FORCE (AEF), BACKDOOR TO WAR, CIRCUS, ENTENTE, FREE TRADE, FREE

WORLD, GERMANOPHOBIA, MI5, MI6, and NORTH ATLANTIC TREATY ORGANIZATION (NATO).

ANGLOPHOBE—Literally, "England hater," or a person whose emotional, financial, and political commitments are opposed to those of Britain. Victims of English nationalism (i.e., the Irish and other Keltic peoples), Continental rivals (i.e., the Germans and French), allies who were later betrayed by British governments (i.e., the French and the Arabs), races enslaved through English imperialism (i.e., Africans) and neutrals favoring an even-handed policy (i.e., ISOLATIONISTs in the United States) tend to historically exhibit frequent outbreaks of Anglophobia. See also AMERICA FIRST, ANGLOPHILE, CENTRAL POWERS, FAIR TRADE, and PERFIDIOUS ALBION.

ANIMAL RIGHTS MOVEMENT—A coalition of organized groups which hold that animals are the moral equivalent to humans. Eschewing meat, fur, leather, and products derived from, or based on, animal experimentation, animal rightists argue for the abolition of all "speciesism" distinctions that contribute to the "exploitation" of animals. To stop the scientific use of animals and the wearing of fur, ACTIVISTS in the Animal Liberation Front have proved willing to engage in TERRORIST tactics with which related FRONT GROUPS/SATELLITE ORGANIZATIONS, such as People for the Ethical Treatment of Animals (PETA), cannot be legally identified. See also MOVEMENT.

ANTIAUTHORITARIANISM—An IDEOLOGY that opposes centralized state domination of social and political life. As a political category, it is comprised of an alphabet soup of groups so large that one can literally "fill in the blanks." Antiauthoritarians include anarcho-communists, anarcho feminists, anarcho-Marxists, anarcho-syndicalists, anticommunists, bandits, Christian anarchists, council communists, counterculturists, democratic socialists, free speech advocates, Jeffersonian constitutionalists, LIBERTARIAN socialists, pagan anarchists, post-situationists, rebels, situationists, social anarchists, social democrats, social ecologists, street gangs, syndicalists, undisciplined rabble, and still others. See also ACTIVISTS, ANARCHISM/ANARCHIST, AUTONOMIST, BILL OF RIGHTS, BOLSHEVIK/BOLSHEVIKI, COMMUNISM/COMMUNIST, COMMUNITARIAN SOCIETY, FREE SPEECH, GLOBALISM, and TOTALITARIANISM.

ANTI-DEFAMATION LEAGUE OF B'NAI B'RITH (ADL)—The Anti-Defamation League of B'nai B'rith is a prominent civil rights organization founded in 1913 to defend Jews and other minority groups from discrimination. Over the years, the ADL has had four basic missions:
1. Monitor prejudice and "expose those who are anti-Jewish, racist, antidemocratic, and violence-prone" through information gathering, publications, educational programs, lobbying, and other activities.
2. Speak out for Jews suffering from false accusations and social discrimination.
3. Provide support to the nation of Israel and defend the actions of that

nation from its critics.

4. Share information with appropriate governmental agencies (including law enforcement) relating to anti-Semitism and "EXTREMISM" in the United States and abroad.

The ADL courageously led the fight against fascist and racist organizations ranging from the American Nazi party to the Ku Klux Klan. During the 1960s, the ADL also championed the civil rights MOVEMENT. Today, the ADL maintains one of the most extensive privately controlled information collection agencies in the world. The Jacob Alson Memorial Library and the Braun Center for Holocaust Studies are major on-site resources at the New York City headquarters. ADL intelligence operatives have also long maintained close contact with police and other investigative agencies. As a result, the ADL is widely seen as the definitive source for materials documenting EXTREMIST groups. The ADL's Fact Finding Department, working under the direction of Irwin Saul, has proved particularly successful in using undercover informants to penetrate highly secretive ANTI-SEMITIC organizations. In 1993, however, the ADL became engulfed in a national burglary, theft, and conspiracy scandal that tarnished its reputation. FBI and San Francisco police investigations revealed the existence of an intelligence network operated by the Anti-Defamation League that not only targeted known HATE GROUPS (both RIGHT-WING/CONSERVATIVE and LEFT-WING/LIBERAL) but also may have illegally obtained confidential data on hundreds of organizations and thousands of individuals considered nonviolent, progressive, and mainstream. Critics allege that the Anti-Defamation League and other pro-Israel LOBBYING/LOBBYIST groups have gone overboard by taking on the role of censoring, intimidating, and otherwise stifling public criticism of Israel in the United States. See also CENSORSHIP, GENOCIDE, SPIRAL OF SILENCE, and ZIONISM/ZIONIST.

ANTI-SEMITIC—The term literally means "against Semitic people" (i.e., the descendants of Noah's son Shem), which today would include most Arabs and Jews. However, it has widely been employed to mean bias and persecution specifically "against Jews." Some commentators have sought (mostly unsuccessfully) to clarify this issue by making a distinction between "anti-Semitism" (referring to any Semite—Arab or Jew) and "antisemitism" (meaning the specific targeting of Jews). Anti-Judaism is sometimes used when referring to the views of those who attack Judaism as a religion, but not Jews as individuals. Some scholars, for example, say Martin Luther's EXTREMIST views stem from his apocalyptic understanding of history and are religious, not racial, so technically they would fall under the category of anti-Judaism or antisemitism as compared to anti-Semitism. Confusion in terminology persists and, by extension, many people also equate anti-Semitism/antisemitism/anti-Judaism with anti-Zionism (criticism of the Zionist movement and opposition to the notion of an independent Jewish-controlled nation of Israel). This tends to involve an "if you are not for me, you are against me" view which sees someone as being at least latently anti-Semitic if they hold pro-Palestinian viewpoints or even express neutral opinions to the idea of a modern secular Israel. Those who dispute this broad interpretation of what "anti-Semitism" means point to the historical

opposition of many Orthodox Jews on religious grounds to Zionism. There is
no doubt that both Jew and Arab hatred continues to infect the modern world,
with forms of anti-Semitism persisting in many countries on an institutional
level as well as through personal prejudice. Anti-Semitic/antisemitic
PROPAGANDA in the twentieth-century is part of this broader phenomenon,
much of it closely linked to perceptions of alleged Jewish control over money
and media. Among the most widely circulated propaganda tracts has been the
Protocols of the Learned Elders of Zion, a DOCUMENT forged in the early
1900s by czarist secret police to supposedly reveal an internationalist Jewish
conspiracy to seize world power. The much translated and reprinted booklet
continues to circulate through the efforts of extremist groups despite being
thoroughly discredited by scholars, largely because such DISINFORMATION
(*DEZINFORMATSIA*) plays to prejudices found within POPULAR
OPINION. Contained are rather extensive sections which purport to describe
how Jews have access to the public mind through their control of the PRESS
and can use this influence to disseminate lies and half-truths designed to divide
and conquer through artificially maneuvering nations into needless wars and
conflicts. Such views were used to justify severe persecutions by the Nazi
regime in Germany and the European territories it conquered during World War
II. See also ANTI-DEFAMATION LEAGUE OF B'NAI B'RITH (ADL), BIG
LIE, CONSPIRACY THEORIES, GENOCIDE, HATE SPEECH,
HEGEMONY, MEDIA/MEDIUM, NATIONAL SOCIALISM/NAZISM,
NESHER, RACIST/RACIALIST/RACIAL DISCRIMINATION, RADICAL,
REACTIONARY, REVISIONISM/REVISIONIST, THOUGHT-STOPPING
CLICHÉ, ZIONISM/ZIONIST, and ZOG.

ANTITERRORISM—Defensive measures used to reduce the vulnerability of
individuals and property to TERRORIST acts, including limited response and
containment by local military forces. See also COUNTERTERRORISM.

ARGUMENTATION—The National Developmental Conference on Forensics
has suggested that argumentation is "reason given in communicative
situations by people whose purpose is the justification of acts, beliefs, and
values." See also POLEMIC, PURPOSEFUL PERSUASION, and
RHETORIC.

ARMED PROPAGANDA—Selective use of murderous violence ("implicit
and explicit terror") in a guerrilla revolutionary war by AGITPROP cadres so
as to neutralize opponents and establish psychological control of the masses.
Ho Chi Minh, in the early stages of the conflict to remove the French from
Vietnam, for example, followed this TERRORIST strategy in asserting that
"political activities were more important than military activities" and "fighting
[was] less important than propaganda." See also ARMED STRUGGLE,
INSURRECTION/INSURRECTIONARY, PROPAGANDA OF THE DEED,
and TERRORISM.

ARMED STRUGGLE—The use of weapons in guerrilla warfare and other
forms of militant resistance designed to undermine, and eventually overthrow,
those in power. The Chinese model propagated by Mao Tse-tung distinguished

between two types of "contradictions" (the Chinese Communist term for political struggles): one was defined as "antagonistic" and pitted oppressor against oppressed. It could be resolved only through struggle, often armed. The second was defined as a contradiction among the oppressed, and could be resolved peacefully by consultation, discussion, compromise, mutual agreement, and diplomacy. Resort to armed struggle has been employed in decolonialism efforts as well as in civil conflicts fraught with POLITICAL PATHOLOGY. The contest for power, which must inevitably accompany paramilitary and military pressure, generally involves the widespread implementation of PROPAGANDA messages. Tactical considerations underlying armed struggle may range from seeking a negotiated settlement to complete victory in forcing an occupying government to withdraw troops. On the other hand, a beleaguered regime may seek to justify its actions in international forums by propagandistically denouncing the "atrocities" committed by the armed resistance as HUMAN RIGHTS violations. Government forces typically increase the repression, engaging in surveillance, incommunicado detention, interrogation, and indoctrination. In the case where the resistance cadre has been driven out of the country, a propaganda goal of the government is to isolate the rebel leadership from those they purport to represent on the ground. However, even when key opposition leaders are captured, the RHETORIC of armed struggle may remain if only for symbolic propagandistic reasons to show resistance persists. Armed struggle may be abandoned when a cause is lost or it is in the interest of those involved. Either side may engage in a "peace offensive" to build public support. Once a genuine peace process is underway, talks among the parties involved are necessary to determine clearly what comes next. A unilaterally declared cease fire with troops in place is the simplest form of tactical abandonment of armed struggle. An unfair and imposed peace may result in new injustices which fan the flames for renewal of violent resistance against the state by guerrillas who fight on and refuse to surrender. See also COMMUNISM/COMMUNIST and INTIFADA.

ASSASSIN—A person willing to use violence, especially murder, to achieve political ends. People who band together for such purposes are usually referred to by their enemies as TERRORISTs. The term *assassin* dates back to an eleventh-century Shiite Muslim sect led by Hasan-i-Sabbah known as the Hashishans or Assassins. CULT members saw themselves as an elite group of warriors, willing to sacrifice their lives if necessary in order to defeat the schemes of non-believers. Two views as to the original meaning of the word are common. One asserts it to have evolved from the Arabic *hashshasin* ("hemp eater"), a reference to the use of PSYCHEDELICS in SACRED TERRORISM rituals connected with promises of paradise for those who die as martyrs. The other viewpoint believes *hashish* (meaning "dry fodder") was first used as a form of contempt for Muslims by the early Christian Crusaders who fought and came to fear them. Whatever the origins, centuries later many of the same issues that led to the creation of the Hashishans still influence us today. The United States government, for example, alleges the Islamic Republic of Iran (whose government is completely controlled by Shiite Muslim clergy) to be the world's leading international practitioner of STATE

TERRORISM. See also CENSORSHIP BY ASSASSINATION and PROPAGANDA OF THE DEED.

ASSETS—Journalists, government employees, professors, and others in key positions who can be mobilized as "agents of influence" on behalf of the propagandist. See also AGENTS/AGENCIES OF INFLUENCE.

AUTONOMIST—A form of ANTIAUTHORITARIANISM associated with modern anarchist/antiimperialist groups having socialist and communist leanings, yet proudly maintaining their autonomy from old-line Communist party control. As a result, "autonomous" still covers a wide range of perspectives, particularly in Europe where the "autonomes" of Germany are well known. The term "autonomist" has evolved in response to the perceived distinctions made between younger, more contemporary antiauthoritarian ACTIVISTS and "classical" anarchists keeping alive many varied, older political ideologies once thought to be headed for extinction. See also ANARCHISM/ANARCHIST, IDEOLOGY, and LEFT-WING/LIBERAL.

BACKDOOR CONTACT—Phillip Knightly, a former investigative journalist for the *London Sunday Times* and authority on propaganda, in 1989 revealed that FDR ran "his own personal intelligence service" prior to World War II using influential friends. Wealthy ANGLOPHILEs such as Vincent Astor, a director of the Western Union Cable Company, monitored international messages and held CLANDESTINE meetings as part of a secret society known as "the Room." Members met monthly in an empty New York City apartment especially rented for the purpose. Others tracked banking movements, and even engaged in secret cloak-and-dagger espionage missions for the president.

BACKDOOR TO WAR—Famous phrase that exemplifies charges, by revisionist historians (such as Charles Callan Tansill) and military men (led by Rear Admiral Robert A. Theobald), that President Franklin D. Roosevelt used his position to provoke Japan to strike first against U.S. territory in order to precipitate American entry into World War II. They argue that the record shows FDR was willing to take material losses and innocent deaths in order to change isolationist PUBLIC OPINION and spark open intervention in the European and Asian conflicts. After failing to provoke a war with Germany in the Atlantic, the revisionists assert Roosevelt lied about his true intentions and opted for a secret "backdoor" strategy of putting intolerable pressures on Japan in order to incite them to make a preemptive move on American positions in the Pacific. This, they say, gave him a war crimes atrocity pretext to wage all-out war based on the false but comforting conviction—reinforced by unrelenting, "Day of Infamy" administration-inspired propaganda—that the United States and allied governments were morally superior to those of the enemy nations. Some scholars have argued that it was British Prime Minister Winston Churchill who had advance intelligence from his codebreakers that the Japanese leadership were decided upon war in the Pacific, but withheld this information from Roosevelt in order to ensure American entry. Still other researchers dispute the entire premise. See also CONSPIRACY THEORIES and REVISIONISM/REVISIONIST.

BACKGROUND—Widely utilized NEWS MEDIA convention where a source agrees to provide quotable information to journalists on condition that direct attribution not be made (i.e., "A high administration official revealed today," etc.). See also DEEP BACKGROUND and OFF THE RECORD.

BACKGROUNDER—A PUBLIC RELATIONS release distributed by an organization to appropriate journalists, usually as part of a MEDIA KIT. Backgrounders neutrally and factually summarize pertinent facts about a subject of current PUBLIC INTEREST. Typically, backgrounders start with a historical overview of the topic, incorporate a situation review of the present situation, and conclude with a straight-forward discussion outlining the implications of the facts presented.

BELTWAY BANDITS—Negative term for Washington, D.C., INSIDERS—government MANDARINS, lobbyists, media workers and other influentials—whose efforts are better spent at advancing their own private interests than those of the country at large. The parochialism of the Washington cognosci "inside the beltway" describe those whose mental world is restricted to what happens within the confines of the freeway system surrounding the capital.

BENCHMARK STUDY—Social science measurements of audience attitudes before and after a persuasive communications campaign, performed in order to determine the effectiveness of the PROPAGANDA effort. See also TRACKING POLLS.

BIG LIE—Term associated with Adolf Hitler who argued that lies by one's opponents may have to be countered by still bigger lies, and that the larger and more widely repeated the lie, the more believable it becomes to the masses. Hitler's "big lie" technique is usually expressed something like this: "Lie often enough and boldly enough, and people will find it difficult not to believe you. . . . History never asks the victor whether he's told the truth." Hitler's use of this analogy was originally in connection with a description of his growing anti-Semitism over what he saw as the political character assassination practiced by the Social Democratic PRESS in pre-World War I Austria. Although most commonly linked to the National Socialist regime in Germany dominated by Hitler and his Minister of Propaganda and Popular Enlightenment, Joseph Goebbels, we now know that the widespread use of very big lies and other forms of DISINFORMATION (*DEZINFORMATSIA*) are regular features of most government propaganda apparatuses. See also BLACK PROPAGANDA, DEMAGOGUE/DEMOGOGISM, FASCISM/FASCIST, and NATIONAL SOCIALISM/NAZISM.

BILDERBERGER GROUP—A loose organization of powerful industrialists, political figures, bankers, media leaders, and intellectual policy advisors who meet quietly on an annual basis to discuss international issues. The term stems from the Bilderberg Hotel in the Netherlands where the first meeting was held in the 1950s. Proponents argue the protective security measures are necessary to prevent TERRORIST attacks and the lack of PUBLICITY is vital to encourage free-ranging discussion and desirable coordination by leading individuals responsible for key sectors of the world economy. Critics see the participants as a forum for elite internationalists who, as part of a global SHADOW GOVERNMENT, conspire to manipulate events from behind the scenes. See also CONSPIRACY THEORIES, COUNCIL ON FOREIGN RELATIONS (CFR), ELITE THEORY, and INVISIBLE GOVERNMENT.

BILL OF RIGHTS—The first ten amendments approved to the U.S. Constitution. Anti-Federalists successfully held up adoption of the new charter for government until the Bill of Rights was included by arguing that written guarantees were needed to secure individual citizens from potential abuses by federal authorities.

BINGO CARDS—Preaddressed postal cards inserted in magazines with numbers the reader can circle in order to subscribe to the publication and request more direct information from specific advertisers or article authors. See also BOUNCEBACK CARDS.

BLACK PROPAGANDA—The use of fabrications, deceptions, BIG LIEs, and false source attributions. During wartime, lying "black propaganda" stories of atrocities are commonly manufactured by the belligerents to discredit the other side. During World War I, for example, the allies said (falsely) that the Germans were chopping off the hands of Belgian babies and turning corpses into soap. See also BLOWBACK, DEMONIZING THE OPPOSITION, DISINFORMATION (*DEZINFORMATSIA*), and SNUGGLING.

BLACKLISTING—A subtle form of political screening in which individuals are denied work for their beliefs and associations, often without knowing explicitly why. Although the term is most often associated with the decade-long harassment of alleged communists and their sympathizers in motion pictures (beginning in the late 1940s), broadcasting (beginning in 1950), and other professions, it has more generic implications for anyone who is perceived to be "politically incorrect" by a majority of the day.

BLACKOUT BOYS—A derisive term used by revisionist historian Harry Elmer Barnes to categorize progovernment apologists who propagandistically "explain away" events to cover-up the truth about official misdeeds and hard social realities. See also COURT HISTORIANS, ORWELLIAN TACTICS, and REVISIONISM/REVISIONIST.

BLACK PROGRAM—A secret governmental project or effort, using off-budget (non-reported) funding. See also COVERT.

BLOWBACK—Propaganda planted in foreign NEWS organs that is picked up and repeated by domestic media. Sometimes this blowback is unintentional or even counterproductive if the purpose was to only influence events in the other country; other times, the appearance of PROPAGANDA in another nation serves a dual purpose by also providing seemingly independent cover for STRUCTURED LEAKS of information that legitimizes its pickup and reuse by unwitting journalists at home. The CENTRAL INTELLIGENCE AGENCY (CIA), which ostensibly is prevented from domestic actions, has reportedly used this technique numerous times by supporting friendly NEWS MEDIA types overseas to publicize a particular storyline that was subsequently parroted by American journalists. See also DISINFORMATION (*DEZINFORMATSIA*) and PARROTING THE PARTY LINE.

BLOWING SMOKE—A strategy to avoid telling the whole truth by using DISINFORMATION (*DEZINFORMATSIA*) and STRUCTURED LEAKS to misleadingly slant public perceptions.

BOLSHEVIK/BOLSHEVIKI—At the Second Congress of the Russian Social Democratic party in 1903, the delegates split into the Bolsheviks ("the larger" group of hard-liners) and Mensheviks ("the smaller" number of Communists accused of being compromisers). The Bolsheviks, led by Nicolai (V.I.) Lenin, insisted on a revolutionary Marxism based on the "interpenetration of scientific socialism and the labor movement." Finally, on October 25 (November 7 by the Gregorian calendar), 1917, the Third Russian Revolution led to the formation of a Bolshevik government in what would soon be renamed the Union of Soviet Socialist Republics. The specter of Communists ("reds") taking power in the name of "world revolution" threatened the monarchies and democracies who were Russia's former allies and foes. The Russian empire erupted into civil war, with the Bolshevik reds opposed by pro-czarist "whites" and LIBERTARIAN "greens." Hysterical pro- and anti-Bolshevik propaganda was widely disseminated internally and externally, culminating in an "intervention" beginning in summer 1918 by foreign troops (including American forces) that sought to undo the revolution by fighting COMMUNISM/COMMUNIST subversion. Eventually, the Red Army under the direction of Leon Trotsky (who had earlier lived in the United States) was reorganized into an efficient fighting machine. By November 1920, Western forces were withdrawn from European Russia and the civil war decided in favor of the Communists. Finally, in October 1922, Japanese and other troops left Asian Russia, bringing to a close this chapter in Soviet history. The triumph of Lenin and his Bolshevik supporters, however, proved short-lived. Following Lenin's death on January 21, 1924, power eventually passed to the ruthless Joseph Stalin, who inaugurated numerous purges that lead to the mass murder of "true believer" Bolshevik ideologues and counterrevolutionaries alike. Stalin then authorized a continuing, and often successful program, of foreign subversion and PROPAGANDA designed to build support for "the Soviet experiment." The term Bolshevik at this point largely disappeared, to be replaced with various socialist and communist references. In 1933, the United States finally established diplomatic relations with the Soviet Union.

BORKING—A word coined by conservatives after the rough going-over Senate liberals gave Judge Robert Bork during his confirmation hearings for a seat on the Supreme Court in 1987. The term refers to a politically-motivated inquisition that smeared—"borked"—the nominee's character and is equivalent to liberal usage of Senator Joseph McCarthy as a hated political symbol. See also McCARTHYISM.

BOUNCEBACK CARDS—Pre-addressed postal cards accompanying direct mail solicitations (or enclosed in plastic-wrap "card packs") that enables recipients to order offered merchandise, request further information, respond to PUBLIC OPINION polls, and make membership/fundraising commitments. Sometimes bouncebacks are used by direct marketers as tagalongs with the fulfillment of another offer. See also BINGO CARDS and DIRECT MARKETING (DM).

BOURGEOIS—A term frequently employed by leftist propagandists to refer to the writings or attitudes of anyone who accepts "capitalist" IDEOLOGY. It is most associated with members of the middle class. The inference is often made (though not often proven) that one with bourgeois attitudes is stolidly dull, petty, and resistant to creativeness. See also CAPITALISM/CAPITALIST, COMMUNISM/COMMUNIST, ELITE THEORY, and FOURTH ESTATE.

BRAINWASHING—A specialized use of ideological coercion and INDOCTRINATION. According to Austin Freeley, author of *Argumentation and Debate*, brainwashing occurs

> in combination with a blend of sound and specious argument, persuasion, propaganda, and rigidly controlled group discussion in a situation where intensive and unremitting pressure is applied by a controlling group—an army, secret police organization, or a band of terrorists—to controlled individuals—prisoners—for the purpose of securing from the prisoners a decision to profess publicly the ideas dictated by their captors. As an essential ingredient of brainwashing the captors punish any "wrong" statement or attitude by physical or mental torture, or conditioning, and reward a "right" statement or attitude by granting some desirable privilege.

Although the practice of brainwashing is very old, the term first came into prominence during the Korean War when American prisoners of war (POWs) underwent "political reeducation" and has resurfaced with lurid tales of religious sect and cult "programming" of followers. Various governments, and notably those of nations caught up in the Cold War (such as the former USSR, the United States, Britain, and Canada), have authorized mind control experiments and torturings. Among the most notorious were those funded by American authorities through the CENTRAL INTELLIGENCE AGENCY (CIA) under the MKULTRA classification. See also COVERT ACTION, PSYCHEDELICS, PSYCHOLOGICAL WARFARE (PSYWAR), and TAVISTOCK METHOD, and TERRORIST.

BROADCAST STANDARDS DEPARTMENTS—Divisions within the major television, cable, and radio networks employing individuals who review all programming (other than NEWScasts) and commercials aired to ensure they meet the networks' guidelines for content acceptability. While the network censors have historically been concerned primarily with broadcast portrayals of sexual behavior, race, and violence, they also have regularly restricted ISSUE ADVERTISING by organizations with a social change message seeking access to audiences. In recent years, as a cost saving measure, many of these functions have been turned over to program suppliers. See also CENSORSHIP, FAIRNESS DOCTRINE, MASS COMMUNICATION, and PUBLIC SERVICE ANNOUNCEMENTS (PSAs).

BROADCASTING—In a generic sense, broadcasting refers to efforts to reach the largest possible audience through mediated, group, and interpersonal communication. However, broadcasting is generally understood to refer to electronic media such as radio (originally known as "wireless"), television, and other related new technologies which utilize assigned levels of power and channel frequencies from the TELECOMMUNICATIONS radio wave portion of the electromagnetic spectrum. According to the Communications Act of 1934 passed by the United States Congress, broadcasting "means the dissemination of radio communications intended to be received by the public, directly or by means of intermediary relay stations." See also BROADCAST STANDARDS DEPARTMENTS, FAIRNESS DOCTRINE, FEDERAL COMMUNICATIONS COMMISSION (FCC), HOT SWITCHING, LEAST OBJECTIONABLE PROGRAMMING (LOP) THEORY, MEDIA/MEDIUM, PUBLIC SERVICE ANNOUNCEMENTS (PSAs), PULLOUTS, STRIP PROGRAMMING, STUNTING, and TABLOID JOURNALISM.

CADRE—The leadership element in any organization. In Communist party practice, the cadres are usually organized into three-person "CELLs" or operating groups (also called cadres) to foil informers and penetration by COUNTERREVOLUTIONARY forces bent on subverting or destroying the MOVEMENT. See also COMMUNISM/COMMUNIST, TREASON, and THE VANGUARD.

CAPITALISM/CAPITALIST—A system involving private ownership of manufacturing and trade, which are operated as businesses in a society where intervention by government in the marketplace of goods and services generally does not occur. True capitalism of this type is rare and generally localized. In practice, the state often intervenes, to the benefit of some interests and the detriment of others. Capitalists are practitioners of, believers in, or supporters of capitalism. The emphasis on private property and individualistic choice in capitalistic philosophy has often resulted in denunciations from those favoring more overtly collective approaches to social organization, particularly activist individuals and groups promoting various forms of socialistic economic structure and governance. See also BOURGEOIS, CLASSICAL LIBERALISM, COMMUNISM/COMMUNIST, FASCISM/FASCIST, FAIR TRADE, FREE TRADE, NATIONAL SOCIALISM/NAZISM, REACTIONARY, and SOCIALISM/SOCIALIST.

CAPITALIST ROADER—A term of approbation made by hard-line communists to denounce fellow communists who may favor implementing market reforms to socialism and pursuing more conciliatory national policies when dealing with Western nations, such as the United States.

CARPETBAGGERS—Northerners who descended upon the prostrate South immediately following the Civil War to unscrupulously seek their fortunes during the corrupt military occupation. These exploiters traveled lightly, often accompanied only by their hastily packed suitcases ("carpetbags"). The analogy has been extended to political candidates who take unfair advantage of their name, wealth, or notoriety to run for an elected office outside their home area to which they otherwise would not be entitled.

CELL—The smallest unit of an organization, usually made up of a few persons. The terminology is linked with the notion of subversion. In undertaking CLANDESTINE activities ranging from propaganda to violence, as has been common in communist underground movements, loyalty and secrecy are paramount considerations. Cell members are insulated from knowing others in the organization beyond their own circle so that if arrested by the authorities they cannot name a trail of fellow coconspirators.

CENSORSHIP—Official controls on media, influencing content and distribution, and designed to ensure coverage favorable to the censoring organization. The purpose is to limit the expression of ideas before they are publicized. Generally, censorship is seen as a function of government when officials seek to monitor content and suppress objectionable elements on military, political, or moral grounds. However, private organizations also engage in the practice when they shape information presented to their members or employees. See also BROADCAST STANDARDS DEPARTMENTS, CHILLING EFFECT, EXTRALEGAL CENSORSHIP, FREE SPEECH, FREETHINKERS, OFFICE OF CENSORSHIP, RITUAL DEFAMATION, SEDITIOUS LIBEL, and SPIKE.

CENSORSHIP BY ASSASSINATION—TERRORIST murders of journalists and other outspoken crusaders in order to silence them permanently, intimidate others from speaking out, and cripple the opposition leadership. See also ASSASSIN, PROPAGANDA OF THE DEED, and TERRORISM.

CENTRAL INTELLIGENCE AGENCY (CIA)—The principal foreign intelligence-gathering organization of the U.S. government, formed under the National Security Act of 1947. The CIA has no authority to operate domestically in the United States, nor does it have arrest powers. The head of the CIA also serves as director of central intelligence (DCI), providing advice to the president while managing to oversee and coordinate the many diverse services comprising America's INTELLIGENCE COMMUNITY. See also BLACK PROGRAM, BRAINWASHING, CLANDESTINE, COMPANY, COVERT ACTION, ESPIONAGE, IRAN-CONTRA INVESTIGATIONS, NATIONAL INTELLIGENCE COUNCIL (NIC), NATIONAL SECURITY COUNCIL (NSC), and SPYING/SPYCRAFT.

CENTRAL POWERS—The alliance of Germany, Austria-Hungary, and several smaller states in World War I.

CENTRIST—According to the definition used by Advocates for Self-Government, Inc. (1995), "Centrists favor selective governmental intervention and temporary affiliations with others. They take a strong stance on few issues, preferring the middle position in most matters. Centrists emphasize practical solutions to current public issues" rather than rely on a consistent ideological decision-making framework.

CHAUVINISM/CHAUVINIST—The display of unreasoning patriotism for a country or ideology taken to the extreme. Chauvinism usually exalts one group at the expense of another. A person practicing chauvinism is known as a chauvinist—named for Nicholas Chauvin, a Frenchman whose fanaticism for the cause of Napoleon Bonaparte proved excessive.

CHECKBOOK JOURNALISM—See TABLOID JOURNALISM.

CHILLING EFFECT—Practices by governments or private organizations that serve to restrict or inhibit otherwise lawful behavior. Typically used are regulations and other indirect controls—rather than an outright ban—to restrict choice and direct actions. The exercise of FREE SPEECH rights is just one practice often subject to chilling effects. However, supporters of such restrictions often justify them as being in the "PUBLIC INTEREST." See also RITUAL DEFAMATION and SPIKE.

CIA—See CENTRAL INTELLIGENCE AGENCY (CIA).

CIRCUS, THE—Nickname for British intelligence. See also INTELLIGENCE COMMUNITY, MI5, MI6, and VETTING.

CITIZENS FOR AMERICA (CFA)—A political action organization founded by corporate leaders such as financier Ivan Boesky "to win support on the local level for key Reagan administration initiatives" (*New York Times,* May 5, 1985). CFA served as one of several FRONT GROUPS/SATELLITE ORGANIZATIONS attempting to mobilize GRASSROOTS POLITICAL ACTION for the executive branch's foreign policy agenda, sponsoring pro-Contra speeches by Marine Lt. Colonel Oliver North while he served as a Reagan/Bush staffer. According to DOCUMENTs later released by Congress, CFA emerged in 1983 as part of a broader "Project Democracy" PUBLIC DIPLOMACY effort by the White House and the NATIONAL SECURITY COUNCIL (NSC) to enlist the help of influential private individuals in raising funds and providing other help to bypass congressional restrictions on COVERT operations overseas. See also CONTRAS and IRAN-CONTRA INVESTIGATIONS.

CIVIL RELIGION—According to Jay M. Shafritz's *The Dorsey Dictionary of American Government and Politics* (p. 100), civil religion is a

belief in the "American way of life" and an acceptance of and reverence for its sacred icons (such as the flag), symbols (such as the Constitution), rituals (such as the pledge of allegiance), and secular saints (such as George Washington and Abraham Lincoln). Civil religion, which exists in parallel harmony with traditional religious beliefs, provides a society with a common set of unifying ideals that give an overarching political culture cohesiveness and form. While the concept was first used by Jean Jacques Rousseau in *The Social Contract* (1762), it was revived by American sociologists in the 1960s.

A second meaning pointed out by Shafritz is "a state sponsored secular religion designed to replace the 'corrupting' aspects of traditional religious practices, such as was implemented after the French Revolution of 1789 and the Russian Revolution of 1917."

CLANDESTINE—The term is often associated with surreptitious activities, particularly SPYING/SPYCRAFT. Unlike COVERT ops which try to conceal the sponsor but not the operation itself, clandestine activities intend to keep the names of intelligence agents and other sensitive sources of information secret indefinitely.

CLANDESTINE RADIO STATIONS—Propagandistic radio broadcasts maintained by insurgent guerrillas, foreign intelligence agencies, and other forces seeking to keep the location of their transmitters secret. These stations' are a prestige way to program information, manifestos, NEWS analysis, and entertainment messages supportive of their cause. Sometimes broadcasters on one side seek to mislead by mimicking the style of their opponents' station(s). To draw in new listeners, say those who regularly tune into a popular government-sponsored news program, rebels will skillfully air their substitute show on adjacent frequencies. See also CLANDESTINE, INTELLIGENCE COMMUNITY, and SNUGGLING.

CLASSICAL LIBERALISM—Principles personified by George Mason and many other Founding Fathers of the United States. As the Institute for Humane Studies observes, these principles share a commitment to liberty and the practice of freedom. They typically include:
- recognition of inalienable individual rights and the dignity and worth of each individual;
- protection of those rights through the institutions of individual private property, contract, and the rule of law;
- voluntarism in all human relations; and
- participation in the self-ordering market through free trade, free migration, and peaceful conduct.

Some of the nation's early leaders, such as Alexander Hamilton, however rejected FREE TRADE in favor of PROTECTIONISM designed to build up American business and manufacturing. See also HUMAN NATURE and LIBERTARIAN.

COALITION—The temporary joining together of independent individuals and organizations for a common cause—often to promote social change through the election of particular candidates, passage of new legislation, or defeat of egregious proposals by the opposition. Even though the participants may have wide-ranging disagreements, such informal alliances generally emerge when cooperation is vital to success on certain major issues considered overriding.

CODE WORDS—Stylistic use of WEASEL WORDS to indirectly imply or infer something else without actually coming out and saying it. When it is politically unpopular to say one favors higher taxes before a national TV audience, the propagandist may speak about the need for a stable financial system and a balanced budget. Similarly, politicians opposed to equal participation by blacks in their states often avoided voicing explicit support for segregation by using the code words "states' rights" instead. See also DOUBLESPEAK, EUPHEMISM, and HIDDEN AGENDA.

COERCIVE DIPLOMACY—Coordinated attempts to influence individuals, organizations, or nations by "sending signals" through traditional diplomatic means coupled with force or threats of force. See also STATE TERRORISM and SPEAK AND RETREAT.

COGNITIVE DISSONANCE—Formulated by famed psychological researcher Leon Festinger, cognitive dissonance is the most widely known of the consistency theories that hold that people prefer to avoid tension or stress-producing situations by maintaining consonance. As a result, individuals tend to avoid paying attention to or retaining information which conflicts with their belief system. Festinger starts with the premise that cognitive elements such as attitudes, knowledge and perceptions influence behavior. To take advantage of cognitive dissonance in modifying actions by members of targeted audiences, propagandists either have to offer new information designed to reduce tension or provide rewards that justify new behavior. See also PERCEPTION MANAGEMENT.

COINTELPRO—Government political counterintelligence programs, a number of which were secretly conducted to neutralize opposition to administration policies. Today, the best known are the COINTELPRO efforts by the Federal Bureau of Investigation, begun in 1956 to monitor and disrupt radical political groups. As the American involvement in Vietnam grew, so did illegal COINTELPRO actions to counteract the antiwar movement. Ironically, the government spy program was exposed in 1971 when one of the targeted organizations turned the tables by breaking into an FBI office and seizing more than a thousand classified DOCUMENTs detailing how COINTELPRO worked. See also VENONA.

COLD WAR—The more than forty-year "super-power" rivalry between the United States and the Union of Soviet Socialist Republics for international dominance which began following World War II and ended with the breakup of the Soviet bloc. See also INTELLIGENCE COMMUNITY, MKULTRA, and USSR or U.S.S.R./CCCP or C.C.C.P.

COMINTERN—The Communist International, or "headquarters of the worldwide communist revolution," formed by Lenin and his supporters to unite all the various Communist political parties and activist organizations across the globe under the controlling banner of Moscow's hammer and sickle. By proclaiming a particular policy, the Comintern could be assured that thousands of communist supporters in a variety of nations would be quickly mobilized. See also ACTIVISTS, COMMUNISM/COMMUNIST, FRONT

GROUPS/SATELLITE ORGANIZATIONS, PARROTING THE PARTY LINE, PAWNS, and POPULAR FRONT/PEOPLE'S FRONT.

COMMAND PROPAGANDA—A type of PROPAGANDA that seeks immediate, specific audience responses. See also DIVERT/REFOCUS STRATEGY.

COMMERCIAL SPEECH—Strongly influenced by Enlightenment thinking, the American Founding Fathers believed political expression to be the purest form of speech and accorded it important constitutional protections. Indeed, so concerned were they that there be an informed citizenry, the authors of what became the FIRST AMENDMENT wrote in absolutist language that provided very broad brush support for all forms of PUBLIC COMMUNICATION. Since ADVERTISING was prevalent in the late 1700s, even though there were relatively few media outlets, the question of whether or not regulatory distinctions should be made between different "types" of speech continues to excite debate. In the United States, political speech (expression concerning government operations or dealing with questions of governance and policy) has often been contrasted with commercial speech (advertisements, PUBLIC RELATIONS and other forms of sponsored communications directly or indirectly supporting a for-profit organization's economic activity). Despite the failure of the Constitution to make such distinctions, American courts have generally held advertisements for commercial products enjoy fewer protections than ads for political candidates. Many nonabsolutists continue to be troubled by the fact that the underlying basis for advertising is persuasion brought about through paid promotional messages designed to stimulate consumer actions and bring economic gain. The regulatory political-commercial distinction is linked to a wide-ranging set of PUBLIC INTEREST considerations involving health, children, safety, finance, and other social factors which have been used to justify the imposition of advertising regulations which impinge on message design and claims. Beginning in the 1970s, the Supreme Court began granting greater protection to advertising and related forms of commercial speech when they contained information important to public decision-making. A four-part test for evaluating the constitutionality of restrictions on commercial free speech was established by the Supreme Court in *Central Hudson Gas & Electric Corp. v. Public Service Commission of New York* (1980). To be entitled to protection, (1) such speech must concern lawful activity and not be misleading. Regulatory considerations include whether (2) the asserted governmental interest is substantial, (3) the restrictions imposed directly advance the alleged government interest, and (4) their application is too excessive.

COMMITTEE ON PUBLIC INFORMATION (CPI or "CREEL COMMITTEE")—U.S. World War I propaganda agency created in 1917 by executive order of President Woodrow Wilson. The CPI proved effective in mobilizing support for the war effort, and many of its staff members later went on to distinguished careers in ADVERTISING, PUBLIC RELATIONS, and media.

COMMUNICATIONS INTELLIGENCE (COMINT)—The process of electronic monitoring, interception, deciphering, analysis, and disruption of telephone, satellite and other telecommunications data from domestic and foreign intelligence purposes. Although private eavesdropping occurs, COMINT is generally considered a government function providing information of assistance to policy makers and military strategists. DISINFORMATION (*DEZINFORMATSIA*) and FALSE FLAG OPERATIONS can also occur when another nation's supposedly secure communications nets are penetrated by outside agencies and misleading signals surreptitiously inserted. In the United States, COMINT is coordinated by the National Security Agency (NSA). COMINT is formally defined in a National Security Council Intelligence Directive as "technical and intelligence information derived from foreign communications by other than the intended recipient." See also INTELLIGENCE COMMUNITY and NATIONAL SECURITY COUNCIL (NSC).

COMMUNICOLOGY—The study of communication by scientists and social scientists.

COMMUNISM/COMMUNIST—An economic and social system whose adherents oppose capitalistic free enterprise and other private property rights-based forms of governance and seek to create an ideal COMMUNITARIAN SOCIETY. Communism has been advocated most forcefully as "scientific socialism" by Karl Marx in *Das Kapital*, whose views were later adopted in other countries such as Russia by Lenin and in China by Mao Tse-tung. A believer in and supporter of one of the forms of communist activism is known as a communist, while a member of a particular party organization would be referred to as a Communist. Communists are authoritarians who seek to create a "New Man" and a "New Society" by replacing all preexisting governments, economies, and societies. In *Das Kapital*, Marx uttered the famous dictum that urged "working men of all nations to unite" in overthrowing the exploitive capitalists. He said that by seizing the means of production, abolishing private property, ending class distinctions, and replacing the family unit, a utopian world would emerge through an enlightened "Dictatorship of the Proletariat" exercised by the working class. Eventually, the need for this central dictatorship would "wither away" with communism evolving into a "Worker's State" in which an abundance of material goods, full equality, and complete social justice would prevail. This belief forms a kind of secular (rather than sacred) religion. The reality, however, is that a communist government is ruled by a rather small VANGUARD who take total power to dictate almost every phase of the people's lives. As Aida Parker, publisher of *The Aida Parker Newsletter* in South Africa, points out:

Communist philosophy (thoughts and ideas) teaches that there are two opposing groups in all (non-communist) societies. First, there is the "bourgeoisie" (middle class), the property owners and those owning and controlling the productive and distributive processes. These, it is taught, are the cause of all problems and conflicts. "There can be no peace until they are overthrown and destroyed." Next are the "proletariat," the workers, those who labour and "really create the wealth."

As "labour creates all the wealth," it is argued, labour is therefore entitled to whatever rewards are available.

As dialectical materialists, Communists believe that life is the result of a natural, evolutionary process rather than any form of divine intervention. For them, morals are a bourgeois invention, God a myth, sin nonexistent, and humanity simply "matter in motion." This view holds that the achievement of the final goal of a utopian state means the elimination of those counterrevolutionary forces and individuals unwilling to be re-educated. Only the Communist party and final victory count. Thus disciplined Communists are able to lie, create hatred, stir unrest, engage in ruthless TERRORIST violence and even condone mass murder without moralistic qualms, should it prove necessary. However, personalities, local conditions, and differing philosophical emphases among adherents of Marxism (termed MARXISTs) have led to splits within the MOVEMENT between Marxist-Leninists, Maoists, Stalinists, Trotskyists, Castroists, Sandinistas, Democratic Socialists etc. See also AGITPROP, ARMED STRUGGLE, AUTONOMIST, BOLSHEVIK/BOLSHEVIKI, BOURGEOIS, BRAINWASHING, CADRE, CAPITALISM/CAPITALIST, CAPITALIST ROADER, CELL, COLD WAR, COMINTERN, COMMUNITARIAN SOCIETY, DYSTOPIA, EXTREMISM, EXTREMIST, MASS TERROR, *PERESTROIKA*, RED-BAITING, RED DECADE, SOCIALISM/SOCIALIST, USSR or U.S.S.R./CCCP or C.C.C.P., VANGUARD, and VENONA.

COMMUNITARIAN SOCIETY—An alternative social organization in which goods are held in common. Mostly, they have been localized and humane utopian experiments undertaken for religious or ideological purposes. Small-scale communities have a mixed record of success in creating new societies, with groups such as the Mennonites proving very able practitioners. No nation has turned entirely to communitarianism, except in the case of mass misery imposed by authoritarian tyrants. When Socialist or Communist political parties have seized the state apparatus, their RHETORIC often invokes the notion of equality through communitarian-sounding slogans. However, they have proved unable to fully implement their programs.

COMPANY, THE—Nickname for the CENTRAL INTELLIGENCE AGENCY (CIA). See also INTELLIGENCE COMMUNITY.

COMPOSITE REPORTING—A journalistic practice that uses the historical novelist's technique of combining elements of various people into a single fictional person "representative" of the issues the reporter or columnist is covering, but presents the story as being documentarily real and true. In May 1984, for example, essayist Alastair Reid of *New Yorker* magazine denied he had violated ethical standards while admitting he regularly fabricated "nonfiction" articles by attributing quotations to people who never made them, detailed places he had never seen, and made up experiences he never had.

COMPUTER-AIDED DESIGN (CAD)—Through the use of CAD technologies, artificial and "real" images can be generated, fabricated, edited, distorted, and otherwise manipulated to create very convincing photographs. Although the practice is most widespread in ADVERTISING, where various elements are typically integrated into eye-catching ads and commercials, CAD is also used in photojournalism to "enhance" images. The impact is that no picture, even a supposedly untouched photograph, can be believed to be authentic. See also DIGITIZED PHOTOGRAPHY and VIRTUAL REALITY.

COMPUTER-MEDIATED COMMUNICATION (CMC)—Through an exploding assortment of technologies (personal computers, faxes, international computer networks, bulletin board systems, conferencing systems, etc.), individuals are now able to communicate with others in the GLOBAL VILLAGE whom, due to geography, time, or financial constraints, they otherwise might not meet. Possibly the most important technological innovation of the latter half of the twentieth century, "computer-mediated communication" is revolutionizing business, governmental, and other interactions. Beyond the convenience of faster and more efficient message exchange, this technology has created a demonstrably novel form of multimedia CYBERSPACE communication, transcending the distinction between written and oral discourse and posing interesting possibilities for dialogue and VIRTUAL REALITY. Furthermore, computer-mediated communication invites us to reconceive existing social relationships and forge new relationships between individuals at school, at work, in political life, and in our increasingly worldwide community. While we know that computer-mediated communication will affect our lives in even more dramatic and profound ways, our efforts to understand this new invention defy segmentation by disciplinary boundaries. The downside is that enhanced communications can also make propaganda and government regulatory controls even more intrusive. See also INFORMATION AGE/INFORMATION SOCIETY and NATIONAL INFORMATION INFRASTRUCTURE (NII).

CONDITIONING PROPAGANDA—A type of PROPAGANDA, says Hugh Rank, author of *The Pep Talk: How to Analyze Political Language*, "which seeks to mold public opinions, assumptions and attitudes on a long-term widespread basis, often as a prelude for later command propaganda." See also PUBLIC OPINION and COMMAND PROPAGANDA.

CONFLICT RESOLUTION—According to the Center for the Advancement of Applied Ethics at Carnegie Mellon University, conflict resolution is "the application of a set of skills and techniques that de-escalates conflicts, opens lines of communication, disentangles values, personalities and substantive issues, and generates integrative solutions." As a form of peacemaking, conflict resolution requires command of a repertoire of theoretical and practical tools in order to successfully analyze and manage complex real world situations. Conflict resolution models often focus on major public controversies which may arise from grievances over inequitable distribution of resources or when access to power is denied. When conflicts also stem from deep-seated cultural differences, the clash of conflicting ideologies can lead to lethal threats. See also IDEOLOGY, ISSUES MANAGEMENT, PUBLIC INTEREST, PUBLIC POLICY PROCESS, PUBLIC RELATIONS

MODELS, and TERRORISM.

CONFORMISTS—Politically active individuals who are opposed to unseemly protest and violence. They prefer to work within the system through attending community meetings, writing letters to the editor of the local newspaper, participating in "good government" committees, contacting officials, and campaigning for candidates.

CONSPIRACY THEORIES—A conspiracy involves an agreement by individuals to work in concert, typically in violation of law. Most often the laws involving conspiracy have been applied to prosecute those engaging in ordinary criminal behavior, but have also been used to limit the activities of those advocating political ideas threatening to the status quo. Actually, all governments tend to be conspiratorial since the real decision-makers prefer to work in private even if they have to put up with a facade of DEMOCRACY. Certainly the allied governments dominated by Britain and France during World War I effectively resisted Woodrow Wilson's RADICAL proposal that they make "open covenants, openly arrived at." Case studies abound of the numerous ACTIVISTS and fringe political groups on the right and left who have suffered from government agencies engaging in often successful COVERT ACTIONs designed to discredit them.

Separating the real from the paranoid, however, is often problematic—particularly since the genuine conspiracists are largely successful in planting false trails and misleading PUBLIC OPINION. Much disputed allegations about grander conspiracies ranging from the murder of presidents to plots to institute a one-world government have been linked to communists, corporate cartels, drug-runners, intelligence agencies, international bankers, Islamic terrorists, Jews, Mafioso, Masons, media moguls, Mormons, Nazis, New Age cultists, racial supremacists, Roman Catholics, Satanists, and members of other controversial groups. The Reverend Dr. Martin Luther King was said to be "part of a Communist conspiracy" by many opponents of integration, while his murder may well have been conspired to by others.

Skeptics such as Steven Emerson ("No October Surprise," 1993) suggest at least seven reasons that allegations of conspiracy should be treated to strong doses of "common sense" before they are believed: (1) check out the claims thoroughly and dispassionately when conspiracy theorists insist they arrived at their beliefs only reluctantly, since this may not in fact be the case; (2) ask "how?" if conspiratorialists say they have independently verified the conspiracy; (3) recognize that conspiracies and beliefs in conspiracies thrive when they serve political ends; (4) understand that journalists will often uncritically repeat unproven allegations and "recklessly invoke 'conspiracy' and 'cover up' in the absence of corroborative evidence"; (5) remember that even if conspiracy charges are completely debunked, the original allegations have staying power and can tar the reputations of individuals and institutions for years to come; (6) realize that conspiracies "are good business, often promoted by people with hidden agendas"; and (7) expect more conspiracy allegations to flourish since the penalties are minimal or nonexistent for those who bring false charges, even if the result is a futile and expensive congressional investigation.

Even assuming a true desire to establish and maintain a successful long-term conspiracy, this is particularly difficult given the necessity of a certain level of CLANDESTINE control. All organizations are susceptible to decline and disappearance. Finding people of like mind is possible, but successfully taking advantage of circumstances is difficult—especially since any new conspiracy starts with many potential enemies and uncertain continuity of internal organizational. Conspirators need to be ruthless in maintaining their secrets, since disloyalty or exposure may damage their organization. Fortunately for conspirators, being part of something bigger than oneself and lying to others appeals to human nature. Thus, intelligence gathering on real or suspected enemies is widely employed. Deception (even self-delusion) is also common, particularly among lower-level recruits. Even murder of opponents or dissenters is eventually condoned as a distasteful necessity, but not marqueed. Rather, continued emphasis is placed on one or more binding purposes that are strong enough to supersede moral qualms and hold appeal to more than a single generation. Indeed, a conspiracy may employ numerous FRONT GROUPS/SATELLITE ORGANIZATIONS having interlocking layers of responsibility which supposedly represent multiple purposes, with only the inner leadership understanding the real goals (or HIDDEN AGENDA) of the entire picture. These organizational purposes need not necessarily be ideological, but must be overtly moral in how they are packaged, for even the most evil persons need to see themselves in an emotionally positive light that provides psychological justification for their actions.

To maintain a conspiracy once begun, one also needs fresh recruits as the older founding members die off. Dynastic succession is possible but not certain, given the differing personalities and abilities of descendants. This means outsiders with real talents must also be added or co-opted over time. Access to power, money, sex, and other allures can be powerful incentives. Use of propaganda or blackmail may work on some. Also required are continuing financial resources, since successful conspiracies must be able to finance their activities if they are to have any impact. Similarly, conspiracies must be able to access and influence key centers of power from the inside (government, media, banking, business, education, etc.) Without such access, it is impossible to stir mass action except through grassroots lobbying or support by powerful outside interests (i.e., the German transport of Lenin and other Bolshevik leaders back to Russia at a critical moment of civil unrest).

Exercising power may be the ultimate goal, but maintaining full or partial control once a conspiracy is successful requires quite a bit of subtlety and agility, given unexpected (even unpredictable) developments in cultures and technologies. This means a long and successful conspiracy must have something going for it. See also ANTI-SEMITIC, BILDERBERGER GROUP, BLACKOUT BOYS, BOLSHEVIK/BOLSHEVIKI, COINTELPRO, COMMUNISM/COMMUNIST, COPPERHEADS, COUNCIL ON FOREIGN RELATIONS (CFR), CULT, ELITE THEORY, ESTABLISHMENT, INSIDERS, INVISIBLE GOVERNMENT, MEDIA ELITE, NESHER, OCTOBER SURPRISE, PROPAGANDA-2 (P-2), SECRET GOVERNMENT, TERRORIST, WHITEWASH, and ZOG.

CONTAGION—Terrorist events are symbolic communicative acts, staged to attract international media attention in an attempt to affect the agendas, attitudes, and perceptions of audiences worldwide. Contagion is the process by which media coverage of TERRORIST events encourages others to also use political violence as part of their own "theater of terror." See also TERRORISM.

CONTRAS—Armed Nicaraguan counterrevolutionaries supported by the U.S. government who waged anti-Sandinista guerrilla operations. President Reagan referred to the "democratic resistance" MOVEMENT of Contra "freedom fighters" as morally equivalent to the founding fathers of the United States. However, Congress became concerned over the antidemocratic nature exhibited by the Contra leadership. Well-documented evidence of TERRORIST atrocities committed by the Contras finally convinced Congress to stop funding the flow of weapons and ammunition. Remaining support was limited to "humanitarian" aid. Reagan administration figures, most notably Elliott Abrams and Marine Lt. Colonel Oliver North, acted to subvert these restrictions by conducting a convoluted fundraising effort engineered by North, waging a PUBLIC RELATIONS (PR) campaign using government resources under the guise of PUBLIC DIPLOMACY and continuing to illicitly supply the rebels in their jungle hideaways. This set of policy decisions, damaging NEWS stories about the continuing COVERT assistance by the CENTRAL INTELLIGENCE AGENCY (CIA), and resulting cover-up eventually created one of the most serious constitutional scandals of modern times, culminating in the IRAN-CONTRA INVESTIGATIONS. See also CITIZENS FOR AMERICA (CFA), CLANDESTINE, CRIMINALIZATION OF POLICY DIFFERENCES, NEOLIBERALISM, REVOLUTION/REVOLUTIONARY, STATE TERRORISM, and UNCONVENTIONAL WARFARE.

CONTROLLED MEDIA—Those communication organs under the direct control of an organization. Examples include employee magazines, brochures, closed-circuit video systems, and newsletters distributed to external audiences.

CONVENTIONAL WISDOM—The PRESS is not entirely objective, due to a variety of factors, including that collection of assumptions, prejudices and pressures contributing to the decision to cover or not report particular issues. Some potential controversies are not considered debatable because "everybody already agrees"—an informal type of POLITICALLY CORRECT (PC) thinking. For example, Robert Parry's book about Washington, D.C., INSIDERS, (*Fooling America*, 1992), argues that the conventional wisdom often serves to hold back hard-hitting investigative journalism for fear of being seen as "too tough." So beat reporters (i.e., the White House press corps) wait for leaders and spokespersons to define the issues, a common form of AGENDA SETTING. The conventional wisdom means the press only goes after many important, underreported stories when goaded into doing more investigation by those personages the working journalists consider significant. Typically, these sources are not unbiased, but rather are promoting their own agenda in ways designed to meet media expectations and fulfill reporter's weakness for HANDOUT JOURNALISM. See also BELTWAY BANDITS and MEDIA BIAS.

COPPERHEADS—Northern opponents of Lincoln's Civil War policy to maintain the Union at all costs, often portrayed as treasonous sympathizers of the Confederacy. Some copperheads, of course, were influenced by racist Knights of the Golden Circle divide-and-weaken conspiracies, which were secretly hatched by British interests active in the United States. However, many antiwar ACTIVISTS were motivated by sincere pacifistic principles, dedicated to free speech, and influenced by their abhorrence of the wholesale violations of civil liberties committed by the Lincoln administration.

CORPORATE CAMPAIGN—A union strategy whose purpose is to create pressure so that the corporate parent of a targeted company will force its subsidiary to make concessions to the union in order to avoid potential adverse publicity. Coupled with media relations efforts designed to rally support for the union and its positions, the effort can include secondary boycotts, shareholder challenges, worker slowdowns, selective strikes, and other mechanisms. In 1985, the United Mine Workers of America organized a boycott of Shell Oil Company, then a partial owner of A.T. Massey Coal Company, accusing Shell of "fueling the wheels of the racist apartheid system" in South Africa. During the bitter Pittston strike in 1989-1990, a union shareholders group attempted to replace Pittston management. The union also pressured Pittston's bankers and disrupted board meetings at other companies whose boards include some of Pittston's directors. The PUBLIC RELATIONS (PR) component incorporates many of the elements found in a presidential election effort: campaign trips to key areas of support, attention-getting speeches, GRASSROOTS LOBBYING endorsements, media NEWS RELEASEs, and coordinated electronic and print ADVERTISING. These longer-term negotiating tactics have proved most successful when used as an alternative to traditional industry-wide economic strikes and acts of violence against replacement ("scab") workers which now tend to backfire by causing an erosion in public and congressional support necessary to achieve a political resolution to the dispute.

CORPORATE COMMUNICATIONS—Large- and mid-sized American businesses commonly house the PUBLIC RELATIONS (PR) function responsible for contact with internal and external audiences such as the PRESS in a formal department called Corporate Communications.

CORPORATE SOCIAL RESPONSIBILITY (CSR)—Organizations face increasing scrutiny of the actions they take. Larger businesses, in particular, may be subjected to a barrage of TOXIC INFORMATION publicized by pesky ACTIVISTS, a series of unfavorable NEWS MEDIA reports, and increased regulatory scrutiny if management fails to act ethically by fully taking into account the direct and indirect concerns of their various STAKEHOLDERS. Thus, strategic planners involved in the process of ISSUES MANAGEMENT recognize they must factor in changing social expectations if their institutions are to survive.

COUNCIL ON FOREIGN RELATIONS (CFR)—An influential

international affairs organization whose members are drawn from government, finance, media, academia and the professions. The council was established in New York City in 1921 as an independent, sister organization to the London-based Royal Institute of International Affairs. Over the years, the CFR has served as a virtual employment bureau for staffing high- and mid-level U.S. State Department and foreign policy positions, including the presidency. Many of these recruits have tended to favor INTERVENTIONIST foreign policy stands, despite the natural isolationist inclinations of the American public. Because of this continuing role irrespective of administration, some critics have warned of a more sinister HIDDEN AGENDA linking members of the CFR to a global conspiracy promoting world federalism. See also ANGLOPHILE, BILDERBERGER GROUP, CONSPIRACY THEORIES, ELITE THEORY, SECRET GOVERNMENT, and TRILATERAL COMMISSION.

COUNTERINSURGENCY—Political, economic, social/civic, judicial, psychological, military, and paramilitary attempts by governments to defeat armed rebellion against the state. Counterinsurgency strategy is a continuing and overlapping process aimed at:
1. Identifying the enemy and their reasons for existence;
2. Coordinating the resources and personnel of all sections of the ESTABLISHMENT against insurgents and their supporters;
3. Containing enemy forces and wearing them down tactically;
4. Isolating and frustrating opponents in every way; and ultimately,
5. Destroying identifiable resistance.

Defining what problems are is an important part of counterinsurgency strategy, because not only does it dictate how people see each side of the conflict, but it also sets the agenda on which a "solution" will be based. Counterinsurgency/counterrevolutionary strategies cannot remain static if they are to be effective. They must fluidly evolve with developments and mirror opposing revolutionary strategies in that they, too, have to be progressive. This may entail appeasement of certain interests and the enactment of limited reforms, but these changes occur only when those who hold power are forced to grant them in order to maintain that control.

When faced with an insurgency and other forms of UNCONVENTIONAL WARFARE, the leaders of smaller governments will very often turn to bigger ones for assistance. For example, from the 1960s onwards, the aim of U.S. military aid to the Latin America was to create proxy armies to fight the "enemy within." As a result, in its ideological war against international communism, the United States sanctioned the use of various COERCIVE DIPLOMACY and COVERT ACTION efforts throughout the region, including (but not limited to) BLACK PROPAGANDA, COUNTERPROPAGANDA, PSYCHOLOGICAL OPERATIONS (PSYOPS), COUNTERTERRORISM, and STATE TERRORISM. Despite what the military action plans were called at the time, whether defined as counterinsurgency or LOW-INTENSITY CONFLICT (LIC)/LOW-INTENSITY WARFARE (LIW), the results were generally mixed—with the unpleasant side effects of DEATH SQUADS and revolutionary violence leading to the massacre and brutalization of hundreds and thousands of innocent civilians caught in the cross fire.

Domestic counterinsurgency programs are more widespread than many people think, even though they operate on the classic dual principle of force followed by co-optation, since their militarization is typically cloaked in "War on Crime" or "War on Drugs" terms. One such effort initiated by the Bush administration in 1991, the Operation Weed and Seed program targeted at high-crime ghetto areas, now operates in more than twenty cities. The program subordinates social spending to Justice Department-established criteria by creating a "public-private partnership" involving law enforcement and approved community organizations. The purpose is to establish "liberated" inner city areas "weeded" of criminals and "seeded" with federal grants to "prevent crime's reoccurrence." In fighting crime, however, the effort involves civil liberties restrictions similar to the "strategic hamlet" efforts employed as part of the HEARTS AND MINDS CAMPAIGNs by the military in Vietnam. Critics also see the effort as pandering to racism, by dehumanizing Latino and African-American youth as "weeds" needing incarceration/eradication. See also COMMUNISM/COMMUNIST and CONTRAS.

COUNTERINTELLIGENCE PROGRAM—See COINTELPRO.

COUNTERPROPAGANDA—The use of PROPAGANDA DEVICES, methods and appeals to oppose and neutralize PROPAGANDA emanating from competing governments, organizations, and INTEREST GROUPS. According to Hugh Rank (1984), counterpropaganda also encompasses educational efforts designed to expose the propaganda process. He sees counterpropaganda as "an attempt to inoculate or to immunize individuals in advance of any particular propaganda blitz or campaign by any organized persuaders (whether from various advertisers, from politicians Left or Right, from governments domestic or foreign) by teaching the common patterns and techniques of persuasion."

COUNTERREVOLUTIONARY—Once a revolution successfully occurs, anyone who opposes the actions of the new leadership is considered "counterrevolutionary." Over time, even the best intended governments tend to dislike criticism. Indeed, staging pro-DEMOCRACY public events is considered a counterrevolutionary "antigovernment activity" in many nations. When PROPAGANDA fails to quell dissent, governments turn to violence, including STATE TERRORISM. As a result, arbitrary arrests which are neither officially reported nor acknowledged are common of dissidents in authoritarian countries. The counterrevolutionaries may be imprisoned for a long list of supposed political "crimes," generally involving the peaceful exercise of fundamental HUMAN RIGHTS, as well as overt violent rebellion. It is not uncommon for unfortunates seeking to exercise the right to freedom of expression or association to receive prison terms or even execution. Thousands of political dissidents are, at this moment, detained across the planet in various nations' jails for taking part in underground dissident organizations, circulating political posters, participating in banned religious activities, attempting to stage peaceful demonstrations, or otherwise expressing their conscience. See also COUNTERINSURGENCY,

REVOLUTION/REVOLUTIONARY, and WARS OF LIBERATION.

COUNTERTERRORISM—According to Harold J. Vetter and Gary R. Perlstein, authors of *Perspectives on Terrorism*, counterterrorism involves "Measures emphasizing the tactical forces option, for prevention, preemption, or retaliation against terrorist acts." Organized offensive efforts to effectively combat TERRORISM cannot rely on traditional police practices and so have resulted in the formation of specialized counterterrorist units. Although private teams exist, for the most part these elite forces are government-created, have access to top secret information, undergo extensive training in ANTITERRORISM tactics, and are well armed. Their goal is to actively "oppose terrorism throughout the entire threat spectrum": neutralize the TERRORIST potential when possible, avoid the unpopular repression terrorists seek to provoke, control media access during times of crisis, and ultimately mold PUBLIC OPINION in support of the governing authorities. See also COUNTERINSURGENCY.

COURT HISTORIANS—A derisive term used by revisionist Harry Elmer Barnes to categorize selected academics given special privileges and access to restricted information by those in power in return for writing authorized progovernment PROPAGANDA masquerading as definitive "official histories." See also BLACKOUT BOYS and REVISIONISM/REVISIONIST.

COURT OF PUBLIC OPINION—Long before an ISSUE arrives in a court of law, it receives widespread PUBLICITY and discussion in NEWS MEDIA coverage and other public forums. How these controversies are interpreted, which sides appear to have a more moral position, and who is seen as right or wrong in the public mind can have important implications. Propagandists are heavily involved in trying to shape these impressions, through ORCHESTRATED PROPAGANDA CAMPAIGNs (also referred to as JUSTICE BY NEWS RELEASE). Sometimes governments or organizations in dicey situations even simply declare VICTORY BY NEWS RELEASE. See also ISSUES MANAGEMENT, NEWS RELEASE, PACK JOURNALISM, PLANTING STORIES, PUBLIC OPINION, SPIN DOCTORS, SPIRAL OF SILENCE, STRUCTURED LEAKS, and TOXIC INFORMATION.

COVER STORY—A plausible explanation released to NEWS MEDIA, influentials, and other target groups in order to mask the truth. Very often, cover stories are prepared as part of contingency plans to be used when operations prove unsuccessful. The broader related term, *cover*, refers to false identifies assumed by spies to conceal their real CLANDESTINE purposes. See also PLAUSIBLE DENIABILITY and RESIDENCY.

COVERT—A word meaning secret, hidden, undercover, or CLANDESTINE. Typically, COVERT ACTIONs are undertaken to disguise the real purpose of an agent's mission. This is done to avoid alerting the enemy, protect operatives' lives, and avoid having to tell embarrassing truths.

COVERT ACTION—President Truman authorized National Security Directive

NSC 10/2 in 1948 which defines covert action as "propaganda; economic warfare; preventive direct action, including sabotage, anti-sabotage, demolition and evacuation measures; subversion against hostile states, including assistance to underground resistance movements, guerrillas and refugee liberation groups, and support of indigenous anti-communist elements." More recently, the Intelligence Authorization Act for Fiscal Year 1991 interpreted covert action to mean "an activity or activities conducted by an element of the United States Government to influence political, economic, or military conditions abroad so that the role of the United States Government is not intended to be apparent or acknowledged publicly." While covert actions attempt to remain secret, they have a public manifestation. For example, if the CENTRAL INTELLIGENCE AGENCY (CIA) supplies newsprint for an opposition newspaper in a Latin American country, readers will be exposed to the product even though they will not know of the CIA involvement. Similarly, it was only many years later that CIA support for Radio Liberty and Radio Free Europe became widely known. Covert action by governments depends on a willingness to engage in BIG LIEs about true intentions and the freedom to operate through a series of compartmentalized action departments. These FRONT GROUPS/SATELLITE ORGANIZATIONS can include government agencies, dummy corporations, spokesperson "cutouts," friendly media, and others making up a working network of hidden connections that give the true decision-makers the option of "PLAUSIBLE DENIABILITY." Critics include former U.S. Senator Frank Church (D-Idaho) who said, in 1982, that covert action is nothing more than "a semantic disguise for murder, coercion, blackmail, bribery, the spreading of lies, whatever is deemed useful to bending other countries to our will." See also DIRTY TRICKS CAMPAIGN and FINDING.

COVER-UP CROWD—Term popularized by columnist William Safire in 1992 to refer to higher-ups in government administration caught in lies and CENSORSHIP. To avoid taking responsibility for their own wrongdoing, they seek to discredit others, divert PRESS coverage, and deflect congressional attention by setting up innocent underlings to take the fall. See also COVER STORY, LIGHTENING RODS, OUT OF THE LOOP, PLAUSIBLE DENIABILITY, and WHITEWASH.

COWBOY OPERATION—A COVERT propaganda or intelligence activity carried on outside normal channels by a limited number of people, undertaken with (or sometimes without) the tacit approval of higher-ups. See also COVERT ACTION, DEATH SQUADS, and PLAUSIBLE DENIABILITY.

CRIMINALIZATION OF POLICY DIFFERENCES—Term coined by Elliott Abrams, a State Department official responsible for Latin American policy in the Reagan administration, to decry criminal prosecutions of illicit acts he and other high officials committed for political purposes. Abrams and other coconspirators in the Reagan administration skirted legal restrictions by their actions, lied to Congress under oath, and conspired to continue funding the Contra rebels through a number of backdoor mechanisms. In justifying his subsequent pardon of defendants caught up in the IRAN-CONTRA

INVESTIGATIONS, President George Bush used the occasion to attack the special prosecutor's motivations in taking the cases to court. The prosecutions, according to the president, represented the "criminalization of policy differences." See also CONTRAS and PUBLIC DIPLOMACY.

CRITICAL ISSUE—As defined by Joseph Nagelschmidt in the glossary of *The Public Affairs Handbook* (1982, p. 288), a critical issue is "an important emerging trend or problem that is reaching its resolution point in the public policy process."

C-SPAN—The Cable-Satellite Public Affairs Network, a scrupulously neutral information source privately funded by the cable industry, is based in Washington, D.C. C-SPAN now operates several cable television and radio services which broadcast unedited government proceedings, hearings, NEWS interviews, conferences, journalist roundtables, call-in shows, and other public policy-oriented programming. Unlike conventional networks, C-SPAN has avoided being tagged as a source of media bias.

CULT—Any authoritarian organization or movement which dominates members' attention and rigidly prescribes their daily conduct. *Cult* is a very value-laden word, with many different (often negative) meanings depending on the source. The term is usually associated with manipulative religious groups, although one may be part of a political cult or even TERRORIST cult. It is most often used by members of one group to describe a competing or heretical sect with which they disagree. All such organizations have five main characteristics: (1) a dominant living leader; (2) an authoritarian governing structure; (3) a seemingly new and unorthodox set of beliefs, doctrines and practices that distances members from mainstream society; (4) an insular social climate—often intensified by physical isolation—in which paranoia and secrecy may thrive if not moderated; and (5) an internal dynamic which leads to splits between more "accommodationist" and "fundamentalist" elements. Because of the total loyalty and commitment demanded, particularly when the leader exudes charismatic charm and is skilled in psychological "mind control" techniques that give identity and purpose to followers, cults are usually seen as bizarre, extreme, and potentially dangerous by outsiders. Some NEW AGE MOVEMENT cults employ coercive and deceptive techniques to recruit new members and maintain loyalty among the converts. However, most cults provide a benign nonviolent, alternative life-style that serves as a social release mechanism and home for the disaffected and dissenting.

Christian Research Institute president Hendrik "Hank" Hanegraaff, in the video *Secrets of Mind Control*, upheld the traditional view of a literal Satanic conspiracy seeking to enslave humanity through a self-centered counterfeit message to that of true love and sacrifice. The diabolical formula for cultic mind control is encapsulated by Hanegraaff's descriptions for the acronym *FLESH*:

F=fear, involving control through physical intimidation and psychological dependency that chains victims to the environment holding them captive,

L=love, involving "displaced devotion" to the leader in which reason and rationality are abandoned and replaced by a blind obedience willing to commit any act, even criminal,

E=*emptiness*, in which, through "dynamic meditation" and other consciousness-altering techniques, the mind becomes a blank slate for the cult to imprint a happily mindless form of spiritual slavery,

S=*sex*, through license and/or restrictions which manipulate the minds and behavior of the followers; and

H=*hatred*, in which suspicion and hatred of outsiders are inculcated to limit external influences and unify the cultists.

For an alternative viewpoint using irony to demonstrate the difficulty of distinguishing a cult from a noncult, note the following bumper sticker by members of War Resisters League distributed in the Donnelly/Colt catalogue:

WARNING —Beware of weird cult which:
- Uses promises of money, a job, and other favors to recruit people;
- Indoctrinates beginners in an armed camp until they're thoroughly brainwashed;
- Employs terror, assassination, murder, and threats thereof;
- Is particularly interested in the young, and those who follow orders without question;
- Holds against their will members who wish to leave;
- Goes by many names, e.g., The Service, military, Armed Forces, ROTC, JROTC, recruiters, Defense, Army, Navy, Air Force, Marines, National Guard, Green Berets.

See also BRAINWASHING, COGNITIVE DISSONANCE, CONSPIRACY THEORIES, and FUNDAMENTALISM/FUNDAMENTALIST.

CULT OF PERSONALITY—A form of secular worship in which the organization's or nation's power and authority is concentrated in one person because of that individual's charismatic personality and/or ruthlessness. This cultivation of the great leader, rather than the official office, is typically excessive and accompanied by widespread PROPAGANDA. The term came into general use following the 1956 Communist party meeting in Moscow which denounced former Soviet leader Joseph Stalin (1879-1953), now safely dead, for his dictatorial abuses.

CULTURAL IMPERIALISM—The worldwide popularity of American, British and French entertainment media, fashions, foods, literature, life-styles, and political philosophies means that certain western social values are transplanted to other cultures. In the case of television shows, for example, it is cheaper to buy recycled American imports than to locally produce alternative programming. Some critics decry this influence because they see the one-way international communication flow as preempting indigenous cultural sovereignty, ultimately creating a subversive form of psychic dependency likened to neocolonialism. See also AMERICA BASHING, FRIENDLY SUBVERSION, IMPERIALISM/IMPERIALIST, NEOLIBERALISM, and TRANSNATIONAL CORPORATIONS (TNCs).

CYBERNETICS—The comparative study of artificial mechanical-electrical communication systems and the automatic control system in humans and other animals formed by the brain and nervous system. Cybernetics as the science of communication and control theory developed from the work supervised by Norbert Wiener at the Massachusetts Institute of Technology during World War II in developing swivel and turret systems for antiaircraft gun platforms. He conceived of the feedback loop as an essential component in all communication systems for informing the control mechanism about the impact of its decisions. Cybernetics (taken from the Greek term *kybernetes* for "helmsman," the one who pilots or steers) has also proved critical to the design of modern digital computers. In military circles, the cybernetic doctrine of C3I (or Command, Control, Communication, and Intelligence) was employed as a way to enhance top-down vertical management of everything from the deployment of battle forces to the launching of space shuttles.

CYBERSPACE—The futuristic "data highways" that make up "cyberspace" are comprised of national and global voice, picture, data, and other computerized TELECOMMUNICATIONS links. This environment spans multiple sources and multiple users, with each computer acting as a window into the information that defines the cyberspace. On this interconnect are educational, business, government and other subscribers, sometimes romantically referred to as "cybernauts" pioneering the new world of VIRTUAL REALITY. See also CYBERNETICS, INFORMATION AGE/INFORMATION SOCIETY, INTERNET, and NATIONAL INFORMATION INFRASTRUCTURE (NII).

DARK HORSE—A racing analogy used to describe a relatively unknown or surprise long-shot candidate nominated for public office. Such individuals typically emerge when the leading contenders are unable to secure enough ballots to nail down the nomination and their supporters look for a compromise alternative acceptable to all the major competing factions. Electoral reforms restricting the influence of political party bosses and other INSIDERS secretly meeting in "smoke-filled backrooms" have lessened the number of—but not eliminated—such candidates.

DEATH SQUADS—Regular army members, police units, and other armed government agents operating under orders who "unofficially" kidnap, torture, and kill opponents of the regime. The victims often simply disappear without a trace. These extrajudicial executions are privately approved but publicly deplored in order to shield government leaders from accountability for human rights violations committed in their name. Death squads have been most often associated in recent years with rightist governments in Argentina, Chile, and El Salvador. However, the practice has proven widespread historically, with many regimes preferring murder to pluralistic democracy (such as happened to Catholics in North Vietnam following World War II).

DEEP BACKGROUND—A NEWS MEDIA convention where an influential source agrees to provide confidential information to journalists on what is happening with the condition that it not be quoted or used except in the most general and indirect manner (i.e., Knowledgeable "Washington sources speculate that," etc.). See also BACKGROUND, DYSJOURNALISM,

INSIDERS, JOURNALISM/ JOURNALIST, MEDIA BIAS, ME-
DIA/MEDIUM, NEWS, OFF THE RECORD, PARROTING THE PARTY
LINE, PAWNS, and PRESS.

DEEP POCKETS SPENDING—The rationale behind some legislative
constraints on COMMERCIAL SPEECH is the belief that corporations have
"deep pockets" and through GRASSROOTS LOBBYING can unduly influence
public perceptions, particularly in referendum campaigns or pending
legislation. In contrast, legislators believe that no such influence can prevail
in direct lobbying because they have experience in dealing with such efforts.
See also LOBBYING/LOBBYIST.

DEMAGOGUE/DEMAGOGISM—Originally, the Greek word *demagogos*
referred to a leader of the people. Now, the term is a negative one applied to
political leaders accused of using their knowledge of RHETORIC and
oratorical skills to win popular support by pandering to the baser instincts.
The implication is that demagogues resort to flattery, hyperbole, spurious
reasoning, exaggerations, and outright lies to curry favor. However, the word
is most often used by the failed opponents of a successful politician, angry
about their inability to defeat or counter that individual's successes.
Demagogism is the practice of demagoguery.

DEMOCRACY—As popularized by the Greeks, democracy referred to *direct
self-rule* by the public at large. Since their city-states countenanced slavery,
this public originally was quite limited and generally meant wealthy land-
owning males. Over time, however, the idea began to include more ordinary
members of the middle class and plebeian populace. Even then, the number of
people involved in self rule was small. A hybrid form of government called
"representative democracy" uses *indirect representation* and has been adopted in
form by the United States and many other countries where the national
institutions have been framed by elites.

In the modern era, the notion of pure democracy has again been
championed by a variety of political ideologies ranging from socialist to
populist. As a result, advocacy of democracy has often been seen as
RADICAL. For example, in *Federalist 10* James Madison concludes:

a pure democracy, by which I mean a society consisting of a small number of
citizens who assemble and administer the government in person, can admit of no
cure for the mischiefs of faction. A common passion or interest will, in almost
every case, be felt by a majority of the whole; a communication and concert results
from the form of government itself; and there is nothing to check the inducements
to sacrifice the weaker party or an obnoxious individual. Hence it is that such
democracies have ever been spectacles of turbulence and contention; have ever
been found incompatible with personal security or the rights of property; and have
in general been as short in their lives as they have been violent in their deaths.
Theoretic politicians, who have patronized this species of government, have
erroneously supposed that by reducing mankind to a perfect equality in their
political rights, they would at the same time be perfectly equalized and assimilated
in their possessions, their opinions and their passions.

Taking a similar view that genuine democracy is a dangerous phenomenon was the U.S. War Department. In *Army Training Manual No. 2000-25*, used for instructing American armed forces between 1928 and 1932 (until the book was withdrawn due to PRESS criticism), the definition is as follows:

A government of the masses. Authority derived through mass meetings or any other form of direct expression. Results in mobocracy. Attitude towards property is communistic—negating property rights. Attitude towards law is that the will of the majority shall regulate. . . . Result is demagogism, license, agitation, discontent, anarchy.

Radicals often assert the opposite: that democracy has been "hijacked—stolen from the people" by fascist RIGHT-WING/CONSERVATIVEs to the point that, for them, democracy today means letting the few elite in power make political decisions and a small number of conglomerates and multinationals make economic choices for the people. Unfortunately, the state and the institutions which claim to constitute "democracy" cannot be relied upon to bring about HUMAN RIGHTS, peace, and justice. Genuine democracy is a grassroots process that results in the expression of universal human rights through the empowerment of people to self-governance. This necessitates decentralizing power to the point where persons and community organizations are actively encouraged to freely participate in making decisions affecting their lives and future. As the Declaration of Independence eloquently articulated, in a democracy the people (rich or poor, comfortable or oppressed), have a natural right to criticize, seek peaceful change, to resist, and even overthrow repressive regimes. See also DEMAGOGUE/DEMAGOGISM, DOGMA, ELECTRONIC DEMOCRACY, ELITE THEORY, FACTION, FASCISM/FASCIST, GRASSROOTS POLITICAL ACTION, IDEOLOGY, INTEREST GROUPS, LOBBYING/LOBBYIST, POPULISM/POPULIST, and SOCIALISM/SOCIALIST.

DEMOCRATIC PARTY—One of the two major national political organizations in the United States, often abbreviated by the capital letter D. According to Jay M. Shafritz's *The Dorsey Dictionary of American Government and Politics* (p. 165):

The Democratic party traces its origins to the Democratic-Republican party of Thomas Jefferson. In 1828, under Andrew Jackson, the party took its current name. The ideals of the party have from the beginning tended toward greater egalitarianism and the abolition of special privilege, but it had difficulty living up to its ideals. . . Ever since the New Deal, the Democratic party has had a reputation for being liberal, for appealing to low-income groups, for expanding civil rights protection, and for believing that government is a legitimate vehicle for solving social problems.

Democrats frequently use a donkey symbol and party officeholders are often identified by the capital letter *D*. See also FEDERAL ELECTION COMMISSION (FEC), REPUBLICAN PARTY, and WATERGATE SCANDAL.

DEMOGRAPHICS—Useful vital statistics of a segment of the population defined by attributes such as age, educational level, gender, income, marital status, and race. These demographic measures are often derived from census data and used in identifying target publics for persuasive media campaigns. See also DIRECT MARKETING (DM), PSYCHOGRAPHICS, PUBLIC, and STAKEHOLDERS.

DEMONIZING THE OPPOSITION—Effectively blackening the reputation of one's opponents by linking them to sets of negative images. This is very often done by government propagandists using domestic media and control over the levers of power to create hatred for leaders and peoples of other nations in order to prepare the population for war. See also AD HOMINEM ATTACK, DESERT SHIELD, FACT SLINGING, FRAMING DEVICES, HATE CAMPAIGNS, POLISPOT, PUSH POLLS, RITUAL DEFAMATION, THOUGHT-STOPPING CLICHÉ, and WEAPONS ON THE WALL.

DESERT SHIELD—Code name for the massive military, political, economic, and propaganda effort led by the United States government to establish an international coalition, build up forces in the Middle East, and prevent further gains by the Iraqi government following its occupation of Kuwait in August 1990. Iraqi President Saddam Hussein was compared to Hitler by President George Bush (who also deliberately mispronounced "Saddam" and engaged in other insults) as part of a classically successful, no-holds-barred DEMONIZING THE OPPOSITION campaign, which was orchestrated to build support in America and overseas for an invasion. Even organizations supposedly committed to HUMAN RIGHTS, such as the Congressional Human Rights Foundation and Amnesty International, were taken in by the PROPAGANDA of HIDDEN PERSUADERS seeking to use them as FRONT GROUPS/SATELLITE ORGANIZATIONS. Ultimately, thirty-four coalition member countries contributed materials or manpower to Desert Shield, which enjoyed widespread media and popular backing in the U.S. under the banner of "Support Our Troops." See also DESERT STORM, DIRTY TRICKS CAMPAIGN, FOREIGN AGENTS REGISTRATION ACT (FARA), HATE CAMPAIGNS, SIDLE COMMISSION, and VIDEO NEWS RELEASE (VNR).

DESERT STORM—Code name for the full-scale Persian Gulf War launched on January 17, 1991, with permission of the United Nations Security Council and the U.S. Congress. Desert Storm's mission was to expel Iraqi forces from Kuwait. Within forty-three days, the U.S.-led military coalition successfully routed the enemy. See also DESERT SHIELD and UNITED NATIONS ORGANIZATION (UNO or UN).

DIAL GROUP—A form of audience pretest research used by marketers and political consultants in which respondents are given a electronic meter and asked to turn the dial up for approval or down for disapproval depending on their reaction to what is being shown and said. This is often used to hone message strategies to maximize the positive impact of key ideas (also known as media talking points) placed in finalized ADVERTISING copy.

DIGITIZED PHOTOGRAPHY—Virtually undetectable computerized translation of still photographs and moving pictures into images that can be electronically manipulated, restructured, and reproduced in various formats. By altering reality at a time when images carry much of a story's message, this electronic sleight-of-hand is causing a debate in journalism about the ethics of using digital technology. The implication of these incredible breakthroughs for students of PROPAGANDA is that seeing is no longer necessarily believing, since the DOCUMENTARY aspect of photography is so compromised as to herald the end of the photograph as evidence. Recent examples of altering or combining photographs include a 1994 *Time* cover making O.J. Simpson look more guilty in the aftermath of his celebrated arrest and a New York *Newsday* picture doctored to make it appear that ice skaters Tonya Harding and Nancy Kerrigan were practicing together when, in fact, they were not. See also COMPUTER-AIDED DESIGN (CAD) and VIRTUAL REALITY.

DIRECT ACTION—Legal obstructionism, street demonstrations, created PSEUDO-EVENT/PSEUDO-NEWS efforts designed to attract media attention, and extralegal violence designed to force social change, usually stemming from long-standing grievances held by committed political believers frustrated over their inability to otherwise effect reform. For example, many labor militants are committed to direct intervention by workers to obtain their demands. Rather than allowing professional negotiators to speak for them, many unions have long engaged in tactics first perfected by the WOBBLIES which undercut or "sabotage" the system through "the conscious withdrawal of efficiency" by direct actions they could control themselves—strikes, slow downs, and strict adherence to work rules. Although anarchists involved in direct actions have often been accused of using arson and dynamite as means of intimidation, most RADICAL workers movements such as the IWW have never advocated violence. Often the real violence has been either perpetrated against them by various legal and quasi-legal police forces defending the status quo, or by AGENTS PROVOCATEURS covertly seeking to discredit the worker's movements. See also CORPORATE CAMPAIGN.

DIRECT CONFRONTATION—When militant supporters of opposing organizations come face-to-face in counterdemonstrations at flashpoint locations, such as abortion clinics, the direct confrontation battle is less concerned with on-the-spot persuasion than with securing sympathetic media coverage.

DIRECT LOBBYING—See LOBBYING/LOBBYIST.

DIRECT MARKETING (DM)—The offering of products or services by organizations through "targeted" media such as telephones and faxes (telemarketing), postal delivery (direct mail), and so on. Direct marketers maintain their own databases of current and prospective customers or rent lists of prospective customers identified by the DEMOGRAPHICS and PSYCHOGRAPHICS of their life-style profiles from firms specializing in such information. See also DIRECT-RESPONSE (DR) ADVERTISING and SPECIALTY ADVERTISING.

DIRECT-RESPONSE (DR) ADVERTISING—A marketing strategy that utilizes any medium (such as direct mail, telemarketing, television, etc.) to spur an immediate action response by customers. All direct-response ADVERTISING is structured around three basic elements: (1) the message communicates a definite offer, (2) the recipient is given information necessary to make a decision, and (3) the ad makes it easy to say "yes" immediately by including one or more response devices (a coupon; 1-800 or 1-900 telephone exchange number; preaddressed order form, envelope, and/or BOUNCEBACK CARD, etc.). INFOMERCIALs are one of the most popular direct-response television formats. See also ADVERTORIAL, DIRECT MARKETING (DM), and INFOTAINMENT.

DIRTY TRICKS CAMPAIGN—The unscrupulous use of STRUCTURED LEAKS, pressure tactics, threats, intimidation, deception, innuendo, fraud, outright lies and other smears to damage the credibility of an opposition individual or organization. Usually, the real sources of these harmful attacks prefer to remain HIDDEN PERSUADERS out of the spotlight, using third-party FRONT GROUPS/SATELLITE ORGANIZATIONS to do the dirty work so as to remain insulated from criticism through the mechanism of PLAUSIBLE DENIABILITY.

DISINFORMATION (*DEZINFORMATSIA*)—The systematic application of pressure designed to exploit and amplify the weaknesses of an opponent, particularly by distributing lies and other distorted information. This process involves corrupting communication channels so as to mislead, inflame, or confound PUBLIC OPINION as part of a campaign to achieve strategic objectives. Disinformation operations differ from conventional PROPAGANDA in that their true origins are concealed, and they usually involve some form of CLANDESTINE action. The Russians define disinformation as "the dissemination of false and provocative information," a translation of the word *dezinformatsia*, which involved the infiltration of the Western PRESS to spread distortions, myths and other misleading information of advantage to the Communist government. According to the description proposed by attendees at the Conference on Contemporary Soviet Propaganda and Disinformation sponsored by the U.S. Department of State and the CENTRAL INTELLIGENCE AGENCY (CIA) in 1985, disinformation is:

a broad concept that includes any communication in which deliberately misleading information is passed to targeted individuals, groups, or governments with the purpose of influencing foreign elite or public opinion. It can take the form of overt propaganda, as well as such things as forgeries, rumors, and covert placements of unattributed articles in foreign media. Instruments used in disinformation operations include both open media and clandestine radios, agents of influence, international front organizations, and espionage agents.

These "phantom groups" effectively disguise the source of the fraudulent information leaks as they enter into an opponent's communication system. Former Czechoslovak deputy minister for disinformation Ladislav Bittman author of several insider books on the topic, says these "grand deceptions" and "subterfuges," are "often designed to exploit legitimate popular concerns about world problems or issues" in order to further deceive the decision-making elite or the public at large. "Demonstrations, strikes and riots organized to debilitate morale and discredit public policies also fall within the Soviet concept of disinformation." However, he points out, as perfected during the days of the KGB, disinformation proved "far more complex than the definition implies." Bittman's experience included the distribution of literacy hoaxes (forged or fabricated DOCUMENTs, letters, manuscripts, and photographs); the propagation of misleading or malicious rumors and erroneous intelligence by agents; the duping of foreign visitors; and the commission of physical acts such as sabotage and murder for psychological effect.

The underlying purposes of disinformation are to disrupt relations among nations, influence policies of other governments, undermine the confidence of opposition groups, deceive foreigners about one's real intentions and conditions, and cover-up embarrassing blunders. "The reason disinformation works so well is that it is deliberately designed to confirm the recipients' darkest suspicions. It plays on prejudice and bias" which ultimately lead us to believe what we want to believe.

See also AGENTS/AGENCIES OF INFLUENCE, AGENTS PROVOCATEUR, BIG LIE, BLOWBACK, CLANDESTINE RADIO STATIONS, DIRTY TRICKS CAMPAIGN, FALSE FLAG OPERATIONS, FRONT GROUPS/SATELLITE ORGANIZATIONS, INSIDERS, KGB (*Komitet po Gosudarstvennoy Bezopasnosti*), PLANTING STORIES, and STRUCTURED LEAKS.

DIVERT/REFOCUS STRATEGY—Political marketing mechanism by which a political leader or organization creates favorable media events or provokes a new crisis capable of easy victory to shift attention away from uncomfortable realities. Political advisors conduct PUBLIC OPINION polls, psychological studies using Jungian archetypes, "power phrase" message-response and values tests, focus-group interviews, and other data gathering using social science techniques. These are then repackaged into phrases and symbols designed specifically to evoke favorable media coverage through the substitution of nice looking and sounding slogan metaphors in place of much more difficult concrete achievements. President Bush proved himself a master at such political marketing through the use of emotionally charged symbolic language and spectacle designed to position him as an environmental, education, "war on drugs" leader, despite the lack of substantive programs to achieve anything meaningful in these areas. His emphasis on foreign affairs, particularly in dealing with the changes in the Soviet Union and easy military victories in Panama (OPERATION JUST CAUSE) and Iraq (DESERT SHIELD and DESERT STORM), for several years successfully co-opted media attention and served to obscure weaknesses domestically.

DOCUDRAMA—Film and video mixtures of DOCUMENTARY fact and dramatic fiction. The docudrama on American television can clearly locate its roots in theater, books, motion pictures, radio, and journalism. Many specific docudrama programs illustrate the positive potential of the genre for public affairs educational enlightenment. On the other hand, one can argue that the dramatic trivialization common to many less pure forms of docudrama can also lead to sensationalism and distortion which have little to contribute to the "PUBLIC INTEREST." This is because the repetitive nature of media and the continuing reliance on stereotypes and genre ("formulaic media conventions") reinforces cultural ideology that limits rather than enhances thought. The result is biased interpretations of historical and contemporary events. Reconstructing too accurately can lack intensity or excitement, with the docudramatist (like the documentarist) often hampered by reality's lack of direct conflict. Fact has a way of receding in importance as you get closer to an event, particularly if something that is supposed to be dramatic fails to provide some essential elements. For example, dramatists often are forced to resort to conventions of fiction, playing up the most exceptional rather than the most representative moments in trials, lives, and so forth to create a story with a satisfying beginning, middle, and end. Biographical films (for years in Hollywood called "biopics") are especially susceptible to fictionalizing and falsifying history because of the traditional focus on heroes and villains and the need to dramatically condense.

According to Hoffer Musburger, and Nelson (1985, based on earlier work by Hoffer and Nelson, 1978), documentary-dramas, (or docudramas) are simply accurate recreations of events in the lives of actual persons based on articles, diaries, transcripts and other documentary materials. The key words are *recreations*, *events*, and *lives of actual persons*. Implied within the term *recreation* are all the dramatic elements used to depict factual events. These include film/video techniques such as constructive editing, in which events are "recreated" on the editing bench instead of the time frame of the original photography. Add to such restructuring, even if the picture is thoroughly "factual," a musical theme (which usually superimposes emotional consistency or counterpoint not present in the original photography of the event) and post-recorded sound effects (which establish new continuities not present when the material was shot), and new problems in documentary classification arise. Their general definition seems to provide a more logical extension to the variations encountered later, enables separation into monologues, event-oriented programs, personality-oriented programs, religious docudramas, partial docudramas or fictionalized documentaries, INFOMERCIAL aberrations, and other types, while remaining close to the docudrama "family." In the United States, public television and cable have provided a home for serious documentary and docudrama programming that would not have otherwise aired in the commercial marketplace.

DOCUMENT—A written, pictorial, and/or sound informational record used as proof or evidence. Propagandists often selectively use such materials to enhance their case, sometimes resorting to forgeries. Governments often form investigative commissions to interview witnesses, review documents, and issue what are known as WHITE PAPERS to explain away, or WHITEWASH, a political failure or scandal.

DOCUMENTARY—For Raymond Carroll, author of "Factual Television in America," (1978), as well as other scholars, "The documentary has been defined as a reconstruction of reality, using real people and events in a socially-meaningful structure, and recorded at the time and place of their occurrence. Its purpose is to inform, perhaps motivate, the audience." Carroll expanded his definition to include a program which "deals with actual events and circumstances in a manner that maintains fidelity to fact, and uses the actual geographic locations and participants in the situation, is based on a 'purposive' point of view, conveys 'knowledge about' a situation and is a delayed analysis—recorded on film or video tape—of the circumstance or event." While the term has been most associated with audio-visual media, work by print journalists is often described as documentary reporting. See also BROADCASTING, COMPOSITE REPORTING, DIGITIZED PHOTOGRAPHY, DOCUDRAMA, INFOMERCIAL, and STUNTING.

DOCUMERCIAL—See INFOMERCIAL.

DOGMA—A fundamental principle, or set of principles (also referred to as a body of doctrines or tenets), held by an individual or group. The term is often associated with the propagation of religious beliefs. For example, in Catholicism, a dogma is declared to be a truth solemnly formulated either by an ecumenical council or by the Pope's "infallible magisterium." See also CULT and FREETHINKERS.

DOUBLESPEAK—Euphemistic use of words for propagandistic purposes with pernicious social consequences. The language used by individuals, private groups, and governmental agencies is often designed to mislead and divert from the truth, even meaning the opposite of what the words sound like in order to cover-up an unpleasant reality. Doublespeak includes double-talk, gobbledygook, officialese, and all other forms of deceptive language, and is a hybrid based on the combination of DOUBLETHINK and NEWSPEAK (from George Orwell's novel, *1984*). Examples include "air support" instead of "bombing"; and "rescue mission" or the more obtuse "pre-dawn vertical insertion" instead of the much plainer "invasion." See also CODE WORDS, EUPHEMISM, MEMORY HOLE, ORWELLIAN TACTICS, and WEASEL WORDS.

DOUBLETHINK—Term invented by George Orwell to describe self-contradictory use of language to create a "vast system of mental cheating, where the lie is always one step ahead of the truth." In other words, doublethink is a system in which one says one thing and means another. See also BIG LIE, DOUBLESPEAK, ORWELLIAN TACTICS, THOUGHT-STOPPING CLICHÉ, and WEASEL WORDS.

DUAL LOYALIST—A person whose allegiances are given to more than one cause or nation on the basis of ideological, ethnic, religious, or other reasons. These loyalties may coincide but often conflict, presenting a dilemma for those employed in sensitive positions where they may be forced to choose sides and enter into TREASON.

DYSJOURNALISM—The prefix *dys* is derived from Greek and Latin roots and refers to an abnormal, diseased, faulty, impaired, bad, or unfavorable phenomenon. As applied to journalism, the system of self-serving STRUCTURED LEAKS and opportunistic disclosure of partial truths that often characterizes the NEWS reporter-government official relationship commonly leads to speculation passing as fact. When for whatever reason reporters draw the wrong conclusions or erroneously characterize motivations ("character assassination," "poisonous lies") in their stories, they commit dysjournalism. See also DEEP BACKGROUND, FEEDING FRENZY, MEDIA BIAS, MEDIA EFFECTS, MEDIA/MEDIUM, NEW JOURNALISM, JOURNALISM/JOURNALIST, JUSTICE BY NEWS RELEASE, PLANTING STORIES, PRESS, TABLOID JOURNALISM, and YELLOW JOURNALISM.

DYSTOPIA—The negative alternative to a futuristic utopia of joy, where instead life becomes a fearful experience and social organizations such as governments discover inventive ways to use deception to control the unhappy populace.

88—A numerical salutation referring to the eighth letter of the English alphabet (H), often used by neo-Nazis to disguise that they really mean "Heil Hitler."

ELECTRONIC COMMUNITY NETWORK—A computer-based system providing a broad spectrum of one-way and interactive community-based information services to local subscribers for little or no cost. Some "freenets" are reachable by telnet on INTERNET, others only by direct-dial telephone. See also CYBERSPACE, ELECTRONIC DEMOCRACY, FLAME POSTS, and NATIONAL INFORMATION INFRASTRUCTURE (NII).

ELECTRONIC DEMOCRACY—A form of direct DEMOCRACY utilizing television and radio talk shows, ELECTRONIC COMMUNITY NETWORKs, and other forms of TELECOMMUNICATIONS to create "electronic town meetings," which influence the PUBLIC POLICY PROCESS by putting pressure on government representatives through GRASSROOTS LOBBYING or bypassing them entirely.

ELECTRONIC PUBLISHING—Production and distribution of DOCUMENTs from a single source to many readers at remote electronic sites by commercial publishers, corporate users, educators, activist groups, and governments.

ELITE THEORY—A system of political analysis that argues DEMOCRACY is mostly an illusion. Elite theorists stress that in every human society there is the iron law of oligarchy, with many historians and sociologists concluding that there are basically two broad categories of people: the class that rules and the class that is ruled. Included in the latter are those whose skills and resources give them some measure of comfort and independence. The larger and better off financially this group ("the BOURGEOIS middle class"), the more indirect the control of the elites. An erosion of the middle class then portends a growing trend to authoritarianism. As political scientist Harold Lasswell noted in *World Politics and Personal Insecurity* (1950), "The few who get the most of any value are the *elite*; the rest are the rank and file. An elite preserves its ascendancy by manipulating symbols, controlling supplies, and applying violence. Less formally expressed, politics is the study of *who gets what, when, and how*." Sociologist C. Wright Mills further popularized these views with his eye-opening study, *The Power Elite* (1956), describing an America dominated by a self-perpetuating establishment of corporate, legal, military and political leaders. Those social scientists who dispute this view tend to argue in favor of pluralism with many competing groups providing checks and balances for a more decentralized decision-making structure. For example, Lichter, Rothman, and Lichter in *The Media Elite: America's New Powerbrokers* (1986) suggested that Mills'

notion that a few people with common social backgrounds and political outlooks made the key decisions that determined America's destiny was always overdrawn. Thirty years later, it has been completely overtaken by rapid change at the top. Today, the traditional elites are challenged by new opinion leaders and institutions that have gained immensely in influence since the 1960s. Among the emerging elites are the public interest movement, a vastly expanded federal bureaucracy, and a national media network that serves as a watchdog over other social institutions.

Those holding to traditional elite theory, however, would argue that these changes represent more an illusory choice than a real one and are actually effecting a consolidation of influence rather than its demise. See also CONSPIRACY THEORIES, ESTABLISHMENT, MEDIA ELITE, MOVEMENT, and PUBLIC INTEREST.

ENGINEERING OF CONSENT—The process by which an organization seeks to consider the PUBLIC OPINION climate, build support, and reach an understanding that proves beneficial to all involved parties. This is usually associated with the notion of linking private interests with a broader PUBLIC INTEREST. The term was originated in the 1920s by public relations counsel Edward L. Bernays. The more recently coined MANUFACTURING OF CONSENT (or CONSENSUS) has a similar, if at times more sinister, connotation.

ENTENTE—The allied powers opposed to Germany and Austria-Hungary in what became World War I, including Britain, France, Russia, and Italy, which were later joined by Japan, the United States, and other national governments.

ESPIONAGE—According to the *Intelligence Community Staff Glossary* prepared by the CENTRAL INTELLIGENCE AGENCY (CIA) in 1978, espionage is "Intelligence activity directed toward the acquisition of information through CLANDESTINE means and proscribed by the laws of the country against which it is committed." See also INTELLIGENCE COMMUNITY and SPYING/SPYCRAFT.

ESTABLISHMENT, THE—An alleged alliance of PRESSURE GROUPS which own and/or control the major media, dominate banking and finance, underwrite most of the key FOUNDATIONS and THINK TANKS, dominate both major political parties, employ propagandists and lobbyists, and effectively control government at the federal and state levels by using the powers to tax for their own selfish purposes. See also BILDERBERGER GROUP, CONSPIRACY THEORIES, COUNCIL ON FOREIGN RELATIONS (CFR), ELITE THEORY, INVISIBLE GOVERNMENT, MEDIA ELITE, PROPAGANDA-2 (P-2), and SECRET GOVERNMENT.

ETHNIC CLEANSING—Term created in 1992 by the U.S. State Department to describe forced removals of one group of people by another based on their differing linguistic, religious, ethnic, or racial heritages. The purpose of "ethnic cleansing" is to establish new boundaries without "disruptive" minorities. The removals are typically accomplished by atrocities involving military conquest, forced relocation, rape, pillage, starvation, murder, and attempted GENOCIDE as in the massacres by Serbian and Croatian forces occurring in Bosnia-Herzegovina during 1992-1995. See also CODE WORDS, DOUBLESPEAK, EUPHEMISM, EXTREMISM, MEMORY HOLE, RACIST/RACIALIST/RACIAL DISCRIMINATION, SCAPEGOAT/ SCAPEGOATING, and WEASEL WORDS.

EUPHEMISM—Substituting an inoffensive word for a possibly harsh or crude one, often with the intent to soften meaning or mislead. See also WEASEL WORDS.

EXTRALEGAL CENSORSHIP—Practices by those in power (governments, business, and even media) in which alternatives to law are used to deny access to information and slant NEWS coverage of events. Numerous examples of hidden threats or harassment resulting in self-CENSORSHIP range from mild forms such as telephone calls by government officials to journalists to more extreme methods of intimidation involving assassinations of independent editors by government DEATH SQUADS.

EXTREMISM—Several useful definitions of extremism are found in Roger Scruton's *A Dictionary of Political Thought* (1982). These include:

1. Talking a political idea to its limits, regardless of unfortunate repercussions, impracticalities, argument, and feelings to the contrary, and with the intention not only to confront, but to eliminate opposition. 2. Intolerance toward all views other than one's own. 3. Adoption of means to political ends which show disregard for the life, liberty, and human rights of others.

EXTREMIST—A term most often used as an epithet to characterize views that conflict with our own, or are advocated by someone we dislike (but probably do not know personally) and whose interests are seen as contrary to ours. As researcher Laird Wilcox observed in an important essay on the topic, the word extremist is generally associated with "fringe" positions. However, he argues that EXTREMISM "is more an issue of style than of content" since those defining themselves as "centrist" or "middle-of-the-road" may prove

far more dogmatic and prejudiced than someone who adopts more radical views but does so in an open and tolerant manner. . . In fact, it could be argued that those beliefs that are accorded legitimacy by consensus, which is to say that everyone unthinkingly accepts them, may even be more prone to appear on the extremist agenda and more difficult to challenge or effectively debate.

See also RADICAL and ZEALOTS.

FACTION—Has three major meanings: (1) self-serving INTEREST GROUPS, condemned by James Madison, in the *Federalist Papers* number 10, as "a number of citizens, whether amounting to a majority or minority of the whole, who are united and actuated by some common impulse of passion or other interest, adverse to the rights of other citizens, or to the permanent and aggregate interests of the community"; (2) subgroups of organizations, such as the liberal wing of the Republican party; and (3) a fictionalized DOCUDRAMA, such as *Roots* (1977, ABC-TV), in which actual persons' lives are recreated but the events become telescoped, with fictional elements added because of the lack of DOCUMENTARY material, cast against a historical mosaic largely based on fact. See also DEMOCRACY and PRESSURE GROUPS.

FACT SLINGING—Negative ADVERTISING messages in which the opponent's own words are used to discredit. In television POLISPOTs, for example, videotape NEWS statements by the incumbent can be used by the challenger to deflate extravagant claims ("no new taxes") with authoritative-sounding data highlighting the less-than-perfect results ("taxes went up 28 percent in the last sixteen months according to the Congressional Budget Office"). See also AD HOMINEM ATTACK and DEMONIZING THE OPPOSITION.

FAIRNESS DOCTRINE—Through the Fairness Doctrine and related regulations the FEDERAL COMMUNICATIONS COMMISSION (FCC) long influenced individual, organizational, and even advertiser access to broadcasting channels in the United States. By overseeing licensee performance, the ostensible purpose of the Fairness Doctrine was to assure balanced presentation on controversial issues of PUBLIC INTEREST, but critics argued that the result was a form of CENSORSHIP. While Section 326 of the Federal Communications Act of 1934 as amended forbids the national government from overtly censoring broadcast programming, Section 307 directs the FCC to grant and renew licenses "based on its assessment of the licensee's ability to serve the public convenience, interest, or necessity." Under the Fairness Doctrine, the FCC required stations "to devote a reasonable amount of broadcast time to the discussion of controversial issues" and "to do so fairly, in order to afford reasonable opportunity for opposing viewpoints." Although the doctrine emerged first as an administrative policy of the FCC, Congress in 1959 incorporated amendments in Section 315(a) of the

Communications Act which imposed an "obligation" on licensees "to operate in the public interest and to afford reasonable opportunity for the discussion of conflicting views on issues of public importance."

In keeping with this mandate, broadcasters were encouraged to air various sides, but as a practical matter the FCC has consistently ruled that broadcasters have great editorial latitude when deciding how an issue will be discussed and who gets access to the public airwaves. One reason for the failure of the Fairness Doctrine is that the first provision—the need for proactive involvement by licensees—has been rarely invoked in legal disputes. Rather, the remedial aspect—the emphasis on the opportunity to reply—has been the central question in all but a handful of cases. The constitutionality of content regulation of electronic media was upheld in the *Red Lion Broadcasting Co., Inc. v. FCC* decision of 1969. In *Red Lion*, the Supreme Court theoretically narrowed the prerogatives of broadcasters when it affirmed "the right of the public to receive suitable access to social, political, esthetic, moral, and other ideas and experiences."

In practice, however, the decision signaled broadcasters that license renewals were going to be less a problem if they relied on their regulated PRESS status and the Fairness Doctrine to avoid controversy—resulting in the widespread exclusion of persons, organizations, and views deemed too RADICAL. On the other hand, those groups already successfully on the air very often praised the doctrine precisely because it protected their interests. Statistical analyses of the actions taken by the FCC in responding to filed complaints raised new questions over the inability of the Fairness Doctrine to actually bring about real openness in NEWS and ADVERTISING access.

The commission and the Supreme Court both subsequently indicated a willingness to review the seminal *Red Lion* decision if it could be shown that the Doctrine had "the effect of reducing rather than enhancing speech." In 1987, despite congressional complaints, the commission boldly moved to rescind the Fairness Doctrine as part of its ongoing deregulation efforts. Congress and the president so far have proved unsuccessful in agreeing to legislation restoring the doctrine, although the constitutionality of commission's action and the premises behind the fairness mandate itself are undergoing continuing challenges.

FAIR TRADE—Euphemism for "managed competition" and other protectionist policies by economic nationalists who assert that FREE TRADE is destructive to the interests of the productive sector. Historically, the FEDERALIST PARTY, the later WHIG PARTY, and many other prominent U.S. political leaders have endorsed an AMERICA FIRST protective tariff (also referred to as the "American System") to build domestic manufacturing.

FALSE FLAG OPERATIONS—A technique often utilized by governments and organizations which recruit informers and agents to work for their cause by hiding who they really are or what they actually stand for. In a false flag operation, the target is convinced he or she will actually be working for some other nation or interest altogether. Their motives range from the patriotic to the mercenary, but victims remain unaware of who or what their efforts are really assisting. The Soviet Union, for example, secretly recruited Americans and Britons friendly to apartheid proponents in South Africa to provide helpful intelligence by pretending to be South African government representatives. A technological disinformation application of false flag strategies involves the secret manipulation/distortion of supposedly secure radio/satellite signals. These efforts not only disrupt the opposition but also can be leaked to the PRESS by official sources to mislead PUBLIC OPINION for propaganda purposes. See also COMMUNICATIONS INTELLIGENCE (COMINT) and DISINFORMATION (*DEZINFORMATSIA*).

FASCISM/FASCIST—A system of government which first emerged in Italy in 1922 under Benito Mussolini and came to be applied in various forms such as the National Socialist regime in Germany led by Adolf Hitler (1933-1945) and Vichy France under General Henri Pétain (1940-1944). Fascists believe in:
- a strong leader at the head of a rigid one-party popular dictatorship,
- the forcible co-optation or suppression of opposition groups (such as dissenting churches, unions, political parties, and media),
- a type of state CAPITALISM in which private ownership of the means of production occurs under the guidance of centralized government planners, and
- fervent nationalism or racism that glorifies past history and emphasizes military might.

The fasces symbol (which is prominently featured on the dais of the U.S. Congress and appeared on the back of Mercury-head dimes) is made up of a bundle of rods bound around a projecting axe blade. This was used anciently by the Roman magistrates to demonstrate their authority. See also FIFTH COLUMN and NATIONAL SOCIALISM/NAZISM.

FDR—Franklin Delano Roosevelt, U.S. president from 1933 to 1945, who dominated domestic politics during the Depression and World War II and proved a masterful public communicator. Roosevelt was disliked by RADICAL members of the RIGHT-WING/CONSERVATIVE camp in American politics, who subjected him to much vilification for his policies and ancestry.

FEDERAL COMMUNICATIONS COMMISSION (FCC)—The national government agency which regulates BROADCASTING, cablecasting, and telecommunications in the United States. The FCC was established in 1934 by Congress, assuming the duties of the previous Federal Radio Commission created in 1927. See also FAIRNESS DOCTRINE.

FEDERAL ELECTION COMMISSION (FEC)—The U.S. national government agency created by the Federal Election Campaign Act (FECA) of 1971, as subsequently amended, which serves as the basic regulatory agency overseeing election laws involving federal offices. The act provides for "disclosure, limitations, prohibitions, and public funding related to candidates for federal office and to party and nonparty political committees, among others."

FEDERALIST PARTY—Those favoring ratification of the U.S. Constitution in the 1780s and a strong central government were known as Federalists, while their opponents who sought to maintain state powers and a BILL OF RIGHTS were referred to as "anti-Federalists." Their widely publicized debate was followed by compromises which eventually resulted in formation of the new government in 1789. Although FACTIONs existed, political parties were not at first considered proper and are not even mentioned in the Constitution. However, George Washington, John Adams, Alexander Hamilton and their supporters enacted policies which coalesced in the formation of the Federalist party. Gradually, their ideological opponents grouped around Thomas Jefferson and became known as Democratic-Republicans. Antidemocratic excesses during the presidency of Adams eroded popular support for the Federalists. The election of Jefferson in 1800 marks the end of the Federalist era and the party completely disappears from national life following the contests of 1816. See also FIRST AMENDMENT.

FEDERAL TRADE COMMISSION (FTC)—An independent regulatory agency created by the Federal Trade Commission Act of 1914 (contained in 15 USC § 45). The commission is charged with preventing monopolies or other restraints on trade. FTC enforcement authority derives from Section 5 of the FTC Act, which now reads: "Unfair methods of competition in or affecting commerce, and unfair or deceptive acts or practices in or affecting commerce, are declared unlawful." The commission is thus empowered to regulate the substance of commercial communication, oversees much of American ADVERTISING, and retains broad power to monitor and punish false or misleading ad claims.

FEEDING FRENZY—Much like sharks unable to control themselves when they sense blood in the water, journalists often cannot master their urge to "get the story" when a sensational news event occurs. They flock to where sources are thought to be, waiting in groups to literally ambush newsmakers by shouting questions and muscling in to obtain interviews and pictures of people then temporarily in the spotlight. A good example involves the excesses committed when hundreds of reporters and support staffs were assigned to cover the O.J. Simpson murder investigation beginning in mid-1994. In response to the feeding frenzy, *New York Times* columnist A.M. Rosenthal that year was prompted to ask, "Are we journalists or garbage collectors?" The answer is a little of both, since competition drives many reporters to publish or broadcast material before it is confirmed. Desperate for NEWS, journalists pounced on dozens of unverified rumors as they surfaced. Many stemmed from STRUCTURED LEAKS crafted by prosecutors and defense attorneys to sway PUBLIC OPINION before the case got to trial. MEDIA BIAS remains a continuing concern in such instances because there are no clear-cut ethical boundaries for journalists to repair to when covering an event of this magnitude. As stories such as these unfold, the media eventually tend to get their facts straight. But the impact of this later information tends to be less than occurs during the first white heat of breaking news. See also DYSJOURNALISM, JOURNALISM/JOURNALIST, MEDIA/MEDIUM, PACK JOURNALISM, STONEWALLING, TABLOID JOURNALISM, and YELLOW JOURNALISM.

FENIAN BROTHERHOOD—Irish rebels engaged in fundraising, arms procurement, and DIRECT ACTIONs supportive of independence from Britain, active in United States during the nineteenth-century. The Fenians enjoyed support among a segment of the Irish population (including Irish-Americans) and serve as an ideological predecessor to modern revolutionaries such as the Irish Republican Army (IRA). See also IRISH NORTHERN AID COMMITTEE (NORAID).

FIFTH COLUMN—Suspected TRAITORs on the homefront, willing to assist "the enemy" occupying forces if they come. The term has a pro-fascist connotation, entering popular usage during the hard-fought Spanish Civil War of the 1930s when a rebel general proclaimed he had four columns of troops marching on republican Madrid and a fifth column of citizens waiting for his arrival in the city. During World War II, *fifth columnist* was a reproach applied to anyone thought to have secret sympathies for the Nazi regime. See also DUAL LOYALIST, FASCISM/FASCIST, and NATIONAL SOCIALISM/NAZISM.

FIGHTING WORDS—Provocative language designed to incite an immediate breach of the peace, such as a public speaker urging violence before a crowd tending toward riot. In the United States, the Supreme Court has held the protections of the FIRST AMENDMENT do not extend to such AGITATION, but laws banning such expression must be narrowly drawn.

FINDING—Policy statements providing authorization for COVERT ACTIONs by departments, agencies, or entities of the United States Government in which the president "finds" that a specific operation in a foreign country is important to the national security. Findings list the "scope" (nation or area of operation) and provide a "description" of what plan of action is intended. Findings are in writing "unless immediate action by the United States is required and time does not permit the preparation of a written finding, in which case a written record of the President's decision shall be contemporaneously made and shall be reduced to a written finding as soon as possible but in no event more than 48 hours after the decision is made." That tortured syntax is from the Intelligence Authorization Act for Fiscal Year 1991. Each finding must be signed and dated by the president personally (although sometimes prepared after the fact), "Pursuant to Section 662 of the Foreign Assistance Act of 1961 as Amended, Concerning Operations Undertaken by the Central Intelligence Agency in Foreign Countries, Other than Those Intended Solely for the Purpose of Intelligence Collection." See also CENTRAL INTELLIGENCE AGENCY (CIA), ESPIONAGE, and INTELLIGENCE COMMUNITY.

FIRST AMENDMENT—The First Amendment was part of a package of ten modifications to the proposed U.S. Constitution, approved in 1791 to mollify anti-Federalists who were opposed to a strong central government. These amendments (the BILL OF RIGHTS) were crafted to break a political deadlock holding up ratification of the new constitutional structure to replace the failed

Articles of Confederation by clearly limiting federal government powers. The First Amendment is particularly important in its protections for individual liberty and reads: "Congress shall make no law respecting an establishment of religion, or prohibiting the free exercise thereof; or abridging the freedom of speech, or of the press; or the right of the people peaceably to assemble, and to petition the government for a redress of grievances." Propagandists argue that under the First Amendment's clear language they enjoy the right to lobby government, engage in grassroots communication, and utilize mass media to agitate for change. See also AGITATION, CENSORSHIP, CIVIL RELIGION, COMMERCIAL SPEECH, FEDERALIST PARTY, FLAME POSTS, FREE SPEECH, GRASSROOTS LOBBYING, HUMAN RIGHTS, LIBERTARIAN, LOBBYING/LOBBYIST, MEDIA/MEDIUM, and PRESS.

FLACK—Derogatory term for a PUBLIC RELATIONS (PR) practitioner. Also used as a verb: "to flack for a client." Derives from either the indiscriminate bombardments in wartime that explode high in the air above to wreak havoc on the unprotected below, and/or "flak catchers" who absorb the shrapnel meant for more important higher-ups.

FLAG WAVING—To proclaim their patriotic intent, many individuals and groups attempt to symbolically (and even literally) cloak their PROPAGANDA efforts in the flag. While this practice cuts across the political spectrum, it tends to be more common among RIGHT-WING/CONSERVATIVE proponents. In emphasizing their belief in traditional values, for example, members of the Christian Right often invoke images of the Bible in one hand and OLD GLORY in the other.

FLAME POSTS—Bombastic tirades and other forms of personal attack against others occurring on computer electronic mail (e-mail) lists and bulletin boards. Social scientists are now studying the sociological phenomenon that leads people to express their views more aggressively and openly ("to flame") in on-line contexts than they would if interpersonally communicating face-to-face. See also CYBERSPACE, ELECTRONIC COMMUNITY NETWORK, ELECTRONIC DEMOCRACY, and FREE SPEECH.

FLOPPYBACK—A book published on computer diskette.

FLUFF EVENTS—Rallies, movie premières, concerts, and other PSEUDO-EVENT/PSEUDO-NEWS activities that are not particularly informative and have little or no redeeming social value but gain favorable PUBLICITY for an organization to make it better known. See also PUBLIC SERVICE EVENTS.

FLUTTER—Polygraph tests given by intelligence agencies as part of ongoing investigative efforts, including loyalty checks of their own employees. See also INTELLIGENCE COMMUNITY and VETTING.

FOREIGN AGENTS REGISTRATION ACT (FARA)—Congress originally passed the Foreign Agents Registration Act in 1938 in response to the growing influence of Communist, Fascist, and National Socialist (Nazi) regimes through PROPAGANDA that they circulated within the United States. The act (1) defines who must register with the Department of Justice as a foreign agent; (2) specifies how such agents are to register and report on their activities; (3) exempts certain types of foreign agents from registration; (4) outlines specific filing and labeling requirements for political propaganda disseminated by registered agents; (5) requires all registered agents to preserve account books and other records on all their activities which must be made available for inspection to officials responsible for enforcing the act; (6) provides for public examination of all agents' registration statements, reports, and political propaganda filed with the department; (7) imposes penalties for willful violations of the act or related regulations; and (8) specifies administrative and judicial enforcement procedures available to the attorney general in bringing about compliance with the requirements of the act. Even though those regulations appear to be very restrictive, the Justice Department has estimated that between 30 and 60 percent of foreign lobbyists avoid registration. Since 1966, federal law has also prohibited any representative acting for a foreign interest from making or promising to make any contribution to U.S. elections.

The Foreign Agents Registration Act (FARA) as amended is now found in 22 USC § 611-618 (1982) and imposes potentially burdensome restrictions on the dissemination of foreign media in the United States. The definition of political propaganda subject to FARA controls is set forth at 22 USC 611(j) (1982) which provides:

The term "political propaganda" includes any oral, visual, graphic, written, pictorial, or other communication or expression by any person (1) which is reasonably adopted to, or which the person disseminating the same believes will, or which he intends to, prevail upon, indoctrinate, convert, induce, or in any other way influence a recipient or any section of the public within the United States with reference to the political or public interests, policies, or relations of a government of a foreign country or a foreign political party or with reference to foreign policies of the United States or to promote in the United States racial, religious, or social dissensions, or (2) which advocates, advises, instigates, or promotes any racial, social, political, or religious disorder, civil riot, or other conflict involving the use of force or violence. As used in this subsection the term "disseminating" includes transmitting or causing to be transmitted in the United States mails or by means of instrumentality of interstate or foreign commerce or offering or causing to be offered in the United States mails.

Despite FARA, the number of lobbyists engaged in political PUBLIC RELATIONS (PR) operations on behalf of foreign countries has continued to increase, although the registered numbers are not impressive (in 1944 an average of 160 foreign lobbyists were on the rolls, with 850 in 1985). The largest influence peddling blitz's linked to foreign governments have been costly—but effective. In a scandal that American NEWS organizations touted as "Koreagate," South Korean rice broker Tongsun Park admitted he had close relations with thirty-one members of Congress, who received an estimated $850,000 in gifts and cash from him between 1967 and 1977. In 1987, after a Japanese firm illegally exported high-technology equipment to the Soviet Union, other Japanese corporations spent $9 million as part of a

LOBBYING/LOBBYIST drive to prevent legislative retaliation by Congress. The largest public relations agency in Washington, D.C. (Hill & Knowlton) was given $10 million by the Kuwaiti government in 1990 through a front group known as "Citizens for a Free Kuwait." The real purpose for such spending was to persuade Americans to throw their support behind military intervention in the Persian Gulf in order to restore the Kuwaiti monarchy. The pro-NAFTA campaign spearheaded by Mexican government and Mexican business groups in 1993 spent over $25 million in persuading Congress to endorse the NAFTA trade pact. Because of instances such as these and many others of lesser magnitude, General Accounting Office (GAO) investigators recently concluded that the U.S. Justice Department has been negligent in enforcing the FARA. The GAO said that Justice officials lacked the will to meaningfully prosecute violators and thus failed to appropriate needed resources to adequately monitor foreign agents' activities. See also ADVOCACY ADVERTISING, AGENDA SETTING, AGENTS/AGENCIES OF INFLUENCE, AGITATION, AGITPROP, ASSETS, BLOWBACK, COMMUNISM/COMMUNIST, DEMONIZING THE OPPOSITION, DESERT SHIELD, DISINFORMATION (*DEZINFORMATSIA*), FALSE FLAG OPERATIONS, FASCISM/FASCIST, FIRST AMENDMENT, FRONT GROUPS/SATELLITE ORGANIZATIONS, GERMANOPHOBIA, GRASSROOTS LOBBYING, HIDDEN AGENDA, HOUSE UN-AMERICAN ACTIVITIES COMMITTEE (HUAC), INDOCTRINATION, INTELLIGENCE COMMUNITY, IRISH NORTHERN AID COMMITTEE (NORAID), ISOLATIONIST, NATIONAL SOCIALISM/NAZISM, PUBLIC INTEREST, and VIDEO NEWS RELEASE (VNR).

FOREIGN AID—The provision of "humanitarian" and military resources from one nation to assist another in pursuit of foreign policy goals. Included are monetary grants, loans, gifts and sales of military equipment, advisors, volunteers, and cultural exchanges. COVERT activities and COUNTERINSURGENCY aid are often cloaked under these transactions, which also are noted for their waste and fraud. The "B.C." comic strip only half-jokingly refers to the practice as "the transfer of money from poor people in rich countries to rich people in poor countries." See also COVERT ACTION, GLOBALISM, and NEOLIBERALISM.

FOUNDATIONS—Tax-free entities authorized under law for charitable and educational purposes, funded by wealthy individuals, families, multiple contributors, organizations, or corporations. Earnings from investments are distributed through research grants, seminars, communications programs, and other mechanisms. Because they tend to have resources, focus on a specific issue or cause, are ACTIVISTS involved in the PUBLIC POLICY PROCESS, and provide respectable SOCIAL ENGINEERING fronts for other interests, foundations are often highly effective as PROPAGANDA vehicles. See also AGENDA SETTING, AGENTS/AGENCIES OF INFLUENCE, ASSETS, BELTWAY BANDITS, FRONT GROUPS/SATELLITE ORGANIZATIONS, HIDDEN AGENDA, THINK TANKS, and UMBRELLA ORGANIZATIONS.

FOUR P's OF THE MARKETING MIX—Classification scheme popularized by E. Jerome McCarthy used by marketers as the framework for much of their decision-making. The categories include: *Product* (its design and development, branding, and packaging), *Place* (including available distribution channels and extent of market coverage), *Price* (its cost to produce, selling price, and profitability), and *Promotion* (incorporating personal selling, ADVERTISING, sales PROMOTION, direct-response, PUBLICITY, and public relations as forms of integrated marketing communications). This, unfortunately, tends to overemphasize product marketing to the neglect of SOCIAL MARKETING, ISSUES MANAGEMENT, and ADVOCACY ADVERTISING. PUBLIC RELATIONS (PR) practitioners are particularly critical of this schema as well, since public relations is treated simply as a promotional subset of marketing communications in the minds of many advertisers, neglecting the practice's much broader range of purposes and activities. Also lacking is the critical fifth "P" of *Public Policy* (more evidence of the neglect in this model of many advocacy and regulatory concerns). See also DIRECT MARKETING (DM), DIRECT-RESPONSE (DR) ADVERTISING, and PUBLIC POLICY PROCESS.

FOURTH ESTATE—The NEWS MEDIA as a check on government. Its usage dates back to eighteenth-century Britain when Irish statesman Edmund Burke, during one of his masterly debate orations in the House of Commons, turned to the Reporters Gallery in Parliament, pointed, and dramatically declared: "There is an Estate more potent than any!" This speech delivered in 1780 led others to use the term "Fourth Estate" to refer to the journalistic profession. The other three classes or "estates" of English society were the Lords Spiritual (the clergy), the Lords Temporal (the nobility), and the Commons (the bourgeoisie middle class and laboring lower classes).

FRAMING DEVICES—According to Todd Gitlin in *The Whole World Is Watching: Mass Media in the Making and Unmaking of the New Left* (1980, p. 7), frames are "persistent patterns of cognition, interpretation, and presentation, or selection, emphasis, and exclusion, by which symbol-handlers routinely organize discourse, whether verbal or visual." Framing devices then are narrative mechanisms which condition audience reactions to particular NEWS, information, or entertainment media programming. They include *contextualizing* (how fully the background is developed and through which interpretive lens this information is filtered), *demonizing* (how pervasive the use of "good versus evil" categorizing language and images are in elevating or deflating particular persons, organizations, MOVEMENTs, ideas, or nations), *equalizing* (how puffed up or deflated are the sides in terms of their implicit strength or importance, especially when contrasted with one another), *excising* (what information is left in or taken out and why), *ordering* (how the narrative is organized to favor one or another side) *personalizing* (how humanly are the protagonists developed and are they portrayed as "others" or "like us"), *sanitizing* (how censored is negative information about real costs in damaged lives and social devastation); and *timing* (how much attention is devoted to a particular agenda, issue, or group). See also AD HOMINEM ATTACK, AGENDA SETTING, CENSORSHIP, CONVENTIONAL WISDOM,

DEMONIZING THE OPPOSITION, DESERT SHIELD, FACT SLINGING, HATE CAMPAIGNS, MEDIA BIAS, NEWS VALUES, OFF THE NEWS, PREFERENTIAL SOURCING, PROPAGANDA DEVICES, RITUAL DEFAMATION, and THOUGHT-STOPPING CLICHÉ.

FREEDOM OF THE PRESS—See FIRST AMENDMENT and FREE SPEECH.

FREE SPEECH—The right to express oneself without fear of governmental harassment or violence is an essential component of true individual freedom. This ideal is part of America's CIVIL RELIGION but has rarely been achieved anywhere in the world, largely because humans do not particularly enjoy criticism. Certainly not everyone believes in unfettered speech, even though the FIRST AMENDMENT to the U.S. Constitution clearly reads, "Congress shall make no law . . . abridging the freedom of speech, or of the press." This absolutist language has been undercut by the courts and members of other institutions willing to accept the notion that a "compelling" government or PUBLIC INTEREST can legitimately override certain forms of expression and regulate media. Laws and regulations dealing with SEDITION, libel, pornography, ADVERTISING, copyright and a host of other areas are examples of the widespread nature of restrictions on what can be communicated. In fact, surveys show most people are willing to grant free speech privileges to those individuals and groups espousing views they favor, but prefer CENSORSHIP of expression they disagree with. Many of those preferring some form of restriction on speech and the PRESS do so on the basis of righting an inequity by taking a *receiver rights*-oriented (rather than the traditional *sender rights*-oriented) approach to controversial issues. For example, it has been argued that "traditionally oppressed groups" which undergo continuing "symbolic abuse" through derogatory social stereotypes are effectively de-legitimized as "social actors." This view believes that not only are members of such groups socially devalued, but their efforts to overcome prejudices are irreparably hampered in a free speech environment. This is because outsiders/nonmembers targeted by the disenfranchised already hold pre-existing mental stigmas which limit their ability to respond fairly and openly to the pleas of the "oppressed." The implication is that by granting complete freedom of speech to everyone, vulnerable groups will be made even more susceptible to marginalization as their attempts to communicate are tainted by social stereotypes and limited resources. This bleak view is countered by those arguing that the only way to avoid new inequities and oppression is through a truly free "marketplace of ideas" which will eventually allow better and truer speech to emerge than any government-regulated one. As John Stuart Mill wrote in his classic *On Liberty*, "If all mankind minus one, were of one opinion, and only one person were of the contrary opinion, mankind would be no more justified in silencing that one person, than he, if he had the power, would be justified in silencing mankind." See also FRAMING DEVICES, FREETHINKERS, HATE SPEECH, LIBERTARIAN, MEDIA/MEDIUM, and SEDITIOUS LIBEL.

FREETHINKERS—Individuals who reject DOGMA and the imposition of arbitrary authority, particularly in the areas of religion and social policy. Most prominent American freethinkers of the eighteenth-century were deists, such as Thomas Paine, who affirmed belief in natural religion but rejected a personal God of divine revelation. Later leaders of the American freethought MOVEMENT, such as Abner Kneeland and Robert Ingersoll, consistently urged political and religious tolerance, weighing in on the side of FREE SPEECH rights and church-state separation. Such LIBERTARIAN views have often been treated as a type of POLITICAL CRIME, with freethinkers in the United States and elsewhere subjected to prosecution under blasphemy, seditious blasphemy, and SEDITIOUS LIBEL laws. Freethinkers of all stripes can be found today, although many define themselves as atheists, agnostics, secular humanists, or libertarians. See also CENSORSHIP, CIVIL RELIGION, HUMAN NATURE, HUMAN RIGHTS, IDEOLOGY, and LIBERTARIAN.

FREE TRADE—Political and economic philosophy in the laissez-faire CAPITALISM/CAPITALIST tradition that supports cross-border investments favorable to TRANSNATIONAL CORPORATIONS (TNCs) and favors the elimination of government-imposed border restrictions such as import licenses, quotas, and tariffs on imported goods. The classic proponent of such views was Adam Smith, whose *An Inquiry into the Nature and Causes of the Wealth of Nations* (first published in 1776) is still widely read. Those who advocate the alternative philosophy of "FAIR TRADE" want to maintain protectionism barriers in order to protect domestic manufacturing and jobs from cheaper imports.

FREE WORLD—A PROPAGANDA slogan used to refer to the United States and its allies, whether democracies or benevolent dictatorships, when comparing the regimes in these countries to Communist or Fascist opponents. Generally, when leaders of the "Free World" speak of "freedom" or "DEMOCRACY," what is generally meant is the PROMOTION of values and policies conducive to their international interests. See also COMMUNISM/COMMUNIST and FASCISM/FASCIST.

FRIENDLY SUBVERSION—An ideological and cultural "invasion" ranging from language to politics, music to Coca-Cola, that occurs when the values and systems used by another country (often more economically or militarily powerful) appear domestically in another nation under the guise of education and entertainment. This co-optation may be a form of purposeful development, but often results from the intersection that occurs when a dynamic society actively exports a culture which proves popular beyond its borders. Those that oppose adapting themselves seek to "decipher the codes" in order to propagandize the fight against such CULTURAL IMPERIALISM.

FRONT GROUPS/SATELLITE ORGANIZATIONS—Various legal entities, FOUNDATIONS, THINK TANKS, citizens committees, COALITIONs, and "innocents"—any independent organization that becomes an "agency of influence" to its constituencies by unwittingly coming under the dominance of others holding a different HIDDEN AGENDA. See also

AGENTS/AGENCIES OF INFLUENCE, PAWNS, POLITICAL ACTION COMMITTEES (PACs), POPULAR FRONT/PEOPLE'S FRONT, PRESSURE GROUPS, and UMBRELLA ORGANIZATIONS.

FUNDAMENTALISM/FUNDAMENTALIST—The term *fundamentalism* stems from U.S. religious history, specifically an early twentieth-century publication called *The Fundamentals: A Testimony to Truth*, edited by George M. Marsden. This reflected the views of conservative Protestants who believed their churches had strayed too far from belief in the literal truth of the Bible. Today, fundamentalism has come to be applied to any religious group whose leaders hearken back to presumed fundamental principles in order to combat the negative influences of modernism, relativism, pluralism, and/or the imperialism that accompanied Westernization. Generally, the term is applied negatively to imply antiscientific bigotry. For example, members of the Christian Right have received widespread media criticism for allegedly utilizing EXTREMIST methods that synthesize Old Testament ethics and sophisticated PROPAGANDA techniques, all in the name of pursuing good intentions.

However, it can be equally argued that fundamentalists are making positive moral contributions at a time when there is a growing loss of confidence over the roles played by the dominant scientific and technological establishments. Indeed, the criticisms of modern society articulated by the more militant fundamentalists have proven attractive to many people, with the membership in such organizations on the upswing. See also CIVIL RELIGION, DEMONIZING THE OPPOSITION, IDEOLOGUES, IMPERIALISM/IMPERIALIST, and POLITICALLY CORRECT (PC).

GATEKEEPER—Person in an influential position to bottleneck or pass through information. In a media context, a gatekeeper is someone with editorial control over what is printed or aired. See also AGENDA SETTING.

GENOCIDE—A word invented in 1943 by Polish Jewish legalist Raphael Lemkin to describe state destruction, in whole or in part, of an identifiable ethnic, racial, or religious group. This has come to be equated with mass murder. See also ETHNIC CLEANSING, HATE CRIME LEGISLATION, and SCAPEGOAT/SCAPEGOATING.

GERMANOPHOBIA—Hatred or fear of Germany, German culture, and the German people. Germanophobia is a form of scapegoating often fanned by PROPAGANDA emanating from other nations and ethnic groups whose economic and political interests conflict with those of Germany. See also SCAPEGOAT/SCAPEGOATING.

GLASNOST—A Russian term having the dual meaning of "openness" and "PUBLICITY," *Glasnost* was employed by Soviet leader Mikhail Gorbachev during his term of office as part of the *PERESTROIKA* ("restructuring") effort to save communism by allowing limited internal reforms and more public participation in decision-making. Gorbachev also used *glasnost* to describe his approach to creating a new dialogue with other countries. Anti-MARXISTs warned that the "openness" was part of a PUBLIC RELATIONS (PR) campaign to gain moral equivalency with the FREE WORLD rather than reflective of any desire by the Soviet leadership for deep-seated changes in their totalitarian society. The forces unleashed, however, took on a life of their own. See also COLD WAR, COMMUNISM/COMMUNIST, and TOTALITARIANISM.

GLITTERING GENERALITY—See PROPAGANDA DEVICES.

GLOBALISM—In anarchist thought, a decentralized social and economic system where nation states will become a thing of the past that will come about through righteous antiauthoritarian struggle and an evolving culture of mutual understanding. Constitutionalists, nationalists, and some conspiracists, on the other hand, define globalism differently. They see it as a dangerous internationalist philosophy promoted by those who would subvert individual liberty for their own gain since many in the world federalism MOVEMENT are committed to the "selective withering" of national sovereignty. As a result, globalist promises to create a "new world order" with a transnational government whose powers supersede those of nation states often take on an Orwellian "Big Brother" rather than utopian tone. Ironically, the terms *new order* and *new world order* have been used by politicians ranging from Nazis to Republicans. For example, when U.S. officials promote a "new world order," they are really speaking of the acceptance of a transnational power with its headquarters in Washington, D.C. See also ANARCHISM/ANARCHIST, ANTIAUTHORITARIANISM, BILDERBERGER GROUP, CONSPIRACY THEORIES, COUNCIL ON FOREIGN RELATIONS (CFR), DYSTOPIA, INTERVENTIONIST, NAFTA, NATIONAL SOCIALISM/NAZISM, NEOLIBERALISM, ORWELLIAN TACTICS, SURRENDER LOBBY, TRANSNATIONAL CORPORATIONS (TNCs), and TRILATERAL COMMISSION.

GLOBAL VILLAGE—A famous pop culture phrase created by Canadian media theorist Marshall McLuhan to refer to technological advances which make the transfer of communication messages around the world as easy as sending them across town.

GOVERNMENT RELATIONS—See PUBLIC AFFAIRS.

GRANFALLOONS—Term created by novelist Kurt Vonnegut, and now being used by social psychologists, to refer to "proud and meaningless associations of human beings." The implication for PROPAGANDA involves a willingness of people to give preferences to others based on a sense of common association, even when such linkages are artificial and lack long-term importance. See also INTEREST GROUPS.

GRASSROOTS LOBBYING—Attempts by corporations, PUBLIC INTEREST groups, and other advocacy organizations to influence the PUBLIC POLICY PROCESS by reaching out to a broad spectrum of individuals, providing useful information, building awareness via appearances in media, and encouraging communication by affected publics with their legislators. The U.S. Congress has made a distinction between such indirect lobbying through grassroots contact (which members do not like much) and more conventional direct interaction with professional lobbyists (which they clearly prefer). Linked to this are worries over DEEP POCKETS SPENDING by business interests and continuing congressional attempts to reimpose regulatory content controls on broadcasting, such as the FAIRNESS DOCTRINE, in order to promote the HIDDEN AGENDA of suppressing RADICAL speech and reining in political criticism from local and national radio talk show hosts such as Rush Limbaugh.

Controversy also springs from the inherent conflict within Internal Revenue Service Regulations based on IRS Code Section 162(e)(2) between paragraph (a) which allows the deduction of expenses to present "views on economic, financial, social, or other subjects of a general nature" and (b) which specifically prohibits the deduction of any amount paid or incurred "in connection with any attempt to influence the general public, or segments thereof, with respect to legislative matters, elections or referendums." This code language is translated by the authorities into IRS Regulation 162-20 (b) as nondeductible if "for the promotion or defeat of legislation, for political campaign purposes . . . , or for carrying on propaganda (including advertising) related to any of the foregoing purposes." The regulations further provide that "no deduction shall be allowed for any expenses incurred in connection with 'grassroots' campaigns or any other attempts to urge or encourage the public to contact members of a legislative body for the purpose of proposing, supporting or opposing legislation." Legislative matters are not defined, but "legislation or proposed legislation" is described as bills and resolutions which are the business of Congress, state, or local legislatures.

Various forms of indirect lobbying through GRASSROOTS POLITICAL ACTION continue to be popular communications strategies because they provide a vehicle which any organization can use to mobilize important third-party endorsements if it successfully taps into popular feelings. Some PUBLIC RELATIONS firms even specialize in creating "astroturf" (or bogus grassroots citizen) campaigns to push for legislation. See also ADVOCACY ADVERTISING, COALITION, GRASSTOPS, ISSUES MANAGEMENT, and LOBBYING/LOBBYIST.

GRASSROOTS POLITICAL ACTION—As defined by Joseph Nagelschmidt in the glossary of *The Public Affairs Handbook* (1982, p. 289), grassroots political action involves "Providing elected officials or candidates for elective office practical assistance in their home constituencies; communicating with elective or appointive officials on issues that affect their home constituency; involvement in the political process at the local level." See also GRASSROOTS LOBBYING and LOBBYING/LOBBYIST.

GRASSTOPS—Individuals who contract their services to lobby members of Congress or state government on their home turf rather than in Washington, D.C., or the state capital. Typically, grasstops work for a major national corporation or trade association. They perform many duties, especially arranging meetings between legislators and members of various local organizations in their districts friendly to the agenda of the grasstops' employer. See also COALITION, GRASSROOTS LOBBYING and LOBBYING/LOBBYIST.

GRAY/GREY LITERATURE—For those interested in being at the forefront of the emerging INFORMATION AGE/INFORMATION SOCIETY, being able to find, analyze, and implement knowledge becomes a key factor in determining success. This is especially true for governments, organizations, and individuals seeking to supplement their other efforts designed to establish and maintain HEGEMONY. Intelligence gathering today is thus less a matter of penetrating secrets and more a matter of separating useful information from the flood of published materials that are available legally and cheaply. Within the INTELLIGENCE COMMUNITY this is known as open source intelligence or OSCINT. Open (unclassified) electronic data, such as that available through the INTERNET and related file servers and on-line newsgroups, is also included in OSCINT. The vast majority of information, including scientific and technical reports, used in OSCINT and other forms of intelligence is designated as *gray literature*. While the term has many definitions, that by Robert D. Steele, president of Open Source Solutions, Inc., given in a talk to the Foreign Acquisition Workshop (1993) is among the most cogent. Gray literature, he says, is "All material, in whatever medium and whatever language, that is unclassified in all respects, but published in a limited edition for a limited audience. It is the demilitarized zone, the DMZ, between a national intelligence community in the throes of dissolution, and the 'rest of government.'"

GRAY/GREY PROPAGANDA—Forms of PROPAGANDA located between WHITE PROPAGANDA and BLACK PROPAGANDA in which truth and falsity are mixed. The source may or may not be accurately presented and the correctness of the information promulgated is not ascertainable.

GREAT WAR—What we now refer to as World War I (1914-1918) was originally called the "Great War" by contemporaries.

GROSS RATINGS POINTS (GRPs)—Term used by the ADVERTISING industry to measure the total number of impressions delivered by a media schedule, expressed as a percentage of the targeted population. A collective total of one-hundred GRPs is not equal to the entire market audience, however, since the figure includes multiple duplicate exposures. See also REACH.

GRU (*Glavnoye Razvedyvatelnoye Upravlenie*)—The Chief Intelligence Directorate of the Soviet General Staff, the military counterpart to the KGB (*Komitet po Gosudarstvennoy Bezopasnosti*) or Committee for State Security.

HANDLERS—Professional consultants whose job it is to shape their clients' public persona and keep them from making gaffes. Often used in the context of political campaign advisors. See also SPIN CONTROL and SPIN DOCTORS.

HANDOUT JOURNALISM—Derogatory term referring to journalists serving as a PROPAGANDA conduit because of their dependency upon government and other sources to feed them information requiring little original reporting skills. See also JOURNALISM/JOURNALIST and PACK JOURNALISM.

HATE CAMPAIGN—The POLEMICal shaping of PUBLIC OPINION by emphasizing negative elements about organizations or individuals opposed to the propagandist while also stressing one's own moral correctness. Hate campaigns are about DEMONIZING THE OPPOSITION, neutralizing the potential impact of the targeted victim, and using calumny, half-truths and negative associations to effectively engage in AGENDA SETTING on one's own terms. See also HATE SPEECH, SPIRAL OF SILENCE, and THOUGHT-STOPPING CLICHÉ.

HATE CRIME LEGISLATION—Laws in many countries ranging from Argentina to Canada provide for fines and imprisonment for anyone who commits a "hate crime." Obvious TERRORIST acts by HATE GROUPS based on racial, religious, or ideological creed are banned. However, such legislation typically also lists as "hate crimes" the act of distributing any publication or belonging to any organization which promotes the superiority of one race or religion over another. Despite pressure by powerful LOBBYING/LOBBYIST groups such as the ANTI-DEFAMATION LEAGUE OF B'NAI B'RITH (ADL), similar sweeping provisions have not been enacted in the United States. The major reason is that restrictions on belief, association, and speech (as compared to other more overt acts) conflict with FIRST AMENDMENT guarantees embedded in the U.S. Constitution, which protect the expression of minority and extremist viewpoints. In a series of cases, the Supreme Court has made a clear distinction between thought and peaceful expression (protected speech) and criminal applications of prejudicial motivations resulting in violent acts (not protected). See also ETHNIC CLEANSING, GENOCIDE, HATE CAMPAIGN, HATE SPEECH, REVISIONISM/REVISIONIST, and SCAPEGOAT/SCAPEGOATING.

HATE GROUPS—Advocacy organization largely defined by who or what its members oppose in contrast to what they favor. Ironically, many hate groups are identified, monitored, and criticized by other hate groups (which would be outraged at the label, but nevertheless feed off the hardened hearts they carry, their desire for vengeance, and the continued hatred they feel toward their opponents). See also HATE CRIME LEGISLATION, HATE SPEECH, INTEREST GROUPS, POLITICALLY CORRECT (PC), and PRESSURE GROUPS.

HATE SPEECH—Proponents of "hate speech" regulation regard it as verbal, written, or physical behavior attacking an individual or group on the basis of who they are. The distinctions between thought and action and between the peaceful and the violent are irrelevant to many favoring enactment of such regulations, but have proved crucial to U.S. courts concerned about the FIRST AMENDMENT or Canadian courts charged with interpreting that nation's Charter of Rights. The more narrowly drawn, but still controversial, FREE

SPEECH and harassment policy adopted by Stanford University in June 1990 said:

Speech or any other expression constitutes harassment by personal vilification if it: (a) is intended to insult or stigmatize an individual or a small number of individuals on the basis of their sex, race, color, handicap, religion, sexual orientation, or national and ethnic origin, and (b) is addressed directly to the individual or individuals whom it insults or stigmatizes, and (c) makes use of insulting or fighting words or non-verbal symbols.

Such speech, by its very utterance, inflicts injury or tends to incite an immediate breach of the peace. These are words commonly understood to convey hatred or contempt toward people. However, after judicial review, even the Stanford policy was overturned. The decision followed an earlier U.S. District Court ruling which struck down a similar "speech rule" at the University of Wisconsin in 1991 as a too draconian extension of CENSORSHIP beyond the present scope of the "fighting words" doctrine. In several recent cases the U.S. Supreme Court has made a distinction between expression (which is protected) and criminal acts (which are not). Speech becomes unprotected—punishable by law—when a causal link to unlawful conduct can be established. Thus burning a cross or painting a swastika on one's own property, for example, are likely legal statements of political opinion while committing those same acts on someone else's property without permission are not. See also ANTI-SEMITIC, HATE CRIME LEGISLATION, HATE CAMPAIGN, HATE GROUPS, HEGEMONY, HUMAN RIGHTS, INDOCTRINATION, POLITICALLY CORRECT (PC), REVISIONISM/REVISIONIST, SCAPEGOAT/SCAPEGOATING, and SPIRAL OF SILENCE.

HEARTS AND MINDS CAMPAIGN—A COUNTERINSURGENCY strategy utilized by the U.S. military in Vietnam and subsequently applied through military assistance programs to other nations facing armed guerrilla operations. The winning of the populace's "hearts and minds" typically involves the setting up of strategic village safe havens in the conflict zones, particularly in the countryside where the majority of the people often live. Progovernment/antirebel AGITATION and PROPAGANDA "educational" communications are pronounced, supplemented by special government-supported social service programs. These efforts help to cut "enemy" access and force the insurgents into violence and other brutalities which turn the people against them. In recent years, the private evangelism and relief efforts of Christian fundamentalists active in Latin America and other regions have been supported by authoritarian and fledgling democratic governments to achieve the same objective by serving as a barrier against inroads by communist propaganda. See also ACTIVE MEASURES, AGITPROP, ARMED PROPAGANDA, COMMUNISM/COMMUNIST, COVERT ACTION, FUNDAMENTALISM/FUNDAMENTALIST, HEGEMONY, HUMAN RIGHTS, and INSURRECTION/ INSURRECTIONARY.

HEGEMONY—The processes by which ruling classes or groups ("the elite") shape popular consent. They do this by influencing the production and diffusion of meanings, values, and beliefs through control of the major informational institutions. Theorists in this area often assert that the mass media in particular reflect the interests of the powerful. Ideological determinists believe that the system of mass-distributed NEWS, for example, is structurally aligned to allow government and dominant private interests to get their messages out to the public. See also ANTI-SEMITIC and ELITE THEORY.

HEURISTIC—A heuristic, according to the definition by Anthony Pratkanis and Elliot Aronson in their *Age of Propaganda: The Everyday Use and Abuse of Persuasion* (1992), is "a simple cue or rule for solving a problem." In social psychology, the mass persuader uses heuristics such as the implied credibility of the message sender, the use of audience-appropriate buzzwords, and/or the band wagoning effect of social consensus as aids for increasing the likelihood the PROPAGANDA will be believed. See also PROPAGANDA DEVICES.

HIDDEN AGENDA—A COVERT motive or set of motivations masked for public consumption by an ostensibly moral purpose.

HIDDEN PERSUADERS—A term coined by Vance Packard in his book, *The Hidden Persuaders* (1957), to refer to the background psychological and social role played by PUBLIC RELATIONS (PR) in creating information HOOKS and influencing the PUBLIC POLICY PROCESS.

HILL, THE—Colloquial expression meaning the U.S. Congress, from Capitol Hill where the Senate and House of Representatives meet.

HOOKS—Those elements of a persuasive message that attract the attention and build the interest of target audience members. This can be centered around a "Unique Selling Proposition" that differentiates the sender from competitors by pointing to a compelling benefit important to the receiver and specific to the advertised product, service or idea. Alternatively, spectacular imagery, sound effects, and/or other attention-getting PROPAGANDA DEVICES can be used to break through media clutter and play upon psychological motives. Later, other confidence-building elements can be built in to reinforce credibility as the persuasive appeal builds momentum to a call for action. See also ADVERTISING, A-I-D-C-A FORMULA, and PSYCHOGRAPHICS.

HOT SWITCHING—The relatively recent BROADCASTING practice of immediately transferring from one television program to another without commercial interruption. The purpose of hot switching is to maintain audience "flow" from one time period to another by avoiding a break which could result in audience tune-out. In radio, this is known as "segue." See also LEAST OBJECTIONABLE PROGRAMMING (LOP) THEORY.

HOUSE UN-AMERICAN ACTIVITIES COMMITTEE (HUAC)—An investigative body of the U.S. Congress, most active from the 1930s through the 1960s, which served as a COLD WAR forum for those opposed to communism, fascism, and proponents of other "isms" besides 100 percent Americanism. Many of the reports it issued are useful and authoritative references, but the Committee's work was often sidetracked by grandstanding Congressmen into circus-like hearings on the HILL. At first the media attention given these investigations successfully spawned anticommunist repression, but wild allegations and bullying abuses ultimately proved so excessive that HUAC was downgraded and eventually disbanded. See also AMERICA FIRST, BILL OF RIGHTS, COMMUNISM/COMMUNIST, DEMAGOGUE/DEMAGOGISM, FASCISM/FASCIST, McCARTHYISM, and PROFESSIONAL PATRIOTS.

HUMAN NATURE—One reason for differing political traditions stems from a conflicting understanding of human motivations. Proponents of various ideologies disagree over whether people are basically good, basically evil, or a flawed mixture of contradictory impulses and behaviors. For example, Nigel Ashford and Stephen Davies, the editors of *A Dictionary of Conservative and Libertarian Thought* (1991), observed:

Classical liberalism and conservatism exemplify sharply contrasting views of human nature. Indeed, it could be said that the differences between the two political philosophies resolve into differences in beliefs about the powers, limitations, and prospects of human beings. On the view of the classical liberal, in order to flourish human nature needs to be emancipated from a multiplicity of social, cultural, and religious hindrances. Among the most noteworthy of these are restrictions on free trade, class structure, national boundaries, and religious dogmatism. The fact that such hindrances have grown up as a result of human activity, and therefore show human nature at work, is only partly recognized by the [classical] liberal.

See also CLASSICAL LIBERAL, FREE TRADE, HUMAN RIGHTS, LEFT-WING/LIBERAL, LIBERTARIAN, MACHIAVELLIAN, and RIGHT-WING/CONSERVATIVE.

HUMAN RIGHTS—Universal principles and specific constitutional protections involving the exercise of freedom of association and related behaviors without having to first receive government approval. At present there are no effective hemispheric, let alone global, bills of rights to protect such actions. For while human rights policies and practices by governments are subject to law, enforcement is often lax unless publicity is evident. Violations are most evident in states where political opposition is not tolerated and dissent in any form is repressed. People engaging in activities deemed to be detrimental to the "stability and unity" of the country—such as political dissidents and members of ethnic or religious groups—continue to be harassed by police, detained or imprisoned, and often badly treated and subject to torture. The Arms Export Control Act prohibits the U.S. government from selling weapons or granting licenses for commercial arms sales to countries with a consistent pattern of gross violations of human rights.

Principles of human rights protection have been established in international law, including agreements such as the International Covenant on Civil and Political Rights (ICCPR) and UNIVERSAL DECLARATION OF HUMAN RIGHTS adopted by the UNITED NATIONS ORGANIZATION

(UNO or UN) and the American Convention on Human Rights of the Organization of American States. These instruments stipulate that even in time of war, public danger, or other emergency that threatens the independence or security of a party state, governments are obliged to protect certain fundamental rights, including the rights to life, physical security and judicial guarantees essential to maintain these rights, such as habeas corpus.

Other agreements of note include the International Covenant on Economic, Social and Cultural Rights and three other treaties drafted by the International Labor Organization pertaining to international due process which would guarantee workers the right to organize free labor unions and engage in collective bargaining without suffering discrimination from either the state or management. The European Convention for the Protection of Human Rights and Fundamental Freedoms (first signed in 1950, effective from 1953 onward) falls short of provisions found in the FIRST AMENDMENT, but nevertheless guarantees freedom of expression under Article 10, including the right "to hold opinions and to receive and impart information and ideas without interference by public authority and regardless of frontiers."

Independent human rights watchdog NONGOVERNMENTAL ORGANIZATIONS (NGOs) noted for their activism include the American Civil Liberties Union (ACLU), Amnesty International (AI), ARTICLE 19 International Centre Against Censorship, Center for Constitutional Rights, the Congressional Human Rights Foundation, Freedom House, Helsinki Watch, Human Rights Advocates, International Human Rights Law Group, International League for Human Rights, Meiklejohn Civil Liberties Institute, and Minnesota Advocates for Human Rights. Amnesty International, for example, urges governments to ensure that these basic human rights are not abrogated and to guarantee the personal safety of any persons already detained, including protecting them from extrajudicial executions, "disappearance," and torture or other cruel, inhuman or degrading treatment. AI encourages the immediate and unconditional release of anyone arrested for their conscientiously held beliefs and who are known not to have used or advocated violence. Toward this end, AI strongly urges political leaderships after coups or during states of emergency to immediately issue a public directive to the security forces stating that the human rights of all citizens, including human rights defenders, are to be fully protected and that any infractions of human rights standards are intolerable and will be severely punished. Amnesty International also calls for information to be made public concerning all those detained, and for any individuals in custody to be permitted access to their families and to legal representation.

According to traditional human rights analysis, only the state violates human rights. This notion is being increasingly challenged by human rights ACTIVISTS and organizations, particularly from developing nations of the THIRD WORLD. One area of human rights work where this is changing rapidly is that of economic and social rights. Organizations such as Radio For Peace International argue that not only does the state have the capacity to violate these rights, but this is also true of large TRANSNATIONAL CORPORATIONS (TNCs), international private banks, and inter-governmental institutions such as the World Bank (WB), Inter-American Development Bank (IADB), and the International Monetary Fund (IMF) based in Washington, D.C. The reason that these international commercial and financial "actors" must be considered as potential human rights violators is that in many, if not most, developing world nations in which they operate, have more economic and commercial power than the dependent nation. Holding such resources, they can effectively demand changes in national policies with the possibility for increased violations of human rights. While development is generally seen as good, there are instances where intensive military operations, propagandistic deceit and harassment have been employed by governments and foreign investors to pave the way for corrupt practices in the name of countrywide "economic progress." Unless "First World" watchdogs, media organizations and politicians become actively interested in reporting the real power and actions of these institutions, there is little or no built-in direct accountability to the people of the countries they operate in. See also BILL OF RIGHTS, DESERT SHIELD, HATE CRIME LEGISLATION, HATE SPEECH, NEOLIBERALISM, NEW WORLD INFORMATION AND COMMUNICATION ORDER (NWICO) DEBATE, PAWNS, and UNIVERSAL DECLARATION OF HUMAN RIGHTS.

HYPE—Bombastic hoopla and oversell, often associated with the excesses of PRESS AGENTRY and PUBLICITY.

HYPODERMIC NEEDLE THEORY—Early studies of MEDIA EFFECTS suggested they could greatly influence audiences, "injecting" readers, listeners, and viewers with a prepackaged set of beliefs and behavior. Scholars now believe this is only possible when the messages conform to public predispositions and where no competing arguments are found. See also COGNITIVE DISSONANCE and MAGIC BULLET THEORY.

IDEODYNAMICS—The name given by David P. Fan to his process of calculating the impact of persuasive information on a population. Using a physical science atomic structure analogy, he postulates that the MEDIA EFFECTS of persuasive messages can be coded as INFONs.

IDEOLOGUES—Individuals who formulate IDEOLOGY and/or reproduce social conventions (patterned codes of behavior) in an ideological package (book, article, poster, film, TV show, etc.) for mass consumption. According to Harold J. Vetter and Gary R. Perlstein's *Perspectives on Terrorism* (1991), ideologues are "individuals belonging to groups whose purpose is to bring about change in the social, economic, or political status quo"—although a conservative ideologue could just as well be committed to maintaining the status quo.

IDEOLOGY—This is a term used by authors in so many different ways that it causes tremendous confusion. There is general agreement, however, that the concept of ideology involves the use of ideas in the service of an interest. Giovani Sartori, in his essay "Politics, Ideology and Belief Systems" (*American Political Science Review*, June 1969, p. 411) highlights the importance of ideologies since they are the crucial lever at the disposal of elites for obtaining political mobilization and for maximizing the possibilities of mass manipulation. This, it seems . . . [is] the single major reason that ideology is so important. We are concerned about ideology because we are concerned, in the final analysis, with the power of man over man, with how populations and nations can be mobilized and manipulated all the along the way that leads to political messianism and fanaticism.

MARXISTs, for example, consider ideology a form of class-based BRAINWASHING in which the dominant power structure abuses its cultural HEGEMONY to propagate an illusory "false consciousness" to maintain its supremacy. They do this through direct and indirect control of key social institutions ranging from schools, political parties, and labor unions to churches and the media. The awareness of inequality is blunted when these instruments manufacture consensus by legitimizing as valid certain commonly accepted cultural "norms" and simultaneously suppressing alternative systems of thought. The exploited classes can break the political and economic "chains" controlling them only through resistance, including deconstruction of the "FRAMING DEVICES" and "codes" making up bourgeois ideology. Once the false ideology is demystified and the hegemonic PROPAGANDA becomes transparent, liberation can occur.

Non-Marxists tend to see ideology in terms of the foundational doctrines (values, beliefs, and governmental policies) which prevail in a society at a given time. Thus, the components of an ideology include a society's cultural traits, religious values, political institutions, and laws as they are historically formed. *Contemporary Political Ideologies* by Lyman Tower Sargent (1972) summarizes by defining an ideology as:

a value or belief system that is accepted as fact or truth by some group. It is composed of sets of attitudes toward the various institutions and processes of society. It provides the believer with a picture of the world both as it is and as it should be, and in so doing, it organizes the tremendous complexity of the world into something fairly simple and understandable.

Other scholars who have studied ideology and competitiveness suggest that every nation has at a minimum one dominant ideology, with several other alternative or congruent ideologies of importance also possible. Such a national ideology generally has the greatest influence over the way technology is developed and adopted. As Harold J. Vetter and Gary R. Perlstein conclude in their *Perspectives on Terrorism* (1991):

Ideology is a central element in the complex patterns of political change and stability. The term *ideology* has many meanings, but we use it here merely to refer to a set of general and abstract beliefs or assumptions about the proper state of things, particularly with regard to moral order and political arrangements, that shape one's positions on specific issues.

Ideologies wax and wane, but rarely die out completely. Indeed, governmental systems may well collapse, but principles live on. See also AGENDA SETTING, CULTURAL IMPERIALISM, ELITE THEORY, EXTREMISM, EXTREMIST, FACTION, FREE SPEECH, IDEOLOGUES,

INDOCTRINATION, ISSUE, MANUFACTURING OF CONSENT (or CONSENSUS), OFFICIAL IDEOLOGY, and PROPAGANDA DEVICES.

IMAGE ADVERTISING—Because images and ISSUEs are closely associated, Robert L. Heath and Richard Alan Nelson, authors of *Issues Management: Corporate Public Policymaking in an Information Society* (1986), suggest that the concept of image ADVERTISING should be treated as a circular continuum. The following list based on corporate examples points to the variety in types of advertisements created by sponsoring organizations:

- *Direct image*, through a favorable description of the company's products or services.
- *Direct image*, by providing facts about the company's or industry's operation.
- *Direct image*, through a favorable description of how a company's activities and policies agree with public expectations of acceptable corporate behavior.
- *Indirect image*, through a favorable description of the company's support of charitable, community service activities.
- *Indirect image*, by providing noncontroversial information of value to the public.
- *Indirect image*, through association with traditional values.
- *Indirect image*, through stands on social, economic, or financial issues by favoring a noncontroversial or popular point of view.
- *Indirect image*, through a favorable discussion of the need for corporations in general (implying the value of the sponsoring company in specific).
- *Indirect image*, through challenge of facts reported about a company or industry, attacking critics and answering criticism.
- *Indirect or direct image in issues idea advertisements*, by taking controversial stands on facts, values, or policy.
- *Indirect or direct image in issues action advertisements*, through calling for participation in the legislative and/or regulatory process.

These messages can appear in any MEDIA/MEDIUM.

IMPERIALISM/IMPERIALIST—Classical imperialism refers to the colonization of territories by subjecting indigenous people to foreign rule, often through military conquest and deception. While the phenomenon has existed ever since one nation lusted after another's wealth, imperialism is most associated with the efforts by the European powers to dominate the world. This can be traced to rivalries and disputes over Spanish claims in the Americas devolving from the expeditions of Columbus and other adventurers. The process of imperialistic expansion continued for over 450 years until well into the twentieth-century when, weakened by two world wars, a growing domestic commitment to democratic principles, and increasingly costly revolts by subjected peoples, the colonial empires of Britain, France, Spain, Italy, Germany, Belgium, and Portugal were dismantled. Political decolonialism, however, did not entirely lessen the interdependence of the newly freed states from "the mother/father lands." The United States tended to devote most of its expansionism in the nineteenth-century to continental MANIFEST DESTINY efforts evidenced by the Mexican War of 1848, war to prevent the secession of the Confederate States in the 1860s, and the purchase of Alaska. Later, though, the annexation of Hawaii, territories acquired as a result of the Spanish-American War of 1898, purchase of the Virgin Islands, and continuing interventions in Latin America pointed to homegrown "jingoistic" imperialist impulses. See also CULTURAL IMPERIALISM, HUMAN RIGHTS, IRISH NORTHERN AID COMMITTEE (NORAID), and PROGRESSIVE/PROGRESSIVISM.

INACTIVES—Persons who do not participate in social or political action, typically not even voting.

INDIRECT LOBBYING—See GRASSROOTS LOBBYING and LOBBYING/LOBBYIST.

INDOCTRINATION—The systematic presentation of a particular set of beliefs, often through control of schools, media, and so forth, by individuals, groups, and government agencies seeking to propagandize their ideologies. The aim of the indoctrination is to ensure that those exposed to it derive the proper attitudes and the proper conditioned reflexes. For example, school textbooks are crammed with manipulative materials mandated to be read by students that are designed to promote compliance with social "norms" of citizenship, belief and behavior. Positive indoctrination is an educational PROPAGANDA approach that when successful inoculates a population to competitive ideologies and thus frees the state from having to baldly emphasize coercion and repression as major pillars propping up the organization or government. See also BIG LIE, BRAINWASHING, COGNITIVE DISSONANCE, IDEOLOGUES, IDEOLOGY, PSYCHEDELICS, PSYCHOLOGICAL WARFARE (PSYWAR), and TAVISTOCK METHOD.

INDUSTRIAL THEATER—A form of marketing designed to motivate business people at corporate meetings and conventions, utilizing full-scale Broadway-style theatrical performances, complete with multi-image lasers and fireworks.

INDUSTRIAL WORKERS OF THE WORLD (IWW)—See WOBBLIES.

INFOMERCIAL—A program-length direct-response ADVERTORIAL aired on broadcast and cable stations. Informercials run fifteen minutes or more, with the half-hour time frame the most common. They usually use a NEWS, DOCUMENTARY, or talk show INFOTAINMENT format to interest viewers or listeners into purchasing the product/service being sold. The programs also feature complete ordering information, pricing and other incentives to "call *now*," and demonstrations/testimonials to reinforce credibility. When the same format is used to market an organization's image or an IDEOLOGY, the program is known as a "documercial." Political documercial formats are also specialized types of POLISPOTS. See also DIRECT-RESPONSE ADVERTISING, IMAGE ADVERTISING, INFOTAINMENT, and

PROPAGANDA DEVICES.

INFON—A measure of the persuasive impact of messages, used by David P. Fan in his IDEODYNAMICS process.

INFORMATION AGE/INFORMATION SOCIETY—These continue to be imprecise terms because they are used differently by various authors. One of the better attempts at definition remains that by Jerry L. Salvaggio, editor of *Telecommunications: Issues and Choices for Society* (1983, pp. 2-3), of a nation in which more than 50 percent of the adult population is tied into a "vast electronic telecommunications network" at home as well as at work. This means such individuals must be able to "transmit and receive NEWS, data, and entertainment through home telecommunications centers" and where "telebanking, telecourses, televoting, telemetering, telecommuting, telegames, and teleshopping are common." See also BROADCASTING, COMPUTER-MEDIATED COMMUNICATION (CMC), CYBERSPACE, ELECTRONIC COMMUNITY NETWORK, ELECTRONIC DEMOCRACY, GLOBAL VILLAGE, INFOMERCIAL, INTERNET, NATIONAL INFORMATION INFRASTRUCTURE (NII), and TELECOMMUNICATIONS.

INFOSHOPS—An infoshop is a hybrid between a RADICAL bookstore and a MOVEMENT archive. They are more prevalent in Europe, but have found a toehold in the United States. According to a media release by the progressive left-wing organization Slingshot (distributed on-line via the NY Transfer News Collective in 1994), ACTIVISTS go to infoshops to

> read or buy movement literature; buy paraphernalia such as stickers, masks and spray paint; attend meetings, lectures or films; or just plain hang out. . . . Many papers are produced at infoshops and distributed through the infoshop network. When urgent communication is needed, in cases of a state crackdown or fascist attack, infoshops can call or fax other infoshops who can then mobilize local activists. The infoshop network is an important part of autonomist left movements in many European countries. Infoshops meet twice a year [to] see what other groups are doing, exchange information, and discuss strategy and theory. Most infoshops rent their space, but many are in squats. Others use part of a cafe or center. Some are run by one collective, while others have a different group in charge each day. None of them have paid positions. Most infoshops have a women-only day either weekly or monthly. In addition to the groups running the infoshop, other groups use it as a meeting place, and as a mailing address. The latter is especially useful for security reasons. . . . because of fascists and police repression. . . . If the group has problems with their mail being opened or stolen, they can use a double envelope: inner addressed to the group and outer to the infoshop.

Given the diffuse nature of contemporary leftist activism in North America, infoshops are beginning to emerge from radical bookshops and group offices to play a similarly useful role in the United States and Canada. In addition to distributing a broad range of literature, the new infoshops are serving as ELECTRONIC DEMOCRACY community action centers housing the latest in computer, telephone, and fax technologies, which makes communications that much easier between individuals and organizations.

INFOTAINMENT—Mixing information and entertainment into one format, most commonly found in television programs utilizing NEWS stylistic conventions such as on-the-scene "reporters," interviews with "experts," and other DOCUMENTARY elements to give greater credibility to what is being presented. The format can be compelling, but critics assert such programs lack rigorous fact checking and are often dependent on sensationalism to boost viewer ratings. Indeed, many infotainment programs appear to commercially plug a particular product being advertised, promote pseudo-scientific occult beliefs, or devolve into a form of PROPAGANDA glorifying various official agencies. See also ADVOCACY ADVERTISING and INFOMERCIAL.

INK—See PUBLICITY.

INSIDERS—Persons with special access, knowledge, and/or influence. The term is often used pejoratively to refer to key members of an alleged conspiracy or powerful opponents one dislikes because of their IDEOLOGY and successes. See also CONSPIRACY THEORIES and MANDARINS.

INSURRECTION/INSURRECTIONARY—An insurgent revolt against a governing authority. Insurrectionaries are those who participate in the rebellion. See also ARMED PROPAGANDA and ARMED STRUGGLE.

INTELLIGENCE COMMUNITY—All governments utilize information-gathering, analysis, PROPAGANDA, ESPIONAGE, and COVERT ACTION operatives to protect national security. A number of foreign intelligence organizations such as MI6 in Britain, MOSSAD ("INSTITUTE") in Israel, and the KGB (*Komitet po Gosudarstvennoy Bezopasnosti*), or Committee for State Security, in the former Soviet Union are famed internationally. To disguise their identify, intelligence agents often publicly operate through FRONT GROUPS/SATELLITE ORGANIZATIONS. In the United States, the intelligence community refers to the eleven publicly known federal agencies and departments responsible for SPYING/SPYCRAFT, some of which hold more important roles. Included in these are representatives from the CENTRAL INTELLIGENCE AGENCY (CIA), Defense Intelligence Agency (in the Department of Defense, having overall responsibilities for military concerns), National Reconnaissance Office (satellite/aerial intelligence), National Security Agency (telephone eavesdropping and the deciphering of worldwide signals, called SIGINT for signal intelligence), Federal Bureau of Investigation (FBI), and intelligence specialists from the Air Force, Army, Marine Corps, Navy, and Departments of Energy, State, and Treasury. The National Foreign Intelligence Board (NFIB), chaired by the director of central intelligence, works much like a board of directors to coordinate their efforts and approve written forecasts with recommendations to the president known as National Intelligence Estimates (NIEs). The activities and personnel of intelligence community staff are subject to the provisions of the National Security Act of 1947, the Central Intelligence Agency Act of 1949, and other pertinent legislation. Private organizations, such as the Lyndon LaRouche

MOVEMENT and the ANTI-DEFAMATION LEAGUE OF B'NAI B'RITH (ADL), also maintain intelligence capabilities that often unofficially liaison with government intelligence community operatives. See also ACTIVE MEASURES, AGENTS/AGENCIES OF INFLUENCE, AGENTS PROVOCATEUR, ASSETS, BACKDOOR CONTACT, BLACK PROPAGANDA, BRAINWASHING, CELL, CENSORSHIP BY ASSASSINATION, CIRCUS, CLANDESTINE, CLANDESTINE RADIO STATIONS, COERCIVE DIPLOMACY, COINTELPRO, COLD WAR, COMINTERN, COMMAND PROPAGANDA, COMMUNICATIONS INTELLIGENCE (COMINT), COMMUNISM/COMMUNIST, COMPANY, CONDITIONING PROPAGANDA, CONSPIRACY THEORIES, CONTAGION, CONTRAS, COUNCIL ON FOREIGN RELATIONS (CFR), COUNTERINSURGENCY, COUNTERTERRORISM, COVER STORY, COVERT, COWBOY OPERATION, CRIMINALIZATION OF POLICY DIFFERENCES, DEATH SQUADS, DEMONIZING THE OPPOSITION, DESERT SHIELD, DIAL GROUP, DIRECT ACTION, DIRTY TRICKS CAMPAIGN, DISINFORMATION (*DEZINFORMATSIA*), DOGMA, DOUBLESPEAK, DUAL LOYALIST, ESTABLISHMENT, EXTRALEGAL CENSORSHIP, FALSE FLAG OPERATIONS, FIFTH COLUMN, FINDING, FLUTTER, FOREIGN AID, FOUNDATIONS, FREE WORLD, GERMANOPHOBIA, *GLASNOST*, GLOBALISM, GRAY/GREY LITERATURE, GRU (*Glavnoye Razvedyvatelnoye Upravlenie*), HATE CAMPAIGN, HEARTS AND MINDS CAMPAIGN, HEGEMONY, IDEOLOGY, IMPERIALISM/IMPERIALIST, INDOCTRINATION, INFON, INSIDERS, INSURRECTION/INSURRECTIONARY, INTERVENTIONIST, INVISIBLE GOVERNMENT, IRAN-CONTRA INVESTIGATIONS, IRISH NORTHERN AID COMMITTEE (NORAID), ISOLATIONIST, JOINT U.S. PUBLIC AFFAIRS OFFICE (JUSPAO), LOW-INTENSITY CONFLICT (LIC)/LOW-INTENSITY WARFARE (LIW), LOYALTY OATH, MACHIAVELLIAN, MANDARINS, MANUFACTURING OF CONSENT (or CONSENSUS), MARXIST, MASS COMMUNICATION, MASS TERROR, MEDIA BIAS, MEDIA EFFECTS, MI5, MILITARISM, MKULTRA, MOSCOW CENTER, NATIONAL INTELLIGENCE COUNCIL (NIC), NATIONAL SECURITY COUNCIL (NSC), NATIONAL SECURITY PLANNING GROUP (NSPG), NEOLIBERALISM, NESHER, NORTH ATLANTIC TREATY ORGANIZATION (NATO), OFFICE OF STRATEGIC SERVICES (OSS), OFFICIAL IDEOLOGY, OPERATION JUST CAUSE, ORCHESTRATED PROPAGANDA CAMPAIGN, PAPER TIGER, PARROTING THE PARTY LINE, PAWNS, PEACEKEEPING, PERSUASION INDUSTRIES, PLANTING STORIES, PLAUSIBLE DENIABILITY, PRESIDENT'S FOREIGN INTELLIGENCE ADVISORY BOARD (PFIAB), PROFESSIONAL PATRIOTS, PROPAGANDA DEVICES, PROPAGANDA ENVIRONMENT, PROPAGANDA MODEL (HERMAN AND CHOMSKY), PROPAGANDA-2 (P-2), PSYCHEDELICS, PSYCHOLOGICAL OPERATIONS (PSYOPS), PSYCHOLOGICAL WARFARE (PSYWAR), PUBLIC DIPLOMACY, RESIDENCY, SACRED TERRORISM, SECRET GOVERNMENT, SECRET TEAM, SHADOW GOVERNMENT, SOMALIAZATION, SPEAK AND RETREAT, SPIKE, STATE TERRORISM, STEALTH TACTICS, SUB-

PROPAGANDA, SUBVERSION/SUBVERSIVES, SURRENDER LOBBY, SVR (*Suzhba vneshnogo razvedky*), TAVISTOCK METHOD, TERROR GROUP, TERRORISM, TERRORIST, THIRD WORLD, UNCONVENTIONAL WARFARE, VENONA, VETTING, and WHITEHALL.

INTEREST GROUPS—As defined by Joseph Nagelschmidt in the glossary of *The Public Affairs Handbook* (1982, p. 289), interest groups are "Organizations of people in which members share common views and objectives and actively carry on programs designed to influence government officials and policies." All interest groups utilize PROPAGANDA which attempts to link the private interests they promote with broader PUBLIC INTERESTs. The "special interest" label is applied by one FACTION actively seeking to advance specified political and social goals in order to discredit and neutralize the effectiveness of opposing PRESSURE GROUPS. Because of the growing impact of government regulation, the number of interest groups involved in the PUBLIC POLICY PROCESS continues to multiply. Internationally, most such groups are known as NONGOVERNMENTAL ORGANIZATIONS (NGOs). Whether or not an interest group in successful in getting more NEWS MEDIA attention depends on its level of resources and the creativity of its leadership in framing ISSUEs. Generally, an organization perceived as only pursuing narrowly self-interested behavior is less interesting to the media—a posture that may ultimately prove self-defeating. See also AGITATION, DEMONIZING THE OPPOSITION, FOUNDATIONS, FRAMING DEVICES, FRONT GROUPS/SATELLITE ORGANIZATIONS, GRANFALLOONS, GRASSROOTS LOBBYING, LOBBYING/LOBBYIST, POLITICAL ANALYSTS, PUBLIC AFFAIRS, THINK TANKS, and UMBRELLA ORGANIZATIONS.

INTERNET—The global Internet is a loosely organized information system (or "web") of approximately 14,000 voluntarily interconnected computer data networks, reaching more than one-hundred countries and serving over 15 million individual users in various government agencies, universities, FOUNDATIONS, THINK TANKS, corporations, and other sites. By 1995, more than 3 million computers, terminals, and other devices were accessible on the Internet, making it the fastest-growing on-line service. CYBERSPACE differs from BROADCASTING where those in charge of the studios and distribution networks can dictate content. Unlike conventional commercial systems, which depend on individually paying customers, the Internet is run as a cooperative without centralized ownership. Because the Internet has no center, various viewpoints find expression through a process of interaction by communicators who are both a receiving center and a broadcaster. This freedom and inexpensive cost are opening up new vistas for numerous local ELECTRONIC COMMUNITY NETWORKs, even though "moderators" and "list owners" on some of the thousands of newsgroups on the Internet are now more frequently exercising some forms of AGENDA SETTING and editorial control. Advertisers have also become increasingly interested in the DEMOGRAPHICS of Internet users and so a number of commercial services such as CompuServe®, Prodigy®, and America Online® now are connected. New copyrighted but free versions of software programs ("freeware") such as

Mosaic® and NetScape® feature colorful graphics and help screens, simplifying TELECOMMUNICATIONS access to the ever growing World Wide Web®.

INTERVENTIONIST—A person who is willing to use whatever means necessary, including war, to achieve strategic geopolitical advantage in furtherance of national foreign policy aims. Major powers tend to impose their own surrogate administrations, by force if necessary, on "client states" in order to secure order, usually accompanied by a PROPAGANDA blitz about supposedly restoring DEMOCRACY. However, interventionists are also willing to destabilize truly independent regimes (which by asserting their independence thereby became "unfriendly"). The emergence of revolutionary or COUNTERREVOLUTIONARY situations in less developed THIRD WORLD and even worse off Fourth World countries now often lead to such outside interventions. Although traditionally concerned with hemispheric affairs involving MANIFEST DESTINY, as the United States grew more powerful its officials have generally adopted increasingly interventionist policies punctuated by complacent returns to "normalcy." Although not a conquering imperialist power in the same way that Britain and France were, the United States government has sent armed forces abroad numerous times in the nineteenth and twentieth century. See also BACKDOOR TO WAR, IMPERIALISM/IMPERIALIST, ISOLATIONIST, STATE TERRORISM, and UNITED NATIONS ORGANIZATION (UNO or UN).

INTIFADA—The ARMED STRUGGLE against Israel by Arabs (many of them youths) seeking termination of the Zionist occupation of Palestine. See also ZIONISM/ZIONIST.

INVISIBLE GOVERNMENT—Critical term used to describe unelected high government officials, key presidential advisors, media leaders, and others exercising great continuing influence over the PUBLIC POLICY PROCESS irrespective of which political party is in power. Often these persons are identified as members of the COUNCIL ON FOREIGN RELATIONS (CFR), TRILATERAL COMMISSION, and other interlocking organizations who secretly attend BILDERBERGER GROUP conferences, Bohemian Grove retreats, and similar largely unpublicized meetings. See also CONSPIRACY THEORIES, DUAL LOYALIST, ELITE THEORY, ESTABLISHMENT, and SECRET GOVERNMENT.

IRAN-CONTRA INVESTIGATIONS—Congressional hearings centering on a scandal involving the reported sale of U.S. weapons to Iran, amid suspicions of accompanying help from Tehran in securing the release of U.S. nationals taken hostage in Lebanon, and the diversion of profits from the weapons sales to the funding of the U.S.-backed rebels (the CONTRAS) in Nicaragua. The investigations also turned up links between U.S. COVERT operations and the sale of illegal drugs by the CENTRAL INTELLIGENCE AGENCY (CIA) as a convenient source of "off-budget" COUNTERINSURGENCY income abroad. See also CRIMINALIZATION OF POLICY DIFFERENCES, MOSSAD ("INSTITUTE"),

NEOLIBERALISM, OCTOBER SURPRISE, SECRET TEAM, STATE TERRORISM, and WHITE PAPERS.

IRISH NORTHERN AID COMMITTEE (NORAID)—According to a NEWS RELEASE issued by supporters:

> The Irish Northern Aid Committee is the largest American humanitarian organization concerned with the conflict in Ireland which is open to men and women of any race, nationality or religion. . . . [It was] formed in 1970 to alleviate the suffering of the dependents of Irish political prisoners. Today the families of more than 700 political prisoners in Ireland, Britain and Europe rely on our all-volunteer fundraising across American conducted on behalf of the charitable trusts, An Cumann Cabrach in Dublin and Green Cross in Belfast. Irish Northern Aid chapters are based in all metropolitan areas in the country and work with Irish American, labor, religious, human and civil rights groups and concerned individuals to promote an end to the conflict, the release of prisoners, and an end to the undemocratic British occupation in the north of Ireland through the exercise of the democratic right to national self-determination. Irish Northern Aid promotes an American awareness of the nature of British rule in Ireland and will highlight the colonial and sectarian nature of partition and the British occupation as the inevitable cause of the ongoing conflict in the north of Ireland. Irish Northern Aid seeks support for a free and independent, thirty-two county Irish Republic governed in accordance with the Proclamation of the Irish Republic issued on Easter 1916.

Critics often raise the charge, not yet proven in a U.S. court of law, that contributions to NORAID are also used to finance the COVERT supply of military equipment to the Irish Republican Army. See also FENIAN BROTHERHOOD, HUMAN RIGHTS, and TERRORISM.

ISOLATIONIST—A person who is generally opposed to participation in foreign military alliances and the use of military force overseas for foreign policy aims, unless directly attacked. In giving his Farewell Address in 1796, a talk often quoted by later isolationists, President George Washington warned against entangling foreign alliances. "Europe has a set of primary interests which to us have none or a very remote relation. Hence she must be engaged in frequent controversies, the causes of which are essentially foreign to our concerns," he told Americans in prescient remarks later ignored by INTERVENTIONIST politicians. "Hence, therefore, it must be unwise in us to implicate ourselves by artificial ties in the ordinary vicissitudes of her politics or the ordinary combinations and collisions of her friendships or enmities." See also AMERICA FIRST and SLIPPERY SLOPE.

ISSUE—A trend, development, or controversy that has the capacity to affect an organization's performance or survival. Often the perceptual gap between an organization's performance and its STAKEHOLDERS' expectations is at the heart of the matter. See also CRITICAL ISSUE, ISSUE ACTION PLANS, and subsequent issue-related entries.

ISSUE ACTION PLANS—As defined by Joseph Nagelschmidt in the glossary of *The Public Affairs Handbook* (1982, p. 289), issue action plans are DOCUMENTs "that incorporate descriptions of the issue, its evaluation, and both strategic and tactical corporate public affairs responses." See also ISSUE CAMPAIGNS and PUBLIC AFFAIRS.

ISSUE ADVERTISING—Also known as ADVOCACY ADVERTISING or controversy ADVERTISING, in which a sponsoring organization uses paid media to discuss social problems rather than products. This would seem to advance the PUBLIC INTEREST, since the expertise brought to bear by advocacy ads helps define, clarify, and focus attention on local, regional and national issues needing to be dealt with. However, politicians have not been as open to such indirect GRASSROOTS LOBBYING communication, preferring their comfortable and cozy traditional relationship to conventional LOBBYING/LOBBYISTs over the pressures engendered by popular mobilization. Not surprisingly, federal tax regulations have been interpreted as favoring the former and discouraging the latter.

Individual stations and publications accept some issue ads. However, broadcast as well as print media have long asserted their editorial right to restrict such ads as part of their social responsibility role. With exceptions for ballot ISSUE and political candidate advertisements (POLISPOTS), the major television networks in particular have long been universally antagonistic to such messages. For example, ABC in 1992 reiterated its long-standing policy through lawyer-worded language to refuse any ad "that directly addresses a controversial issue of public importance and takes an explicit position thereon, or if the advertisement presents information or makes statements that have the effect of paralleling (and therefore advancing) the positions taken by partisans in the controversy." Similarly, CBS will not sell time for "advocacy of viewpoints on controversial issues of public importance." Indeed the CBS policy (unchanged since 1986) openly states: "A commercial announcement will be considered unacceptable if it either (1) explicitly takes a position on such an issue, or (2) without taking an explicit position, presents arguments parallel to those being made by one side or the other in the debate concerning the issue, so as to constitute implicit advocacy." For many years, this opposition was couched in FIRST AMENDMENT concerns over the possible triggering of FAIRNESS DOCTRINE litigation as "protectors of the public interest," but that proved to be largely a stalking horse for the larger fear that controversy would cut into profits. Without clear financial gain or the imposition by the FEDERAL COMMUNICATIONS COMMISSION (FCC) of common carrier regulatory provisions to broadcast advertising, it is unlikely that networks and stations will opt to provide LIBERTARIAN access to their channels for ISSUE CAMPAIGNS.

ISSUE CAMPAIGNS—Issues do not have a life of their own, but are framed by propagandists pushing their own either overt or HIDDEN AGENDA. Organizations engage in issue campaigns when they build coalitions of INTEREST GROUPS to influence the PUBLIC POLICY PROCESS. ISSUE campaigns concentrate on several kinds of activities, incorporating direct and indirect image/issues appeals. In monitoring socio-political trends and providing communication related to a narrow, but important range of topic areas, they (1) call to targeted publics to be involved in the creation, passage and/or defeat of legislation; (2) seek to blunt or enhance regulatory activities; (3) rebut disputed facts about an industry's or organization's operations, services, or products; (4) discuss contested norms and values of behavior; and (5) champion ideologies (as when a business group promotes capitalism and FREE TRADE). See also ADVOCACY ADVERTISING, CAPITALISM/ CAPITALIST, IDEOLOGY, IMAGE ADVERTISING, ISSUE EVALUATION, ISSUE SCANNING, ISSUES MANAGEMENT, OFF THE NEWS, SWOT ANALYSIS, and TRACKING POLLS.

ISSUE EVALUATION—As defined by Joseph Nagelschmidt in the glossary of *The Public Affairs Handbook* (1982, p. 289), issue evaluation is "the process of systematically reviewing public affairs issues, detected in issue scanning, to determine their potential impact on the corporation" or organization. See also ISSUE SCANNING, ISSUES MANAGEMENT, PUBLIC AFFAIRS, SWOT ANALYSIS, and TRACKING POLLS.

ISSUE SCANNING—Organizations involved in ISSUES MANAGEMENT systematically examine a broad range of PUBLIC AFFAIRS issues. Trend studies undertaken by issues managers look at the patterns of events, conditions, and attitudes that help shape PUBLIC OPINION, rank CRITICAL ISSUEs in importance to their impact on the organization, and monitor their status, direction, and momentum. See also AGENDA SETTING, ISSUE, PUBLIC POLICY PROCESS, SWOT ANALYSIS, and TRACKING POLLS.

ISSUES MANAGEMENT—The process of predicting and shaping PUBLIC OPINION through proactively participating in the events that directly affect an organization is called issues management. The whole idea behind issues management is not to fabricate a false public image, but rather establish honest and effective dialogue with important audiences to eliminate misunderstanding and establish a basis for long-term cooperation. For example, issues managers at Fortune 500 businesses often gather intelligence and coordinate efforts to deal with regulators, lobbyists, INTEREST GROUPS, consumers, and other important constituencies.

Functions of a comprehensive issues management program include (1) integrating PUBLIC POLICY PROCESS issues analysis and audits into the organizational leadership's strategic planning, (2) monitoring standards of organizational performance to discover the opinions and values held by key publics that may affect operations, (3) developing and implementing ethical codes of organizational social accountability, (4) assisting senior management decision-making, particularly in readjusting goals and operating policies vis-à-vis public opinion, (5) identifying, defining, prioritizing and analyzing empirically those ISSUEs of greatest operational, financial and political significance to the organization, (6) creating multidimensional proactive and reactive institutional response plans from among the range of available issue change strategy options, (7) establishing grassroots contact with potential cooperators (including media), (8) communicating on those issues identified as most important to the organization *and* its various key publics to establish an agenda and build external support, (9) directing opinion to stall or mitigate the development and effects of undesirable legislation or regulation, and (10) evaluating the impact of these efforts to determine whether objectives were achieved, to direct ongoing improvements, and to make further recommendations to management.

In a 1988 article in *Public Relations Review* (pp. 28-29), Brad Hainsworth and Max Meng offered an industry-wide explanation of issues management, which they define as an:

action oriented management function which seeks to identify potential or emerging issues (legislative, regulatory, political, or social) that may impact the organization, and then mobilizes and coordinates organizational resources to strategically influence the development of those issues. The ultimate goal of issues management should be to shape public policy to the benefit of the organization.

No model of issues communication should treat it as merely a matter of disagreement or misunderstanding. At heart, it centers on a power struggle between corporate interests and public interests as interpreted by social MOVEMENT agitators and media coverage. Despite the goal of CONFLICT RESOLUTION, the popularity of the advocacy over adversary approach is understandable given the reality that successful persuasive campaigns typically mobilize or reinforce supporters rather than convert opponents. See also CORPORATE SOCIAL RESPONSIBILITY (CSR), ISSUE ADVERTISING, ISSUE CAMPAIGNS, ISSUE EVALUATION, ISSUE SCANNING, PUBLIC INTEREST, SWOT ANALYSIS, and TRACKING POLLS.

JAPAN BASHING—When it is to their advantage, propagandists in other countries play upon existing anti-Japanese prejudices to elicit the expression of unfavorable opinions about the country and its people. They do this by publicizing selective negative interpretations that present a distorted and one-sided view of Japanese ethnic origins, governmental policies, economic activities, and/or cultural practices. See also AD HOMINEM ATTACK, AMERICA BASHING, DEMONIZING THE OPPOSITION, HATE SPEECH, RACIST/RACIALIST/RACIAL DISCRIMINATION, RITUAL DEFAMATION, and SPIRAL OF SILENCE.

JOINT U.S. PUBLIC AFFAIRS OFFICE (JUSPAO)—A government entity formed in 1965 to coordinate American propaganda efforts in Vietnam.

JOURNALISM/JOURNALIST—Very imprecise terms covering a broad-range of activities since journalism is self-defined ("news is what journalists say is news"). In the United States, the FIRST AMENDMENT gives the PRESS special protections, and unlike some countries, there are no government-imposed licensing or certification requirements. Libertarians tend to promote absolutist FREE SPEECH interpretations of the FOURTH ESTATE that extend to protection of COMMERCIAL SPEECH rights. Despite the plain language of the U.S. Constitution, however, legislatures and courts have justified imposing a number of restrictions on American journalists. These range from libel to national security concerns.

The problem over exactly what constitutes "a journalist" is especially difficult since, technically, everyone from a radio talk show host to a locally published political commentator to the editor of a photocopied monthly newsletter to a network DOCUMENTARY producer of "reality" television programs can call themselves journalists if their work is seen as NEWS. Even the majority of journalism texts neglect to describe the field succinctly, either in the introductory chapters or a glossary. A more detailed social responsibility definition can be gleaned from the report of the Commission on Freedom of the Press entitled *A Free and Responsible Press*, issued in 1947. The commission members suggest that journalism serves a public good when presenting:

- a truthful, comprehensive and intelligent account of the day's events in a context that gives them meaning,
- a forum for the exchange of comment and criticism,
- a means of projecting the opinions and attitudes of members of the society to one another, and
- a method for clarifying the goals and values of the society.

More recently, G. Stuart Adam, in *Notes towards a Definition of Journalism: Understanding an Old Craft as an Art Form* (Poynter Institute for Media Studies, 1993), makes the case that "journalism is an invention or a form of expression used to report and comment in the public media on the events and ideas of the here and now."

Generally, journalists work for print and electronic NEWS MEDIA organizations that employ them as news gatherers, editors, and reporters rather than as PUBLIC RELATIONS (PR) practitioners. These organizations are "public" in the sense that many media products are widely circulated. In the United States, however, only a minority of media outlets are actually "publicly owned" rather than privately controlled (i.e., most are profit-making corporations). Information comes to journalists from numerous self-interested sources and is skewed towards those interests and organizations considered most important (such as government).

The work of journalists is periodically packaged and edited into stories, pictures, and sounds whose purpose is ostensibly to meet a social obligation involving a "right to know." However, when "published," this information is not neutral since it also has the potential to affect the economic bottom-line of the media employers journalists work for—plus educate, entertain, socialize, persuade, and mobilize news consumers (whether readers, viewers, and/or listeners). The notion that journalists should be objective is a twentieth-century one, which is most popular in the United States. Proponents of various alternative "new" forms of journalism prefer to express their commitment for change through reporting that attempts to be accurate, critical, moral and polemical. Electronic technologies are making possible a more populist and democratic "interactive journalism" which focuses on issues not addressed by the mainstream media and incorporates two-way contact in which both the communicator and the audience learn from each other. See also ADVOCACY JOURNALISM, BLOWBACK, COMPUTER-MEDIATED COMMUNICATION (CMC), DYSJOURNALISM, ELITE THEORY, FEEDING FRENZY, HEGEMONY, LIBERTARIAN, MEDIA BIAS, MEDIA/MEDIUM, MUCKRAKERS, NEW JOURNALISM, OFF THE

RECORD, OP-ED, PACK JOURNALISM, POLEMIC, TABLOID JOUR-
NALISM, and YELLOW JOURNALISM.

JUSTICE BY NEWS RELEASE—Massive PUBLICITY about a
government investigation before any charges are bought, through
STRUCTURED LEAKS designed to "get" the target, whether or not a
successful prosecution results. See also FEEDING FRENZY,
ORCHESTRATED PROPAGANDA CAMPAIGN, PACK JOURNALISM,
PLANTING STORIES, TOXIC INFORMATION, and VICTORY BY NEWS
RELEASE.

KGB (*Komitet po Gosudarstvennoy Bezopasnosti*)—The Bolsheviks
formed what was to become the Committee for State Security upon taking
control of Russia in 1917. This secret police organization, originally known
as the Cheka or Vecheka, was noted for its ruthlessness and efficiency. Later
incarnations were the GPU, OGPU, NKVD, and MVD. In 1954, the
CLANDESTINE Soviet security service was reorganized as the Committee for
State Security (KGB), also known as "the committee" or "the organs." The
KGB performed the functions equivalent to more than twenty-five different
U.S. intelligence, security, and law enforcement agencies. Western analysts
believe the KGB, at its height in the late 1980s, had between 400,000 and
700,000 employees. In late 1991, the KGB was reorganized by the post-
Communist regime, with external responsibilities located in the Russian
Foreign Intelligence Service known as the SVR (*Suzhba vneshnogo razvedky*).
While some of the top leadership are new, most rank-and-file agents continue
on as before. See also COMMUNISM/COMMUNIST, INTELLIGENCE
COMMUNITY, and *PERESTROIKA*.

KNEE-CAPPING—Shooting a person in both knees to permanently maim that
individual as a form of graphic punishment by governments or armed
opposition groups. Such TERRORIST shootings, maimings, and continuing
threats of death are HUMAN RIGHTS abuses designed to stifle dissent by the
victim and serve as a warning to others.

LAUNCHING A NUKE—Airing highly negative POLISPOTS very late in an
election campaign that allege serious wrongdoing by one's opponent, giving
no time for reply ADVERTISING to be prepared.

LEAKS—See STRUCTURED LEAKS.

LEAST OBJECTIONABLE PROGRAMMING (LOP) THEORY—
Belief by broadcasters that individuals often turn on their sets just to watch
television rather than preplan their viewing. The theory holds that people will
then cancel out program types they don't care for and settle for the channel
airing a show that meets minimal expectations. As a result, network and
station programmers often design their program schedules to avoid driving
away viewers. See also BROADCASTING, HOT SWITCHING, and STRIP
PROGRAMMING.

LEFT-WING/LIBERAL—According to the definition used by Advocates for Self-Government, Inc. (1995):

Left/Liberals like personal choice in civil matters and central decision-making in economics. They want government to serve the disadvantaged and promote equality. Left/Liberals place high value on good intentions. They accept diversity in social behavior but seek more equality in economics. They work with libertarians in defending civil liberties and with socialists in advancing economic central planning.

Those who more stridently distance themselves from centrist positions are occasionally pejoratively referred to as RADICAL left, far left, ultra left, or extreme left. Opponents of those holding liberal values—as reflected in the promotion of gay rights, abortion rights, pornography, and other causes often associated with elements of the national DEMOCRATIC PARTY—regularly use the terms as a slur. See also EXTREMISM, IDEOLOGUES, IDEOLOGY, LIBERTARIAN, NEOLIBERALISM, POPULISM/POPULIST, RIGHT-WING/CONSERVATIVE, and SOCIALISM/ SOCIALIST.

LIBERATION MOVEMENT—Sloganistic term to refer to the collective effort by dissidents to eliminate oppressive government actions. If these requests for change are not addressed, the MOVEMENT may turn to ARMED STRUGGLE and seek the aid of outside powers. In time, the local population often turn out to be PAWNS in a bigger geopolitical chessboard. Soviet strategy in seeking to win victory for socialism in Africa, for example, held that political power had to be wielded exclusively by the VANGUARD of the liberation movement. As a practical matter, this meant that alliances could be formed only with those political groups that accepted the Soviet-endorsed leadership. This policy was ruthlessly followed by Angola's ruling MPLA party, Mozambique's FRELIMO party, and the former Marxist dictatorship in Ethiopia, all with tragic consequences. As a practical matter, it is easier to gain support and sympathy at home and abroad for groups which shun violence in seeking to change harsh realities and turn instead to courageous social struggle in behalf of their peoples. See also ARMED PROPAGANDA, COMMUNISM/COMMUNIST, COUNTERINSURGENCY, LIBERATION THEOLOGY, PEOPLE'S WAR, REVOLUTION/REVOLUTIONARY, SOCIALISM/SOCIALIST, and WAR OF LIBERATION.

LIBERATION THEOLOGY—A philosophy that combines Marxism and Christianity by arguing that Jesus was a revolutionary who supported the "class struggle" between rich and poor or oppressor and oppressed. Liberation theology (also referred to as "social theology" and "black theology") is an IDEOLOGY that asserts the need for church leaders to be involved in directly working with the masses of people inhabiting developing countries. It goes beyond traditional missionary work and hunger/relief efforts, however, by emphasizing a politicized "social gospel" in which violent revolutionary action is permitted and even encouraged.

LIBERTARIAN—Individuals (also referred to as "classical liberals") who seek to limit the power of government to rule by coercion. Libertarians thus value tolerance and individual responsibility and prefer that government interference in civil and economic matters be supplanted by voluntary agreements and private contract. Government's singular responsibility is to safeguard one against the violent designs of others. "The right of personal freedom," to quote Thomas Jefferson, limits government paternalism and the popular sovereignty of DEMOCRACY so that what one chooses to do with one's own life, liberty and property in pursuit of self-happiness is no one else's business, least of all government. Attempts to undercut such personal freedom and erode constitutional protections *against* government (especially the Ninth Amendment) would inevitably result in "liberticide," a term often used by Jefferson in describing coercive intrusions into the realm of legitimate liberties. According to Gilbert Harman's essay "Libertarianism and Morality" (in Tibor R. Machan, ed., *The Libertarian Reader*, 1982, p. 226):

Libertarianism is in part a thesis about the limits of governmental action. In its strictest form, it holds that government may legitimately protect people from each other but may not legitimately impose taxes and other restrictions merely for the sake of projects aimed at advancing general welfare. Governments may prevent people from injuring each other, they may protect property rights, they may enforce contracts. But they may not prevent people from injuring themselves, they may not interfere with immoral acts that do not affect others, and they may not require those who are better off to help those who are worse off.

See also ANTIAUTHORITARIANISM, CLASSICAL LIBERALISM, FREE-THINKERS, HUMAN NATURE, and RIGHT-WING/CONSERVATIVE.

LIGHTENING RODS—Organizational officials in and out of government who, either through intent or circumstance, divert criticism and deflect blame away from their leader. See also PLAUSIBLE DENIABILITY.

LOBBYING/LOBBYIST—A lobbyist is a person who directly represents an individual's or organization's point of view to elected representatives, appointed regulators, their staffs, and other key constituencies. The purpose of such lobbying is the enactment of favorable governmental policies or quashing of harmful legislation. Because of the stakes involved, this is often accomplished through use of paid advocates—professional lobbyists—skilled in the legislative system and RHETORIC. Congress and the states have enacted regulations requiring registration and mandating filing of activities reports, but loopholes mean that many lobbyists escape these provisions. Attempts in 1994 to tighten these restrictions—particularly by cutting out tax deductions—have resulted in cases still wending their way through the courts. New federal legislation which took effect on January 1, 1996, will lead to increased registration and reporting. Lobbying may also be supplemented by indirect mobilization efforts via GRASSROOTS POLITICAL ACTION and coalition participation with a variety of FRONT GROUPS/SATELLITE ORGANIZATIONS, UMBRELLA ORGANIZATIONS, and independent third parties (including media contacts, linkups to INTEREST GROUPS, etc.). The goal is to build support helpful to furthering one's influence over the direction of government actions, including the passage, defeat, or modification of particular legislative bills and regulations. The FIRST AMENDMENT includes lobbying when it says: "Congress shall make no law . . . abridging the freedom of speech, or . . . the right of the people peaceably to assemble, and to petition the government for a redress of grievances." See also ADVOCACY ADVERTISING, BELTWAY BANDITS, FREE SPEECH, FOREIGN AGENTS REGISTRATION ACT (FARA), GRASSROOTS LOBBYING, GRASSTOPS, ISSUE, ISSUE ACTION PLANS, ISSUE ADVERTISING, ISSUE CAMPAIGNS, ISSUE EVALUATION, ISSUE SCANNING, ISSUES MANAGEMENT, PUBLIC POLICY PROCESS, and PUBLIC RELATIONS (PR).

LOW-INTENSITY CONFLICT (LIC)/LOW-INTENSITY WARFARE (LIW)—The U.S. Army definition for a low-intensity conflict, issued in 1986, describes one as:

a limited politico-military struggle to achieve political, social, economic, or psychological objectives. It is often protracted and ranges from diplomatic, economic, and psychosocial pressures through terrorism and insurgency. Low-intensity conflict is generally confined to a geographic area and is often characterized by constraints on the weaponry, tactics, and level of violence. . . . It is, in essence, an environment in which political concerns predominate."

LIC/LIW campaigns involve:
- coordinating indirect pressures,
- manipulating economic and humanitarian aid,
- disseminating overt PROPAGANDA and COVERT types of DISINFORMATION (*DEZINFORMATSIA*),
- implementing political organizing efforts, and
- arming of surrogate "freedom fighters" in place of more open military intervention.

While TERRORISM, torture, and upheavals in the targeted country perpetrated by the various sides may cause great misery to the indigenous population, the conflict is low intensity from the point of view of the intervening power. The downside costs of STATE TERRORISM are minimal in terms of investment and possible casualties. The rewards can be great, however, in terms of achieving long-term foreign policy goals without exciting much unwanted homefront NEWS MEDIA attention. See also ANTITERRORISM, ARMED STRUGGLE, CADRE, CELL, CONTAGION, COUNTERINSURGENCY, COUNTERPROPAGANDA, COUNTERTERRORISM, HEARTS AND MINDS CAMPAIGN, HEGEMONY, HUMAN RIGHTS, INSURRECTION/INSURRECTIONARY, INTELLIGENCE COMMUNITY, INTERVENTIONIST, LIBERATION MOVEMENT, NEOLIBERALISM, PEOPLE'S WAR, PROPAGANDA OF THE DEED, PSYCHOLOGICAL WARFARE (PSYWAR), REVOLUTION/REVOLUTIONARY, and WAR OF LIBERATION.

LOYALIST—The approximately one-third of all American colonists who remained loyal supporters of the British Crown in the late eighteenth-century and opposed the revolutionaries. Following Britain's defeat in the Revolutionary War, Loyalists were denied the ostensible freedoms and liberties the overthrow of government was supposedly fought to secure. As a result, at war's end many returned to Britain or joined the more than 100,000 Loyalists who migrated to Canada.

LOYALTY OATH—A sworn statement made by an individual to affirm his or her support of the organization. The oath generally involves a commitment not to join specified subversive organizations no advocate certain unpatriotic ideas. In U.S. history, such oaths have often been mandated by policy or law in order to secure government employment. See also DUAL LOYALIST, HOUSE UN-AMERICAN ACTIVITIES COMMITTEE (HUAC), McCARTHYISM, OFFICIAL IDEOLOGY, ORWELLIAN TACTICS, POLITICAL CRIME, PROFESSIONAL PATRIOTS, REACTIONARY, RED-BAITING, and SCAPEGOAT/SCAPEGOATING.

McCARTHYISM—Tactics using the power of government investigations, highly publicized NEWS MEDIA charges larded with innuendo, and other "witch-hunt" and "fishing expedition" methods to accuse individuals of disloyalty. The truth or innocence of the victim are often less important than using such smear tactics to advance the interests of the accusers. The term is named after Senator Joseph McCarthy (R-Wisc.) who alleged that Communist party members and other RADICAL left-wing political ACTIVISTS had infiltrated the federal government. While some wrongdoing pinpointed by McCarthy occurred, U.S. Senate and other related government hearings in the 1940s and 1950s uncovered very little tangible evidence documenting widespread domestic subversion. See also BIG LIE, CENSORSHIP, COMMUNISM/COMMUNIST, HOUSE UN-AMERICAN ACTIVITIES COMMITTEE (HUAC), LEFT-WING/LIBERAL, LOYALTY OATH, OFFICIAL IDEOLOGY, ORWELLIAN TACTICS, POLITICAL CRIME, POLITICALLY CORRECT (PC), PROFESSIONAL PATRIOTS, PROPAGANDA DEVICES, REACTIONARY, RED-BAITING, RIGHT-WING/CONSERVATIVE, RITUAL DEFAMATION, SCAPE-GOAT/SCAPEGOATING, SEDITION, and WHISPERING CAMPAIGN.

MACHIAVELLIAN—The unethical pursuit of one's own selfish aims, particularly in using unscrupulous means to achieve governing power. Named after Niccolò Machiavelli (1469-1527), an Italian statesman and author of *The Prince*, *The Discourses*, and other works that separated political action from ethical considerations. Machiavelli held that HUMAN NATURE is fundamentally bad, insisted that morals have no place in politics, and declared that the end justifies the means. He is considered by many to be the founder of modern political science. See also STEALTH TACTICS.

MAGIC BULLET THEORY—Similar to HYPODERMIC NEEDLE THEORY in arguing that media have great powers to influence every exposed individual in a more or less uniform way. Those critics most concerned about MEDIA BIAS often speak of "the power of MASS COMMUNICATION" in rather uncritical endorsement of this theory. The belief that media have an automatic and direct causal relationship to behavior has been largely abandoned by many social scientists who study MEDIA EFFECTS because of inaccurate assumptions its proponents have often made about human motivations. On the other hand, instances exist in which media have proven their ability to quickly mobilize mass belief and/or behavior, and consequently the theory cannot be entirely dismissed.

MANDARINS—Senior government officials wielding great influence, who are capable of affecting the PUBLIC POLICY PROCESS and deflecting the efforts of their opponents within the system. See also BELTWAY BANDITS, COVER-UP CROWD, INSIDERS, and NESHER.

MANIFEST DESTINY—The doctrine, most actively promoted in the nineteenth-century, which asserted the historical inevitability of the Anglo-Saxon domination of North America from sea to sea. The term was first coined by newspaper editor John L. O'Sullivan in 1845 and it soon found echo from those promoting the westward expansion of the United States, while simultaneously justifying exploitation of racial minorities. Proponents held that the "racially-superior" white race, had a moral duty handed down by God to take control of the entire Western hemisphere in order to civilize" the "backward peoples" found there—namely black slaves, Mexicans, and Native Americans. This alleged providential favor resulted in a number of INTERVENTIONIST wars of conquest and other military adventures. While the overt RACIST/RACIALIST/RACIAL DISCRIMINATION aspects of Manifest Destiny have been largely abandoned, the view that the United States should control Latin America still finds echoes in "DEMOCRACY building" policies associated with NEOLIBERALISM. See also DEMOCRACY, IMPERIALISM/IMPERIALIST, and MILITARISM.

MANUFACTURING OF CONSENT (or CONSENSUS)—Terms used by linguist and political theorist Noam Chomsky in describing the national role of PROPAGANDA in bringing about social compliance. They are very similar to the phrase earlier popularized by Edward L. Bernays, ENGINEERING OF CONSENT.

MARCH OF PROVOCATION—Parades, marches, and other forms of street demonstrations designed to create confrontation and provoke a response (often violent) from opposition elements. This then serves to "justify" the sponsoring organization's purpose and acts to generate favorable NEWS MEDIA coverage for one's cause. See also AGITATION and AGITPROP.

MARXIST—An admirer of Karl Marx, the nineteenth-century founder of modern socialism. The term is inclusive in that not all Marxists, for example, are Communists with a capital C. Marx's public reputation as a loving humanistic figure is at odds with his private behavior. At the time Marx died in 1883, he was seen largely as a failure and only six people attended his funeral. Although Marx's parents were Jews who converted to Christianity largely for business reasons when he was a child, as an adult he exhibited strong ANTI-SEMITIC feelings and harbored negative attitudes toward the working classes ("proletariat"). His scholarship and theoretical work to "uplift the downtrodden" led the cofounder of modern communism to strangely neglect his own family. Three of Marx's six children died of starvation when young and two of his daughters and a son-in-law committed suicide.

The portrayal of Marx is a myth largely created after his death, but he nevertheless proved a brilliant RADICAL social critic and writer. Many Americans have been attracted to Marx's political analyses, often making their own contributions. Daniel De Leon (1852-1914), for example, was one of the leading U.S. Marxist ACTIVISTS and theoreticians. In 1886, while a law professor at Columbia University, De Leon became involved in worker MOVEMENT issues as an ally of labor. He subsequently became a famed orator with many published speeches and served as editor of *The People*, the newspaper of the Socialist Labor party. De Leon articulated a humanistic—yet militant—Marxism, arguing that:

> Between the working class and the capitalist class there is an irrepressible conflict, a class struggle for life. No glib-tongued politician can vault over it, no capitalist professor or official statistician can argue it away; no capitalist parson can veil it; no labor faker can straddle it; no reform architect can bridge it over. It crops up in all manner of ways, in ways that disconcert all the plans and all the schemes of those who would deny or ignore it. It is a struggle that will not down, and must be ended, only by either the total subjugation of the working class, or the abolition of the capitalist class.

See also COMMUNISM/COMMUNIST and SOCIALISM/SOCIALIST.

MASS COMMUNICATION—Process in which ideas emanating from various sources are collated and then transmitted through a media system capable of reaching many people. The mass communication phenomenon is characterized by: (1) complex formal organizations; (2) divisions of labor and sub-specializations; (3) technological channels in various media; (4) large (often heterogeneous) audiences widely separated from and anonymous to the source and to each other; (5) reception of simultaneous or nearly simultaneous dissemination of the mediated content from the communicator organization; and (6) formal audience responses to the message(s). Historically, the mass communication process has been dominated by one-way sender-to-receiver messages such as ADVERTISING. More recently, researchers have begun analyzing the implications of establishing genuine two-way communication relationships in which audience feedback is integral to future decision-making partnerships. See also MEDIA/MEDIUM and TELECOMMUNICATIONS.

MASS TERROR—Policy of the ruthless use of force adopted by Lenin as official Communist party strategy in 1918, who argued that "we can achieve nothing unless we use terror." Lenin based his views of "popular revolution" on the need to employ extreme violence—which he said was "the meaning and essence of Red Terror." See also COMMUNISM/COMMUNIST and TERRORISM.

MEDIA BIAS—Entertainment and information content of media have to be selected from a welter of alternative sources. Bias is the predisposition for or against a particular point of view. Whenever the positions or interests of a portion of the audience are overlooked, distorted, or censored the problem of bias is found. Bias may result from unintentional or deliberate decisions on the part of media GATEKEEPERs, but nevertheless subjects audiences to a skewed reality potentially detrimental to their best interests. The problem of AGENDA SETTING is compounded by the increasing centralization of information supply created from the rise of big media owned by interlocking conglomerates. The influence of the MEDIA ELITE is so pervasive that many organizations and their social ideas are effectively disenfranchised by their exclusion from the mainstream channels of distribution. On the other hand, favored viewpoints and groups can receive a boost from biased coverage promoting their cause.

Most media industries, including journalism, ostensibly operate under codes of ethics designed to protect against unfairness and bias. However, these provisos lack grounding in ethical theory and tend to reflect antinomian thinking based on an ad hoc approach to moral decision-making using only the situation for guidance. Unlike codes found in other professions such as medicine and law, MASS COMMUNICATION codes of ethics in the United States are also voluntary and have no real mechanisms to punish wrong-doers. Similarly, most watchdog organizations are private entities without enforcement power—other than PUBLICITY—to call attention to questionable behavior. Congress and government regulatory agencies such as the FEDERAL COMMUNICATIONS COMMISSION (FCC), FEDERAL TRADE COMMISSION (FTC), and the Securities and Exchange Commission (SEC) entrusted with specific aspects of media performance oversight are hemmed in by FIRST AMENDMENT considerations. In practice, this means what is constitutionally lawful is generally treated as what is ethical.

Whether or not media bias exists is a seemingly endless debate. Yet valid questions remain about media performance and the role of PUBLIC COMMUNICATION practitioners in shaping perception. There are some researchers who use a "social construction of reality" framework to analyze American media and the ways in which information is filtered. Their MEDIA EFFECTS findings suggest that when bias occurs it stems from combination of factors:

- The media are neither objective nor completely honest in their portrayal of important ISSUEs.
- FRAMING DEVICES are employed in stories by featuring some angles and downplaying others.
- The NEWS is a product not only of deliberate manipulation, but of the ideological and economic conditions under which the media operate.
- While appearing independent, the NEWS MEDIA are institutions that are controlled or heavily influenced by government and business interests experienced with MANUFACTURING OF CONSENT (or CONSENSUS).
- Reporters' sources frequently dominate the flow of information as a way of furthering their own overt and HIDDEN AGENDAs. In particular, the heavy reliance on political officials and other-

government related experts occurs through a PREFERENTIAL
SOURCING selection process which excludes dissident voices.

- Journalists widely accept the "faulty premise" that Washington's
  collective intentions are benevolent, despite occasional mistakes.
- The regular use of the word "we" by journalists in referring to U.S.
  government actions implies nationalistic complicity with those
  policies.
- There is an absence of historical context and contemporary
  comparisons in reportage which would make news more meaningful.
- The failure to provide follow up assessment is further evidence of a
  PACK JOURNALISM mentality that at the conclusion of a
  "FEEDING FRENZY" wants to move on to other stories.
- Americans must maintain a critical perspective on the media in order
  to make informed choices and participate effectively in the PUBLIC
  POLICY PROCESS.

Typical of such critics is Edward S. Herman who says in a "Balance a
Foreign Concept in International News" (special issue of *Extra!*, October
1991, p. 1):

Perhaps the most important source of bias is the hidden and implicit political basis
of what is "newsworthy." These choices often reflect a fairly mechanical
transmission of what the [U.S.] government chooses to emphasize. . . . Iraq's
human rights abuses suddenly became newsworthy after August 2, 1990, as the
Bush administration readied the public for military action against Iraq, while the
same abuses were essentially ignored in prior years when the administration was
building friendly relations with Saddam Hussein. Where the worth of victims, as
measured by intensity of focus and indignation, is so closely tied to the
government's political agenda, media bias seems evident.

Two polemical—but informative—books help further clarify this issue.
As RIGHT-WING/CONSERVATIVE stalwarts L. Brent Bozell III and Brent
H. Baker note in *And That's the Way It Isn't: A Reference Guide to Media Bias*
(1990):

By exercising control over the nation's agenda—picking and choosing which
issues are fit for public debate, which news is "fit to print"—the news media can
greatly influence the political direction of this country. They can ignore or ridicule
some ideas and promote others. They can wreck a politician's career by taking a
quote or two out of context or by spotlighting a weakness in his background. They
can make winners look like losers and vice versa, known that, in the political
world, appearance easily supplants reality.

Bozell and Baker describe seven methods used to analyze the existence of
and quantify bias:

- Surveys of the political/cultural attitudes of journalists, particularly
  members of the media elite, and of journalism students.
- Studies of journalists' previous professional connections.
- Collections of quotations in which prominent journalists reveal their
  beliefs about politics and/or the proper role of their profession.
- Computer word-use and topic analysis searches to determine content

and labeling.
- Studies of policies recommended in news stories.
- Comparisons of the agenda of the news and entertainment media with agendas of political candidates or other ACTIVISTS.
- Analyses of positive/negative coverage.

Their LEFT-WING/LIBERAL counterparts, Martin A. Lee and Norman Solomon in *Unreliable Sources: A Guide to Detecting Bias in News Media* (1991), adopt a different starting point, but one can nonetheless extrapolate from their well-documented work at least four additional strategies, such as:

- Reviews of the personal DEMOGRAPHICS of media decision-makers.
- Comparisons of ADVERTISING sources/content that influence information/entertainment content.
- Analyses of the extent of government PROPAGANDA and PUBLIC RELATIONS (PR) industry impact on media.
- Studies of the use of experts and spokespersons etc. by media vs. those not selected to determine the INTEREST GROUPS and IDEOLOGUES represented vs. those excluded.

Reports using these methodologies are appearing more regularly from monitoring groups ranging across the political spectrum from Fairness and Accuracy in Reporting (FAIR) and the Institute for Media Analysis (IMA) on the left to Accuracy in Media (AIM) and the Center for Media and Public Affairs on the right. Even though disagreeing on specifics and IDEOLOGY, they are making valuable contributions to our understanding of the communications process. See also ADVOCACY ADVERTISING, ADVOCACY JOURNALISM, BIG LIE, CENSORSHIP, CONVENTIONAL WISDOM, DESERT SHIELD, DOUBLESPEAK, DYSJOURNALISM, EXTRALEGAL CENSORSHIP, HIDDEN PERSUADERS, ISSUES MANAGEMENT, MEDIACRACY, MEMORY HOLE, MUCKRAKERS, NEW JOURNALISM, NEW WORLD INFORMATION AND COMMUNICATION ORDER (NWICO) DEBATE, OFF THE NEWS, ORCHESTRATED PROPAGANDA CAMPAIGN, PLANTING STORIES, POLEMIC, POLITICALLY CORRECT (PC), PRESS BASHING, SPIKE, and WORKING THE REFS.

MEDIACRACY—Term coined by RIGHT-WING/CONSERVATIVE political theorist Kevin Phillips in 1975 to disparage the power of the "LEFT-WING/LIBERAL national PRESS." Columnist John Walcott ("Land of Hype and Glory: Spin Doctors on Parade," *U.S. News & World Report*, 1992, pp. 6-7) argues that Phillips'

definition falls short: Mediacracy is not rule by the media but rule by those who know how to manipulate symbols, information and the media. It is rule by spin doctors, spokesmodels and celebrities. Its creed is spelled out by tennis player Andre Agassi in a television commercial: "Image is Everything."

See also PERCEPTION MANAGEMENT and SPIN DOCTORS.

MEDIA EFFECTS—Communication studies analyzing the impact of media whose methodologies borrow heavily from sociology and psychology. Most research can be grouped under "powerful effects" proponents, who argue that media have a strong influence on the public mind, and "minimal effects" findings, which dispute that the media alone have significant power to persuade or motivate. Scholars, noting that there are examples of each, currently tend to lean towards the middle in believing that media can be particularly effective but only in certain situations. See also AGENDA SETTING, CENSORSHIP, COGNITIVE DISSONANCE, HYPODERMIC NEEDLE THEORY, IDEODYNAMICS, MAGIC BULLET THEORY, MEDIACRACY, MEDIA BIAS, MEDIA LITERACY, SALIENCE, SPIKE, SPIRAL OF SILENCE, and TWO-STEP FLOW (MULTI-STEP FLOW).

MEDIA ELITE—The preponderance of American NEWS and entertainment comes from an interlocking cartel of less than twenty-five group ownership sources. In U.S. journalism this would include the *New York Times* and its syndicated news service, *Washington Post* (plus *Newsweek* and other properties), Dow Jones (owners of *Wall Street Journal* and other media), Gannett (*USA Today* and many other newspapers), Time-Warner (*Time, People Weekly*, books, cable, and other media), Turner Broadcasting (Cable News Network, *Turner Network Television*, WTBS-TV, and other media), ABC-Capitol Cities (ABC Network, etc.), General Electric (NBC Network, etc.), Loew's Inc. (CBS Network, movie interests, etc.), Fox (Fox TV Network, FX cable service, TV production, movies, etc.), TCI Cable, Public Broadcasting Service, plus other major news sources and syndicators such as the Associated Press, the *Los Angeles Times* and Tribune Media (*Chicago Tribune*, WGN-TV, radio etc.). Prestige NEWS MEDIA also includes *Christian Science Monitor*, *U.S News & World Report*, and several important journals of opinion (*Nation, National Review, New Republic*, etc.) In terms of entertainment television, cable, and films, again a limited number of production and distribution companies dominate. ANTI-SEMITIC propagandists have long claimed that Jews "control" the major media, but evidence is inconclusive and tainted by their other EXTREMIST views. See also BIG LIE, CONSPIRACY THEORIES, ELITE THEORY, MEDIA BIAS, PACK JOURNALISM, REVISIONISM/REVISIONIST, and SIDLE COMMISSION.

MEDIA KIT—Package of information containing NEWS RELEASEs, fact sheets, BACKGROUNDERs, photographs, POSITION PAPERS, reprints and other materials given to NEWS MEDIA representatives so as to simplify their jobs and maximize the possibility the supplying organization's "story" will be covered. Also known as a PRESS kit. See also FACT SLINGING, NEWS EMBARGO, and PUBLIC RELATIONS (PR).

MEDIA LITERACY—People of all ages are learning to apply a variety of critical thinking skills to the thousands of images, words and sounds that bombard us daily. A 1992 report from The Aspen Institute notes that the media literacy MOVEMENT seeks "to expand notions of literacy to include the powerful post-print media that dominate our informational landscape." According to Elizabeth Thoman of the Center for Media and Values, independent research shows that media literacy can be taught and, through guided practice, become everyday habits for both children and adults. For example, a fact sheet her organization distributes says:

Media literacy education into the influences of television empowers viewers to ask hard questions of themselves, of others and of society, to "make the connections" between what they see on the screen and what they experience at home, at work, at school. In formal classrooms as well as informal groups, media literacy activities are beginning to be integrated into every form of learning environment—schools, churches and temples, after-school groups and clubs. Although well established in many other countries, media literacy education is just beginning to emerge in the United States.

MEDIA MANIPULATION—See MEDIA BIAS and MEDIA EFFECTS.

MEDIA/MEDIUM—Any print, electronic, or other communication "vehicle" that serves to extend and amplify the reach of the communicator beyond that of small group communication. In simple terms, this might include a microphone, bull horn, telephone, or photocopied notice. The word *media* is the plural form (*medium* is the singular form). Thus, even though one commonly hears phrases such as, "the media has" or "the media is," these are incorrect and should be changed to "the media have" or "the media are." Print media include newspapers, magazines, newsletters, other periodicals, billboards, broadsides, books, pamphlets, brochures, tracts, handbills, lithographs, sheet music and a variety of items capable of carrying an imprinted message (even coffee cups and T-shirts with SPECIALTY ADVERTISING logos qualify). Filmic media include chemical-based photographs and motion pictures. Electronic media include radio, over-the-air broadcast television (TV), cable television, satellite direct broadcast systems, various electronic mail and other computerized message services, telephonic communication, recordings, videos, and related types of electromagnetic forms of communication. New advances, however, are blurring these distinctions (for example, DIGITIZED PHOTOGRAPHY and satellite delivery of newspapers). Generally, U.S. media are owned by businesses and may be grouped into industries.

There is no single guideline which determines when a technology becomes a MASS COMMUNICATION medium, and the whole concept is undergoing renewed scrutiny because of concerns by marketers about cost-effective targeting to the "right" demographic and/or psychographic audience profile. For example, in the United States there are:
- over 1,300 television and 10,000 radio stations,
- more than 1,600 daily newspapers,
- about 26,000 newsletters, magazines, and similar periodicals,
- thousands of other publications,
- hundreds of syndication sources, and
- a wide range of alternative media.

Despite this diversity, however, most of the major media in terms of prestige and circulation are owned by a shrinking list of conglomerate companies. Media performance is often a subject of controversy, particularly when they move beyond the role of objective sources of information into becoming promoters of personalities, events, ISSUEs, and cultural icons. See also ADVERTISING, BROADCASTING, CENSORSHIP, CONTROLLED MEDIA, C-SPAN, FREE SPEECH, JOURNALISM/JOURNALIST, MEDIA BIAS, MEDIA ELITE, NEWS MEDIA, OUTDOOR ADVERTISING, PRESS, TELECOMMUNICATIONS, VOICE OF AMERICA (VOA), and WEAPONS ON THE WALL.

MEMORY HOLE—Term used by George Orwell, in his satirical political commentary, *1984*, to describe the deliberate forgetting of inconvenient individuals and facts, particularly by governments which constantly shift alliances so that foreign powers switch from being bad guys, to good guys, and back to bad guys once again. In the novel, history is rewritten by workers in the Ministry of Truth who with regularity dispatch "nonpersons" to the "Memory Hole." See also ORWELLIAN TACTICS and PSEUDO-REALISM.

MI5—The British Security Service, largely responsible for domestic intelligence involving national security matters; U.K. counterpart to the Federal Bureau of Investigation (FBI) in the United States. See also FLUTTER, INTELLIGENCE COMMUNITY, MI6, UK or U.K., and WHITEHALL.

MILITARISM—The glorification of armed might and the role of the military in national history. Honest patriotism and respect for the sacrifices of members of the armed services during war is often cruelly exploited by PRESSURE GROUPS and jingoist PROFESSIONAL PATRIOTS who desire to foment new wars. PROPAGANDA is trotted out to prove the new "police action" or other "PEACEKEEPING" intervention to "halt aggression" derives from ostensibly noble and humanitarian purposes. An outpouring of HYPE, lies, and deliberate obfuscations usually masks the real reason: Powerful FACTIONs ranging from the so-called "defense industries" to the moneylenders make financial and political profit from war. The loser is truth and, of course, the working-class families whose flesh and blood is left on the front lines. Antimilitarism includes individuals and groups promoting everything from true pacifism (those who conscientiously object to participation in any war), to those objecting to government involvement in a specific conflict (as was the case for many antiwar PROTESTERS during the Vietnam War era). See also GLOBALISM, NEOLIBERALISM, SOMALIAZATION, and UNOSOM I/UNOSOM II/UNITAF.

MI6—The British Secret Intelligence Service, largely responsible for foreign intelligence and COVERT ACTIONs involving national security matters; U.K. counterpart to the CENTRAL INTELLIGENCE AGENCY (CIA) in the United States. See also ANGLOPHILE, BACKDOOR TO WAR, CIRCUS, ENTENTE, ESPIONAGE, FLUTTER, FREE WORLD, INTELLIGENCE COMMUNITY, MI5, NORTH ATLANTIC TREATY ORGANIZATION (NATO), PROPAGANDA, SPYING/SPYCRAFT, UK or U.K., and VETTING.

MKULTRA—The long-running COLD WAR mind- and behavior-control program created by scientists working for the CENTRAL INTELLIGENCE AGENCY (CIA) and Defense Department through a series of research FRONT GROUPS/SATELLITE ORGANIZATIONS typified by the Society for the Investigation of Human Ecology. As early as 1947, the Navy tested "speech-inducing drugs" to interrogate "enemy or subversive personnel" in what was called Operation Chatter. By 1952, the U.S. government's Psychological Strategy Board outlined an agenda to counteract Communist BRAINWASHING successes in Korea. This urged that a range of drug, electric shock, lobotomy, sensory deprivation, and other clinical studies be conducted by federal authorities "in a remote situation." The MKULTRA experiments involved exposing individuals to LSD and other powerful perception-altering drugs (PSYCHEDELICS) surreptitiously or without full explanations as to the potentially damaging side effects. CIA Director Richard Helms ordered the destruction of most MKULTRA DOCUMENTs in 1973 to prevent them becoming public. More recent government BLACK PROGRAM efforts have involved the creation of high-tech LTL (less than lethal) armaments designed to disorient militant protesters, subdue rioters, and quell other public disturbances without bloodshed See also PSYCHOLOGICAL WARFARE (PSYWAR).

MOSCOW CENTER—Nickname for the Soviet KGB intelligence apparatus based in Moscow, headquartered at 2 Dzerzhinsky Square. See also COLD WAR, COMMUNISM/COMMUNIST, ESPIONAGE, GRU (*Glavnoye Razvedyvatelnoye Upravlenie*), INTELLIGENCE COMMUNITY, KGB (*Komitet po Gosudarstvennoy Bezopasnosti*), SPYING/SPYCRAFT, and SVR (*Suzhba vneshnogo razvedky*).

MOSSAD ("INSTITUTE")—The most famous of the Israeli intelligence organizations, created on September 1, 1951, by a directive from Prime Minister David Ben-Gurion ordering that the Mossad be independent from Israel's Ministry of Foreign Affairs. The official Hebrew designation is *Ha Mossad, le Modiyn ve le Tafkidim Mayuhadim* ("The Institute for Intelligence and Special Operations"). The Mossad is generally considered one of the most effective ESPIONAGE and PROPAGANDA agencies in the world, but it has received negative publicity in the United States for its alleged involvement in the Iran-Contra, Banca Nazionale de Lavora, and other COVERT ACTION/spying scandals. See also INTELLIGENCE COMMUNITY, IRAN-CONTRA INVESTIGATIONS, NESHER, SPYING/SPYCRAFT, and ZIONISM/ZIONIST.

MOUTHPIECE—Derogatory term sometimes used to refer to an opposition's spokesperson—such as a lawyer or PUBLIC RELATIONS (PR) practitioner.

MOVEMENT—There is no common definition of this vague and often loosely applied term. This book defines a movement as a coalition of formally organized INTEREST GROUPS/PRESSURE GROUPS whose followers share a common goal and work to promote or resist change through collective action. The constituent groups usually each have a form of structure ranging from highly centralized to semi-autonomous, a written statement of purpose or

IDEOLOGY articulating their proposed blueprint for change, a leadership CADRE, followers/members, and a logistical support base.

Charles J. Stewart, Craig Allen Smith, and Robert E. Denton, Jr., in the second edition of *Persuasion and Social Movements* (1989), say a movement "is an organized, uninstitutionalized, and significantly large collectivity that emerges to bring about or to resist a program for change in societal norms and values, operates primarily through persuasive strategies, and encounters opposition in what becomes a moral struggle."

Daniel A. Foss and Ralph Larkin seek to distinguish social movements from reform politics and cultural or religious movements by arguing, in *Beyond Revolution: A New Theory of Social Movements* (1986), that "nonroutinized countercoercive physical force" is the "decisive criterion" for a social movement. They propose that

a social movement is the developing collective action of a significant portion of the members of a major social category, involving at some point the use of physical force or violence against members of other social categories, their possessions, or their institutionalized instrumentalities, and interfering at least temporarily—whether by design or unintended consequence—with the political and cultural reproduction of society.

However, Frances Fox Piven and Richard Cloward observe, in *Poor People's Movements: Why They Succeed, How They Fail* (1977), that "the substantial record of violence associated with protest movements in the United States is a record composed overwhelmingly of the casualties suffered by protesters at the hands of public or private armies." Focusing on violence also obviously excludes the possibility of a pacifistic action, a point made by Herbert W. Simons, Elizabeth W. Mechling, and Howard N. Schreier. The alternative definition preferred by these researchers in their essay on "The Functions of Human Communication in Mobilizing for Action from the Bottom Up," (1984) sees social movements as "sustained efforts by noninstitutionalized collectivities to mobilize resources, resist counter-pressures, and exert external influence in behalf of a cause."

See also ACTION GROUP, ACTIVISTS, ADVOCACY ADVERTISING, AGAINST THE MAIL, AGENDA SETTING, AGENTS/AGENCIES OF INFLUENCE, AGITATION, AGITPROP, ANARCHISM/ANARCHIST, ANIMAL RIGHTS MOVEMENT, ANTIAUTHORITARIANISM, ARMED PROPAGANDA, ARMED STRUGGLE, ASSETS, AUTONOMIST, CAPI-TALISM/CAPITALIST, CITIZENS FOR AMERICA (CFA), COALITION, COMMUNISM/COMMUNIST, CONFLICT RESOLUTION, COPPER-HEADS, DIRECT CONFRONTATION, ELECTRONIC COMMUNITY NETWORK, ELECTRONIC DEMOCRACY, ESTABLISHMENT, EX-TREMISM, FACTION, FASCISM/FASCIST, FIFTH COLUMN, FIRST AMENDMENT, FOREIGN AGENTS REGISTRATION ACT (FARA), FOUNDATIONS, FREE SPEECH, FREETHINKERS, FRONT GROUPS/ SATELLITE ORGANIZATIONS, FUNDAMENTALISM/FUNDAMENTAL-ISTS, GRANFALLOONS, GRASSROOTS LOBBYING, GRASSROOTS POLITICAL ACTION, GRASSTOPS, HATE GROUPS, IDEOLOGUES,

ISOLATIONIST, LEFT-WING/LIBERAL, LIBERATION MOVEMENT, LOYALIST, MANUFACTURING OF CONSENT (or CONSENSUS), MARCH OF PROVOCATION, MARXIST, MASS COMMUNICATION, MOUTHPIECE, MUCKRAKERS, NATIONAL SOCIALISM/NAZISM, NEOLIBERALISM, NEW AGE MOVEMENT, ORCHESTRATED PROPAGANDA CAMPAIGN, ORGANIZATIONS WITHOUT FORM, PAWNS, PEOPLE'S PARTY, PEOPLE'S WAR, POLEMIC, POLITICAL ACTION COMMITTEES (PACs), POLITICALLY CORRECT (PC), POPULAR OPINION, POPULAR FRONT/PEOPLE'S FRONT, POPULISM/POPULIST, PRESS, PROGRESSIVE/PROGRESSIVISM, PROTESTERS, PSEUDO-EVENT/PSEUDO-NEWS, PUBLIC, PUBLIC COMMUNICATION, PUBLIC INTEREST, PUBLICITY, PUBLIC OPINION, PUBLIC POLICY PROCESS, PUBLIC RELATIONS (PR), PUBLIC SERVICE ANNOUNCEMENTS (PSAs), PUBLIC SERVICE EVENTS, PURPOSEFUL PERSUASION, RACIST/RACIALIST/RACIAL DISCRIMINATION, RADICAL, REACTIONARY, RED-BAITING, RED DECADE, RESCUE OPERATION, REVISIONISM/REVISIONIST, REVOLUTION/REVOLUTIONARY, RIGHT-WING/CONSERVATIVE, RITUAL DEFAMATION, *SAMIZDAT*, SCAPEGOAT/SCAPEGOATING, SOCIALISM/SOCIALIST, SOCIAL MARKETING, SPIN DOCTORS, SPOKESMANSHIP/SPOKESPERSON TRAINING, STAKEHOLDERS, STRATEGIC LAWSUITS AGAINST PUBLIC PARTICIPATION (SLAPP), SUBVERSION/SUBVERSIVES, SUFFRAGETTES, TEMPERANCE MOVEMENT, TERROR GROUP, TERRORISM, TERRORIST, UMBRELLA ORGANIZATIONS, UNCONVENTIONAL WARFARE, VANGUARD, WHISPERING CAMPAIGN, WOBBLIES, WOMEN'S MOVEMENT, ZAPATISTAS, ZEALOTS, and ZIONISM/ZIONIST.

MUCKRAKERS—Investigative writers, most active in the 1902-1912 period, who exposed government corruption and the "money power" exercised by corporate "trusts" and other "vested interests" controlled by "the ruling families." Their work documenting the misconduct of prominent individuals and institutions appeared more frequently in magazines and books than in newspapers. Ida M. Tarbell and Lincoln Steffens were among the most prominent muckrakers of the early twentieth-century. Later journalists, such as Seymour Hersh and Bob Woodward, and critics, such as George Seldes and Ralph Nader, have continued the muckraking tradition. An important contemporary source is *Muckraker*, the journal of the Center for Investigative Reporting. See also ACTIVISTS, CONSPIRACY THEORIES, JOURNALISM/JOURNALIST, MEDIA BIAS, RADICAL, and SOCIALISM/SOCIALIST.

NAFTA—The North American Free Trade Agreement, a formal pact to reduce tariffs and other trade barriers between Canada, the United States, Mexico, and other future participants. In the largest known media and lobbying campaign conducted in the United States by foreign interests, the Mexican government and Mexican business groups spent more than $25 million persuading Congress to approve NAFTA in 1993. See also FOREIGN AGENTS REGISTRATION ACT (FARA), FREE TRADE, LOBBYING/LOBBYIST,

NEOLIBERALISM, and ZAPATISTAS.

NARROWCASTING—Instead of reaching out to the broadest possible general audience, this practice involves directing messages to a more highly differentiated and narrowly defined marketing niche. This occurs through very selective buying in mass media and increase use of specialized or targeted media. See also BINGO CARDS, BROADCASTING, DIRECT MARKETING (DM), and SPECIALTY ADVERTISING.

NATIONAL INFORMATION INFRASTRUCTURE (NII)—Proposals to form interactive high speed electronic networks that bring together into one national system various TELECOMMUNICATIONS technologies and information sources ranging from raw data providers to schools to entertainment services. As envisioned by the Clinton administration, the National Information Infrastructure (NII) will consist of thousands of interconnected, interoperable media sites containing:
  • computer systems;
  • consumer electronics such as television monitors, fax machines, telephones, and other "information appliances";
  • software, database, and information/library services; and
  • trained people who can build, maintain, and operate these systems.
   Vice President Al Gore, in particular, has put political muscle behind "information highway" efforts to forge agreements between government and industry. Proponents argue the emerging advanced NII "digital superhighway" needs such a public-private partnership if the United States is to effectively tie available electronic resources together into a seamless on-line web that will conveniently put vast amounts of information at users' fingertips. They see this linkup as not only a necessary good for its own sake, but point to the potential for economic growth and improved social performance. Development of the NII can help unleash an information revolution that will change forever the way people live, work, and interact with each other. The ultimate goal is enhanced delivery of electronic information in a "knowledge-based DEMOCRACY" or "teledemocracy," which uses technologies more creatively so that citizens can easily access and influence government and private services.
   The initiatives to form a coherent national information infrastructure stem from breakthrough commercial developments. With the enactment of the High Performance Computer and Communications Initiative (HPCCI), discussions currently have the purpose of building coalitions to further support the PUBLIC POLICY PROCESS framework essential to creating such an advanced information-based interconnect. What this net will actually turn out to be is mostly speculation at this point. Critics warn that what may result is a corporate system supported by government which crowds out ACTIVISTS and other independent voices by relying too heavily on existing media conglomerate models of control. Among the federal agencies involved in coordinating various proposals is the National Telecommunications and Information Administration.

See also COMPUTER-MEDIATED COMMUNICATION (CMC), CYBER-

SPACE, ELECTRONIC COMMUNITY NETWORK, ELECTRONIC DEMOCRACY, INFORMATION AGE/INFORMATION SOCIETY, INTERNET, NATIONAL RESEARCH AND EDUCATION NETWORK (NREN), and TELCO.

NATIONAL INTELLIGENCE COUNCIL (NIC)—A federal advisory group of academic and other specialists who coordinate with the director of central intelligence in establishing overall U.S. intelligence policy. See also CENTRAL INTELLIGENCE AGENCY (CIA) and NATIONAL SECURITY COUNCIL (NSC).

NATIONAL RESEARCH AND EDUCATION NETWORK (NREN)—NREN was originally conceived as the government-owned and supported high-speed computer gigabit communications "backbone" for the proposed NATIONAL INFORMATION INFRASTRUCTURE (NII). The program has evolved so that NREN is now seen as unifying many "technologies without boundaries" to form the "INFORMATION AGE/INFORMATION SOCIETY interstate." Recent focus has been on setting policies and subsidizing various organizations in the research and education communities to encourage accelerated development of the network. It is being sold as a tool for advancing the U.S. national interest by promoting technological (and thus economic) competitiveness.

NATIONAL SECURITY COUNCIL (NSC)—A very senior executive branch body consisting of the president, the president's assistant for national security affairs (commonly called the national security advisor), the vice president, the secretaries of defense and state, and designated staff members. The director of central intelligence and the chairman of the Joint Chiefs of Staff have advisory responsibilities. The primary function of the NSC is to counsel the president on domestic, foreign, and military planning related to the security of the nation. The NSC has served as a convenient vehicle to design and order implementation of administration foreign policies, including COVERT ACTIONs. See also INTELLIGENCE COMMUNITY and NATIONAL SECURITY PLANNING GROUP (NSPG).

NATIONAL SECURITY PLANNING GROUP (NSPG)—During the Reagan administration, the NSPG served as a convenient decision-making vehicle to bypass the NATIONAL SECURITY COUNCIL (NSC) when implementing even more COVERT plans. Included were the president, a small number of trusted top international-policy advisors, and the director of central intelligence.

NATIONAL SOCIALISM/NAZISM—The international fascist political MOVEMENT led by the National-Sozialistische Deutsche Arbeiter Partei (NSDAP, NAZI, NS, or National Socialist German Workers party) founded in 1919. Under the direction of charismatic leader (or *führer*) Adolf Hitler, the Nazis grew in influence. Benefiting from the economic destabilization of the Weimar Republic caused by the unequal treatment of the Versailles Treaty and the worldwide spread of the Great Depression, by the early 1930s his followers contested for control of Germany. Because of Hitler's experiences in the German Army during World War I where he saw first-hand the impact of British disinformation campaigns, he incorporated PROPAGANDA as an essential component of NSDAP's IDEOLOGY. Soon after the Nazis achieved power in Germany in 1933, the government created an active Ministry of Propaganda and Public Enlightenment run by another charismatic National Socialist leader, Dr. Joseph Goebbels. Aryan racism that loudly declared Germans as "the master race" was linked to a growing persecution of Jews, Jehovah's Witnesses, and other minorities. Nazi economic policies involved large public works projects and rearmament, eventually leading to the repudiation of the Versailles Treaty and the outbreak of World War II.

The defeat of Germany along with its "Axis" partners ended the Nazi regime and led to the banning of Nazi or Nazi-like fascist political movements in many countries. In recent years, however, the impact of historical revisionism, the continued underground distribution of pro-Nazi materials, and appearance of alienated youth spouting neo-Nazi slogans while engaging in skinhead violence has raised new concerns from Jewish and other anti-Nazi INTEREST GROUPS. See also ANGLOPHOBE, ANTI-SEMITIC, BIG LIE, CENTRAL POWERS, DISINFORMATION (*DEZINFORMATSIA*), FASCISM/ FASCIST, FIFTH COLUMN, GERMANOPHOBIA, GREAT WAR, REVISIONISM/REVISIONIST, RIGHT-WING/CONSERVATIVE, and SOCIALISM/SOCIALIST.

NEOLIBERALISM—A term used by leftist commentators and other critics of U.S. foreign policy efforts. While neoliberalism is a very new word in North America, it is widely used elsewhere to refer to the exportation of classic laissez-faire economic policies into their countries. In the nineteenth-century, for example, liberalism was the capitalist IDEOLOGY before the age of monopolies. In the struggle between liberal and conservative forces, liberalism and nationalism generally triumphed. This proved a mixed blessing, particularly in Latin America, where the elite social and financial sectors enjoyed broad-based links to international markets but their nations remained essentially dependent to interests in the United States and Europe. Even while ostensibly benefiting from decolonialization, the results also included the weakening of indigenous communities, imposition of imported cultural norms, the expropriation of peasant and church lands by the wealthier classes who controlled the state apparatus, and the danger of military intervention by powerful countries under the guise of "stability." Neoliberalism is also dressed up in "fair play" and "competitiveness" language, but it remains the same ideology and economic doctrine in this age of worldwide cartels and monopolies. International FREE TRADE proposals emanating from the United States, including TELECOMMUNICATIONS developments, are seen as "the siren song of the sharks seeking to eat the sardines. Now the aim is to wipe out every industrial development in our countries, to make cheapest the labour force, and to use the Latin American markets as a shelter for the USA against Europe and Japan," wrote activist Victor Ahaya in an on-line memorandum widely distributed in 1993 during the NAFTA debate.

The International Monetary Fund is instrumental for that policy of collective pain.

They ask that so-called "structural adjustments" to be implemented before providing loans. This means, basically, to reduce public expenses by closing state-run departments and enterprises (creating unemployment) or privatizing them; to reduce expenditures in education and health, and so on. When the loans come, they are to pay interest for the astronomical foreign debt, which is now around $400 billion.

See also CAPITALISM/CAPITALIST, CLASSICAL LIBERALISM, COMMUNISM/COMMUNIST, CULTURAL IMPERIALISM, ELITE THEORY, FOREIGN AID, FREE WORLD, FRIENDLY SUBVERSION, GLOBALISM, HUMAN RIGHTS, IMPERIALISM/IMPERIALIST, INTERVENTIONIST, IRAN-CONTRA INVESTIGATIONS, LEFT-WING/LIBERAL, LIBERATION THEOLOGY, MILITARISM, NEW WORLD INFORMATION AND COMMUNICATION ORDER (NWICO) DEBATE, PEACE-KEEPING, PUBLIC DIPLOMACY, RIGHT-WING/CONSERVATIVE, SOMALIAZATION, THIRD WORLD, TRANSNATIONAL CORPORATIONS, TRILATERAL COMMISSION, UNIVERSAL DECLARATION OF HUMAN RIGHTS, and UNOSOM I/UNOSOM II/UNITAF.

NESHER—A secretive, behind-the-scenes group, whose name means "Eagle" in Hebrew, which was founded by high-ranking officials in the Reagan administration to "promote and protect" Israel's interests in U.S. government decision-making. By the late 1980s, more than one-hundred influential members of the national security ESTABLISHMENT belonged to the loose-knit "club" which maintained close links to the MEDIA ELITE, INTELLIGENCE COMMUNITY, and the powerful Israel lobby. Despite the change from Republican to Democratic control of the White House, some analysts attribute the influence of Nesher and its allied organizations to the orchestrated downfall of FBI Director William Sessions in 1993. He was allegedly targeted not so much because of conflict-of-interest allegations but for his failures to "contain" politically sensitive information linking the MOSSAD ("INSTITUTE") and prominent U.S. political figures to the IRAN-CONTRA INVESTIGATIONS and the Banca Nazionale de Lavora scandal. See also ANTI-DEFAMATION LEAGUE OF B'NAI B'RITH (ADL), DUAL-LOYALIST, INSIDERS, LOBBYING/LOBBYIST, MANDARINS, ZIONISM/ZIONIST, and ZOG.

NEW AGE MOVEMENT—A loose collection of nonorthodox alternative life-styles and religious groups that encourage people to look within themselves for spiritual growth, search for a higher consciousness, and discover answers to life's problems. The MOVEMENT is a collage of various organizations with widely divergent outward emphases—including Eastern religionists, astrologists, mother earthists, occultists, para-normalists, mystics, pop psychologists, psychics, tarot card readers, Scientologists, shamanists, spiritualists, theosophists, and wiccaists to name a few. Many of these ACTIVISTS employ media-savvy communication techniques, often benefiting from celebrity members, such as Shirley MacLaine, who appear on their behalf. Although there has been a backlash against the "New Age" label because of excesses by EXTREMIST fringe elements, growing acceptance of

New Age IDEOLOGY by the culture at large is occurring. The impact of the movement is supplemented by thousands of New Age books and other paraphernalia available from specialized stores. While the range of practices under such a large umbrella is great, New Age groups tend to share the following beliefs in common:

- There is a "universal oneness" that unites everything—seen and unseen, living and inanimate—in a single essence.
- Because we are all one, there are no ultimate rights and wrongs. The physical world, including our current bodies, is largely an illusion.
- Death is not final, since every living thing is on a path of evolutionary enlightenment and undergoes rebirth in new forms through reincarnation.
- We are gods. Humans, by being part of the universal oneness, are divine. Even though we suffer from spiritual amnesia of our past existences, we can rediscover ourselves and the oneness through various means. Advanced "masters" and gurus will serve as spiritual guides to help "channel" messages and lead us to higher truths, aided by our studying esoteric knowledge, meditating, playing special musical harmonies, chanting mantras, manipulating body positions, crystal healing, altering mind-sets through ingestion of PSYCHEDELICS, and other practices.

Ironically, none of these ideas or experiences are particularly new, with much that is taught being a variant of Hindu and other Eastern belief systems that are thousands of years old. Sometimes, New Age beliefs are presented as a form of religion compatible with Christianity. Opponents consider them dangerous counterfeit mystic delusions propagated by Satanically inspired anti-Judeo-Christian cultists and money-grubbing con artists. See also ANTI-SEMITE, CULT, and PROPAGANDA DEVICES.

NEW JOURNALISM—New journalism is a loose MOVEMENT which rejects the importance of objectivity in news coverage and instead embraces an activist commitment to promoting various forms of social responsibility. As Richard Kallan observed in the mid-1970s, one of the major premises of "new journalism" is that there are not always two equal sides for each story. New journalists are proud to be biased in the types of reports they favor and the specific reforms and/or ideologies they advocate. The technique of presenting the facts from a personal perspective is at the heart of concurrent developments in television programming (typified by widespread implementation of eyewitness NEWS, TABLOID JOURNALISM, and some contemporary DOCUDRAMA formats). There is also increasing acceptance of "new journalism" by mainstream publications seeking to generate interest and controversy important to funding bottom-line profits. Other terms have also described this mix of literary form and NEWS MEDIA reporting: ADVOCACY JOURNALISM, participatory journalism, saturation reporting, and so on. See also ACTIVISTS, JOURNALISM/JOURNALIST, and MEDIA BIAS.

NEWS—Technically, news is anything a journalist reports. There is no universally accepted definition, although conventions promoted by U.S.-based trade organizations and textbooks typically assert that news is an accurate, fair, balanced, and objective report of current developments appearing in a journalistic medium. Such a report incorporates certain NEWS VALUES based on criteria such as prominence, impact, timeliness, proximity, human interest, and conflict. See also JOURNALISM/JOURNALIST, NEW JOURNALISM, and NEWS MEDIA.

NEWS EMBARGO—Informal agreement under which journalists are given advance copies of important information (speeches, public policy statements, and research reports) by PUBLIC AFFAIRS and PUBLIC RELATIONS (PR) sources on the understanding these will not be publicly utilized until a specified day and time set by the releasing organization. Offering desirable information and access to newsmakers on an exclusive basis to influential NEWS outlets increases the likelihood those holding the exclusive (the "feeding favorites") will give it greater play. An alternative strategy is for sources to release news items close to the reporters' deadline ("controlled timing"), making it difficult for them to obtain independent verification or alternative commentary. When very bad news (TOXIC INFORMATION) has to be faced, some organizations pretend they are acting in a timely manner by scheduling its release after deadline or on weekends to minimize the negative impact and get it OFF THE NEWS.

NEWS FEED—A grouping of syndicated or network NEWS reports and VIDEO NEWS RELEASE (VNR) story packages sent via satellite to affiliates for airing and editing as the recipients see fit.

NEWS HOLE—The amount of space or time left over for NEWS in a publication or broadcast after the ADVERTISING and other nonnews elements are included.

NEWS MEDIA—Those print, electronic, and other media which define their principle role as the supplying of information about current events and processes, or whose journalistic units have an important impact on public awareness (i.e., the television network NEWS arms). See also JOURNALISM/JOURNALIST and MEDIA/MEDIUM.

NEWSPEAK—Term created by George Orwell where the communicator's intention is to uncouple rational thought from action by making speech as nearly as possible independent of consciousness. Commonly used by spokespersons for business, education, government, military and other groups. See also DOUBLESPEAK, ORWELLIAN TACTICS, PROPAGANDA DEVICES, SOCIOLINGUISTICS, and WEASEL WORDS.

NEWS RELEASE—Information distributed in print or electronic form by an organization designed to elicit NEWS MEDIA coverage; same as "PRESS release" or "media release." See also COURT OF PUBLIC OPINION, MEDIA KIT, VICTORY BY NEWS RELEASE, and VIDEO NEWS RELEASE (VNR).

NEWS VALUES—Out of the whole panorama of life, certain events, trends, organizations, and individuals are singled out by journalists as more newsworthy than others. Reporting textbooks generally point to the presence of certain "news values" as important determinants in this process. Five of the most widely cited include:

- *impact/consequence*, or what numbers of people are affected and to what degree will their lives be influenced by the events,
- *prominence*, or how well-known are the people and institutions involved,
- *currency*, or how relevant is the story to today's social conditions,
- *conflict*, so that dramatic differences between two or more sides to an ISSUE can be presented, and
- *uniqueness*, or how deviant or unusual are the events from everyday norms.

See also FRAMING DEVICES, JOURNALISM/JOURNALIST, and SHIRT-TAILING.

NEW WORLD INFORMATION AND COMMUNICATION ORDER (NWICO) DEBATE—International efforts by THIRD WORLD nations to break the stranglehold of European and American media organizations in control of information. One of the more important mechanisms furthering the NWICO agenda to massively redistribute wealth and resources was the work of the International Commission for the Study of Communication Problems. The resulting study, *Many Voices One World* (the *"MacBride Report,"* 1980), provoked renewed controversy when it argued for a powerful MEDIA EFFECTS model. Representatives of many nations now question the business-oriented FREE TRADE communications model promoted by the United States since it seems to leave their countries permanently in a second class position. While AMERICA BASHING is still popular among LEFT-WING/LIBERAL critics of NEOLIBERALISM, many suspect that a key reason for the continued dominance of Western media is that, for all their faults, they are more credible than the craven, propagandistic "palaver" emanating from state-sponsored information departments.

NON-DENIAL DENIAL—A diversion tactic to avoid directly responding to harmful allegations (especially when they are true). Instead, the smoke screen effort is characterized by resorting to coordinated attacks on the character of opponents, assailing their credibility, focusing on the small picture of minor inconsistencies in their case, and responding with condemnatory phrases ("outrageous," "inappropriate," "terrible," "incredible," etc.) which imply but never quite make a categorical denial. See also DEMONIZING THE OPPOSITION, NEWSPEAK, and WEASEL WORDS.

NONGOVERNMENTAL ORGANIZATIONS (NGOs)—Private groups that:

- provide specific advice, expertise and assistance,
- monitor government practices,
- mobilize support for HUMAN RIGHTS and other causes, and/or
- lobby for public policy changes before national legislatures, the

UNITED NATIONS ORGANIZATION (UNO or UN) and its agencies, and at other international forums.

For example, the International Labour Office (ILO), the World Intellectual Property Organization (WIPO), the Economic and Social Council of the United Nations, and the United Nations Educational, Scientific, and Cultural Organization (UNESCO) all officially work with NGOs. UNESCO awards "consultative status A" to a restricted number of nongovernmental organizations which are broadly international in membership, of proven competence in an important field of education, science or culture, and have a record of making regular major contributions to UNESCO's programs. There are literally hundreds of NGOs, with Amnesty International and the American Friends Service Committee being among the best known for their human rights efforts. In the United States, such organizations often seek section 501(c)(3) status under the Internal Revenue Code in order to preserve tax deductible status for donated contributions, but may be precluded if seen as too partisan or political. See also COUNCIL ON FOREIGN RELATIONS (CFR), INTEREST GROUPS, LOBBYING/LOBBYIST, PRESSURE GROUPS, and TRILATERAL COMMISSION.

NORTH AMERICAN FREE TRADE AGREEMENT—See NAFTA.

NORTH ATLANTIC TREATY ORGANIZATION (NATO)—The North Atlantic Treaty of 1949, a multinational agreement, formed NATO as an anticommunist, geopolitical military alliance led by the United States. The COLD WAR pact was signed by Belgium, Britain, Canada, Denmark, France, Holland, Iceland, Italy, Luxembourg, Norway, Portugal, and the U.S. In 1951, Greece and Turkey joined, and the former West Germany became a member in 1955. NATO headquarters are in Brussels, Belgium. French insistence on an independent nuclear force and refusal to participate in some of NATO's maneuvers weakened the organization in the mid-1960s. With the collapse of the old Soviet Union and the breakup of its Eastern Bloc Warsaw Pact military alliance, NATO's role is undergoing reevaluation with new "partners for peace" initiatives to former adversaries in central and eastern Europe. NATO strategists seem to repositioning the organization to serve as a broader, international, political, public policy forum as well as a military alliance capable of intervening in smaller localized conflicts stemming from renewed ethnic fighting in the former Yugoslavia and other parts of the world.

OCTOBER SURPRISE—Theory that members of Ronald Reagan's 1980 campaign team, led by William Casey and George Bush, engaged in secret negotiations with Iranian representatives to delay the return from Tehran of fifty-two U.S. hostages until after the November elections. The purpose of the alleged conspiracy was to ensure a Reagan-Bush victory by denying President Jimmy Carter any political advantage a last-minute release might create for the beleaguered incumbent. The allegations, if proved true, would imply not only illegality but TREASON. However, later congressional investigations dismissed most of the charges as false. See also CONSPIRACY THEORIES.

OFFICE OF CENSORSHIP—U.S. government agency in World War II responsible for preventing sensitive information from appearing publicly. For example, stories about nuclear research were monitored to prevent speculation or more serious accidental NEWS leaks involving the super-secret nuclear bomb research program known as the Manhattan Project. See also CENSORSHIP.

OFFICE OF STRATEGIC SERVICES (OSS)—The American intelligence agency established in World War II to coordinate SPYING/SPYCRAFT and COVERT ACTION, headed by William J. "Wild Bill" Donovan. The OSS was the predecessor to the CENTRAL INTELLIGENCE AGENCY (CIA). See also ESPIONAGE and INTELLIGENCE COMMUNITY.

OFFICE OF WAR INFORMATION (OWI)—U.S. World War II PUBLIC RELATIONS (PR) effort headed by veteran journalist Elmer Davis.

OFFICIAL IDEOLOGY—Particularly in totalitarian nations, the set of values and beliefs imposed by the centralized bureaucracy and the party apparatus make up the official IDEOLOGY. State power is often projected through instruments of CENSORSHIP and other organs that reinforce the voice of ideological control. See also ORWELLIAN TACTICS.

OFF THE NEWS—Issues that fail to receive much NEWS MEDIA coverage or "play" are considered off the news. There are a number of reasons why potential stories do not break through into print or on air. However, savvy NEWS sources can successfully define the agenda of stories that are reported and influence the type of coverage by spoon feeding the PRESS.

OFF THE RECORD—The practice of providing confidential information to journalists on the understanding that it will not be openly published or broadcast with attribution. Sometimes the information is leaked simply as BACKGROUND so the reporter has a better understanding of the process and ISSUEs being addressed by the source. In other cases, the materials can be used in preparing stories, but no linkage is to be made to the source. These explanatory briefings give authorities a chance to present their official point of view without fear of being held accountable should the resulting report prove controversial or incorrect. Journalists occasionally violate these conventions, particularly when they have not given assent as part of the ground rules established at the beginning of their researches. However, when reporters break a verbal contract state courts have ruled they can be legally held accountable. In practice, most journalists accept off-the-record agreements because their access to inside information (particularly from government sources) would dry up without them.

OLD GLORY—The U.S. national flag, also commonly known as the Stars and Stripes. See also FLAG WAVING.

OMNIBUS WORDS—Words or phrases, such as *peace* and *freedom*, that are emotionally charged but obscure real communication by meaning all things to all people. Theologian Francis Shaeffer referred to these as "contentless banners." The use of omnibus words is widespread in PROPAGANDA and diplomacy. See also CODE WORDS, DOUBLESPEAK, ETHNIC CLEANSING, EUPHEMISM, NEWSPEAK, THOUGHT-STOPPING CLICHÉ, and WEASEL WORDS.

OP-ED—Journalistic shorthand for "opposite-editorial page." According to *The Why, Who and How of the Editorial Page*, by Kenneth Rystrom (1983, pp. 290-291), the term first appeared in the early 1920s. Herbert Swope, the executive editor for Joseph Pulitzer's *New York World*, reputedly said of his innovation: "I devised a method of cleaning off the page opposite the editorial page . . . and thereon I decided to print opinions, ignoring facts."

OPEN SOURCE INTELLIGENCE (OSCINT)—See GRAY/GREY LITERATURE.

OPERATION JUST CAUSE—The code name for the December 1989 invasion of Panama by U.S. military forces, including PSYCHOLOGICAL WARFARE (PSYWAR) specialists. See also SIDLE COMMISSION.

OPPO RESEARCH—A political campaign term, referring to the systematic creation of a computerized record of information about the opposition. The database tracks NEWS MEDIA accounts, financial dealings, public statements, speeches, voting records, and other materials that may later prove useful in PLANTING STORIES and designing attack advertisements to undercut the other side. Political aides routinely leak such potentially damaging information about their opponents to reporters on BACKGROUND, a condition that the source not be identified. The practice of such intelligence gathering and active counterthrusts, however, is not limited to candidates and is widespread in other institutions. See also HANDLERS, POLISPOTS, POLITICAL ANALYSTS, SPIN CONTROL, and SPIN DOCTORS.

ORCHESTRATED PROPAGANDA CAMPAIGN—Continuing series of accusations (truth or falsity is usually irrelevant) using various media to create a TOXIC INFORMATION barrage or blitz that drives home a single point. The moralistic branding and tone of outrage that often accompanies such charges is designed to be preemptive, minimizing the effect of the opposition's COUNTERPROPAGANDA by setting the ISSUE agenda and boxing them into a defensive position. The PROPAGANDA person, organization, IDEOLOGY, or country is portrayed in such a villainous way that a TRIAL BY NEWS RELEASE occurs long before legal action may be instituted, directing the treatment of the topic so that the third-party recipients of the propaganda react in a preconditioned manner. See also AGENDA SETTING and PACK JOURNALISM.

ORGANIZATIONS WITHOUT FORM—An amorphous network of underground ACTIVISTS and organizations united against the government in power but differing in their goals and strategies. These groups range from nonviolent CLANDESTINE resistance forces and HUMAN RIGHTS monitors to militant guerrillas committed to ARMED STRUGGLE.

ORWELLIAN TACTICS—Systematic distortion, lying, and fakery are essential PROPAGANDA DEVICES of state control. Orwellian tactics, named for the practices exposed in George Orwell's nightmarish novel, *1984*, refer to an ends-justify-the-means approach whereby reality is distorted. For example, Central American ACTIVISTS in the 1980s pointed out numerous examples where government officials imposed "institutionalized lies" upon society through "the systematic screening of reality." This screening of reality takes various forms: it begins with an ORCHESTRATED PROPAGANDA CAMPAIGN aggressively supported by all the public and private instruments at the command of government to create an "official story" which ignores crucial aspects of reality, distorts others, and even falsifies or invents still others. This institutionalized lying has the added advantage of allowing those in power to loot the public treasury and conceal the high levels of corruption within the government. An "imposed silence" is placed upon inconvenient facts which challenge the institutionalized lie and cannot be entirely concealed by the state; such facts are simply ignored and forgotten over time. Independent reporting that actually unmasks the government's repressive measures is considered "subversive" and subjects the journalist or other whistleblower to legal harassment—with the most troublesome targeted for assassination or "disappearance" by DEATH SQUADS.

OUTDOOR ADVERTISING—A communication medium noted for its message displays that target drivers, individuals using public transportation, and pedestrians. The sheer dominating size of many billboards creates impact and helps maintain awareness. As a form of ADVERTISING, outdoor also offers marketing flexibility ranging from mass coverage to ethnic and geographic targeting. It provides a long-term, day-in/day-out presence that reminds viewers of other ad efforts, generates high levels of message recall, and does so affordably. Among the common forms of outdoor advertising are:
  - *painted bulletins*, large signs (often 14 by 48 feet) in which the copy is reproduced by painting directly on the surface,
  - *posters*, standard billboards containing preprinted paper sheets with messages and artwork,
  - *illuminateds*, displays which can be seen at night, including *backlights*, where the ad appears on polyvinylchloride (PVC) sheets and is illuminated from behind,
  - *spectaculars*, longer-term displays using incandescent lamps, luminous flashers, oversize inflatable objects, board movement, overlays, and other devices to attract attention, and
  - *transits*, message cards and smaller posters appearing on busses, trains, subways, transit stops, shopping malls, and other out-of-automobile locations.

The Outdoor Advertising Association of America, Inc. (OAAA) is the trade association which recommends industry-wide business standards for display structures, services, market coverage measurements, and public policy initiatives in the United States. See also POLITICAL GRAPHICS and WEAPONS ON THE WALL.

OUT OF THE LOOP—Claims made that a person was not part of the decision-making chain of command, generally asserted when some action goes awry. See also INSIDERS and PLAUSIBLE DENIABILITY.

PACK JOURNALISM—Journalists often consult each other for reassurance, relying on consensus as a guard against individual error. Contrary to their image as investigators whose "job is to comfort the afflicted and to afflict the comfortable" (quoting veteran newspaperman James Gordon Bennett of the old *New York Herald*), most producers, editors, and reporters today tend to "run with the herd." Outside of the handful of NEWS enterprises with their own correspondents, the Associated Press singularly dominates national coverage by U.S. broadcasters and smaller market newspapers. MEDIA ELITE such as the *New York Times* and *Washington Post*, are powerful in that they influence not only policymakers and readers in key markets, but also the story selection lineup for thousands of other print and broadcast outlets across the country. They further reinforce this interpretive slant through articles, columns and features distributed and reprinted through their syndicated news services. This creates a circular flow of information in which later "research" by reporters typically entails a quick review of existing information in clip files and electronic databases. For an individual or organization either attacked or promoted, this recycled background check is often superficial and serves to reinforce existing attitudes and prejudices. Reporters and editors also tend to judge their success by the praise of their peers. While some MUCKRAKERS still find work, taking an idiosyncratic or contrary approach is rarely attempted in the mainstream PRESS. Publishers fear the "wrong kind" of controversy can threaten ADVERTISING and their community standing. Working journalists too far from the pack consensus also worry about being marginalized, with those "stepping across the line" facing dismissive ridicule from other newspeople whose opinions they value.

PAMPHLETEERING—The distribution of pamphlets, manifestoes, posters and other materials designed to arouse opinion and mobilize public action—usually against "the established order" currently in power. American revolutionary Tom Paine was an early proponent of pamphleteering, a tradition continued by *SAMIZDAT* (self-publishing) writers. Modern communication advances have opened up new outlets. Radio and television already cross national boundaries, with profound effects, but have been dominated by governments and large private interests. These are facing legal challenges from a growing number of community-minded micro broadcasters operating low power stations without regulatory sanction. New electronic technology systems are proving even more populist. INTERNET, for example, features thousands of on-line forums devoted to political and social issues on an ever-changing international data stream, making it increasingly difficult for governments to suppress their peoples.

PAPER TIGER—A term popularized by the Maoist regime in China to refer to an impotent United States, whose REACTIONARY government engaged in propagandistic bravado but little concrete COUNTERREVOLUTIONARY action. In a talk with American NEWS correspondent Anna Louise Strong in August 1946, Mao Tse-tung observed: "All reactionaries are paper tigers. In appearance, the reactionaries are terrifying, but in reality they are not so powerful. From a long-term point of view, it is not the reactionaries but the people who are really powerful" (See *Quotations from Chairman Mao Tse-tung*, 1972 edition, p. 72).

PARROTING THE PARTY LINE—The repeating of one organization's particular ideological interpretation of a factual event or ISSUE to a third-party audience by supposedly independent AGENTS/AGENCIES OF INFLUENCE.

PAWNS—Individuals used for propagandistic purposes who can easily be cast aside when their usefulness ends. Examples include those lured by intelligence agencies into FALSE FLAG OPERATIONS and gullible journalists corrupted when PLANTING STORIES occurs. FRONT GROUPS/SATELLITE ORGANIZATIONS serve a similar purpose at the institutional level. Pawns may be motivated by any of a number of causes. In developing countries, however, massive refugee movements are proving a particularly fertile recruiting ground for such persons in ways that challenge the integrity and security of sending and receiving nations alike. In the 1960s and early 1970s, refugees were largely confined to the THIRD WORLD—mainly Africa—as large numbers of persons sought to escape the turmoil created by the ARMED STRUGGLEs being waged against colonialism. Since the late 1970s, poverty and limited resources have led to new hostility, repression, and violence for those living in developing nations. Intensified by superpower COLD WAR rivalries, these root problems resulted in conflicts—inflamed by propagandists—which continue to influence domestic as well as international politics. Armed exiles have been instrumental pawns, both as "freedom fighters" and guerrillas used to wage PEOPLE'S WARs not yet snuffed out by COUNTERINSURGENCY efforts. "Humanitarian" international assistance programs designed to aid refugees have in some instances served to sustain these rebel LIBERATION MOVEMENTs and contributed to political instability. See also HUMAN RIGHTS and LIBERATION THEOLOGY.

PEACEKEEPING—According to a U.S. Army definition released in 1986, peacekeeping refers to "military operations conducted in support of diplomatic efforts to achieve, restore, or maintain peace in areas of potential or actual conflict." The UNITED NATIONS ORGANIZATION (UNO or UN) intervention in Somalia during 1993 has been defined as such a peacekeeping mission, although this is seen by some as a euphemism for waging war to make peace favorable to the occupying powers. See also COERCIVE DIPLOMACY, HIDDEN AGENDA, INTERVENTIONIST, MILITARISM, SOMALIAZATION, STATE TERRORISM, UNOSOM I/UNOSOM II/UNITAF, and UNPROFOR.

PEOPLE'S PARTY—Political party, emerging from the rise of the populist MOVEMENT, which contested local, state, and national elections in the United States from 1892 into the early 1900s. See also POPULISM/ POPULIST.

PEOPLE'S WAR—A form of MARXIST "class struggle" to transform an oppressive society and its structures through the application of "just violence" in conjunction with the twin policies of PROPAGANDA and political AGITATION so as to bring about revolutionary liberation. The term is most often associated with proxy wars waged to install or reestablish a Communist party government. As early as 1916, Lenin defined any Soviet-initiated military conflict, whether offensive or defensive, as a just "revolutionary struggle." See also ARMED STRUGGLE, BOLSHEVIK/BOLSHEVIKI, COMMUNISM/COMMUNIST, LIBERATION MOVEMENT, and REVOLUTION/REVOLUTIONARY.

PERCEPTION MANAGEMENT—Efforts by SPIN DOCTORS and other propagandists to control popular understanding in the belief that perception is more important than reality.

PERESTROIKA—Meaning *restructuring*, the term was widely utilized by former Soviet leader Mikhail Gorbachev but was actually conceived by his predecessor, Yuri Andropov. Given the crises facing the Soviet Union in domestic and foreign policy, Andropov, who previously headed the KGB (*Komitet po Gosudarstvennoy Bezopasnosti*), concluded that to save the Communist party's leadership position it would be necessary to modernize communism. He opted for a more flexible, "super-détente" approach to international diplomacy and the introduction of limited internal reforms highly publicized through a policy of "frank speaking and openness" known as *GLASNOST*. International PRESS coverage proved very favorable to both leaders, even leading to "Gorbymania," in which the Soviet secretary-general was portrayed as more humane and progressive than COLD WAR leaders of Western countries such as Britain and the United States. The reforms, however, proved ineffective domestically and had the unintended effect of unleashing forces seeking to overthrow Communist party rule. See also COMMUNISM/COMMUNIST.

PERFIDIOUS ALBION—A negative reference to Britain, alluding to its untrustworthiness as an ally and imperial "divide and dominate" attitude towards continental Europe (particularly France). See also ANGLOPHOBE.

PERSUASION INDUSTRIES—Practitioners in ADVERTISING, PUBLIC RELATIONS (PR), political communications, and related social psychology-based fields whose economic success is linked to their ability to persuade others on behalf of their clients' interests. See also HANDLERS, PURPOSEFUL PERSUASION, and SPIN DOCTORS.

PLANTING STORIES—Deliberate STRUCTURED LEAKS and placement of "NEWS" designed to support a particular organization's interests. Governments often do this by giving favored reporters BACKGROUND access to inside thinking about policy decisions or other information with headline potential. Undetected by the NEWS MEDIA representatives, such stories may include DISINFORMATION (*DEZINFORMATSIA*) and other PROPA-

GANDA elements. See also JUSTICE BY NEWS RELEASE and PLAU-
SIBLE DENIABILITY.

PLAUSIBLE DENIABILITY—The ability to state credibly that one is unaware of something ("OUT OF THE LOOP"), even though one is directly
responsible for a PROPAGANDA action. This may take the form of having a
prearranged COVER STORY ready for release, if needed, to serve a
misdirection function by diverting attention or suspicion to someone else. A
strategy for disseminating such fictions involves the mechanism of
PLANTING STORIES. See also COVER-UP CROWD, LIGHTENING
RODS, and WHITEWASH.

POLEMIC—A controversial discussion or argument made in public debate by a
skilled communicator (or polemicist). The term is derived from an ancient
Greek word meaning *war*. See also ARGUMENTATION and RHETORIC.

POLISPOTS—Political campaign radio and television commercials, ranging in
length from 10 seconds to full-length half hour or more INFOMERCIALs
("documercials"). FEDERAL COMMUNICATIONS COMMISSION (FCC)
regulations require all broadcast political ADVERTISING include information
citing who sponsored or paid for the messages. With the growing involvement
of POLITICAL ACTION COMMITTEES (PACs) beginning in the 1970s,
such disclosure revealed that many polispots—particularly at the presidential
level—were paid for by independent organizations instead of by the candidates
themselves. Campaigns often supplement their ads with PUSH POLLS and
other communication strategies designed to maximize the impact of their
message. See also WAVE FRONT.

POLITICAL ACTION COMMITTEES (PACs)—Campaign committees
established by organizations of like-minded individuals for political purposes
under the watchful eye of the FEDERAL ELECTION COMMISSION (FEC)
are now part of the American political system. As defined by Joseph
Nagelschmidt in the glossary of *The Public Affairs Handbook* (1982, p. 289),
PACs may be

organized by a business, labor, professional, agrarian, ideological or issue group
to raise political funds voluntarily from members, stockholders or employees to
aggregate numerous, smaller contributions into larger, more meaningful amounts
that are then contributed to favored candidates, multicandidate committees, or
political party committees.

The proliferation of PACs prove they are needed as part of the democratic
process, but also results in criticism from opponents who charge they
undermine America's traditional representative DEMOCRACY by making
candidates more beholden to narrow INTEREST GROUPS rather than to their
constituents. Following the WATERGATE SCANDAL, Congress in 1974
amended federal election laws to formalize the role of PACs as a well-regulated
way to fund candidates and end secret payoffs by business interests and unions,
plus limit the influence of outside wealthy contributors.

POLITICAL ANALYSTS—Individuals whose expertise gives them a media forum to interpret political events and shape campaign NEWS accounts. Analysts include "SPIN DOCTORS" employed to represent a particular organization or candidate, former spin doctors now retired from active campaign planning or between assignments, pollsters, policy/communications analysts drawn from industry and academia, and "pundits" who have all-around credentials as political INSIDERS—journalists and ex-journalists, lobbyists, political party professionals, consultants at THINK TANKS, ex-office holders, INTEREST GROUP leaders, ADVERTISING/PUBLIC RELATIONS (PR) practitioners, and so on. See also HANDLERS, OPPO RESEARCH, PREFERENTIAL SOURCING, PUBLIC POLICY PROCESS, and SPIN CONTROL.

POLITICAL CRIME—One meaning refers to the abuse of authority by political office holders (ranging from the comparatively minor WATERGATE SCANDAL to crimes against humanity such as GENOCIDE). The term *political crime*, however, is more commonly applied to mean violation of the law in order to bring about political change. Tactics range from the use of civil disobedience to subversion, assassination and TREASON. Even though the TERRORIST act of REPRESENTATIVE VIOLENCE may be the same (robbing a bank), the purposes (seeking to raise money for weapons and PROPAGANDA rather than simply get rich) differ from those of "common" criminals. Officials sometimes find it convenient to arrest dissidents for simple association (see RED-BAITING and SEDITIOUS LIBEL) or trivial violations of law (such as trespassing), even though the real reason may be to dampen a challenge to their authority. Many persons jailed for heinous crimes (murder of a political figure or blowing up of an airliner) prefer to be seen as political prisoners (claiming that their ideological convictions are the real reason they are imprisoned), while representatives of the state generally try to paint a much darker picture that disconnects any legitimate HUMAN RIGHTS political motive to the attack.

POLITICAL GRAPHICS—Commercial posters which, when displayed, turn art works into ideological tools, or WEAPONS ON THE WALL.

POLITICALLY CORRECT (PC)—Generically, the term refers to following what is considered acceptable in terms of political discussion by the majority of the day. It describes individuals who, and organizations that, resort to TOTALITARIANISM when attempting to prevent views they find unpalatable from being heard. In recent years, RIGHT-WING/CONSERVATIVEs and LIBERTARIANs have applied it to mean a secular indoctrination program by LEFT-WING/LIBERALs which seeks to suppress open debate about race-based affirmative action quota systems, expand feminist and homosexual civil rights, urge multicultural educational curricula reforms that link Western civilization with "white imperialism," and promote other ISSUEs in which the PC agenda is equated with "the PUBLIC INTEREST." Opponents of such "sensitivity training" are often shouted down with low-intelligence RHETORIC proclaiming, "No FREE SPEECH for . . . " whatever insensitive view the "do-gooder" PC fanatics wish to quash. Ironically, conservatives have their own politically correct set of issues and would with equal relish SPIKE the influence and IDEOLOGY of the left in such matters. An alternative view is provided by Jamin Raskin in "The Fallacies of 'Political Correctness,'" appearing in *Z Magazine* (January 1993). Raskin asserted:

"Political correctness" does not exist, and has never existed, as a body of political ideas. It is not an ideology, like socialism, liberalism, or nationalism, nor is it an organized (or disorganized) social movement. Nor is it a world view, a moral philosophy, a partisan organization, an intellectual trend, or even an academic faction. As a description of political ideas, "political correctness" expresses, literally, nothing. It is an empty vessel of a signifier into which meaning is poured on a purely expedient and ad hominem basis. . . . Enforcers of today's brittle status quo now employ "politically correct" to describe any political position which disputes the soundness of economic life, the validity of the assertion that racism and sexism no longer influence our society, the infallibility of corporate power, the nobility of right-wing culture, the value of militarism, or the wisdom of any given policy of the Reagan-Bush tenure.

See also AD HOMINEM ATTACK, CENSORSHIP, DEMONIZING THE OPPOSITION, FACTION, HATE SPEECH, HOUSE UN-AMERICAN ACTIVITIES COMMITTEE (HUAC), LOYALTY OATH, McCARTHYISM, MILITARISM, MOVEMENT, OFFICIAL IDEOLOGY, IMPERIALISM/IMPERIALIST, ORWELLIAN TACTICS, POLITICAL CRIME, PROFESSIONAL PATRIOTS, REACTIONARY, RED-BAITING, RITUAL DEFAMATION, SCAPEGOAT/SCAPEGOATING, SOCIAL MOVEMENT, and SPIRAL OF SILENCE.

POLITICAL PATHOLOGY—Political pathology may be manifested in two key ways: One is found in the formation of paramilitary organizations with a small number of ruthless and determined TERRORISTs in the VANGUARD of ARMED STRUGGLE. The other is the continuous breakdown of constitutionally-formulated negotiations representing a common middle ground because of pressure from EXTREMISTs on various sides pushing for more RADICAL measures. Moderates are forced into hiding or murdered (CENSORSHIP BY ASSASSINATION and PROPAGANDA OF THE DEED). They are replaced on the public scene by demagogues seeking to use the opportunity to further destabilize the society until it is reconstructed under their new model. See also DEMAGOGUE/DEMAGOGISM and REPRESENTATIVE VIOLENCE.

POPULAR FRONT/PEOPLE'S FRONT—Cooperation by Communist party members with socialists and liberal INTEREST GROUPS to fight a greater threat. The term is most often associated with the 1935-1939 period, when the tactic of direct revolutionary activism was temporarily abandoned by the Seventh Congress of the Communist International (COMINTERN) to concentrate on the growing menace of fascism. See also ACTIVISTS, CADRE, COALITION, COMMUNISM/COMMUNIST, FASCISM/FASCIST, FRONT GROUPS/SATELLITE ORGANIZATIONS, LEFT-WING/LIBERAL, and SOCIALISM/SOCIALIST.

POPULAR OPINION—A transitory form of PUBLIC OPINION, which is usually very volatile and subject to propagandistic manipulation.

POPULISM/POPULIST—Any organization claiming to represent "the people" can raise the banner of populism. The terms are most associated with the MOVEMENT for U.S. economic and political reform growing out of the National Farmer's Alliance and Industrial Union in the late nineteenth-century. Populism became an important political force in the 1890s for rural Americans, fielding candidates under the PEOPLE'S PARTY name for more than a decade and continuing as a factor in the makeup of the major parties. The IDEOLOGY of populism is somewhat difficult to classify, since it crosses conventional partisanship. The particular programs advocated by populists often differ from those promoted by LEFT-WING/LIBERALs and RIGHT-WING/CONSERVATIVEs, but they actually share much in the way of a RADICAL common analysis and RHETORIC about the underlying problems facing the nation. Populists are not especially antigovernment and have much in common with others expressing SOCIALISM/SOCIALIST leanings, since they support intervention by constituted authorities to remedy social "wrongs." Populists also tend to favor FAIR TRADE efforts designed to promote economic nationalism (protectionism), promulgate an AMERICA FIRST foreign policy, and pay homage to fundamentalist religious values. A common theme in populist PROPAGANDA is the defense of the common person ("the real America") against big institutions controlled by the powerful and wealthy (often representing "alien" ideologies). In recent years, the attempt to found a new Populist party has floundered, in part because of its affiliation with individuals such as David Duke (R-La.). Leading contemporary populist organizations in the United States include For the People (led by Chuck Harder) and Liberty Lobby (founded by Willis Carto). Many other persons exhibit populist attitudes, even though they may not identify themselves as such. Among those who do is former Kansas Governor Joan Finney (D, 1991-1995). See also FUNDAMENTALISM/FUNDAMENTALIST.

POSITION PAPERS—NEWS RELEASEs outlining an organization's official position on a particular public policy ISSUE. They may be distributed in answer to a journalist's request, incorporated in MEDIA KITs, entered on internal and external computer bulletin boards, or proactively mailed directly to key NEWS MEDIA representatives. Government-issued position papers are often called WHITE PAPERS.

POSITIVE INDOCTRINATION—See INDOCTRINATION.

PREFERENTIAL SOURCING—By selecting certain people to act as sources and ignoring others, NEWS reports are slanted. Sometimes this skewing is purposefully done, but often preferential sourcing reflects an over-reliance on government officials and other "influentials" who have proved "reliable" in the past in helping the journalist file stories. The resulting news coverage greatly affects not only the perspective reported, but also distorts the baseline of what is considered "factual" when widely conflicting claims are put forward by the protagonists. For example, numbers of deaths attributed to the September 1991 military coup in Haiti ran from "dozens" (U.S. embassy officials), to 500 for the week (international HUMAN RIGHTS groups), to 1,000 (deposed President Bertrand Aristide, citing unreported mass graves). Most mainstream media, relying for the most part on U.S. State Department sources, opted for the U.S. government-provided statistics. By actively applying epithets and allusions in an unbalanced manner, selectively focusing on only certain topics to the neglect of others, and unrelentingly branding political stereotypes, a person, corporation, interest group, MOVEMENT, religion, or nation can be rather quickly demonized or angelized in the public mind. The labels and adjectives linked to many public figures and countries often subtlety play into existing prejudices, evidenced by the U.S.-centric or Eurocentric focus of most international stories about THIRD WORLD development. See also ANTI-SEMITIC, DEMONIZING THE OPPOSITION, DISINFORMATION (*DEZINFORMATSIA*), FRAMING DEVICES, INTEREST GROUPS, MEDIA BIAS, and PROPAGANDA MODEL (HERMAN AND CHOMSKY).

PRESIDENT'S FOREIGN INTELLIGENCE ADVISORY BOARD (PFIAB)—A nonpartisan panel made up of fourteen experienced policymakers, the President's Foreign Intelligence Advisory Board monitors American COVERT efforts and provides advice to the commander-in-chief. Due to the sensitive nature of intelligence, sometimes the PFIAB is caught up in controversy.

PRESS—The term *press* (often referred to as *the press*) historically referred to printed media, but is now commonly used generically to include all forms of MASS COMMUNICATION in which an expression of ideas occurs: books, pamphlets, periodicals, newspapers, comics, posters, motion pictures, recordings, radio, television, cable, and, to a limited extent, stage plays. Some court rulings have attempted to make a distinction between print and newer forms of media, as well as between "political speech" and "COMMERCIAL SPEECH." The effect has been a watering down of FIRST AMENDMENT protections for freedom of expression. See also FOURTH ESTATE, FREE SPEECH, INTERNET, JOURNALISM/JOURNALIST, MEDIA/MEDIUM, and PRESS BASHING.

PRESS AGENTRY—Heavy handed, but shrewd, PUBLICITY efforts often associated with the PROMOTION of entertainment industry figures and products. See also HYPE.

PRESS BASHING—Sensationalist charges that the NEWS MEDIA are acting in a biased, propagandistic way. These are usually made by a public figure or organization able to command PRESS attention for these views, ironically using the messenger to criticize the messenger. The ORCHESTRATED PROPAGANDA CAMPAIGN seeks to exploit the public's distrust of media, and is often linked to fundraising or other appeals designed to advance the political or economic interests of those making the attack. It is also not uncommon to have one element of the press leadership hypocritically attack another for their reporting (as when so-called "legitimate" NEWS organizations name call populist tabloid publications such as the *Star* and *National Enquirer* "sleazy" or refer to television programs such as *A Current Affair* as "contemptible"). See also MEDIA BIAS, MEDIACRACY, and TABLOID JOURNALISM.

PRESS KIT—See MEDIA KIT.

PRESS RELEASE—See JUSTICE BY NEWS RELEASE and NEWS RELEASE.

PRESSURE GROUPS—Organized INTEREST GROUPS or factions that seek to influence the PUBLIC POLICY PROCESS of political decision-making without actually electing or appointing their members to official governmental capacities. Wrote James Madison in the *Federalist Papers* number 10:

The most common and durable source of factions has been the various distributions of property, the landed interest, the manufacturing interest, the mercantile interest, the money interest with many lesser interests, grow up of necessity in civilized nations and divide themselves into different classes; the regulation of these interfering interests forms the principal task of modern legislation and involves the spirit of party and faction in the necessary and ordinary operations of the government.

While all organizations may potentially become pressure groups, they do not do so unless they lobby. Conflicts among pressure groups most often involve competition for resources requiring subsidies and taxation. The social utility of pressure groups is that they represent a variety of views and their competition for public attention and legislative remedy acts to ameliorate unnecessary regulation and poor legislation where the social cost is too high. See also AGITATION, FACTION, GRASSROOTS LOBBYING, HATE GROUPS, LOBBYING/LOBBYIST, NONGOVERNMENTAL ORGANIZATIONS (NGOs), and POLITICAL ANALYSTS.

PROFESSIONAL PATRIOTS—Also known as *sunshine patriots* and *100 percenters*, often derisory terms referring to those who use patriotic themes to advance their own political or commercial interests but who in reality could care less about honor, integrity, selflessness and the other ideals true patriotism encompasses. The phrase is utilized in the same context as the famous dictum, "Patriotism is the last refuge of scoundrels." See also HOUSE UN-AMERICAN ACTIVITIES COMMITTEE (HUAC).

PROGRESSIVE/PROGRESSIVISM—A political reform MOVEMENT that was significant in defining early twentieth-century liberalism, whose roots (unlike those of populism) were urban. Progressives, especially, believed in implementing new legislation and using other government powers to correct what they believed to be social and economic inequities. Its appeal was such that members of both major political parties, the Socialist party, the "Bull

Moose" coalition headed by ex-President Theodore Roosevelt, and other ACTIVISTS were at times classified as progressives. Today, the designation of progressive is most likely to be utilized by LEFT-WING/LIBERAL individuals and groups.

PROMOTION—A PUBLIC RELATIONS (PR) function in which a range of special activities or events are created to stimulate popular interest in a person, product, or organization. Promotions include sponsored PUBLICITY events such as open house tours, public entertainments, and other sales/marketing/communications support efforts. Participants typically receive free samples, SPECIALTY ADVERTISING gifts, discount coupons, and other promotional allowances. See also ADVERTISING.

PROPAGANDA—There is a need for a deeper understanding of the usage and context of the term propaganda itself. According to the definition proposed by attendees at the Conference on Contemporary Soviet Propaganda and Disinformation sponsored by the U.S. Department of State and the CENTRAL INTELLIGENCE AGENCY (CIA) in 1985, propaganda involves

the dissemination of information—facts, arguments, rumors, half-truths, or lies— to influence public opinion. As a systematic effort to persuade, it is an act of advocacy in mass communications, involving the making of deliberately one-sided statements to a mass audience. In this, it is not necessarily deceptive.

Propaganda, then, is a process—a form of manipulative communication designed to elicit some predetermined response—"the organized spreading of special doctrines, information, ideas or beliefs to promote or injure a cause, group, nation, etc." Propaganda is also an artifact, the MASS COMMUNICATION products that contain the facts, ideas, or allegations distributed for such a purpose. Propaganda, in Communist party terms, is additionally associated with the notion of one-sided education (the propagating of many ideas) to a few people, usually the leadership elements known as the CADRE.

To accomplish their goals, modern propagandists use media to target specific groups of people, give them a set of plausible and compelling reasons as to why they should lend their support. Propaganda can be conveniently separated into those messages which encourage us to buy a commercial product and those which seek to direct our belief structure and personality in a more fundamental way. Not all propaganda is equally embracive, pervasive, or effective in motivating people to think or do certain things. In many cases, the job of today's propagandist involves not so much changing minds as in finding the right audiences and psychological HOOKS so as to reinforce and extend existing prejudices and attitudes. Those who interpret propaganda as a negative phenomenon tend to see it as a form of RHETORIC designed to persuade without revealing the true intentions or even strategies of the communicator. For purposes of this book, propaganda is neutrally defined as a systematic form of PURPOSEFUL PERSUASION that attempts to influence the emotions, attitudes, opinions, and actions of specified target audiences for ideological, political or commercial purposes through the controlled transmission of one-sided messages (which may or may not be factual) via mass and direct media channels. A propaganda organization employs *propagandists* who engage in *propagandism*—the applied creation and distribution of such forms of persuasion.

See also ACTIVE MEASURES, ADVERTISING, AGENTS/AGENCIES OF INFLUENCE, AGENTS PROVOCATEUR, AGITPROP, A-I-D-C-A FORMULA, ARMED PROPAGANDA, ASSETS, BACKDOOR CONTACT, BLACK PROPAGANDA, BRAINWASHING, CODE WORDS, COMMAND PROPAGANDA, CONDITIONING PROPAGANDA, CONSPIRACY THEORIES, COUNTERPROPAGANDA, COVERT, COVERT ACTION, COVER-UP CROWD, CULT OF PERSONALITY, DEMONIZING THE OPPOSITION, DIAL GROUP, DIRECT ACTION, DIRTY TRICKS CAMPAIGN, DISINFORMATION (*DEZINFORMATSIA*), DOGMA, DOUBLESPEAK, DOUBLETHINK, ELITE THEORY, EXTREMISM, GRAY/GREY PROPAGANDA, HATE CAMPAIGN, HEARTS AND MINDS CAMPAIGN, HIDDEN AGENDA, IDEOLOGY, INDOCTRINATION, INFOSHOPS, INTELLIGENCE COMMUNITY, MACHIAVELLIAN, MANUFACTURING OF CONSENT (or CONSENSUS), MARXIST, MEDIA/MEDIUM, OFFICIAL IDEOLOGY, ORCHESTRATED PROPAGANDA CAMPAIGN, PARROTING THE PARTY LINE, PAWNS, PERSUASION INDUSTRIES, PLANTING STORIES, PLAUSIBLE DENIABILITY, PROFESSIONAL PATRIOTS, PROPAGANDA ANALYSIS, PROPAGANDA DEVICES, PROPAGANDA ENVIRONMENT, PROPAGANDA OF THE DEED, PROPAGANDA MODEL (HERMAN AND CHOMSKY), PROPAGANDA MODEL (JOWETT AND O'DONNELL), PROPAGANDA PHONY, PROPAGANDA-2 (P-2), PROTESTERS, PSYCHOLOGICAL OPERATIONS (PSYOPS), PSYCHOLOGICAL WARFARE (PSYWAR), PUBLIC DIPLOMACY, PUBLIC OPINION, PUBLIC RELATIONS (PR), PUBLIC RELATIONS MODELS, SALIENCE, STATE TERRORISM, STEALTH TACTICS, SUBPROPAGANDA, SUBVERSION/SUBVERSIVES, TAVISTOCK METHOD, TERROR GROUP, TERRORISM, and WHITE PROPAGANDA.

PROPAGANDA ANALYSIS—A critical and historical approach to better understanding PROPAGANDA patterns shaping social influence. This line of inquiry, drawing upon earlier paradigms common to RHETORICal scholarship and later incorporated in progressive IDEOLOGY, was most common to research of the 1920s and 1930s. It was largely impressionistic, pacifistic, and aimed at educating a broad PUBLIC about the continuing dangers presented by the PERSUASION INDUSTRIES. This presented a problem for those who sought to more dispassionately investigate the PROPAGANDA ENVIRONMENT. Gradually, as they were influenced by the increasing precision of the social sciences, those researchers in this competing MASS COMMUNICATION tradition turned to statistical and experimental methodologies.

PROPAGANDA DEVICES—Techniques described in *The Fine Art of Propaganda: A Study of Father Coughlin's Speeches*, prepared by Alfred

McClung Lee and Elizabeth Briant Lee, for the Institute for Propaganda Analysis, Inc., prior to American entry in World War II. The book is often referred to as "The ABC's of Propaganda Analysis." Though their work is flawed by selective interpretations of fact and uncritical acceptance of a powerful MEDIA EFFECTS model, the Lees' approach to PROPAGANDA studies has proved highly influential. They catalogued seven ways professional propagandists try to manipulate others, terms which have entered popular culture. The devices identified by the Lees (pp. 22-25) include:

- *name calling* —giving an idea a bad label,
- *glittering generality*—using virtuous sounding words to get the target to accept or approve of someone or something without examining the evidence,
- *transfer*—associating the authority and prestige of something or someone to another in order to make the latter more acceptable,
- *testimonial*—"having some respected or hated person say that a given idea or program or product or person is good or bad,"
- *plain folks*—attempting to convince audience members that the propagandist and his or her ideas are good because they reflect the views of people just like them,
- *card stacking*—selecting and using "facts or falsehoods, illustrations or distractions, and logical or illogical statements in order to give the best or worst possible case for an idea, program, person, or product," and
- *band wagon*—emphasizing that since everybody else is joining, doing etc. what the propagandist advocates, targeted audience members should also get with it by following the crowd and jumping on the bandwagon.

See also HEURISTIC, PERCEPTION MANAGEMENT, PERSUASION INDUSTRIES, PUBLIC RELATIONS MODELS, RITUAL DEFAMATION, and SELECTIVE PERCEPTION.

PROPAGANDA ENVIRONMENT—A pervasive cultural condition in which opinion and belief are manipulated by social managers more interested in control than freedom. While the illusion of choice is maintained, truly independent thought is discouraged. The result is a channeling away from broadly participatory democratic processes into more predictable intermittent rituals rubber stamping prepackaged commodities ranging from candidates to products. See also MANUFACTURING OF CONSENT (or CONSENSUS) and PROPAGANDA MODEL (HERMAN AND CHOMSKY).

PROPAGANDA MODEL (HERMAN AND CHOMSKY)—In an analysis extending far beyond Edward Bernays' ENGINEERING OF CONSENT (or CONSENSUS) guidelines, Edward S. Herman and Noam Chomsky assert that the entire media system in the United States is deterministically analogous to authoritarian regimes, except that control is shared by the government with corrupting interests such as big business. The cynical short circuiting of critical thinking and subversion of political discourse that make up the PROPAGANDA ENVIRONMENT are "the outcome of large-scale social and historical trends—mass society, mass media, mass production depending on compulsive consumerism. The propaganda environment is nurtured in every state—people's republic or capitalist democracy—that draws its legitimacy from the consent of the governed while it devotes vast resources to manufacturing that consent." The authors' propaganda model published in *Manufacturing Consent: The Political Economy of the Mass Media* (1988, p. 2) focuses on:

(1) the size, concentrated ownership, owner wealth and profit orientation of the dominant mass media firms; (2) advertising as the primary income source of the mass media; (3) the reliance of the media on information provided by government, business and "experts" funded and approved by these primary sources and agents of power; (4) "flak" as a means of disciplining the media; and (5) "anti-communism'" as a national religion and control mechanism.

Herman and Chomsky assert these elements

interact with and reinforce one another. The raw material of news must pass through successive filters, leaving only the cleaned residue fit to print. They fix the premises of discourse and interpretation, and the definition of what is newsworthy in the first place, and they explain the basis and operations of what amount to propaganda campaigns.

See also ADVERTISING, DEMOCRACY, MEDIA BIAS, PROPAGANDA, and PROPAGANDA ANALYSIS.

PROPAGANDA MODEL (JOWETT AND O'DONNELL)—Defining propaganda in terms of process also is useful, and the work of Garth Jowett and Victoria O'Donnell has proven especially helpful in developing a comprehensive analytical "Purpose Model of Propaganda" which can be applied to the various PROPAGANDA stages. As they describe in their book, *Propaganda and Persuasion*, there are ten such stages that encompasses all the elements of propaganda:
- The IDEOLOGY and purpose of the ORCHESTRATED PROPAGANDA CAMPAIGN,
- the context in which the propaganda occurs,
- identification of the propagandist,
- the structure of the propaganda organization,
- the target audience,
- media utilization techniques,
- special techniques used to maximize effect,
- audience reaction to various techniques,
- COUNTERPROPAGANDA, if present, and
- effects and evaluation.

Once each element has been identified, Jowett and O'Donnell (p. 213) point out that this information can in turn be analyzed via their model to more comprehensively answer the following questions:

To what ends, in the context of the times, does a propaganda agent, working through an organization, reach an audience through the media while using special symbols to get a desired reaction? Further, if there is opposition to the propaganda, what form does it take? Finally, how successful is the propaganda in achieving its purpose?

See also PUBLIC RELATIONS MODELS and SCAME.

PROPAGANDA OF THE DEED—The use of DIRECT ACTION including violence to make a political point, usually because the organization employing terror cannot attract sufficient support for their cause through open political processes. To many TERRORISTs and armed anarchists, a single decisive "deed" is better PROPAGANDA than a thousand pamphlets. "Politics by murder" thus can be traced to early history and is something which predates contemporary preoccupation with "Islamic terrorists." Governments, too, often are willing to dispense with legalities such as a trial on the evidence when vengeance can be justified after the fact. There are many examples of unilateral willingness to resort to STATE TERRORISM by democracies as well as dictatorships under cover of moralistic-sounding propaganda. Examples from recent history include the murderous Allied firebombing of Dresden in World War II, which was done without real military objective other than "punishment" of German civilians; the infamous "Phoenix Program" in South Vietnam, under which tens of thousands of Vietnamese were assassinated because of suspicions they worked with the Communists; the killing of a number of civilians in Tripoli when the Reagan administration "retaliated" for alleged Libyan TERRORISM; the death of a great many noncombatants in Panama when the Bush administration moved to "liberate" that country through the mechanism of OPERATION JUST CAUSE; and the "smart bomb" attack on Iraqi intelligence headquarters ordered by the Clinton administration with the "unfortunate" side effect of "spillover" into residential areas. See also ANARCHISM/ANARCHIST, ARMED PROPAGANDA, ASSASSIN, CENSORSHIP BY ASSASSINATION, PROTESTERS, REPRESENTATIVE VIOLENCE, and TERROR GROUP.

PROPAGANDA PHONY—Persons or organizations with a favorable public image created through media relations wholly at odds with their true nature.

PROPAGANDA-2 (P-2)—A secretive Masonic lodge, based in Italy, whose membership proved to be a "Who's Who" roster of Italian government officials, banking moguls, media owners, businessmen, internationalists, and other influential INSIDERS. The scandal that resulted from P-2's public exposure in the 1980s served merely to open a small window into the extent to which public trust is often abused by those wielding power behind the scenes. See also CONSPIRACY THEORIES and ELITE THEORY.

PROTESTERS—Dissidents who resort to demonstrations and other overt forms of political action to express their desire for change. Reformists tend to engage in "moderate levels" of protest such as lawful demonstrations and boycotts, while zealots are willing to turn to more EXTREMIST measures (including TERRORISM) if thwarted.

PSEUDO-EVENT/PSEUDO-NEWS—Terms invented by social historian

Daniel Boorstein in referring to the staging of NEWS for PUBLICITY purposes by experienced PUBLIC RELATIONS (PR) practitioners. Pseudo-events include dramatized rallies, open houses, PRESS conferences, and photo opportunities. See also FLUFF EVENTS and PUBLIC SERVICE EVENTS.

PSEUDO-REALISM—The mediated mimicking of reality by NEWS organizations and others who rarely look at the long term causes of events because they fail to penetrate beyond the surface appearances of social behavior. Generally, the approach is nonpolitically centrist (excluding many facts outside an artificially determined normality), with lowest-common-denominator appeals.

PSYCHEDELICS—Mind-altering substances and narcotics (including marijuana, cocaine, heroine, and LSD) which change a person's perception of surroundings to produce hallucinations and delusions. These drugs were studied at universities and military installations for their usefulness as PSYCHOLOGICAL OPERATIONS (PSYOPS)/BRAINWASHING weapons under U.S. Department of Defense contracts beginning in the 1950s. Ironically, the pleasant and mentally stimulating side effects experienced by many users helped contribute to the hippie and antiwar MOVEMENTs. See also MKULTRA and NEW AGE MOVEMENT.

PSYCHOGRAPHICS—Advertisers and other persuasive communicators recognized that traditional reliance on DEMOGRAPHICS and related characteristics of their potential audience did not take into account personality traits and other psychologically based motivational factors. The psychological variables that influence "buying behavior" are many but generally have to take into account the attitudes, experiences, interests, mental decision processes, needs, opinions, and values of the targeted PUBLICs. Methods such as PRIZM (Potential Rating Index by Zip Market), which classifies communities and neighborhoods into homogeneous population clusters, and the VALS (Values and Life-styles System) developed by Stanford Research Institute, are popular program formats for integrating psychographic principles into campaign design. See also SELECTIVE PERCEPTION.

PSYCHOLOGICAL OPERATIONS (PSYOPS)—The application of psychological principles to discredit, demoralize, and intimidate. Psyops may well reflect the continuing domestic PROPAGANDA practices found in nations dominated by TOTALITARIANISM, but the term is most commonly applied in a military context. All PSYCHOLOGICAL WARFARE (PSYWAR) activities have the purpose of sowing confusion and encouraging the enemy to become divided, desert, surrender readily, or fight without enthusiasm. Psyops principles are typically used not only in full-scale wars, but also in UNCONVENTIONAL WARFARE situations where they prove integral to COUNTERINSURGENCY and COUNTERTERRORISM efforts designed to break the link between the enemy's fighting forces and the people who provide them support and shelter. Brigadier Frank Kitson, author of the British Army's counterinsurgency' bible, *Low Intensity Operations*, accepted the analysis by Mao Tse-tung of what motivates guerrillas/insurgents, that it is in individual's minds that wars of subversion must be fought and decided. Thus psyops or psych-ops are frequently referred to as HEARTS AND MINDS CAMPAIGNs. Often, appeals are made to "law and order." Psyops treats this rather cynically, since the practice ranges from the most basic BLACK PROPAGANDA to cold-blooded murder. Essentially, in Kitson's own words, the law is "just another weapon in the government's arsenal" which "becomes little more than a propaganda cover for the disposal of unwanted members of the public." The Americans, British and other major combatants conducted psychological operations in World War II with some skill, with more advanced techniques coming out of subsequent COLD WAR, Vietnam, and anticolonial experiences. Modern psychological warfare principles were codified in the 1960s by Kitson and his counterparts. Examples of their practical use have been made PUBLIC in the revelations of ex-U.S., British, and Soviet intelligence agents and military personnel. In a civilian context, the same approach can be used to disrupt the opposition, often through resort to DIRTY TRICKS CAMPAIGNs.

PSYCHOLOGICAL WARFARE (PSYWAR)—According to Paul Linebarger's classic definition (*Psychological Warfare*, 1948 edition, p. 39), psywar "Comprises the use of propaganda against an enemy, together with such other operational measures of a military, economic or political nature as may be required to supplement propaganda." See also COUNTER-PROPAGANDA and PSYCHOLOGICAL OPERATIONS (PSYOPS).

PUBLIC—From the standpoint of PUBLIC OPINION, a public is a group of people with common interests or similar opinions on an ISSUE capable of controversy. Generally, publics are not so much self-defined by their background and life-style profiles, as measured by DEMOGRAPHICS and PSYCHOGRAPHICS, but rather identified as STAKEHOLDERS by an organization seeking to influence them as a "target audience." Something can be "made public" if it appears in the NEWS. See also GRANFALLOONS.

PUBLIC ACCESS PROGRAMMING—Local governments usually hold the rights to award a monopoly to commercial cable companies seeking the right to serve a particular locality. The contracts they enter into generally include provisions stipulating certain channels be set aside for community programming and further mandating that residents have low cost access to production equipment in order to produce their own shows. Public access channels offer more than the juvenile *Wayne's World*. also featuring sometimes amateurish but always vibrant alternative cable television vehicles such as *Calandario Latino*, *Local Union News*, *Paper Tiger TV*, *Artist's Television Access*, and other programs designed to appeal to specific elements of a community. These include artistic, ethnic, linguistic, sexual, political, and other FACTIONs whose access to mainstream media may otherwise be limited. True public access prohibits either the city or cable company from imposing CENSORSHIP, serving to create a FREE SPEECH forum which further encourages controversial programming by minority interests. Policymakers in some localities made uncomfortable by unfettered speech (which includes pornography and racist recruiting messages) have renegotiated contracts to undercut public access by imposing editorial responsibilities on the cablecaster licensee in order to limit "unsettling" EXTREMIST voices.

PUBLIC AFFAIRS—The Conference Board, representing major American corporations, defines public affairs as "a significant and substantial concern and involvement by individuals, business, labor, foundations, private institutions, and government with the social, economic, and political forces that singly or through interaction shape the environment within which the free enterprise system exists." According to *The Public Affairs Handbook* edited by Joseph S. Nagelschmidt (1982, glossary, p. 290), public affairs is "A management function concerned with the relationship between the organization and its external environment, and involving the key tasks of intelligence gathering and analysis, internal communication, and external action programs directed at government, communities, and the general public." PUBLIC RELATIONS (PR) practitioners often call this process "government relations." Military PUBLIC COMMUNICATION efforts are also generally conducted by Public Affairs Officers (PAOs). See also CORPORATE SOCIAL RESPONSIBILITY (CSR), ISSUES MANAGEMENT, and SIDLE COMMISSION.

PUBLIC COMMUNICATION—Interpersonal, organizational, and mass-mediated use of information and influence to shape the thoughts and judgments of others. See also PUBLIC AFFAIRS, PUBLIC DIPLOMACY, PUBLIC INFORMATION CAMPAIGNS, PUBLICITY, and PUBLIC RELATIONS (PR).

PUBLIC DIPLOMACY—According to a United States Commission on Public Diplomacy report, entitled *Diplomacy in the Information Age* (1993, inside cover):

Public Diplomacy describes activities that foster dialogue and open communication between the United States and the people of other countries. It complements and strengthens traditional diplomacy, conducted between governments. Through public diplomacy, the U.S. government communicates it views to people around the world, together with information about the United States that puts them in perspective. By enabling Americans to observe other cultures, and by bringing others here to see the American democratic experience for themselves, public diplomacy helps to build relationships and mutual understandings that support the nation's long-term interests. press and information activities of U.S. missions overseas, educational and cultural exchanges, and international radio and television broadcasting are essential elements of public diplomacy. The United States Information Agency (USIA) has primary responsibility for a wide range of public diplomacy activities, and for advising the government on the policy implications of foreign public opinion. USIA's Director reports to the President and receives policy guidance from the Secretary of State.

See also CITIZENS FOR AMERICA (CFA), CONTRAS, NEOLIBERAL-ISM, and UNITED STATES INFORMATION AGENCY (USIA).

PUBLIC INFORMATION CAMPAIGNS—Organized communication

programs intended to influence opinions on public policy issues. Typically, these are conducted by nonprofit organizations, INTEREST GROUPS, other ACTIVISTS, government agencies, and corporate interests involved in "educational" image building, social reform, and political referendum efforts. The emphasis on supposed social good and altruistic purpose differentiates so-called public information campaigns from other forms of persuasive communication, although they equally embrace the use of PROPAGANDA DEVICES and appeals. Many such public information campaigns have proved failures because the real goal is propagandistic behavioral change, not objective information gathering or neutral knowledge transfer. See also PUBLIC AFFAIRS, PUBLIC RELATIONS (PR), and PUBLIC RELATIONS MODELS.

PUBLIC INFORMATION OFFICER (PIO)—To avoid the abuse of position, federal and state regulations generally restrict communications by government officials for ADVERTISING, PROPAGANDA, or PUBLIC RELATIONS (PR) purposes. Those terms are symbolically avoided, even though the need to provide two-way information is inherent within a DEMOCRACY. As a result, many employees in government service are described euphemistically as public information officers, PUBLIC AFFAIRS specialists, administrative aides, or counselors.

PUBLIC INTEREST—A widely misused term with an illusive definition since no single *the public interest* exists. Propagandists usually seek to mask their private special interests by proclaiming their goal as one of serving the public interest. They do this even while selectively presenting their case, couching their policies and proposals in terms of being morally superior, and manipulating reaction to their messages. As a result, there has been an attempt to reinterpret the public interest as an overarching construct that links everyone together. Burton A. Weisbrod, Joel F. Handler, and Neil K. Komesar, the coauthors of *Public Interest Law: An Economic and Institutional Analysis* (1978, p. 26), note that "many definitions of the public interest emphasize some kind of commonalty of interest, a single interest that all citizens are presumed to share." For example, the public interest:
- is the "common interest";
- "serves the ends of the whole public rather than those of some sector of the public";
- is "the sum total of all interests in the community . . . which are balanced for the common good"; and
- is "a consensus [that] constitutes the public interest within the frame of reference."

Seldom do the actions of one or a few benefit the whole of society. The widespread equating of the public interest "consensus" with the results of TRACKING POLLS measuring PUBLIC OPINION is fine for those in agreement with social trends of the day. This approach can prove unsatisfactory to some critics, however, especially when POPULAR OPINION is considered particularly intolerant, xenophobic, nationalistic, racist, religiously biased and so forth. Balancing HATE SPEECH limitations against the downsides of CENSORSHIP is thus a concern. While constraining some media from making some social problems worse, it can certainly also be argued that regulatory "public interest provisions" such as the FAIRNESS DOCTRINE (which usually turn out to be "protect-the-interests-of-those-in-power provisions") sometimes prevent a medium from achieving its potential for positive change.

However, a compromise or balance of interests may be achieved. Barry M. Mitnick's *The Political Economy of Regulation* (1980, pp. 92-93) incorporates various options in describing the five major interrelated concepts for achieving "the public interest" as follows:

1. A *particular*, *paternal*, or *personal dictate* concept, unitary in character, emerges when the public interest is equated with the preferences of a particular person, organization, or system.
2. A *trade-off* concept applies when interests affected by regulation are made to provide some costly service or other benefit judged to be in the public interest in exchange for certain private benefits to these parties.
3. A *compromise* concept develops when interests are made to concede part of what they desire so that the public policy product is seen to be in the general "public interest."
4. A *balance* concept of the public interest results from the simultaneous satisfaction of selected aspects important to several different interests.
5. An overriding *national or societal goals* concept occurs when countrywide social objectives are defined and held to supersede private interests.

On organizations trying to claim they represent the public interest, see HATE GROUPS, INTEREST GROUPS, LOBBYING/LOBBYIST, and PRESSURE GROUPS.

PUBLICITY—Information about an individual, organization, event, product, or other marketable commodity disseminated through NEWS MEDIA and other channels to attract PUBLIC notice. Often publicists resort to PRESS AGENTRY and HYPE to promote their clients. Normally, this PUBLIC COMMUNICATION is designed to bring about positive coverage or "ink." Sometimes, however, backdoor DISINFORMATION (*DEZINFORMATSIA*) strategies are utilized to attack opponents and force them into the spotlight of unfavorable publicity. See also FLUFF EVENTS, PROMOTION, PSEUDO-EVENT/PSEUDO-NEWS, PUBLIC RELATIONS (PR), PUBLIC SERVICE ANNOUNCEMENTS (PSAs), PUBLIC SERVICE EVENTS, PURPOSE-FUL PERSUASION, and SPECIALTY ADVERTISING.

PUBLIC OPINION—Oral and visual expression of individual views about ISSUEs of common concern that collectively contribute to the steady stream of competing ideas. Public opinion involves arousal of latent attitudes to the point that they affect internal thought or external behavior. Even totalitarian societies need to take into account public opinion, although more frequently it is seen as characteristic of a free society. Public opinion is usually measured by TRACKING POLLS, ranging from intercept studies in which citizens are buttonholed on the street to more sophisticated random surveys designed to scientifically measure their views within a predetermined range of error. The results play an important role in formulating public policy.

A relatively new form of "deliberative polling" involves exposing a demographically-representative group of people to experts, followed by a chance for them all to interact in discussing the issues. Polling occurs on the before-and-after opinions expressed by "citizens." According to Cynthia Crossen's *Tainted Truth: The Manipulation of Fact in America* (1994):

> Tactical research has dominated contemporary debates about abortion, gun control, family leave, recycling, school choice and the speed limit. Each issue has its dueling polls. The timber industry has its polls showing most people wouldn't sacrifice a single job to save an endangered species. Proponents of school choice have surveys showing that people want it, and opponents have their surveys showing that people do not. Gun control activists have surveys showing that many people want increased regulation of guns; the National Rifle Association has surveys showing the opposite.

Sponsored public opinion polling and policy research studies are especially subject to unconscious self-CENSORSHIP and subtle finagling of results to please the client, Crossen says. He observes:

> Whatever their affiliation, academics and other researchers can be susceptible to sponsors' pressures. Without any words being spoken, researchers know what outcome would most likely result in another research contract. . . That the understanding is implicit, is one of the most dangerous aspects of sponsored research.

Some social scientists make a distinction between long-term public opinion which exhibits stability and shorter-term POPULAR OPINION, which is volatile and more subject to propagandistic manipulation. This dichotomy, however, is not fully accepted. See also AGENDA SETTING, COURT OF PUBLIC OPINION, DEMOGRAPHICS, PUBLIC INTEREST, and PUBLIC POLICY PROCESS.

PUBLIC POLICY PROCESS—At the nexus of politics and policy development lies persistent conflict over problem definition: where issues come from, what they signify for PUBLIC OPINION, and what kinds of solutions should be pursued. The greater the impact a proposed governmental action may have on particular individuals and institutions, the more likely an ISSUE is to be contested. In a representative DEMOCRACY, the public policy process thus involves the resolution of the toughest issues through lobbying, debate, and compromise between INTEREST GROUPS, government officials, journalists, POLITICAL ANALYSTS, and other ACTIVISTS. The consensus eventually reached is reflected in laws and regulations that members of a society are expected to obey. See also CRITICAL ISSUE, LOBBYING/LOBBYIST and ISSUES MANAGEMENT.

PUBLIC RELATIONS (PR)—Reflecting the fragmented nature of the many components that comprise what is loosely referred to as the practice of "public relations," there are numerous widely promoted definitions outlining the operating philosophy and set of techniques used by integrate organizations and the people they depend upon. The British Institute of Public Opinion states in its promotional literature that "public relations is the deliberate, planned, and sustained effort to establish and maintain mutual understanding between an organization and its publics." Denny Griswold, founder of *Public Relations News*, says that public relations is "the management function which evaluates public attitudes, identifies the policies and procedures of an individual or organization with the public interest, and plans and executes a program of action [incorporating communication] to earn public understanding and acceptance." The World Assembly of Public Relations meeting in Mexico City in 1978 adopted the following definition: "Public relations practice is the art and social science of analyzing trends, predicting their consequences, counseling organization leaders, and implementing planned programs of action which serve both the organization's and the public's interest." On the other hand, the editors of *Inside PR* magazine in targeting a corporate audience see public relations as

a philosophy that guides a company to act in the interests of those people—employees, customers, shareholders, communities, regulators, and others—upon whom it depends for its success, recognizing that reputation is an asset that must be protected, nurtured and managed if long-term success is to be achieved. . . Public relations is a management discipline that encompasses a wide range of activities, from marketing and advertising to investor relations and government affairs.

Whatever the definition, good public relations does not so much involve avoiding controversy as addressing it in a credible manner. Note that the term is also used as a verb: "They worked hard to PR the potentially damaging miscue." In addition to the organizations mentioned above, there are numerous other professional groups of importance in the persuasive communications field, notably the PUBLIC RELATIONS SOCIETY OF AMERICA (PRSA), International Public Relations Association (IPRA), and International Association of Business Communicators (IABC). See also FLACK, FLUFF EVENTS, HIDDEN PERSUADERS, HYPE, ISSUES MANAGEMENT, OFF THE NEWS, PRESS AGENTRY, PROMOTION, PSEUDO-EVENT/PSEUDO-NEWS, PUBLIC AFFAIRS, PUBLICITY, PUBLIC RELATIONS MODELS, PUBLIC SERVICE EVENTS, REACH, SPIN DOCTORS, SPOKESMANSHIP/SPOKESPERSON TRAINING, and STAKEHOLDERS.

PUBLIC RELATIONS MODELS—Conceptualizing the process of PUBLIC RELATIONS (PR) has led to many theories of PUBLIC COMMUNICATION. Some researchers stress the role of public relations in determining whether it primarily involves a management counseling or technician-oriented communications. The most influential theory in recent years has been the four management models approach first devised by James E. Grunig and Todd Hunt in their book *Managing Public Relations* (1984) and subsequently elaborated on. Using a systems theory approach, they analyzed the organizational structures and communications strategies most widely used by practitioners to derive the following categories:

- *One-way PRESS AGENTRY model*, emphasizing the generation of favorable PUBLICITY in the mass media.
- *One-way public information model*, stressing more journalistic dissemination of relatively objective information through controlled media (brochures, newsletters, direct mail) as well as MASS COMMUNICATION vehicles.
- *Two-way asymmetrical or PROPAGANDA MODEL*, involving greater use of social science research so the organization becomes better at persuasion.
- *Two-way symmetrical or CONFLICT RESOLUTION model*, engaging in caring research-based dialogue to establish mutually-beneficial partnerships with strategic publics. This latter approach is the only one in which the negative implications of manipulation is minimized.

Connected with this four-part outline has been the notion that each model represents an ethical stage in the evolution of public relations, from primitive to advanced. However, scholars recently have begun to dispute this Darwinistic assumption. See also CORPORATE SOCIAL RESPONSIBILITY (CSR), SALIENCY, and SCAME.

PUBLIC RELATIONS SOCIETY OF AMERICA (PRSA), THE—Of all the professional organizations in the field of PUBLIC RELATIONS (PR), this is the largest with more than 14,000 members. It operates a national professional development and awards program, has a number of special interest sections, maintains a reference library, publishes *Public Relations Strategist*, sponsors the PUBLIC RELATIONS STUDENT SOCIETY OF AMERICA (PRSSA), and provides other services.

PUBLIC RELATIONS STUDENT SOCIETY OF AMERICA (PRSSA), THE—A college organization with more than 150 chapters, founded in 1968 as an affiliate of the PUBLIC RELATIONS SOCIETY OF AMERICA (PRSA) to promote PUBLIC RELATIONS (PR) education.

PUBLIC SERVICE ANNOUNCEMENTS (PSAs)—In order to better serve the PUBLIC INTEREST, BROADCASTING networks/stations, cable systems, magazines, newspapers, and OUTDOOR ADVERTISING companies voluntarily donate airtime and space to worthy groups. Charitable, educational, and other nonprofit organizations with limited funds often rely on these ADVERTISING- or NEWS-like PUBLICITY messages to tell their story. The most influential supplier of PSAs in the United States is the ADVERTISING COUNCIL.

PUBLIC SERVICE EVENTS—Organizations need the cooperation of STAKEHOLDERS to be successful. Public service events implement a variety of PUBLICITY activities designed to tell others what an organization is all about and solicit support. Events may include informational meetings, public speeches, seminars, table displays, PSEUDO-EVENT/PSEUDO-NEWS presentations, and other forms of PUBLIC COMMUNICATION that facilitate direct networking. See also FLUFF EVENTS.

PULLOUTS—Cancellations by advertisers of purchased media time in response to boycotts by PRESSURE GROUPS incensed about a particular broadcast program theme, article topic, or other controversial media policy decision. Sponsor withdrawals of ADVERTISING for all reasons, for example, cost the major television networks between 10 and 20 million dollars annually in the early 1990s.

PURPOSEFUL PERSUASION—According to a useful text by Austin Freeley, *Argumentation and Debate* (1986), purposeful persuasion is:

communication intended to influence the acts, beliefs, attitudes, and values of others. Clearly one method of persuasion is debate. Persuasion is not, however, limited to seeking reasoned judgments, as is debate, nor does persuasion required reasoned arguments both for and against a given proposition. . . . Persuaders reach a decision on the problem before they begin the process of persuasion. They continue the process of persuasion until they solve the problem by persuading others to accept the decision or until they are convinced that further efforts at persuasion are pointless. In their efforts to influence others, they may find it necessary or advantageous to join with other persuaders and become propagandists or face the opposition and become debaters. . . Unintended persuasion occurs when one receives a message not intended for that particular receiver . . . or when a person unknowingly communicates to and influences others in an unintended way.

See also PERSUASION INDUSTRIES and RHETORIC.

PUSH POLLS—A political tool, couched in the language of supposedly legitimate survey research, push polls emanate from a usually anonymous telemarketer phone bank working for one candidate in a hotly contested campaign. The callers utilize a scripted questionnaire carefully designed to probe the weaknesses of opponents and spread often-misleading PROPAGANDA. One widely used form of such "advocacy phoning" involves contacting thousands of registered voters just before an election to make damning allegations and smears. Selected likely voters for the opponent will typically be asked pointedly critical questions along these lines: "Are you more or less likely to vote for candidate X if you knew he voted to spend $10 million to promote trade to communist Cuba or $75 million to fund a special pension plan open only to members of Congress?" In such cases the push polls, even though draped in the authority of a PUBLIC OPINION survey, are short in duration and the responses are not recorded. Other, more positive, push poll efforts are designed to provide encouragement to supporters of a campaign in order to reinforce their commitment and mobilize them into the voting booths. See also BENCHMARK STUDY, HANDLERS, POLISPOTS, TOXIC INFORMATION, and TRACKING POLLS.

RACIST/RACIALIST/RACIAL DISCRIMINATION—A person engaging in discrimination solely on the basis of race or related factors (such as skin color) is a racist. Nationalistic fervor is often associated with racist trappings, particularly when one ethnic group defines itself in terms of *not* being from some other group. Many critics of racist ideologies link them to this "hate" of others phenomenon since racists subjectively tend to rank races, with their own typically being the best. Racists often attempt to defend their views by denying hatred of others, asserting they simply love their own kin and kith. The related term *racialist* is often used interchangeably with *racist*, although some scholars have asserted this should be more properly applied to the objective scientific study of race differences without a pejorative connotation.

Article 1 of the International Convention on the Elimination of All Forms of Racial Discrimination adopted by the General Assembly of the UNITED NATIONS ORGANIZATION (UNO or UN) in 1965, defines the term racial discrimination as

any distinction, exclusion, restriction or preference based on race, colour, descent, or national or ethnic origin which has the purpose or effect of nullifying or impairing the recognition, enjoyment or exercise, on an equal footing, of human rights and fundamental freedoms in the political, economic, social, cultural or any other field of public life.

The convention, while inequitably enforced, further proscribes specific obligations of ratifying member states to encourage nations to outlaw racial discrimination and establish penalties for actions which stir up racial incitement. These provisions may be broadly interpreted. For example, despite the fact that Jews do not constitute a specific race, the Nazi use of *racialism* in the context of ANTI-SEMITIC pogroms has been widely condemned as a form of racial persecution. See also CENSORSHIP, ETHNIC CLEANSING, EXTREMISM, GENOCIDE, HATE GROUPS, HATE SPEECH, HUMAN RIGHTS, JAPAN BASHING, NATIONAL SOCIALISM/NAZISM, and ZIONISM/ZIONIST.

RADICAL—The word means the seeking of fundamental or extreme change by "going to the root" of an issue. For example, as Karl Marx observed in *Critique of Hegel's "Philosophy of Right"* (1970, originally published in 1843), "To be radical is to grasp things by the root." Because of varying interpretations of what is or is not radical, the label is often applied pejoratively to more than EXTREMISTs and ZEALOTS, particularly when domestic or foreign policy challenges arise. U.S. policymakers typically refer to individuals, organizations, or regimes as radical when their behavior is perceived as unfriendly or threatening to American governmental interests. For example, women who fought to end child-labor abuses were called radicals. An irony is that revolutionary MOVEMENTs in other countries, which often couch their own "fight for freedom against tyranny" in language drawn from the 1776 Declaration of Independence, tend to be opposed by the U.S. government. Historian Gene Clanton, author of *Populism: The Humane Preference in America* (1991), preferred to define radical in terms of "efforts to advance political, economic, and social democracy which often, though not always, see the capitalist system as the cause of the problems" by those struggling "to create their own special version of the cooperative commonwealth."

REACH—An ADVERTISING term, the same as "cume" or cumulative audience, which refers to the total number of persons exposed to a particular COMMERCIAL SPEECH message. It is estimated that the average American each day is confronted by 1,200 selling attempts. These range from interpersonal word-of-mouth sources to slick television spots. Since any single exposure is unlikely to break through this "clutter" to have a measurable behavioral effect, marketing communications specialists design their campaigns to have multiple "impressions." Through frequency of repetition, the advertised message has a chance to sink in. Effective reach refers to exposing the audience enough times to a message so as to create "top-of-mind awareness." When designing a media schedule, the audiences delivered through circulation, readership, listenership, viewership and so forth are quantified in various ways for comparison purposes, such as:

- Their DEMOGRAPHICS and PSYCHOGRAPHICS;
- Cost per thousand impressions (abbreviated CPM, with the M referring to the Roman numeral for 1,000); and
- Cost per point (CPP, with one point being the equivalent of one percent of the total audience). The points are often added to give the GROSS RATINGS POINTS (GRPs).

REACTIONARY—As American socialist Daniel De Leon observed, "Where a social revolution is pending and, for whatever reason, is not accomplished, reaction is the alternative." Reactionaries generally favor the status quo or an economic and political return to more RIGHT-WING/CONSERVATIVE policies. The term is often negatively applied by progressives on the left to label their opponents and is even applied by MARXISTs and other revolutionaries to refer to those in their ranks opting for more moderate policies. See also CAPITALIST ROADER, COMMUNISM/COMMUNIST, CONFORMISTS, DOGMA, EXTREMIST, LEFT-WING/LIBERAL, POPULAR OPINION, PROGRESSIVE/PROGRESSIVISM, RADICAL, REVOLUTION/REVOLUTIONARY, and SOCIALISM/SOCIALIST.

RED-BAITING—Attacks either in person or via media calling individuals and organizations communists, reds, and related "slurs" in order to publicly discredit them because of their political beliefs. While sometimes true, such widely voiced denunciations often included innocent victims whose only "crime" was to exercise their FIRST AMENDMENT freedoms of association and dissent. See also COMMUNISM/COMMUNIST, HOUSE UN-AMERICAN ACTIVITIES COMMITTEE (HUAC), McCARTHYISM, POLITICAL CRIME, PROPAGANDA DEVICES, and RITUAL DEFAMATION.

RED DECADE—Somewhat inaccurate term sometimes applied to the 1930s to highlight a period of growing Communist party influence in the United States.

REPRESENTATIVE VIOLENCE—A TERRORIST tactic used to make a political point. During and after a breakdown of social order, people are assaulted or killed merely because they belong to an opposing group. Deteriorating conditions lead to incremental violence found first in extra-legal activities, followed by vigilantism. These increase as the state becomes more ineffective in dealing with challenges to the existing order from those practicing selective TERRORISM and other POLITICAL CRIMEs. Such instability is followed either by a restoration of confidence or a final breakdown marked by indiscriminate violence and leading to some new order. See also ASSASSIN and PROPAGANDA OF THE DEED.

REPUBLICAN PARTY—Political organization founded in 1854 as a northern antislavery FACTION composed of disgruntled Whigs, dissident Free Soilers, and "Know-Nothings" from the AMERICAN PARTY, dropouts from the DEMOCRATIC PARTY, and others reacting to sectional stresses threatening the Union. Under Lincoln and his successors, the Republicans became the only political organization to evolve from "third party" status into a major partisan force that continues to shape the levers of government in America. Republicans frequently use an elephant symbol and the initials GOP when referring to themselves, meaning they are members of a "Grand Old Party." Republican officeholders are often identified by the capital letter *R*. See also FEDERAL ELECTION COMMISSION (FEC) and WATERGATE SCANDAL.

RESCUE OPERATION—A military EUPHEMISM designed to disguise that what really is occurring is a military invasion to overthrow another government, as in Grenada. The term is also used by antiabortionists to refer to civil disobedience designed to save unborn children by shutting down abortion clinics.

RESIDENCY—A government intelligence organization operating in another nation, often out of the embassy. An "illegal resident" is an intelligence representative working abroad under unofficial cover designed to further disguise the individual's true rank and purpose. See also COVER STORY and INTELLIGENCE COMMUNITY.

REVISIONISM/REVISIONIST—The term *revisionism* (or *Revisionism* as favored by many in the MOVEMENT) has several meanings, with both positive and negative connotations. One of the leading proponents of revisionist research, Harry Elmer Barnes, observed that revisionism is "nothing more or less than the effort to correct the historical record in the light of a more complete collection of historical facts, a more calm political atmosphere, and a more objective attitude." However, Barnes noted,

During the last forty years or so, Revisionism has become a fighting term. To so-called Revisionists, it implies an honest search for historical truth and the discrediting of misleading myths that are a barrier to peace and good will among nations. In the minds of the anti-Revisionists, the term savors of malice, vindictiveness, and an unholy desire to smear the saviors of mankind.

Members of the revisionist movement tend to be LIBERTARIAN in challenging the use of secrecy by governments, but are not easily classified in terms of the "right-left" political spectrum. The term is most often associated today with writers advocating various CONSPIRACY THEORIES to explain events and questioning the standard histories of such sensitive topics as the Holocaust. The body of revisionist studies material is quite large. However, as a result of their courage (or stupidity) in challenging the conventional wisdom, many of the works by these authors are not mass distributed and so cannot be found in leading book stores, most libraries, or other outlets available to the more conventional.

As Tom Marcellus, director of the controversial Institute for Historical Review, pointed out in a pamphlet called *The Tradition of Historical Revision*:

The term originated with a group of scholars (French, British, American, German and others) whose researches undermined the presumption of unique German responsibility for the outbreak of the First World War in 1914. Although the term Revisionist originally was used to apply only to the question of guilt for WWI, it has subsequently come to include all historical findings at odds with the establishment version. Revisionism is freedom of speech in history. Those early Revisionists and those who followed the tradition recognized a fact of life pertaining to the writing of history: in the case of wars, historians of the victorious nations tended to write historical accounts that ignore relevant facts not favorable to the victor, while, at the same time, misrepresenting or inventing other facts in order to cast the loser in an unfavorable light. Most of these historians had played an active role in World War I, many in propaganda and intelligence; after the Second World War, it was not uncommon for them to continue to have links with intelligence agencies. The efforts of Establishment historians to remain on the good side of the powers-that-be (like the court historians who served kings and emperors of old) created a historical record that oftentimes resembled wartime propaganda more than independent scholarship.

Civil libertarians believe revisionist researchers have always performed a useful service even when it is easy to disagree with them. As radicals, they help define the outer limits of an issue and force those in the center to be more thorough. When they are right, revisionists help clarify fact. And when they are wrong, their failures to displace the truths they unsuccessfully challenged have made those renewed truths ever more precious and secure.

Those facing the brunt of revisionist attack are often less charitable. Organizations such as the ANTI-DEFAMATION LEAGUE OF B'NAI B'RITH (ADL) have issued a number of works which equate revisionism with EXTREMISM. The concerns of antirevisionists revolve around World War II researches humanizing the German National Socialist regime and questioning the "Final Solution" GENOCIDE policies the Nazis are associated with. Typical of studies attacking the "Holocaust deniers and debunkers" is a recent monograph compiled by the ADL entitled *Hitler's Apologists: The Anti-Semitic Propaganda of Holocaust "Revisionism."*

Marxists have also often been in the antirevisionist camp, attacking such dissenters whether outside or inside the Communist party as "right opportunist" counterrevolutionaries. In *Quotations from Chairman Mao Tse-tung* (1972 edition, pp. 20-22), the Chinese revolutionary leader observed:

It is revisionism to negate the basic principles of Marxism and to negate its universal truth. Revisionism is one form of bourgeois ideology. The revisionists deny the differences between socialism and capitalism, between the dictatorship of the proletariat and the dictatorship of the bourgeoisie. What they advocate is in fact not the socialist line but the capitalist line. In present circumstances, revisionism is more pernicious than dogmatism. One of our current important tasks on the ideological front is to unfold criticism of revisionism. . . . There are still a number of people who vainly hope to restore the capitalist system and fight the working class on every front, including the ideological one. And their right-hand men in the struggle are the revisionists.

See also ACTIVISTS, ANTI-SEMITIC, BIG LIE, BLACKOUT BOYS, CAPITALISM/CAPITALIST, CAPITALIST ROADER, COMMUNISM/ COMMUNIST, COUNTERREVOLUTIONARY, ESTABLISHMENT, FAS-CISM/FASCIST, FIGHTING WORDS, FREE SPEECH, IDEOLOGY, MARXIST, NATIONAL SOCIALISM/NAZISM, RADICAL, REVOLU-TION/REVOLUTIONARY, and SOCIALISM/ SOCIALIST.

REVOLUTION/REVOLUTIONARY—The overthrow of one system of governance by adherents of another. Revolutions typically involve some violence, although they can also successfully occur through the peaceful/nonviolent withdrawal of support. Indicative of successful revolutionary thought is the TOTALITARIANISM espoused in the collected *Quotations from Chairman Mao Tse-tung*. This was translated into English by order of the Chinese government and widely distributed in red-covered book form across the United States during the 1970s. Mao said:

A revolution is not a dinner party, or writing an essay, or painting a picture, or doing embroidery; it cannot be so refined, so leisurely and gentle, so temperate, kind, courteous, restrained and magnanimous. A revolution is an insurrection, an act of violence by which one class overthrows another.

Later, Mao reflected that

whoever sides with the revolutionary people is a revolutionary. Whoever sides with imperialism, feudalism and bureaucrat-capitalism is a counterrevolutionary. Whoever sides with the revolutionary people in words only but acts otherwise is a revolutionary in speech. Whoever sides with the revolutionary people in deed as well as in word is a revolutionary in the full sense.

See also ARMED PROPAGANDA, ARMED STRUGGLE, CADRE, COMMUNISM/COMMUNIST, DIVERT/REFOCUS STRATEGY, DOG-MA, IDEOLOGY, IMPERIALISM/IMPERIALIST, INSURRECTION/IN-SURRECTIONARY, LIBERATION THEOLOGY, and MARXIST.

RHETORIC—The language by which people move other people to action; "the management of symbols in order to coordinate social action." Plato, in the *Phaedrus*, defines rhetoric as "a universal art of winning the mind by arguments, which means not merely arguments in the courts of justice and all other sorts of public councils, but in private conference as well." See also ARGUMENTATION, CLASSICAL LIBERALISM, POLEMIC, PURPOSE-FUL PERSUASION, and SPEAK AND RETREAT.

RIGHT-WING/CONSERVATIVE—Technically, a conservative is a person who prefers the status quo and is willing to accept only limited change. The term takes on a somewhat different meaning when political views are discussed. According to the definition by Advocates for Self-Government, Inc. (1995):

Right/Conservatives like personal choices in economics and central decision-making in civil matters. They want government to defend the community from threats to its moral fiber. Right/Conservatives place high value on laws and legislation. They accept diversity in economics but seek similarity in social behavior. They work with libertarians in defending economic freedoms and populists in enforcing community standards in social matters.

Conservatives are frequently described as advocates of limited government and a free marketplace, but that more properly refers to libertarianism. Rather, conservatives often favor state intervention through mechanisms such as a mandatory draft to support a strong military, enhanced police powers to restrict "deviant" sexuality, censorship of a wide range of artistic and literary expression they find disturbing, regulatory economic practices which aid big business, and other controls over private and public behavior. Some modern conservatives in the United States go further, however, and seek RADICAL changes to hearken back to an era free from the "dangerous liberalism," "secular humanism," and "decayed moralism" they see as "rampant" in American society. Those who more stridently distance themselves from centrist positions are occasionally pejoratively referred to as radical right, far right, ultra right, or extreme right. Opponents of those holding conservative values—as reflected in the promotion of religious issues such as prayer in schools, antiabortion and antipornography crusades, and other causes often associated with elements of the national REPUBLICAN PARTY—regularly use the terms as a slur.

See also CAPITALISM/CAPITALIST, CLASSICAL LIBERAL, EXTREM-ISM, FUNDAMENTALISM/FUNDAMENTALIST, HUMAN NATURE, IDEOLOGUES, LEFT-WING/LIBERAL, LIBERTARIAN, NEOLIBERAL-ISM, POPULISM/ POPULIST, and REACTIONARY.

RITUAL DEFAMATION—Term used by EXTREMISM researcher Laird Wilcox to describe the process of intimidation that relies on name calling, guilt-by-association, and resort to outright threats. Governments, HATE GROUPS, CULTs, and other POLITICALLY CORRECT (PC) organizations are often successful in applying such PROPAGANDA DEVICES to SPIKE criticisms of their activities and beliefs. See also AD HOMINEM ATTACK, AMERICA BASHING, ANTI-SEMITIC, CENSORSHIP, DEMONIZING THE OPPOSITION, JAPAN BASHING, RACIST/RACIALIST/RACIAL DISCRIMINATION, RED-BAITING, SCAPEGOAT/SCAPEGOATING, SLIPPERY SLOPE, SMOKING GUN, SPIRAL OF SILENCE, and TOXIC INFORMATION.

ROOSEVELT, FRANKLIN DELANO—See FDR.

SACRED TERRORISM—The use of religious appeals to justify vigilantism and legitimize state use of force against one's "enemies." Moral justifications are more loudly proclaimed the more brutal the reprisal, the more savage the revenge. Murders in the name of God (or a Jihad to defend the honor of Allah) become easier, more acceptable, even desirable when the instinctive social breaks against the cycle of violence are removed. See also ASSASSIN, ETHNIC CLEANSING, FUNDAMENTALISM/FUNDAMENTALIST, GENOCIDE, HATE GROUPS, IDEOLOGY, LIBERATION THEOLOGY, PROPAGANDA OF THE DEED, SCAPEGOAT/SCAPEGOATING, STATE TERRORISM, and TERRORISM.

SALIENCE—All propagandists have to answer two basic questions that people naturally ask when faced with persuasive messages: (1) "What does this mean to me?" and (2) "Why should I care?" A failure to understand the real nature of the targeted audience means the propagandist's main ideas will likely be "off message." On the other hand, the more the key points emphasized by the propagandist relate to the interests and needs of the target audience—an indication of salience—the more effective and meaningful the messages are likely to be perceived. See also AGENDA SETTING, MEDIA EFFECTS, and OFF THE NEWS.

SAMIZDAT—Governments often will maintain tight controls and registration on typewriters, mimeograph machines, photocopiers, and computers to limit independent contacts. *Samizdat* is a Russian-language term literally meaning "self-publishing." Included are PAMPHLETEERING and other forms of underground literature circulated in defiance of a regime's ban on private communication. The word also means the process or system for the COVERT distribution of materials suppressed by government.

SCAME—A formula for analyzing PROPAGANDA that takes into account *S*ource, *C*ontent, *A*udience, *M*edia, and *E*ffects.

SCAPEGOAT/SCAPEGOATING—A person, ethnic group, organization, or thing that is blamed for the mistakes, disasters, misfortunes or problems of others. The notion of the scapegoat derives from Jewish history where the high priest confessed the people's sins on Yom Kippur (the Day of Atonement), killed a goat without blemish, and asked Yahweh (God) for national and individual forgiveness. By accepting the sacrifice in this ritual, Yahweh created a symbol of the forthcoming messiah. This lesson, however, has been misappropriated and used to justify persecution and mass murder. See also ETHNIC CLEANSING, GENOCIDE, RACIST/RACIALIST/RACIAL DISCRIMINATION, RED-BAITING, RITUAL DEFAMATION, and SACRED TERRORISM.

SECRET GOVERNMENT—A term sometimes used to refer to those directing COVERT ACTIONs in the CENTRAL INTELLIGENCE AGENCY (CIA) and other government departments. At other times, *secret government* is used synonymously to mean the ESTABLISHMENT and SHADOW

GOVERNMENT. Proponents of this viewpoint argue that irrespective of which political party is in office, real power is held by a small cabal of wealthy internationalists. The alleged conspiracists are believed to already control the major centers of influence in the United States and other countries and are said to now be actively seeking to create a "new world order" under their domination. Conspiracy researchers often cite as proof for such secret government allegations the links maintained by these powerful individuals through their memberships in elite organizations such as the COUNCIL ON FOREIGN RELATIONS (CFR), the TRILATERAL COMMISSION, the BILDERBERGER GROUP, and other related global interests. See also CONSPIRACY THEORIES, ELITE THEORY, GLOBALISM, and MEDIA ELITE.

SECRET TEAM—Term used by some authors to refer to a conspiracy by rogue intelligence and military operatives using their positions to advance an unauthorized and undemocratic private ideological and political agenda. The members of the secret team allegedly finance themselves through manipulation of COVERT bank accounts, drug deals, arms smuggling, and even murder for hire. Daniel Sheehan, General Counsel of the Christic Institute, publicly asserted the existence of a secret team of former CENTRAL INTELLIGENCE AGENCY (CIA) operatives, retired military officers, and anti-Castro Cubans with connections to the Reagan-Bush White House as at the core of the Iran-Contra scandal. These allegations were denied by the accused. See also CONSPIRACY THEORIES, COWBOY OPERATION, INTELLIGENCE COMMUNITY, and IRAN-CONTRA INVESTIGATIONS.

SECT—See CULT.

SEDITION—Subversive acts against the government which fall short of TREASON. See also ANARCHISM/ANARCHIST, SEDITIOUS LIBEL, and SUBVERSION/SUBVERSIVES.

SEDITIOUS LIBEL—An imprecise term used by ruling authorities to define a POLITICAL CRIME. The real purpose is to prosecute social dissenters who are too aggressive in questioning government policies and pointing to official misdeeds. See also FREETHINKERS and SEDITION.

SEGUE—See HOT SWITCHING.

SELECTIVE PERCEPTION—The concept that different individuals interpret the same messages and other sense-based stimuli differently depending on their interest, attention, and PSYCHOGRAPHICS makeup. In effect, we see what we prefer to see, hear what we want to hear, and remember what we choose to remember in ways we wish to.

SHADOW GOVERNMENT—In Britain, the opposition parties' designates for office. As used in the U.S., however, *shadow government* is a term loosely bandied about by conspiracy theorists who tend to equate it with vested SECRET GOVERNMENT interests and the illegal SECRET TEAM operations used to support them. See also CONSPIRACY THEORIES.

SHIRTTAILING—Journalistic practice of following up on a NEWS story, usually by seeking a local angle. Often the follow-up has diminished importance, being aired or printed in a less prominent position with reduced time or space.

SIDLE COMMISSION—An advisory panel consisting of former senior military officers and eminent journalists, set up in 1984 by the secretary of defense, and chaired by Major General Winant Sidle (retired). The panelists examined the relationship between the armed forces and NEWS MEDIA following the 1983 American military mission in Grenada. Following their review, the commissioners made a series of policy recommendations which proposed establishing new media ground rules, including a blueprint for a cooperative "pool system" to be activated in a conflict situation. The plan, agreed to by major American NEWS organizations, designated a small number of select professional journalists to provide surrogate reports to a much larger group of print and electronic outlets. The pool system was subsequently utilized with varying degrees of success in the OPERATION JUST CAUSE invasion of Panama and the DESERT SHIELD/DESERT STORM operations in the Persian Gulf area of the Middle East (Southwest Asia).

SIGNAL-TO-NOISE RATIO—A term adapted from electronic engineering to describe interference in the MASS COMMUNICATION distribution and feedback process. It refers to the relationship between the amount of useful information in a given environment and the ever-present nonsense, misinformation, and deliberate DISINFORMATION (*DEZINFORMATSIA*)—often referred to as "HYPE," "noise," and "clutter"—that inevitably accompanies, and even threatens to drown out, the valuable input.

SLIPPERY SLOPE—A term used by one side to disparage an opponent's proposal by warning that, while seemingly moderate or innocuous, if enacted it would result in later decisions considered dangerous. The fear is that once a precedent is approved, ACTIVISTS will not be content until further more far-reaching, public policy changes occur. *Slippery slope* also describes the process that occurs when one's own actions and mistakes, once publicized by the NEWS MEDIA, lead to ultimate failure. Despite making what amounts to a public confession *mea culpa* (referred to by Washington, D.C., BELTWAY BANDITS as "eating the carpet"), the focus of attention often remains so negative that the juggernaut of events and loss of credibility takes the individual, organization, or idea down.

SMOKING GUN—Evidence that contradicts public claims or otherwise demonstrates guilt. Often such damaging TOXIC INFORMATION is released or publicized by one's opponents in order to inflict harm on the unfortunate target. See also WATERGATE SCANDAL.

SNUGGLING—A BLACK PROPAGANDA strategy in which an insurgent PROPAGANDA broadcast is aired on a radio frequency adjacent to that of a government station. The rebel mimics the style and tone of the official announcer to insert DISINFORMATION (*DEZINFORMATSIA*) and confuse unwary listeners. A similar tactic is accomplished in print with the production of ersatz newspapers and other materials distributed in place of the genuine publications whose look they are copying. See also CLANDESTINE RADIO STATIONS and INSURRECTION/ INSURRECTIONARY.

SOCIALISM/SOCIALIST—Adherents of socialist beliefs tend to see socialism as a principled philosophy that seeks the just redistribution of wealth, privilege and responsibilities at all levels of society. According to the definition by Advocates for Self-Government, Inc. (1995), socialists

favor central decision-making in both civil and economic matters. They believe the needs of the individual are subordinate to the needs of society. They want government to 'correct wrongs.' While they strongly differ [from populists] on particular programs, both prefer equality in economic and personal matters.

Right socialists tend to favor variants of fascism, while left socialists tend to express their commitment to worker control and the abolition of capitalism. Actually, the word socialism has been much distorted in our time, with many political parties and regimes claiming socialism as their IDEOLOGY enacting very little of it in their programs once in power.

SOCIAL MARKETING—A term popularized by Philip Kotler and Gerald Zaltman in 1971 to refer to ISSUES MANAGEMENT attempts by nonprofit organizations, business trade associations, and other INTEREST GROUPS. This is also known as "cause-related marketing" because these groups seek to bring about planned social change through their PUBLIC INFORMATION CAMPAIGNS.

SOCIAL MOVEMENT—See MOVEMENT.

SOCIOLINGUISTICS—The study of the complex relationship between language and society, including how words influence behavior.

SOFT MONEY—Large financial contributions made by corporate and other donors for political party-building activities, monitored by the FEDERAL ELECTION COMMISSION (FEC). The U.S. Congress has been more lenient in this aspect of the political process than when legislating restrictions on monies given directly to candidates by POLITICAL ACTION COMMITTEES (PACs). See also DEMOCRATIC PARTY and REPUB-LICAN PARTY.

SOMALIAZATION—Assumption that once another country is deemed un-governable, U.S. officials therefore have the right, either unilaterally or as part of an international force, to send in troops to "restore peace and DEMOCRACY"—as was the case in the December 1992 intervention within Somalia and the more recent occupation of Haiti. See also INTERVENTIONIST, MILITARISM, PEACEKEEPING, UNOSOM

I/UNOSOM II/UNITAF, and VICTORY BY NEWS RELEASE.

SOUND BITE—See ACTUALITY.

SPEAK AND RETREAT—When one side of a dispute makes public threats to others, but fails to back up those warnings with concrete actions, it not only undermines the credibility of the specific ultimatums but also lessens the leverage remaining to those issuing the demands. If the empty threats continue, the failure to move beyond symbolic RHETORIC only serves to embolden offending parties. A classic example of speak and retreat statements occurred in mid-1995 when UNITED NATIONS ORGANIZATION (UNO or UN) officials told ethnic Serb rebels in Bosnia that they faced "massive retaliation" and "devastating airstrikes" if certain "safe areas" were attacked. Because of internal political differences between the United States and its NORTH ATLANTIC TREATY ORGANIZATION (NATO) allies over which policy to pursue in support of the UNO, however, these efforts at saber rattling generally proved hollow and fueled Serbian contempt for their PAPER TIGER opponents.

SPECIAL INTEREST GROUPS—See INTEREST GROUPS and PUBLIC INTEREST.

SPECIALTY ADVERTISING—The Promotional Products Association International (formerly Specialty Advertising Association International) defines specialty advertising as an ADVERTISING, sales PROMOTION, PUBLICITY, and motivational communication medium that displays the sponsoring organization's name, logo, or message on useful articles of merchandise. The imprinted products, called "ad specialties" or "adcentives" when given away free, or "premiums" when recipients have to make a purchase or contribution before receiving the item, are often personalized to better target those people who are most important to the sender.

Four major business groupings make up the specialty advertising/promotional products industry: Suppliers; Distributors; Direct-Selling Houses; and Trade Organizations. Over 15,000 different specialty advertising items are now offered through the industry. In recent years, the top five product categories have been wearables, writing instruments, business accessories, calendars, and glassware/ceramics.

There has been a debate on whether advertising specialties constitute advertising or sales promotion. Actually, specialty advertising items can be both and more simultaneously. For example, consider the person who occasionally drinks a particular brand of soda and, responding to a sales promotion campaign, receives a T-shirt complete with commercial art message. He or she wears the shirt when out with friends, providing more exposure for the brand. Additionally, according to research in psychology, the consumer's positive attitude toward the brand will be strengthened as a result of publicly wearing the shirt. Regardless of the advertising/sales promotion labels, ad specialties have the potential of providing high impact to a tightly targeted market niche. They can also deliver long-term advertising value beyond short-term sales promotion objectives. The key to success in such endeavors is in matching the adcentive-based elements to the interests of the audience segment—that is, targeting true prospects rather than suspects. See also DIRECT MARKETING (DM).

SPIKE—The deliberate suppression of a potentially controversial NEWS story before it becomes public knowledge by a media GATEKEEPER responding to political, economic, or other CENSORSHIP pressures. A second meaning refers to the CLANDESTINE use of recording equipment (bugging) to monitor rooms, telephones, and so forth.

SPIN CONTROL—A manipulation technique practiced by HANDLERS or SPIN DOCTORS designed to influence the NEWS MEDIA process. Spin controllers promote perceptions and nuances they hope will be conveyed within the tone of subsequent reporting and commentary beyond the bare facts of hard news. By using their insider positions to provide certain interpretations of events they know will appeal to journalists seeking SOUND BITE quotes, the handlers expect the media to incorporate the spin in ways leading to acceptance by viewers, listeners, and readers. See also AGENDA SETTING, GATEKEEPER, INSIDERS, MEDIACRACY, OPPO RESEARCH, ORCHESTRATED PROPAGANDA CAMPAIGN, PACK JOURNALISM, PERCEPTION MANAGEMENT, TOXIC INFORMATION, and TWO-STEP FLOW (MULTI-STEP FLOW).

SPIN DOCTORS—Professional communicators whose job it is to see that a pre-determined interpretation is given to NEWS events. They are often employed by political organizations and INTEREST GROUPS to get favorable coverage or insulate their employer from probing questions. Retired spin doctors or those temporarily between assignments (for example, when their candidate drops out of the race) often go to work for the NEWS MEDIA as POLITICAL ANALYSTS. Political figures opt for maximum control, although experience shows that presidential image in particular is more shaped by likable personality than IDEOLOGY. The term "spin doctors" was first used by the *New York Times* on October 21, 1984, to refer to appearances in the PRESS room by senior campaign advisors after the Reagan-Mondale televised debates. See also HANDLERS, IMAGE ADVERTISING, and SPIN CONTROL.

SPIRAL OF SILENCE—German scholar Elisabeth Noelle-Neumann has suggested that MASS COMMUNICATION and POLITICAL ANALYSTS must take into account the "cumulative effects" of media which, she claims, impose a "spiral of silence." The ubiquitous, redundant, and propagandistic nature of many of the messages, she observes, are important in terms of defining choice—particularly in terms of the PUBLIC POLICY PROCESS. She argues that one of the outcomes of media AGENDA SETTING is that certain favored views become even more dominant while minority viewpoints are shunted into obscurity. This CENSORSHIP involves intimidation and ideational TERRORISM. Corporate DEEP POCKETS SPENDING is one way that some views are overwhelmed. Another is through catering to "the offended" who vociferously seek to ban any form of expression which invokes discomfort to them. See also COURT OF PUBLIC OPINION, FREE SPEECH, HATE SPEECH, MEDIA EFFECTS, POLITICALLY CORRECT (PC), and SPIKE.

SPOKESMANSHIP/SPOKESPERSON TRAINING—A number of so-called "imagemaker" consultants design effectiveness programs to educate clients in the ways of media diplomacy, particularly in how to conduct oneself in interviews responding to crisis situations. One leading media training firm is Fairchild/LeMaster of Dallas, Texas, which helped ready brewery executives Joseph and Bill Coors to neutralize CBS newsman Mike Wallace's hardball questions when *60 Minutes* did a probing story alleging that the Adolph Coors Brewing Company mistreated its employees.

SPYING/SPYCRAFT—The CLANDESTINE obtaining of information by governments, businesses, and other organizations through ESPIONAGE. Many spies remain undetected, but the profession is a risky one. According to the venerable *Encyclopedia Britannica* of 1771, a spy is "a person hired to watch the actions, motions, etc. of another, particularly of what passes in a camp. When a spy is discovered, he is hanged immediately." In the United States today, a person convicted of spying is more likely to be imprisoned.

STAKEHOLDERS—Constituent groups defined in terms of whether or not they are affected by or have the power to influence the activities of an organization. Stakeholders for businesses would include employees, stockholders, distributors, customers, retirees, suppliers, royalty holders, taxing authorities, INTEREST GROUPS, and community residents. Many stakeholders are essentially passive, particularly in public policy ISSUEs. As stakeholders become more involved, their activism makes them more important target PUBLICs. See also ACTIVISTS and PRESSURE GROUPS.

STATE TERRORISM—When government regimes go beyond their legal authority by committing acts of lawless violence against their political opponents (which can either be domestic or foreign), then the state itself engages in *state terrorism*. This often involves the limited use of military intervention (a blockade or bombing strike) that technically is an act of war but is not intended to lead to full-scale conflict. Rather the resort to force is undertaken unilaterally or in concert with other national partners for short-term geopolitical purposes. *State-directed terrorism* is less overt—it features TERRORISTs who operate as agents of a sponsoring government, which then also provides substantial organizational, intelligence, logistical, and operational support. State-directed terrorism may involve the use of surrogate violence against another country's government, often again without a formal declaration of war against "the enemy" (as occurred with the CIA-directed CONTRAS in Nicaragua during the 1980s). A variant specialists call *state-supported terrorism* involves TERROR GROUPs that generally operate independently, but receive backing from one or more governments because of their usefulness.

There is much hypocrisy in this whole phenomenon. Typically, one nation will accuse another of state-directed terrorism or state-sponsored terrorism as a way to justify its own use of "retaliatory" violence in "sending a message." Because of NEWS MEDIA and PUBLIC OPINION concerns, even aggressors committed to violence will often seek the cloak of legal justification through some form of multinational approval. This can cut two ways. Powerful governments often react unfavorably when smaller countries decide to pursue independent policies, as has been the case with the U.S. response to the installation of more RADICAL regimes, not just in Nicaragua, but also in Cuba, Panama, Iraq, Libya, North Korea, and elsewhere. To advance its own (often hidden) political agenda, the bigger state has an advantage in that it may be able to intimidate, bribe, or otherwise coerce representatives from other countries at the United Nations, Organization of American States, or similarly convenient international forum into voting for resolutions condemning the targeted nation. These propagandistic "sanitizing" efforts provide the necessary "window dressing" to publicly position the administration and sanction the forms of violence it favors.

The concept of "retaliation" has dubious standing in international law, with preemptive violence often justified as being in accord with Article 51 of the UNO Charter, which says, in part that "Nothing in the present Charter shall impair the inherent right of individual or collective self defense if an armed attack occurs against a member of the United Nations." See also CENTRAL INTELLIGENCE AGENCY (CIA), COERCIVE DIPLOMACY, COLD WAR, HIDDEN AGENDA, INTERVENTIONIST, MILITARISM, PEACEKEEPING, SOMALIAZATION, SPEAK AND RETREAT, TERRORISM, UNOSOM I/UNOSOM II/UNITAF, and UNPROFOR.

STEALTH TACTICS—Practice of disguising one's true purposes while seeking power, by focusing on only safe ISSUEs and using popular terminology to hide the true IDEOLOGY one really seeks to promote. Opponents of Christian RIGHT-WING/CONSERVATIVE candidates for elective office often attempt to paint them as EXTREMIST by asserting that they are concealing or playing down their positions on controversial issues in order to fool voters before an election. In reality, however, many individuals, organizations, and governments maintain a HIDDEN AGENDA and engage in DISINFORMATION (*DEZINFORMATSIA*) or noninformation campaigns to mask their real goals. See also FUNDAMENTALISM/FUNDAMENTALIST.

STONEWALLING—Refusing to answer allegations, resorting to overt "no comment" responses, denying access to written DOCUMENTs, and otherwise actively hindering outside access to information make up the strategy of stonewalling. Stonewalling usually occurs when an individual or organization is accused of wrongdoing, has suffered some catastrophic reversal ("bad NEWS"), or is threatened with an unpleasant investigation. The idea is that by drying up the flow of information to media, regulators, or other investigative bodies, they will eventually give up their attack and move on to another target. Sometimes stonewalling works to stop the "FEEDING FRENZY," but in other instances such intransigence only serves to exacerbate attention and maximize the potential downside once the process wends its way to completion.

STRATEGIC LAWSUITS AGAINST PUBLIC PARTICIPATION (SLAPP)—Tactic which emerged in the 1970s designed to intimidate ACTIVISTS from exercising their political rights and muzzle criticism by punishing those who have done so through the filing of libel and related lawsuits. The SLAPP action term was coined by University of Denver law professor George W. Pring and sociology professor Penelope Canan in 1988 in referring to civil complaints or counterclaims for monetary damages and/or injunctions. Plaintiffs are typically large commercial enterprises while the defendants are generally individual citizens or small community NONGOVERNMENTAL ORGANIZATIONS (NGOs). SLAPP actions stem from dislike by the plaintiffs of the views expressed by their opponents on an issue of some PUBLIC INTEREST or concern. The growing success of such defamation, trade libel, contract interference, economic damage and related common-law torts has weakened direct FIRST AMENDMENT protections. Defendants often win their case or settle out of court, but are faced with heavy litigation expenses which may prove similarly crippling to future activism. Evidence shows that even the threat of SLAPP lawsuits has led many vocal critics to curtail their efforts via conventional and grassroots lobbying, interviews, NEWS RELEASEs, media commentaries, and even individual letters to the editor. See also CHILLING EFFECT, DEEP POCKETS SPENDING, and LOBBYING/LOBBYIST.

STRIP PROGRAMMING—Television viewing has strong hourly, daily, weekly and seasonal patterns. "Strip" scheduling airs the same program series over several nights or weeks, encouraging repeat viewer tune-ins.

STRUCTURED LEAKS—Orchestrating NEWS tips, lining up endorsements from key outside leaders and/or celebrities, lobbying behind the scenes, and otherwise engaging in preliminary staging to build up "good news" and support prior to major policy announcements. See also COURT OF PUBLIC OPINION, FEEDING FRENZY, JUSTICE BY NEWS RELEASE, LAUNCHING A NUKE, LOBBYING/LOBBYIST, MEDIA BIAS, ORCHESTRATED PROPAGANDA CAMPAIGN, PLANTING STORIES, and PROPAGANDA DEVICES.

STUNT—A one-time PUBLICITY action or event, often of questionable taste and legality, that is designed to attract attention.

STUNTING—The BROADCASTING practice of scheduling many specials and miniseries in the lineup. These shows take the place of more regular series programming, opening the door for continued exploitation of NEWS specials, popularized documentaries, and DOCUDRAMAs.

SUBLIMINAL MESSAGES—Communication designed to influence behavior by entering the mind below the threshold of consciousness. Despite much popular media attention as well as serious research, the general conclusion is that subliminal ADVERTISING, backward song masking in music recordings, and self-help audiotapes and videos do not work.

SUBPROPAGANDA—Long-term approach to creating an environment of confidence and trust, particularly by a propagandist who is working for a newly created organization or promoting an unfamiliar message. The goal of such subpropaganda is not immediate, but rather cumulative. The PUBLIC RELATIONS (PR) process involves so-called "facilitative communications" which work to establish social contacts with the PRESS and other constituencies, build goodwill, and evolve into comfortable working relationships maintained between the propagandist and members of these groups. Activities include cultural exhibits, language classes/educational exchange programs, informational seminars/lectures, media relations research help, parties, and other services. Subpropaganda often is incorporated in government-run PUBLIC DIPLOMACY efforts by organizations such as the UNITED STATES INFORMATION AGENCY (USIA).

SUBVERSION/SUBVERSIVES—The British government's broadened redefinition, adopted by the home secretary in 1984, classifies subversion as "activities which threaten the safety or well-being of the State and which are intended to undermine or overthrow Parliamentary democracy by political, industrial or violent means." The term has been generally used in a similar way in the United States, although the imprecise language leaves open the door to suppression of legitimate dissent. For example, business and government interests have often labeled as subversive those labor organizers seeking to exercise the right to unionize, the right to leaflet, the right to strike, and other forms of FREE SPEECH and expression that we take for granted today. See also CORPORATE CAMPAIGN, DEMOCRACY, HUMAN RIGHTS, SEDITION, TERROR GROUP, TERRORISM, and TREASON.

SUFFRAGETTES—Members of the MOVEMENT to achieve the vote for women in Britain, the United States, and other countries. Some scholars prefer to use the gender neutral term *suffragists*. See also TEMPERANCE MOVEMENT and WOMEN'S MOVEMENT.

SUNSHINE PATRIOTS—See PROFESSIONAL PATRIOTS.

SURRENDER LOBBY—A term of derision used by some U.S. RIGHT-WING/CONSERVATIVE pundits to refer to pro-UNITED NATIONS ORGANIZATION (UNO or UN) internationalists, unilateral disarmament supporters, and those LEFT-WING/LIBERALs who sought to appease Soviet interests. *Surrender lobby* is often associated with those attending the series of Pugwash Conferences hosted by industrialist Cyrus Eaton.

SVR (*Suzhba vneshnogo razvedky*)—The Russian Foreign Intelligence Service created in late 1991 by the post-Communist government to partially replace the former KGB (*Komitet po Gosudarstvennoy Bezopasnosti*).

SWOT ANALYSIS—A tool used by strategic planners to analyze the *S*trengths, *W*eaknesses, *O*pportunities, and *T*hreats facing their organization. See also ISSUE SCANNING and ISSUES MANAGEMENT.

TABLOID JOURNALISM—Generally refers to newspapers printed in an easy-to-hold, 12 by 16 inch or similar format with an editorial policy characterized by an emphasis on celebrity NEWS, many pictorial elements, and sensationalist copy. The term *tabloid* has also been applied in recent years to broadcast programs that emulate their print counterparts by employing a style of journalism dominated by entertainment considerations (what critics call "sleaze TV" or the newest form of YELLOW JOURNALISM). The tabloids are also criticized for engaging in "checkbook journalism" by paying for inside information, story leads, and exclusive interviews. Some of the tabloids are totally unreliable and make no pretense at telling the truth. On the other hand, important stories neglected or even suppressed by the more traditional PRESS have often been revealed only because of the willingness of the tabloids to courageously take on the topic. See also FIRST AMENDMENT, JOURNALISM/JOURNALIST, MEDIA BIAS, and PRESS BASHING.

TARGET GROUPS—See PUBLIC and STAKEHOLDERS.

TAVISTOCK METHOD—The Tavistock Institute of Human Relations in London, England, is a leading center for psychological control studies. Originally founded as a clinic in 1921, Tavistock has evolved into an important PSYCHOLOGICAL WARFARE (PSYWAR) and PROPAGANDA think tank with close relations to the British intelligence services. Particularly influential in shaping government interest in BRAINWASHING techniques was Brigadier-General John Rawlings Rees, who became the clinic's director in 1932. Rees promoted what has been called by critics the "Tavistock method of retrogressive psychology" for inducing controlled forms of mass psychosis in wartime. Government-sponsored studies undertaken by Tavistock researchers, many of which remain secret, have seen COVERT applications by a network of psychological warriors. Numerous professionals and students affiliated with Tavistock have also gone on to influence commercial MASS COMMUNICATION, especially ADVERTISING to "target populations." See also MI5, MI6, PSYCHOLOGICAL OPERATIONS (PSYOPS), and THINK TANKS.

TELCO—A service provider in the TELECOMMUNICATIONS industry. The term is most associated with telephone companies such as the "Baby Bells," the former AT&T local carriers spun off in an antitrust agreement, that are now beginning to offer other information and entertainment services.

TELECOMMUNICATIONS—Literally "distance communications," but in reality, *telecommunications* refers to electronic media such as cable services, computer interconnects, telephonic distributors, satellite delivery firms, and radio/television BROADCASTING operations. In the United States, Congress has awarded jurisdiction for most telecommunications regulation to the FEDERAL COMMUNICATIONS COMMISSION (FCC). Telemarketers are specialized firms which rely on sophisticated phone banks and computerized data sources to sell products, ideas, and political candidates. See also COM-

PUTER-MEDIATED COMMUNICATION (CMC), CENSORSHIP, CY-
BERSPACE, ELECTRONIC COMMUNITY NETWORK, ELECTRONIC
DEMOCRACY, ELECTRONIC PUBLISHING, INTERNET, MASS COM-
MUNICATION, MEDIA ELITE, MEDIA/MEDIUM, NATIONAL IN-
FORMATION INFRASTRUCTURE (NII), PUSH POLLS, TELCO, and TV.

TEMPERANCE MOVEMENT—Social and political efforts by prohibi-
tionists, more pronounced in the late nineteenth- and early twentieth-centuries,
seeking to restrict the sale and consumption of alcoholic beverages. Many of
the temperance MOVEMENT leaders were women also active as
SUFFRAGETTES.

TERROR GROUP—Organization extralegally seeking major policy changes or
the overthrow of entrenched authority through the use of any means, including
ARMED STRUGGLE involving PROPAGANDA OF THE DEED.

TERRORISM—A low-budget form of warfare, usually guerrilla revolutionary
activity involving the deliberate use of violence or threats of violence (often
against innocent people) with the purpose of producing fear for political ends.
In analyzing international terrorism, the purpose of the act, the nationalities of
the victims, and/or the resolution of the incident are factors to be considered.
Terror can be utilized by individuals or organizations so as to dramatize a
political cause, generate media attention, obtain funds, embarrass the dominant
leadership, secure the release of convicted terrorists, and/or accomplish other
propagandistic purposes. Terrorism is generally defined by the state under siege
as criminal and treasonous. The definition used by the U.S. State Department,
in *Patterns of Global Terrorism* (1984) and subsequent publications, states
"Terrorism is premeditated, politically-motivated violence perpetrated against
noncombatant targets by subnational groups or clandestine state agents,
usually intended to influence an audience."

Many MOVEMENTs throughout history have resorted to TERRORIST
tactics, including:

- the *nihilists* in czarist Russia;
- *partisans* in World War II;
- anticolonialist *national liberation* struggles of the 1950s and 1960s;
- *nationalistic freedom fighters* seeking well defined ethnic, linguistic, or
  religious objectives as in Palestine, Ireland, or Bosnia;
- *single-issue groups*, typified by the more fanatic of the antiabortion
  ACTIVISTS; and
- *ideological groups* with less clear-cut goals other than destabilization,
  such as Peru's Shining Path or Italy's Red Brigades.

When governments utilize lawless violence against their political opponents,
this is known as STATE TERRORISM. Although rarely willing to
acknowledge the fact, democracies (including the United States) regularly
engage in or support terrorist attacks on other "unfriendly" nations and
movements. WHITEHALL, the Pentagon, and major Western NEWS MEDIA
prefer to label these operations as COUNTERTERRORISM, as evidenced by
coverage given British and U.S. actions in the Middle East, North Africa,
Latin America, East Timor, and elsewhere. In fact, the truth is that terrorism

is terrorism, whether ordered from some safe house in Baghdad, Berlin, Cairo, London, Moscow, Paris, Tehran, Tel Aviv, or even deep from within the White House itself.

Terrorist acts are usually planned to attract widespread PUBLICITY and are designed to focus attention on the existence, cause, or demands of the terrorists. The relationship between terrorists and mass media is a complex one, although the spectacular nature of terrorist violence generally results in NEWS coverage and would seem to serve as a catalyst for additional acts of terrorism. However, except in the case of state terrorism benefiting from media acquiescence, the emphasis on the sensational also works to undermine the event's (and in turn, the terrorists') legitimacy.

See also ANTITERRORISM, ARMED PROPAGANDA, CENSORSHIP BY ASSASSINATION, CLANDESTINE, CONTAGION, INTIFADA, LIBERA-TION MOVEMENT, LOW-INTENSITY CONFLICT (LIC)/LOW-INTEN-SITY WARFARE (LIW), MASS TERROR, POLITICAL CRIME, PRO-PAGANDA OF THE DEED, REPRESENTATIVE VIOLENCE, SACRED TERRORISM, SUBVERSION/SUBVERSIVES, TERROR GROUP, and UNCONVENTIONAL WARFARE.

TERRORIST—A person willing to use terror for political purposes. Selecting this term rather than *freedom fighter*, *member of a liberation front*, *resistance leader*, or even *guerrilla*, implies that the specific action is illegitimate or criminal. Use of one of the alternative labels in media coverage encourages the reader, viewer or listener to accept a particular incident—even if it involves kidnapping, bombing or killing—as a legitimate tactic in an unequal "struggle for social justice." See also ANTITERRORISM, ARMED STRUGGLE, ASSASSIN, INSURRECTION/INSURRECTIONARY, and TERRORISM.

THINK TANKS—Research centers and institutes involved in behavioral science planning, often with a particular topical or ideological focus. They tend to:
- conduct original research;
- produce reports and position papers;
- engage in PUBLIC RELATIONS (PR) media campaigns, complete with OP-EDs, radio interviews, and television appearances;
- work with INTEREST GROUPS in mobilizing their constituencies; and
- lobby governments by providing expert testimony which clarifies the agenda subject to debate.

Think tanks are often funded by FOUNDATIONS or universities and typically peopled by former government officials, scholars, media practitioners, and other POLITICAL ANALYSTS concerned with social ISSUEs. Through their advocacy efforts to push ideas and persuade opinion leaders, think tanks help shape the PUBLIC POLICY PROCESS.

THIRD WORLD—Decolonialization after World War II and the onset of COLD WAR super-power rivalries put pressure on the leaders of newly independent countries to choose sides. Many of those who wanted to remain nonaligned sought a third way for political and social development as an alternative to the models forged by the Western alliance democracies of North America, Europe, and Japan (the "First World") or the competing Soviet bloc (the "Second World"). The *Third World* slogan first appeared at the 1955 Bandung Conference, hosted by President Sukarno of Indonesia, who called the gathering "the first intercontinental conference of the so-called colored peoples in the history of mankind." Some writers have referred to a "Fourth World" of nations whose economies and social infrastructure are so impoverished that it is unlikely their peoples ever will enjoy an improved quality of life. Because of the negative connotations sometimes given to Third World and Fourth World classification, many specialists prefer the term *developing nations*. See also HUMAN RIGHTS and LOW-INTENSITY CONFLICT (LIC)/LOW-INTENSITY WARFARE (LIW).

THOUGHT-STOPPING CLICHÉ—Phrase used by Robert Jay Lifton and others to describe how politically loaded words such as *racist, hatemonger, crackpot, un-American, anti-Semite, EXTREMIST, Nazi, bigot, subversive,* and *commie* are used in campaigns designed to inflict damage on the reputation and psyche of a targeted individual or group. Debate over the facts is usually not desired by the person or organization making the charges, since the existence of the RITUAL DEFAMATION is usually enough to effectively neutralize their opponent's credibility. The powerful images and feelings unleashed are believed because they have been publicized and play into the pre-existing belief patterns of the audience. The goal is to shut down the opposition's PROPAGANDA by discrediting it and intimidating potential supporters through dehumanizing character assassinations that shift the context from the rational to the emotional. See also DEMONIZING THE OPPOSITION and HATE CAMPAIGN.

TOTALITARIANISM—A form of authoritarianism in which the goal is not simply acquiescence, but voluntary participation in which neutrality is not permitted. Totalitarians allow no rival parties or loyalties. The expression, "You are either for us or against us," is an example of this thinking. The behavioral effect of "doing" and "participating" can build intensity of belief and support by plugging into the powerful psychological mechanism referred to as "commitment." Self-indoctrination (even the illusion of voluntary participation) is a goal of totalitarian states, which have life and death powers. Totalitarian nations are saturated with symbols and rituals designed to reinforce statist authority by undermining independent thought and FREE SPEECH. This phenomenon can even extend to less inherently coercive organizations (such as universities where freedom of inquiry has long been enshrined), when a segment of the institution applies pressure to conform to "socially desirable goals." Sometimes, the purpose of a totalitarian reward and punishment system is even more banal—to provide a justification for the existence of a particular bureaucracy. Other times, totalitarian rituals degenerate into a politics of vengeance, in which those deemed not POLITICALLY CORRECT (PC) are required to suffer through sensitivity sessions designed to provide psychological gratification for their tormentors. In such instances, the fact that coercion may lead to resentment rather than commitment is largely irrelevant to those in power since their control of the system is secure enough to effectively intimidate the resistors and preclude overt expression of dissident views. See also ANTIAUTHORITARIANISM and BRAINWASHING.

TOXIC INFORMATION—The marketplace of ideas is fettered by media self-CENSORSHIP and timidity, economic vulnerability to pressure points, and the relative abundance of questionable information. True facts, innuendoes, DISINFORMATION (*DEZINFORMATSIA*), and outright lies can all negatively influence PUBLIC OPINION. Such toxic information about an individual or organization can stem from several sources: (1) failure to behave ethically or communicate clearly to begin with; (2) accidental misunderstanding caused by SELECTIVE PERCEPTION on the part of audiences who often "get it wrong"; (3) misuse of technical terms and jargon which sows confusion and contributes to negative effects; (4) deliberate release of damaging facts and/or false leads by opposing forces designed to weaken or discredit (market sabotage) through rumor and negative NEWS coverage; and (5) the echoing effect that harmful information has once it enters the marketplace, particularly when repeatedly recycled through TRAWLING journalistic databases as "research" for future stories. Sometimes organization officials will try to preempt bad news and deflect attention from themselves ("head off stories") by using the mechanism of STRUCTURED LEAKS to issue self-serving information. Governments typically want to WHITEWASH embarrassing disclosures by overly classifying such matters "top secret" in the often misused name of national security.

TRACKING POLLS—Series of scientific PUBLIC OPINION measurements taken over time to determine the effect of particular media messages (ads, NEWS RELEASEs, etc.) and events on a political or commercial campaign. See also BENCHMARK STUDY, DIVERT/REFOCUS STRATEGY, and PUSH POLLS.

TRAITOR—A person guilty of TREASON, although the term is widely bandied about to impugn one's ideological opponents. Whether one is a traitor or not usually depends on which side prevails in a particular controversy or war, since the winner invariably interprets events. Members of the American Civil Liberties Union and others who opposed the internment-camp rounding up of Japanese-Americans during World War II on constitutional grounds, for example, were labeled "traitors" for their FREE SPEECH efforts. See also AGENTS/AGENCIES OF INFLUENCE, DUAL LOYALIST, and FIFTH COLUMN.

TRANSNATIONAL CORPORATIONS (TNCs)—Business firms that own or control production or service facilities outside the country in which they are based. Traditionally, most TNCs were American, but that has been changing with the shift of economic power to Asia and Europe. In the past, TNCs were accepted as a necessary part of the world system and often were commended for their role in bringing modernization, technological innovation, management skills and economic well-being to developing countries. At the same time they have been credited with being a force for peace and stability, since their far-flung business interests for the most part depend on cooperation and stability befitting their GLOBALISM. These benign views have come under challenge, particularly when TNCs are seen to undermine national sovereignty by aligning themselves with corrupt dictatorships or racist regimes, exploiting rather than enhancing THIRD WORLD economies, and substituting CULTURAL IMPERIALISM and Western NEOLIBERALISM for local custom. Membership by transnational corporation leaders in elite internationalist organizations such as the TRILATERAL COMMISSION have also proved controversial. The United Nations Centre on Transnational Corporations (UNTNC) was created in the mid-1970s to study the international performance and social impact of TNCs.

TRAWLING—Quick search of computer databases (including INTERNET) by journalists and other researchers to compile data and source quotes in fleshing out a story idea or report. Trawling is considered "questionable netiquette" because of the possible infringement on "private" communications and other potential abuses.

TREASON—Generally means a level of disloyalty resulting in attempts to illicitly overturn the lawful government, but treason also is widely used to refer to any organized dissent to authority. Because the writers of the U.S. Constitution feared that federal authorities would use their powers against treason to restrict legitimate political opposition, the practice is defined more narrowly under Article 3, section 3: "Treason against the United States, shall consist only in levying war against them, or in adhering to their enemies, giving them aid and comfort." The latter concept would be referred to as "high treason" if it occurred in Britain. See also SUBVERSION/SUBVERSIVES, TERRORISM, and TRAITOR.

TREND—See ISSUE SCANNING.

TRIALS BY NEWS RELEASE—See COURT OF PUBLIC OPINION.

TRILATERAL COMMISSION—One of several elite planning organizations with immense influence on the international PUBLIC POLICY PROCESS. One of banker David Rockefeller's goals in launching the Trilateral Commission in July 1973 was to bring insular Japan into a discussion of world affairs. As a result, the commission is comprised of 325 "private" individuals committed to GLOBALISM who are drawn from the FREE WORLD's three largest industrial, financial, and cultural centers: North America, Japan, and Western Europe. Its members are primarily leading chief executive officers of international corporations, bankers, politicians, and a smattering of academics with broad experience in government, business, media, and research. The Trilateral Commission promotes agreements such as NAFTA that help create a borderless FREE TRADE world in which TRANSNATIONAL CORPORATIONS (TNCS) would be free of "interference from nation-states." Critics see the commission as a vehicle for the ruling classes to co-opt the THIRD WORLD and maintain HEGEMONY over the world economy. The commission's activist "global agenda" and links to other "new world order" proponents such as the COUNCIL ON FOREIGN

RELATIONS (CFR) and the BILDERBERGER GROUP have also ensured controversy, particularly from those who see the Trilaterals as part of "the Conspiracy." See also CONSPIRACY THEORIES, ELITE THEORY, and NEOLIBERALISM.

TURNING THE QUESTION—A media tactic that diverts a reporter's question with a response such as, "That's not what really matters. The real concern is . . . ," to establish a point that the newsmaking interviewee wants to make.

TV—The most common abbreviation for television in the United States. See also MEDIA/MEDIUM.

TWO-STEP FLOW (MULTI-STEP FLOW)—Successful suppliers of information and ideas influence many more people than those exposed directly to the original communications. Essentially, the two-step/multi-step flow is a PROPAGANDA conveyor belt useful in the AGENDA SETTING and PUBLIC OPINION processes. Messages transmitted via media are picked up by opinion leaders who then pass them onto their family and friends, who do the same thing to others, and so forth. While there is lessening of message control the further removed one is from the source, an interpersonal "word of mouth" WHISPERING CAMPAIGN can have great credibility and impact. See also AGITATION and TOXIC INFORMATION.

UK or U.K.—Standard abbreviations for what is currently the United Kingdom of Great Britain and Northern Ireland. England is a distinct part of Britain (which also includes Scotland, Wales, the Isle of Man, and other political jurisdictions). The *British Isles* is sometimes synonymously used, but this is imprecise since many citizens of independent Ireland/Eire dislike being associated with the imposed term *British*.

UMBRELLA ORGANIZATIONS—Although the term can be applied to any coalition group, it is generally taken to mean large trade associations representing diverse Fortune 500 businesses typified by the National Association of Manufacturers, U.S. Chamber of Commerce, Business Roundtable, and other influentials. See also FRONT GROUPS/SATELLITE ORGANIZATIONS.

UNCONVENTIONAL WARFARE—According to Major General (retired) John K. Singlaub (1982), the term *unconventional warfare* "includes, in addition to terrorism, subversion and guerrilla warfare, such covert and nonmilitary activities as sabotage, economic warfare, support to resistance groups, black and gray psychological operations, disinformation activities, and political warfare."

UNITED NATIONS ORGANIZATION (UNO or UN)—In World War II, the coalition of forces led by the United States and Britain was often referred to in government NEWS RELEASEs as the United Nations. President Franklin D. Roosevelt (FDR) is credited with creating the phrase which was first used on January 1, 1942, in the Declaration of the United Nations. With victory, a post-war peace conference was held in San Francisco, which led to treaties establishing the United Nations Organization as an official entity on October 24, 1945. Over the years, the UNO has engaged in numerous PUBLIC RELATIONS (PR) campaigns in support of world federalism, attracting strong support and opposition for its policies. During the COLD WAR era, the UNO General Assembly primarily served as a forum to discuss world issues, with the more powerful Security Council often remaining deadlocked because of U.S.-Soviet rivalries. Beginning with the Korean crisis in 1950, however, the council authorized troops from member nations to intervene in numerous localized conflicts and hot spots typified by the UNPROFOR and UNOSOM I/UNOSOM II/UNITAF missions. The UNO leadership has also recently attempted to create its own standing army in order to give the organization more clout. Affiliated agencies such as the World Health Organization (WHO) and United Nations Educational, Scientific, and Cultural Organization (UNESCO) have proven more effective in their own spheres. See also INTERVENTIONIST, NONGOVERNMENTAL ORGANIZATIONS (NGOs), UNIVERSAL DECLARATION OF HUMAN RIGHTS, and ZIONISM/ZIONIST.

UNITED STATES INFORMATION AGENCY (USIA)—The official government department with primary responsibility for a wide range of PUBLIC DIPLOMACY activities, and for advising on the policy implications of foreign PUBLIC OPINION. USIA's director reports to the president and receives policy guidance from the secretary of state. The agency explains America to foreign audiences through media, cultural exchanges, and other communication efforts. Among USIA's broadcast operations are the Voice of America (which transmits NEWS, entertainment, and PROPAGANDA worldwide in dozens of languages), Radio Free Europe/Radio Liberty (which are being redefined in the wake of developments caused by the end of the COLD WAR), and the anti-Castro Radio Marti and TV Marti services directed at Cubans. A proposed Radio Free Asia remains under discussion. See also BLOWBACK, CRIMINALIZATION OF POLICY DIFFERENCES, PUBLIC DIPLOMACY, SUBPROPAGANDA, and VOICE OF AMERICA (VOA).

UNIVERSAL DECLARATION OF HUMAN RIGHTS—A statement of principles adopted in 1948 by the UNITED NATIONS ORGANIZATION (UNO or UN) outlining fundamental freedoms that should apply to all human beings irrespective of country or government. For example, Article 19 declares: "Everyone has the right to freedom of opinion and expression; this right includes freedom to hold opinions without interference and to seek, receive and impart information and ideas through any media regardless of frontiers." See also HUMAN RIGHTS.

UNOSOM I/UNOSOM II/UNITAF—A coalition of troops acting under UNITED NATIONS ORGANIZATION (UNO or UN) command in 1992 moved to occupy Somalia following the breakdown of domestic political control in that country. UNOSOM I (United Nations Operation in Somalia I) occurred in the period April 1992 to April 1993. These UNOSOM I forces were inserted to relieve widespread starvation under Chapter 6 of the United Nations Charter, which makes provisions for "peacekeeper" interventions. However, when the UNOSOM I commanders found they could not maintain order, U.S. Marines spearheading the American-led Unified Task Force in Somalia (called UNITAF) were deployed to the beaches of Somalia and occupied the capital city of Mogadishu in December 1992, amid the media blare of officially sponsored photo opportunities. At first, the occupation led to successful food deliveries, but attempts to impose a "democratic" political solution proved futile. As the UNITAF mission turned more to COVERT military actions, a disastrous series of commando raids led to the brutal deaths of American soldiers. Graphic photos and television NEWS accounts turned U.S. PUBLIC OPINION and led President Bill Clinton to order a phase-out of American involvement. UNOSOM II (United Nations Operation in Somalia II) was a mission involving 9,412 military and civilian police personnel (who suffered 134 fatalities), which operated from May 1993 to March 1995, with an estimated annual cost to the UNO of $942.4 million. The twenty-eight nation UNOSOM II force took over for UNITAF under the never-before-used Chapter 7 of the United Nations Charter, which provides for "peacemakers." As defined by the charter, "peacekeepers" are only allowed to use their weapons in self-defense, while "peacemakers" are allowed to go on the offensive and attack what they perceive to be threats to the peace. As a result, UNOSOM II was criticized by those who saw the occupation as part of an attempt to impose a militaristic "new world order" solution on people of color. The failure of the UNO forces to establish stabilized conditions in Somalia eventually led to their complete withdrawal. See also INTERVENTIONIST, MILITARISM, PEACEKEEPING, SOMALIAZATION, and VICTORY BY NEWS RELEASE.

UNPROFOR—Official abbreviation for the UNITED NATIONS ORGA-NIZATION (UNO or UN) "Protection Force" in Croatia whose operations began in 1992 and were phased out with the arrival of NORTH ATLANTIC TREATY ORGANIZATION (NATO) troops in late 1995. See also PEACEKEEPING.

US or U.S./USA or U.S.A.—Standard abbreviations for the United States of America, also often called "the States" by English-speaking Europeans.

USSR or U.S.S.R./CCCP or C.C.C.P.—Standard abbreviations for the Union of Soviet Socialist Republics, created in 1917 when the Communist party took power in Russia and extended its control over annexed territories. The fall of a number of European Communist regimes ultimately led to the demise of the Soviet Union as an official state in late 1991.

VANGUARD—The leadership CADRE (key members surrounding a supreme leader) who determine policy and communication strategies of a MOVEMENT, widely found in communist terminology. Each member of the vanguard rises to the top through charisma, ideological commitment, intelligence, or ruthlessness.

VENONA—A classified counter-spy program initiated by the U.S. Army's Signal Intelligence organization beginning in 1943 and continued by the National Security Agency until 1980. Intercepted Soviet cables were secretly deciphered using cryptanalysis and cross-checked with FBI field investigations. Recently revealed cables corroborate the existence of a well-organized Soviet spy program and support earlier allegations that Alger Hiss, the Rosenbergs, and other prominent COLD WAR figures were indeed CLANDESTINE American supporters of the communist regime. See also COMMUNISM/COMMUNIST, SPYING/SPYCRAFT, and SUBVERSION/SUBVERSIVES.

VETTING—British INTELLIGENCE COMMUNITY term for supposedly thorough background checks scrutinizing the bona fides, loyalty, and factual accuracy of claims made by individuals and classified DOCUMENTs obtained by CLANDESTINE means. See also FLUTTER, MI5, MI6, SPYING/SPYCRAFT, and WHITEHALL.

VICTORY BY NEWS RELEASE—Long-distance DISINFORMATION (*DEZINFORMATSIA*) variant of the BIG LIE technique, in which harsh realities away from home are smothered under syrupy praise. Instead of admitting failures, SPIN DOCTORS loudly trumpet alleged successes to domestic media by focusing on only the most favorable interpretations of events. So many examples of the military claiming of victory by NEWS RELEASE stem from the Vietnam conflict that it has become a classic case study of self-delusion. However, the practice is so widespread that one can find daily incidents torn directly from the headlines. A recent example involved the failed commando raid in Somalia of late August 1993 where the arrest of UNO workers rather than the alleged "warlord" was declared "no mistake" and a "complete success." See also SPEAK AND RETREAT.

VIDEO NEWS RELEASE (VNR)—A prepackaged, audio-visual NEWS story, with accompanying interview sound bites, supporting pictorial elements (called "B-roll"), script suggestions, and additional useful materials distributed for PUBLIC RELATIONS (PR) purposes on videotape without charge or restriction to television news operations. Many video news releases are created for individual clients (businesses, trade associations, government agencies, INTEREST GROUPS, universities, and other organizations) by specialized VNR production and distribution companies. The sponsors pay to distribute these video news releases to advance their goals. Most VNRs in the United States are sent by satellite, although a number are mailed or hand-delivered here and abroad. Generally, these VNR story packages may be aired as is, completely reedited with other inserts, or simply discarded, depending on the editorial judgment of station and network news producers. However, in instances where live coverage is provided to news organizations by government organizations—the National Aeronautics and Space Administration (NASA) space shoots come to mind—the potential for propagandistic control increases. Monitoring of potential viewership is measured by special embedded codes in some VNRs picked up by ratings firms and through off-air "clipping" services, station self-reports, and other means.

Similar ad hoc syndication services to media also exist for audio only and print NEWS RELEASEs. VNRs and their counterparts for other media are controversial because they often run as news stories without the audience being told of their true commercial or political nature. For example, for several months the only video images from inside Kuwait available to U.S. broadcasters following the invasion by Iraq were those provided by the public relations firm of Hill & Knowlton on behalf of Citizens for a Free Kuwait. Most television stations did not identify the source nor indicate the self-interested PROPAGANDA value such VNRs had in shaping PUBLIC OPINION across the United States to support military intervention in Kuwait. Defenders of the practice point to the added information VNRs bring to the marketplace and the entirely voluntary nature of their use by the BROADCASTING industry. See also DESERT SHIELD, FOREIGN AGENTS REGISTRATION ACT (FARA), FRONT GROUPS/SATELLITE ORGANIZATIONS, INTERVENTIONIST, and PUBLIC SERVICE ANNOUNCEMENTS (PSAs).

VIRTUAL REALITY—Computer-generated artificial experiences that merge multimedia, three-dimensional, and interactive technologies to create a fantasy environment that seems incredibly real. See also COMPUTER-AIDED DESIGN, COMPUTER-MEDIATED COMMUNICATION (CMC), and CYBERSPACE.

VOICE OF AMERICA (VOA)—The Voice of America is the international radio service of the UNITED STATES INFORMATION AGENCY (USIA), broadcasting almost a thousand hours a week in forty-six languages. According to the Charter of the Voice of America (U.S. Public Law 94-30):

The long-range interests of the United States are served by communicating directly with the people of the world by radio. To be effective, the Voice of America . . . must win the attention and respect of listeners. These principles will therefore govern Voice of America (VOA) broadcasts:
1. VOA will serve as a consistently reliable and authoritative source of news. VOA news will be accurate, objective and comprehensive.
2. VOA will represent America, not any single segment of American society, and will therefore present a balanced and comprehensive projection of significant American thought and institutions.
3. VOA will present the policies of the United States clearly and effectively, and will also present responsible discussion and opinion on those policies.

In the post-COLD WAR era, VOA direct short-wave and medium wave broadcasts reach approximately 92 million listeners each week (1994 figures). This estimate does not include listeners who tune in VOA programs rebroadcast by approximately 1,100 affiliate radio stations around the world which greatly expands VOA's REACH. Geographically, the audience to VOA direct BROADCASTING breaks out as follows: Africa, 20 million; Latin America, 6 million; China, 19 million; other East Asia and Pacific countries, 1 million; Europe, including the former Soviet Union, 21 million; and Near East and South Asia, 25 million. About one in five listeners tune in VOA

Worldwide English programs; the rest listen to VOA's language service airings.

WAR OF LIBERATION—See ARMED STRUGGLE and PEOPLE'S WAR.

WATERGATE SCANDAL—Refers to bungled political burglary operations conducted in 1972 by REPUBLICAN PARTY operatives and the subsequent "damage control" attempted by President Richard M. Nixon and key figures in his administration once they learned of the operation. There is still dispute over the purposes of the CLANDESTINE activity, who really authorized it, and whether the men caught were actually set up as fall guys. What is known is that anti-Castro Cuban refugees were used by the Committee to Reelect the President to illegally break into the offices of the Democratic National Committee, then housed in the Watergate hotel-apartment-office complex in Washington, D.C. The operation was discovered and gained momentum as a ongoing NEWS story once the Nixon administration resorted to STONEWALLING rather than cooperating with congressional investigators. Although Nixon easily won the election, less than two years later he was forced to resign in disgrace. What many consider the "smoking gun" proving Nixon's culpability are White House audiotape recordings contradicting the president's claims that he had not been part of the cover-up. The term *Watergate* and the suffix "gate" are now generically applied to any POLITICAL CRIME or crisis involving abuse of office and bureaucratic corruption which is severe enough to challenge the fundamental authority of governing institutions.

WAVE FRONT—A computer program that converts swirling dots into a coherent portrait, increasingly used in POLISPOTS to present a candidate as the answer to a seeming jumble of problems.

WEAPONS ON THE WALL—Propaganda posters that have just six seconds or less to communicate their message. They are widely used both in peacetime by governments and other organizations, but proliferate during extended armed conflicts requiring total wartime commitment. According to PROPAGANDA analyst Zbynek Zeman (1978), wartime posters concentrate on five basic military and humanistic themes: exhorting patriotism through emotive appeals directed at the troops, warning of domestic threats to national security, boosting homefront morale to make sacrifices in support of the war effort, promoting brave and steadfast national allies, and castigating the enemy as a subject worthy only of vilification.

WEASEL WORDS—Vague, innocuous, or pretentious language used by individuals and organizations to avoid saying what they mean and meaning what they say. Because such words do not really mean anything substantive at all, they can be used as a form of NEWSPEAK to imply a moral position without much risk of disagreement. See also CODE WORDS, DOUBLES-PEAK, ETHNIC CLEANSING, EUPHEMISM, OMNIBUS WORDS, OR-WELLIAN TACTICS, RESCUE OPERATION, and THOUGHT-STOPPING CLICHÉ.

WHIG PARTY—In the United States, opponents of Andrew Jackson formed the Whig party in 1836. Henry Clay and other Whig leaders promoted "American System" FAIR TRADE economic policies emphasizing public works and a protective tariff. The Whigs quickly proved successful at the national level by electing presidents in 1840 (William Henry Harrison) and 1848 (Zachary Taylor). However, compromises in selecting non-Whig vice presidential candidates to bolster the ticket's popularity backfired with the early deaths of Harrison and Taylor. By 1852, divisions over the slavery question so weakened the Whigs that the party literally disintegrated, with many former supporters joining the new REPUBLICAN PARTY. *Whig* is a shortened form of *whiggamore* (applied to Scottish Covenanters who marched on Edinburgh in 1648), which in turn is a form of West Scots *whiggamaire* (*whig*, a cry to urge on horses, plus *maire*, a horse). The American political organization was named after the seventeenth-century political party in England, which sought the elevation of a parliament as compared to the king. In the modern era, Lyndon LaRouche has described his policy proposals as Whig.

WHISPERING CAMPAIGN—Person-to-person AGITATION using gossip and the private conversational grapevine to convey key persuasive messages.

WHITEHALL—The British government and its ministries based in London. See also ANGLOPHILE, ANGLOPHOBE, BACKDOOR TO WAR, CIRCUS, ENTENTE, FREE WORLD, MI5, MI6, NORTH ATLANTIC TREATY ORGANIZATION (NATO), UK or U.K., and VETTING.

WHITE PAPERS—Official government reports usually designed to explain some policy shift or political failure. Although objectively packaged, particularly when issued by some ostensibly independent commission, White Papers are invariably sanitized interpretations of events—meaning that they often contain lies, distortions, and evasions. White Papers are then promoted by government PUBLIC INFORMATION OFFICER (PIO)s and generally reported as unbiased "fact" by the government- or corporate-controlled PRESS. There is another propagandistic purpose to White Papers—they will be subsequently used by COURT HISTORIANS in their writings and thus to influence future generations.

WHITE PROPAGANDA—Forms of PROPAGANDA in which the source of the message is correctly identified and what is said also tends to be truthful. Persuaders who have facts or events on their side often rely on a white propaganda approach utilizing straightforward, honest communication to make the case.

WHITEWASH—A cover-up. Governments often lay down a "security blanket" by suppressing embarrassing information. In Britain, for example, where there is an Official Secrets Act, authorities in WHITEHALL have the right to precensor anything thought to imperil national security. See also COVER-UP CROWD and TOXIC INFORMATION.

WOBBLIES—Members of the Industrial Workers of the World (IWW or I.W.W.), the "one big union" founded in 1905. Many of the founders of the IWW, such as Eugene Debs and "Big Bill" Haywood, were also active in SOCIALISM/SOCIALIST politics.

WOMEN'S MOVEMENT—The modern extension of early feminists who were active in the suffrage and temperance causes. Contemporary efforts involve equality in the marketplace, sexual freedom, and abortion rights ISSUEs. The MOVEMENT suffered a setback with the failure of the proposed Equal Rights Amendment to place legal prohibitions against discrimination on the basis of sex in the U.S. Constitution. See also SUFFRAGETTES and TEMPERANCE MOVEMENT.

WORKING THE REFS—A political analogy drawn from sports. Just as coaches complain to the referees about real and imagined infractions in the expectation that later on they may be given a break, political strategists and other so-called HANDLERS often raise the issue of MEDIA BIAS or incomplete reporting. Their purpose in doing so is to set up future NEWS coverage that may be more favorable.

YELLOW JOURNALISM—News coverage characterized by an emphasis on profit over accuracy, a crusading editorial policy more adept at controversy than truth, an emphasis on human interest and gossip features rather than hard NEWS, and sensationalistic excess rather than sober storytelling. The term evolved from the competitive efforts in the late nineteenth- and early twentieth-centuries by rival newspaper publishers Joseph Pulitzer (whose flagship was the *New York World*) and William Randolph Hearst (owner of the *New York Journal*) to combine exciting editorial matter and PROMOTION with the latest in graphic technologies in order to outdo one another for market dominance. The antithesis of yellow journalism is the reasoned reporting one finds in the *Christian Science Monitor* and similar prestige publications. See also FIRST AMENDMENT, JOURNALISM/JOURNALIST, MEDIA BIAS, MEDIA ELITE, NEWS MEDIA, PRESS, PSEUDO-EVENT/PSEUDO-NEWS, and TABLOID JOURNALISM.

ZAPATISTAS—A recently formed Mexican revolutionary organization made up mainly of indigenous people and named after Emiliano Zapata—one of the leaders of the Revolution of 1910. The Frente Zapatista de Liberacion Nacional (FZLN) demands land, DEMOCRACY, and an end to the military repression carried out by the Mexican government against the peasantry. Zapatistas made worldwide headlines on January 1, 1994, following an armed uprising in which they took over three strategic towns in the state of Chiapas near Guatemala. Subsequent developments raised questions about the ability of the national governing authorities in Mexico to maintain social stability and fully implement the NAFTA trade pact.

ZEALOTS—Individuals who are single-mindedly absorbed with one ISSUE of such overriding importance that they are motivated to action, often by joining others of like views to form a MOVEMENT. Also referred to as "single-issue

ACTIVISTS" and "single-issue voters," zealots can turn to EXTREMISM and even TERRORISM if they fail through more democratic means.

ZIONISM/ZIONIST—A political and cultural MOVEMENT that encourages the return of Jews to the ancient land of Israel. The First Zionist Congress met as a organizational entity in Basle, Switzerland in August 1897, under the leadership of Theodore Herzl and other Jewish ACTIVISTS. Zionist efforts proved successful with the formation of the state of Israel in 1948 out of parts of the former British mandate in Palestine administered by the UNITED NATIONS ORGANIZATION (UNO or UN). Twentieth-century Zionist groups are very effective advocates of their position and hold great influence in the United States. Numerous organizations raise funds, lobby, provide expert testimony, distribute educational materials, work with media, and otherwise promote their cause. Some, such as the ANTI-DEFAMATION LEAGUE OF B'NAI B'RITH (ADL) and the American Israeli Public Affairs Committee (AIPAC), also operate private intelligence units. AIPAC's "Policy Analysis" group maintains dossiers on a variety of ISSUEs and individuals deemed to be anti-Israel. This information is selectively provided to friendly journalists and public officials in order to advance policies favored by AIPAC and discredit opponents of the Zionist movement. See also ANTI-SEMITIC, DEMO-NIZING THE OPPOSITION, DUAL LOYALIST, INTIFADA, INTELLI-GENCE COMMUNITY, IRAN-CONTRA INVESTIGATIONS, MOSSAD ("INSTITUTE"), NESHER, and ZOG.

ZOG—A term used by RADICAL anti-Zionists such as the Freemen militia group based in Montana involved in the 1996 altercation with the FBI. It alludes to alleged Jewish domination of U.S. political administrations by lobbyists and INSIDERS committed to a so-called "Zionist Occupation Government" policy of dual loyalism in which Israel's interests are placed ahead of those of America. See also ANTI-SEMITIC, DUAL LOYALIST, NESHER, and ZIONISM/ZIONIST.

SELECTED REFERENCES

Adam, G. Stuart. *Notes towards a Definition of Journalism: Understanding an Old Craft as an Art Form*. St. Petersburg, Fla.: The Poynter Institute for Media Studies, 1993.

Advocates for Self-Government, Inc. *Political Definitions*. Chart. Atlanta, Ga.: Author, 1995 and earlier versions.

American Business Consultants. *Red Channels: The Report of Communist Influence in Radio and Television*. New York: Author, 1950.

Amnesty International. *1993 Annual Report*. London: Author, 1993.

"An American." *Imminent Dangers to the Free Institutions of the United States through Foreign Immigration, and the Present State of the Naturalization Laws. A Series of Numbers Originally Published in the New York Journal of Commerce by an American*. Rev. and corrected, with additions. New York: E. B. Clayton, 1835.

Anti-Defamation League of B'nai B'rith. *Hitler's Apologists: The Anti-Semitic Propaganda of Holocaust "Revisionism."* New York: Author, 1993.

Anti-Defamation League of B'nai B'rith. *Pro-Arab Propaganda in America: Vehicles and Voices*. New York: Author, 1983.

Aristotle. *On Rhetoric: A Theory of Civic Discourse*. Newly trans. with an introduction, notes, and appendixes, George A. Kennedy. New York: Oxford University Press, 1991. Paperback ed., 1992. Originally composed circa 335 B.C.E.

Armour, J. Ogden. "The Packers and the People." *Saturday Evening Post* 178 (10 March 1906): 6.

Ashford, Nigel, and Stephen Davies, eds. *A Dictionary of Conservative and Libertarian Thought*. London and New York: Routledge, 1991.

Ashworth, William. *Under the Influence: Congress, Lobbies, and the American Pork-Barrel System*. New York: Hawthorn/Dutton, 1981.

Bagdikian, Ben H. *The Media Monopoly*. Boston: Beacon Press, 1983. 4th ed., rev. and expanded, 1993.

Bailyn, Bernard. *Ideological Origins of the American Revolution*. Cambridge, Mass.: Belknap Press of Harvard University Press, 1967.

Bailyn, Bernard, ed. *Federalist and Antifederalist Speeches, Articles, and Letters during the Struggle over Ratification*. 2 vols. New York: Library of America, 1994.

Bailyn, Bernard, ed. *Pamphlets of the American Revolution, 1750-1776*. Cambridge, Mass.: Belknap Press of Harvard University Press, 1965.

Baird, Jay W. *The Mythical World of Nazi War Propaganda, 1939-1945*. Minneapolis: University of Minnesota Press, 1974.

Baker, C. Edwin. *Advertising and a Democratic Press*. Princeton, N.J.: Princeton University Press, 1994.

Bamford, James. *The Puzzle Palace: A Report on NSA, America's Most Secret Agency*. Paperback ed., with new afterward. New York: Penguin Books, 1983.

Baradat, Leon P. *Political Ideologies: Their Origins and Impact*. Englewood Cliffs, N.J.: Prentice-Hall, 1979.

Barghoorn, Frederick C. *Soviet Foreign Propaganda*. Princeton, N.J.: Princeton University Press, 1964.

Barnes, Harry Elmer. *Selected Revisionist Pamphlets*. New York: Arno Press, 1972. Includes his privately printed "Blasting the Historical Blackout" and "Revisionism and Brainwashing: A Survey of the War Guilt Question in Germany after Two World Wars," along with other key works.

Barnet, F.R., and C. Lord, eds. *Political Warfare and Psychological Operations*. Washington, D.C.: National Defense University Press, 1989.

Barnouw, Erik. *Documentary: A History of the Non-Fiction Film*. New York: Oxford University Press, 1974. 2d rev. ed., 1993.

Barnouw, Erik. *Tube of Plenty: The Evolution of American Television*. New York: Oxford University Press, 1975. 2d rev. ed., 1990.

Barnouw, Erik, ed.-in-chief. *The International Encyclopedia of Communications*. 4 vols. New York: Oxford University Press, 1989.

Bennett, James T., and Thomas J. DiLorenzo. *Official Lies: How Washington Misleads Us*. Alexandria, Va.: Groom Books, 1992.

Berger, Carl. *Broadsides and Bayonets: The Propaganda War of the American Revolution*. Rev. ed., San Rafael, Calif.: Presidio Press, 1976.

Bernays, Edward L. *Crystallizing Public Opinion*. New York: Boni and Liveright, 1923. 2d ed., New York: Liveright, 1961.

Bernays, Edward L. *Propaganda*. New York: Horace Liveright, 1928.

Biocca, Frank, ed. *Television and Political Advertising*. Volume 1: *Psychological Processes*. Hillsdale, N.J.: Lawrence Erlbaum Associates, 1991.

Biocca, Frank, ed. *Television and Political Advertising*. Volume 2: *Signs, Codes, and Images*. Hillsdale, N.J.: Lawrence Erlbaum Associates, 1991.

Bird, Stewart, Dan Georgakas, and Deborah Shaffer. *Solidarity Forever: An Oral History of the IWW*. Chicago: Lake View Press, 1985.

Bishop, Robert Lee. *Public Relations: A Comprehensive Bibliography—Articles and Books on Public Relations, Communication Theory, Public Opinion, and Propaganda, 1964-1972*. Ann Arbor: University of Michigan Press, 1974.

Bittman, Ladislav. *The Deception Game*. Syracuse, N.Y.: Syracuse University Research Corporation, 1972.

Bittman, Ladislav. *The KGB and Soviet Disinformation: An Insider's View*. Washington, D.C.: Pergamon-Brassey's, 1985.

Bittman, Ladislav. *The New Image Makers: Soviet Propaganda and Disinformation Today*. Washington, D.C.: Pergamon-Brassey's, 1988.

Blakey, George T. *Historians on the Homefront: American Propagandists for the Great War*. Lexington: University of Kentucky Press, 1970.

Blanco, Richard L., ed. *The American Revolution, 1775-1783: An Encyclopedia*. 2 vols. New York: Garland Publishing, 1993.

Bohn, Thomas. *An Historical and Descriptive Analysis of the "Why We Fight" Series*. New York: Arno Press, 1977.

Boorstin, Daniel J. *The Image: A Guide to Pseudo-Events in America*. 25th anniversary ed., with a new foreword by the author. New York: Atheneum, 1987.

Bozell, L. Brent III, and Brent H. Baker. *And That's the Way It Isn't: A Reference Guide to Media Bias*. Alexandria, Va.: Media Research Center, 1990.

Brinkley, David. *Washington Goes to War*. New York: Alfred A. Knopf, 1988.

Paperback ed., New York: Ballantine Books, 1989.

Burns, Emile. *A Handbook of Marxism; Being a Collection of Extracts from the Writings of Marx, Engels, and the Greatest of their Followers*. New York: Random House/International Publishers, 1935; London: Victor Gollancz, 1935. Reprint, New York: Haskell House, 1970.

Carawan, Guy, and Carawan, Candie, comps. and eds. *Sing for Freedom: The Story of the Civil Rights Movement Told through Its Songs*. Santa Cruz, Calif.: New Society Publishers, 1990.

Carlsnaes, Walter. *The Concept of Ideology and Political Analysis: A Critical Examination of Its Usage by Marx, Lenin, and Mannheim*. Westport, Conn.: Greenwood Press, 1981.

Carlson, John Roy (pseud.). *Under Cover: My Four Years in the Nazi Underworld in America—The Amazing Revelation of How Axis Agents and Our Enemies Within Are Now Plotting to Destroy the United States*. New York: E. P. Dutton and Co., 1943.

Carroll, Raymond L. "Factual Television in America: An Analysis of Network Television Documentary Programs, 1948-1975." Ph.D. dissertation, University of Wisconsin—Madison, 1978.

Carruth, Gorton, and associates, eds. *The Encyclopedia of American Facts and Dates*. 7th ed. New York: Thomas Y. Crowell, 1979.

Chagall, David. *New Kingmakers: An Inside Look at the Powerful Men behind America's Political Campaigns*. New York: Harcourt Brace Jovanovich, 1981.

Chaitkin, Anton. *Treason in America From Aaron Burr to Averell Harriman*. 2d ed. New York: New Benjamin Franklin House, 1984.

Chalmers, David M. *Hooded Americanism: The History of the Ku Klux Klan*. New York: Franklin Watts, 1981. 3d ed., rev. Durham, N.C.: Duke University Press, 1987.

Chalou, George C., ed. *The Secrets War: The Office of Strategic Services in World War II*. Washington, D.C.: National Archives and Records Administration, 1992.

Chamorro, Edgar. *Packaging the Contras: A Case of CIA Disinformation*. New York: Institute for Media Analysis, 1987.

Chandler, Robert W. *War of Ideas: The U.S. Propaganda Campaign in Vietnam*. Boulder, Colo.: Westview Press, 1981.

Chase, Stuart, in conjunction with the Labor Bureau, Inc. *The Tragedy of Waste*. New York: Macmillan, 1925.

Chesterton, A[rthur] K[Kenneth]. *The New Unhappy Lords: An Exposure of Power Politics*. 4th ed., rev. Liss Forest, England: Candour Publishing Co., 1972.

Childs, Harwood L. *A Reference Guide to the Study of Public Opinion*. Princeton, N.J.: Princeton University Press, 1934. Reprint, Ann Arbor, Mich.: Gryphon Books, 1971.

Childs, Harwood L., and John B. Whitton, eds. *Propaganda by Short Wave* [1942]. Bound with C.A. Rigby's *The War on Short Waves* [1943] in a joint reprint edition as part of the International Propaganda and Communication series. New York: Arno Press, 1972.

Choate, Pat. *Agents of Influence: How Japan Manipulates America's Political and Economic System*. New York: A. A. Knopf, 1990.

Chomsky, Noam. *Necessary Illusions: Thought Control in Democratic Societies*. Boston: South End Press, 1989.

Churchill, Ward, and James Vander Wall. *COINTELPRO Papers: Documents from the FBI's Secret Wars against Domestic Dissent*. Boston: South End Press, 1990.

Clanton, Gene. *Populism: The Humane Preference in America, 1890-1900*. Boston: Twayne Publishers, 1991.

Clark, Eric. *The Want Makers—The World of Advertising: How They Make You Buy*. New York: Viking, 1989.

Clark, Ramsey. *The Fire This Time: U.S. War Crimes in the Gulf.* New York: Thunder's Mouth Press, 1992.

Clements, Kendrick A. *William Jennings Bryan: Missionary Isolationist.* Knoxville: University of Tennessee Press, 1982.

Coben, Stanley. *A. Mitchell Palmer: Politician.* New York: Columbia University Press, 1963.

Cohn, Norman. *Warrant for Genocide: The Myth of the Jewish World-Conspiracy and the Protocols of the Elders of Zion.* 3d ed. Brown Judaic Studies series, no. 23. Chico, Calif.: Scholars Press, 1981.

Colodny, Len, and Robert Gettlin. *Silent Coup: The Removal of a President.* New York: St. Martin's Press, 1991.

Combs, James E., and Dan Nimmo. *The New Propaganda: The Dictatorship of Palaver in Contemporary Politics.* New York: Longman, 1993.

Committee of Coal Mine Managers. *Facts Concerning the Struggle in Colorado for Industrial Freedom.* Denver, Colo.: Author, 1914. Series of news releases prepared by Ivy Ledbetter Lee, issued for the Rockefeller interests during a mining strike.

Conlin, Joseph R., ed. *The American Radical Press: 1880-1960.* Multiple vols. Westport, Conn.: Greenwood Press, 1974.

Creel, George. *How We Advertised America: The First Telling of The Amazing Story of the Committee on Public Information That Carried the Gospel of Americanism to Every Corner of the Globe.* New York: Harper and Brothers, 1920. Reprint, New York: Arno Press, 1972.

Crossen, Cynthia. *Tainted Truth: The Manipulation of Fact in America.* New York: Simon and Schuster, 1994.

Culbert, David, ed.-in-chief. *Film and Propaganda in America: A Documentary History.* 5 vols. Westport, Conn.: Greenwood Press, 1990-1993. *See* individual entries under David Culbert, Lawrence H. Suid, and Richard Wood.

Culbert, David, ed. *Film and Propaganda in America: A Documentary History.* Volume 2: *World War II, Part 1.* Documentary Reference Collections series. Westport, Conn: Greenwood Press, 1990.

Culbert, David, ed. *Film and Propaganda in America: A Documentary History.* Volume 3: *World War II, Part 2.* Documentary Reference Collections series. Westport, Conn: Greenwood Press, 1990.

Culbert, David, ed. *Film and Propaganda in America: A Documentary History.* Volume 5: *Microfiche Supplement, 1939-1979.* Documentary Reference Collections series. Westport, Conn: Greenwood Press, 1993.

Cullop, Charles P. *Confederate Propaganda in Europe, 1861-1865.* Coral Gables, Fla.: University of Miami Press, 1969.

Cunningham, Raymond J., ed. *The Populists in Historical Perspective.* Boston: Heath, 1968.

Cutlip, Scott M. *The Unseen Power: Public Relations, a History.* Hillsdale, N.J.: Lawrence Erlbaum Associates, 1994.

Darracott, Joseph, ed. *The First World War in Posters.* New York: Dover, 1974.

Darracott, Joseph, and Belinda Loftus. *Second World War Posters.* London: Imperial War Museum, 1972.

Darwin, Charles. *On the Origin of Species by Means of Natural Selection, or, The Preservation of Favoured Races in the Struggle for Life.* London: J. Murray, 1859.

Daugherty, William E., and Morris Janowitz, eds. *A Psychological Warfare Casebook.* Baltimore, Md.: Operations Research Office of the Johns Hopkins University, Johns Hopkins Press, 1958.

Davidson, Philip. *Propaganda and the American Revolution, 1763-1783.* Chapel Hill: University of North Carolina Press, 1941. Reprinted as *Propaganda in the American Revolution,* New York: Norton, 1973.

Denton, Robert E., Jr., and Gary C. Woodward. *Political Communication in America.* New York: Praeger, 1985.

Diamond, Edwin, and Stephen Bates. *The Spot: The Rise of Political Advertising on Television.* Cambridge, Mass.: MIT Press, 1984. Rev. ed., 1988. 3d ed., 1992.

Documents from the Nest of Spies, also known as *Revelations from the Nest of Espionage* and *Documents from the U.S. Espionage Den.* 71 vols. Tehran, Islamic Republic of Iran: Daftar-i Intisharat-i Islami, 1981-1989.

Doenecke, Justus. *Anti-Interventionism: A Bibliographical Introduction to Isolationism and Pacifism from World War I to the Early Cold War.* New York: Garland, 1987.

Doob, Leonard W. *Propaganda: Its Psychology and Technique.* New York: Holt, 1935.

Doob, Leonard W. *Public Opinion and Propaganda.* 2d ed. Hamden, Conn.: Archon Books, 1966.

Douglas, Sara U. *Labor's New Voice: Unions and the Mass Media.* Norwood, N.J.: Ablex, 1986.

Draper, Theodore. *The Roots of American Communism.* New York: Viking Press, 1957.

Dubofsky, Melvyn. *We Shall All Be: A History of the Industrial Workers of the World.* Chicago: Quadrangle Books, 1969.

Dumond, Dwight Lowell. *Antislavery: The Crusade for Freedom in America.* New York: W.W. Norton and Company, 1966.

Duus, Masayo. *Tokyo Rose: Orphan of the Pacific.* Tokyo, New York, and San Francisco: Kodansha International Ltd., 1979. Paperback ed., 1983.

Dyer, Murray. *The Weapon on the Wall: Rethinking Psychological Warfare.* Baltimore, Md.: Johns Hopkins University Press, 1959.

East Timor Action Network/US. *East Timor: Turning a Blind Eye.* Video. New York: Paper Tiger Television, 1993.

Ebon, Martin. *The Soviet Propaganda Machine.* New York: McGraw-Hill, 1987.

Edmondson, Robert Edward. *"I Testify": Amazing Memoir-Exposure of Anti-National War Plotting.* Bend, Ore.: Author, 1953, 1954.

Edwards, Samuel. *Rebel! A Biography of Tom Paine.* New York: Praeger, 1974.

Ellul, Jacques. *Propaganda: The Formation of Men's Attitudes.* New York: Knopf, 1965. Reprint, New York: Vintage Books, 1973.

Emerson, Steven. "No October Surprise." *Wall Street Journal,* 14 January 1993, p. A16.

Evans, Sara. *Personal Politics: The Roots of Women's Liberation in the Civil Rights Movement and the New Left.* New York: Alfred Knopf, 1979.

Eyerman, Ron, and Andrew Jamison. *Social Movements: A Cognitive Approach.* University Park: Pennsylvania State University Press, 1991.

Fagan, Myron C. *Red Treason in Hollywood.* Hollywood, Calif.: Cinema Educational Guild, 1949.

Fan, David P. *Predictions of Public Opinion from the Mass Media: Computer Content Analysis and Mathematical Modeling.* Westport, Conn.: Greenwood Press, 1988.

Festinger, Leon. *A Theory of Cognitive Dissonance.* Stanford, Calif.: Stanford University Press, 1957.

Fielding, Raymond. *The American Newsreel: 1911-1967.* Norman: University of Oklahoma Press, 1972.

Fight for Freedom, Inc. "In Hitler's Own Words: Shut up, Yank — learn to speak NAZI!" Advertisement, *New York Times,* October 19, 1941.

Filler, Louis. *Progressivism and Muckraking.* New York: Bowker, 1976.

Fischer, Roger A. *Tippecanoe and Trinkets Too: The Material Culture of American Presidential Campaigns, 1828-1984.* Urbana: University of Illinois Press, 1988.

Fishbein, Martin, and Icek Ajzen. *Understanding Attitudes and Predicting Social Behavior.* Englewood Cliffs, N.J.: Prentice-Hall, 1980.

Fleener-Marzec, Nickieann. *D.W. Griffith's "The Birth of a Nation": Controversy,*

Suppression, and the First Amendment as it Applies to Filmic Expression, 1915-1973. Dissertations on film series. New York: Arno Press, 1980.

Foner, Philip S. *History of the Labor Movement in the United States.* 6 vols. New York: International Publishers, 1947-1982.

Foner, Philip S., ed. *American Labor Songs of the Nineteenth Century.* Urbana: University of Illinois Press, 1975.

Foner, Philip S., ed. *The Democratic-Republican Societies, 1790-1800.* Westport, Conn.: Greenwood Press, 1976.

Foner, Philip S., ed. *Fellow Workers and Friends: I.W.W. Free-Speech Fights as Told by Participants.* Westport, Conn.: Greenwood Press, 1981.

Ford, Glen. *The Big Lie: Analysis of U.S. Press Coverage of the Grenada Invasion.* Prague, Czechoslovakia: International Organization of Journalists, in cooperation with the National Alliance of Third World Journalists, 1985.

Foss, Daniel A., and Ralph Larkin. *Beyond Revolution: A New Theory of Social Movements.* South Hadley, Mass.: Bergin and Garvey, 1986.

Foster, William Z. *Toward Soviet America.* New York: Coward-McCann, 1932.

Frankel, Benjamin, ed. *The Cold War, 1945-1991.* 3 vols. Detroit: Gale Research, 1992.

Fraser, James. *The American Billboard: 100 Years.* New York: Harry N. Abrams, 1991.

Frederick, Howard H. *Cuban-American Radio Wars: Ideology in International Telecommunications.* Norwood, N.J.: Ablex, 1986.

Freeley, Austin J. *Argumentation and Debate: Critical Thinking for Reasoned Decision Making.* 6th ed. Belmont, Calif.: Wadsworth, 1986.

Freeman, Jo, ed. *Social Movements of the Sixties and Seventies.* New York: Longman, 1983.

French, Roderick Stuart. "The Trials of Abner Kneeland: A Study in the Rejection of Democratic Secular Humanism." Ph.D. thesis, George Washington University, 1971. Available on microfilm (1 reel) from Ann Arbor, Mich.: University Microfilms, 1971. Includes bibliography.

Freud, Sigmund. *The Interpretation of Dreams.* Trans. from the German and ed., James Strachey. 3d rev. English ed. New York: Basic Books, 1960.

Friedman, I[saac] K[ahn]. *By Bread Alone: A Novel.* New York: McClure, Phillips and Co., 1901.

Friendly, Fred W. *The Good Guys, the Bad Guys, and the First Amendment: Free Speech vs. Fairness in Broadcasting.* New York: Vintage Books, 1977.

Full Texts of Secret Treaties as Revealed at Petrograd. New York: *New York Evening Post,* 1918.

Furhammer, Leif, and Folke Isaksson. *Politics and Film.* New York: Praeger, 1971.

Galambos, Louis. *The Public Image of Big Business in America, 1880-1940: A Quantitative Study of Social Change.* Baltimore, Md.: John Hopkins University Press, 1975.

Galvin, John R. *Three Men of Boston.* New York: Crowell, 1976.

Gandy, Oscar H., Jr. *Beyond Agenda Setting: Information Subsidies and Public Policy.* Norwood, N.J.: Ablex Publishing, 1982.

Gans, Herbert J. *Deciding What's News: A Study of CBS Evening News, NBC Nightly News, Newsweek, and Time.* New York: Pantheon Books/Random House, 1979. Paperback ed., New York: Vintage, 1980.

Garis, Roy Lawrence. *Immigration Restriction: A Study of the Opposition to and Regulation of Immigration into the United States.* New York: Macmillan, 1927.

Gartner, Michael G. *Advertising and the First Amendment.* A Twentieth Century Fund Paper. New York: Priority Press, 1989.

Garvey, Marcus. *Aims and Objects of Movement for Solution of Negro Problem Outlined: Asks White Race to be Considerate and Sympathetic; Help Negroes to*

Have a Nation of their Own in Africa; Friendly Appeal of Negro for His Race. New York: Universal Negro Improvement Association, 1924. Reprint, 1969.

Garvey, Marcus. *Philosophy and Opinions of Marcus Garvey*. Comp., Amy Jacques-Garvey. 2d ed. New York: Universal Publishing House, 1926. Reprint, with new preface by Hollis R. Lynch, New York, Atheneum, 1969.

George, Alexander L. *Forceful Persuasion: Coercive Diplomacy as an Alternative to War*. Foreword, Samuel W. Lewis. Washington, D.C.: United States Institute of Peace Press, 1991.

Giffard, C. Anthony. *UNESCO and the Media*. White Plains, N.Y.: Longman, 1988.

Gillman, Howard. *The Constitution Besieged: The Rise and Demise of Lochner Era Police Power Jurisprudence*. Durham, N.C.: Duke University Press, 1993.

Ginger, Ann Fagan, Beverly Wilson, and Linton Hale, eds. *Human Rights Organizations and Periodicals Directory*. 7th ed. Berkeley, Calif.: Meiklejohn Civil Liberties Institute, 1993.

Ginsberg, Benjamin. *The Captive Public: How Mass Opinion Promotes State Power*. New York: Basic Books, 1986.

Gitlin, Todd. *The Whole World Is Watching: Mass Media in the Making and Unmaking of the New Left*. Berkeley: University of California Press, 1980.

Goddard, Arthur, ed. *Harry Elmer Barnes, Learned Crusader: The New History in Action*. Colorado Springs, Colo.: Ralph Myles Publisher, 1968.

Godwin, Mary [Wollstonecraft]. *A Vindication of the Rights of Women, with Strictures on Political and Moral Subjects*. Philadelphia: William Gibbons, 1792. Orig. pub. in England, 1790. Enlarged ed., slightly different title, Boston: Peter Edes, 1792.

Golitsyn, Anatoliy. *New Lies for Old: The Communist Strategy of Deception and Disinformation*. New York: Dodd, Mead and Company, 1984.

Goodman, Walter. *The Committee: The Extraordinary Career of the House Committee on Un-American Activities*. New York: Farrar, Straus and Giroux, 1968. Reprint, New York: Penguin Books, 1969.

Goodrich, Leland M., and Edvard Hambro. *Charter of the United Nations: Commentary and Documents*. Boston: World Peace Foundation, 1946.

Goodrum, Charles, and Helen Dalrymple. *Advertising in America: The First 200 Years*. New York: Abrams, 1991, with 566 illustrations.

Goodwyn, Lawrence. *Democratic Promise: The Populist Movement in America*. New York: Oxford University Press, 1976.

Graber, Doris A. *Mass Media and American Politics*. 3d ed. Washington, D.C.: Congressional Quarterly Books, 1988.

Graham, John, ed. *"Yours for the Revolution": The Appeal to Reason, 1895-1922*. Lincoln: University of Nebraska Press, 1990.

Green, Jonathon. *The Encyclopedia of Censorship*. New York: Facts on File, 1990.

Greider, William. *Who Will Tell the People? The Betrayal of American Democracy*. New York: Simon and Schuster, 1992.

Grunig, James E., and Todd Hunt. *Managing Public Relations*. New York: Holt, Rinehart, and Winston, 1984.

Gunderson, Robert Gray. *The Log-Cabin Campaign*. Lexington: University of Kentucky Press, 1957.

Gunter, John D. *Taken at the Flood: The Story of Albert D. Lasker*. New York: Harper, 1960.

Gustainis, J. Justin. *American Rhetoric and the Vietnam War*. Westport, Conn.: Praeger, 1993.

Hachten, William A. *The World News Prism: Changing Media, Clashing Ideologies*. 2d ed. Ames: Iowa State University Press, 1987.

Haiman, Franklyn S. *"Speech Acts" and the First Amendment*. Carbondale: Southern Illinois University Press, 1994.

Hainsworth, Brad, and Max Meng. "How Corporations Define Issues Management." *Public Relations Review* 14,4 (Winter 1988): 18-30.

Hale, Julian. *Radio Power: Propaganda and International Broadcasting.* Philadelphia: Temple University Press, 1975.

Hall, Stuart. "The Rediscovery of 'Ideology': Return of the Repressed in Media Studies." In Michael Gurevitch, T. Bennett, J. Curran, and J. Woollacott, eds., *Culture, Society and the Media.* London and New York: Methuen, 1982, pp. 56-90.

Hallin, Daniel C. *The "Uncensored War"—The Media and Vietnam.* New York: Oxford University Press, 1986.

Hamilton, Alexander, James Madison, and John Jay. *The Federalist Papers.* Intro. by Clinton Rossiter. New York: New American Library/Mentor Books, 1961.

Hanegraaff, Hendrik "Hank." *Secrets of Mind Control.* Video. San Juan Capistrano, Calif.: Christian Research Institute, 1991.

Hapgood, Norman, ed. *Professional Patriots: An Exposure of the Personalities, Methods and Objectives Involved in the Organized Effort to Exploit Patriotic Impulses in These United States during and after the Late War.* New York: Boni, 1927.

Harlow, Ralph Volney. *Samuel Adams, Promoter of the American Revolution: A Study in Psychology and Politics.* New York: Holt, 1923.

Harman, Gilbert. "Libertarianism and Morality." In Tibor R. Machan, ed., *The Libertarian Reader.* Totowa, N.J.: Rowman and Allanheld, 1982, pp. 226+ .

Harty, Sheila. *Hucksters in the Classroom: A Review of Industry Propaganda in Schools.* Washington, D.C.: Center for the Study of Responsive Law, 1980.

Harwood, Richard (pseud., Richard Verrall). *Did Six Million Really Die?* Richmond, England: Historical Review Press, 1974.

Hawthorn, Jeremy, ed. *Propaganda, Persuasion, and Polemic.* Baltimore, Md.: Edward Arnold, 1987.

Hays, Will H. *The Memoirs of Will H. Hays.* Garden City, N.Y.: Doubleday and Company, 1955.

Haywood, William D. *Bill Haywood's Book: The Autobiography of William D. Haywood.* New York: International Publishers, 1929.

Heath, Robert L., and associates. *Strategic Issues Management: How Organizations Influence and Respond to Public Interests and Policies.* San Francisco: Jossey-Bass, Inc., 1988.

Heath, Robert L., and Jennings Bryant. *Human Communication Theory and Research: Concepts, Contexts, and Challenges.* Hillsdale, N.J.: Lawrence Erlbaum Associates, 1992.

Heath, Robert L., and Richard Alan Nelson. *Issues Management: Corporate Public Policymaking in an Information Society.* Beverly Hills, Calif.: Sage Publications, 1986. Paperback ed., Newbury Park, Calif.: Sage Publications, 1989.

Heise, Juergen Arthur. *Minimum Disclosure: How the Pentagon Manipulates the News.* New York: Norton, 1979.

Heller, John. "The Selling of the Constitution: The Federalist Papers Viewed as an Advertising Campaign." MAJC thesis, University of Florida, 1974.

Hellinger, Daniel, and Dennis R. Judd. *The Democratic Facade.* Pacific Grove, Calif.: Brooks/Cole, 1991.

Herman, Edward S. "Balance a Foreign Concept in International News." *Extra!* 4,7 (October 1991): 1, 3.

Herman, Edward S. *Beyond Hypocrisy: Decoding the News in an Age of Propaganda, Including a Doublespeak Dictionary for the 1990s.* Cartoons by Matt Wuerker. Boston: South End Press, 1992.

Herman, Edward S. *The Real Terror Network: Terrorism in Fact and Propaganda.* Boston: South End Press, 1982.

Herman, Edward S., and Frank Brodhead. *Demonstration Elections: U.S.-Staged Elections in the Dominican Republic, Vietnam, and El Salvador*. Boston: South End Press, 1984.

Herman, Edward S., and Noam Chomsky. *Manufacturing Consent: The Political Economy of the Mass Media*. New York: Pantheon, 1988.

Herman, Edward S., and Gerry O'Sullivan. *The "Terrorism" Industry: The Experts and Institutions That Shape our View of Terror*. New York: Pantheon Books, 1989.

Herring, E. Pendleton. *Group Representation before Congress*. Washington, D.C.: Brookings Institution, 1929.

Hersh, Seymour M. *"The Target is Destroyed"—What Really Happened to Flight OO7 and What America Knew about It*. Updated ed., with new preface. New York: Vintage Books, 1987.

Hertsgaard, Mark. *On Bended Knee: The Press and the Reagan Presidency*. New York: Farrar Straus Giroux, 1988.

Hess, Stephen. *The Government/Press Connection*. Washington, D.C.: Brookings Institution, 1984.

Hess, Stephen, and Milton Kaplan. *The Ungentlemanly Art: A History of American Political Cartoons*. New York: Macmillan, 1968.

Heuvel, Jon Vanden. *Untapped Sources: America's Newspaper Archives and Histories*. LaMay, Craig, and Martha FitzSimon, eds. Prepared for the American Society of Newspaper Editors' Newspaper History Task Force. New York: Gannett Foundation Media Center, Columbia University, April 1991.

Heywood, Ezra H. *Uncivil Liberty*. Intro. James J. Martin. Colorado Springs, Colo.: Ralph Myles Publisher, 1978; orig. ed., 1873.

Hiebert, Ray Eldon. *Courtier to the Crowd: The Life Story of Ivy Lee and the Development of Public Relations*. Ames: Iowa State University Press, 1966.

Higham, John. *Strangers in the Land: Patterns of American Nativism 1860-1925*. 2d ed., corrected with a new preface. New York: Atheneum, 1970.

Hill, Christopher. *Milton and the English Revolution*. New York: Viking Press, 1977, 1978.

Hitler, Adolf. *Mein Kampf*. Unexpurgated, annotated trans. New York: Reynal and Hitchcock, 1940. Sentry ed., trans., Ralph Manheim. Boston: Houghton Mifflin, 1943. Originally published in Germany by Franz Eher Verlag.

Hoffer, Eric. *The True Believer: Thoughts on the Nature of Mass Movements*. New York: Harper and Row, 1951.

Hoffer, Thomas W., Robert Musburger, and Richard Alan Nelson. "Docudrama." In Brian G. Rose, ed., *TV Genres: A Handbook and Reference Guide*. Westport, Conn.: Greenwood Press, 1985, pp. 181-211.

Hoffer, Thomas W., and Richard Alan Nelson. "Docudrama on American Television." *Journal of the University Film Association* 30,2 (Spring 1978): 21-27.

Honey, Maureen. *Creating Rosie the Riveter: Class, Gender, and Propaganda during World War II*. Amherst: University of Massachusetts Press, 1984.

Horwitt, Sanford D. *Let Them Call Me Rebel: Saul Alinsky, His Life and Legacy*. New York: Knopf, 1989.

House, Edward Mandell. *Philip Dru: Administrator; a Story of Tomorrow, 1920-1935*. New York: B.W. Huebsch, 1912.

Hovland, Carl I., Irving L. Janis, and Harold H. Kelly. *Communication and Persuasion: Psychological Studies of Opinion Change*. New Haven, Conn.: Yale University Press, 1953.

Howe, Quincy. *England Expects Every American to Do His Duty*. New York: Simon and Schuster, 1937.

Howe, Russell Warren. *The Hunt for "Tokyo Rose."* Lanham, Md.: University Press of America, 1990.

Howe, Russell Warren, and Sarah Hays Trott. *The Power Peddlers: How Lobbyists Mold America's Foreign Policy*. Garden City, N.Y.: Doubleday, 1977.

Hudson, Michael C., and Ronald G. Wolfe, eds. *The American Media and the Arabs*. Washington, D.C.: Center for Contemporary Arab Studies, Georgetown University, 1980.

Hudson, Robert V. *Mass Media: A Chronological Encyclopedia of Television, Radio, Motion Pictures, Magazines, Newspapers, and Books in the United States*. New York: Garland Publishing, 1987.

Hummel, William, and Keith Huntress. *The Analysis of Propaganda*. New York: William Sloane/Holt, Rinehart, and Winston, 1949.

Hunter, Edward. *Brainwashing: The Story of the Men Who Defied It*. New York: Farrar, Straus and Cudahy, 1956.

Huxley, Aldous. *Brave New World Revisited*. New York: Perennial Library, 1958.

Ickes, Harold L *America's House of Lords: An Inquiry into the Freedom of the Press*. New York: Harcourt, Brace and Company, 1939.

Immerman, Richard. *The CIA in Guatemala: The Foreign Policy of Intervention*. Austin: University of Texas Press, 1982.

Information Control and Propaganda: Records of the Office of War Information. Part I: The Director's Central Files, 1942-1945. Frederick, Md.: University Publications of America, 1987. 35-mm (12 reels), with printed guide.

Information Control and Propaganda: Records of the Office of War Information. Part II: Office Policy Coordination, Series A: Propaganda and Policy Directives for Overseas Programs, 1942-1945. Frederick, Md.: University Publications of America, 1987. 35-mm (15 reels), with printed guide.

Information Freedom and Censorship: World Report 1991/Article 19. Pref. by William Shawcross; intro. by Frances D'Souza. Chicago: American Library Association, 1991.

Ingelhart, Louis Edward. *Press Freedoms: A Descriptive Calendar of Concepts, Interpretations, Events, and Court Actions, from 4000 B.C. to the Present*. New York: Greenwood Press, 1987.

International Propaganda/Communications: Selections from the Public Opinion Quarterly. New York: Arno Press, 1972.

Irwin, Will. *Propaganda and the News; or, What Makes You Think So?* New York: McGraw-Hill, 1936. Reprint, Westport, Conn.: Greenwood Press, 1970.

Jamieson, Kathleen Hall. *Packaging the Presidency: A History and Criticism of Presidential Campaign Advertising*. New York: Oxford University Press, 1984. 2d ed., 1992.

Jamieson, Kathleen Hall, and Karlyn Kohrs Campbell. *The Interplay of Influence: News, Advertising, Politics, and the Mass Media*. 3d ed. Belmont, Calif.: Wadsworth, 1992.

Jansen, Sue Curry. *Censorship: The Knot That Binds Power and Knowledge*. New York: Oxford University Press, 1988. Paperback ed., 1991.

Jeffreys-Jones, Rhodri. *The CIA and American Democracy*. New Haven, Conn.: Yale University Press, 1989.

Jenkins, William. *Pro-Slavery Thought in the Old South*. Chapel Hill: University of North Carolina Press, 1935.

Jensen, Joan M. *Army Surveillance in America, 1775-1980*. New Haven, Conn.: Yale University Press, 1991.

Jensen, Joan M. *The Price of Vigilance*. New York: Rand-McNally, 1968.

Johnson, Walter. *The Battle Against Isolation*. Chicago: University of Chicago Press, 1944.

Johnston, Winifred. *Memo on the Movies: War Propaganda, 1914-1939*. Norman, Okla.: Cooperative Books, 1939.

Jones, Winfield. *Story of the Ku Klux Klan*. Washington, D.C.: American Newspaper Syndicate, 1921.

Jowett, Garth S., and Victoria O'Donnell. *Propaganda and Persuasion*. Newbury Park, Calif.: Sage, 1986. 2d rev. ed., 1992.

Kahn, Gordon. *Hollywood on Trial*. New York: Boni and Gaer, 1948.

Kaid, Lynda Lee, Dan Nimmo, and Keith R. Sanders. *New Perspectives on Political Advertising*. Carbondale: Southern Illinois University Press, 1986.

Kaid, Lynda Lee, Keith R. Sanders, and Robert O. Hirsch. *Political Campaign Communications: A Bibliography and Guide to the Literature*. Metuchen, N.J.: Scarecrow Press, 1974.

Kaid, Lynda Lee, and Anne J. Wadsworth. *Political Campaign Communications: A Bibliography and Guide to the Literature, 1973-1982*. Metuchen, N.J.: Scarecrow Press, 1985.

Kalven, Harry. *A Worthy Tradition: Freedom of Speech in America*. New York: Harper and Row, 1988.

Kaplar, Richard T. *Advertising Rights: The Neglected Freedom—Toward a New Doctrine of Commercial Speech*. Washington, D.C.: The Media Institute, 1991.

Katz, Daniel, Dorwin Cartwright, Samuel J. Eldersveld, and Alfred McClung Lee, eds. *Public Opinion and Propaganda: A Book of Readings*. New York: Dryden/Henry Holt, 1954.

Katz, Phillip Paul. *A Systematic Approach to Psyop Information*. Washington, D.C.: Center for Research in Social Systems, 1970.

Kautilya. *Kautilya's Arthas'ästra*. Trans. R. Shamasastry. 8th ed. Mysore, India: Mysore Printing and Publishing House, 1967. Originally written circa 321-296 B.C.E.

Keller, Morton. *The Art and Politics of Thomas Nast*. New York: Oxford University Press, 1968.

Kenneally, Finbar. *United States Documents in the Propaganda Fide Archives: A Calendar*. 11 vols. Washington, D.C.: Academy of American Franciscan History, 1966-1987.

Kerber, Linda K. *Federalists in Dissent: Imagery and Ideology in Jeffersonian America*. Ithaca, N.Y.: Cornell University Press, 1980.

Kerr, K. Austin. *Organized for Prohibition: A New History of the Anti-Saloon League*. New Haven, Conn.: Yale University Press, 1985.

Key, Wilson Bryan. *The Subliminal Seduction: Ad Media's Manipulation of a Not So Innocent America*. Englewood Cliffs, N.J.: Prentice-Hall, 1973. Paperback ed., New York: New American Library, 1974.

Khaldun, ibn. *The Muqaddimah: An Introduction to History*. Trans. from the Arabic by Franz Rosenthal. New York: Pantheon Books, 1958.

Kincade, William H., and Priscilla Hayner, eds. *The ACCESS Resource Guide: An International Directory of Information on War, Peace, and Security*. New York: Ballinger, 1988.

King, Dennis. *Lyndon LaRouche and the New American Fascism*. New York: Doubleday, 1989.

Kitson, Frank. *Low Intensity Operations*. London: Faber and Faber, 1971.

Klare, Michael, and Peter Kornbluh, eds. *Low Intensity Warfare: Counterinsurgency, Proinsurgency, and Antiterrorism in the 80s*. New York: Random House/Pantheon, 1988.

Klehr, Harvey. *The Heyday of American Communism: The Depression Years*. New York: Basic Books, 1984.

Klein, Walter. *The Sponsored Film*. New York: Hastings House, 1976.

Klement, Frank L. *The Limits of Dissent: Clement L. Vallandigham and the Civil War*. Lexington: University Press of Kentucky, 1970.

Klingender, F.D., and Stuart Legg. *Money behind the Screen*. London: Lawrence and Wishart, 1937.

Knightley, Phillip. *The First Casualty—From the Crimea to Vietnam: The War Correspondent as Hero, Propagandist, and Myth Maker*. New York: Harcourt Brace Jovanovich, 1975. Paperback ed., 1976.

"A Know Nothing." *The Satanic Plot, or Awful Crimes of Popery in High and Low Places. By a Know Nothing*. Boston: N. B. Parsons, 1855.

Koppes, Clayton R., and Gregory D. Black. *Hollywood Goes to War: How Politics, Profits, and Propaganda Shaped World War II Movies*. New York: Free Press, 1987. Berkeley: University of California Press, 1990.

Kornbluh, Joyce L., ed. *Rebel Voices, an IWW Anthology*. Ann Arbor: University of Michigan Press, 1964. Rev. ed., Chicago: Charles H. Kerr, 1985.

Kornbluh, Peter, and Malcolm Byrne, ed. *The Iran-Contra Scandal: The Declassified History*. New York: New Press, 1993.

Kotler, Philip, and Alan Andreasen. *Strategic Marketing for Nonprofit Organizations*. Englewood Cliffs, N.J.: Prentice-Hall, 1991.

Kotler, Philip, and Gerald Zaltman. "Social Marketing: An Approach to Planned Social Change." *Journal of Marketing* 35 (July 1971): 3-12.

Kraditor, Aileen S. *The Radical Persuasion, 1880-1917: Aspects of the Intellectual History and Historiography of Three American Radical Organizations*. Baton Rouge: Louisiana State University Press, 1981.

Kreuter, Kent, and Gretchen Kreuter. *An American Dissenter: The Life of Algie Martin Simons, 1870-1950*. Lexington: University of Kentucky Press, 1969.

Kwitny, Jonathan. *The Crimes of Patriots: A True Tale of Dope, Dirty Money, and the CIA*. New York: W.W. Norton and Co., 1987.

Labunski, Richard E. *The First Amendment under Siege: The Politics of Broadcast Regulation*. Westport, Conn.: Greenwood Press, 1981.

Lacqueur, Walter, and Yonah Alexander, eds. *The Terrorism Reader*. Rev. ed., New York: NAL Penguin, 1987.

LaMay, Craig, Martha FitzSimon, and Jeanne Sahadi, eds. *The Media at War: The Press and the Persian Gulf Conflict*. New York: Gannett Foundation Media Center, June 1991.

Lasswell, Harold D. *Propaganda Technique in the World War*. London: Kegan Paul, Trench, Trubner, 1927. New York: Knopf, 1927. Reprinted as *Propaganda Technique in World War I*. Cambridge, Mass.: MIT Press, 1971.

Lasswell, Harold D. *World Politics and Personal Insecurity*. New York: Free Press of Glencoe, 1950.

Lasswell, Harold D., and Dorothy Blumenstock. *World Revolutionary Propaganda*. New York: Knopf, 1939.

Lasswell, Harold D., Ralph D. Casey, and Bruce L. Smith. *Propaganda and Promotional Activities: An Annotated Bibliography*. Minneapolis: University of Minnesota Press, 1935. Reprint, Chicago: University of Chicago Press, 1969.

Lasswell, Harold D., Daniel Lerner, and Hans Speier, eds. *Propaganda and Communication in World History*. Volume 1: *The Symbolic Instrument in Early Times*. Honolulu: University Press of Hawaii, 1979.

Lasswell, Harold D., Daniel Lerner, and Hans Speier, eds. *Propaganda and Communication in World History*. Volume 2: *The Emergence of Public Opinion in the West*. Honolulu: University Press of Hawaii, 1979.

Lasswell, Harold D., Daniel Lerner, and Hans Speier, eds. *Propaganda and Communication in World History*. Volume 3: *A Pluralizing World in Formation*. Honolulu: University Press of Hawaii, 1980.

Latimer, H.T. *U.S. Psychological Operations in Vietnam*. Monographs on National Security Affairs. Providence, R.I.: Brown University, 1973.

Lavine, Harold, and James Wechsler. *War Propaganda and the United States*. New Haven: Yale University Press for the Institute for Propaganda Analysis, 1940. Reprint, New York: Arno Press, 1972.

Lawyers Committee for Human Rights. *A Chronicle of a Death Foretold: The Jesuit Murders in El Salvador*. New York: Author, 1993.

Leab, Daniel, ed. *Communist Activity in the Entertainment Industry. FBI Surveillance Files on Hollywood, 1942-1958*. Frederick, Md.: University Publications of America, 1992. 35-mm microfilm (14 reels), with printed guide.

Leary, William M., ed. *The Central Intelligence Agency: History and Documents*. University, Ala.: University of Alabama Press, 1984.

LeBon, Gustave. *The Crowd: A Study of the Popular Mind*. New York: Macmillan, 1925.

Lederman, Jim. *Battle Lines: The American Media and the Intifada*. New York: Henry Holt and Co., 1992.

Lee, Alfred McClung. *How to Understand Propaganda*. New York: Holt, Rinehart, 1952.

Lee, Alfred McClung, and Elizabeth Briant Lee. *The Fine Art of Propaganda: A Study of Father Coughlin's Speeches*. New York: Harcourt, Brace and Company, 1939. Reprint, New York: Octagon, 1972; San Francisco: International Society for General Semantics, 1979.

Lee, Ivy Ledbetter. "Declaration of Principles." New York: Parker and Lee, 1906. The declaration is cited in full in Sherman Morse, "An Awakening on Wall Street." *The American Magazine*, 62 (September 1906): 460.

Lee, Ivy Ledbetter. "Indirect Service of Railroads." *Moody's Magazine* 2 (November 1907): 580-584.

Lee, Ivy Ledbetter. *Publicity; Some of the Things It Is and Is Not*. New York: Industries Publishing Co., 1925.

Lee, Ivy Ledbetter. *See also* Committee of Coal Mine Managers.

Lee, Martin A., and Norman Solomon. *Unreliable Sources: A Guide to Detecting Bias in News Media*. New York: Lyle Stuart, 1990. Revised ed., 1991.

Leighton, Marian K. *Soviet Propaganda as a Foreign Policy Tool*. New York: Random House, 1991.

Leiss, William, Stephen Kline, and Sut Jhally. *Social Communication in Advertising: Persons, Products, and Images of Well-Being*. New York: Methuen, 1986.

Lens, Sidney. *Radicalism in America*. New York: Crowell, 1969.

Lenski, Robert. *The Holocaust on Trial: The Case of Ernst Zündel*. Decatur, Ala.: Reporter Press, 1990.

Leonard, Thomas C. *The Power of the Press: The Birth of American Political Reporting*. New York: Oxford, 1986. Paperback ed., 1987.

Lerner, Daniel. *Sykewar: Psychological Warfare Against Germany, D-Day to VE-Day*. New York: George W. Stewart, 1949.

Lerner, Daniel, ed. *Propaganda in War and Crisis: Materials for American Foreign Policy*. New York: George W. Stewart, 1951. Reprint, New York: Arno Press, 1972.

Lerner, Max. "Media Have Four Themes—and Why They Do." Nationally syndicated column. *Houston Chronicle*, 8 February 1980, section 1, p. 22.

Levy, Leonard W. *Emergence of a Free Press*. New York: Oxford University Press, 1985. Paperback ed., 1987.

Levy, Leonard Williams, comp. *Blasphemy in Massachusetts: Freedom of Conscience and the Abner Kneeland Case, a Documentary Record*. New York: DaCapo Press, 1973.

Lewis, Dio. *Prohibition a Failure: Or, the True Solution of the Temperance Question*. Boston: J.R. Osgood and Co., 1875.

Liberty Lobby. *Spotlight on the Bilderbergers*. Washington, D.C.: Author. First published in 1975 and frequently updated.

Lichter, S. Robert, Stanley Rothman, and Linda S. Lichter. *The Media Elite: America's New Powerbrokers*. Bethesda, Md.: Adler and Adler, 1986.

Lichty, Lawrence W., and Malachi C. Topping, eds. *American Broadcasting: A Source Book on the History of Radio and Television*. New York: Hastings House, 1975.

Lillich, Richard B., ed. *International Human Rights Instruments*. 2d ed. Buffalo, N.Y.: William H. Hein Co., 1990.

Linebarger, Paul. *Psychological Warfare*. Washington, D.C.: Infantry Journal Press, 1948. 2d ed. Washington, D.C.: Combat Forces Press, 1954; New York: Duell, Sloan, and Pearce, 1954. Reprint, New York: Arno Press, 1972.

Linfield, Michael. *Freedom under Fire: U.S. Civil Liberties in Times of War*. Pref. Ramsey Clark. Boston: South End Press, 1990.

Lingeman, Richard R. *Don't You Know There's a War On? The American Home Front, 1941-1945*. New York: Putnam's, 1970.

Linsky, Martin. *Impact: How the Press Affects Federal Policymaking*. New York: W.W. Norton and Company, 1986.

Lippmann, Walter. *The Cold War*. Boston: Little, Brown, 1947.

Lippmann, Walter. *Drift and Mastery: An Attempt to Diagnose the Current Unrest*. New York: Mitchell Kennerley, 1914. Reprint, Englewood Cliffs, N.J.: Prentice-Hall, 1961.

Lippmann, Walter. *Public Opinion*. New York: Harcourt, Brace and Company, 1922. Reprint, New York: Macmillan, 1949. Rev. ed., New York: Free Press, 1965.

Lipset, Seymour Martin, and Earl Raab. *The Politics of Unreason: Right-Wing Extremism in America, 1790-1970*. New York: Harper and Row, 1970.

Lipstadt, Deborah E. *Denying the Holocaust: The Growing Assault on Truth and Memory*. New York: Free Press, 1993.

Lisann, Maury. *Broadcasting to the Soviet Union: International Politics and Radio*. New York: Praeger, 1975.

Livingstone, Neil C. *The Cult of Counterterrorism: The "Weird World" of Spooks, Counterterrorists, Adventurers, and the Not Quite Professionals*. Lexington, Mass.: Lexington Books, 1990.

Lowenthal, Leo, and Norbert Guterman. *Prophets of Deceit; a Study of the Techniques of the American Agitator*. 2d ed. Palo Alto, Calif.: Pacific Books, 1970.

Lukaszewski, James E. *Influencing Public Attitudes: Direct Communication Strategies that Reduce the Media's Influence on Public Decision-Making*. Leesburg, Va.: Issue Action Publications, 1992.

Lumley, Frederick E. *The Propaganda Menace*. New York: Century, 1933.

Lumpkin, Grace. *A Sign for Cain*. Novel. New York: Lee Furman, Inc., 1935.

Luntz, Frank I. *Candidates, Consultants, and Campaigns*. New York: Basil Blackwell, 1988.

Luther, Martin. *The Jews and Their Lies*. Los Angeles, Calif.: Christian Nationalist Crusade, 1948. Originally published in Germany in 1543.

Luther, Martin. *Luther's Ninety-Five Theses*. Trans., C.M. Jacobs; rev., Harold J. Grimm. Philadelphia: Fortress Press, 1957.

MacArthur, John R. *Second Front: Censorship and Propaganda in the Gulf War*. New York: Hill and Wang, 1992.

MacBride, Sean, chair. *Many Voices One World: Report of the MacBride Commission*. Paris: UNESCO, 1980.

MacCann, Richard Dyer. *The People's Films: A Political History of U.S. Government Motion Pictures*. New York: Hastings House, 1973.

McClellan, David. *Ideology*. Stony Stratford, England: Open University Press, 1986; Minneapolis: University of Minnesota Press, 1986.

McGovern, George S., and Leonard F. Guttridge. *The Great Coalfield War*. Boston: Houghton Mifflin, 1972. Based on McGovern's Ph.D. dissertation.

McGuire, William J. "Persuasion, Resistance and Attitude Change." In Ithiel de Sola Pool, Wilbur Schramm, et al., eds., *Handbook of Communication.* Chicago: Rand McNally, 1973, pp. 216-252.

Machiavelli, Niccolò. *The Portable Machiavelli.* Ed. and trans., Peter Bondanella and Mark Musa. New York: Penguin Books, 1979.

MacKay, Lamar. "Domestic Operations of the Office of War Information in World War II." Ph.D. dissertation, University of Wisconsin, 1966.

McLaughlin, Barry, ed. *Studies In Social Movements: A Social Psychological Perspective.* New York: Free Press, 1969.

McLaurin, Ron D., ed. *Military Propaganda: Psychological Warfare and Operations.* New York: Praeger, 1982.

McLuhan, Marshall. *The Gutenberg Galaxy.* New York: Signet, 1969.

McLuhan, Marshall. *Understanding Media.* New York: Signet, 1964.

McLuhan, Marshall, and Bruce R. Powers. *The Global Village: Transformations in World Life and Media in the 21st Century.* New York: Oxford University Press, 1989. Paperback ed., 1992.

McPhail, Thomas L. *Electronic Colonialism: The Future of International Broadcasting and Communication.* 2d ed. Newbury Park, Calif.: Sage Publications, 1986.

Maddoux, Marlin. *Free Speech or Propaganda: How the Media Distorts the Truth.* Nashville: Thomas Nelson Publishers, 1990.

Maddox, William S., and Stuart A. Lilie. *Beyond Liberal and Conservative.* Washington, D.C.: Cato Institute, 1984.

Magel, Charles R. *Keyguide to Information Sources on Animal Rights.* Jefferson, N.C.: McFarland, 1989.

Mahood, H.R. *Interest Group Politics in America: A New Intensity.* Englewood Cliffs, N.J.: Prentice Hall, 1990.

Mahood, H.R. *Pressure Groups in American Politics.* New York: Scribner's, 1967.

Mao, Tse-tung. *Quotations from Chairman Mao Tse-tung* ("The Little Red Book"). 2d ed. Peking, People's Republic of China: Foreign Languages Press, 1976; 1st ed., 1967, 1972.

Marcellus, Tom. *The Tradition of Historical Revision.* Pamphlet. Costa Mesa, Calif.: Institute for Historical Review, nd.

Marchetti, Victor, and John D. Marks. *The CIA and the Cult of Intelligence.* Updated paperback ed. New York: Laurel/Dell Publishing Co., 1983.

Marks, Barry. "The Idea of Propaganda in America." Ph.D. dissertation, University of Minnesota, 1957.

Marks, John. *The Search for the "Manchurian Candidate": The CIA and Mind Control—The Story of the Agency's Secret Efforts to Control Human Behavior.* New York: Times Books, 1979.

Marsden, George M., ed. *The Fundamentals: A Testimony to Truth.* Reprint. New York: Garland, 1988. Original pub., Chicago, Ill.: Testimony Publishing Co., 1910-1915.

Marshall, Jonathan, Peter Dale Scott, and Jane Hunter. *The Iran-Contra Connection: Secret Teams and Covert Operations in the Reagan Era.* Boston: South End Press, 1987.

Martin, James J. *Men against the State: The Expositors of Individualist Anarchism in America, 1827-1908.* Colorado Springs, Colo.: Ralph Myles Publisher, 1970. Originally pub., 1953.

Martin, L. John. "Disinformation as a Form of Propaganda: An Instrumentality in the Propaganda Arsenal." *Political Communication and Persuasion* 2 (1982): 57-58.

Marx, Karl. *Capital.* Ed., Frederick Engels. Trans. from the definitive 3d German edition of *Das Kapital.,* Samuel Moore and Edward Aveling. London: Lawrence and Wishart, 1974.

Marx, Karl. *Critique of Hegel's "Philosophy of Right."* Trans. from the German, Annette Jolin and Joseph O'Malley. Ed. with an intro. and notes, Joseph O'Malley. Cambridge, England: Cambridge University Press, 1970. Originally pub., 1843.

Marx, Karl, and Friedrich Engels. *The Communist Manifesto.* Ed. with an intro., David McLellan. Oxford, England: Oxford University Press, 1992. This is an updated, corrected edition of the 1888 translation by Samuel Moore, including authors' prefaces written subsequent to the original German edition, which was published anonymously in 1848 as *Manifest der Kommunistischen Partei.* The first complete U.S. publication in English occurred in *Woodhull and Claflin's Weekly,* New York, 1872.

Matasar, Ann B. *Corporate PACs and Federal Campaign Financing Laws: Use or Abuse of Power?* Westport, Conn.: Greenwood, 1986.

Maynard, Richard A. *Propaganda on Film: A Nation at War.* Rochelle Park, N.J.: Hayden Books, 1975.

Meadow, Robert G. *Politics as Communication.* Norwood, N.J.: Ablex, 1980.

Meadow, Robert G., ed. *New Communication Technologies in Politics.* Washington, D.C.: Annenberg School of Communications, 1985.

Melder, Keith E. *Hail to the Candidate: Presidential Campaigns from Banners to Broadsides.* Washington, D.C.: Smithsonian Institution Press, 1992.

Meng, Max Byron. "Issues Management Theory." M.A. thesis, Brigham Young University, August 1987.

Meyer, Robert S. *Peace Organizations Past and Present: A Survey and Directory.* Jefferson, N.C.: McFarland, 1988.

Meyers, William. *The Image Makers.* New York: Times Books, 1984.

Michael, George. *Handout.* New York: G.P. Putnam's Sons, 1935.

Mickelson, Sig. *America's Other Voice: The Story of Radio Free Europe and Radio Liberty.* New York: Praeger, 1983.

Mill, John Stuart. *On Liberty.* Indianapolis, Ind.: Bobbs-Merrill, 1956. First pub., London: Parker and Son, 1859.

Miller, John C. *Sam Adams: Pioneer in Propaganda.* Stanford, Calif.: Stanford University Press, 1936.

Mills, C. Wright. *The Power Elite.* New York: Oxford University Press, 1956.

Milton, John. *The Portable Milton.* Ed., Douglas Bush. Includes "Areopagitica, a speech of Mr John Milton for the liberty of unlicens'd printing to the Parlament [sic] of England" (London, 1644) and his other major works. New York: Penguin Books, 1976.

Mintz, Frank P. *The Liberty Lobby and the American Right: Race, Conspiracy, and Culture.* Westport, Conn.: Greenwood Press, 1985.

Mitchell, Greg. *The Campaign of the Century.* New York: Random House, 1992.

Mitchell, Malcolm G. *Propaganda, Polls and Public Opinion: Are the People Manipulated?* Englewood Cliffs, N.J.: Prentice-Hall, 1970.

Mitchell, W. J. Thomas. *Iconology: Image, Text, Ideology.* Chicago: University of Chicago Press, 1986.

Mitnick, Barry M. *The Political Economy of Regulation: Creating, Designing, and Removing Regulatory Forms.* New York: Columbia University Press, 1980.

Mitroff, Ian I., and Warren Bennis. *The Unreality Industry: The Deliberate Manufacturing of Falsehood and What it is Doing to Our Lives.* New York: Oxford University Press, 1993.

Mock, James R., and Cedric Larson. *Words that Won the War: The Story of the Committee on Public Information, 1917-1919.* Princeton, N.J.: Princeton University Press, 1939. Reprint, New York: Russell and Russell, 1968; Meriden, Conn.: Cobden Press, 1984.

Molella, Arthur P. *FDR, the Intimate Presidency: Franklin Delano Roosevelt, Communication, and the Mass Media in the 1930s*. Washington, D.C.: Smithsonian Institution, 1982.

Montgomery, Kathryn C. *Target: Prime Time—Advocacy Groups and the Struggle Over Entertainment Television*. New York: Oxford University Press, 1989. Paperback ed., 1990.

The Mormons; or, Knavery Exposed. Frankfort, Pa.: E.G. Lee, [etc., etc.], 1841.

Morreale, Joanne. *The Presidential Campaign Film: A Critical History*. Westport, Conn.: Praeger Publishers, 1993.

Morris, Warren B., Jr. *The Revisionist Historians and German War Guilt*. Brooklyn, N.Y.: Revisionist Press, 1977.

Morse, Richard L. D., ed. *The Consumer Movement: Lectures by Colston E. Warne*. Manhattan, Kan.: Family Economics Trust Press, 1993.

Morse, Samuel F. B. *Imminent Dangers to the Free Institutions of the United States through Foreign Immigration, and the Present State of the Naturalization Laws*. New York: E. B. Clayton, 1835.

Motion Picture Producers and Distributors of America, Inc. "Code to Govern the Making of Talking, Synchronized and Silent Motion Pictures." New York: Author, 1930, 19 pp. Popularly known as the "Hays Office Motion Picture Production Code." Versions remained in effect in the U.S. until 1968, when a new Motion Picture Association of America (MPAA) ratings system replaced the Production Code.

Mowlana, Hamid, George Gerbner, and Herbert I. Schiller, eds. *Triumph of the Image: The Media's War in the Persian Gulf—A Global Perspective*. Boulder, Colo.: Westview Press, 1992.

Munson, Wayne. *All Talk: The Talkshow in Media Culture*. Philadelphia: Temple University Press, 1993.

Murray, Robert. *Red Scare: A Study in National Hysteria, 1919-1920*. Minneapolis: University of Minnesota Press, 1955. Reprint, New York: McGraw-Hill, 1964.

Murty, B.S. *The International Law of Propaganda: The Ideological Instrument and World Public Order*. New Haven, Conn.: New Haven Press, 1989.

Myers, Gustavus. *History of Bigotry in the United States*. Rev. ed., New York: Capricorn Books, 1960.

Myers, Larry Ross. "The Idea of Propaganda in America, 1917-1941." M.A. thesis, University of Maryland, 1975.

Nader, Ralph, and Donald Ross. *Action for a Change*. New York: Crown Publishing, 1971. Rev. ed., 1972.

Nagelschmidt, Joseph S., ed. *The Public Affairs Handbook*. New York: AMACOM, a Division of American Management Associations, 1982.

"A Native American." *"Young Sam" or, Native Americans' Own Book! Containing the Principles and Platform on Which the Order Stands; accompanied by an Array of some of the Most Thrilling Facts Ever Published. Shall Foreign Influence Rule? NEVER!!! By a Native American*. New York: American Family Publication Establishment, 1855.

Navarro, Peter. *The Policy Game: How Special Interests And Ideologues Are Stealing America*. New York: Wiley, 1984.

Neilson, Francis. *Escort of Lies: War Propaganda*. Brooklyn, N.Y.: Revisionist Press, 1979.

Nelson, Derek. *The Ads that Won the War*. Osceola, Wisc.: Motorbooks International, 1992.

Nelson, Derek. *The Posters that Won the War: The Production, Recruitment and War Bond Posters of WWII*. Osceola, Wisc.: Motorbooks International, 1991.

Newby, I.A. *Jim Crow's Defense: Anti-Negro Thought in America, 1900-1930*. Baton Rouge: Louisiana State University Press, 1965.

Nieburg, H.L. *Public Opinion: Tracking and Targeting*. New York: Praeger, 1984.

Nimmo, Dan D. *The Political Persuaders: The Techniques of Modern Election Campaigns*. Englewood Cliffs, N.J.: Prentice-Hall, 1970.

Noelle-Neumann, Elisabeth. *The Spiral of Silence: Public Opinion—Our Social Skin*. Chicago: University of Chicago Press, 1984.

Nolan, David. "Nolan Chart." Np: Author, 1970.

Nordenstreng, Kaarle, E.G. Manet, and W. Kleinwachter. *New International Information and Communication Order*. Prague, Czechoslovakia: International Organization of Journalists, 1987.

Nordenstreng, Kaarle, and Herbert I. Schiller, eds. *Beyond National Sovereignty*. Norwood, N.J.: Ablex Publishing, 1993.

Norman, Albert. *Our German Policy: Propaganda and Culture*. New York: Vintage Press, 1951.

Norris, Frank. *The Pit: A Story of Chicago*. New York: Doubleday, Page and Co., 1903.

Nowlan, Stephen E., D.R. Shayon, and Contributing Editors from Human Resources Network. *Leveraging the Impact of Public Affairs: A Guidebook Based on Practical Experience for Corporate Affairs Executives*. Philadelphia: Human Resources Network, 1984.

O'Connor, John. *Image as Artifact: The Historical Analysis of Film and Television*. Malabar, Fla.: R.E. Krieger Publishing Co., 1990.

Odegard, Peter. *Pressure Politics: The Story of the Anti-Saloon League*. New York: Columbia University Press, 1928.

Ogilvy, David. *Confessions of an Advertising Man*. New York: Atheneum, 1960.

Olasky, Marvin N. *Corporate Public Relations: A New Historical Perspective*. Hillsdale, N.J.: Lawrence Erlbaum Associates, 1987.

Olasky, Marvin N. *Prodigal Press: The Anti-Christian Bias of the American News Media*. Westchester, Ill.: Crossway Books, 1988.

Olson, James S. *Dictionary of the Vietnam War*. New York: Greenwood Press, 1988.

"On Propaganda." *Etc.: A Review of General Semantics* [special issue], 36 (Summer 1979).

Ontiveros, Suzanne, and Susan Kinnell. *Corporate Social Responsibility: Contemporary Viewpoints*. Santa Barbara, Calif.: ABC-Clio Information Services, 1986.

Orwell, George. *Orwell's Nineteen Eighty-Four*. 2d ed. New York: Harcourt Brace Jovanovich, 1983. Orig. pub., England, 1948.

O'Toole, G.J.A. *Honorable Treachery: A History of U.S. Intelligence, Espionage and Covert Action from the American Revolution to the C.I.A.* New York: Atlantic Monthly Press, 1991.

Packard, Vance. *The Hidden Persuaders*. New York: McKay, 1957. Rev. ed., New York: Pocket Books, 1980.

Paine, Thomas. *The Writings of Thomas Paine*. Ed., Moncure Daniel Conway. 4 vols. New York: Putnam's, 1894-1896. Reprint, New York: AMS Press, 1967.

Parekh, Bhikhu C. *Marx's Theory of Ideology*. Baltimore, Md.: Johns Hopkins University Press, 1982.

Parenti, Michael. *Inventing Reality: The Politics of the Mass Media*. New York: St. Martin's Press, 1986. 2d ed. *Inventing Reality: The Politics of News Media*, New York: St. Martin's Press, 1992.

Paret, Peter, Beth Irwin Lewis, and Paul Paret. *Persuasive Images: Posters of War and Revolution from the Hoover Institution Archives*. Princeton, N.J.: Princeton University Press, 1992.

Parry, Robert. *Fooling America: How Washington Insiders Twist the Truth and Manufacture the Conventional Wisdom*. New York: William Morrow, 1992.

Peck, Abe. *Uncovering the Sixties: The Life and Times of the Underground Press*. New York: Pantheon, 1985.

Perot, H. Ross, with Pat Choate. *Save Your Job, Save Our Country. Why NAFTA Must Be Stopped—Now!* New York, Hyperion, 1993.

Perris, Arnold. *Music as Propaganda.* Westport, Conn.: Greenwood Press, 1985.

Peterson, Horace C. *Propaganda for War: The Campaign Against American Neutrality, 1914-1917.* Norman: University of Oklahoma Press, 1939. Reprint, Port Washington, N.Y.: Kennikat Press, 1968.

Petty, Richard E., and John T. Cacioppo. *Communication and Persuasion: Central and Peripheral Routes to Attitude Change.* New York: Springer-Verlag, 1986.

Philbrick, Herbert A. *I Led Three Lives.* New York: McGraw-Hill, 1952.

Philippe, Robert. *Political Graphics: Art as a Weapon.* New York: Abbeville Press, 1982.

Piven, Frances Fox, and Richard Cloward. *Poor People's Movements: Why They Succeed, How They Fail.* New York: Pantheon, 1977.

Plato. *The Dialogues of Plato.* Trans. with comment., R.E. Allen. 2 vols. New Haven, Conn.: Yale University Press, 1984-1991. Originally recorded circa 385 B.C.E.

Plato. *Phaedrus.* Ed. with notes, R. Hackworth. Cambridge, England: Cambridge University Press, 1972.

Pollay, Richard W., ed. *Information Sources in Advertising History.* Westport, Conn.: Greenwood Press, 1979.

Ponsonby, Arthur. *Falsehood in War-Time: Containing an Assortment of Lies Circulated Throughout the Nations During the Great War.* New York: E. P. Dutton and Co., 1928. Paperback reprint ed., *Falsehood in Wartime.* Torrance, Calif.: Institute for Historical Review, 1980.

Pool, Ithiel de Sola. *Technologies of Freedom.* Cambridge, Mass.: Belknap Press of Harvard University Press, 1983.

Post, James E. *Corporate Behavior and Social Change.* Reston, Va.: Reston Publishing Co., 1978.

Post, Louis F. *The Deportations Delirium of Nineteen-Twenty; A Personal Narrative of an Historic Official Experience.* Chicago: Charles H. Kerr and Co., 1923. Reprint, New York: DaCapo Press, 1970.

Powe, Lucas A., Jr. *American Broadcasting and the First Amendment.* Berkeley, Calif.: University of California Press, 1987.

Prados, John. *Keepers of the Keys: A History of the National Security Council from Truman to Bush.* New York: William Morrow, 1991.

Prados, John. *Presidents' Secret Wars: CIA and Pentagon Covert Operations Since World War II.* New York: William Morrow, 1986.

Pratkanis, Anthony, and Elliot Aronson. *Age of Propaganda: The Everyday Use and Abuse of Persuasion.* New York: W. H. Freeman and Company, 1992.

Presby, Frank. *The History and Development of Advertising.* New York: Glenwood Press, 1929.

Preston, William, Jr. *Aliens and Dissenters: Federal Suppression of Radicals, 1903-1933.* Cambridge, Mass.: Harvard University Press, 1963. Reprint, New York: Harper and Row, 1963.

Preston, William, Jr., Edward S. Herman, and Herbert I. Schiller. *Hope and Folly: The United States and UNESCO, 1945-1985.* Minneapolis: University of Minnesota Press, 1989.

Progressive Periodicals Directory. 2d ed. Nashville, Tenn.: Progressive Education, 1989.

Pronay, Nicholas, and D. W. Spring, eds. *Propaganda, Politics and Film, 1918-1945.* London: Macmillan, 1982. Atlantic Highlands, N.J.: Humanities Press, 1982.

Protocols of the Learned Elders of Zion. Trans. from the 1905 Russian text of Sergiei A. Nilus by Victor E. Marsden. Studies in Antisemitism series. New York: Gordon Press, 1978.

Puette, William J. *Through Jaundiced Eyes: How the Media View Organized Labor.* Ithaca, N.Y.: ILR Press, Cornell University, 1992.

Qualter, Terence H. *Opinion Control in the Democracies.* New York: St. Martin's Press, 1985.

Qualter, Terence H. *Propaganda and Psychological Warfare.* New York: Random House, 1962.

Rank, Hugh. *The Pep Talk: How to Analyze Political Language.* Park Forest, Ill.: Counter-Propaganda Press, 1984.

Rank, Hugh. *The Pitch: How to Analyze Advertising.* Park Forest, Ill.: Counter-Propaganda Press, 1982.

Raucher, Alan R. *Public Relations and Business, 1900-1929.* Baltimore, Md.: Johns Hopkins University Press, 1968.

Read, James M. *Atrocity Propaganda, 1914-1919.* New Haven, Conn.: Yale University Press, 1941. Reprint, New York: Arno Press, 1972.

Reed, John. *Ten Days That Shook the World.* New York: Boni and Liveright, 1919 Reprint ed., with new intro. and notes, Bertram D. Wolfe. Foreword, V.I. Lenin. New York: Vintage Books, 1960.

Reed, Rebecca Theresa. *Six Months in a Convent.* Boston: Rusell, Odiorne and Metcalf, 1835.

Rees, David. *Soviet Active Measures, the Propaganda War.* London: Institute for the Study of Conflict, 1984.

Reichley, A. James. *The Life of the Parties: A History of American Political Parties.* New York: Free Press, 1992.

Reisman, W. Michael, and James E. Baker. *Regulating Covert Action: Practices, Contexts, and Policies of Covert Coercion Abroad in International and American Law.* New Haven, Conn.: Yale University Press, 1992.

Revel, Jean-François. *The Flight From Truth: The Reign of Deceit in the Age of Information.* Trans. from the original French, Curtis Cate. New York: Random House, 1992.

Rhodes, Anthony. *Propaganda—The Art of Persuasion: World War II.* New York: Chelsea House, 1976. Reprint, Secaucus, N.J.: Wellfleet Press, 1987.

Rice, Ronald E., and Charles K. Atkin, eds. *Public Communication Campaigns.* 2d ed. Newbury Park, Calif.: Sage Publications, 1989.

Rice, Ronald E., and William J. Paisley, eds. *Public Communication Campaigns.* Beverly Hills, Calif.: Sage Publications, 1981.

Richelson, Jeffrey T. *The U.S. Intelligence Community.* Cambridge, Mass.: Ballinger, 1985.

Rideout, Walter B. *The Radical Novel in the United States 1900-1954: Some Interrelations of Literature and Society.* Cambridge, Mass.: Harvard University Press, 1965.

Riegel, Oscar W. *Mobilizing for Chaos: The Story of the New Propaganda.* New Haven, Conn.: Yale University Press, 1934. Reprint, New York: Arno Press, 1972.

Ries, Al, and Jack Trout. *Positioning: The Battle for Your Mind.* New York: McGraw-Hill, 1981.

Riff, Michael A., ed. *Dictionary of Modern Political Ideologies.* New York: St. Martin's Press, 1987.

The Right Guide 1995: The Comprehensive Directory of Conservative, Free Market and Traditional Values Organizations. Ann Arbor, Michigan: Economics America, Inc., 1995.

Robison, John. *Proofs of a Conspiracy Against All the Religions and Governments of Europe, Carried on in the Secret Meetings of Free Masons, Illuminati, and Reading Societies, Collected from Good Authorities.* 4th ed. New York: George Forman, 1798. Reprint, with new intro., Boston: Western Islands, 1967.

Rochester, Anna. *Rulers of America: A Study of Finance Capital*. New York: International Publishers, 1936.

Roeder, George H., Jr. *The Censored War*. New Haven, Conn.: Yale University Press, 1993.

Roetter, Charles. *The Art of Psychological Warfare 1914-1945*. New York: Stein and Day, 1974.

Rogers, Daniel T. *Contested Truths: Keywords in American Politics since Independence*. New York: Basic Books, 1987.

Roloff, Michael, and Gerald R. Miller, eds. *Persuasion: New Directions in Theory and Research*. Beverly Hills, Calif.: Sage Publications, 1980.

Rome, Edwin P., and William H. Roberts. *Corporate and Commercial Free Speech: First Amendment Protection of Expression in Business*. Westport, Conn.: Quorum Books, 1985.

Rousseau, Jean Jacques. *The Social Contract, and Discourses*. Trans. from the original French with a new intro., G.D.H. Cole. New York: Dutton, 1950. *The Social Contract* first appeared in 1762.

Ruch, William V. *International Handbook of Corporate Communication*. Jefferson, N.C.: McFarland, 1989.

Rudé, George. *Ideology and Popular Protest*. London: Lawrence and Wishart, 1980.

Rupp, Leila J. *Mobilizing Women for War: German and American Propaganda, 1939-1945*. Princeton, N.J.: Princeton University Press, 1978.

Ryan, Charlotte. *Prime Time Activism: Media Strategies for Grassroots Organizing*. Boston: South End Press, 1991.

Rystrom, Kenneth. *The Why, Who and How of the Editorial Page*. New York: Random House, 1983.

Sabato, Larry J. *PAC Power: Inside the World of Political Action Committees*. New York: William Morrow, 1984.

Sabato, Larry J. *The Rise of the Political Consultants: New Ways of Winning Elections*. New York: Basic Books, 1981.

Salmon, Charles T., ed. *Information Campaigns: Balancing Social Values and Social Change*. Newbury Park, Calif.: Sage, 1989.

Salvaggio, Jerry L., ed. *Telecommunications: Issues and Choices for Society*. New York: Longman, 1983. Reprint ed., *The Information Society: Economic, Social, and Structural issues*. Hillsdale, N.J.: Lawrence Erlbaum Associates, 1989.

Savage, Robert L., and Dan Nimmo, eds. *Politics in Familiar Contexts: Projecting Politics Through Popular Media*. Norwood, N.J.: Ablex Publishing, 1990.

Sargent, Lyman Tower. *Contemporary Political Ideologies*. Homewood, Ill.: Dorsey Press, 1972.

Sartori, Giovani. "Politics, Ideology and Belief Systems." *American Political Science Review* 63,2 (June 1969): 411+.

Schein, Edgar H., Inge Schneier, and Curtis H. Barker. *Coercive Persuasion: A Socio-Psychological Analysis of the "Brainwashing" of American Civilian Prisoners by the Chinese Communists*. New York: Norton, 1961.

Schiller, Herbert I. *Information and the Crisis Economy*. New York: Oxford University Press, 1986.

Schiller, Herbert I. *The Mind Managers*. Boston: Beacon Press, 1973.

Schlesinger, Stephen, and Stephen Kinzer. *Bitter Fruit: The Untold Story of the American Coup in Guatemala*. Garden City, N.Y.: Doubleday, 1982. Paperback ed., Garden City, N.Y.: Anchor Press/Doubleday, 1984.

Schmertz, H. *Good-Bye to the Low Profile: The Art of Creative Confrontation*. Boston: Little, Brown, and Company, 1986.

Schmid, Alex P. *Political Terrorism: A Research Guide to Concepts, Theories, Data Bases and Literature*. New Brunswick, N.J.: Transaction Books, 1983.

Schmid, Alex P., and Janny de Graaf. *Violence as Communication: Insurgent Terrorism and the Western News Media*. Beverly Hills, Calif.: Sage, 1982.

Schudson, Michael. *Advertising, the Uneasy Persuasion*. New York: Basic Books, 1985.

Schwar, Jane. "Interventionist Propaganda and Pressure Groups in the United States, 1937-1941." Ph.D. dissertation, Ohio State University, 1973.

Scruton, Roger. *A Dictionary of Political Thought*. New York: Harper and Row, 1982.

Seldes, George. *The Facts Are . . . A Guide to Falsehood and Propaganda in the Press and Radio*. New York: In Fact, 1942.

Seldes, George. *Witness to a Century: Encounters with the Noted, the Notorious, and the Three SOBs*. New York: Ballantine Books, 1987. Paperback ed., 1988.

Sethi, S. Prakash. *Handbook of Advocacy Advertising: Concepts, Strategies, and Applications*. Cambridge, Mass.: Ballinger/Harper and Row, 1987.

Severin, Werner J., and James W. Tankard, Jr. *Communication Theories: Origins, Methods, and Uses in the Mass Media*. New York: Longman, 1992. Expanded from an earlier ed. published in New York: Hastings House, 1979.

Shafritz, Jay M. *The Dorsey Dictionary of American Government and Politics*. Chicago: Dorsey Press, 1988.

Shalom, Stephen R. *Imperial Alibis: Rationalizing U.S. Intervention after the Cold War*. Boston: South End Press, 1993.

Shannon, Claude, and Warren Weaver. *The Mathematical Theory of Communication*. Urbana: University of Illinois Press, 1949.

Shannon, David A. *The Socialist Party in America: A History*. Chicago: Quadrangle Books, 1955.

Shapiro, Andrew L. *We're Number One, Where America Stands—and Falls—in the New World Order*. New York: Vintage Books, 1992.

Shaw, Donald L., and Maxwell E. McCombs. *The Emergence of American Political Issues: The Agenda-Setting Function of the Press*. St. Paul, Minn.: West, 1977.

Sherif, Carolyn, Muzafer Sherif, and Roger E. Nebergall. *Attitude and Attitude Change: The Social Judgment-Involvement Approach*. Philadelphia: W.B. Saunders, 1965.

Shoemaker, Pamela A., ed. *Communication Campaigns about Drugs: Government, Media, and the Public*. Hillsdale, N.J.: Lawrence Erlbaum Associates, 1989.

Short, K.R.M., ed. *Western Broadcasting over the Iron Curtain*. London: Croom Helm, 1986.

Shulman, Holly Cowan. *The Voice of America: Propaganda and Democracy, 1941-1945*. Madison: University of Wisconsin Press, 1990.

Shultz, Richard H., and Roy Godson. *Dezinformatsia: Active Measures in Soviet Strategy*. Washington, D.C.: Pergamon-Brassey's, 1984.

Shulzinger, Robert D. *The Wise Men of Foreign Affairs: The History of the Council of Foreign Relations*. New York: Columbia University Press, 1984.

Shumate, T. Daniel, ed. *The First Amendment: The Legacy of George Mason*. Fairfax, Va.: George Mason University Press, 1985.

Siddiqui, Dilnawaz A., and Abbass F. Alkhafaji, et al. *The Gulf War: Implications for Global Business and Media*. Apollo, Pa.: Closson Press, 1992.

Simons, Herbert W. *Persuasion: Understanding, Practice and Analysis*. 2d ed. New York: Random House, 1986.

Simons, Herbert W., ed. *Rhetoric in the Human Sciences*. Inquiries in Social Construction series. Newbury Park, Calif.: Sage Publications, 1989.

Simons, Herbert W., Elizabeth W. Mechling, and Howard N. Schreier. "The Functions of Human Communication in Mobilizing for Action from the Botton Up: The Rhetoric of Social Movements." In Carroll C. Arnold and John Waite Bowers, eds., *Handbook of Rhetorical and Communication Theory*. Boston: Allyn and Bacon, 1984, pp. 792-867.

Simpson, Christopher. *Science of Coercion: Communication Research and Psychological Warfare, 1945-1960*. New York: Oxford University Press, 1994.

Simpson, Colin. *The Lusitania*. Boston: Little, Brown, 1972.

Sinclair, Upton. *The Brass Check: A Study in American Journalism*. Pasadena, Calif.: Author, 1919. Reprint, New York: Arno Press, 1974.

Sinclair, Upton. *The Jungle*. New York: Doubleday, Page and Company, 1906.

Singerman, Robert. *Antisemitic Propaganda: An Annotated Bibliography and Research Guide*. New York: Garland, 1982.

Singlaub, [Major General (retired)] John K. "A New Strategy for the 1980's." Address before the United States Council for World Freedom and the North American Region of the World Anti-Communist League meeting in Phoenix, Arizona, 23 April 1982; reprinted in *ABN Correspondence* (New York) 33,4/5 (July-October 1982): 25-28; and excerpted in Scott Anderson and John Lee Anderson, *Inside the League: The Shocking Expose of How Terrorists, Nazi, and Latin American Death Squads Have Infiltrated The World Anti-Communist League*. New York: Dodd, Mead and Company, 1986, p. 150.

Skinner, James M. *The Cross and the Cinema: The Legion of Decency and the National Catholic Office for Motion Pictures*. New York: Praeger, 1993.

Sklar, Holly. *Washington's War on Nicaragua*. Boston: South End Press, 1988.

Sklar, Holly, ed. *Trilateralism*. Boston: South End Press, 1982.

Skvortsov, L. *The Ideology and Tactics of Anti-Communism*. Moscow: Progress, 1969.

Sloan, William David. *American Journalism History: An Annotated Bibliography*. Westport, Conn.: Greenwood Press, 1989.

Small, William. *Political Power and the Press*. New York: Norton, 1972.

Smith, Adam. *An Inquiry into the Nature and Causes of the Wealth of Nations*. London: W. Strahan and T. Cadell, 1776. New ed., Philadelphia: Thomas Dobson, 1789. New 11th London ed.; with notes, supplementary chapters, and a life of Dr. Smith by William Playfair. Hartford, Conn.: O.D. Cooke, 1811. Another new ed., with notes and supplementary chapters, by William Playfair, and an account of Dr. Smith's life, by Dugald Stewart. Early American imprints, second series, no. 45724. Hartford, Conn.: Cooke and Hale/George Goodwin and Sons, 1818. Reprint ed., with an intro., notes, marginal summary, and enlarged index, Edwin Cannan. New York: Modern Library, 1993.

Smith, Anthony. *The Geopolitics of Information: How Western Culture Dominates the World*. New York: Oxford University Press, 1980. Paperback ed., 1981.

Smith, Bradley F. *The Shadow Warriors: O.S.S. and the Origins of the C.I.A.* New York: Basic Books, 1983.

Smith, Bruce L., Harold D. Lasswell, and Ralph D. Casey. *Propaganda, Communication, and Public Opinion: A Comprehensive Reference Guide*. Princeton, N.J.: Princeton University Press, 1946.

Smith, Bruce L., and Chitra M. Smith. *International Communication and Political Opinion: A Guide to the Literature*. Princeton, N.J.: Princeton University Press, 1956. Reprint, Westport, Conn.: Greenwood Press, 1972.

Smith, Craig R. *The Fight for Freedom of Expression: Three Case Studies*. Washington, D.C.: Institute for Freedom of Communication, 1985.

Smith, Jeffery A. *Printers and Press Freedom: The Ideology of Early American Journalism*. New York: Oxford University Press, 1988. Paperback ed., 1990.

Smith, Ted J., III, ed. *Propaganda: A Pluralistic Perspective*. New York: Praeger, 1989.

Smoller, Frederic T. *The Six O'Clock Presidency: A Theory of Presidential Press Relations in the Age of Television*. Westport, Conn.: Praeger, 1990.

Snyder, Robert L. *Pare Lorentz and the Documentary Film*. Norman: Oklahoma University Press, 1968.

Soley, Lawrence C. *Radio Warfare*. New York: Praeger, 1989.

Sorauf, Frank J. *Party Politics in America*. 4th ed. Boston: Little Brown, 1989.

Sorensen, Thomas C. *The Word War: The Story of American Propaganda*. New York: Harper and Row, 1968.

Splichal, Slavko, and Janet Wasko, eds. *Communication and Democracy*. Norwood, N.J.: Ablex Publishing, 1993.

Spooner, Lysander. *Vices Are Not Crimes: A Vindication of Moral Liberty*. Cupertino, Calif.: Tanstaafl Publishing Co., 1977. Originally published anonymously as a section in Dio Lewis, *Prohibition a Failure: Or, the True Solution of the Temperance Question*. Boston: J.R. Osgood and Co., 1875.

"'The Spotlight': Liberty Lobby's Voice of Hate." *Facts* (New York and Washington, D.C., Anti-Defamation League of B'nai B'rith) 26,1 (June 1980). 10-page report.

Springen, Donald K. *William Jennings Bryan: Orator of Small-Town America*. Great American Orators: Critical Studies, Speeches and Sources series, no. 11. Westport, Conn.: Greenwood Press, 1991.

Sproule, J. Michael. "Propaganda Studies in American Social Science: The Rise and Fall of the Critical Paradigm." *Quarterly Journal of Speech* 73,1 (February 1987): 60-78.

Squires, James D. *British Propaganda at Home and in the United States from 1914 to 1917*. Cambridge, Mass.: Harvard University Press, 1935.

Stalin, Joseph. *Foundations of Leninism*. 10th anniversary ed. New York: International Publishers, 1934.

Stanton, Bill. *Klanwatch*. New York: Grove Weidenfeld Press, 1991.

Steel, Ronald. *Walter Lippmann and the American Century*. Boston: Little, Brown and Co., 1980. Paperback ed., New York: Vintage Books, 1981.

Steele, Janet E. *The "Sun" Shines for All: Journalism and Ideology in the Life of Charles A. Dana*. Syracuse, N.Y.: Syracuse University Press, 1993.

Steele, Richard W. *Propaganda in an Open Society: The Roosevelt Administration and the Media, 1933-41*. Westport, Conn.: Greenwood Press, 1985.

Steele, Robert D. "The Role of Grey Literature and Non-Traditional Agencies in Informing Policy Makers and Improving National Competitiveness." Transcript of spontaneous remarks to the 1993 Foreign Acquisition Workshop, 21 September 1993, Washington, D.C. Available for free on-line retrieval via the database at <ftp://ftp.oss.net/pub/oss/steeler/greylit.txt>

Stein-Schneider, Herbert. "Versailles on the Potomac." *France Magazine*, no. 7 (Winter 1986-87): 42-43.

Steinberg, Peter. *The Great "Red Menace": United States Prosecution of American Communists, 1947-1952*. Westport, Conn.: Greenwood Press, 1984.

Stenejhem, Michele Flynn. *An American First: John T. Flynn and the America First Committee*. New Rochelle, N.Y.: Arlington House, 1976.

Stevenson, William. *A Man Called Intrepid: The Secret War*. New York: Harcourt Brace Jovanovich, 1976.

Stewart, Charles J., Craig Allen Smith, and Robert E. Denton, Jr. *Persuasion and Social Movements*. 2d ed. Prospect Heights, Ill.: Waveland Press, 1989.

Stowe, Harriet Beecher. *The Annotated Uncle Tom's Cabin*. Ed., with an intro., Phillip Van Doren Stern. New York: Eriksson, 1964.

Suid, Lawrence H., ed. *Film and Propaganda in America: A Documentary History*. Volume 4: *1945 and After*. Documentary Reference Collections series. Westport, Conn: Greenwood Press, 1991.

Suleiman, Michael W. *The Arabs in the Mind of America*. Brattleboro, Vt.: Amana Books, 1988.

Swan, John, and Noel Peattie. *The Freedom to Lie: A Debate about Democracy*. Jefferson, N.C.: McFarland, 1989.

Swanson, David L., and Dan Nimmo, eds. *New Directions in Political Communication: A Resource Book*. Newbury Park, Calif.: Sage Publications, 1990.

Szatmary, David P. *Shays' Rebellion: The Making of an Agrarian Insurrection*. Amherst: University of Massachusetts Press, 1980.

Taheri, Amir. *Nest of Spies: America's Journey to Disaster in Iran*. New York: Pantheon Books, 1988.

Tarde, Gabriel de. *On Communication and Social Influence: Selected Papers*. Ed. with an intro., Terry N. Clark. Chicago: University of Chicago Press, 1969.

Taylor, Philip M. *War and the Media: Propaganda and Persuasion in the Gulf War*. Manchester, U.K.: Manchester University Press, 1992.

Taylor, Robert. *Film Propaganda*. New York: Barnes and Noble, 1979.

Tedford, Thomas L. *Freedom of Speech in the United States*. New York: Random House, 1985. Carbondale: Southern Illinois University Press, 1985.

Terry, Randall A. *Higher Laws*. Dallas, Tx: Operation Rescue, 1987.

Theoharis, Athan. *Spying on Americans: Political Surveillance from Hoover to the Huston Plan*. Philadelphia: Temple University Press, 1978.

Thompson, Fred, and Patrick Murfin. *The I.W.W., Its First Seventy Years, 1905-1975*. Chicago: Industrial Workers of the World, 1976.

Thomson, Oliver. *Mass Persuasion in History: A Historical Analysis of the Development of Propaganda Techniques*. Edinburgh, Scotland: Paul Harris Publishing, 1977.

Thoreau, Henry David. *Walden, and Civil Disobedience*. Intro., Michael Meyer. New York: Penguin Books, 1983. Reproduces the text of the first ed., *Walden, or Life in the Woods*. Boston: Ticknor and Fields, 1854, which also includes the essay "On the Duty of Civil Disobedience," penned in 1849.

Thum, Gladys, and Marcella Thum. *The Persuaders: Propaganda in War and Peace*. New York: Atheneum, 1974.

Timberlake, James. *Prohibition and the Progressive Movement, 1900-1920*. Cambridge, Mass.: Harvard University Press, 1963.

Tompkins, E. Berkeley. *Anti-Imperialism in the United States: The Great Debate, 1890-1920*. Philadelphia: University of Pennsylvania Press, 1970.

Trento, Susan B. *The Power House: Robert Keith Gray and the Selling of Access and Influence in Washington*. New York: St. Martin's Press, 1992.

Treverton, Gregory F. *Covert Action: The Limits of Intervention in the Postwar World*. New York: Basic Books, 1987.

Tyson, James L. *Target America: The Influence of Communist Propaganda on U.S. Media*. Chicago: Regnery Gateway, 1981.

Tzu, Sun. *Sun Tzu, The Art of War*. Trans., Samuel Griffith. London: Oxford University Press, 1963. Originally written in China during the mid-fourth-century B.C.E.

Unger, Irwin. *The Movement: A History of the American New Left, 1959-1972*. New York: Dodd, Mead and Co., 1974.

United Nations Organization (UNO). *Discrimination Against Indigenous Peoples: Draft Declaration on the Rights of Indigenous Peoples*. New York: Author, 1993.

United States Central Intelligence Agency (CIA). *Intelligence Community Staff Glossary*. Washington, D.C.: Author, June 1978.

United States Congress. Senate. Committee on the Judiciary. *Brewing and Liquor Interests and German and Bolshevik Propaganda*. Report, Doc. No. 61. Washington, D.C.: Government Printing Office, 1919.

United States Congress. Senate. Committee on the Judiciary. *The Technique of Soviet Propaganda. A Study Presented by the Subcommittee to Investigate the Administration of the Internal Security Act and Other Internal Security Laws of the Committee on the Judiciary*, by Suzanne Labin. Washington, D.C.: Government Printing Office, 1960.

United States Congress. Senate. Committee on the Judiciary. Subcommittee on Administrative Practice and Procedure. *Sourcebook on Corporate Image and Corporate Advocacy Advertising.* Committee Print, 95th Cong., 2nd sess. Washington, D.C.: Government Printing Office, 1978.

United States Congress. Senate. Committee on the Judiciary. Subcommittee on Constitutional Rights. *Freedom of the Press.* 92nd Cong., 1st and 2nd sess. Washington, D.C.: Government Printing Office, 1972.

United States Congress. Senate. Select Committee on Secret Military Assistance to Iran and the Nicaraguan Opposition. *Hearings.* Washington, D.C.: Government Printing Office, 1988.

United States Congress. Senate. Select Committee to Study Government Operations with Respect to Intelligence Activities of the United States Senate. (The "Church Committee"). *Alleged Assassination Plots Involving Foreign Leaders: Interim Report of the Senate Select Committee to Study . . . Intelligence Activities.* Staff Report. 94th Cong., 1st sess. Washington, D.C.: Government Printing Office, 20 November 1975.

United States Congress. Senate. Select Committee to Study Government Operations with Respect to Intelligence Activities of the United States Senate. (The "Church Committee"). *Covert Action in Chile, 1963-1973.* Staff Report. 94th Cong., 1st sess. Washington, D.C.: Government Printing Office, 18 December 1975.

United States Congress. Senate. Select Committee to Study Government Operations with Respect to Intelligence Activities of the United States Senate. (The "Church Committee"). *Final Report of the Senate Select Committee to Study . . . Intelligence Activities.* 4 vols. 94th Cong., 2nd sess. Washington, D.C.: Government Printing Office, 23-26 April 1976.

United States Congress. Senate. Select Committee to Study Government Operations with Respect to Intelligence Activities of the United States Senate. (The "Church Committee"). *Hearings.* September 23, 24, and 25, 1975. Multiple volumes. 94th Cong., 1st sess. Washington: Government Printing Office, 1975.

United States Congress. Senate. Committee on Interstate Commerce. *Propaganda in Motion Pictures. Hearings Before a Subcommittee of the Senate Committee on Interstate Commerce Pursuant to S. Res. 152.* 77th Cong., 1st sess. Washington, D.C.: Government Printing Office (Committee Print), 1942.

United States Department of State. *Patterns of Global Terrorism: 1983.* Washington, D.C.: Government Printing Office, September 1984.

United States Information Agency (USIA). *Propaganda and Information: An Annotated Bibliography.* Washington, D.C.: USIA Library, July 1973.

United States. Kerner Commission. *Report of the National Advisory Commission on Civil Disorders.* New York: Bantam Books, 1968.

United States Library of Congress. *A List of Bibliographies on Propaganda.* Comp., Grace Hadley Fuller, under the direction of Florence S. Hellman. Washington, D.C.: Library of Congress, Division of Bibliography, 1940.

United States. National Archives and Records Service. *Sounds of History from the National Archives: World War 2.* Washington, D.C.: National Archives Trust Fund Board, 1980.

United States. Surgeon General's Scientific Advisory Committee on Television and Social Behavior. *Television and Growing Up: The Impact of Televised Violence; Report to the Surgeon General.* Washington, D.C.: U.S. Government Printing Office, 1972.

Vankin, Jonathan. *Conspiracies, Cover-ups and Crimes: Political Manipulation and Mind Control in America.* New York: Paragon House, 1991. Rev. paperback ed., *Conspiracies, Cover-ups and Crimes: From JFK to the CIA Terrorist Connection.* New York: Dell Publishing, 1992.

Vaughn, Stephen L. *Holding Fast the Inner Lines: Democracy, Nationalism, and the Committee on Public Information*. Chapel Hill: University of North Carolina Press, 1980.

Vercellin, Giorgio. *A Guide to Documents from the Nest of Spies*. Occasional paper (Afghanistan Forum), no. 26. New York: Afghanistan Forum, [1986].

Vetter, Harold J., and Gary R. Perlstein. *Perspectives on Terrorism*. Pacific Grove, Calif.: Brooks/Cole Publishing Co., 1991.

Viereck, George S. *Spreading Germs of Hate*. New York: Horace Liveright, 1930.

Villard, Oswald Garrison. *Fighting Years: An Autobiography*. New York: Harcourt, Brace and Company, 1939.

Volkman, Ernest. *A Legacy of Hate: Anti-Semitism in America*. New York: Franklin Watts, 1982.

Walcott, John. "Land of Hype and Glory: Spin Doctors on Parade." *U.S. News and World Report* (10 February 1992): 6-7.

Walker, David. *David Walker's Appeal, in Four Articles; Together with a Preamble to the Colored Citizens of the World, But in Particular, and Very Expressly, to Those of the United States of America*. Boston: Author, September 1829. 3d ed., March 1830.

Walker, Mabel Gregory. *The Fenian Movement*. Colorado Springs, Colo.: Ralph Myles Publisher, 1969.

Walker, Martin. *The Cold War: A History*. New York: Henry Holt and Company, 1993.

Walker, Robert H. *Reform in America: The Continuous Frontier*. Lexington: University Press of Kentucky, 1985.

Ward, Larry W. *The Motion Picture Goes to War: The U.S. Government Film Effort During World War I*. Ann Arbor, Michigan: University Microfilms, 1985.

Washburn, Patrick S. *A Question of Sedition: The Federal Government's Investigation of the Black Press during World War II*. New York: Oxford University Press, 1987.

Washington, George. *Address of George Washington, to the People of the United States, Announcing his Resolution to Retire from Public Life: Containing an Invaluable Legacy of Good Advice*. Early American imprints, first series, no. 31550. Providence, R.I.: Carter and Wilkinson, 1796. Reprint, *Washington's Farewell Address, in Facsimile, with Transliterations of All the Drafts of Washington, Madison, and Hamilton, Together with Their Correspondence and other Supporting Documents*. New York: New York Public Library, 1935.

Wasko, Janet, and Vincent Mosco. *Democratic Communications in the Information Age*. Norwood, N.J.: Ablex Publishing, 1992.

Watson, John B. *Psychology, from the Standpoint of a Behaviorist*. Philadelphia: J.B. Lippincott Co., 1919.

Weatherford, Doris. *American Women's History: An A to Z of People, Organizations, Issues, and Events*. New York: Prentice Hall General Reference, 1994.

Weatherwax, Clara. *Marching! Marching!* New York: John Day Company, 1935.

Webster, Nesta Helen (Mrs. Arthur Webster). *Secret Societies and Subversive Movements*. New York: E.P. Dutton and Company, 1924. 4th ed., London: Boswell Printing and Publishing Co. Ltd., 1928. 9th ed., Hawthorne, Calif.: Christian Book Club of America, 1967.

Weisbrod, Burton A., Joel F. Handler, and Neil K. Komesar. *Public Interest Law: An Economic and Institutional Analysis*. Berkeley and Los Angeles, Calif.: University of California Press, 1978.

Wiebe, Robert H. *The Search for Order: 1877-1920*. New York: Hill and Wang, 1967.

Wilcox, Dennis L., Phillip H. Ault, and Warren K. Agee. *Public Relations Strategies and Tactics*. 4th ed. New York: Harper and Row, 1995.

Wilcox, Laird. *The Hoaxer Project Report—Racist and Anti-Semitic Graffiti, Harassment and Violence: An Essay on Hoaxes and Fabricated Incidents*. Olathe,

Kan.: Editorial Research Service, December 1990. Includes the essays "What is 'Political Extremism'?" and "The Practice of Ritual Defamation: How Values, Opinions and Beliefs are Controlled in Democratic Societies."

Wilcox, Laird, ed. *Guide to the American Left: Directory and Bibliography*. Rev. and updated ed. Olathe, Kan.: Editorial Research Service, 1990.

Wilcox, Laird, ed. *Guide to the American Right: Directory and Bibliography*. Rev. and updated ed. Olathe, Kan.: Editorial Research Service, 1990.

Wilcox, Laird, ed. *Terrorism, Assassination, Espionage and Propaganda: A Master Bibliography*. Rev. and enlarged ed. Olathe, Kan.: Editorial Research Service, 1989.

Wildmon, Donald. *The Home Invaders*. Wheaton, Ill.: Victor Books, 1986.

Wilkerson, Marcus. *Public Opinion and the Spanish-American War: A Study in War Propaganda*. Baton Rouge: Louisiana State University Press, 1932.

Williamson, Audrey. *Thomas Paine: His Life, Work and Times*. London: Allen and Unwin, 1973.

Wilmer, Lambert A. *Our Press Gang; or, a Complete Exposition of the Corruptions and Crimes of the American Newspapers*. Philadelphia: J.T. Lloyd, 1859. Reprint, New York: Arno Press, 1970.

Wilson, Woodrow. *In Our First Year of War; Messages and Addresses to the Congress and the People, March 5, 1917, to April 6, 1918*. New and enl. ed. New York, Harper, 1918. Includes the famous "Fourteen Points" presidential address outlining American war aims (largely authored by advisor Walter Lippmann) delivered to a joint session of the U.S. Congress, January 8, 1918.

Winfield, Betty Houchin. *FDR and the News Media*. Urbana and Chicago: University of Illinois Press, 1991.

Winkler, Allan M. *The Politics of Propaganda: The Office of War Information, 1942-1945*. New Haven, Conn.: Yale University Press, 1978.

Winters, Donald E., Jr. *The Soul of the Wobblies: The I.W.W., Religion, and American Culture in the Progressive Era, 1905-1917*. Westport, Conn.: Greenwood Press, 1985.

Wise, David. *The Politics of Lying: Government Deception, Secrecy and Power*. New York: Vintage Books, 1973.

Wolfe, Alan. *The Seamy Side of Democracy: Repression in America*. 2d ed. White Plains, N.Y.: Longman, 1978.

Wolfe, Gregory. *Right Minds: A Sourcebook of American Conservative Thought*. Chicago: Regnery Gateway, 1987.

Wood, Richard, ed. *Film and Propaganda in America: A Documentary History*. Volume 1: *World War I*. Documentary Reference Collections series. Westport, Conn: Greenwood Press, 1990.

Woodward, Gary C., and Robert E. Denton, Jr. *Persuasion and Influence in American Life*. Prospect Heights, Ill.: Waveland Press, 1988.

Zeman, Zbynek. *Selling the War: Art and Propaganda in World War II*. London: Orbis, 1978.

Zimbardo, Philip, Ebbe B. Ebbesen, and Christina Maslach. *Influencing Attitudes and Changing Behavior*. 2d ed. New York: Random House, 1977.

INDEX*

ABC-Capitol Cities, 206
ABC Network: acquired by Capital Cities
  Communications, 91; formed from part
  of NBC, 61; and issue advertising,
  192; as MEDIA ELITE, 206; and public
  service announcements, 94; radio
  division realignment, 80
abortion, 82, 94, 96, 101, 103
Abourezk, James G., 86
Abrams, Elliott, 108, 142, 147
Abrams v. United States (court case), 43
Academy of Motion Picture Arts and
  Sciences 63, 88; Academy Awards, 63,
  74, 87, 96
Academy of Television Arts and
  Sciences, 84; Emmy Awards, 91
Accuracy in Media (AIM), 205
ACTION GROUP, 115
ACTIVE MEASURES, 115. *See also*
  COVERT
ACTIVISTS, 115-16, 215
Acts and Monuments of the Martyrs
  (book), xvi
ACTUALITY, 116
Adam, G. Stuart, 195
Adams, John, 4, 7, 8, 165

Adams, John Quincy, 9, 10
AD HOMINEM ATTACK, 116
ADVERTISING, 26, 59, 100, 117, 165;
  of cigarettes, 80; OUTDOOR
  ADVERTISING, 222
Advertising Age (magazine), 100
ADVERTISING COUNCIL, 60-61, 93,
  117
ADVERTORIAL, 117-18
ADVOCACY ADVERTISING, 118
ADVOCACY JOURNALISM, 118
Advocates for Self-Government, 132-33,
  197, 251, 255
Africa, 197
African-American men, March on
  Washington (1995), 113
African Masonic Lodge, 4
African National Congress (ANC), 94
AGAINST THE MAIL, 118
Agency for International Development
  (AID), 77
AGENDA SETTING, 118-19, 257
AGENTS/AGENCIES OF INFLUENCE,
  119, 172
AGENTS PROVOCATEUR, 119
AGITATION, 119-20

---

* NOTE: Terms listed in CAPITAL LETTERS (with the exception of acronyms) indicate
glossary main entries.

Agitational propaganda. *See* AGITPROP
AGITPROP, 120, 185
Aguinaldo, Emilio, 29
Ahaya, Victor, 214-15
A-I-D-C-A FORMULA, 120
Aideed, Mohamed Farah, 110
Alar (pesticide), 96
Al-Azhar University (Cairo, Egypt), xii
Alexander Bill (radio broadcasting
     regulation), 40
Alien and Sedition Acts, 7-8
Allende, Salvador, 82
Allied Control Council, 62
Allies (in World War II), 60
Aloisi, Baron, 54
Alson, Jacob Memorial Library, 123
Alternating current (AC), 24
Alternative Index (newspaper), 98
Amerasia (magazine), 62
America (song), 11
America, xvi; discovery of, 1. *See also*
     United States of America
AMERICA BASHING, 120
AMERICA FIRST, 120, 191
America First Committee, 58, 120
America First (poster), 36
American Antislavery Society, 11
American-Arab Anti-Discrimination
     Committee, 86
American Bar Association, 102
American Broadcasting Companies. *See*
     ABC Network
American China Policy Association,
     Inc., 63
American Civil Liberties Bureau,
     established, 38; name changed, 44
American Civil Liberties Union (ACLU),
     181; formerly American Civil
     Liberties Bureau, 44; and Japanese
     internment during World War II, 266;
     and Nazi parade (Skokie, Illinois), 83;
     opposition to Robert Bork Supreme
     Court nomination, 93; and Palestinian
     Information Office, 95
American Civil War, 18-20, 143
American Colonization Society, 9. *See
     also* slavery
American Committee for Cultural
     Freedom, 66
American Communist party, 62. *See also*
     Communist Party of the United States
     of America (CPUSA)
American Convention on Human Rights

of the Organization of American
     States, 181
American Convention for Promoting the
     Abolition of Slavery, 8
American Crisis, The (booklet), 4
AMERICAN EXPEDITIONARY FORCE
     (AEF), 39, 120
American Family Association (AFA),
     106
American Farm Bureau Federation, 43
American Federation of Labor, 27, 29, 50
American Free Trade League, 19
American Friends Service Committee,
     219
American Institute for Free Labor
     Development (AIFLD), 74
American Institute of Public Opinion, 55
American Israeli Public Affairs
     Committee (AIPAC), 276
American Jewish Committee, 109
American Legion, 43
American Medical Association, 101
American Missionary Society, 9
American Newspaper Guild, 52
AMERICAN PARTY, 16, 120, 248. *See
     also* POPULISM/POPULIST; RIGHT-
     WING/CONSERVATIVE
American Peace Mobilization, 58
American Protective League, 41-42
American Railway Union, 26
American Red Cross, 23
American Relief Administration, 46
*American Remembrancer, and Universal
     Tablet of Memory, The* (book), 6
American Revolution, 2-3, 4
American Socialist, The (magazine), 33
American Society of Newspaper Editors,
     51
American Telephone and Telegraph
     Company (AT&T), 32, 48, 90
American-Whig party, 17
American Writers' Conference, 53
*America's House of Lords: An Inquiry
     into the Freedom of the Press* (book),
     57
Ames, Aldrich, 113
Amir, Yigal, 113
Amnesty International (AI), 110, 153,
     181, 219
Amos n' Andy (radio show), 49
Ampex Corporation, 72
ANARCHISM/ANARCHIST, 33, 120-21.
     See also specific types

anarchy, 120-21
ANC: The Inside Story (booklet), 94
ANCHORS, 121
Anderson, Jane, 55, 61
Andropov, Yuri, 225
ANGLOPHILE, 121-22
ANGLOPHOBE, 122
Angola, 197
ANIMAL RIGHTS MOVEMENT, 122
ANTIAUTHORITARIANISM, 122
ANTI-DEFAMATION LEAGUE OF B'NAI
    B'RITH (ADL), 87, 88, 105, 112, 122-
    23; formed in Chicago, 34;
    intelligence operations of, 188, 276;
    opposed to Liberty Lobby
    organization, 73; opposed to Louis
    Farrrakhan, 89; opposed to *Oliver
    Twist* (motion picture), 66; and
    revisionism, 249; spying operation
    of, 108-9
Anti-Imperialist League, 29, 44
Anti-Judaism, 123
Anti-Masonic party, 10, 11
Antimilitarism, 208
Anti-Popery Union, 12
Anti-Racist Action (ARA), 110
Antisaloon League, 26
ANTI-SEMITIC, 123-24. *See also*
    ZIONISM/ZIONIST
ANTITERRRORISM, 124. *See also*
    COUNTERTERRORISM
anti-Zionism, 123
Apocalypse Now (motion picture), 85
Appeal to Reason, The (booklet), 27, 33,
    46, 98
Appomattox Court House, 19
Aptheker, Herbert, 73, 102
Arab League, 62, 63, 71
Arabs, 123, 124, 190
Arbeiter-Zeitung (newspaper), 23
Arbenz, Jacobo, 70
ARENA party, 108
Areopagitica (book), 1
Argentina, 97, 150
ARGUMENTATION, 124
Aristide, Jean-Bertrand, 102, 112
Aristotle, x
ARMED PROPAGANDA, 124
ARMED STRUGGLE, 124-125
Arms Export Control Act, 180
Armstrong Circle Theater (television
    program), 67, 72
Armstrong, Edwin, 56

Arnett, Peter, 101
Arnold, Benedict, 3
Aronson, Elliot, 179
Aronson, James, 65
Article 19 International Centre against
    Censorship, 100
Articles of Confederation, 4, 167. *See
    also* United States Constitution
Aryan Nations Hour (radio show), 95
Ashford, Nigel, 180
Aspen Institute, 66, 206
ASSASSIN, 125-26. *See also*
    TERRORIST
assembly, freedom of, 6. *See also* FIRST
    AMENDMENT
ASSETS, 126. *See also* AGENTS/
    AGENCIES OF INFLUENCE
Associated Press (AP), 34, 223, 206
Association of Motion Picture Producers,
    65
Astor, Vincent, 126
AT&T. *See* American Telephone &
    Telegraph
Atlantic Charter, 59
Attucks, Crispus, 3
Audion tube, 31
Auschwitz, Poland, 62, 87
AUTONOMIST, 126. *See also*
    ANTIAUTHORITARIANISM, 126
Axis powers (in World War II), 58, 60
"Axis Sally," 66

BACKDOOR CONTACT, 126
BACKDOOR TO WAR, 126. *See also*
    CONSPIRACY THEORIES
BACKGROUND, 127, 220, 221. *See also*
    DEEP BACKGROUND
BACKGROUNDER, 127
Baker, Brent H., 204-5
Baker, Newton D., 39
Baldwin, Roger, 38
Balfour Declaration, 40
Baltimore and Ohio Railroad, 10, 22
Bandung Conference, 265
Bar-Cochba, xi
Barnes, Harry Elmer, 128, 146, 248
Barton, Clara, 23
Bass, Mrs. George, 38
Batista, Fulgencio, 73
Batten, Barton, Durstine & Osborn
    (BBDO), 59, 70, 90, 96
Battle Cry of Peace, The (motion
    picture), 36

Battle of Hastings, xiii
Battleship Potemkin (motion picture), 47
Bay of Pigs, Cuba, 74, 111
BBDO (advertising agency). See Batten, Barton, Durstine & Osborn
Beach, Henry L., 79
Beadle, Irwin P. (publisher), 18
Beam, Louis, 89-90
Beck, James, 51
Beijing, China, 97
Belfrage, Cedric, 65, 72
Belgium, 219
Bell, Alexander Graham, 22, 35
Bell, John, 18
Bell Operating Companies (BOCs), 90, 100
Belmont, August, 15
BELTWAY BANDITS, 127
BENCHMARK STUDY, 127. *See also* TRACKING POLLS
Ben-Gurion, David, 69, 209
Bennett, James Gordon, 13, 223
Berg, Alan, 90
Berkman, Alexander, 44
Berlin Wall, 98
Berliner, Emile, 24
Bernays, Edward L.: beginnings as public relations counsel, 43; celebration of invention of electric light bulb, 50; as counsel for United Fruit Company, 71; *Crystallizing Public Opinion* (book) published, 46; death of, 113; and term "engineering of consent," 160, 201, 234; work for COMMITTEE ON PUBLIC INFORMATION, 39
Bernhard, Prince (Netherlands), 72
Bernstein, Carl, 81
Betamax, 83
bias, 202-5
Bible, King James, 1
Biblical Recorder (magazine), 34-35
BIG LIE, 127
Bilbo, Theodore, 46
BILDERBERGER GROUP, 72, 127-28
BILL OF RIGHTS, 5-6, 128. *See also* United States Constitution
BINGO CARDS, 128. *See also* BOUNCEBACK CARDS
Birth of a Nation, The (motion picture), 21, 37
Bishop, Maurice, 91
Bittman, Ladislav, 119, 156

BLACKLISTING, 128
BLACKOUT BOYS, 128
Black Panthers, 79
BLACK PROGRAM, 128. *See also* COVERT
BLACK PROPAGANDA, 128
Black theology, 197
Black Warrior (ship), 16
Blaine, James G., 23
Blair, Eric, 67
BLOWBACK, 128-29
BLOWING SMOKE, 129
Blue Book (FCC), 63
B'nai B'rith, 13. *See also* ANTI-DEFAMATION LEAGUE OF B'NAI B'RITH
Board of Censorship, 32
Boesky, Ivan, 133
Bogardus, Emory S., 47
BOLSHEVIK/BOLSHEVIKI, 129; and KGB, 196; portrayed in *Battleship Potemkin* (motion picture), 47; and Russian Revolution (1917), 39; tried for holding anti-Stalinist views (1936), 55; in World War I, 41, 42
bonds, sale of during World War II, 61
Bone, Homer T., 59
Bonner, Raymond, 87
Book of Mormon, The, 11
Book-of-the-Month Club, 48
book publishing industry, xiv, 56
Book Union, 53
Boorstein, Daniel, 237
Booth, John Wilkes, 19
BORKING, 129. *See also* McCARTHYISM
Bork, Robert, 92, 129
Bosnia-Herzegovina, 113, 161, 256
Boston Investigator (newspaper), 11, 12, 29-30
"Boston Massacre," 3
Boston News-Letter (newspaper), 2
Boston Port Act, 3
Boston Tea Party, 3
BOUNCEBACK CARDS, 130. *See also* BINGO CARDS; DIRECT MARKETING (DM)
BOURGEOIS, 130. *See also* CAPITALISM/CAPITALIST; FOURTH ESTATE
Bozell, L. Brent III, 204-5
BRAINWASHING, 130, 262. *See also* PSYCHOLOGICAL WARFARE

(PSYWAR)
Branch Davidians, 107
Brandywine-Main Line v. FCC (court case), 81
Brass Check, The (book), 44
Braun Center for Holocaust Studies, 123
Bremer, Arthur, 81
Breslin, Jimmy, 74
Brinkley, David, 59
Brinkley, John R., 51
Britain, 225; and American Revolution, 199-200; and Ireland, 191; and North Atlantic Treaty Organization, 219; as part of United Kingdom, 268; Statute of Jewry, xiii; and United States in World War II, 60; in World War I, 36, 140, 160; and Zimmerman telegram, 38. *See also* England; UK (or U.K.)
British Broadcasting Corporation (BBC), 96
British Institute of Public Opinion, 243
British Isles, 268
British Parliament, 3
British Secret Intelligence Service (SIS), 57, 208
British Security Service, 208
BROADCASTING, 49, 62, 131. *See also* Radio; TELECOMMUNICATIONS; TV
BROADCAST STANDARDS DEPARTMENTS, 130-31. *See also* CENSORSHIP
Bronstein, Lev, 39
Brooks, C. Wayland, 59
Broun, Heywood, 52
Browder, Earl, 47, 50, 54
Brown, Henry, 17
Brown, James Sutherland "Buster," 45
Brown, John, 18
Brownson, Orestes, 14
Bryan, William Jennings, 27, 28, 37
Bryant, Louise, 44
Buchanan Committee, 67
Buchanan, James, 17
"Bull Moose party," 33-34
Bulloch, James A., 16
Bullock, Roy, 109
Bureau of Alcohol, Tobacco and Firearms (BATF), 107
Bureau of Corporations Bill, 29
Burke, Edmund, 170
Burke, Kenneth, 53
Burns, Emile, 54
Burr, Aaron, 8

Burson, Harold, 71
Burson-Marsteller (public relations firm), 71
Burstyn v. Wilson (Supreme Court case), 69
Busch, Wilhelm, 19
Bush, George: 1980 election, 86; 1984 election, 90; 1988 election, 95; 1992 election, 105; assassination plot against, 110; and China, 97; and declaration of war on Kuwait, 100; and DESERT SHIELD, 153; and disinformation, 113; and DIVERT/ REFOCUS STRATEGY, 156; and IRAN-CONTRA INVESTIGATIONS, 148; and Iran hostage crisis, 106, 219; and International Covenant on Civil and Political Rights, 104; and Operation Weed and Seed, 145; and Panama, 97, 98; and Persian Gulf War, 100, 101, 103; and public access to information, 100, 103, 107; in public opinion polls, 100; and Somalia, 106
Butterfield Overland Mail, 18
Byoir, Carl, 39

Cable News Network (CNN), 85-86, 101, 112, 206
Cable Satellite Public Affairs Network (C-SPAN), 84, 148
Caddell, Mike, 98
Cadillac Motor Company, 36-37
CADRE, 131. *See also* VANGUARD
Caesar, Galerius, xi
California, gold rush, 14
Calvin, xv
camera marketed, 24
campaign, first popular political, 10
Canada, 3, 20, 21, 89, 104, 219; Conservative party in, 32; independence from Britain, 45; invasion by United States, 45; Liberal party in, 32
Canan, Penelope, 260
Cannibals All, or Slaves without Masters (book), 17
"Cannons of Journalism," 51
Capital Cities Communications, 91
CAPITALISM/CAPITALIST, 4, 131, 164
CAPITALIST ROADER, 131
Capra, Frank, 60, 91
Carmichael, Stokely, 76
Carnegie Commission, 77

Carnegie Endowment for International
  Peace, 32
Carnegie Steel Company, 26
CARPETBAGGERS, 131-32
Carroll, Raymond, 158
Carter, Jimmy: 1976 election, 83; 1980
  election, 86; and International
  Covenant on Civil and Political
  Rights, 104; and Iran hostage crisis,
  106, 219; on television (with Walter
  Cronkite), 84
cartoons, 46
Carto, Willis, 72-73, 229
Casey, William, 86, 219
Castro, Fidel, 73
Catholic Church, xiii, xv. *See also*
  Roman Catholic Church
Cato's Letters (newspaper
  commentaries), 2
Caxton, William, xiv
CBS Network, 49, 63, 94, 192, 206
Ceefax (teletext system), 81
CELL, 132
celluloid photofilm, invention of, 22
CENSORSHIP, 132, 257; and Abraham
  Lincoln, 19; in motion picture
  industry, 27, 32, 46, 50, 71; and
  public access, 238; and Radio Act of
  1927, 49; report on (1991), 100; and
  Smith Act, 58; *See also* FREE
  SPEECH; OFFICE OF CENSORSHIP;
  SPIKE; SPIRAL OF SILENCE
CENSORSHIP BY ASSASSINATION,
  132, 228
Center for the Advancement of Applied
  Ethics (Carnegie Mellon University),
  139-40
Center for Constitutional Rights, 181
Center for Investigative Reporting, 211
Center for Media and Public Affairs, 205
Center on Speech, Equality and Harm,
  108
Central America, 70-71, 84, 87, 93, 98,
  108, 222
*Central Hudson Gas & Electric Corp. v.
  Public Service Commission of New
  York*, 136
Central Intelligence Agency Act of 1949,
  187
CENTRAL INTELLIGENCE AGENCY
  (CIA), 132, 138, 187; and Alfredo
  Stroessner, 106; Conference on
  Contemporary Soviet Propaganda and

Disinformation, 232; and Congress of
  Cultural Freedom (CCF), 67; and
  espionage, 160; established (1947),
  64; examples of covert action, 147;
  and Manuel Noriega, 97; as member of
  intelligence community, 187; and
  MI6, 208; and nonprofit organizations
  as fronts, 77; and OFFICE OF
  STRATEGIC SERVICES (OSS), 220;
  and publishing agencies as fronts, 83;
  release of declassified Cold War-era
  documents, 111
CENTRAL POWERS, 132
CENTRIST, 132-33
Chamber of Commerce (national), 33
Chambers, Whittaker, 65-66
Chamorro, Violeta, 98, 109
Charlemagne, xii
Chase, Stuart, 47
"Chatham House," 43
Chauvin, Nicholas, 133
CHAUVINISM/CHAUVINIST, 133
CHECKBOOK JOURNALISM. *See*
  TABLOID JOURNALISM
Cheka (later KGB), 196
Chernenko, Konstantin, 91
Chesapeake & Ohio Railway--Nickel
  Plate Road, 62
Chiang Kai-shek, 63
Chicago, Haymarket Square Riot, 23
Chicago Tribune (newspaper), 38, 206
Chile, 74, 82, 150; elections, 80
CHILLING EFFECT, 133
China, xiv, 59, 64, 97, 223-24; and
  Communism, 137
Choctaw Nation, 11
Chomsky, Noam, 201, 234-35
Christianity, x, xi, xii, 197
Christian Leaders for Responsible
  Television (CLeaR-TV), 106
Christian Science Monitor (newspaper),
  206, 275
Christic Institute, 85
*Chronicle of a Death Foretold, A: The
  Jesuit Murders in El Salvador* (report),
  107
Church of Christ, 11
Church, Frank, 78, 147
Churchill, Winston, 37, 59, 62, 63, 126
CIA. *See* CENTRAL INTELLIGENCE
  AGENCY
CIRCUS, THE, 133
CITIZENS FOR AMERICA (CFA), 133

Citizens band (CB) radio, 83
Citizens for a Free Kuwait, 99, 103, 272
CIVIL RELIGION, 133-34
civil rights, 75, 96, 107-8, 122-23
Civil Rights Act (1968), 75, 78
Civil War (United States), 18-20, 143
Claflin, Tennessee, 22
CLANDESTINE, 134
CLANDESTINE RADIO STATIONS, 134
Clansman, The (motion picture), 37
Clanton, Gene, 246
Clark, D. Worth, 59
CLASSICAL LIBERALISM, 134
Clay, Henry, 9, 11, 12, 13-14, 274
Clayton Antitrust Act, 35
Clement, xiii
Cleveland, Grover, 23, 26
Clinton, Bill Interactive Kiosk, 104
Clinton, Bill (William Jefferson): 1992
    election, 105; first presidential
    Internet message, 108; inauguration,
    106; and lobbying regulation, 114;
    and NAFTA, 112; and NATIONAL
    INFORMATION INFRASTRUCTURE
    (NII), 212; and preservation of
    electronic messages (opposition to),
    111; and scandal (1992), 103; and U.S.
    troops in Somalia, 270
Cloward, Richard, 210
Clune, W.H., 37
CNN, 85-86, 101, 112, 206
COALITION, 134
Coalitions for America, 96
Code to Govern the Making of Talking,
    Synchronized and Silent Motion
    Pictures (booklet), 50
CODE WORDS, 134-35. *See also*
    EUPHEMISM; HIDDEN AGENDA;
    WEASEL WORDS
COERCIVE DIPLOMACY, 135
"Coercive and Intolerable Acts," 3
COGNITIVE DISSONANCE, 135
Cohan, George M., 39
Cohen, Jeff, 97
COINTELPRO (Counterintelligence
    Program), 73, 78, 81, 135
Colby, Bainbridge, 44
COLD WAR, 64, 98, 135
Cold War, The (book), 64
Collier's (magazine), 73
Colodny, Len, 103
Columbia Broadcasting System. *See* CBS
    Network

Columbus, Christopher, xiv-xv, 1
comic strips, 27, 31
Cominform, 64
COMINTERN, 43, 61, 64, 135-36, 228;
    Seventh Convention, 50; Sixth
    Convention, 49. *See also*
    COMMUNISM/COMMUNIST
COMMAND PROPAGANDA, 136
commerce, 165. *See also* FEDERAL
    TRADE COMMISSION (FTC)
COMMERCIAL SPEECH, 136
Commission on Freedom of the Press,
    195
Committee of Coal Mine Managers, 36
Committee on Interstate Commerce, 59
Committee on Patriotism through
    Education, 40
Committee on Public Doublespeak, 82
COMMITTEE ON PUBLIC
    INFORMATION (CPI or "CREEL
    COMMITTEE"), 39, 43, 136
Committee to Reelect the President, 273
Committee in Solidarity with the People
    of El Salvador (CISPES), 87
Committee for State Security, 196. *See*
    also KGB
Committees of Correspondence, 3, 102
Common Sense (pamphlet/book), 4
communication, early developments in,
    xiv
Communications Act of 1934, 131
COMMUNICATIONS INTELLIGENCE
    (COMINT), 137
COMMUNICOLOGY, 137
COMMUNISM/COMMUNIST, 44, 65,
    101, 119, 129, 137-8, 201-2. *See also*
    BOLSHEVIK/BOLSHEVIKI;
    Communist party; Communist Party of
    the United States of America (CPUSA);
    SOCIALISM/SOCIALIST
Communist (magazine), 49
Communist International. *See*
    COMINTERN
Communist Manifesto, The
    (pamphlet/book), 14, 21-22
Communist party members, 43, 45, 47,
    50, 68, 70, 131, 228; in film industry,
    52
Communist Party of the United States of
    America (CPUSA), 50, 58, 66, 101,
    104; membership, 52, 53. *See also*
    Communist party members
COMMUNITARIAN SOCIETY, 138

COMPANY, THE, 138
COMPOSITE REPORTING, 138
Comprehensive Anti-Apartheid Act
    (1986), 101
COMPUTER-AIDED DESIGN (CAD),
    138-39
COMPUTER-MEDIATED
    COMMUNICATION (CMC), 111, 139
Computers, used in typesetting, 74
Comrade (magazine), 29
CONDITIONING PROPAGANDA, 139.
    See also COMMAND PROPAGANDA
Confederate State of America, 18;
    Constitution of, 19
Conference Committee on
    Telecommunications Reform, 113-14
Conference on Contemporary Soviet
    Propaganda and Disinformation, 155,
    232
Confessions of a Nazi Spy (motion
    picture), 57
confidential information, 220
conflict, 199
CONFLICT RESOLUTION, 139-40, 244
CONFORMISTS, 140
confrontation, 116
Congress of the Communist
    International. *See* COMINTERN
Congress of Cultural Freedom (CCF), 67,
    77
Congress of Industrial Organizations
    (CIO), 52
Congressional Black Caucus, 112
Congressional Human Rights
    Foundation, 103, 153, 181
Conrad, Robert, 74
CONSPIRACY THEORIES, 140-41
Constitution Besieged, The (book), 25
Constitutional Union party, 18
consumer regulation, 26
Consumers Union of the United States,
    54
CONTAGION, 142-43. *See also*
    TERRORISM
Continental Congress, 3; Second, 4
CONTRAS, 109, 142, 147-48. *See also*
    IRAN-CONTRA INVESTIGATIONS
CONTROLLED MEDIA, 142
CONVENTIONAL WISDOM, 142. *See
    also* MEDIA BIAS
Cooley, Charles, 29
Coolidge, Calvin, 45, 46, 47, 48
Coors, Adolph Brewing Company, 258

Coors, Bill, 258
Coors, Joseph, 258
COPPERHEADS, 16, 143
Coppola, Francis Ford, 85
Cornwallis, Charles, 4
CORPORATE CAMPAIGN, 143
CORPORATE COMMUNICATIONS, 143.
    See also PUBLIC RELATIONS (PR)
CORPORATE SOCIAL RESPONSIBILITY
    (CSR), 143. *See also* ISSUES
    MANAGEMENT
Corporation for Public Broadcasting
    (CPB), 77, 79
Costello, Robert, 72
Coughlin, Charles Edward, 25, 55, 59,
    60, 84
COUNCIL ON FOREIGN RELATIONS
    (CFR), 45, 143-44
Council of Toulouse, xiii
Council of Trent, xv
COUNTERINSURGENCY, 144-45. *See
    also* rebellion
COUNTERINTELLIGENCE PROGRAM.
    See COINTELPRO
COUNTERPROPAGANDA, 145, 221
Counter-Reformation, xvi
COUNTERREVOLUTIONARY, 145-46.
    See also COUNTERINSURGENCY;
    REVOLUTION/REVOLUTIONARY
COUNTERTERRORISM, 146. *See also*
    ANTITERRORISM;
    COUNTERINSURGENCY;
    TERRORISM
COURT HISTORIANS, 146. *See also*
    PROPAGANDA
COURT OF PUBLIC OPINION, 146, 221.
    See also JUSTICE BY NEWS RELEASE
Cousins, Norman, 73
COVER STORY, 146
COVERT ACTION, 146-47
Covert Action (book), 74
COVERT, 146; compared to
    CLANDESTINE, 134
COVER-UP CROWD, 147
COWBOY OPERATION, 147
Cox, Earnest Sevier, 46
Cox, James M., 45
Crane, Stephen, 28
Crawford, William H., 9
"Creel Committee," 39, 43. *See also*
    COMMITTEE ON PUBLIC
    INFORMATION (CPI or "CREEL
    COMMITTEE")

Creel, George. *See* "Creel Committee"
Creelman, James, 28
CRIMINALIZATION OF POLICY
    DIFFERENCES, 147-48
CRITICAL ISSUE, 148
"Crittenden Compromise," 18
Croatia, 270
Croly, Herbert, 36
Cronkite, Walter, 78, 84
Crossen, Cynthia, 242
Crossley, Archibald, 51
Crusades, xii
Crystallizing Public Opinion (book), 46
C-SPAN (Cable Satellite Public Affairs
    Network), 84, 148
C-SPAN II, 92
Cuba, 16, 17, 74, 75, 83, 98-99
Cuban Missile Crisis, 75, 83. *See also*
    Bay of Pigs, Cuba
CULT, 148-49. *See also*
    BRAINWASHING
CULT OF PERSONALITY, 149
CULTURAL IMPERIALISM, 149
Cushing, Caleb, 16
Custer, George A., 22
CYBERNETICS, 149-150
CYBERSPACE, 150. *See also*
    INFORMATION AGE/INFORMATION
    SOCIETY; INTERNET;
    TELECOMMUNICATIONS
Cyrus, xi
Czolgosz, Leon, 29

Daley, Richard, 78
Dall, Caroline H., 16
DARK HORSE, 150
Darwin, Charles, 18
Das Kapital (book), 137
D'Aubuisson, Roberto, 108
David Walker's Appeal, in Four Articles
    (book), 10
Davies, Stephen, 180
Davis, Angela, 102
Davis, Elmer, 61, 220
Davis, Jefferson, 15, 18, 20
Davis, Paulina Wright, 16
Davis, Richard Harding, 28
Day, Benjamin, 12
Day, Stephen, 1
D-Day, Allied (World War II), 62
Dean, John, 103
DEATH SQUADS, 150
Debs, Eugene, 26, 40, 42, 275; 1900

election, 28; 1904 election, 30; 1912
    election, 34; 1920 election, 45
Declaration of Independence, 4, 6, 152
Declaration of Principles (news release)
    31
*Declaration of the Rights of Man and of
    the Citizen* (proclamation) 5
Declaration of the United Nations, 269
Deep Dish TV Network, 92
DEEP BACKGROUND, 150-51. *See also*
    OFF THE RECORD
DEEP POCKETS SPENDING, 151
Defense Intelligence Agency, 187
Deforest, Lee, 31
De Leon, Daniel, 25, 202, 247
Dellinger, David, 79
Delorita in the Passion Dance (motion
    picture), 27
DEMAGOGUE/DEMAGOGISM, 151. *See
    also* RHETORIC
DEMOCRACY, 151-52
Democratic National Committee (DNC),
    93, 273
Democratic National Convention (1968),
    78
DEMOCRATIC PARTY, 17, 152, 197,
    248; 1840 election, 13; 1860
    election, 18; 1884 election, 23; 1896
    election, 27; donkey symbol, 21; and
    women, 38
Democratic-Republican party, 6, 152,
    165
DEMOGRAPHICS, 153
DEMONIZING THE OPPOSITION, 152.
    See also FACT SLINGING
Denmark, 219
Dennis, Eugene, 61
Denton, Robert E., Jr., 210
Depression (1893), 26
Depression (1930s), 50, 213
Deseret, State of, 14-15
DESERT SHIELD, 99, 153, 254
DESERT STORM, 101, 153, 254
Design for Death (motion picture), 63
Deutch, John, 113
Developing nations, 265
Dewey, Thomas E., 66
DIAL GROUP, 153-54
Diamond Match Company, 25
Diamond Sutra (book), xiv
Dictes and Sayings of the Philosophers
    (book), xiv
Did Six Million Really Die? (booklet),

88
Dies, Martin, 56, 57
DIGITIZED PHOTOGRAPHY, 154. *See also* COMPUTER-AIDED DESIGN (CAD)
Diocletian, Emperor, xi
direct current (DC) electricity, 24
DIRECT ACTION, 154, 236
DIRECT CONFRONTATION, 154
DIRECT LOBBYING. *See* LOBBYING/LOBBYIST
DIRECT MARKETING (DM), 154-55
DIRECT-RESPONSE (DR) ADVERTISING, 155. *See also* BOUNCEBACK CARDS; INFOMERCIAL
DIRTY TRICKS CAMPAIGN, 155. *See also* STRUCTURED LEAKS
Discrimination Against Indigenous Peoples (report), 110
DISINFORMATION (DEZINFORMATSIA), 155-56, 271
DIVERT/REFOCUS STRATEGY, 156
Dixon, Thomas, 37
DOCUDRAMA, 156-57. *See also* DOCUMENTARY
DOCUMENT, 157. *See also* WHITE PAPERS
DOCUMENTARY, 60, 116, 158
Documercial, 185
Dodd, Christopher, 111
DOGMA, 158
Donation of Constantine (manuscript), xiii
Donnelly, Ignatius, 26
Donovan, William J. "Wild Bill," 220
Doonesbury (comic strip), 80
DOUBLESPEAK, 158. *See also* CODE WORDS; EUPHEMISM
DOUBLETHINK, 158
Douglas, Frederick, 119
Douglas, Stephen A., 17, 18
Dow Jones, 206
Dragnet (television program), 67
Dred Scott (court case), 17
Dreiser, Theodore, 51
Dresden, Germany, 236
DUAL LOYALIST, 158-59
DuBois, W.E.B., 73
Duffy, Ben, 70
Dukakis, Michael, 95
Duke, David, 86, 229
Dusenberry, Phil, 90

Dwight, Theodore, 9
DYSJOURNALISM, 159
DYSTOPIA, 159
Dzhugashvili, Joseph, 47. *See also* Stalin, Joseph

Eagleburger, Lawrence, 97
Early Bird (communication satellite), 76
East Timor Action Network/US, 107
East Timor: Turning a Blind Eye (video), 107
Eastman, George, 22
Eastman, Max, 33
Eaton, Cyrus, 261
Ebony (magazine), 62
Economic and Social Council of the United Nations, 219
Edison Company, 24
Edison, Thomas Alva, 22, 24, 26, 50
Edmondson, Robert Edward, 51
Educational Television and Radio Center, 69
Edward I (King of England), xiii
Edwards, Charles, 2
88 (neo-Nazi greeting meaning Heil Hitler), 159
Eisenhower, Dwight D., 70, 73
Eisenstein, Sergei, 47
El Mozote (El Salvador), 87, 108
El Salvador: civil war, 84, 87, 103, 108, 111; and DEATH SQUADS, 150; and Guatemala, 70; murder of Jesuit priests (1989), 98, 107; and Nicaragua, 109; United States involvement in, 84, 98, 107, 108
electricity, 24
electronic communication, 111, 139
ELECTRONIC COMMUNITY NETWORK, 159
ELECTRONIC DEMOCRACY, 159
ELECTRONIC PUBLISHING, 159
ELITE THEORY, 159-60
Emancipation Proclamation, 19
Emerson, Steven, 140
Emotional Development System, 96
Encyclopedia of American Facts and Dates (book), 36
ENGINEERING OF CONSENT, 160, 201
England, 121, 122. *See also* Britain
English Channel, 14
Enlightenment, xvi
ENTENTE, 160
Equal Rights Amendment, 275

ESPIONAGE, 160, 209. *See also*
  SPYING/SPYCRAFT
Essex, England, xiii-xiv
ESTABLISHMENT, THE, 161, 252. *See
  also* ELITE THEORY
ethics, 51, 92, 173; ethical concerns,
  30, 84, 143, 165, 200, 244, 266;
  ethical codes and standards, 138, 193
Ethiopia, 197; Italian invasion of, 54
ETHNIC CLEANSING, 161; ethnocide,
  110. *See also* GENOCIDE
ethnicity, 46, 99; ethnic cohesion, 46,
  ethnic fighting, 219; ethnic origins
  and group identity, 14, 32, 38, 158,
  161, 173, 180, 194, 222, 238, 245,
  246, 252, 256, 263
EUPHEMISM, 161. *See also* WEASEL
  WORDS
European Convention for the Protection
  of Human Rights and Fundamental
  Freedoms, 181
Executive Order 9835, 64
EXTRALEGAL CENSORSHIP, 161
EXTREMIST, 161-62. *See also*
  RADICAL; ZEALOTS

Fabian Society, 43
fabrications, 128
fact checking, 187
FACTION, 162; factions, 5, 7, 8, 11, 79,
  82, 150, 151, 162, 165, 189, 208,
  228, 231, 238, 248. *See also*
  INTEREST GROUPS/PRESSURE
  GROUPS
*Facts Concerning the Struggle in
  Colorado* (series of news releases), 36
Factsheet Five, viii
fact sheets, 206
FACT SLINGING, 162. *See also* AD
  HOMINEM ATTACK; DEMONIZING
  THE OPPOSITION
FAIR TRADE, 163. *See also* AMERICA
  FIRST; FREE TRADE
Fairchild/LeMaster (media training firm),
  258
Fairness and Accuracy in Reporting
  (FAIR), 97, 205
FAIRNESS DOCTRINE, 94, 162-63
FALSE FLAG OPERATIONS, 163-64. *See
  also* DISINFORMATION
  (DEZINFORRMATSIA)
Fan, David P., 182, 186
Faneuil Hall (Boston), 2

Faneuil, Peter, 2
Farabundo Marti National Liberation
  Front (FMLN), 103, 109, 111
Farnsworth, Philo, 49
Farrakhan, Louis, 48, 84, 89, 112, 113.
  See also Nation of Islam
FASCISM/FASCIST, 46, 55, 56, 164.
  See also FIFTH COLUMN; NATIONAL
  SOCIALISM/NAZISM
FDR (Franklin Delano Roosevelt), 61,
  164; 1920 election, 45; 1932
  election, 51; 1936 election, 55; 1944
  election, 62; and Atlantic Charter, 59;
  and British Secret Intelligence Service,
  57; death of, 63; and fireside chats, 52;
  New Deal, 52, 54; and UNITED
  NATIONS ORGANIZATION, 268-69;
  and World War II, 58, 60, 126; at
  Yalta, 62
Federal Bureau of Investigation (FBI),
  46, 73, 83, 187, 203
Federal Communications Act of 1934,
  162-63
FEDERAL COMMUNICATIONS
  COMMISSION (FCC), 58, 63, 90,
  164, 203, 262; and *Aryan Nations
  Hour* (radio program), 95; editorial
  policies, 67; established (1934), 52;
  and FAIRNESS DOCTRINE, 94, 162-
  63; and political advertising, 226; and
  radio, 85, 103, 106; and television
  development, 62, 65, 69, 104
Federal Council of Churches, 31-32, 67
Federal Election Campaign Act (FECA),
  164
FEDERAL ELECTION COMMISSION
  (FEC), 164, 226
Federal Emergency Management Agency
  (FEMA), 89
Federal Espionage Act, 39-40
Federal Radio Commission (FRC), 49,
  51, 164
Federal Reserve Act, 34
Federal Theater Project, 54, 57
Federal Trade Commission Act (1914),
  35, 165
FEDERAL TRADE COMMISSION (FTC),
  112, 165, 203
Federalist Papers (newspaper columns
  later collected into a book), 4-5
FEDERALIST PARTY, 4-5, 9, 164-65
FEEDING FRENZY, 165, 259. *See also*
  DYSJOURNALISM;

JOURNALISM/JOURNALIST
Fellowes, George W., 51
FENIAN BROTHERHOOD, 17, 20, 166
Fenton Communications, 96
Ferdinand V (King of Spain), xiv-xv
Ferraro, Geraldine, 90
Fessenden, Reginald, 31
Festinger, Leon, 73, 135
FIFTH COLUMN, 166. *See also*
    TRAITOR
Fight for Freedom Committee, 58, 59
FIGHTING WORDS, 166. *See also*
    AGITATION
Figueredo, Reinaldo, 108
Fillmore, Millard, 17
film, 35, 50; 16-millimeter, 48;
    industry, 58; invention of, 22. *See*
    also motion pictures
Film and Photo Leagues, 50
FINDING, 166
Finney, Joan, 229
FIRST AMENDMENT, 6, 37, 102, 166-
    67, 199, 203. *See also* CENSORSHIP;
    FREE SPEECH
First International, 22
First Zionist Congress, 276
Fisher, H.C. "Bud," 31
Fish, Hamilton, Sr., 60
Fitzhugh, George, 17
FLACK, 167
flag burning, 96
Flagg, James Montgomery, 39
FLAG WAVING, 167
Flaherty, Robert, 46
FLAME POSTS, 167
Flanagan, Hallie, 57
Fleishman, Doris, 43
FLOPPYBACK, 167
FLUFF EVENTS, 167
FLUTTER, 167
FM (frequency modulation) radio, 56, 62
Fogli d' Avvisi (newsletter), xvi
Ford Foundation, 69, 77
Ford, Gerald R., 83
Ford, James, 51
FOREIGN AGENTS REGISTRATION ACT
    (FARA), 56, 83, 168-69
FOREIGN AID, 169
Foreign Assistance Act of 1961, 166
For the People, 229
For the Rule of the Church Militant
    (papal bull), xv
Fort Erie, 20

Fort Henry, 9
Fort Sumter, 18
'49er Gold Rush, 14-15
Foss, Daniel A., 210
Foster, William Z., 50, 51
FOUNDATIONS, 169
Foundations of Leninism (book), 52
fountain pen, 23
"Four Freedoms," 59
FOUR P's OF THE MARKETING MIX,
    170
"Fourteen Points," 40
FOURTH ESTATE, 170
Fourth World, 265
Fox, John, xvi
Foxman, Abraham, 105
Fox TV Network, 206
FRAMING DEVICES, 170-71
Franco, Francisco, 54
France, 4, 6, 140, 160, 164, 219;
    revolution, 5
France, Vichy, 164
Franklin, Benjamin, 2, 14
Franklin, James, 2
Freedom House, 181
FREEDOM OF THE PRESS. *See* FIRST
    AMENDMENT; FREE SPEECH; PRESS
Freedom's Journal (newspaper), 9
Freeley, Austin, 130, 245
Freemasonry, 2, 3, 4. *See also* Scottish
    Rite of Freemasonry
Freeman (magazine), 68
Freemen, 276
Freenet, 159
free press, 2. *See also* FIRST
    AMENDMENT; PRESS
Free Radio Berkeley, 105
Free Soil party, 13, 17, 248
FREE SPEECH, 2, 6, 75, 102, 136, 171,
    238. *See also* FIRST AMENDMENT
FREETHINKERS, 171-72. *See also*
    LIBERTARIAN
FREE TRADE, 172, 267. *See also* FAIR
    TRADE
FREE WORLD, 172
Fremont, John C., 17
French Revolution, 6
Frente Zapatista de Liberacion Nacional
    (FZLN), 275
Freud, Sigmund, 28
Friendly, Fred, 69
FRIENDLY SUBVERSION, 172
Friends of Animals, 93-94

FRONT GROUPS/SATELLITE
ORGANIZATIONS, 119, 172
FSLN. *See* Sandinista National
Liberation Front (FSLN)
*Full Texts of Secret Treaties as Revealed
at Petrograd* (pamphlet), 41
FUNDAMENTALISM/FUNDAMENTAL-
IST, 173
"Fundamental Standard Interpretation:
Free Expression and Discriminatory
Harassment" (speech code), 99
Future Shock (book), 80

Gage, Lyman, 22
Galambos, Louis, 42
Gallup, George, 53
Gallup poll, 55, 57, 75, 84
Gannett Corporation, 31, 87, 206
Gardner, Henry J., 16
Garrison, William Lloyd, 10, 11
Garvey, Marcus Moziah, 46, 47-48
GATEKEEPER, 173
Gates, Robert, 111
GATT (General Agreement on Trade and
Tariffs), 111, 113
gay rights movement, 79
Gazeta (newspaper), xvi
Geisel, Theodor Seuss, 60, 63
General Agreement on Trade and Tariffs
(GATT), 111, 113
General Allotment Act, 24
General Electric Corp., 50, 206
Genêt, Edmond, 6
GENOCIDE, 61, 173. *See also* ETHNIC
CLEANSING
Gentiles, xi
George, Henry, 23-24
Gerard, Thomas J., 109
German Democratic Republic, 100
GERMANOPHOBIA, 173
Germany, 51, 56, 173; and FASCISM,
164; and NATIONAL
SOCIALISM/NAZISM, 213-14;
reunification, 98, 100; Weimar
Republic, 42; in World War I, 36; and
World War II, 57, 58, 60, 63
Gettlin, Robert, 103
Gibbons, Floyd, 38
Gillars, Mildred, 66
Gillman, Howard, 25
Gitlin, Todd, 170
Gitlow, Benjamin, 43
GLASNOST, 173-74, 225

GLITTERING GENERALITY. *See*
PROPAGANDA DEVICES
GLOBAL VILLAGE, 174
GLOBALISM, 174, 267. *See also*
ORWELLIAN TACTICS
Godwin, Mary Wollstonecraft, 6
Goebbels, Joseph, 50, 51, 63, 127, 214
Goldman, Emma ("Red Emma"), 31, 40,
44, 121
Goldwater, Barry, 76
Goldwyn, Sam, 65
Gorbachev, Mikhail, 91, 173, 225
Gordon, Thomas, 2
Gore, Al, 105, 112, 212
GOVERNMENT RELATIONS. *See*
PUBLIC AFFAIRS
GPU (formerly KGB), 196
gramophone disk, 24
"Grand Old Party (GOP)," 22, 248. *See
also* REPUBLICAN PARTY
GRANFALLOONS, 174
Grangers, 20
Grant, Ulysses S., 19, 21
GRASSROOTS LOBBYING, 174-75. *See
also* LOBBYING/LOBBYIST
GRASSROOTS POLITICAL ACTION, 175
GRASSTOPS, 175-76. *See also*
GRASSROOTS LOBBYING
GRAY/GREY LITERATURE, 176
GRAY/GREY PROPAGANDA, 176. *See
also* BLACK PROPAGANDA; WHITE
PROPAGANDA
Gray, Harold, 46
"Great Awakening," 2
Great Britain. *See* Britain; England
Great Depression, 50, 213
"Great Famine" (in Ireland), 14
Great Peace Marchers, 91
GREAT WAR, 176. *See also* World War I
Greece, 219
Greeley, Horace, 13
Greenback party, 22
Greenpeace, 104
Gregory the Great, xiii
Gregory XV (Pope), xvi
Grenada, 89, 248, 254
Griffith, D.W., 37
Griswold, Denny, 243
GROSS RATINGS POINTS (GRPs), 176.
See also REACH
GRU (Glavnoye Razvedyvatelnoye
Upravlenie), 176
Grunig, James E., 243-44

Guardian (newspaper), 65, 72, 104
Guatemala, 70-71, 109-110
Gulf of Tonkin, 75
Gutenberg, Johann, xiv

Hadrian, Emperor, xi
Hagglund, Joel, 37
Hainsworth, Brad, 194
Haiti, 37, 102, 104-5, 112, 230, 255
Hale, Ruth, 52
Haley, Alex, 84
Haley, Bill and the Comets, 72
Hall, Gus, 102
Hall, Prince, 4
Hamilton, Alexander, 4, 134, 165
Hamilton, Andrew, 2
Hamilton, Lee, 106
Hammer, Armand, 104
Handbook of Marxism, A (book), 54
Handler, Joel F., 240
HANDLERS, 176
HANDOUT JOURNALISM, 177
Hanegraaff, Hendrik "Hank," 148
Hannah, John, 77
Hanna, Mark, 27-28
Harder, Chuck, 229
Hardie, James, 6
Harding, Warren G., 45, 46
Harman, Gilbert, 198
Harper Brothers, 9
Harpers Ferry, Virginia, 18
Harper's Weekly (magazine), 25
Harrison, William Henry, 12-13, 274
Hartford Convention, 9
Harvard College, 1
Harvard University, 32
Harwood, Richard, 88
Hashishans, 125
HATE CAMPAIGN, 177. *See also*
   DEMONIZING THE OPPOSITION
HATE CRIME LEGISLATION, 177
Hate Crimes Statistics Act, 99
HATE GROUPS, 177
HATE SPEECH, 102, 177-78. *See also*
   FREE SPEECH; FIRST AMENDMENT
Hayden, Tom, 79
Haymarket Square Riot (Chicago), 23, 24
Hays, Will H., 50; and "Hays Office"
   representing motion picture industry,
   46, 53
Haywood, "Big Bill," 30, 45, 49, 275
HBO (Home Box Office), 81
health care issue, 101

Hearst, William Randolph, 27, 31, 32,
   275
HEARTS AND MINDS CAMPAIGN, 178
Heath/Nelson Model of Activist
   Movement Development, 115-16
Heath, Robert L., 115-16, 184
Hebrews, Diaspora of, xi
Hefner, Hugh, 71
HEGEMONY, 178-79
Heinrichs, E.H., 24
Heinz, Henry J., 26
Helms, Richard, 209
Helsinki Watch, 181
Hennock, Frieda, 69
Hepburn Act, 30
Heritage Front Hotline, 110
Herman, Edward S., 204, 234-35
Hersh, Seymour, 211
Herzl, Theodore, 276
Hess, Rudolf, 46
HEURISTIC, 179. *See also*
   PROPAGANDA DEVICES
Heywood, Ezra H., 22
HIDDEN AGENDA, 179
HIDDEN PERSUADERS, 179. *See also*
   PUBLIC RELATIONS (PR)
Higher Laws (pamphlet), 94
High Performance Computer and
   Communications Initiative (HPCCI),
   212
Highway Beautification Act, 76
Hill & Knowlton (public relations
   agency), 99, 103, 169, 272
Hill, Joe, 37-38
Hill, Lewis, 66-67
HILL, THE, 179
Hippler, Fritz, 91
Hiroshima, Japan, 63
Hiss, Alger, 65-66, 67-68, 89, 105, 271
Hitler, Adolf, 44, 46, 51, 56, 127, 159,
   213
Hitler Lives (motion picture), 63
Ho Chi Minh, 124
Hoffman, Abbie, 79
Hoffman, Julius, 79
"Hogan's Alley" (comic strip), 27
Hogan, William, 16
Holland, 219
Hollywood Anti-Nazi League, 55, 56
Holocaust, 84, 88, 109, 112, 249
Holocaust Memorial Museum, 109
Home Box Office (HBO), 81
Homestead Strike (against Carnegie Steel

Company), 26
homosexuality, 106
Honduras, 70
Honest Money League, 22
HOOKS, 179. See also ADVERTISING
Hook, Sydney, 66
Hoover, Herbert, 49, 51
Hoover, J. Edgar, 46, 75
Horton, Willie, 95
Hostage crisis (in Iran), 86, 106, 219
HOT SWITCHING, 179
House, Edward Mandel, 33, 39
HOUSE UN-AMERICAN ACTIVITIES
    COMMITTEE (HUAC), 64, 65, 73,
    179-80; and Alger Hiss, 65, 67; and
    Federal Theater Project, 57; and
    motion picture industry, 56, 58, 64;
    and radio programming, 73; and
    Whittaker Chambers, 65
Hughes, Charles Evans, 38
Hughes, David, 17
HUMAN NATURE, 180
HUMAN RIGHTS, 180-82. See also
    UNIVERSAL DECLARATION OF
    HUMAN RIGHTS
Human Rights Advocates, 181
Humphrey, Hubert H., 78-79
Hungers Lodges, 12
Hunt, E. Howard, 81
Hunt, Todd, 243-44
Hurley, Edward N., 35
Hussein, Saddam, 99, 100, 101, 110,
    153, 204
Huxley, Aldous, 75
Hyde, Henry, 106
HYPE, 182
HYPODERMIC NEEDLE THEORY, 182

Iceland, 219
Ickes, Harold, 57
Iconoscope tube, 46
IDEODYNAMICS, 182
IDEOLOGUES, 182
IDEOLOGY, 182-84. See also OFFICIAL
    IDEOLOGY
I.F. Stone's Weekly
    (newsletter/magazine), 71
If You Love This Planet (motion picture),
    88
Ignatius of Loyola, xv
I Led Three Lives (book and television
    program), 70
Illinois, 1858 Senate debates, 17

Illuminati Order, 3, 9
Illustrations of Freemasonry (book), 9
IMAGE ADVERTISING, 184. See also
    ADVERTISING
immigration (to America), 14, 21
Imminent Dangers to the Free
    Institutions of the United States
    through Foreign Immigration (book),
    12
Impartial Administration of Justice Act,
    3
IMPERIALISM/IMPERIALIST, 184-85.
    See also MANIFEST DESTINY
INACTIVES, 185
incandescent lamp, 23
Independence party, 32
Independent National party, 22
"Indian Wars," 21
INDIRECT LOBBYING. See
    GRASSROOTS LOBBYING;
    LOBBYING/LOBBYIST
Indochina, 59
INDOCTRINATION, 130, 185
Indonesia, 107
Industrial Revolution, 4
INDUSTRIAL THEATER, 185
Industrial Union, 26, 229
INDUSTRIAL WORKERS OF THE
    WORLD (IWW). See WOBBLIES
industrialism, 20
Infact (newsletter), 58, 68
INFOMERCIAL, 185-86. See also
    DIRECT-RESPONSE ADVERTISING
INFON, 186
INFORMATION AGE/INFORMATION
    SOCIETY, 186, 213. See also GLOBAL
    VILLAGE
information highway, 212. See also
    INTERNET; NATIONAL
    INFORMATION INFRASTRUCURE
    (NII)
INFOSHOPS, 186-87
INFOTAINMENT, 187
Ingersoll, Robert G., 12, 24, 172
INK. See PUBLICITY
Inquiry into the Nature and Causes of the
    Wealth of Nations, An (book), 4
Inside PR (magazine), 243
INSIDERS, 187
Institute of Communication Research, 64
Institute for Historical Review, 84, 87,
    90
Institute for Humane Studies, 134

Institute of International Affairs, 43
Institute for Media Analysis (IMA), 205
Institute of Pacific Relations (IRP), 69,
    70
Institute for Policy Innovation, 106
INSURRECTION/INSURRECTIONARY,
    187
Intelligence Authorization Act for Fiscal
    Year 1991, 147, 166
INTELLIGENCE COMMUNITY, 132,
    187-89
Intercollegiate Socialist Society, 30
INTEREST GROUPS/PRESSURE
    GROUPS, 115, 189, 209, 231
Internal Revenue Code, 219
Internal Revenue Service (IRS), 93;
    Regulations, 175, 219
International Association of Business
    Communicators (IABC), 243
International Association for Cultural
    Freedom, 77
International Bible Students
    Association, 34-35
International Centre Against
    Censorship, 181
International Commission for the Study
    of Communication Problems, 218
International Convention on the
    Elimination of All Forms of Racial
    Discrimination, 246
International Covenant on Civil and
    Political Rights (ICCPR), 104, 180
International Covenant on Economic,
    Social and Cultural Rights, 181
International Frequency Registration
    Board (IFRB), 99
International Human Rights Law Group,
    181
International Jewish Boycott
    Conference, 52
International Labor Organization, 181
International Labour Office (ILO), 219
International League for Human Rights,
    181
International Military Tribunal, 63
International Monetary Fund, 214-15
International News Service, 73
International Organization of Journalists
    (IOJ), 91
International Public Relations
    Association (IPRA), 243
International Publishers, 47, 50, 52, 54
International Socialist Review

(magazine), 28-29, 33
International Telecommunication Union
    (ITU), 19, 99
International Working People's
    Association, 23
INTERNET, 108, 114, 159, 189-90. See
    also CYBERSPACE;
    TELECOMMUNICATIONS
Internet Service Providers, 114
Interpretation of Dreams (book), 28
Interstate Commerce Act (1887), 24, 44
Interstate Commerce Commission, 24
INTERVENTIONIST, 190. See also
    IMPERIALISM/IMPERIALIST
INTIFADA, 190. See also
    ZIONISM/ZIONIST
INVISIBLE GOVERNMENT, 190. See
    also ELITE THEORY;
    ESTABLISHMENT
Iran, 71, 85, 92, 219; hostage crisis, 86,
    106, 219
IRAN-CONTRA INVESTIGATIONS, 86,
    88, 91, 92, 190-91, 253; and George
    Bush, 147-48; public support for
    Oliver North, 93. See also CONTRAS
Iraq: assassination plot against former
    President George Bush, 110; and
    MEDIA BIAS, 204; Persian Gulf War,
    99, 100, 101, 110, 153; and
    PROPAGANDA OF THE DEED, 236
Ireland, xii, 14, 17, 166, 191; potato
    crops, 14
Irish Church, xii
IRISH NORTHERN AID COMMITTEE
    (NORAID), 80, 191
Irish Republic, 191
Irish Republican Army (IRA), 166
"Iron Curtain," 63
Irwin, Will, 32-33
Isabella I (Queen of Spain), xiv-xv
Islam, x, xii. See also Nation of Islam
Isle of Man, 268
ISOLATIONIST, 120, 191
Israel, 66, 92; and ANTI-DEFAMATION
    LEAGUE OF B'NAI B'RITH, 122-23;
    attack on U.S.S. Liberty (ship), 77;
    conquered by Assyrians, x-xi;
    foundations of, 40; and INTIFADA,
    190; and MOSSAD, 69, 209; and
    NESHER, 215; and Palestinian
    Liberation Organization, 111; and
    ZIONISM, 276
Israelites, x

ISSUE, 191
ISSUE ACTION PLANS, 191-92
ISSUE ADVERTISING, 192
ISSUE CAMPAIGNS, 192-93
ISSUE EVALUATION, 193. *See also*
  PUBLIC AFFAIRS
ISSUE SCANNING, 193. *See also* SWOT
  ANALYSIS
ISSUES MANAGEMENT, 193-94. *See*
  also PUBLIC OPINION
Italy: and Benito Mussolini, 46; and
  FASCISM, 164; invasion of Ethiopia,
  54; and NORTH ATLANTIC TREATY
  ORGANIZATION, 219; and
  PROPAGANDA-2, 236; Renaissance
  in, xiii; and World War I, 160; and
  World War II, 58, 60, 63
IWW. *See* WOBBLIES

Jackson, Andrew, 9, 10, 11, 152, 274
Jackson, Jesse, 89
Jacobins, 6
James I (King), xiii
Japan, 56, 58, 59, 63, 160, 168-69; U.S.
  embargo, 59
JAPAN BASHING, 194. *See also* AD
  HOMINEM ATTACK; DEMONIZING
  THE OPPOSITION;
  RACIST/RACIALIST/RACIAL
  DISCRIMINATION
Japanese-Americans, relocation during
  World War II, 61
Jay, John, 4
Jazz Singer, The (motion picture), 49
Jefferson, Thomas, 6, 7, 8, 152, 165,
  198
Jehovah's Witnesses, 38, 40
Jerome, V.J., 120
Jerusalem, xi, xii
Jesuits, xv, 107, 108
Jesus Christ, xi, 197
Jewish Defense League, 87, 90
Jewish organizations, 51-52
Jews, x-xi; and ANTI-DEFAMATION
  LEAGUE OF B'NAI B'RITH, 34, 122-
  23; and ANTI-SEMITISM, 123-24; and
  Khalid Abdul Muhammad, 112; public
  opinion of, 105; and SCAPEGOATING
  (origin of the term), 252; and
  ZIONISM, 276
Jews and Their Lies, The (book), xv
J.F.K. (motion picture), 102
Jim Crow laws, 21

Joan of Arc, xiv
John (King of England), xiii
John Reed Clubs, 49-50, 53
Johnson, Andrew, 20
Johnson, Hiram, 39
Johnson, Lyndon B., 75, 76, 78
"Joint Committee on Reconstruction,"
  20
JOINT U.S. PUBLIC AFFAIRS OFFICE
  (JUSPAO), 76, 194
JOURNALISM/JOURNALIST, 194-96.
  See also PRESS
Jowett, Garth, 235-36
Joyce, William, 31
Judah, xi
Judaism, x, xi
Judea, xi
JUSTICE BY NEWS RELEASE, 196. *See*
  also ORCHESTRATED PROPAGANDA
  CAMPAIGN

Kahl, Gordon, 88-89
KAL 007 (Korean Airlines), 88, 105
Kallan, Richard, 216
Kansas-Nebraska Act (1854), 16
Kautilya (Indian strategist), x
KAYE-AM radio (Payallup, Washington),
  82
Kaye, Danny, 87
KDKA-AM radio (Pittsburgh), 45
Keller, Helen, 30
Kelley, Jack, 74
Kendall, Amos, 10
Kennedy, John F., 73, 74, 75, 82, 102
Kennedy, Joseph, 57
Kennedy, Robert, 78
Kennen, George, 64
Kent, England, xiii-xiv
Kent State University (Ohio), 80
Kerensky, Alexander, 38
Kerner Commission, 78
Kerr, Charles H. and Company, 29
Key, Francis Scott, 9
Keynes, John Maynard, 43
KGB (Komitet po Gosudarstvennoy
  Bezopasnosti), 73, 187, 196, 261
Khaldun, ibn, xii
Khrushchev, Nikita, 82
Kinetoscope, 24
King, Martin Luther, Jr., 72, 75, 78,
  113, 140; "I Have a Dream" speech, 75
King, Rufus, 9
Kirk, Russell, 14

Kitson, Frank, 237-38
Klan, The: A Legacy of Hate in America
   (motion picture), 87
Klanwatch Project, 84, 87
KNEE-CAPPING, 196
Kneeland, Abner, 11, 12, 172
Knights of the Golden Circle, 16, 20,
   143
Know-Nothing party, 16, 120, 248
Kodak (company), 48
Koenig, Friedrich, 8
Kohlberg, Alfred, 63, 68
Komesar, Neil D., 240
Koran (book), xii
Korea, lobbyists from, 168
Korean War, 71, 130; American
   prisoners of war, 69, 104; United
   States casualties, 71
Koresh, David, 107
Koster & Bial's Music Hall, 28
Kotler, Philip, 255
KPPC-FM radio (Los Angeles), 76
Kristallnacht, 56
KSAN-FM radio (San Francisco), 76
Kuhn, Loeb & Company, 45
KUHT-TV (Houston), 71
Ku Klux Klan (KKK): and *Birth of a
   Nation* (motion picture), 37; founded
   (1867), 20-21; and Klanwatch Project,
   84, 87; membership in, 48, 75, 77,
   88, 98; in Oklahoma, 46
Kuwait, 99, 100, 101, 110, 153, 169,
   272
KZZI radio (Utah), 95

Labor Herald (magazine), 47
Labor Reform party, 21
Laconia (ship), 38
Lafayette, Marquis de, 7
Landon, Alf, 55
Land Reform party, 17
Larkin, Ralph, 210
LaRouche, Lyndon, 90, 95, 187-88, 274
Larry King Show (radio and television
   program), 112
Lasker, Albert, 45
Lasswell, Harold Dwight, 49, 66, 160
Latin America, and United States, 144
Latter-day Saints. *See* Mormon Church
LAUNCHING A NUKE, 196. *See also*
   POLISPOTS
Laurier, Wilfrid, 32
Law No. 191, 62

Lawyers Committee for Human Rights,
   106-7
Laxalt, Paul, 92
League of American Writers, 53
League to Enforce Peace, 38
League of Nations, 38
League of United Latin American Citizens
   (LULAC), 50
Leahy, Patrick, 111
LEAKS. *See* STRUCTURED LEAKS
Lear, William, 49
Lease, Mary Ellen, 26
LEAST OBJECTIONABLE
   PROGRAMMING (LOP) THEORY,
   196. *See also* BROADCASTING; TV
Lebanon, 190
Lee, Alfred McClung, 234
Lee, Elizabeth, Briant, 234
Lee, Ivy, 29, 30-31, 35-36, 52
Lee, Martin A., 205
Lee, Robert E., 19
LEFT-WING/LIBERAL, 197, 232
Lemkin, Raphael, 61, 173
L'Enfant, Pierre Charles, 5
Lenin, Nicolai (V.I.), 25, 225; and
   Bolshevik revolution (1917), 39, 129;
   and COMINTERN, 135; and
   Communism, 137; death of, 46-47;
   and Joseph Stalin, 46-47; and terror,
   202
Leo III (Pope), xii
Leuchter, Fred, 88, 112
Levaco, Ron, 97
Lewis, John L., 57
Liberal party, 25
Liberalism, 231
LIBERATION MOVEMENT, 197. *See
   also* ARMED STRUGGLE
LIBERATION THEOLOGY, 197
Liberator, The (magazine), 11, 41, 47
Liberia, 9. *See also* slavery
LIBERTARIAN, 197-98, 251. *See also*
   REVISIONISM/REVISIONIST
Liberty Lobby, 72-73, 229
Liberty Magazine, 23, 55
Liberty party, 13
Liddy, G. Gordon, 103
Life (magazine), 55, 81
Lifton, Robert Jay, 265
light bulb, electric, 50
LIGHTENING RODS, 198
Limbaugh, Rush, 175
Lincoln, Abraham, 17-19, 22, 143, 248

Lindbergh, Charles A., Sr., 34
Lindbergh, Charles, Jr., 49, 57-58, 59
Linebarger, Paul, 238
Lippmann, Walter, 46; *The Cold War*
    (book), 64; death of, 83; *New Republic*
    (magazine), 36; organization of first
    Socialist Club (Harvard), 32; *Public
    Opinion* (book), 46; and WOBBLIES,
    30; and Woodrow Wilson's "Fourteen
    Points," 40
lithography, 8
Little Big Horn, Battle of, 22
Little, Frank, 41
Little Katy; or, the Hot Corn Girl (play),
    16-17
"Little Orphan Annie" (comic strip), 46
Live Aid (concert), 91
Living Newspaper, The (theatrical
    group), 54
LOBBYING/LOBBYIST, 73, 112, 114,
    115, 198-99. *See also* ADVOCACY
    ADVERTISING; FOREIGN AGENTS
    REGISTRATION ACT (FARA);
    GRASSROOTS LOBBYING
Loew's Inc., 206
Log Cabin (newspaper), 13
London, Jack, 30
Long, Huey, 54
long-playing records (LPs), 65
"Lord Haw Haw," 31
Look (magazine), 55, 81
Lorenz, Pare, 54, 56
Los Angeles Times (newspaper), 206
Lovejoy, Elijah, 12
LOW-INTENSITY CONFLICT (LIC)/LOW-
    INTENSITY WARFARE (LIW), 199
Loyal Publication Society, 19
LOYALIST, 199-200
Loyalty Board, 64
LOYALTY OATH, 200
"Loyalty Order," 64
Luddite Rebellions, 8-9
Ludlow Massacre, 35-36
Lumpkin, Grace, 71
Lusitania (ship), 37
Luther, Martin, xv
Luxembourg, 219
Lyon, Matthew, 7-8

MacArthur, Douglas, 39, 53, 69
MacArthur, John R., 102-3
MacBride, Sean, 86; and *MacBride
    Report* (report), 218

MACHIAVELLIAN, 200
Machiavelli, Niccolo, 200
MacLaine, Shirley, 215
MacLeish, Archibald, 60
Madison, James, 4, 5, 151, 162, 231
magazines, and color printing, 21
MAGIC BULLET THEORY, 200-201. *See
    also* MEDIA EFFECTS
Magna Charta (document), xiii
magnetic audio recording tape, 61
mail, political, 93
mail service, 18, 34
Malan, Magnus, 94
Man with the Golden Arm, The (motion
    picture), 72
"Management of Public Diplomacy
    Relative to National Security
    (SECRET)," 88
MANDARINS, 201
Manhattan Project, 220
MANIFEST DESTINY, 14, 201
MANUFACTURING OF CONSENT (or
    CONSENSUS), 201
*Many Voices One World: Report of the
    MacBride Commission*, 86, 218
Mao Tse-tung, 124-25, 224, 237-38,
    240-50; and Communism, 137
Marcellus, Tom, 248
MARCH OF PROVOCATION, 201. *See
    also* AGITATION
March of Time (broadcast and motion
    picture), 53
"March on Washington for Jobs and
    Freedom," 75
March for Women's Lives, 103
Marconi, Guglielmo, 27, 29
Marsden, George M., 173
Marshall, Edward, 28
Marshall, George C., 60
Marsteller, William, 71
Marvin, Thomas O., 28
Marx, Karl, 23, 137, 201-2, 246
Marxism, 48, 54, 129, 197
MARXIST, 201-2, 225, 249. *See also*
    COMMUNISM/COMMUNIST;
    SOCIALISM/SOCIALIST
Mason Book, 2
Mason, George, 134
Mason, John Y., 17
MASS COMMUNICATION, 118, 202,
    203, 207, 230. *See also* media;
    TELECOMMUNICATIONS; *and related
    topics*

MASS TERROR, 202. *See also*
    COMMUNISM/COMMUNIST;
    TERRORISM
Massachusetts Bay Regulatory Act, 3
Masses, The (magazine), 33, 34, 41
matchbooks (in advertising), 25-26
Matchett, Charles, 26
*Mathematical Theory of Communication,
    The* (book), 66
"Max and Moritz" (comic strip), 19
Mayflower case (FCC decision), 58
Maynard, Bob, 88
McCarran, Pat, 69; and McCarran
    Committee, 69; and McCarran
    (Internal Security) Act, 68; and
    McCarran-Walter Act, 70, 72
McCarthy, Dwight, 95
McCarthy, E. Jerome, 170
McCarthy, Joseph, 63, 68, 72, 200
McCARTHYISM, 200. *See also*
    COMMUNISM/COMMUNIST; HOUSE
    UN-AMERICAN ACTIVITIES
    COMMITTEE; RED-BAITING
McClure, Samuel S., 23
McClure's Magazine, 26, 29, 50
McCombs, Maxwell E., 118
McDonald, John A., 25
McDonald, Larry, 88
McFarland, Ernest W., 59
McFarlane, Robert, 91
McGovern, George, 81
McGraw-Hill (publishing company), 94
McKinley, William, 27, 28, 29
McLuhan, Marshall, 174
McNamara affair, 33
McWilliams, Carey, 73
Mechling, Elizabeth W., 210
media, 5, 200-201. *See also related
    topics*
Media Alliance, 97
MEDIA BIAS, 202-5
MEDIACRACY, 205. *See also*
    PERCEPTION MANAGEMENT; SPIN
    DOCTORS
MEDIA EFFECTS, 205-6. *See also*
    HYPODERMIC NEEDLE THEORY;
    MAGIC BULLET THEORY
MEDIA ELITE, 206
MEDIA KIT, 206
MEDIA LITERACY, 206-7
MEDIA MANIPULATION. *See* MEDIA
    BIAS; MEDIA EFFECTS
MEDIA/MEDIUM, 207-8. *See also*

BROADCASTING;
    JOURNALISM/JOURNALIST
media release, 217
Medina, xii
Medrano, Juan Ramon, 111
Meiklejohn Civil Liberties Institute, 181
Mein Kampf (book), 46
MEMORY HOLE, 208. *See also*
    ORWELLIAN TACTICS
Meng, Max, 194
Mennonites, 21, 138
Mensheviks, 129
Mermelstein, Mel, 87
Merriam, Frank Finley, 52
Methodist Foundation of Social Service,
    31
Metzger, Tom, 88, 89
Mexican-American War, 14
Mexico, 14, 32, 113, 169, 211, 275
Meyers, Cortland, 27
Michaelis, George V.S., 28
Michelman, Kate, 96
Michigan State University, 77
MI5, 208
MILITARISM, 208
Mill, John Stuart, 18
Miller v. California (court case), 82
Million Man March (1995), 113
Mills, C. Wright, 160
Mills, John Stuart, 171
Milton, John, 1
Ministry of Propaganda and Public
    Enlightenment, 51, 214
Minnesota Advocates for Human Rights,
    181
Minnow, Newton, 74
Miracle decision (Supreme Court case),
    69
MI6, 187, 208
Missiles of October (television
    docudrama), 82
Mississippi Burning (motion picture),
    96
Missouri Compromise, 9, 16. *See also*
    Slavery
Mitchell, Alexander, 22
Mitnick, Barry M., 241
MKULTRA, 208-9. *See also*
    PSYCHOLOGICAL WARFARE
    (PSYWAR)
mobilization, 116
Mohammed, xii
Molly Maguires, 14

Mondale, Walter, 86, 90
Monroe Doctrine, 9
Monroe, James, 9
Moody's Magazine, 31
Moon is Blue, The (motion picture), 71
Moon, first manned landing, 79
Morgan, J.P. & Company, 45
Morgan, William, 9
Mormon Church (officially, Church of Jesus Christ of Latter-day Saints), 13-15
Mormons, The; or, Knavery Exposed (book), 13
Morse, Samuel F.B., 12, 13
MOSCOW CENTER, 209
Mossadeq, Mohammed, 71
MOSSAD ("INSTITUTE"), 69, 187, 209
Most, Johan, 23
Mother Earth (magazine), 31, 40
motion picture industry, 32, 53, 56, 59, 64. *See also* motion pictures; *and related topics*
Motion Picture Association of America (MPAA), 111
Motion Picture Producers and Distributors of America, 50
Motion Picture Production Code, 79. *See also* Hays, Will H.
motion pictures, 24, 28, 37, 49, 56; attendance at, 68-69; newsreel, 32. *See also* motion picture industry
MOUTHPIECE, 209
movable metal type, xiv
MOVEMENT, 115, 209-11. *See also specific types*
moving pictures. *See* Motion pictures
Moyers, Bill, 91
Mozambique, 197
Ms. Magazine, 81
MUCKRAKERS, 26, 211
Muhammad, Elijah, 75
Muhammad, Khalid Abdul, 112
Munn v. Illinois (court case), 22
Muqaddimah (book), xii
Murphy, Richard, 111
Murrow, Edward R., 58, 69, 72, 76
Muslims, x, xii. See also Islam
Mussolini, Benito, 46, 164
Mutual Film Corporation v. Industrial Commission of Ohio (Supreme Court case), 37, 69
Mutual Radio Network, 55
"Mutt and Jeff" (comic strip), 31

MVD (formerly KGB), 196

Nader, Ralph, 80, 95, 211
NAFTA, 111-12, 113, 169, 211-12. *See also* FREE TRADE
Nagasaki, Japan, 63
Nagelschmidt, Joseph: and CRITICAL ISSUES, 148; and GRASSROOTS POLITICAL ACTION, 175; and INTEREST GROUPS, 189; and ISSUE ACTION PLANS, 191-92; and ISSUE EVALUATION, 193; and POLITICAL ACTION COMMITTEES, 226; and PUBLIC AFFAIRS, 239
Nanook of the North (motion picture), 46
narcotics, 237
NARROWCASTING, 212. *See also* DIRECT MARKETING (DM); SPECIALTY ADVERTISING
Nast, Thomas, 21, 22
Nation (magazine), 206
Nation of Islam, 84, 89, 113. *See also* Farrakhan, Louis
National Abortion Rights Action League (NARAL), 96
National Advisory Commission on Civil Disorder, 78
National Americanization Committee, 36
National Archives, 90
National Association for the Advancement of Colored People (NAACP), 29, 37, 112
National Association for the Advancement of White People (NAAWP), 86
National Association of Manufacturers (NAM), 27, 35
National Board of Censorship of Motion Pictures/National Board of Review of Motion Pictures, 32
National Board for Historical Service, 40
National Broadcasting Company (NBC), 48, 61, 63, 94, 206
National Commission on the Causes and Prevention of Violence, 78
National Committee to Abolish the House Committee on Un-American Activities, 74
National Committee Against Repressive Legislation (NCARL), 74
National Committee for the Defense of Political Prisoners, 51
National Council of Churches, 67

National Council of Teachers of English, 82

National Developmental Conference on Forensics, 124

National Education Association, 40

National Farmer's Alliance, 26, 229

National Film Board of Canada, 88

National Foreign Intelligence Board (NFIB), 187

National Guardian (newspaper), 65

National Industrial Security Program Operating Manual, 103

NATIONAL INFORMATION INFRASTRUCTURE (NII), 212-13. *See also* COMPUTER-MEDIATED COMMUNICATION (CMC); CYBERSPACE; ELECTRONIC COMMUNITY NETWORK; INTERNET

NATIONAL INTELLIGENCE COUNCIL (NIC), 213. *See also* CENTRAL INTELLIGENCE AGENCY (CIA); NATIONAL SECURITY COUNCIL (NSC)

National Intelligence Estimates (NIEs), 187

National Labor Reform party, 21

National Legion of Decency, 52-53

National Opposition Union (UNO), 98

National Organization for Women, 93, 103

National Popular Government League, 44

National Reconnaissance Office, 187

National Recovery Act, 53-54

National Recovery Administration (NRA), 53

NATIONAL RESEARCH AND EDUCATION NETWORK (NREN), 213

National Review (magazine), 206

National Rip-Saw, The (newspaper), 33

National Security Act (1947), 64, 132, 187

National Security Agency (NSA), 64, 137, 187, 271

NATIONAL SECURITY COUNCIL (NSC), 64, 88, 89, 137, 213

National Security Decision Directives (NSDDs), 77, 88, 89

National Security Directive NSC 10/2, 65, 146-47

National Security League, 40

NATIONAL SECURITY PLANNING GROUP (NSPG), 213

National Security Political Action

Committee, 95

NATIONAL SOCIALISM/NAZISM, 51, 73, 109, 213; and FASCISM, 164; and *Kristallnacht*, 56; National Socialist German Workers party established (1920), 44; and Olympic games (1936), 54; planned march in Skokie, Illinois (1977), 83-84; portrayed in motion pictures, 57, 60, 87. *See also* Goebbels, Joseph; Hitler, Adolf

National Taxpayers Union, 95

National Telecommunications and Information Administration, 212

National Union for Social Justice, 55

Native American party, 16

Native Americans, 22; land rights, 24; relocation of, 21; treaty relations, 24

nativism, 25, 120

NATO (North Atlantic Treaty Organization), 67, 219

Natural Resources Defense Council (NRDC), 96

Nazis. *See* NATIONAL SOCIALISM/NAZISM

Nazi-Soviet Non-Aggression Pact, 57

NBC Network, 48, 61, 63, 94, 206

negotiation, 116

Nelson, Richard Alan, 115-16, 184

NEOLIBERALISM, 214-15. *See also* CLASSICAL LIBERALISM

neon (advertising signs), 36

NESHER, 215

Neutrality Act, 55

NEW AGE MOVEMENT, 215-16

New Beginning, A (motion picture), 90

"New Deal," 52, 53, 54

"New Diplomacy," 40

New England Antislavery Society, 11

New England Courant (newspaper), 2

New England's First Fruits (pamphlet), 1

"New Generations of Resistance Tour," 107

New Hampshire, 5

NEW JOURNALISM, 216. *See also* ADVOCACY JOURNALISM; MEDIA BIAS

New Masses (magazine), 48, 49, 53

New Republic (magazine), 36, 206

NEWS, 216-17. *See also* JOURNALISM/JOURNALIST

news conferences, presidential, 23

NEWS EMBARGO, 217

NEWS FEED, 217

newsfilm, 26
NEWS HOLE, 217
NEWS MEDIA, 203, 217
newspaper syndicate, first, 23
newspapers, 4, 62; earliest, xiv, 1, 2;
    foreign-language, 2, 38. *See also*
    individual newspapers by title
NEWSPEAK, 217. *See also*
    DOUBLESPEAK; ORWELLIAN
    TACTICS; PROPAGANDA DEVICES
NEWS RELEASE, 217, 229; compared to
    ADVERTISING, 117
NEWS VALUES, 218
Newsweek (magazine), 206
New Testament (book), xi
NEW WORLD INFORMATION AND
    COMMUNICATION ORDER (NWICO)
    DEBATE, 82, 218
New York City, draft riots, 19
New Yorker (magazine), 81
New York Evening Post (newspaper), 40-
    41
New York Herald (newspaper), 13
New York Herald Tribune (newspaper), 74
New York Journal (newspaper), 275
New York Morning Journal (newspaper),
    27
New York Times (newspaper), 35, 102-3;
    begins publication, 15; "Fight for
    Freedom" advertisement in, 59; and
    Haiti, 104-5; as MEDIA ELITE, 206,
    223; term *terrorism* first appears in, 80
New York Tribune (newspaper), 28
New York Weekly Journal (newspaper), 2
New York World (newspaper), 23, 27,
    36, 275
Niagara Movement, 29
Nicaragua: Contra rebels in, 91, 142; and
    David Ortega, 85; and El Salvador,
    109; IRAN-CONTRA
    INVESTIGATIONS, 92, 142, 190; and
    National Opposition Union, 98, 109;
    and Sandinista National Liberation
    Front, 85, 98, 109; United Nations
    intervention in, 111; and Violeta
    Chamorro, 98, 109; and William
    Walker, 17
Nicholas II (Russian czar), 38
Nielsen, A.C., ratings, 80
"Night of the Crystals," 56
Niles' Register (magazine), 13
Nineteenth Amendment, 45
"95 theses," xv

Nipkow, Paul, 23
Nixon, Richard, 68, 70, 74, 79, 81, 83,
    273
NKVD (formerly KGB), 196
Nobel, Alfred, 27
Nobel Peace Prize, 27
Noelle-Neumann, Elisabeth, 257
Nolan, David, 80
Non-Aligned Movement (NAM), 82
NON-DENIAL DENIAL, 218. *See also*
    NEWSPEAK; WEASEL WORDS
NONGOVERNMENTAL
    ORGANIZATIONS (NGOs), 218-19.
    See also INTEREST GROUPS
Noriega, Manuel A., 97, 98
NORTH AMERICAN FREE TRADE
    AGREEMENT. *See* NAFTA
NORTH ATLANTIC TREATY
    ORGANIZATION (NATO), 67, 219
North Korea, 68
North, Oliver, 89, 91, 92, 93, 133, 142
Northern Ireland, 268
Norway, 219
Nova Scotia, 3
Nuremberg, Germany, 63
Nuremberg War Trials, 63
Nye, Gerald P., 59; and Nye Committee,
    52

objectivity, 118
OCTOBER SURPRISE, 219
O'Donnell, Victoria, 235-36
OFF THE NEWS, 220
OFF THE RECORD, 220
OFFICE OF CENSORSHIP, 219-20
Office for Combating Terrorism, 81
Office of Facts and Figures, 60, 61
Office of Public Diplomacy, 91
OFFICE OF STRATEGIC SERVICES
    (OSS), 220
OFFICE OF WAR INFORMATION (OWI),
    61, 220
OFFICIAL IDEOLOGY, 220
OGPU (formerly KGB), 196
Oklahoma, 46, 113
Oklahoma City bombing, 113
OLD GLORY, 220. *See also* FLAG
    WAVING
Oliver Twist (motion picture), 66
Olympic Games, 54
OMNIBUS WORDS, 220-21. *See also*
    DOUBLESPEAK; EUPHEMISM;
    NEWSPEAK

On Liberty (essay), 18
On the Duty of Civil Disobedience
    (essay), 15
On the Origin of Species (book), 18
online services, 114
Ontario, 3
OP-ED, 221
OPEN SOURCE INTELLIGENCE
    (OSCINT). *See* GRAY/GREY
    LITERATURE
Operation Chatter, 209
"Operation Desert Shield," 99, 153, 254
"Operation Desert Storm," 101, 153, 254
OPERATION JUST CAUSE, 98, 221, 254
"Operation Rescue," 94, 101
Operation Weed and Seed, 145
Ophuls, Marcel, 79
OPPO RESEARCH, 221
Oracle (teletext system), 81
ORCHESTRATED PROPAGANDA
    CAMPAIGN, 221, 222
Order of the Star Spangled Banner, 15
Order, The, 89, 90
O'Reilly, John Boyle, 22, 25
Organization of Afro-American Unity, 76
ORGANIZATIONS WITHOUT FORM,
    221-22
Ortega, Daniel, 85
Orwell, George, 67, 158, 208, 217, 222
ORWELLIAN TACTICS, 222. *See also*
    PROPAGANDA DEVICES
Ostend Manifesto, 17
O'Sullivan, John L., 201
Otis, James, 2, 4
OUT OF THE LOOP, 223, 226
Outcault, Richard, 27
OUTDOOR ADVERTISING, 222
Outdoor Advertising Association of
    America, Inc. (OAAA), 81, 222
Over There (song), 39
Owen, Robert, 12
Owens, Jesse, 54

Pacifica Foundation, 66-67, 73, 75
Packard, Vance, 179
PACK JOURNALISM, 223
PACs. *See* POLITICAL ACTION
    COMMITTEES
Page, Arthur, 49
Paine, Thomas, 4, 8, 172, 223
Palestine, xi, 65, 190, 276
Palestinian Information Office, 95
Palestinian Information Office v. Schultz

(court case), 95
Palestinian Liberation Organization
    (PLO), 75, 95, 96, 111
Palmer, A. Mitchell, 44
Palmer, Volney, 13
PAMPHLETEERING, 223
Panama, 97, 98, 221, 236, 254
Panic of 1893, 26
Panic of 1907, 31
PAPER TIGER, 223-24
Paper Tiger Television, 107
Paraguay, 106
Parker, Aida, 137-38; *Aida Parker
    Newsletter*, 137
Parker, Dorothy, 58
Parker, George F., 29, 30
Parks, Rosa, 72
PARROTING THE PARTY LINE, 224
Parry, Robert, 142
Pathé Weekly (newsreel), 32
Patrons of Husbandry, 20
Patton, Jerry, 105
PAWNS, 224
PBS (Public Broadcasting Service), 79,
    91, 206
Peace Corps, 74
Peaceful Revolutionist (magazine), 12
PEACEKEEPING, 224
Pearl Harbor, Hawaii, 60
Pearson, Drew, 73
Peasant's Revolt (England), xiii-xiv
Pell, Alfred, 19
pen, ballpoint, 24
pencil, invention of, xvi
Pennsylvania Railroad, 30-31
People for the Ethical Treatment of
    Animals (PETA), 122
PEOPLE'S PARTY, 26, 224. *See also*
    POPULISM/POPULIST
PEOPLE'S WAR, 225. *See also*
    COMMUNISM/COMMUNIST;
    LIBERATION MOVEMENT;
    REVOLUTION/REVOLUTIONARY
People Weekly (magazine), 206
PERCEPTION MANAGEMENT, 225
PERESTROIKA, 173, 225. *See also*
    COMMUNISM/COMMUNIST
PERFIDIOUS ALBION, 225
Perkins, George, 30
Perlstein, Gary R., 146, 182
Perot, Ross, 105, 112
Pershing, John J., 39, 42
Persian Gulf War, 99, 100, 101, 106,

153, 254
PERSUASION INDUSTRIES, 225. *See also* PURPOSEFUL PERSUASION
Petain, Henri, 164
petition, freedom to, 6. *See also* FIRST AMENDMENT
Philadelphia, 5, 8, 9
Philadelphische Zeitung (newspaper), 2
Philbrick, Herbert A., 66, 70
Philip Dru: Administrator (novel), 33
Philippine Islands, 29; independence, 63
Phillips, Kevin, 205
Phillips, Wendell, 15-16
phonograph, 22; phonograph cylinder, 24
Photo-Drama of Creation (motion picture), 35
photography: color, 26; half-tone, 28
Pierce, Franklin, 15
Pike, Albert, 20-21
Pilot, The (newspaper), 22
Pinochet, Augusto, 82
Pi Shen, xiv
Pittston strike (1989-1990), 143
Piven, Frances Fox, 210
plague (Europe, 1348-1352), xiii
Plain Talk (magazine), 63, 68
Planned Parenthood, 96
PLANTING STORIES, 225-26
Plato, x
Platoon (motion picture), 94
PLAUSIBLE DENIABILITY, 226
Playboy (magazine), 71
Playing for Time (television docudrama), 87
Plow that Broke the Plains, The (motion picture), 54
Pocket Books, 56
Poland, 57, 87
POLEMIC, 226. *See also* ARGUMENTATION
POLISPOTS, 226
POLITICAL ACTION COMMITTEES (PACs), 81, 85, 87, 226. *See also* INTEREST GROUPS; WATERGATE SCANDAL
POLITICAL ANALYSTS, 227
political buttons, 28
POLITICAL CRIME, 227. *See also* *specific crimes*
POLITICAL GRAPHICS, 227. *See also* WEAPONS ON THE WALL
political party system, American, 8

POLITICAL PATHOLOGY, 228
POLITICALLY CORRECT (PC), 227-28. *See also* CENSORSHIP
Polk, James K., 14
Pollard, Jonathan Jay, 92
polygamy, 15
Pony Express, 18
Popery! As It Was and As It Is (book), 16
POPULAR FRONT/PEOPLE'S FRONT, 228
Popular Liberation Forces (FPL), 109
POPULAR OPINION, 229. *See also* PUBLIC OPINION
POPULISM/POPULIST, 24-25, 26, 229. *See also* PEOPLE'S PARTY
Port Huron Statement (manifesto), 75
Portugal, 219
POSITION PAPERS, 229
POSITIVE INDOCTRINATION. *See* INDOCTRINATION
Posner, Michael, 107
Posse Comitatus, 79, 88
postage stamps, first, 14
Postal Rate Commission (PRC), 93
postal service, first regular, 2
posters, xiv, xv, 10, 36, 39, 96, 145, 182, 222, 223, 227, 230, 273
Potential Rating Index by Zip Market (PRIZM), 237
Pratkanis, Anthony, 179
PREFERENTIAL SOURCING, 204, 229-30. *See also* MEDIA BIAS
Preminger, Otto, 71, 72
PRESIDENT'S FOREIGN INTELLIGENCE ADVISORY BOARD (PFIAB), 230
PRESS, 1, 206, 230; freedom of, 6, 12. *See also* FIRST AMENDMENT; FREE SPEECH
PRESS AGENTRY, 230, 244
PRESS BASHING, 230-31
PRESS KIT. *See* MEDIA KIT
PRESS RELEASE. *See* JUSTICE BY NEWS RELEASE; NEWS RELEASE
PRESSURE GROUPS, 231, 245. *See also* LOBBYING/LOBBYIST
PRESTEL, 84
Pring, George W., 260
printing, xiv, 8; color, 21
printing presses, 26; first (steam-powered), 8
PRIZM (Potential Rating Index by Zip Market), 237
PROFESSIONAL PATRIOTS, 231

Progress and Poverty (book), 23
Progressive Era, 25, 30
Progressive party, 33-34, 46, 66
PROGRESSIVE/PROGRESSIVISM, 231-32
Prohibition, 42, 263
Prohibition party, 21
Promontory Point, Utah, 21
PROMOTION, 232. *See also* ADVERTISING
Promotional Products Association International, 256
Proofs of a Conspiracy against All the Religions and Governments of Europe (book), 7
PROPAGANDA, 189, 209, 221, 232-33, 262; etymology of the word, ix. *See also* PURPOSEFUL PERSUASION; SCAME
PROPAGANDA ANALYSIS, 233
PROPAGANDA OF THE DEED, 228, 236
PROPAGANDA DEVICES, 233-34
PROPAGANDA ENVIRONMENT, 234
PROPAGANDA MODEL, 244
PROPAGANDA MODEL (HERMAN AND CHOMSKY), 118-19, 234-35
PROPAGANDA MODEL (JOWETT AND O'DONNELL), 235-36
Propaganda in Motion Pictures (book), 59
PROPAGANDA PHONY, 236
PROPAGANDA-2 (P-2), 236
Protestant Reformation, xiv, xv
PROTESTERS, 236
Protocols of the Learned Elders of Zion (book), 124
PSEUDO-EVENT/PSEUDO-NEWS, 236-37. *See also* FLUFF EVENTS
Pseudo-Isidorian Decretals (document), xiii
PSEUDO-REALISM, 237
PSYCHEDELICS, 237
psychoanalysis, 28
PSYCHOGRAPHICS, 237
Psychological Strategy Board, 209
PSYCHOLOGICAL OPERATIONS (PSYOPS), 101, 237-38. *See also* HEARTS AND MINDS CAMPAIGN
PSYCHOLOGICAL WARFARE (PSYWAR), 237, 238, 262
Psychology, from the Standpoint of a Behaviorist (book), 43
"Publius," 4

PUBLIC, 238. *See also* STAKEHOLDERS
PUBLIC ACCESS PROGRAMMING, 238-39
PUBLIC AFFAIRS, 239
Public Affairs Program for the Arab World (confidential document), 82
Public Broadcasting Act (1967), 77
Public Broadcasting Service (PBS), 79, 91, 206
Public Citizen, Inc., 80, 95-96
PUBLIC COMMUNICATION, 239, 241
PUBLIC DIPLOMACY, 239. *See also* UNITED STATES INFORMATION AGENCY (USIA)
PUBLICITY, 241
Publicity Bureau, 28, 30
PUBLIC INFORMATION CAMPAIGNS, 239-40
PUBLIC INFORMATION OFFICER (PIO), 240
PUBLIC INTEREST, 44, 117, 240-41
Public Interest Research Group (PIRG), 80
PUBLIC OPINION, 20, 241-42, 266. *See also* COURT OF PUBLIC OPINION
Public Opinion (book), 46
public opinion polls, 73, 75, 79, 89, 91, 100, 109
PUBLIC POLICY PROCESS, 242
PUBLIC RELATIONS (PR), 35-36, 242-43; corporate, 24. *See also* PUBLICITY; PUBLIC RELATIONS MODELS; STAKEHOLDERS
PUBLIC RELATIONS MODELS, 243-44
PUBLIC RELATIONS SOCIETY OF AMERICA (PRSA), 66, 243, 244
PUBLIC RELATIONS STUDENT SOCIETY OF AMERICA (PRSSA), 244
PUBLIC SERVICE ANNOUNCEMENTS (PSAs), 244. *See also* ADVERTISING COUNCIL
PUBLIC SERVICE EVENTS, 244. *See also* FLUFF EVENTS
Publick Occurrences Both Foreign and Domestick (newspaper), 2
publishing industry, 56; and John Milton, 1; and mass-produced paperbacks, 106
Pugwash Conferences, 261
Pulitzer, Joseph, 23, 27, 98, 275
Pullman Company, 26
PULLOUTS, 245
PURPOSEFUL PERSUASION, 245

PUSH POLLS, 245

Quartering Act, 3
Quayle, Dan, 105
QUBE, 84
Quebec, 3
Quebec Act, 3
Quitman, John A., 15, 16
Qur'an (book), xii

R.A.V. v. St. Paul (Supreme Court case), 102
Rabin, Yitzhak, 113
Race (Race and Reason) (video series), 89
RACIST/RACIALIST/RACIAL DISCRIMINATION, 245-46. *See also* ETHNIC CLEANSING; GENOCIDE; HATE GROUPS
RADICAL, 246
radio: advertising on, 46; and audion tube, 31; car, 49; broadcast of President Coolidge's inauguration, 48; citizens band (CB), 83; clandestine stations, 134; decline of, 68; election coverage on, 45; first congressional broadcast, 60; frequency modulation (FM), 56, 62; micro-stations, 105-6; Olympic Games (1936) coverage, 54; ratings, 51; regulation of, 33, 40; scandal on, 73; short-wave, 43; and television, 62; transistor, 65; wireless, 29, 31
Radio Act of 1912, 33
Radio Act of 1927, 49
Radio Corporation of America (RCA), 43, 48, 56
Radio Free Asia, 269
Radio Free Europe, 66, 147, 269
Radio Liberty, 69, 147, 269
Radio Marti (Cuba), 269
Radio Moscow, 84, 96
Radio for Peace International, 181
"Rafferty Act," 59-60
railroad: first passenger, 10; invention of locomotive trains, 8; regulation of, 24; transcontinental, 21; and use of publicity, 30-31
Railway Executives' Advisory Committee, 38
Rand School of Social Science, 31
Random House (publisher), 54
Rank, Hugh, 139
Raskin, Jamin, 228

Raymond, Walter, 87-88
RCA (Radio Corporation of America), 43, 48, 56
REACH, 246-47. *See also* ADVERTISING; GROSS RATING POINTS (GRPs)
REACTIONARY, 247. *See also* CONFORMISTS
Reader's Digest (magazine), 46
Reagan, Ronald: 1980 election, 86; 1984 election, 90; Central American policies, 91, 108; and CITIZENS FOR AMERICA, 133; and CONTRAS (in Nicaragua), 142; and disinformation, 113; and Iran hostage crisis, 106, 219; and Israel, 215; and national security directives, 88, 89; and NATIONAL SECURITY PLANNING GROUP, 213
rebellion, xiv, 3, 19, 29, 144, 145, 187
rebels, xi, 73, 77, 85, 91, 113, 122, 125, 134, 142, 166, 178, 190, 224, 255.
records (LPs), 65
RED-BAITING, 247. *See also* COMMUNISM/COMMUNIST; McCARTHYISM
Red Channels (book), 68
Red Cross, American, 23
RED DECADE, 247. *See also* COMMUNISM/COMMUNIST
"Red Emma" (Goldman), 31, 40, 44, 121
Red Lion Broadcasting Co., Inc. v. FCC (Supreme Court case), 79, 163
Red Nightmare (motion picture), 74
Redgrave, Vanessa, 87
Reed, Daniel, 69
Reed, John, 34, 41, 43, 44, 104
Reed, Rebecca, 12
Rees, John Rawlings, 262
Reeves, Rosser, 70
Regulation 2666, 99
Reid, Alastair, 138
religion, x; freedom of, 1-2, 6. *See also* FIRST AMENDMENT
Renaissance, xiii
Reno, Janet, 107
Reporters Committee for Freedom of the Press, 100
REPRESENTATIVE VIOLENCE, 247-48
Republican National Committee (RNC), 92, 93, 101
Republican National Convention (1984), 90

REPUBLICAN PARTY, 248, 251; 1860 election, 18; 1884 election, 23; 1896 election, 27-28; 1900 election, 28; 1912 election, 34; 1928 election, 49; 1952 election, 70; and Andrew Johnson, 20; "Contract with America," 113; elephant symbol, 22; established, 13, 17; and Harry Truman, 70; and WHIG PARTY, 274; women's division of, 43. *See also* Bush, George; Reagan, Ronald;

RESCUE OPERATION, 248

RESIDENCY, 248. *See also* INTELLIGENCE COMMUNITY

resolutions, 116, 259

response efforts, 155, 193, 201

restrictions 172, 192, 198. *See also* CENSORSHIP

retirees, 258

return to Africa movement, 47. *See also* Garvey, Marcus Moziah

REVISIONISM/REVISIONIST, 250; examples of revisionism, 73, 84, 90, 104, 126, 128, 146, 214, 248-50. *See also* LIBERTARIAN

REVOLUTION/REVOLUTIONARY, 250; revolts and revolutions, 14, 28, 30, 32, 43, 44, 51, 53, 79, 85, 89, 120, 121, 129, 144, 145, 184, 187, 190, 197, 223, 225, 246, 247, 249, 250, 263, 275; revolutionaries, 5, 166, 200, 247; revolutionary action 41, 197; revolutionary activism, 228; revolutionary art and literature, 49; revolutionary disturbances, 38; revolutionary people, 250; revolutionary romantics, 43

Revolution of 1910, 275

Revolutionary War , 2, 4, 40, 200

"Rex-84 Alpha," 89

Reynolds, Charles B., 24

Rhetoric (book), x

RHETORIC, 250; examples of rhetoric, 76, 84, 90, 113, 138, 151, 198, 227, 229, 232, 233, 250, 256

Rhode Island, 1-2

Richard II (King of England), xiv

Richey, Charles, 95

Rideout, Walter B., 33

Riefenstahl, Leni, 60

RIGHT-WING/CONSERVATIVE, 251. *See also* LIBERTARIAN

RITUAL DEFAMATION, 251

roads, 8

Robison, John, 7

Rochemont, Louis de, 53

Rock Around the Clock (song), 72

Rock Springs Massacre, 23

rock-and-roll music, 72

Rockefeller, David, 82, 267

Rockefeller Foundation, 77

Rockefeller, John D., Jr., 35-36

Roe v. Wade (Supreme Court case), 82

Rojas, Don, 90-91

Roman Catholic Church, xii; Office of Inquisition, xiv

Roman empire, x

Romero, Oscar, 108

Romerstein, Herbert, 96

ROOSEVELT, FRANKLIN DELANO. *See* FDR

Roosevelt, Theodore, 23-24, 27, 28, 29, 30, 32, 33-34, 232

Roots (television miniseries), 84

Roper Organization, 109

Roper poll, 57

Rosenberg, Ethel, 68, 71, 271

Rosenberg, Julius, 68, 71, 271

Ross, F.A., 17

Rossiya (Soviet newspaper), 101

Rousseau, Jean Jacques, 6, 134

Royal Institute of International Affairs (RIIA), 43, 45, 144

Russell, Charles Taze, 22-23, 34-35, 38

Russia, 38-39, 101-2, 160, 196, 270; and Communism, 137. *See also* Soviet Union

Russian Foreign Intelligence Service (SVR), 196, 261

Russian Revolution (1917), 129

Russian Social-Democratic party, 129

Rystrom, Kenneth, 221

S.C. Johnson & Son Inc., 106

Sacco, Nicola, 45, 49

Sacra Congregation de Propaganda Fide, xvi

Sacred Congregation for the Propagation of Faith, xvi

SACRED TERRORISM, 252

Safety Appliance Act, 26

Safety of the Alternating System for Electrical Distribution, The (book), 24

Safire, William, 147

Salem, Massachusetts, witch trials, 2

SALIENCE, 252

Salvaggio, Jerry L., 186
SAMIZDAT, 252
Sandinista National Liberation Front
 (FSLN), 85, 98, 109
Sargent, Lyman Tower, 183
Sartori, Giovani, 182-83
Saturday Evening Post (magazine), 36-
 37, 79
Saudi Arabia, 99
Saul, Irwin, 123
Save Your Job, Save Our Country (book),
 112
SCAME, 252
SCAPEGOAT/SCAPEGOATING, 252
Schary, Dore, 65
Schenk v. United States (Supreme Court
 case), 43
Schiff, Jacob, 29
Schipper, Gary, 110
schools, public (and scientific
 creationism), 92
Schramm, Wilbur, 60, 64
Schreier, Howard N., 210
Scientific American (magazine), 31, 104
Scientific Conference for World Peace,
 66
Scotland, 268
Scott, Dred, 17
Scott, Winfield, 15
Scottish Rite of Freemasonry, 8, 21. *See
 also* Freemasonry
Scowcroft, Brent, 97
Scripps, E.W., 31
Scruton, Roger, 161
Seale, Bobby, 79
Seaver, Horace, 12
Second American Writers' Congress, 55
SECRET GOVERNMENT, 252-53. *See
 also* CONSPIRACY THEORIES; ELITE
 THEORY
SECRET TEAM, 253. *See also*
 CONSPIRACY THEORIES
SECT. *See* CULT
Securities and Exchange Commission
 (SEC), 203
SEDITION, 253. *See also*
 SUBVERSION/SUBVERSIVES
Sedition Act, 41
SEDITIOUS LIBEL, 253
See It Now (television series), 69
SEGUE. *See* HOT SWITCHING
Seldes, George, 32, 42, 58, 68, 211
Select Committee on Lobbying

Activities, 67
SELECTIVE PERCEPTION, 253
Senate Internal Security Subcommittee,
 69, 73
Senefelder, Aloys, 8
sensationalism, 23
Serbs, 256
Serrano, Jorge Elias, 109-10
Sessions, William, 215
Seuss, Dr., 60, 63
Seward, William H., 10
SHADOW GOVERNMENT, 252-54. *See
 also* CONSPIRACY THEORIES
Shaeffer, Francis, 221
Shafritz, Jay M., 133-34, 152
Shannon, Claude, 66
Shapiro, Andrew L., 102
Shaw, Donald L., 118
Shays' Rebellion, 4
Sheehan, Daniel, 253
Sheen, Fulton J., 55
Shell Oil Company, 143
SHIRTTAILING, 254
Sick, Gary, 86
SIDLE COMMISSION, 254
Sidle, Winant, 254
Sign for Cain, A (book), 71
SIGNAL-TO-NOISE RATIO, 254
Simms, Ruth Hanna McCormick, 43
Simons, A.M., 28
Simons, Herbert W., 210
Simpson, Alan, 101
Sinclair, Upton, 30, 44, 52
Sinesky, Jeffrey P., 112
Singlaub, John K., 268
Single Taxers, 23-24
Six Day War, 77
Six Months in a Convent (book), 12
60 Minutes (television series), 258
Sixth Report and Order (report), 69
Skokie (television docudrama), 87
slavery: abolition of, 8; advertisements
 in newspapers, 2; and American
 Antislavery Society, 11; antislavery
 movement, 9, 10; beginnings in
 America (1619), 1; and Crittenden
 Compromise, 18; and Kansas-
 Nebraska Act (1854), 16; number of
 slaves in the United States, 8; and
 Ostend Manifesto, 17; rebellion, 11;
 support of, 15; and WHIG PARTY, 274
Slavery Ordained of God (book), 17
Slidell, John, 16

Slinger, Pierre, 74
Slingshot (organization), 186
SLIPPERY SLOPE, 254
Small, Herbert, 28
Smith Act (1940), 58
Smith, Adam, 4, 172
Smith, Craig Allen, 210
Smith, Gerrit, 17
Smith, James A., 17
Smith, Joseph, Jr., 11, 13
Smith, R.M., 25
SMOKING GUN, 254. See also TOXIC
    INFORMATION
SNUGGLING, 254-55. See also BLACK
    PROPAGANDA; CLANDESTINE
    RADIO STATIONS
Social Democratic party, 28
Social Justice (magazine), 55, 60
SOCIAL MARKETING, 255
SOCIAL MOVEMENT. See MOVEMENT
Social Organization (book), 29
social theology, 197
"Socialism and the Church," 14
SOCIALISM/SOCIALIST, 33, 46, 201,
    255
Socialist Club, 32
Socialist Labor party (SLP), 22, 25, 26,
    66, 202
Socialist party, 29, 30, 33, 38, 45, 46,
    66
Socialist Workers party, 66
Society of Jesus, xv
SOCIOLINGUISTICS, 255
SOFT MONEY, 255
Solomon, Norman, 205
Solzhenitsyn, Aleksandr, 83
Somalia, 106, 110, 224, 255, 269-70,
    271
SOMALIAZATION, 255-56. See also
    INTERVENTIONIST
Somoza, Anastasio, 85
Sony Corporation, 83
Sorrow and the Pity, The (motion
    picture), 79
Soulé, Pierre, 17
SOUND BITE. See ACTUALITY
South Africa, 94, 101
South African Defence Force, 94
South Korea, 68
Southern Poverty Law Center, 87
Soviet Russia Pictorial (magazine), 47
Soviet Union, 73, 104, 270; and Cuban
    Missile Crisis, 75; establishment of,

129; FALSE FLAG OPERATIONS of,
    163-64; and George Bush, 156; and
    NORTH ATLANTIC TREATY
    ORGANIZATION, 219; and
    PERESTROIKA, 225; United States
    recognition of (1933), 52; and World
    War II, 57, 60
Soviet Union Communist party, 91
space program, moon landing, 79
Spain, xiv-xv, 54-55
Spanish-American War, 28
Spanish Civil War, 54-55
Spanish Inquisition, xiv
Spartacus (motion picture), 74
SPEAK AND RETREAT, 256. See also
    PAPER TIGER; RHETORIC
SPECIAL INTEREST GROUPS. See
    INTEREST GROUPS; PUBLIC
    INTEREST
SPECIALTY ADVERTISING, 256-57. See
    also ADVERTISING; DIRECT
    MARKETING; PROMOTION;
    PUBLICITY
Specialty Advertising Association
    International, 256
"Speech, Equality and Harm: Feminist
    Legal Perspectives on Pornography
    and Hate Propaganda," (conference),
    108
speech, freedom of, 6, 102, 136, 171,
    238. See also FIRST AMENDMENT
Spies, August, 23, 24
SPIKE, 257. See also CENSORSHIP;
    GATEKEEPER
SPIN CONTROL, 257. See also AGENDA
    SETTING; ORCHESTRATED
    PROPAGANDA CAMPAIGN
SPIN DOCTORS, 257, 271. See also
    HANDLERS; POLITICAL ANALYSTS
SPIRAL OF SILENCE, 257-58
Spirit of St. Louis (airplane), 49
SPOKESMANSHIP/SPOKESPERSON
    TRAINING, 258
Spotlight, The (newspaper), 73
Sputnik I (satellite), 73
Sputnik II (satellite), 73
SPYING/SPYCRAFT, 220, 258. See also
    CLANDESTINE; ESPIONAGE
STAKEHOLDERS, 258. See also
    INTEREST GROUPS/PRESSURE
    GROUPS
Stalin, Joseph, 44, 47, 129; and
    COMINTERN abolishment, 64; and

CULT OF PERSONALITY, 149;
Foundations of Leninism (book), 52;
and Nazi-Soviet Non-Aggression Pact
(1939), 57; at Yalta, 62
Stamp Act, 2
Standard Oil, 29
Stanford University, 99, 178
Star, The (tabloid newspaper), 103
Star Spangled Banner, The (song), 9, 51
Stars and Stripes (U.S. Army newspaper),
41
STATE TERRORISM, 258-59. *See also*
TERRORISM
STEALTH TACTICS, 259. *See also*
HIDDEN AGENDA
Steele, Robert D., 176
Steffens, Lincoln, 211
Stein-Schneider, Herbert, 5
Stephenson, William "Intrepid," 57
Stevenson, Adlai E., 28, 70, 73
Stewart, Charles J., 210
Stewart, Donald Ogden, 58
Stock market crash (1929), 50
Stone, Isador Feinstein "Izzy," 71, 96,
104
Stone, Oliver, 94, 102
STONEWALLING, 259
Stonewall Inn (New York City), 79
Stout, Fred, 97
Stowe, Harriet Beecher, 15
strain, 115
STRATEGIC LAWSUITS AGAINST
PUBLIC PARTICIPATION (SLAPP),
260. *See also* CHILLING EFFECT
strikes (labor), 22, 26-27, 35, 52, 154.
See also Unions
STRIP PROGRAMMING, 260
Stroessner, Alfredo, 106
Strong, Anna Louise, 224
STRUCTURED LEAKS, 196, 225, 260.
See also ORCHESTRATED
PROPAGANDA CAMPAIGN
Student Nonviolent Coordinating
Committee (SNCC), 76
Students for a Democratic Society (SDS),
75, 76, 77, 79, 80
STUNT, 260. *See also* PUBLICITY
STUNTING, 260
SUBLIMINAL MESSAGES, 260
SUBPROPAGANDA, 261
SUBVERSION/SUBVERSIVES, 261
Subversive Activities Control Act
(1950), 68

Subversive Activities Control Board
(SACB), 68
SUFFRAGETTES, 261. *See also*
TEMPERANCE MOVEMENT;
WOMEN'S MOVEMENT
Sukarno (Indonesian president), 265
Sun, The (newspaper, New York City), 12
Sun Tzu, x
SUNSHINE PATRIOTS. *See*
PROFESSIONAL PATRIOTS
Surles, Alexander D., 53
SURRENDER LOBBY, 261
Susskind, David, 72
SVR (Suzhba vneshnogo razvedky), 261
Swope, Herbert, 221
SWOT ANALYSIS, 261. *See also* ISSUE
SCANNING; ISSUES MANAGEMENT

TABLOID JOURNALISM, 262. *See also*
YELLOW JOURNALISM
Taft, Robert A., 67
Taft, William, 32, 33
Tarbell, Ida M., 29, 211
TARGET GROUPS. *See* PUBLIC;
STAKEHOLDERS
tariffs, 25, 111-12, 211
Tavistock Institute of Human Relations,
262
TAVISTOCK METHOD, 262. *See also*
PSYCHOLOGICAL OPERATIONS
(PSYOPS); THINK TANKS
Taylor, Zachary, 15, 274
TCI Cable, 206
Tecumseh (Shawnee chief), 12
TELCO, 262
TELECOMMUNICATIONS, 19, 186,
212, 262-63. *See also specific types*
telegraph cable, submarine, 14
telegraphy, 13, 15, 18, 19; printing, 17;
wireless, 27
telemarketing, 112
telephone, 22, 35
telephone services, 100, 104;
transatlantic cable, 73
telephone surveys. *See* PUSH POLLS
teletext systems, 81
Televisa SA (Mexico), 112
television. *See* TV
Telstar I (satellite), 74
TEMPERANCE MOVEMENT, 21, 263.
See also SUFFRAGETTES
TERROR GROUP, 263
TERRORISM, 33, 80, 94, 263-64. *See*

also ANTITERRORISM;
COUNTERTERRORISM; STATE
TERRORISM
TERRORIST, 264. *See also* ASSASSIN
Terry, Randall, 94
Texas, 14
Texas v. Johnson (court case), 96
Theory of Cognitive Dissonance, A
(book), 73
THINK TANKS, 264. *See also*
POLITICAL ANALYSTS; PUBLIC
POLICY PROCESS
Third (Communist) International, 43
THIRD WORLD, 264-65
Thoman, Elizabeth, 206
Thomas, J. Parnell, 57
Thomas, Norman, 38, 51
Thompson, Virgil, 54
Thoreau, Henry David, 15
THOUGHT-STOPPING CLICHE, 265. *See
also* RITUAL DEFAMATION
Thurmond, Strom, 66
Tiananmen Square, 97
Time (magazine), 46, 206
Time-Warner, 206
Tippecanoe, Battle of, 12
Titus, xi
Tobey, Charles W., 59
Toffler, Alvin, 80
Tokyo, Japan, 100
Tongsun Park, 168
Tories, 2-3, 8
Toronto, Canada, 9
TOTALITARIANISM, 265-66
Toubon, Jacques, 111
Toward Soviet America (book), 51
TOXIC INFORMATION, 217, 266
Toynbee, Arnold, 36, 43
Trachtenberg, Alexander, 47
TRACKING POLLS, 241-42, 266
trade, 211
trade tariffs, 25, 111-12, 211
Trade Union Educational League, 50
Trade Union Unity League, 50
Tragedy of Waste (book), 47
"Trail of Tears," 11
Trains, invention of, 8. *See also* Railroad
TRAITOR, 266. *See also* DUAL
LOYALIST; FREE SPEECH
TRANSNATIONAL CORPORATIONS
(TNCs), 266-67. *See also* GLOBALISM
Transportation Act (1920), 44
Traute, Henry D., 25

TRAWLING, 267
TREASON, 219, 266, 267
Treaty of Guadalupe-Hidalgo, 14
Trenchard, John, 2
TREND. *See* ISSUE SCANNING
Treverton, Gregory F., 74
TRIALS BY NEWS RELEASE. *See*
COURT OF PUBLIC OPINION
Tribune Media, 206
Tricontinental Film Center, 83
TRILATERAL COMMISSION, 82, 267-
68. *See also* CONSPIRACY
THEORIES; ELITE THEORY
"Tri-partite Pact," 58
Tripoli, Libya, 236
Trotsky, Leon, 39, 49, 58, 129
Trotskyists, 49
Trudeau, Garry, 80
Truman, Harry S.: 1944 election, 62;
1948 election, 66; becomes president
(1945), 63; and Chiang Kai-shek, 63;
and China, 64; and communists, 68;
and Douglas MacArthur, 69; and Korea,
68; "Loyalty Order," 64; and McCarran
(Internal Security) Act, 68; and
McCarran-Walter Act, 70; and National
Security Directive NSC 10/2, 146-47
Trumbo, Dalton, 74
"Truth Commission," 108
Truth Seeker (magazine), 30
Tucker, Benjamin, 23
Turkey, 219
Turner Broadcasting, 206
Turner, Nat, 11
Turner Network Television, 206
Turner, Ted, 85
TURNING THE QUESTION, 268
TV, 268; and Army-McCarthy Senate
hearings (1954), 72; development of,
69; first appearance of term
"television," 31; first cable system,
67; first color, 63; first educational
station, 71; first patent for, 49; first
transatlantic broadcast, 74; and HOT
SWITCHING, 179; number of sets in
United States, 69, 72, 74, 77, 80;
Olympic Games (1936) coverage, 54;
pay cable programming, 81; and radio,
62, 65; ratings of, 94; and scandal on,
73; technological advances, 23, 46;
over telephone lines, 104; violence
on, 81; at World's Fair (1939), 56
TV Guide (magazine), 65

TV Marti (Cuba), 98-99, 269
TWO-STEP FLOW (MULTI-STEP FLOW), 118, 268
Tydings Committee, 68
Tyler, John, 12, 13
Tyler, Wat, xiv
Tyndale, William, xv
Tyner, Kathleen, 97
typewriter, 21
typography, xiv

U.S. News & World Report (magazine), 206
U.S.S. *Liberty* (ship), 77
U.S.S. *Panay* (ship), 56
UK (or U.K.), 268
Ultra high frequency (UHF), 72
Ulyanov, Vladimir Ilich, 39
UMBRELLA ORGANIZATIONS, 268
UN. *See* UNITED NATIONS ORGANIZATION
Una (magazine), 16
Unanue, Manuel, de Dios, 103
Uncivil Liberty (essay), 22
"Uncle Sam," 9, 39
Uncle Tom's Cabin (book), 15
UNCONVENTIONAL WARFARE, 268
Underground Railroad, 12. *See also* slavery
Unified Task Force in Somalia (UNITAF), 270
Union League Board of Publications, 19
Union of Soviet Socialist Republics, 39, 129, 270
Union Pacific Coal, 23
Union Pacific Railroad, 21
unions (labor): American Railway, 26-27; in Colorado, 35-36; CORPORATE CAMPAIGN strategy, 143; and DIRECT ACTION, 154; and free speech, 56-57; Ludlow Massacre, 35-36; membership in 28, 29, 44, 47, 51, 56-57, 67; and WOBBLIES, 30
United Church of Christ (UCC), 76
United Church of Christ v. FCC (court case), 77
United Fruit Company, 71
United Independent Broadcaster (UIP), 49
United Mine Workers of America, 143
United Nations Centre on Transnational Corporations (UNTNC), 267
United Nations Committee on Information, 85

United Nations Educational, Scientific, and Cultural Organization (UNESCO), 82, 86, 91, 219, 269
United Nations General Assembly, 102
United Nations High Commissioner for Refugees (UNHCR), 69
United Nations Operation in Somalia II (UNOSOM II), 270
United Nations Operation in Somalia I (UNOSOM I), 269
UNITED NATIONS ORGANIZATION (UNO or UN), 268-69; Charter, 259; founded (1945), 63; and HUMAN RIGHTS, 180-81; indigenous peoples, report on, 110; and Iraq, 99; and Palestine, 65; Protection Force, 270; and RACIAL DISCRIMINATION, 246; relief in Somalia, 106, 224; "Truth Commission," 108; and ZIONISM, 83
United Nations Security Council, 99
United Nations Universal Declaration of Human Rights, 65
United Nations World Conference on Human Rights, 110
United Press International (UPI), 31, 73, 94
United States of America, xiii, 160, 219, 270; Civil War, 18, 19, 20, 143; Constitution, 4-6, 164-65, 267; Declaration of Independence, 4; in Desert Storm, 101; federal debt, 87; invasion of Canada, 45; and Iraq, 99; and Japan in World War II, 59; Manifest Destiny, 14, 201; neutrality, 6, 7, 8; population, 77; in World War I, 39, 42
United States Army, 199
United States Army Signal Intelligence, 271
United States Brewers Association, 40
United States Bureau of Corporations, 30, 35
United States Bureau of Education, 36
United States Central Intelligence Agency. *See* CENTRAL INTELLIGENCE AGENCY
United States Commission on Public Diplomacy, 239
United States Communist party. *See* Communist Party of the United States of America
United States Congress, 179
United States Constitution, 164-65, 267;

amendments to, 4-6. *See also*
     individual amendments
United States Defense Department, 64,
     89
United States Department of Commerce
     and Labor, 29
United States Division of Cultural
     Relations, 56
United States Film Service, 56
UNITED STATES INFORMATION
     AGENCY (USIA), 269; Express File,
     94; limitation of powers, 100; and
     motion picture industry regulation, 95;
     and PUBLIC DIPLOMACY, 239; and
     United Press International (UPI), 94;
     and Vietnam, 76; VOICE OF
     AMERICA, 71, 272
United States Justice Department, 44
United States Navy, 59
United States Postal Service, 98
United States Senate Select Committee to
     Study Government Operations with
     Respect to Intelligence Activities, 78
United States State Department, 232, 263
United States War Department, 64, 152
UNIVERSAL DECLARATION OF HUMAN
     RIGHTS, 180-81, 269
Universal Negro Improvement
     Association (UNA), 47
University of California-Berkeley, 75
University of Illinois, 64
University of Wisconsin, 178
UNOSOM I/UNOSOM II/UNITAF, 269-
     70. *See also* SOMALIAZATION
UNPROFOR, 270
Untermyer, Samuel, 52
US (or U.S./USA or U.S.A.), 270. *See
     also* United States of America
USA Today (newspaper), 87, 206
USSR (or U.S.S.R./CCCP or C.C.C.P.),
     73, 104, 270
Utah, 15

Valenti, Jack, 111
VALS (Values and Life-styles System),
     237
Van Buren, Martin, 11, 13
Vanderbilt, Cornelius, 17
VANGUARD, 270
Vanzetti, Bartolomeo, 45, 49
Variety (newspaper), 52
Vecheka (later KGB), 196
VE-Day (World War II), 63

Venezuela, 108
VENONA, 271. *See also*
     SPYING/SPYCRAFT
Versailles, France (as inspiration for
     Washington, D.C.), 5
Versailles, Treaty of, 43, 213, 214
Vest, George, 111
Vetter, Harold J., 146, 182
VETTING, 271
VICTORY BY NEWS RELEASE, 271. *See
     also* SPEAK AND RETREAT
Victory at Sea (television documentary
     series), 69
VIDEO NEWS RELEASE (VNR), 271-72
videocassette recorders, 83
videotape, 72, 83
videotext, interactive, 84
Vietnam: American involvement in, 76;
     American prisoners of war, 104; cease-
     fire signed, 82; DEATH SQUADS in,
     150; Gulf of Tonkin incident, 75-76;
     HEARTS AND MINDS CAMPAIGN of
     United States military, 178; and JOINT
     U.S. PUBLIC AFFAIRS OFFICE, 194;
     and *Platoon* (motion picture), 94; and
     PROPAGANDA OF THE DEED, 236;
     Tet offensive, 77-78; and VICTORY
     BY NEWS RELEASE, 271
Village Voice (newspaper), 72
Villard, Oswald Garrison, 41
Vindication of the Rights of Women, A
     (essay), 6
VIRTUAL REALITY, 272
VJ-Day (World War II), 63
VOICE OF AMERICA (VOA), 61, 65, 71,
     92, 96, 269, 272-73; Charter, 83
Voice of the Gulf, 101
Volkogonov, Dmitri A., 105
Vonnegut, Kurt, 174
voting age, 80

Waco, Texas, 107, 113
Walcott, John, 205
"Waldorf Conference," 65
Wales, 268
Walker, David, 10, 11
Walker, William, 17
Wall Street Journal (newspaper), 83, 206
Wallace, George, 81
Wallace, Henry, 62, 66
Wallace, Mike, 258
Wanger, Walter, 65
"War against Northern Aggression," 18-

19
"War between the States," 18-19
War of 1812, 9
War of the Worlds (radio broadcast), 56
War Resisters League, 149
WAR OF LIBERATION. *See* ARMED
    STRUGGLE; PEOPLE'S WAR
Ward, Barbar, 43
Ward, Harry F., 31
Ward, Henry Dana, 10
Warne, Colston, 54
Warner & Swasey Company, 58
Warner, Jack L., 74
Warning, A (book), 24
Warren, Josiah, 12
Washburn, L.K., 29-30
Washington, D.C., 5, 9, 13, 16, 36, 66,
    70, 73, 74, 81, 85, 100, 103, 109,
    113, 127, 142, 148, 169, 174, 182,
    254, 273; and Million Man March
    (1995), 113
Washington, George, 4, 5, 6, 7, 14, 165,
    191; *Farewell Address*, 7
Washington Goes to War (book), 59
Washington Post (newspaper), 81, 206,
    223
Washington Times (newspaper), 40
Watch Tower Society, 22-23, 40
WATERGATE SCANDAL, 81, 83, 273
Watson, John B., 43
Watson, Thomas A., 35
WAVE FRONT, 273
Wayland, J.A., 27, 33
WBAI-FM radio (New York), 75
We the People (organization), 92
*We're Number One, Where America
    Stands--and Falls--in the New World
    Order* (book), 102
WEAF-AM radio (New York), 46
Wealth of Nations (book), 4
weapons, 124-25
WEAPONS ON THE WALL, 273. *See also*
    posters
WEASEL WORDS, 273. *See also* CODE
    WORDS; DOUBLESPEAK; NEWSPEAK
Weathermen, 79, 80
Weaver, James B., 26
Weaver, Warren, 66
Webb, Jack, 74
Weed, Thurlow, 10
Weimar Republic, 42, 213
Weingarten, Reid, 106
Weisbrod, Burton A., 240

Weishaupt, Adam, 3
Well, the, 114
Welles, Orson, 56
West Germany, 219
Westinghouse, 24, 45, 50
Weyl, Walter, 36
Weyrich, Paul, 96
WGN-TV, 206
Wheeler, Burton K., 57
WHIG PARTY, 12, 13, 15, 16, 17, 248,
    274
Whisky Rebellion, 6
WHISPERING CAMPAIGN, 274
White America (book), 46
White American Resistance, 88
White Aryan Resistance (WAR), 88
WHITEHALL, 274. *See also* UK
WHITE PAPERS, 274
WHITE PROPAGANDA, 274
WHITEWASH, 274
Whitewater scandal, 113
Who's Afraid of Virginia Woolf? (motion
    picture), 76
Why Korea? (motion picture
    documentary), 69
Why Viet Nam? (motion picture
    documentary), 76
Why We Fight (motion picture
    documentary series), 60
*Why, Who and How of the Editorial Page,
    The* (book), 221
Wilcox, Laird, 161-62, 251
Wildmon, Donald, 106
Wilkie, Wendell, 59
William the Conqueror, xiii
Williams, Napoleon, 105
Wilshire's Magazine, 33
Wilson, Woodrow: 1912 election, 34;
    and *Birth of a Nation* (motion picture),
    37; and COMMITTEE ON PUBLIC
    INFORMATION, 39, 136; "Fourteen
    Points" address, 40; and League of
    Nations, 38; openness in foreign
    relations, 140; and U.S. troops sent to
    Russia, 42
Winchevsky, Morris, 29
Wing, Simon, 26
Wise, Herbert, 87
Wiseman, William, 39
Witch trials, 2
WOBBLIES, 30, 37, 38, 41, 47, 275
Wolfe, Tom, 74
Women's Bureau, 38

WOMEN'S MOVEMENT, 275. *See also*
    SUFFRAGETTES, TEMPERANCE
    MOVEMENT
Women's suffrage, 6, 21, 34, 45
Woodhull, Victoria, 22
Woodward, Bob, 81, 211
Woolsey, James, 111
Workers (Communist) Party of America,
    45, 47, 49, 50. *See also* Communist
    Party of the Unitet States of America
    (CPUSA)
Workers Monthly (magazine), 47
WORKING THE REFS, 275
Works Progress Administration (WPA),
    54
World Anti-Communist League (WACL),
    98
World Assembly of Public Relations
    (Mexico), 243
World Bank (WB), 181
world federalism, 144, 174, 269
World Health Organization (WHO), 269
World Intellectual Property Organization
    (WIPO), 219
World Jewish Economic Federation, 52
World League for Freedom and
    Democracy, 98
World Peaceways, 54
World Politics and Personal Insecurity
    (book), 160
World Trade Center, 107
World War I (1914-1918), 33, 35, 36,
    39, 40, 41, 42, 43, 48, 54, 55, 65,
    108, 120, 121, 127, 128, 132, 136,
    140, 160, 176, 214, 249; American
    casualties, 42; end of, 43
World War II (1939-1945), 31, 43, 57,
    59, 60, 63, 65, 69, 79, 88, 104, 117,
    120, 124, 126, 135, 150, 164, 166,
    214, 219, 220, 234, 236, 238, 249,
    263, 264, 266, 268; American
    casualties, 63; American prisoners of
    war, 104; D-Day, 62. *See also*
    NATIONAL SOCIALISM/NAZISM
World War II : The Propaganda Battle
    (television episode), 91
World's Columbian Exposition
    (Chicago), 26
Wrigley, William, 25
WTBS-TV (Atlanta), 206
Wyoming, 21, 101

X, Malcolm, 48, 75, 76

xenophobia, 240

Y'shua ben Joseph, xi
Yahweh (God), xi, 252
Yalta, 62
yellow badge, xiii. See also ANTI-
    SEMITIC
YELLOW JOURNALISM, 27, 262, 275.
    See also MEDIA BIAS; TABLOID
    JOURNALISM
"Yellow Kid" (comic strip), 27
Yeltsin, Boris, 105
Yiddisher Cowboy, The (motion picture),
    32
Yippies, 78-79
Yom Kippur, 252
York, Canada, 9
Young, Brigham, 13, 14-15
Yugoslavia, 113, 219

Zaltman, Gerald, 255
Zapata, Emiliano, 275
Zapatista National Liberation Army,
    113, 275
ZAPATISTAS, 113, 275
ZEALOTS, 116, 275-76. *See also*
    ACTIVISTS
Zeman, Zbynek, 273
Zenger, John Peter, 2
Zenith Corporation, 69
Zimmermann telegram, 38
*Zion's Watch Tower and Herald of
    Christ's Presence* (magazine), 22
Zion's Watch Tower Bible and Tract
    Society, 22-23
ZIONISM/ZIONIST, 83, 102, 124, 276
ZOG, 276. *See also* ANTI-SEMITIC
Zorthian, Barry, 76
Zundel, Ernst, 88, 104
Zworykin, Vladimir, 46

About the Author

Richard Alan Nelson is Associate Dean for Graduate Studies and Research and Professor at Louisiana State University's Manship School of Mass Communication in Baton Rouge. From 1989-1994, Nelson headed the Public Relations Sequence at Kansas State University. He previously served as an Associate Director of the International Telecommunications Research Institute and tenured faculty member at the University of Houston.

Nelson is professionally accredited by the Public Relations Society of America and is recognized in the Heritage Foundation's *Annual Guide to Public Policy Experts*. From 1989-1991 he also served on the Advisory Council of The Media Institute's Center for Media Analysis, another Washington, D.C. think tank featuring nationally-known professional and academic leaders. He is president, board member, and public relations track chair for the International Academy of Business Disciplines (IABD), and is past head of the Public Relations Division of the Association for Education in Journalism and Mass Communication (AEJMC).

Nelson's research focuses on public policy, strategic planning, management, and political communications issues. He is the author of more than 40 articles and reports on media industry topics ranging from the public opinion role played by persuasive communicators, to the impact of new communications technologies, to state promotion of motion picture/television industrial development. He has written several books, including *Florida and the American Motion Picture Industry, Lights! Camera! Florida!*, and *Propaganda: A Reference Guide* (forthcoming, Greenwood), and is co-author of *Issues Management: Corporate Public Policymaking in an Information Society*.

His professional background includes work as a weekly newspaper journalist, trade magazine editor, government public information coordinator, television news writer, and management consultant. Nelson is a graduate of Stanford University (A.B., political science), later studied at Brigham Young University (M.A., communications), and completed his Ph.D. in communication at Florida State University.

ISBN 0-313-29261-2

EAN

9 780313 292613

HARDCOVER BAR CODE